American
Jewish
Year Book

American

Jewish

Year Book 1980

VOLUME 80

Prepared by THE AMERICAN JEWISH COMMITTEE

Editors
MILTON HIMMELFARB
DAVID SINGER
Editor Emeritus
MORRIS FINE

THE AMERICAN JEWISH COMMITTEE
NEW YORK
THE JEWISH PUBLICATION SOCIETY OF AMERICA
PHILADELPHIA

ISBN 0-8276-0173-5

Library of Congress Catalogue Number: 99-4040

PRINTED IN THE UNITED STATES OF AMERICA
BY THE HADDON CRAFTSMEN, INC., SCRANTON, PA.

Preface

T he present volume contains three feature articles. In "Jews, Nazis, and Civil Liberties," David Dalin examines the impact on the Jewish community of the revival of neo-Nazi activities in the United States. Steven Cohen's "Trends in Jewish Philanthropy" presents a bleak picture of the outlook for Jewish communal giving. In "Israelis in the United States: Motives, Attitudes, and Intentions," Dov Elizur brings a social-science perspective to bear on an important phenomenon on the current Jewish scene.

The review of developments in the United States includes Murray Friedman's "Intergroup Relations"; George Gruen's "The United States, Israel, and the Middle East"; William Korey's "American Reaction to the Shcharansky Case"; and Walter Ackerman's "Jewish Education Today." Alvin Chenkin and Maynard Miran provide revised U.S. Jewish population estimates, while S.P. Goldberg covers Jewish communal services.

Jewish life around the world is reported on in a series of articles dealing with Israel, Canada, Argentina, Great Britain, France, Germany, the Soviet Union, Poland, Rumania, and South Africa. New estimates for the world Jewish population are given.

Carefully compiled directories of national Jewish organizations, periodicals, and federations and welfare funds, as well as religious calendars and obituary notices, round out the 1980 AMERICAN JEWISH YEAR BOOK.

We are very grateful to our colleague Joan Margules for technical and editorial assistance. Thanks are also due to Cyma M. Horowitz, director of the Blaustein Library, Lotte Zajac, and all our other co-workers in the Information and Research Department.

Morris Fine's association with the YEAR BOOK began some years before 1946–47, when his name first appeared on the title page. Now he has retired as editor. For his colleagues to praise him is to praise themselves by praising the YEAR BOOK, and Solomon said, "Let another praise you, but not your own mouth." On the other hand, Solomon also said, "To tell the truth is to further justice." For close to forty years now, whatever merit the YEAR BOOK has had has been very largely Morris Fine's doing. We shall try to maintain his standards.

THE EDITORS

Contributors

WALTER I. ACKERMAN; Shane Professor of Education; chairman, department of education, Ben Gurion University of the Negev, Beer Sheva, Israel.

BERNARD BASKIN; rabbi, Temple Anshe Sholom, Hamilton, Ont., Canada.

ALVIN CHENKIN; research consultant, Council of Jewish Federations and Welfare Funds.

STEVEN MARTIN COHEN; associate professor of sociology, Queens College, CUNY.

DAVID G. DALIN; assistant director, San Francisco Jewish Community Relations Council.

DENIS DIAMOND; executive director, South African Jewish Board of Deputies, Johannesburg.

DOV ELIZUR; senior lecturer, Bar Ilan University, Ramat Gan, Israel; research director, Israel Institute of Applied Social Research, Jerusalem.

MURRAY FRIEDMAN; director, middle atlantic region, American Jewish Committee.

S.P. GOLDBERG; assistant director, Council of Jewish Federations and Welfare Funds.

GEORGE E. GRUEN; director, Israel and Middle East affairs, foreign affairs department, American Jewish Committee.

LIONEL E. KOCHAN; Bearsted Reader in Jewish history, University of Warwick; honorary fellow, Oxford Centre for Post-graduate Hebrew Studies, England.

MIRIAM KOCHAN; journalist; translator, Oxford, England.

WILLIAM KOREY; director, international policy research, B'nai B'rith.

MISHA LOUVISH; writer; translator; journalist, Jerusalem.

ARNOLD MANDEL; essayist; novelist; reporter and literary critic, *Information Juive* and *L'Arche*, Paris.

NAOMI F. MEYER; co-director, Camp Ramah, Argentina.

MAYNARD MIRAN; research associate, Council of Jewish Federations and Welfare Funds.

FRIEDO SACHSER; political and news editor, *Allgemeine Jüdische Wochezeitung;* German correspondent, London *Jewish Chronicle,* Düsseldorf.

LEON SHAPIRO; professor emeritus, Russian and Soviet Jewish history, Rutgers University.

Table of Contents

Special
Articles

Jews, Nazis, and Civil Liberties

by DAVID G. DALIN

UNTIL THE BEGINNING OF THE 1970's it could be argued that the concern of some Jewish community leaders for the position of Jews in the United States was exaggerated. Antisemitism had largely disappeared in the years following World War II. Reaction to the atrocities of the Nazi era was such that even mildly antisemitic public utterances came to be viewed as unacceptable. The civic status of American Jews seemed more secure than ever before.

This "Golden Age" in American Jewish life has come to an end. American Jews have been experiencing a growing anxiety over various developments in the last decade, including the growth of Black Power, the emergence of quotas in employment and education, and the growth of Arab influence in the United States. The political climate of the country is clearly changing; there appears to be a growing indifference to Jewish concerns. Jews see themselves faced with new threats to their security.

Adding to the renewed sense of insecurity has been the much publicized activities of neo-Nazi groups, activities which the Jewish community has been unable to halt. While few in number,[1] the Nazis, evoking nightmarish memories of the Holocaust, have sent a shudder through American Jewry.

The progenitor of Nazism as we know it in the United States today is the American Nazi party, founded in 1959 by George Lincoln Rockwell. From his national headquarters in Arlington, Virginia, Rockwell controlled a small, but active, organization with units in Chicago, Los Angeles, San Francisco, Boston, Dallas and elsewhere. By the time of his assassination by a disgruntled Nazi party member in August 1967, Rockwell had become the "Fuehrer" of American Nazism.

Following Rockwell's death, a brief but intense leadership struggle took place, with a Milwaukee native, Matt Koehl, emerging as the head of the National Socialist White Peoples' party. (This name had been selected by Rockwell prior to his assassination as being more American and therefore more acceptable.) In 1970 several former Rockwell aides broke away from Koehl to form their own local Nazi groups. Among these men were Allen

---

[1]Total Nazi membership in the United States in 1977 was between 1,500 and 2,000. There were probably no more than 20 activists each in Chicago and San Francisco. See Milton Ellerin, "Intergroup Relations," AJYB, Vol. 79, 1979, p. 117.

Lee Vincent, who founded the National Socialist White Workers party (NSWWP) in San Francisco, and Frank Collin, who organized the National Socialist Party of America (NSPA) near Marquette Park, on Chicago's South Side. In the spring of 1977, it was Collin and Vincent who orchestrated the American Nazi movement's most publicized activities, when the former announced plans for a Nazi march through the predominantly Jewish suburb of Skokie, Illinois and the latter opened a Nazi bookstore across the street from a synagogue in San Francisco.

This article will focus on events in Skokie and San Francisco. In both cities the immediate targets of Nazi provocation were groups of Jewish survivors who had settled in the United States in the aftermath of the Holocaust. These Jews viewed the reappearance of the swastika in their midst as a direct threat to both American democracy and Jewish survival. Jews throughout the United States were outraged by the Nazi activities.

Events in Skokie and San Francisco, as well as other manifestations of neo-Nazism, have posed a painful dilemma for the American Jewish community. On the one hand, there has been a growing consensus among American Jews that Nazism, in any form, must not be allowed to reassert itself, and that the earlier Jewish communal strategy of ignoring the activities of virulently antisemitic groups is inappropriate and outdated. "Never Again" is no longer the slogan of the militant Jewish Defense League alone; as a response to the growing Holocaust consciousness of American Jewry, it is becoming the anti-Nazi rallying cry of the organized Jewish community as a whole.

On the other hand, American Jews have traditionally been staunch supporters of civil liberties, including the right to free speech and expression. In a major public opinion study conducted in 1954, Samuel Stouffer found that Jews were far more supportive of civil liberties than were members of other religious or ethnic groups.[2] This continues to be the case today, as both Everett Carll Ladd, Jr.[3] and Alan Fisher[4] have noted. The civil libertarian propensities of American Jews have resulted in a disproportionate Jewish involvement in the American Civil Liberties Union (ACLU), an organization traditionally committed to protecting and defending the First Amendment rights of all groups, including American Nazis.[5]

---

[2]Samuel Stouffer, *Communism, Conformity and Civil Liberties* (Garden City, 1955), p. 143. See also Lawrence H. Fuchs, *The Political Behavior of American Jews* (Glencoe, 1956), pp. 187–190.

[3]Everett Carll Ladd, Jr., "Jewish Life in the United States: Social and Political Values," paper delivered at YIVO Institute for Jewish Research Colloquium, New York City, May 28–29, 1978, pp. 31–32.

[4]Alan Fisher, "Continuity and Erosion of Jewish Liberalism," *American Jewish Historical Quarterly*, December 1976, pp. 330–334.

[5]Various explanations have been put forward to account for Jewish support for civil liberties. Some have pointed to Jewish religious values derived from biblical and talmudic antecedents

In the public debate over defending the rights of Nazis, many American Jews have been torn between their commitment to the principle of unfettered freedom of expression guaranteed by the First Amendment, and their anguished memory of the Holocaust. This has led them to rethink the meaning of the First Amendment, and the extent of their support of the ACLU. The First Amendment, many Jews now maintain, is not absolute. The public display of the swastika in a community of Holocaust survivors, they assert, constitutes a provocative act that goes far beyond the right to freedom of expression guaranteed by the First Amendment. During the past two years, thousands of American Jews have resigned in protest from the ACLU.

The anger of many Jews over the ACLU role in Skokie cannot be separated from their unhappiness with the general drift of ACLU policy in the last decade—a drift characterized by growing politicization, radical liberalism, and indifference to Jewish concerns. Whereas in the past most Jews supported liberal causes, including free speech for Nazis, even when they seemed to threaten Jewish interests and security, this is no longer the case.

SKOKIE AND SAN FRANCISCO

Skokie

On April 27, 1977 the Illinois chapter of the American Civil Liberties Union agreed to go to court on behalf of Frank Collin, who was seeking to organize a Nazi march through the predominantly Jewish suburb of Skokie. Attorneys for the Village of Skokie had just filed a petition against Collin in the Cook County Circuit Court requesting an injunction to prevent him from organizing the march. Collin claimed that his constitutional rights were being threatened and asked the ACLU to aid him in his legal defense.

A month earlier Collin and his followers had written to the Village of Skokie Park District seeking permission to hold a public rally in the Village park. The trustees of the Park District wrote back informing the Nazis that an insurance requirement for a rally was in force; Collin would have to produce $350,000 in insurance before a permit to hold the rally could be obtained. Since the Nazis were unable to pay this insurance requirement,

---

as the source. Charles S. Liebman has suggested that Jewish liberalism in general, and the Jewish commitment to civil liberties in particular, is rooted "in the search for a universalistic ethic to which a Jew can adhere but which is seemingly irrelevant to specific Jewish concerns . . ." See Charles Liebman, *The Ambivalent American Jew* (Philadelphia, 1973), pp. 135–159.

the permit was refused. To protest the Skokie Park District's requirement of insurance for permits, Collin announced that he and his followers planned to march down the streets of Skokie in full Nazi attire.

Skokie, a middle-class community north of Chicago, has a population of 69,000, approximately 40,000 of whom are Jews. Of these 40,000, about 7,000 are estimated to be Holocaust survivors. It has been said that there are more former concentration camp inmates living in Skokie than in any other single community in the United States. Thus, as Chicago Congressman Abner Mikva pointed out,[6] Skokie is more than a village which happens to be a part of suburban America. Its uniqueness lies not so much in its claim to be the world's largest village, but in the fact that it is a "sanctuary for thousands of Jewish Americans who still bear the scars of Hitler's Germany." For many of these people, the sense of community that they have been able to share has provided important emotional security.

It is not surprising that the ACLU defense of the Nazis aroused a strong reaction among the Jewish residents of Skokie. Frank Collin freely admitted that he and his followers deliberately chose to march "where our concept of white power is most opposed." In doing so, the Nazis hoped to precipitate a violent counter-demonstration, thus making themselves martyrs, and generating wide media attention. Collin compared his strategy to that of the civil rights protestors of the 1960's. Others have noted a similarity between this tactic and that of Great Britain's National Front, which deliberately targeted London's heavily Jewish East End as the site for antisemitic rallies. A spokesman for the Jewish United Fund and Welfare Federation of Metropolitan Chicago (JUF) called the Nazi plan "a deliberate and calculated" affront to the Jewish community of Chicago, an undisguised effort to provoke a violent confrontation. The residents of Skokie filed suit in Circuit Court to obtain an injunction against Collin, contending that even a few jack-booted storm troopers waving swastika flags in their streets threatened imminent violence.

The legal battle[7] over the proposed Nazi march in Skokie—initially scheduled for May 1 and subsequently rescheduled for July 4—officially began on April 28, 1977, when Circuit Court Judge Joseph M. Wosik imposed an injunction banning the march. On April 29 the Appellate Court

---

[6]Abner Mikva, "Skokie is Different," *Moment,* June 1978, p. 43.
[7]The narrative of events in Skokie is developed from a number of sources: Marc Stern, "The Dilemma of Skokie: Protecting Civil Liberties or Curbing the Nazis?" *Research Report,* Institute of Jewish Affairs, London, August 1978, pp. 3–6; David Hamlin, "Swastikas and Survivors: Inside the Skokie-Nazi Free Speech Case," *Civil Liberties Review,* March-April 1978, pp. 8–33; and selected Jewish Telegraphic Agency *Daily News Bulletins,* 1977 and 1978.

of Illinois rejected the Nazi petition to temporarily lift the injunction while Collin and his followers, with the aid of the ACLU, endeavored to appeal the legality of the ban in the courts.

While the ACLU appeal on behalf of the Nazis with regard to the Skokie injunction was pending, the Village of Skokie enacted three new ordinances designed to insure that the Nazis would not be able to march regardless of the outcome of the case. One ordinance required a permit, issued by Village officials, for street or sidewalk parades. In order to obtain such a permit, the applicant had to provide 30 days advance notice and payment of $350,000 in liability insurance against any possible damage. A second ordinance banned the public display of symbols offensive to the community and political rallies or parades in which participants wore "military style" uniforms. A third ordinance banned the dissemination of literature which might "incite or promote hatred against persons of Jewish faith or ancestry" or against persons of any other race or religion, or which in any way constituted "group libel." Once again the ACLU entered the case on the side of the Nazis.

During the same period, Skokie resident Sol Goldstein instituted, with the legal assistance of the Anti-Defamation League of B'nai B'rith, a class action suit seeking a permanent injunction against the Nazis, claiming that he and his fellow Holocaust survivors in the community would suffer "severe emotional distress" and "psychic" harm if the march were held. Goldstein's attorney, Jerome Torshen, argued that "menticide" could create emotional damage every bit as injurious as physical assault. The ACLU, again representing the Nazis, demanded that Goldstein's suit be dismissed, on the grounds that if speech or other expression that was emotionally painful to individuals or abhorrent to the majority were suppressed little would be left of the freedom of expression protected under the First Amendment.[8] While the Illinois Supreme Court subsequently ordered, without the benefit of full written or oral arguments, the dismissal of the Goldstein class action suit, it stayed the order so as to allow Goldstein time to petition the United States Supreme Court for a review of the decision.[9] The Nazis, announcing that they would not march until all legal obstacles had been eliminated, then called off their July 4 demonstration.

Prior to the cancellation of the Nazi rally, the organized Jewish community of metropolitan Chicago had begun to organize itself to combat the Nazis. A special Sub-Committee on Individual Liberty and Jewish Security of the Public Affairs Committee (PAC) of JUF was established to formulate a community response. The chairman of the sub-committee was Sol

---

[8]Stern, *loc. cit.*, p. 3.

[9]The U.S. Supreme Court subsequently refused to review the Illinois Supreme Court's dismissal, thus upholding the lower court's decision in the Goldstein suit.

Goldstein, who, in addition to having instituted the above-mentioned class action suit, was a former president of the Skokie Holocaust Survivors Association. "There is no room in my backyard for such a demonstration," stated Goldstein. "I went through the Holocaust . . . and I thought the war was the end of the Nazi movement." Goldstein and his neighbors in Skokie, active in the newly-formed PAC sub-committee, argued that the First Amendment "can only be stretched so far." Nazism, he stated, "is an idea the whole civilized world has condemned. When the First Amendment was introduced, they never thought of such a thing as genocide."[10] During the next year, Goldstein and his neighbors played a prominent role in Jewish communal decision-making vis-à-vis the Nazis.

With the threatened July 4 Nazi march called off, PAC, in an effort to reduce tensions, cancelled a scheduled counter-demonstration at a Jewish community center in Skokie. Against the wishes of the PAC leadership, however, the militant Jewish Defense League (JDL) went ahead with its own plans to hold a protest rally in Skokie on July 4. Speaking at the rally, Rabbi Meir Kahane, the JDL leader, exhorted a crowd of about 400 to "kill Nazis now." The JDL held its rally in the parking lot of the Jewish Community Center after having been refused permission to use the building. Sol Goldstein denounced the JDL for stirring up fears that the Nazis would eventually win their ongoing court battle to march. Rabbi Lawrence Montrose of the Skokie Central Traditional Congregation, the unofficial chaplain of the Village's death camp survivors, agreed with Goldstein, stating that, although he wanted to confront the Nazis with a "good strong protest," he was opposed to the violent tactics of the Jewish Defense League. By their actions, Montrose argued, the JDL made it more difficult to forge unity within the Jewish community and to form an anti-Nazi coalition with non-Jewish groups.

The court battle over the Nazis' right to march in Skokie continued for more than a year—through June 1978. On March 17, 1978 Judge Bernard M. Decker of the Federal District Court in Chicago ordered a 45-day ban on the proposed march, to allow Skokie officials time to appeal his earlier ruling holding the three anti-Nazi ordinances unconstitutional. On April 2 the Federal Court of Appeals in Chicago upheld the Decker ruling prohibiting the Nazis from marching before May. However, on April 6 the Circuit Court of Appeals reversed the District Court decision and set aside the 45-day stay, stating that there was no reason for such a postponement since it intended to decide promptly on the constitutionality of the three Skokie ordinances. On May 22 the Circuit Court of Appeals ruled that the Skokie ordinances were unconstitutional. Skokie officials then appealed the ruling

---

[10]Kathryn McIntyre, "One Man's War with Nazis," *US Magazine*, April 18, 1978, p. 56.

to the U.S. Supreme Court, which, on June 12, turned down the Village's request for an indefinite postponement of the June 25 march. At the same time, two anti-Nazi bills that had been introduced in the Illinois State Legislature were defeated in the House after being passed in the Senate. The march in Skokie, it seemed, would go on.

On May 31 the Village of Skokie Council had issued a permit to PAC to stage a counter-demonstration in Skokie on June 25. Plans were announced for providing facilities for 50,000 demonstrators. PAC allocated $100,000 to underwrite expenses, including the hiring of staff to administer and coordinate all related activities in Skokie. Eugene DuBow, on leave from his position as midwest regional director of the American Jewish Committee, became the coordinator of the project, working closely with Goldstein and members of the PAC sub-committee. Goldstein announced that after discussions with Skokie officials, PAC had accepted the athletic field of Niles Township East as the site for the Jewish community's counter-demonstration.

A broad-based coalition of Jewish and non-Jewish groups made plans to participate in the demonstration. The American Federation of Jewish Fighters, Camp Inmates and Nazi Victims announced that it would send busloads of its members to Skokie; it publicly urged other Jewish organizations to do likewise. Marvin Morrison, executive director of the New York department of the Jewish War Veterans, sent mailgrams to 100,000 JWV members urging them to be in Skokie on June 25. Congressmen from both major parties announced their intention to join in the anti-Nazi march. Support was also received from labor, veteran, and ethnic groups, among them Polish Catholic army veterans who had fought against the Nazis in World War II. An *ad hoc* coalition of 43 Chicago-area ethnic groups including Poles, Lithuanians, Ukranians, and Byelorussians, announced strong support for the anti-Nazi demonstration. Julian E. Kulas, local Ukranian community leader and spokesman for the coalition, announced that it would stand by the Jews of Skokie "in order to make it crystal clear that Nazism is a threat not only to Jews but to all Americans."[11]

The 25-member planning committee coordinating "Project Skokie" included James Rottman, director of the National Conference of Christians and Jews, and several Christian clergymen from the Skokie area. The committee issued a call to religious leaders to support the march and to condemn Nazism as contrary to the Judaeo-Christian tradition and the ideals of American democracy. Sister Ann Gillen, executive director of the National Interreligious Task Force on Soviet Jewry, convened a meeting of Chicago-area Catholic leaders that pledged "persistent action" against the

---

[11]Chicago *Sun Times,* June 20, 1978, p. 12.

Nazis in Chicago and elsewhere. An editorial in the April issue of *St. Anthony's Messenger,* a national Catholic magazine, urged Christians throughout the United States to don the yellow Star of David that Jews had been forced to wear during the Nazi era, as a way of protesting the march. Groups of evangelical Christians planned to travel to Skokie to join the protest as well.

A few days before the June 25 Nazi march, Collin announced that his group was cancelling its planned demonstration in Skokie and would march instead in the racially-mixed area of Marquette Park. This change in strategy was attributable, ostensibly, to a ruling by a federal judge ordering the Chicago Park District to allow the Nazis to hold a rally in Marquette Park without being forced to pay the $60,000 liability insurance—reduced from an earlier $350,000—required by the district. Marquette Park, Collin now claimed, had been his original target area all along. "My overall goal always was Marquette Park, speaking to my own white people rather than a mob of howling creatures in the streets of Skokie." Few believed him, however, assuming rather that the Nazis had been scared away by the specter of 50,000 counter-demonstrators. PAC called off its counter-demonstration shortly after the Nazis announced cancellation of their plans. When the Nazi rally was held in Marquette Park on July 9, anti-Nazi demonstrators, largely unorganized, were kept two blocks away, and no violence erupted.

San Francisco

Five days before the beginning of Passover, 1977, Rabbi Theodore Alexander of Congregation B'nai Emunah, a small synagogue composed mainly of Holocaust survivors, in the predominantly middle-class Sunset district of San Francisco, arrived at his office to find that a Nazi bookstore had opened across the street. To mark the opening of the store, named after Hitler confidante Rudolf Hess, the Nazis erected a swastika in front of the building and displayed a picture of Hess, other Nazi insignia, and anti-Jewish posters in the store window. Several days later an angry crowd of Jews armed with sledgehammers and crowbars ransacked and destroyed the bookstore. A few hours later, five stained glass windows at Congregation B'nai Emunah were smashed, apparently as an act of retaliation. Morris Weiss, a Holocaust survivor, and his son Allan were subsequently arrested for leading the assault on the Nazi store.

The bookstore incident was by no means the first in which local Nazis were the cause of public confrontation and controversy. Since early 1974 the San Francisco chapter of the National Socialist White People's Party, of which Alan Vincent was the leader, had been disrupting public meetings of the San Francisco Board of Education. The Nazis had organized several rallies at public sites at which virulently antisemitic literature was distributed. Moreover, a local *cause célèbre* had developed around Sandra Silva, an avowed Nazi who was employed as a clerk-typist in the San Francisco Police Department.

On one side of the debate in the Silva case was the ACLU, supported by San Francisco Mayor Joseph Alioto, which strongly defended Silva's constitutional right to "maintain her belief" without jeopardizing her job. On the other side were a number of Jewish and Black groups, led by Jewish city supervisor Quentin Kopp,[12] which argued that Silva's anti-democratic beliefs did conflict with the performance of her job. At first, the possibility was raised that she might be dismissed on the basis of her Nazi ideology alone. But that debate ended when the San Francisco Civil Service Commission came to Silva's defense, stating that her party affiliation did not interfere with her performance at work.[13]

A subsequent public furor developed over the question whether Silva had violated a Civil Service residency law requiring city employees to live in the city and might, therefore, be subject to dismissal. This was the argument of Supervisor Kopp, who claimed that he had hard evidence from several sources, including a private investigator, that Silva had been living in San Mateo. Kopp asked the Civil Service Commission to institute dismissal proceedings against her. Following Kopp's request, the ACLU came to Silva's defense. Ruth Jacobs, an attorney with the local ACLU and the wife of radical author-activist Paul Jacobs, charged that Kopp was raising a totally irrelevant issue—i.e., the residency rule—"in an attempt to deprive Silva of her right to free speech under the First Amendment." The ACLU maintained that Silva was "temporarily" residing with her parents in San Mateo and was therefore not in violation of the city's residency requirement. "If Kopp feels that she should be fired because of political beliefs," suggested Jacobs, "it is his privilege to pursue that unlawful course. But he should not use the dubious device of questioning her residency. What Kopp is attempting through this investigation is to punish Miss Silva, by having her fired, for exercising her First Amendment rights."[14] In response, Kopp charged that the ACLU had "smeared me in exactly the fashion used by Joe McCarthy 20 years ago by ascribing false motives to my actions," and that "the ACLU's statement showed a lack of knowledge of the city's residency law and how it applies to Miss Silva . . . I'm not depriving her

---

[12]Kopp is a former member of the ACLU. He resigned in protest over the organization's growing politicization. Interview with Quentin Kopp, April 24, 1978.

[13]New York *Times,* August 4, 1974, p. 37.

[14]San Francisco *Examiner,* July 16, 1974, p. 1.

of free speech, but acting in response to complaints from constituents who believe the [residency] law should be enforced."[15]

The opening of the Rudolf Hess bookstore, housed ironically in a building owned by a Jewish survivor of Auschwitz, caused great public outrage. "San Francisco is one of the nation's most tolerant cities," editorialized the San Francisco *Examiner*, "but a terminal point was reached when a group of American Nazis tried to revive Hitlerism with all its horrors . . . The ransacking and burning of the store was inevitable . . ."[16] Reacting to the incident, the San Francisco Board of Supervisors unanimously passed a resolution urging the introduction of a bill in the state legislature to outlaw public display of the swastika and the wearing of Nazi uniforms. (Three years earlier, the Board of Supervisors had failed in an attempt to ban the wearing of a Nazi uniform in public. See below pp. 22–3.) Introduced by Supervisor Dianne Feinstein (who in November 1978 became mayor), the resolution stated: "The Board of Supervisors is of the opinion that the wearing of the Nazi uniform and the display of the Nazi swastika will continue to provoke acts of violence and fear for the public safety."[17] Supervisor Feinstein went further in voicing public sympathy for those who destroyed the bookstore: "I conceivably could have done the same thing if it had been in my neighborhood," she said. "In Nazi Germany the same things existed and people laughed. Then suddenly the Nazis were in power."[18] Feinstein's sentiments were echoed in statements by Rabbi Alexander and other leaders of the Jewish community. "I've heard that it would impair the right of free speech and the right of free assembly," noted Rabbi Alexander in urging passage of the bill. "I've heard it should not be voted and should not be passed . . . But when they dispense hate against other Americans, that can no longer fall under the right of free expression. It becomes an entirely different story. It is no longer political. It becomes incitement to hatred and murder."[19]

With the help of the Jewish Community Relations Council (JCRC), the landlord of the building housing the bookstore obtained legal counsel to have the Nazis evicted. The basis of the eviction order was misrepresentation, and they were given until April 15 to vacate the premises. At the same time, friends of the Weiss family hired attorney Ephraim Margolin to represent Morris and Allan Weiss.[20] (They also organized a legal defense fund, the Sunset Anti-Fascist Committee, to raise the money needed to

---

[15]San Francisco *Chronicle*, July 18, 1974, p. 3.
[16]San Francisco *Examiner*, April 5, 1977, p. 26.
[17]San Francisco *Jewish Bulletin*, May 13, 1977, p. 5.
[18]San Francisco *Examiner*, April 5, 1977, p. 5.
[19]*Ibid.*
[20]The charges against the Weisses were subsequently dropped.

# #

cover the Weisses' court expenses.) The choice of Margolin as the Weisses' counsel was significant, since he, a graduate of the Hebrew University and Yale Law School, had become one of the leading civil liberties attorneys in the city. As chairman of the Legal Committee of the Northern California chapter of the ACLU, Margolin had impeccable credentials in the civil liberties field. At the same time, he was an important figure in the organized Jewish community—an officer of the American Jewish Congress, JCRC, Bureau of Jewish Education, and Jewish Welfare Federation.

Adding to the anger in the San Francisco Jewish community over the bookstore incident was the insensitivity shown in some quarters as to the meaning of Nazism. A local television station, in a broadcast editorial about the bookstore confrontation, stated that the "anti-Nazis," i.e., those Jews who had attacked the bookstore, "exhibited a mentality as ruthless and primitive as the one they were attacking." "In that fashion," noted Earl Raab, the director of JCRC, "was the calculated demolition of millions of people equated with the minor property damage done by some of its angry victims. Even those who most disapproved of the trashing knew that there was something pathological about that equation as the main burden of a T.V. editorial."[21] In a televised rebuttal to the station's editorial, noted attorney and JCRC chairman Mathew Weinberg argued that trashing of the bookstore "was not an organized action; it was a spontaneous act of rage against Nazi symbols by relatives of those who were tortured and killed under the aegis of those symbols. I do not defend violence, even against property . . . But to turn the bookstore episode into a primary attack against the principles of Nazi butchery is a strange inversion of values and an affront to our common sense. But more than that, the editorial was a depressing sign that we have forgotten the horror which led America to fight a bloody war."[22]

During the same period, Jewish leaders in San Francisco met with the management of a different local television station to protest another Nazi-related incident. While being interviewed by the station, Nazi party chief Vincent stated that at certain times during the year, American Jews "commit their blood sacrifice" and "Christian children begin to disappear from the streets." The station received a large quantity of mail criticizing its editorial judgement in allowing the infamous "blood libel" to go unchallenged on public television. "By what measure of editorial judgement," asked one Jewish communal leader, "had this hoary and gratuitous slander

[21]Earl Raab, "The Insensitives—'Neutral' on Anti-Semitism," *Midstream*, August-September, 1978, p. 59.
[22]Mathew Weinberg, "Rebuttal," editorial on "Freedom of Speech," May 4–5, 1977, transcribed and reprinted by KGO-T.V., San Francisco.

been allowed to remain in this filmed interview?" The station management's explanation, that there was no "malicious intent" on its part, and that it was merely being "neutral" in reporting the opinions of newsworthy individuals, seemed to many Jews to represent precisely the kind of indifference to antisemitism that made it possible for Nazi activity to continue.

Throughout 1977 and 1978, much time was spent by the San Francisco Jewish Community Relations Council in discussing ways of counteracting Nazi activity while, at the same time, protecting First Amendment guarantees of freedom of speech and assembly. A lawyer's committee began to examine possible legislation which might limit Nazi activity and propaganda in a number of specific situations. In January 1978 a community-wide Committee for Continuing Education Against Nazism was organized under the auspices of the San Francisco Conference on Religion, Race and Social Concerns. The committee was headed by San Francisco Mayor George Moscone and included Protestant, Catholic, and Jewish clergy, as well as civic and business leaders.

FREE SPEECH AND THE NAZIS

The First Amendment to the United States Constitution states that "Congress shall make no law . . . abridging the freedom of speech . . . or the right of the people peacefully to assemble and to petition the government for redress of grievances." The First Amendment, however, is by no means absolute; it has never been so interpreted by a majority of the United States Supreme Court. The view that the Constitution does not protect all forms of speech was most powerfully expressed by Justice Oliver Wendell Holmes, Jr. in his now classic dictum that "the most stringent protection of free speech would not protect a man in falsely shouting fire in a crowded theater." Over the past six decades a substantial body of legal opinion has developed which stresses that those forms of speech and public expression that are "provocative" or injurious can indeed be restricted. Thus, Professor Philip B. Kurland of the University of Chicago Law School, in supporting the constitutionality of Skokie's position vis-à-vis the Nazis, has observed that "no one denies the value of protecting the right to speak. But this does not mean that all speech is protected speech or that the context of the speech is irrelevant to the protection required to be afforded by the State."[23] Indeed, in at least one instance even the ACLU has refused to uphold the rights of Nazis to absolute freedom of speech. In May 1978 the Houston, Texas ACLU chapter voted not to aid

---

[23]Quoted in Mikva, *loc. cit.*, p. 46.

a Nazi group whose recorded telephone message had been cut off by a court injunction. The message had offered a $5,000 bounty for "every non-white killed during an attack on a white person." "Offering a bounty or a tangible incentive for murder," commented ACLU executive director Aryeh Neier, "is not protected by the First Amendment."[24]

The precedent cited most authoritatively by the courts on this matter is the landmark case of *Chaplinsky v. New Hampshire* (1942). As Justice Murphy stated on behalf of the unanimous court:

> There are certain well-defined and narrowly limited classes of speech, the prevention and punishment of which have never been thought to raise any constitutional problem. These include the lewd and obscene, the profane, the libelous, and the insulting or "fighting" words—those which by their utterance inflict injury or tend to incite an immediate breach of the peace. It has been well observed that such utterances are no essential part of any exposition of ideas, and are of such slight social value as a step to truth that any benefit that may derive from them is clearly outweighed by the social interest in order and morality.[25]

Legal precedent for the restriction of provocative and defamatory speech can similarly be found in the 1951 opinion of Justice Robert Jackson in the case of *Kunz v. New York*: Kunz, a Baptist minister, had been convicted and fined for holding a religious meeting on the streets of New York without a permit. Pointing out that Kunz's public meetings had included attacks on Catholics and Jews, Jackson argued that "to blanket hateful and hate-stirring attacks on races and faiths under the protections for freedom of speech may be a noble innovation. On the other hand, it may be a quixotic tilt at windmills which belittles great principles of liberty." It made "a world of difference," Jackson maintained, that Kunz had been speaking in street meetings, since that posed the question whether New York was required to place its streets at his service "to hurl insults at the passerby." Jackson suggested that this case fell within the "fighting words" doctrine of the *Chaplinsky* case.[26]

The legal debate over Skokie has centered around the doctrine of "fighting words" first enunciated in *Chaplinsky*.[27] Opposition to the Nazi march has been based on the fact that the Village of Skokie is heavily Jewish, with a substantial number of "survivors," and that a Nazi march through its streets would thus be a deliberate effort to utter "fighting

---

[24]Interview with Aryeh Neier, April 5, 1978.

[25]*Chaplinsky v. New Hampshire,* 1942. For an interesting discussion of the Chaplinsky ruling see Hadley Arkes, "Civility and the Restriction of Speech: Rediscovering the Defamation of Groups," in Philip B. Kurland (ed.), *Free Speech and Association: The Supreme Court and the First Amendment* (Chicago, 1975), pp. 414–22.

[26]David Fellman, "Constitutional Rights of Association," in Philip B. Kurland, *Ibid.,* p. 44.

[27]See Aryeh Neier, *Defending My Enemy* (New York, 1979), *passim.*

words" and provoke public disorder. Many Jews who agreed with the ACLU on the question of freedom of speech generally—even for Nazis and other antisemites—differed over the proposed march in Skokie. In their opinion, a parade by uniformed stormtroopers, complete with jackboots and swastika armbands, was nothing short of a direct provocation, and thus was excluded from the protective umbrella of the First Amendment.

In July 1977, the Illinois Appellate Court invoked the "fighting words" doctrine to uphold the local injunction barring the Nazi march. "The swastika," the court declared, "is a personal affront to every member of the Jewish faith. It calls to mind the nearly consummated genocide of their people committed within memory by those who used the swastika as their symbol . . . The epithets of racial and religious hatred are not protected speech." Thus, the public display of the swastika, in the view of the Illinois Court, constituted "symbolic speech," which, being the equivalent of "fighting words," could legitimately be curtailed. The ACLU, arguing that the Appellate Court based its decision on a "novel" and entirely unwarranted interpretation of the *Chaplinsky* case, appealed on behalf of the Nazis first to the Illinois Supreme Court and then to the U.S. Supreme Court for a stay of injunction. The swastika, it maintained, is "symbolic speech" just as fully protected by the First Amendment as the wearing of black arm bands during the Vietnam war. The state, the ACLU claimed, does not have the power to decide which symbols are permissible and which are not. In taking this position, the ACLU was following the direction of the Supreme Court in recent years, as a majority of the Court had attempted to narrow the interpretation of *Chaplinsky* by suggesting that there is no way to effectively distinguish between forms of speech—real or symbolic—that are provocative or injurious and those that are neutral or inoffensive. In its 1971 decision in *Cohen v. California,* and in subsequent rulings, the Supreme Court made it more difficult to uphold anti-Nazi municipal ordinances on grounds of "provocative" speech.

The judges who ruled in favor of the Nazis indicated that it was the "burden" of the Skokie residents to avoid "the offensive symbol if they can do so without unreasonable inconvenience." Presumably, then, it would be the responsibility of the Holocaust survivors living in Skokie to stay indoors while the Nazis marched through their village. At the very least they would have to avoid the City Hall area around which the march would be centered. The "burden" of the Holocaust survivors in San Francisco, whose B'nai Emunah synagogue was directly across the street from the Nazi bookstore, would be much greater; they could avoid the public display of the swastika in their midst only by ceasing to attend the synagogue. Would

JEWS, NAZIS, AND CIVIL LIBERTIES / 17

such "inconveniences," some wondered, not constitute an infringement of Jewish civil rights?[28]

The Supreme Court and ACLU opinion that the swastika is "symbolic speech" deserving of protection under the First Amendment was challenged on a variety of grounds. For years the ACLU has argued that the best test of truth is the power of an idea to get itself accepted in the marketplace of ideas. Yet, one may ask, as have George Will, Hadley Arkes, and other critics of the ACLU position, what unresolved issue exists in the marketplace of ideas that the Nazis may help to settle. "If we restrict the speech of Nazis," Arkes has asked, "is it conceivable that we may shield ourselves from ideas that may turn out one day to be valid? Is it possible, for example, that a convincing case could yet be made for genocide if people were given a bit more time to develop the argument?"[29] George Will maintains that the marketplace is not a good place to test truth, since it "measures preferences (popularity), not truth. Liberals say all ideas have an equal right to compete in the market. But the right to compete implies the right to win. So the logic of liberalism is that it is better to be ruled by Nazis than to restrict them."[30]

Those who oppose the ACLU position maintain that the organization's First Amendment rights of Nazis is a betrayal of its basic civil liberties function. "The overriding purpose of the ACLU," argued Florida State University economist Abba P. Lerner in a letter to the New York *Times,* "is to promote and defend a democratic social order in which freedom of speech is secure. If this purpose comes into conflict with the freedom of speech directed at destroying such a social order, their obligation is surely to protect the social order of free speech rather than the free speech of its destroyers."[31] Through its staunch defense of the Nazis, these critics assert, the ACLU is helping to undermine the cause of civil liberties and liberal democracy itself. "The irony," notes Arkes, "is that the ACLU sees itself as defending at this moment the freedom of a minority, but the principles on which it mounts that defense would cut the ground out from under constitutional government itself and, in that sense, would also imperil the freedom of all minorities."

Some of those opposing the ACLU position point out that the Nazis do not merely insist on their right to advocate freely the denial of freedom to others but anticipate, and receive, free legal assistance in support of their

---

[28]This point is made by Marie Syrkin in "Sadat, Skokie and Cosmos 954," *Midstream,* March 1978, pp. 65–66.

[29]Hadley Arkes, "Marching Through Skokie," *National Review,* May 12, 1978, p. 593.

[30]George F. Will, "Nazis: Outside the Constitution," Washington *Post,* February 2, 1978, p. A19.

[31]New York *Times,* March 20, 1978, p. 20.

right to do so. Those taking this position concede that the Nazis have a right to march, but maintain that the ACLU, given its limited resources, should not provide the Nazis with free legal representation. The ACLU, they point out, turns away a number of cases in which civil liberties have been denied simply because it is unable to find the lawyers to handle them and unable to pay the costs of the litigation. Why, therefore, permit any part of the ACLU's scarce funds to be wasted on the Nazis? As one such critic of the ACLU position, labor union leader Victor Gotbaum, has put it: "If you want to ask me if Nazis ought to march through Skokie, I'd say 'Yes,' but if you ask me if the ACLU . . . should put its resources to work for them, I say, 'No.' "[32]

In a reply to a letter by Aryeh Neier in the New York *Jewish Week,* one writer stated: "I cannot agree that it is not 'a clear and present danger' for demonstrators to deliberately provoke an outraged people into violence. It is far too much to expect Jews sensitive to the Nazi Holocaust to react dispassionately to an organized Nazi provocation in a Jewish neighborhood, just as it would be too much to expect the people of Harlem to be judicious about an organized anti-Black provocation in their area. Shouldn't there be a distinction in law and law-enforcement between demonstrators for realization of constitutional rights and demonstrators who seek to destroy constitutional rights for others?"[33] Most American Jews clearly thought there should. Thus, by 1978 the search for an effective anti-Nazi legal strategy was well under way. In both San Francisco and Chicago, lawyers' committees were formed within the Jewish community to explore possible group libel legislation or other legal action that might limit Nazi activity in a number of specific situations. At the May 1978 annual meeting of the American Jewish Committee, Hadley Arkes made an eloquent plea for the desirability of enacting group libel legislation aimed at the Nazis. He sat down to a standing ovation, a far different response from that he would have received from a comparable audience in the 1960's. Maynard Wishner, the AJC Board of Governors chairman, echoed the changing sentiments of many members when he observed: "This proposed march represents an obscenity. Saying 'We aren't finished with you' or 'Hitler was right' goes beyond the pale of what we should expect under the First Amendment."[34] There was a similar shift of opinion within the American Jewish Congress. In 1960 the Congress had agreed that Nazis should be permitted to hold a rally in New York City. In 1978 the Congress, "after long and heated

[32]Quoted in Fred Ferretti, "The Buck Stops With Gotbaum," *New York Times Magazine,* June 4, 1978, p. 89.

[33]Phineas Stone, New York *Jewish Week,* August 7, 1977, p. 14.

[34]Maynard Wishner, "American Nazis and the First Amendment," *Sh'ma,* May 27, 1977, p. 136.

internal discussion," urged the U.S. Supreme Court to prohibit Nazis from marching through Skokie wearing Nazi uniforms "which identify them as implementing the evil objectives of Hitlerism."[35]

THE CRISIS WITHIN THE ACLU

The ACLU's decision to defend Chicago Nazi leader Frank Collin resulted in the most serious crisis in the organization's history, a crisis from which, some believe, it may never recover.[36] ACLU officials indicate that 40,000 members, out of a total membership of 250,000, resigned from the organization in 1977. In 1978 there were additional heavy membership losses. The resulting financial pinch led to a 15 per cent cut in the national ACLU staff, and a corresponding cut on the local level.

Not surprisingly, the loss of membership and income was most dramatic in the Chicago area. David Hamlin, executive director of the ACLU's Illinois affiliate, stated in August 1977: "We've projected that we'll lose 25 per cent of our Illinois membership and our financial support because of this Nazi-Skokie case." It is safe to assume that the majority of those resigning from the ACLU were Jews.[37]

During 1977 and 1978, ACLU staff officials made a concerted effort to broaden support for their position on Skokie within the Jewish community. Executive Director Aryeh Neier, while freely admitting his lack of involvement in Jewish affairs, spoke with pride of his Jewish background and reminded audiences that he and his parents had been refugees from the Nazis. National Chairman Norman Dorsen, a Jewish professor of law at

[35]Stern, *loc. cit.,* p. 6, and American Jewish Congress press release, Feb. 2, 1978, p. 1.

[36]Jim Mann, "Hard Times for the ACLU," *The New Republic,* April 15, 1978, pp. 12–15. The decline in ACLU membership since 1976 is not attributable solely to the Skokie controversy. A good many ACLU members were outraged by the organization's decision to defend Ku Klux Klan members stationed at the Marine Corps base at Camp Pendleton, California, after they were attacked by a group of Black marines in November 1976. See J. Anthony Lukas, "The ACLU Against Itself," *New York Times Magazine,* July 9, 1978, p. 11.

[37]Not all groups in the Jewish community thought it wise for Jews to disassociate themselves. The Union of American Hebrew Congregation's Commission on Social Action of Reform Judaism stated that "one can disagree strongly with the approach of the ACLU, but it would be destructive of our deepest Jewish interests to contribute to the weakening and undermining of the ACLU on the American scene." This position was also supported by the Central Conference of American Rabbis, the Reform rabbinic group. See Albert Vorspan, memo on "Skokie," Commission on Social Action of Reform Judaism, Union of American Hebrew Congregations, June 15, 1978. The UAHC position is further developed in its "Working Paper on Skokie," on file at the Commission on Social Action of Reform Judaism, Union of American Hebrew Congregations, New York City.

New York University, presented the ACLU case to the Domestic Affairs Commission of the American Jewish Committee. Neier, Dorsen and other ACLU leaders indicated that the angry Jewish response to the ACLU role in Skokie took them by surprise, since the organization had a long-standing policy of defending freedom of speech for Nazis.

Why did Jews, both within and outside the organization, react so strongly to the ACLU role in Skokie? Certainly the crucial factor was the burgeoning Holocaust consciousness of American Jews; the feeling that, no matter what, Nazism must never again be permitted to lift its head. At the same time, Jewish anger over the ACLU defense of the Nazis has to be seen in the context of a growing Jewish disillusionment with the general drift of the organization's policies.

Until the early 1960's the ACLU was a relatively small (45,000 members) organization, heavily concentrated in New York and devoted primarily to filing *amicae curiae* briefs in free speech and other First Amendment cases. Since that time, however, the Union has been transformed into a "mass organization with a large professional staff, involved in a wide range of concerns, of which fundamental civil liberties issues such as free speech and free assembly are only a small part."[38] It was the Vietnam war that first thrust the organization into the political and social arena. When Dr. Benjamin Spock was indicted for counseling draft evasion, the national ACLU Board agreed to take the case, although a number of members voiced concern that such a step would result in the organization's defending Spock's politics, rather than his civil liberties. In 1970 Aryeh Neier was elected executive director as the "candidate of the left"; he was responsible for pushing the organization in a more political direction.[39] Following the Cambodian invasion and the Kent State incident the ACLU, under Neier's direction, passed a resolution calling for the "immediate termination" of the war, a popular political stance that won the organization thousands of new members. In 1973, after an acrimonious internal debate, the ACLU became the first major national organization to call for Richard Nixon's impeachment. By the mid-1970's the politicization of the ACLU had, in many respects, become the salient feature of its organizational life.

Jewish involvement in the ACLU had been conspicuous and consistent since the organization's founding in 1920.[40] Among those playing a direct

---

[38]Mann, *loc. cit.,* p. 13. See also Joseph W. Bishop, Jr., "Politics and the ACLU," *Commentary,* December 1971, pp. 50–58.

[39]J. Anthony Lukas, *loc. cit.,* p. 20.

[40]In recounting the history of the ACLU, Roger Baldwin, the guiding spirit behind the organization, stated that he could not "remember a time from when [he] first began when there was not a very strong Jewish presence" in the ACLU. See Interview with Roger Baldwin, November 16, 1973, p. 16, on file at William E. Wiener Oral History Collection, American Jewish Committee.

role in establishing the ACLU were Felix Frankfurter, Stephen Wise, and Arthur Garfield Hayes. Louis Marshall, while not a card-carrying member, argued several cases on the ACLU's behalf during the 1920's, as did his law partner Samuel Untermeyer. Morris Ernst, who was instrumental in organizing both the American Newspaper Guild and National Lawyer's Guild during the 1930's, served as ACLU general counsel for many years. In 1937, when the ACLU first engaged in the legal defense of Nazis, it was Ernst and Hays who urged Mayor La Guardia of New York to approve the use of city property for a Nazi meeting. Hays also aided the attorney for the (Nazi) Friends of New Germany in court proceedings appealing a prohibition of meetings by that group in New Jersey. In 1955 Osmond K. Fraenkel, who had assisted Ernst in preparing the defense for the Scottsboro case, became general counsel to the ACLU. In the 1960's and 1970's Aryeh Neier played a crucial role in the organization. Many staff attorneys and affiliate executives, including David Goldberger in Chicago and David Fishlow and Ruth Jacobs in San Francisco, are Jewish. When Neier resigned as executive director in October 1978, Ira Glasser, a New Yorker, running against Marvin Schacter of Los Angeles, was elected to succeed him.

Despite the large number of Jews in leadership positions in the ACLU during the latter half of the 1960's and throughout the 1970's, the organization manifested a cold indifference to the concerns of the Jewish community. Neier and his Jewish colleagues were representative of a "new politics" oriented group of civil rights attorneys and social policy experts for whom the ethnic concerns of Jews—whether the welfare of the State of Israel, or the institutional needs of the Jewish community, or just the protective comfort of political representation—were at best a peripheral matter. The focus of their attention was the political agenda and rhetoric of the New Left, Black Power and the Third World. Thus, it is not surprising that on issue after issue, between 1966 and 1978, the ACLU took a stand that was seen by many as being inimicable to Jewish interests. The ACLU, for example, supported the proposal by the Lindsay administration in New York City to establish a civilian review board for the police department. During the New York City teachers' strike, the organization backed demands by Black militants for community control of the schools. The ACLU came to the defense of the openly anti-Jewish Black Panthers in their confrontations with the police. Finally, the ACLU opposed Marco De Funis and Alan Bakke in their suits charging reverse discrimination.

Against the background of the ACLU's drift to the left and its indifference to the Jewish communal agenda, the organization's defense of the

Nazis appeared to many Jews as the final insult. Small wonder that the ACLU suffered significant membership losses.

COMBATTING THE NAZIS: THE LEGISLATIVE FRONT

In Jewish communal circles throughout the United States much effort has been made over the past few years to develop a legal strategy to combat Nazism in America. The enactment of effective anti-Nazi legislation, however, has proved to be no simple matter. Indeed, the inability to pass such legislation has been a source of frustration and concern to Jewish communal leaders.

The experience in San Francisco offers insight into the difficulties that arise in attempting to combat Nazis by legal means.[41] During the early months of 1974, as was noted above, Nazi party members began to sit in on public meetings of the city's Board of Education. Despite the heated objections of Jews and Blacks in the audience, to whom the Nazi uniform symbolized both racism and genocide, there was no legal way to halt Nazis. As an official statement of the San Francisco Human Rights Commission issued at the time put it: "The Board of Education must let anyone enter the hall when there is a public meeting in session . . . The Board of Education must let anyone speak . . . The City of San Francisco and San Franciscans detest the Nazis, but we must allow them to speak, within the limits of the First Amendment. The courts would force us to let them speak, if we did not, and the courts would be right."[42] The problem posed by the presence of the Nazis at the Board of Education meetings was similarly articulated by the Jewish Community Relations Council: "The presence of that [Nazi] symbol at the Board of Education meeting is disgusting and disturbing to all of us. It is also frustrating in the extreme because there is no way to ban the presence of these individuals from a public meeting without destroying our most basic principle of liberty, and therefore handing a great victory to the Nazis . . ."[43]

After consulting with Jewish communal leaders, supervisors Quentin Kopp and Robert Mendelsohn proposed a new municipal ordinance which would have made it illegal to wear the uniform or insignia of the Nazi party

---

[41]The discussion which follows is based on David G. Dalin, *Public Affairs and the Jewish Community: The Changing Political World of San Francisco Jews,* unpublished Ph.D. dissertation, Brandeis University, 1977, pp. 152–155.

[42]San Francisco *Jewish Bulletin,* January 25, 1974, p. 1.

[43]*Ibid.*

in public. The proposed ordinance, however, while enjoying widespread popular support, both within the Jewish and the general community, never became law. On May 20 City Attorney O'Connor advised the Board of Supervisors that it could not legally outlaw the wearing of Nazi, or any other, uniforms in public. The United States Supreme Court, he indicated, had in the past consistently ruled that the wearing of political symbols is "symbolic speech" protected by the free speech provisions of the First Amendment. In 1969, for example, the Court ruled *(Tinker v. Des Moines)* that students could not be prevented from wearing black armbands to school in order to protest the Vietnam war. In 1960 a Miami ordinance prohibiting the wearing of Nazi (or Communist) uniforms in public places was struck down by a state court.

In the wake of O'Connor's advisory opinion, the Board's State and National Affairs Committee called upon the state legislature to deal with the matter. During the next three years, however, the legislature in Sacramento failed to enact any anti-Nazi legislation. Hence, at the time of the opening of the Rudolf Hess bookstore in 1977 there was still no legal way to ban the public display of Nazi symbols. It was in response to this legislative void that Supervisor Dianne Feinstein, as was noted above, introduced a new resolution urging the legislature to bar the display of the swastika and the wearing of the Nazi uniform in public. In co-sponsoring this resolution, Supervisor Mendelsohn said that the display of Nazi symbols and uniforms "provokes acts of violence and threatens the public peace." Mendelsohn and the other supervisors, however, expressed doubt about the proposal's chances of being enacted as state law. This in fact proved to be the case.

One other unsuccessful effort at passing anti-Nazi legislation in San Francisco is worth noting. In early 1978 it was revealed that the Nazis were holding meetings at the Wawona Clubhouse, a rented public facility in the city-owned Sigmund Stern Grove. The JCRC issued a statement protesting "the private use of public facilities by Nazi groups, which exclude people on the basis of race and religion." On the basis of a municipal ordinance requiring that there be no discrimination in the rental of city property, Supervisor Kopp sought to evict the Nazis. The City Attorney, backed by the ACLU, ruled in March, however, that the ordinance in question did not apply to the Nazis, because of an amendment stating that rentals of less than 30 days a year would be exempt from the law's provisions. The Jewish community's efforts to combat Nazi activity were thus once again thwarted.

In Chicago the Jewish community has found itself similarly powerless to enact anti-Nazi legislation. Illinois State Senators John Nimrod and Howard Carroll introduced two bills in May 1978; one would have empowered local officials to deny parade permits for demonstrations which might result in defamation of a group because of race, creed, color, or religion; the other would have allowed for the rejection of parade permits if there were "reasonable apprehension" about violence occurring as a result of the display of "quasi-military" uniforms.[44] The first bill, by making group defamation criminally punishable, might have served as a model for similar laws in other states. Illinois, it should be noted, had first enacted group libel legislation in 1917 (it was upheld by the United States Supreme Court in 1952 in a five-to-four decision), but the law had been repealed in 1964.

After the Illinois State Senate adopted the two bills, the state's Assembly Judiciary Committee met to consider the matter. Spokesmen for Skokie's Jewish community, including Rabbi Laurence Montrose and Erna Gans, president of the B'nai B'rith Korczak Lodge in Skokie, testified on the bill's behalf. They urged the legislators to speak out by passing the statutes, just as the residents of Skokie had spoken out by resisting the Nazi demonstration. Joel Sprayregen, a prominent Chicago civil liberties attorney, who had been a staff counsel for the ACLU in the early 1960's and had subsequently served for several years as a member of its board of directors, testified in favor of the proposed bills, while ACLU executive director Aryeh Neier testified in opposition. Following the Sprayregen-Neier debate, the committee voted. To the shock of the many Holocaust survivors in attendance, the anti-Nazi bills were soundly defeated; the Judiciary Committee voted fifteen to five against the group libel bill and sixteen to four against the bill introduced by Carroll. Chicago's Jewish community viewed the defeat of the bills as a moral victory for the Nazis, who called a press conference to celebrate the legislature's inaction.[45]

In Milwaukee efforts at enacting anti-Nazi legislation met with similar results. The Brennan ordinance, patterned on the Illinois bill prohibiting group defamation, won the support of the Milwaukee County Board of Supervisors but was subsequently defeated in the Common Council of the City of Milwaukee. In the view of political observers, the ordinance's defeat was largely due to the efforts of the Wisconsin chapter of the ACLU, which vigorously defended the Nazis' constitutional rights.[46]

[44]JTA *Daily News Bulletin,* May 30, 1978, p. 4.
[45]Neier, *op. cit.,* pp. 62–65.
[46]Zvi Deutsch, "Milwaukee Jews Counter Nazi Threat," *Jewish Currents,* September 1977, p. 6.

COMBATTING THE NAZIS: THE
EDUCATIONAL FRONT

As legislative efforts to combat neo-Nazism proved increasingly ineffective, American Jewry turned its attention to the educational front. There was growing support within the Jewish community for the introduction of Holocaust study courses on both the high school and university levels. During the 1977-78 school year, such courses were in fact mandated in the New York City and Philadelphia school systems. Jews were concerned that the history of the Holocaust was little understood by young people, since most social studies texts and curricula avoided the subject. One survey of the 45 most widely-used high school, social studies textbooks revealed that 15 "omitted any mention of the Nazi persecution of Jews and 22 glossed over the facts."[47]

In April 1977 the San Francisco Conference on Religion, Race and Social Concerns, an interfaith social action group coordinated by JCRC associate director Rita Semel, announced the formation of a city-wide committee for "community education" against Nazism. A cross-section of Protestant, Catholic, and Jewish clergy and civic leaders, including Mayor George Moscone and Supervisors Kopp and Feinstein, agreed to join the committee, whose purpose would be "to focus on educating the public on what is behind the headlines . . . why Nazism is and should be anathema to a democratic society and why the fight against its ideology must be broadened and strengthened." Plans called for the inservice training of teachers, as well as "education for the general public" through the showing of movies such as "Judgment at Nuremburg." "The teaching of social studies," noted Semel, "has changed so that World War II is barely mentioned in many courses now. And we're now in the fourth generation. Not only haven't the kids lived through World War II, many of the teachers haven't either."[48]

Public education concerning Nazism took a significant step forward in April 1978 when NBC televised "Holocaust," a nine-hour, prime-time special dealing with Jewish fate under the Nazis. Jewish and Christian organizations, as well as NBC, developed a variety of discussion guides targeted for different audiences, to be utilized in conjunction with the show. Under the auspices of the National Jewish Welfare Board, 15 Jewish agencies joined together in preparing a "Holocaust Program Package" designed "to transform this TV special into a 'multi-media' educational tool for use in formal and informal Jewish educational settings."[49] The National

---

[47]Judith Herschlag Muffs, "US Teaching on the Holocaust," *Patterns of Prejudice,* May-June 1977, p. 29.

[48]San Francisco *Examiner,* April 7, 1977, p. 4.

[49]"Materials for NBC-TV Holocaust Series," National Jewish Community Relations Advisory Council memo, February 24, 1978, p. 2.

Council of Churches, in cooperation with the National Conference of Catholic Bishops and the American Jewish Committee, produced a four-page interreligious study and discussion guide for use by churches throughout the country. NBC developed its own discussion guide, which it distributed, through its 217 affiliated stations, free of charge to public schools across the nation.

The National Jewish Community Relations Advisory Council asked its constituent agencies to utilize "every possible channel to the non-Jewish community" to encourage public viewing of "Holocaust." In some cities cooperative efforts were undertaken by local NBC affiliates and Jewish community relations councils in arranging a pre-screening of the program for various religious, ethnic, and civic leaders. NJCRAC also encouraged its constituent agencies to organize follow-up programs to "Holocaust" and intergroup dialogues on various aspects of the Holocaust and contemporary neo-Nazism. "We are attempting," one NJCRAC leader noted, "to teach the lessons of the Holocaust to our non-Jewish neighbors. If we cannot stop Nazi appearances, if we must endure the anguish, must we not use every possible means to fasten the general public's attention onto the principles for which the Nazis stand?"[50]

THE LESSONS OF SKOKIE

The threatened Nazi march through Skokie represented a radically new experience for many American Jews, especially those under the age of 35. As Eugene DuBow, organizer of the planned PAC counter-demonstration, noted, it had been many years since American Jewry was faced with the prospect of a major Nazi demonstration in an area heavily populated by Jews. The planned Nazi march in Skokie forced many Jews to weigh their commitment to civil liberties against their concern for Jewish security and abhorrence of Nazism.

There were Jews in Skokie who had the gnawing feeling that history was repeating itself, that Nazism was once again on the rise. "There are the echoes of history rumbling through your mind and ticking off similarities and parallels that are all too uncomfortable," said one Skokie resident. "Absurd analogies you say? Hitler started off small, bluffed and got what he wanted by promoting ideas contrary to what the vast majority of people and countries believed. He radicalized antisemitism. So has Collin. Hitler used the law to promote his 'rights' until he was in a position of power to

---

[50]Theodore R. Mann, address delivered at NJCRAC plenary session, Tucson, Arizona, January 22–23, 1978, p. 5.

have his will alone become law. So has Collin. His violence of words, deed and symbols are protected."[51] There was a determination in the Skokie Jewish community, and among Jews throughout the United States, not to sit idly by in the face of Nazi threats.

This was a much different communal response from that of the 1960's, when the policy of the organized Jewish community had been one of "quarantine," i.e., to ignore most Nazi incidents in the hope that the Nazis, bereft of publicity and media attention, would disappear.[52] By 1978 leaders of the National Jewish Community Relations Advisory Council were seriously reconsidering the wisdom of the quarantine approach. "I am troubled by our 1963 conclusion that public protests against Nazi appearances merely provide them with increased publicity and bolster their image of martyred heroes," stated NJCRAC chairman Theodore Mann. "It seems to me curiously outdated . . . The concept of quarantine as the general rule seems to be an anachronism." On the contrary, Mann argued, "Jewish leadership should be able to fashion a counter-demonstration or protest march or meeting, with signs and literature and releases to the media depicting the bestial acts of Nazi Germany, which would provide both an outlet for Jewish anguish and a lesson for our neighbors as to what the swastika really means."[53] A shift from quietism toward communal activism vis-à-vis the Nazis was apparent in San Francisco, where JCRC urged the "organized Jewish community to speak out vociferously and take prompt and militant action against the Nazis in any way that will hurt the Nazi cause."[54] A reporter noted that in Skokie "Jews, who normally would be appalled at the thought of taking to the streets, now are thinking the unthinkable."[55]

Sol Goldstein, chairman of the PAC Committee on American and Jewish Security, maintained that it was the determination of thousands of people to confront the Nazis that had scared them off. Goldstein emphasized that he regarded Skokie as only "one battlefront" of a much larger "war." "This battlefront gained a victory. But the war is not over . . . We will come to any place the Nazis will appear." The lesson of Skokie, Goldstein maintained, was that the Nazis would back down "when confronted by a determined American public."[56] In commenting on the cancellation of the Nazi

---

[51]Arthur J. Sabin, "Skokie," *Sh'ma,* September 15, 1978, p. 163.

[52]The "quarantine" strategy was first developed in the 1940's. See S. Andhill Fineberg, "Checkmate for Rabble-Rousers," *Commentary,* September 1946, pp. 220–26 and S. Andhill Fineberg, *Deflating the Professional Bigot* (New York, 1960), pp. 8–10.

[53]Theodore R. Mann, address delivered at NJCRAC plenary session, Tucson, Arizona, *loc. cit.,* p. 5. NJCRAC memo to member agencies, February 24, 1978.

[54]*How to Prevent Nazism,* discussion guide, Jewish Community Relations Council, San Francisco, 1978, p. 49.

[55]San Francisco *Examiner,* June 26, 1977.

[56]*JTA Daily News Bulletin,* June 27, 1978, p. 4.

march, National Jewish Community Relations Advisory Council chairman Theodore Mann noted: "The important lesson of Skokie is that the Jewish survivors of the Nazi death camps found that they were not alone as they were 40 years ago."[57]

Skokie's Holocaust survivors had the satisfaction of having kept the Nazis out of their community. Their active opposition helped educate a generation that had grown up with only a dim awareness of what Nazism was all about. "Sure, the Nazis have gotten publicity because of our opposition," said Korczak B'nai B'rith lodge president Erna Gans, "but we've also raised the consciousness of the American people. Schools are beginning to teach courses on the Holocaust. People from around the country are standing with us. When I talk to groups, they all want to know what they can do to keep Nazism from happening here."[58]

---

[57]Theodore R. Mann, NJCRAC plenary address, *op. cit.*
[58]Quoted in John J. Camper, *loc. cit.,* p. 34.

Trends in Jewish Philanthropy

by STEVEN MARTIN COHEN

NEARLY TWO DECADES HAVE PASSED since Marshall Sklare first questioned whether support for Jewish philanthropic giving in the United States was deep and secure.[1] Sklare noted that the charitable drives of Jewish federations (central philanthropic agencies) in the largest communities enlisted the support of no more than a third of Jewish households. Moreover, significant variations in per capita giving from one locale to another implied important differences in the strength of local campaigns. Bemoaning the lack of hard data on various aspects of Jewish philanthropy, Sklare wrote: "None of the leading Jewish fund-raising institutions . . . has done so much as the most rudimentary market research concerning either the financial status of non-givers or the proportion of disposable income being contributed by donors."[2]

Since the time that Sklare wrote, several federations have conducted potentially valuable community surveys. Two such surveys—the 1965 and 1975 Boston studies[3]—are especially useful in answering questions about the past (and, by inference, the future) of American Jewish giving, because they include detailed, virtually identical questions on philanthropic behavior. Secondary analyses of the 1975 data set have already led to the tentative

Note: The critical comments of Samuel C. Heilman, Harold Himmelfarb, Bernard Reisman, Paul Ritterband, and Marshall Sklare are deeply appreciated. The Combined Jewish Philanthropies of Greater Boston made the data available. The research was supported by PSC-BHE Research Award #13031 from the City University of New York Research Foundation. Neither agency bears any responsibility for the interpretations contained herein.

[1]Marshall Sklare, "The Future of Jewish Giving," *Commentary,* November 1962, pp. 416–426. For a more pessimistic view, see Milton Goldin, *Why They Give: American Jews and Their Philanthropies* (New York, 1977). For background on American Jewish philanthropy, see Harry J. Lurie, *A Heritage Affirmed* (Philadelphia, 1961); Daniel J. Elazar, *Community and Polity: The Organizational Dynamics of American Jewry* (Philadelphia, 1976); the June 1977 issue of *Moment*; Marc Lee Raphael, "Jewish Philanthropy and Communal Democracy: In Pursuit of a Phantom," *Response,* Fall 1977, pp. 55–65; S.P. Goldberg, "Jewish Communal Services: Programs and Finances," *AJYB,* Vol. 78, 1978, pp. 172–221; and Charles S. Liebman, "Leadership and Decision-making in a Jewish Federation: The New York Federation of Jewish Philanthropies," *AJYB,* Vol. 79, 1979, pp. 3–76.

[2]*Ibid.,* p. 420.

[3]Morris Axelrod, Floyd T. Fowler, Jr., and Arnold Gurin, *A Community Survey for Long Range Planning: A Study of the Jewish Population of Greater Boston* (Boston, 1967) and Floyd J. Fowler, *1975 Community: A Study of the Jewish Population of Greater Boston* (Boston, 1977).

conclusion that Jewish philanthropic support is likely to decline.[4] This article, analysing results from both the 1965 and 1975 surveys, builds upon and extends the earlier analyses.

THE SIGNIFICANCE OF
JEWISH PHILANTHROPY

Support for Jewish philanthropy is crucial to the financial well-being of a wide variety of beneficiaries: local health and welfare services, camps, Jewish community centers, Jewish schools and supportive services, cultural institutions, national agencies, and, not least, social services in Israel. At the same time, Jewish charitable giving, particularly to the centralized drives of federations, constitutes an important social act in that it affirms the individual's ties to the community.[5] The frequency and generosity of giving, then, have implications which go far beyond the financial security of particular agencies. A strong philanthropic campaign reflects a coherent and well-integrated Jewish community. A weak campaign implies a partial unraveling of the ties that bind Jews together.

The social nature of Jewish charitable giving is reflected in the various fund-raising techniques employed by professional fund-raisers. Most preferred is the face-to-face solicitation.[6] This technique involves pairing a carefully chosen solicitor with a potential donor; often the solicitor and donor are friends or business associates. The solicitor seeks maximal prior knowledge of the prospect's family background, Jewish interests, and financial means, and brings this information to bear in a highly personalized plea for funds. Another effective fund-raising technique which relies on the social bonds between indentified Jews is the testimonial dinner. Here, business colleagues or members of a synagogue or Jewish organization are exhorted to purchase tickets to a reception and publicly pledge donations in honor of a prominent individual. Often, face-to-face solicitation of more affluent and generous givers precedes the dinner, the expectation being that they will serve as pace-setters for less wealthy or less dedicated donors. In recent years, members of an elite philanthropic group, the National UJA

---

[4]Steven Martin Cohen, "Will Jews Keep Giving? Prospects for the Jewish Charitable Community," *Journal of Jewish Communal Service,* Autumn 1978, pp. 59–71; Paul Ritterband and Steven Martin Cohen, "Will the Well Run Dry? The Future of Jewish Giving in America," *Response,* Summer 1979, pp. 9–16.

[5]For the social function of charitable giving in a modern Orthodox synagogue, see Samuel C. Heilman, "The Gift of Alms: Face-to-Face Almsgiving among Orthodox Jews," *Urban Life and Culture,* January 1975, pp. 371–395.

[6]Aryeh Nesher, "Aryeh Nesher, Solicitor-General," *Moment,* June 1977, pp. 27–30, 60–62.

Young Leadership Cabinet (YLC), have taken to making "full financial disclosure" in a group setting. At their annual retreat, YLC members rise individually to describe their incomes and assets, propose a donation, and accept encouragement from friends and colleagues to attain even greater heights of generosity. That this method has proved to be phenomenally effective in generating contributions testifies to Jewish philanthropy's highly social nature.

An understanding of the social dimension of Jewish philanthropy is further enhanced when we note that the multitudinous solicitations of American Jewish donors grow out of a highly elaborate social apparatus. This apparatus is coordinated by professionals who maintain and mobilize a series of interlocking, hierarchically structured networks of lay leaders centered around different loci. Thus, the most prominent givers comprise a continent-wide network. They, in turn, are among the leaders of local networks centered around particular industries, trades, synagogues, Jewish organizations, or residential neighborhoods. These networks are, of course, critical for fund-raising. Equally important, however, they serve as pools from which Jewish communal organizations of every type can draw lay leaders.[7] In addition, the fund-raising apparatus generates a multiplicity of overlapping leadership circles in the Jewish community, thus serving to unite potentially competing factions.[8]

One final aspect of Jewish philanthropy's social dimension that merits attention is its impact in the political sphere. The ability of the organized Jewish community to raise millions of dollars annually cannot help but make a profound impression on political leaders and elected officials. For policy makers, these funds are a tangible measure of the Jewish community's cohesion and the degree of its support for the State of Israel and other Jewish concerns.

In sum, it is clear that the vitality of Jewish philanthropy is crucial to American Jewry in several ways: in terms of social coherence, leadership recruitment, institutional coordination, political impact, and, most obviously, the financial security of beneficiary agencies. Questions about the future of Jewish giving, then, are in reality questions about the future of organized Jewry.

---

[7]Yohanon Manor and Gabriel Sheffer, "L'United Jewish Appeal ou la Métamorphose du Don," *Revue Française Sociologie,* Summer 1977, pp. 3–24.
[8]*Ibid.*

REASONS FOR PESSIMISM

The pessimistic outlook for Jewish giving is based, in the first instance, on what has been happening in terms of the actual dollar amounts collected. From the mid-1960's through the mid-1970's, the annual federation campaigns in the United States raised almost steadily-increasing sums of money. The 1965 nationwide total reached $131 million; in 1974, following the Yom Kippur War, that sum amounted to a record $660 million. In 1975, however, the total amount raised nationwide plummeted to $475 million; it has remained there ever since, even as inflation has eroded the purchasing power of the charitable dollar. The most recent estimate compiled by the Council of Jewish Federations and Welfare Funds places the 1978 total at $480-485 million.

The experience in Boston mirrors that in the nation as a whole. In 1965 $5.3 million was raised; in 1975 the amount was $13.2 million. Then stagnation set in; between 1976 and 1978 collections rose by only one million dollars. In fiscal 1979, a year of nearly double digit inflation, there was a $200,000 decline to $14 million.

Adding to the pessimistic outlook for Jewish philanthropy are certain observed trends which seem to distinguish today's younger Jews. First, and most simply, they may well be less attached to the Jewish community (however it is defined) than their elders were when they were young. They belong to a later generation, and Jews who are generationally removed from the immigrant heritage, like members of other ethnic groups, less frequently undertake expressions of religious or ethnic attachment such as Jewish charitable giving.[9] Secondly, younger Jews have been shifting away from those occupations that have been characteristic for federation stalwarts;

---

[9]Among various American ethnic groups, generation relates directly with several measures of assimilation: friendship and inter-ethnic marriage (See Harold J. Abramson, *Ethnic Diversity in Catholic America*, New York, 1973; Steven Martin Cohen, *Patterns of Interethnic Marriage and Friendship in the United States*, Ph.D. dissertation, Columbia University, 1974; and Richard D. Alba, "Social Assimilation Among American Catholic National-Origin Groups," *American Sociological Review*, December 1976, pp. 637–653); residence outside areas of ethnic concentration (Stanley Lieberson, *Ethnic Patterns in American Cities*, New York, 1963); lower levels of in-group solidarity sentiments (Cohen, *Patterns of Interethnic Marriage, op. cit.*); and less distinctive political orientations (Steven Martin Cohen and Robert E. Kapsis, "Religion, Ethnicity, and Party Affiliation in the United States: Evidence from Pooled Electoral Surveys, 1968–1972," *Social Forces*, December 1977, pp. 657–663).

With reference to Jews specifically, see Sidney Goldstein and Calvin Goldscheider, *Jewish Americans: Three Generations in a Jewish Community* (New Jersey, 1968); Axelrod et al., *op. cit.*; Fowler, *op. cit.*; Marshall Sklare and Joseph Greenblum, *Jewish Identity on the Suburban Frontier* (New York, 1967); Harold Himmelfarb, "The Interaction Effect of Parents, Spouse and Schooling: Comparing the Impact of Jewish and Catholic Schools," *The Sociological Quarterly*, Autumn 1977, pp. 464–477; and Harold Himmelfarb, "The Study of American Jewish Identification: How It is Defined, Measured, Obtained, Sustained, and Lost," *Journal for the Scientific Study of Religion*, forthcoming, 1980.

they are entering the salaried professions rather than becoming independent entrepreneurs.[10] The resulting shifts in type of work (from business to professions) and sources of income (from self-employed to salaried) mean that younger Jews will less often enter the pool of potential multi-millionaires, that group which has most generously supported federation drives in the past. The shift in source of income also means that a smaller fraction of total family income (even if it remains at a high level) will be of the disposable variety. One need not be overly cynical to realize that self-employed entrepreneurs have a greater ability to hide their income from the Internal Revenue Service than do most salaried professionals.

The shift in type of work to the professions also means that less social and economic pressure can be brought to bear on potential contributors. For people in business, charitable giving publically symbolizes success to their peers. As such, they make donations in part to enhance their social esteem. Moreover, when a business person is solicited by a customer, a gift's size can influence his or her commercial prospects. For professionals such as social workers, teachers, or other public employees, however, federation giving entails fewer potential rewards or punishments. A salaried professional's reputation is less firmly tied to public demonstrations of material success. His or her livelihood is not as often dependent on the good will of customers; those in a position to influence a professional's career—principals, editors, supervisors—are constrained by professional norms from making advancement contingent upon acceptable levels of charitable giving. Moreover, certain professions—particularly law, medicine, and college teaching—can become a way of life and thus successfully compete with ethnicity as a basis for self-definition.[11] As a result, individuals in these

---

[10]Sidney Goldstein writes that data pertaining to "future trends in Jewish occupational composition . . . point to a continuing increase in the proportion of Jews engaged in professional work, and to either stability or actual decline for the managerial and proprietor group." See "American Jewry: A Demographic Analysis," in David Sidorsky (ed.), *The Future of the Jewish Community in America,* (Philadelphia, 1973), p. 118.

[11]See Nathan Glazer and Daniel Patrick Moynihan, *Beyond the Melting Pot* (Cambridge, Mass., 1970). In his study of interreligious marriage, Fred Sherrow writes: "Intellectuals have been described as forming a kind of society of their own, even akin to an ethnic community. Thus not only do they reject the significance of such statuses as religion or ethnic origin in their behavior, but they may have little need for such identities, having developed surrogates for them" (Fred Sherrow, *Patterns of Religious Intermarriage Among American College Graduates,* Ph.D. dissertation, Columbia University, 1971, pp. 142–143). On this point Sherrow cites Milton Gordon, *Assimilation in American Life* (New York, 1964) and J. Wilensky and J. Ladinsky, "From Community to Occupational Group: Structural Assimilation Among Professors, Lawyers, and Engineers," *American Sociological Review,* August 1967, pp. 541–561. See also Andrew Greeley, *Why Can't They Be Like Us?* (New York, 1971), especially pp. 120–134; and Steven Martin Cohen, "Sociological Determinants of Interethnic Marriage and Friendship," *Social Forces,* June 1977, pp. 997–1010.

professions may feel less of a need to link themselves to the Jewish community through charitable giving.

Evidence of changes in the Jewish family adds to the pessimism regarding the future of Jewish philanthropy. We know that life cycle affects virtually all forms of voluntary participation.[12] Jewish communal participation, in particular, may be heightened by marriage and is almost certainly increased by the presence of children in the home.[13] At the same time, reliable information about American population trends and impressions about Jewish participation in those trends suggest an increase in what may be termed "alternative" Jewish households: singles, childless couples, and divorced or separated individuals. If the active Jewish community does, in fact, consist disproportionately of those in more conventional households (couples who now have or have raised children, as well as the widowed), and these households are diminishing in number, then Jewish giving will eventually suffer.

A number of trends, then, lead to the expectation that today's younger Jews will emerge less dedicated donors than their counterparts in the past. To test the validity of this expectation, as well as to determine the precise effects of diminishing Jewishness, occupational shift, and the decline of the conventional family on Jewish philanthropy, we turn to an analysis of the Boston data.

DATA AND MEASURES

This study is based on a secondary analysis of two random sample surveys of Jews residing in the Boston metropolitan area. The University of Massachusetts Survey Research Center conducted the surveys on behalf of the Combined Jewish Philanthropies of Greater Boston. The data were collected in face-to-face interviews, totalling 1,569 in 1965 and 932 in 1975. Respondents were chosen in two ways. First, a large number were randomly selected from a master list of Jews known to the organized Jewish community. Due to cost considerations, a much smaller number of Jews were located via a random area sampling procedure. Since the latter group represented a proportion of the universe larger than their proportion in the sample, weighting procedures were used which had the effect of multiplying those respondents not found on the master list.

---

[12]David Knoke and Randall Thomson, "Voluntary Association Membership Trends and the Family Life Cycle," *Social Forces,* September 1977, pp. 45–65.

[13]Himmelfarb, "The Study of American Jewish Identification," *loc. cit.,* and Sklare and Greenblum, *op. cit.*

The special characteristics of Boston's Jews affect the extent to which observations from these data can be generalized to the rest of American Jewry. Greater Boston's Jewish population of 180,000 in the middle 1970's placed it sixth behind New York, Los Angeles, Philadelphia, Chicago, and Miami.[14] The total amount ($13 million) contributed to its annual federation campaign in 1975 (Combined Jewish Philanthropies) was similar to that given in comparably-sized communities (e.g., Baltimore, Cleveland, Detroit, Miami, and San Francisco). As in other metropolitan areas, substantial numbers of Jews have left Boston's central city neighborhoods for the suburbs over the last two decades. An extensive and well-established Jewish institutional infrastructure, as well as a very large number of colleges and universities, distinguish Boston from other cities. As a corollary, Boston Jewry is disproportionately young. In order to adjust for the tremendous increase in the number of students and other young people between 1965 and 1975, the 1975 survey was weighted so that its age distribution replicated that of the earlier survey.

The analysis below focuses on two aspects of giving. First, did the respondent's household contribute to the CJP campaign during the last 12 months? Second, how much did the household contribute to all Jewish causes aside from synagogue-related expenses?

To assess the importance of Jewish orientation in influencing philanthropic behavior, the full range of Jewish identificational items available in both data sets were canvassed. Interestingly, in this sphere, behavior is a much more potent predictor of giving than are attitudes about such matters as the importance of a Jewish education, a preference for Jewish friends and neighbors, hypothetical reactions to an intermarriage in the family, and the salience of the State of Israel. Thus, the Jewishness scale used in this study awards two points if the respondent attends religious services during the high holidays or more often; two points for those who perform at least two of the following rituals: take part in a Passover Seder, light Sabbath candles, keep kosher at home; and one point if the respondent belongs to a Jewish organization. This index will be referred to as the Jewish Activities scale.

Consistent with the rationale advanced above, two aspects of occupation were taken into account: source of income (self-employed or salaried) and type of work (professional or non-professional). Cross-classifying these two aspects yields four distinct occupational categories.

Preliminary analysis of several types of households yielded three clusters. First, there are the conventional households: married couples with children living at home or those with grown children. At the other extreme in terms

---

[14]Alvin Chenkin, "Jewish Population in the United States, 1976," *AJYB,* Vol. 77, 1977, pp. 229–239.

of philanthropic behavior are three household types which can be grouped under the alternative rubric: singles; divorced or separated individuals; and married couples without children. The widowed, a third category, are treated separately since their philanthropic patterns differ from those of the other two groups.

Since about a third of the sample refused to provide information on family income, income was estimated for those respondents by using prediction equations employing education, occupation, and monthly housing costs. Somewhat different equations were used in the two surveys. Since inflation accounted for a large growth in income between 1965 and 1975, both income and the amount contributed to Jewish charity in 1965 were multiplied by 2.395, a factor which was chosen so as to make identical the 1965 and 1975 mean incomes of mature individuals, i.e., those over 30.

Age, the critical independent variable, is that of the male adult member of the household, or that of the female adult if no male is present. Alternative measures, such as averaging male and female ages or giving precedence to the age of the female, resulted in more modest relationships with the dependent variables.

Finally, it should be noted that the household and not the individual is the unit of analysis.

FINDINGS

Age, Period, and Cohort Effects

Table 1, which reports levels of philanthropic activity by age and period, lends itself to three types of comparisons, each of which yields different sorts of inferences. First, we can read the table vertically and examine changes in philanthropic behavior by age while holding period constant. Such a comparison, in conjunction with other comparisons and information, would permit inferences about age or life-cycle effects—how does philanthropic activity rise or fall as people get older? Second, we can read the columns diagonally, from upper left to lower right, to trace various birth cohorts, learning about one of many types of period effects. Of course, each birth cohort not only passes into a new period of history, it also ages by ten years. Inferred period effects, therefore, have to take into account probable age effects. Finally, we can supplement both sorts of comparisons with a horizontal reading of the table to infer cohort effects, i.e., differences in philanthropic behavior arising out of differences in time of birth and socialization. Since there is no clear-cut method for unraveling age, period, and cohort effects, the wisest course is to attempt to achieve a comprehensive

Table 1
Philanthropic Behavior by Age, 1965 and 1975

Age at Time of Survey	Per Cent Giving to CJP			Amount Given[a]			Givers Only[b]		
	1965	1975	Rate[c]	1965	1975	Rate	1965	1975	Rate
20–29	17	12	.71	23	53	2.30	80	321	4.01
30–39	64	25	.39	236	268	1.14	362	607	1.68
40–49	70	46	.66	302	252	.83	453	392	.87
50–59	72	61	.85	413	211	.51	618	282	.46
60+	61	53	.87	247	198	.80	474	326	.69
Total	60	43	.72	263	205	.78	463	367	.80

a. Amount given to all Jewish causes except those connected with the synagogue, in constant (1975) dollars.

b. Amount given to all Jewish causes except those connected with the synagogue, in constant (1975) dollars, excluding those who gave less than $25.

c. "Rate" is the retention rate, the 1975 entry divided by the adjoining 1965 entry for the same age group.

understanding of the data, informed by an intelligent use of side information.[15]

Examining the frequency of giving to the CJP campaign (irrespective of amount donated), we can reasonably infer the broad contours of an age or life-cycle effect. People in their 20's are consistently infrequent contributors. The rate of giving rises until the upper 50's, when it takes a downward turn. It is important to note, however, that there are considerable differences in the age contours of the two samples. In 1965, giving rises sharply (by age 30) to a plateau and largely remains there, whereas in 1975 giving in the 20's starts out quite low (a 12 per cent rate) and rises only gradually in each succeeding cohort, until it peaks in the 50's age group.

There are two plausible explanations for the divergent contours, with very different implications for the future of Jewish philanthropy. The more benign explanation suggests that, for some reason, by 1975 only middle-aged and elderly Jews regarded charitable giving as normative. Thus, although fewer young Jews contributed, as compared with 1965, the overall frequency of donations is likely to remain stable, since they can be expected to increase their rate of giving as they age. Alternately, it is possible that

[15]For an excellent discussion of the need to resolve the ambiguities in cohort data by applying informed theory to the anaysis, see Norval Glenn, *Cohort Analysis* (Beverly Hills, 1977).

the younger cohorts who began to mature between 1965 and 1975 are permanently less inclined to give than their predecessors. In other words, frequent giving is characteristic of only certain birth cohorts (according to these data, those born earlier than 1935).

Diagonal and horizontal comparisons lend support to the birth cohort, as opposed to the age explanation. Diagonally we find that all cohorts but one (the youngest group in 1965) experienced declines in frequency of giving from 1965 to 1975. The youngest group's rate increased from 17 to 25 per cent, but did so only slightly because powerful aging effects barely won out over period and cohort effects. If those in their 20's in 1965 had replicated the behavior of the group ten years older in that year, they would have risen to a 64 per cent level rather than a 25 per cent rate.

A horizontal comparison of each 1975 age group with its predecessor in 1965 is also revealing. We may divide the 1975 rates by the 1965 rates to derive, in effect, a rate of retention. A retention rate of 2.00 would mean that giving doubled for that group over the ten-year interval; a rate of retention of .50 would mean that the frequency was cut in half. Interestingly, the rate of retention is highest among the oldest Jews, and through age 30 declines steadily cohort by cohort. The only reason the retention rate is so high (.71) among those in their 20's is that the base rate of 17 per cent in 1965 is so low to begin with. In other words, the decline in overall frequency of giving between 1965 and 1975 is most directly attributable to declines among the youngest age groups, precisely those Jews whose behavior is most important in terms of the future of Jewish giving.

When we turn to the amounts given to all Jewish causes, a very different picture emerges. Apparently, while younger Jews give less frequently than their predecessors, they contribute much more generously when they do. Retention rates of total dollars given are highest for the youngest groups and decline through age 59, before turning slightly upward for the elderly. (The latter phenomenon is attributable in part to a rather low 1965 base for those 60 and older.) The inference of a shrinking but far more generous donor base is even more clearly supported when we consider only those who made a meaningful ($25 or more per year) contribution. The "givers-only" columns in Table 1 show that the youngest group in 1975 is four times as generous as its predecessor, while the 30–39 group in 1975 is one and two-thirds times as generous as its 1965 counterpart. All other groups are less forthcoming in 1975 than were their predecessors.

The 1965–75 period witnessed changes not only in the rate and extent of Jewish philanthropy, but also in the distribution of those characteristics which influence charitable behavior. Table 2 reports trends in household type, occupation, income, and Jewish orientation.

With reference to household type, "alternative" families are found most frequently in the youngest age category, decline as one moves up the age

Table 2

Distributions of Household and Occupational Types; Mean Family Income
(in constant 1975 dollars) and Jewish Activities by Age, 1965 and 1975

Age	1965					1975				
	20–9	30–9	40–9	50–9	60+	20–9	30–9	40–9	50–9	60+
Household Types (%)										
Alternative[a]	63	18	8	14	19	89	40	12	13	18
Conventional[b]	35	79	86	78	53	11	60	85	83	54
Widowed	2	3	6	8	28	0	0	3	4	28
Occupational Types (%)										
Self-employed Pros	2	11	8	7	12	4	36	28	22	20
Entrepreneurs	5	22	31	36	45	8	17	19	39	30
Salaried Pros	59	35	12	16	8	44	33	24	14	14
Non-pro. Workers	34	31	48	41	35	45	27	42	36	47
Retirees[c]	0	0	0	(5)	(47)	0	0	0	(2)	(51)
Mean Family Income (in $1,000)	18	35	36	32	19	13	37	35	35	17
Mean Jewish Activities	3.6	3.9	4.2	4.2	4.2	3.0	3.1	3.9	3.8	3.8

a. Singles, childless married couples, and divorced and separated who have not remarried.
b. Married couples with children living at home or who have raised children, now away from home.
c. Retirees are excluded from occupational computations.

ladder, and turn slightly upward in the older years as unmarried divorcé(e)s accumulate. Widows and widowers, of course, are concentrated in the later years. Conventional families peak in the 40–59 age range and trail off somewhat above age 60. Most critically, the number of alternative households has grown considerably between 1965 and 1975. In 1965, 63 per cent of family heads in their 20's were living in alternative homes, while in 1975, 89 per cent do so. Among those aged 30–39, the figure for alternative households increases from 18 per cent in 1965 to 40 per cent in 1975, owing largely to a later marrying age and a decline in the birthrate.

The 1965 and 1975 data sets employed different coding schemes for occupation, and it may well be that the latter set is more accurate. In fact, the data for 1975 more clearly illustrate occupational patterns which have been thought to characterize American Jewry in recent years. Reading from older to younger groups, we find a steady growth (through age 30) in the proportion of salaried and self-employed professionals. Commensurately, there is a nearly consistent decline in the percentage of self-employed non-professionals (largely entrepreneurs) and a wavering in the proportion of salaried nonprofessionals (workers). The youngest group, 20–29 in age, must be treated with caution since so many of its members have not yet entered their chosen careers; presumably they will end up confirming the trend toward the professions. The 1965 data show the same patterns, although somewhat less clearly. In short, there is irrefutable evidence of a movement toward the professions and away from entrepreneurship, and a lesser trend toward salaried jobs as opposed to self-employment.

Since the 1965 income figures were multiplied by 2.395, it is not surprising that the two surveys show roughly the same age contours with respect to income. Income is lowest at the oldest and youngest extremes and is at a high plateau between ages 30 and 59. Interestingly, the youngest group's income in 1965 is higher in constant dollars than that of its 1975 counterpart. This finding is consistent with the presumed tendency of the latter to study longer for a professional career and to marry later, actions which would have the effect of postponing high income levels.

Finally, the Jewish Activities index reveals life-cycle, period, and cohort effects. The two surveys display some similarity in their age contours: low Jewish Activity in the 20's and relatively high activity after the age of 40. This pattern is similar to the contour for frequency of giving. However, the leap to a higher plateau of Jewish Activities takes place largely among the 30–39 age group in 1965 and is postponed until the ages 40–49 in the 1975 survey. This finding would seem to indicate a cohort effect: younger Jews in 1975 may well be inherently "less Jewish" on the whole than their elders. While every age group in 1975 reports fewer Jewish Activity means than similarly aged counterparts in 1965, the declines are unevenly distributed: they are smaller (between .3 and .4) for the older (above 40) groups and larger (.6 and .8) for the younger groups.

Younger Jews in 1975 are, then, distinguished from their elders and predecessors in that they more frequently live in alternative households, more often pursue professional careers, and perform fewer Jewish Activities. It is not only the distribution of these characteristics among Jews that has been changing, however, but also the relationship between each trait and charitable activity.

The Growing Importance of Jewishness

Federations were established by the Jewish social elite in various metropolitan areas during the early 20th century. In many communities, New York being a prime example, somewhat assimilated, wealthy Jews of German background were the most active philanthropists. Their aim was to assure that the very foreign, indigent, East European immigrants who were arriving in the United States in large numbers quickly acculturated and moved out of poverty, thus avoiding any embarrassment to their more established coreligionists. While East Europeans eventually replaced German Jews as federation stalwarts, Jewish philanthropic giving remained for many years largely the province of affluent and relatively assimilated Jews. As a result, informed observers held a somewhat accurate stereotype of the Jewish philanthropist: he or she was active in Jewish public affairs but uninvolved in private Jewish behaviors.

In recent years a new group of philanthropists is thought to have replaced the old-line activists, a group motivated less by a sense of *noblesse oblige* than by particularistic religio-ethnic concerns. Thus, Charles Liebman found that the members of New York Federation's most powerful lay body (the Distribution Committee) in 1978 had higher levels of Jewish education, synagogue membership, and survivalist religio-ethnic attitudes than their 1968 predecessors.[16] If a parallel situation were to obtain among Boston Jewry's mass donor base as well, one would expect certain trends to emerge in the survey data. In 1965 private Jewish behaviors should have a limited impact on giving, while public Jewish involvement should significantly influence charitable activity. In 1975, on the other hand, the association of private behaviors with giving should show a marked increase.

Table 3 presents mean rates of CJP donations and annual amounts given by the various items and subindices which make up the Jewish Activities scale. Adjoining the main columns are difference scores, i.e., the difference in giving behavior found by subtracting the scores of the least Jewish category from the most Jewish category in each instance. Thus we can compare the effect, for instance, of having a seder, or lighting Sabbath candles, or keeping kosher in three ways: across years (the most critical comparison), across types of giving behavior (rate and amount), and across activities.

In terms of private and semi-private Jewish behaviors (the three rituals and synagogue attendance, but not organizational membership) we find a consistent pattern: both forms of Jewishness have a much greater impact on giving in 1975 than in 1965. Thus, those performing all three rituals in 1965 were only 11 per cent more likely to give to the CJP than those performing none (interestingly, they were *less* likely to give than those performing two rituals); by 1975, the impact had grown five times to a total of 56 per cent. Similarly, the amount given (in constant dollars) grew from a difference score of $108 to $375. With one exception (the impact of total rituals on the amount given) the growth in impact of rituals and service

---

[16]Liebman, *op. cit.*

Table 3

Philanthropic Behavior by Jewish Activities Items and Indices, 1965 and 1975

	Per Cent Giving to CJP				Amount Given[a]			
	1965	Dif.[b]	1975	Dif.	1965	Dif.	1975	Dif.
Take part in a Seder?								
Yes	62		51		284		240	
No	46	16	10	41	97	187	36	204
Light Sabbath candles?								
Yes	63		51		274		280	
No	55	8	38	13	236	38	135	145
Keep Kosher at home?								
Yes	60		57		195		345	
No	60	0	41	16	248	−89	174	171
Sum of above rituals								
3	59		64		196		401	
2	68		45		333		225	
1	55		48		284		171	
0	47	11	8	56	88	108	36	375
Synagogue attendance[c]								
4+	65		60		345		340	
3	56		52		210		177	
0–2	56	9	23	37	155	190	91	241
Jewish organization memberships								
3+	86		65		750		517	
2	78		53		479		240	
1	55		48		126		180	
0	50	36	31	34	120	630	101	416

a. Amount given to all Jewish causes except those connected with the synagogue, in constant (1975) dollars.

b. Difference in philanthropic behavior between highest and lowest categories of items or indices.

c. Synagogue attendance: 4+ = more often than high holidays; 3 = high holidays; 0–2 = less often than high holidays or never.

attendance upon giving is due to a decline in donations among the less Jewishly active respondents rather than an increase in charity among those most actively committed to Jewish life. It would appear, then, that philanthropic activity is becoming increasingly confined to those Jews who regularly act out their Jewishness; they maintain traditional levels of giving even as growing numbers of less-involved Jews turn away from philanthropy.

While the impact of rituals and service attendance on both the frequency and amount of giving grew significantly between 1965 and 1975, the impact of organizational involvement was of a different sort. In terms of the rate of giving, the influence of organizational membership was largely stable (declining slightly from 36 to 34 per cent), while in terms of the amount given there was a noticeable decline (from $630 to $416). What these data may indicate is that Jewish role specialization is coming to an end. In the past those Jews who were privately religious may not have been very likely to join fraternal organizations or agency boards. At the same time, those who were communally active (and hence likely to give to a communal charitable drive) were not drawn from the most ritually observant sectors of the Jewish community. By 1975, however, the less observant Jews (measured by ritual performance and synagogue attendance) had largely dropped out of organized Jewish life. Consistent with this notion, the various subindices of Jewish Activity display only weak correlations in 1965, but are significantly stronger in 1975 (data not shown). At the present time, then, only those Jews who are committed to living a Jewish life in the private sphere will be likely to express a commitment to Jewish life in the public (communal) sphere.

The changing overall impact of rituals, synagogue attendance, and organizational membership can be understood via an eta correlation ratio, a summary statistic which indicates the influence of the Jewish Activities index on charitable behavior (Table 4).

The correlation ratios essentially confirm the tabular results reported in Table 3. Examining the second row (with controls for the three other independent variables), we find barely any net relationship between Jewish Activities and charitable behavior in 1965 (etas = .13 and .11). In 1975 the comparable relationships between Jewish Activities and giving is much stronger (etas = .31 and .18 respectively).

The increasing impact of Jewish Activities on charitable behavior does not bode well for the future of Jewish philanthropy. The proportion of Jewishly involved Jews is declining, while the growing segment of relatively assimilated Jews is giving less frequently and generously than its counterparts in the past.

Table 4
Effects of Jewish Activities upon Philanthropic Behavior, 1965 and 1975

	Per Cent Giving to CJP[a]		Amount Given[b]	
	1965	1975	1965	1975
Controls				
None	.23	.39	.20	.24
Age, household & income	.13	.31	.11	.18

a. Entries in the first row are etas, or correlation ratios. Entries in the second row are betas. Both are derived from Multiple Classification Analysis.

b. Amount given to all Jewish causes except those connected with the synagogue, in constant (1975) dollars.

Occupational Shift

It was suggested above that charitable behavior should be greater among the self-employed than among the salaried, and greater among those in business than in the professions. Moreover, it was argued that the number of professionals is increasing while the proportion of entrepreneurs is declining. The validity of the above hypotheses remains to be examined.

Table 5 reports frequency of giving and average amounts donated by occupational categories in 1965 and 1975. Since both income and age are related to occupation, controls for these variables are introduced.

The data for 1965 largely support the conventional wisdom regarding differential charitable behavior by occupations. Without controls, we find high rates of giving among the self-employed (81 per cent) and much less frequent giving among salaried non-professionals (60 per cent), salaried professionals (47 per cent), and the retired (40 per cent). These relationships are narrowed somewhat when income and age are held constant (eta, the overall measure of effect, declines from .32 to .18), but the self-employed still lead other occupational groups. In terms of amounts given, the entrepreneurs are most generous ($563 per household per year), followed, rather distantly, by self-employed professionals ($297) and the others. Controls for income and age significantly narrow occupational differences as eta drops from .24 to .10. Relative to their age and income, retirees are as generous as entrepreneurs, who are only slightly more forthcoming than salaried professionals and workers. Interestingly, given their income and, to a lesser

Table 5

Philanthropic Behavior by Occupation, Controlling for Age and Income,
1965 and 1975

Controls	Per Cent Giving to CJP		Amount Given[a]	
	None	Age, Inc.	None	Age, Inc.
1965				
Self-employed pros	81	71	297	164
Entrepreneurs	81	69	563	327
Salaried professionals	47	58	219	285
Non-pro. Workers	60	62	130	222
Retired	40	46	122	324
Eta	.32	.18	.24	.10
1975				
Self-employed pros	50	52	530	384
Entrepreneurs	53	46	261	145
Salaried professionals	43	55	161	227
Non-pro. Workers	34	37	136	215
Retired	45	28	91	88
Eta	.15	.19	.26	.16

a. Amount given to all Jewish causes except those connected with the synagogue, in constant (1975) dollars.

extent, their age, self-employed professionals emerge, in 1965, as the least generous occupational group.

The patterns in 1975 deviate from those in 1965. Once again, without controls the self-employed are the most frequent donors, although only by a small margin. Holding age and income constant, however, self-employed and salaried professionals are the most frequent givers, again by a small margin. Turning to amounts given, we find very high giving among self-employed professionals, amounts that are reduced but remain substantial when income and age are taken into account. Far behind in second place are entrepreneurs. They are about half as generous as self-employed professionals; with controls for age and income they emerge as less charitable than any other non-retired occupational group.

This finding is indeed propitious: self-employed professionals—one of the two growing occupational categories—are apparently fairly frequent donors and, even more importantly, very generous donors. This finding may be peculiar to Boston insofar as the CJP has expended much effort to raise funds among the community's affluent attorneys, a group which makes up a large percentage of the self-employed professionals. Analysis reveals that lawyers are indeed the most generous professionals in the sample, with physicians being the least generous. Even if the Boston findings in this case are not applicable to the rest of the country, they certainly do point to the potential effectiveness of philanthropic campaigns focused on key occupational groups.

Gross categories of the character of work (professional versus non-professional) seem to bear little relationship to the frequency or generosity of giving. The nature of income—both its amount and its disposability as indicated by self-employed or salaried status—seems to be the key factor in mediating occupation's influence on the charitable act.

While self-employed professionals may well be replacing self-employed business people as larger than average donors, their replacement value is limited in two ways. First, the growth increase in the number of self-employed professionals is not as large as the decline in the number of entrepreneurs. The salaried professions are claiming many of those who in previous periods might have gone into business. Second, the data do not embrace people capable of the very highest levels of giving. Fund-raisers report that "superdonors", who are quite rare but extremely crucial to successful campaigns, are invariably drawn from the most affluent business sectors. Thus, while self-employed professionals can perhaps replace entrepreneurs in the second or third echelon of donors, they cannot replenish the thinning ranks of multimillionaire philanthropists.

Alternative Households

The three groups making up the alternative household type—singles, childless married couples, and divorced or separated people—score low on the Jewish Activities scale (data not shown). The reasons for this pattern probably have to do with the Jewish community's family-centeredness. The unmarried and couples without children apparently find little need to become participants in the organized Jewish community until children are born. At that point, parents may become more concerned with ritual observance in the home and may affiliate with a synagogue in order to send their children to religious school. This involvement, in turn, brings the family into a Jewish orbit where it is subject to pressure to support Jewish causes. Divorcé(e)s (with or without children) are as remote from the Jewish community as are singles and non-parents. Those without children apparently feel little need to affiliate; those with children, while making frequent use of such federation services as day-care centers and summer camps, apparently have little time available for voluntary organizations.

These general patterns are portrayed in Table 6, which reports philanthropic behavior for three household categories.

In both 1965 and 1975 alternative households are the least frequent and least generous donors. In 1965 they donated slightly more than half as often as conventional families (37 as against 70 per cent). In 1975 the absolute difference in rates is about the same, but alternative giving is now less than half as frequent as in conventional households (20 as opposed to 52 per cent). Since alternative households tend to be younger and less affluent than conventional households, we need controls for income and age to obtain the net effect of household type on giving. Taking this into account, we find that in 1965 an original difference between alternative and conventional households of 33 percentage points in the giving rate is reduced to 14 points (51 as against 65 per cent); in 1975 the reduction is less dramatic—from 32 to 19 percentage points (30 as opposed to 49 per cent).

Similar patterns are manifested in terms of the amounts given. In both years, large initial differences in amounts given are explained by differences in age and income. Once these controls are introduced, the difference in 1965 between alternative and conventional households shrinks to a mere $54 ($267 as against $213); in 1975 the difference stands at $140 ($245 as against $105).

Table 6
Philanthropic Behavior by Household Type, Controlling for Age and Income, 1965 and 1975.

Controls	Per Cent Giving to CJP		Amount Given[a]	
	None	Age, Inc.	None	Age, Inc.
1965				
Alternative[b]	37	51	90	213
Conventional	70	65	339	267
Widowed	46	48	134	332
Eta	.28	.14	.15	.04
1975				
Alternative	20	30	72	105
Conventional	52	49	273	245
Widowed	52	45	165	265
Eta	.29	.17	.18	.13

a. Amount given to all Jewish causes except those connected with the synagogue.
b. See Table 2 for household type definitions.

Widows and widowers display quite different patterns. In 1965 their giving frequency places them near the alternative households; ten years later, their giving rates approximate that of conventional families. In both years, widow(er)s' contributions are rather small; in light of their reduced income, however, they emerge when controls are introduced as the most generous group.

We have already seen how alternative households grew in number between 1965 and 1975. Now we learn, based on the Jewish Activities scale (not shown), that such households have moved further away from the Jewish community in general and, as demonstrated in Table 6, from philanthropic behavior in particular. The growing estrangement of alternative households from organized Jewry reflects recently developed institutional supports for singles, childless couples, and the divorced. These people can now find many individuals like themselves with whom to associate; they expect and demand greater acceptance of their household status as normative; they may even regard that status as permanent rather than transitory. Members of alternative households, then, are in no great need of the support of the conventional community, and are less likely to seek to emulate the behavior of conventional households.

The Diminishing Importance of Income

The simultaneous impact of the four predictors—age, occupation, income, and Jewish Activities—on giving can be understood by means of regression equations. The standardized regression coefficients (and etas) in Table 7 report the net impact of each predictor on the dependent variable controlling simultaneously for the three other determinants of charitable giving. (Since the impact of household type, once age and income are taken into account, is largely mediated via Jewish Activities, the former is excluded from the integrative analysis presented here.)

Looking first at frequency of CJP giving, we find that income and age are the most important determinants of giving in 1965, with Jewish Activities and occupation displaying smaller but nearly equivalent effects. In 1975 the picture is very different: while age retains its potency, income no longer has any effect on the likelihood of giving; Jewish Activities have become as important as age; and occupation retains a slight but noticeable effect. On the amount given side, we note that in 1965 only income has any appreciable impact on the size of charitable contributions. In 1975 income's influence has diminished while that of Jewish Activities has increased somewhat.

Another way to understand income's changing impact on giving is to consider the unstandardized coefficients (in parentheses) which report the net increase in the dependent variable per thousand dollar increase in income. Thus, in 1965 every $1,000 in income (in 1975 dollars) means a ½

Table 7

Regressions of Philanthropic Behaviors upon Age, Income, Occupation, and
Jewish Activities, 1965 and 1975

Independent Variables	Dependent Variables			
	Gave to CJP[a]		Amount given[b]	
1965				
Age	.28		.14	
Income	.25	(.005)	.56	(17.31)
Occupation	.15		.09	
Jewish Activities	.14		.11	
R	.505		.570	
R²	.255		.324	
1975				
Age	.32		.12	
Income	.00	(.00)	.43	(9.62)
Occupation	.15		.14	
Jewish Activities	.31		.18	
R	.490		.486	
R²	.240		.235	

a. Entries are eta/beta coefficients reported using Multiple Classification Analysis. Entries in parentheses are unstandardized coefficients indicating net unit change in the dependent variable per $1,000 change in income.

b. Amount given to all Jewish causes except those connected with the synagogue.

per cent increase in the likelihood of making a CJP contribution; in 1975 income has no effect on the likelihood of giving. In 1965 every $1,000 means a $17.31 increase in the size of annual contributions to all Jewish causes. By 1975 income's net impact is reduced by almost one-half to $9.62.

The diminishing influence of income and the growing importance of Jewishness reflect a changing rationale for Jewish philanthropy. Whereas in the past philanthropic giving was undertaken as a way of symbolizing economic success and securing social standing, today it is much more a reflection of Jewish commitment. Third- and fourth-generation Jews feel little need to display their wealth or shore up their social standing. Moreover, the breakdown of social barriers against Jewish entry into formerly non-Jewish social circles makes it more likely that they will contribute to non-Jewish charitable causes.

While the act of giving is unaffected by income and very much influenced by Jewishness in 1975, the opposite pattern holds true in terms of the amount given: income retains a major impact on the size of contributions while the influence of Jewishness is much smaller. Putting things crudely, it appears that deciding whether to give is a Jewish decision; deciding what to give is an economic one.

CONCLUSION

This study was initiated to test the validity of a pessimistic prognosis of the future of Jewish philanthropy. This view has been largely borne out by the data, but the picture is far from one-sided. Today's younger Jews are indeed less likely to contribute to organized Jewish philanthropy, but when they give they are more generous than their elders or predecessors.

Several factors underlie these trends. First, today's younger Jews are less Jewishly involved than their predecessors of ten years ago. At the same time, Jewish activity has become a more important predictor of charitable behavior. Second, the decline in Jewishness is itself explained by a shift away from conventional households, toward alternative households. Not only have the latter become much more numerous among the under-40 group, they have moved further away from the Jewish community in general and from Jewish philanthropic giving in particular. Third, Jews are less often entering the business world and are more frequently becoming self-employed and salaried professionals. The shift toward the professions is apparently less consequential than the shift toward salaried occupations. Relatively fewer Jews in the future will amass large fortunes. Also, fewer will have the incentive of the self-employed to contribute to philanthropy of any sort. Fourth, the wealthy can no longer be expected to serve as philanthropic stalwarts. Jewish philanthropy has become less elitist (in financial terms) than in the past.

It is clear that Jewish involvement has become philanthropy's capital stock, and that that stock is badly in need of replenishment. The self-interest of federations, then, requires that they seek to improve Jewish socialization. Moreover, since the Jewishly identified segment of the community is increasingly important in terms of Jewish charitable giving, federations might well want to adopt policies which conform more closely to its values and outlook.

The decline of conventional families, coupled with their importance for the charitable campaigns, implies that federations have an interest in promoting policies favorable to marriage, marital happiness, and fertility. However, given that long-term demographic trends have classically resisted manipulation by public policy, federations will have to address themselves to the growth of singles, childless couples, and the divorced in more immediate terms. Federations can decide to focus on the needs of alternative families and make efforts to better incorporate them into the Jewish community or they can focus fund-raising efforts on those families who have the greatest propensity to give, i.e., conventional households.

The changing Jewish occupational picture implies that fund-raising mechanisms which in the past were constructed around business circles should be replicated in the future around the professions. Indeed, Boston's CJP, as well as other federations, have shifted their organizing efforts to the professions with some apparent success. The declining number of self-employed Jews, however, poses a much greater, if not insurmountable, challenge to professional fund-raisers, since salaried status implies not only lower incomes, but less disposable income as well.

The broadening base of philanthropic support could well mean that the classical preponderance of a small number of wealthy families in each community's philanthropic circle may not obtain in the future. Federation leadership may pass to individuals of more moderate means who have a relatively strong commitment to Jewish life. Indeed, this process appears to be already underway.

Whether these trends will continue, whether policies will be enacted to deal with them, and, if so, whether they will have the desired effects remains, of course, to be seen. What is certain is that fewer donors and decreased giving would have far-reaching implications for the future of American Jewry. Such an eventuality would mean not only weakened financial support for Jewish agencies, but, in addition, lessened unity within the Jewish community, poorer recruitment of lay leaders for all aspects of organizational life, and, quite possibly, diminished Jewish political influence.

Israelis in the United States: Motives, Attitudes, and Intentions

by DOV ELIZUR

ISRAEL AND THE UNITED STATES are nations of immigrants. At the same time, both countries have experienced considerable emigration. Of the 13,000 Jews who arrived in Palestine in 1926, for example, more than half left; in 1927 emigration, for the first time, exceeded immigration.[1] Recent studies indicate that in certain periods as many as one third of the immigrants to the United States re-emigrated.[2] While studies of migration have focused mainly on the adjustment problems of immigrants, recent literature has begun to take note of the movement of emigrants back to their countries of origin. Appleyard and Richmond have investigated British emigrants returning to the United Kingdom from Australia and Canada;[3] Cerase has studied Italians returning from the United States;[4] Engel has examined Americans returning from Israel;[5] and Toren has focused on Israelis returning from the United States and France.[6]

The growing number of Israelis residing abroad is of special significance, because Israel is a small country and its existence depends on a steadily increasing population. Since the inception of the Jewish State, Israeli society has been subjected to unprecedented psychological pressure from the

Note: The author is grateful to Esther Fleishman, Joan Lewis, Miriam Berman, and Shaul Fox for kind cooperation and help; to the Institute of Industrial Relations, the University of California, Berkeley for technical assistance; to the Israeli consulates and student's organizations; to all others who contributed by providing addresses of Israelis living in the U.S.; and to all the Israelis who participated in the study by responding to the questions.

[1]Golda Meir, *My Life* (New York, 1976), p. 82.

[2]A. Antonovsky and A.D. Katz, *From the Golden to the Promised Land,* (Darby, 1979), p. 15; T.J. Samuel, "Migrations of Canadians to the U.S.A.: The Causes," *International Migration,* 1969, pp. 106–116.

[3]R.T. Appleyard, *British Emigration to Australia* (Canberra, 1964), and A.B. Richmond, "Demographic and Family Characteristics of British Immigrants Returning from Canada," *International Migration,* 1966, pp. 21–27.

[4]F. P. Cerase, "Expectations and Reality: A Case Study of Return Migration from the United States to Southern Italy," *International Migration Review,* 1974, pp. 245–262.

[5]G. Engel, "Comparison Between Americans Living in Israel and Those Who Returned to America," *The Journal of Psychology,* 1970, *74,* pp. 195–204; *75,* pp. 243–251; *76,* 117–123.

[6]N. Toren, *Characteristics, Motives for Returning, and Intentions to Stay of Returning Israeli Citizens* (Jerusalem, 1974).

outside. Tension has also resulted from the inter-ethnic strain of the Israeli melting-pot. Thus, some Israelis going abroad want nothing more than to relax; many others, however, have the aim of acquiring education or professional skills, of improving their economic situation, or of exploring life abroad.

Emigration from Israel is frequently stigmatized as unpatriotic; it evokes negative sentiments and even hostility on the part of government officials and the general public. While immigrants who come to Israel are described as *olim* ("going up"), those leaving the country are labelled *yordim* ("going down"). Yet, with a growing number of Israelis residing abroad, the social stigma of being a *yored* has significantly lessened.

Because Israeli emigrants constitute a significant sub-ethnic group among Jews in various countries, including the United States, Canada, South Africa, and parts of Europe, it is possible to investigate their motives, attitudes, and intentions with regard to the choice of a country of residence. The present study, based on data collected from two samples of Israelis residing in the United States, analyzes their reasons for going abroad, their sense of identity (Jewish, Israeli, and American), and their considerations both for and against returning to Israel.

Estimates of the extent of the *yeridah* phenomenon vary. According to official statistics, over 300,000 Israeli citizens are residing abroad.[7] The number of Israelis travelling outside the country is growing from year to year, as is the case in most Western nations. This, however, reflects a rise in the standard of living rather than a migratory trend. In the period 1950–54, when about 30,000 people left the country each year, the difference between the number of departing and returning residents was an average of 11,000, or 37 per cent. In the period 1975–77, when the number of departing residents each year was between 288,000 and 333,000, the difference between those departing and those returning was an average of 14,000, or between 4 and 5 per cent.[8] Despite an enormous increase in population and in the number of departing residents, the proportion and even the absolute number of emigrants was lower in the early 1970's than in the 1950's.

In order to study emigration from Israel, it is necessary to define the population. While it is possible to ask people directly what their intentions are, this method has limited utility. Some departing Israelis have not given any thought to migrating; others have not yet come to a definite decision. Even Israelis who plan to emigrate will probably feel uncomfortable in admitting their intentions. Experience has shown, moreover, that

---

[7]*Statistical Abstract of Israel,* Central Bureau of Statistics, 1978, pp. 126–127.

[8]Z. Rabbi, "Emigration from Israel, 1948–1977," *Monthly Bulletin of Statistics,* Central Bureau of Statistics, 1978, No. 5, pp. 83–96.

declarations of intention are not very reliable; many people who declare their intention to emigrate eventually return.[9]

Various scholars have suggested that an emigrant be defined as a person who changes his or her place of residence and stays there one year or more.[10] This definition, which is employed in United Nations reports on migration, was found to be suitable for the present study. Since "Israelis residing abroad" is more precise than *yordim* or "emigrants", the former term will usually be applied in the following discussion.

THE SAMPLE

The analysis in this study is based on two random samples: a group of 378 Israelis residing in the U.S. for 5 years or more, interviewed in 1972, and a group of 188 Israelis residing in the U.S. for one year or more, interviewed in 1977.[11] The samples were derived from lists provided by Israeli consulates, Israeli student organizations (excluding active students), and other sources. Additional names were obtained through a "snowball" effect, i.e., each respondent was asked to provide names of other Israelis known to him. A questionnaire designed for self-administration was mailed to the subjects. The response rate was about 27 per cent in both samples. While the samples may not be representative of the total population of Israelis residing in the U.S. (difficulties were encountered, for example, in reaching cab drivers), they provide some basis for understanding the group.

Sixty-five per cent of all respondents were male; 55 per cent were single when they arrived in the U.S.; 1 per cent were widowed or divorced. At the time of the investigation, 70 per cent were already married; 27 per cent had remained single and 3 per cent were divorced. In the 1977 sample, 29 per cent of the spouses were born in the U.S.; in the 1972 sample the figure was 24 per cent. Eight per cent of the spouses in the 1977 sample were of non-Jewish origin, as compared with 2 per cent in the 1972 sample. The average age of the 1977 sample was lower than that of the 1972 sample: 61 per cent of the 1977 sample were between 25 and 34 years of age; 68 per cent of the 1972 sample were in the 30–49 age group. About one-third of the 1972 sample and about half of the 1977 sample had higher education.

---

[9]*Ibid.*, p. 84.

[10]W. Petersen, "Migration, Social Aspects," *The International Encyclopedia for the Social Sciences, 10,* (Glencoe, 1968), pp. 186–292.

[11]The 1972 sample is examined in D. Elizur and M. Elizur, *The Long Way Back: Attitudes of Israelis Residing in the U.S. and in France Toward Returning to Israel,* (Israel Institute of Applied Social Research, 1974).

Seventy-four per cent of all respondents were of Ashkenazic background. In terms of religious outlook, in the 1972 sample 29 per cent were Orthodox, 54 per cent traditional, and 18 per cent secular; in the 1977 sample the figures were 16, 56, and 28 per cent, respectively. Sixty per cent of the 1977 sample were born in Israel, while only 40 per cent of the 1972 sample were Israeli-born. This finding supports the contention of many observers that a growing number of *sabras* (Jews born in Israel) are moving abroad.

THE FINDINGS

Motives for Going Abroad

In the past, leaving one's country and going overseas often resulted in a complete break with the country of origin. Technological developments in transportation and communication, however, have considerably altered this situation; travel abroad today need not involve a severing of ties. Nonetheless, migration overseas is still a difficult and risky proposition, and requires strong motivation.

The decision to leave one's home country usually ripens gradually and is the result of a variety of considerations. The scholarly literature on the subject tends to place particular stress on economic factors. What, then, are the considerations motivating Israelis to emigrate? Are there discernible differences between the two population samples in this regard?

Table I

Motives for Moving Abroad

(By Percentage)

Content	Sample	Extent of Influence					
		Very Great	Great	Some	Little	None	Total
1. Level of Income	1977	9	7	16	10	58	100
	1972	19	14	19	10	38	100
2. Standard of living	1977	6	7	18	22	47	100
	1972	15	14	21	10	40	100
3. Quality of life	1977	9	14	16	14	48	100
	1972	—	—	—	—	—	—
4. Chances for suitable employment	1977	18	9	9	10	55	100
	1972	23	16	11	9	41	100

5. Chances of acceptance at university	1977	37	6	3	6	48	100
	1972	22	7	5	2	64	100
6. Children's education	1977	1	1	5	3	91	100
	1972	6	7	5	1	81	100
7. Desire to join family	1977	10	3	5	6	76	100
	1972	15	5	7	5	68	100
8. Chances for professional development	1977	30	15	9	9	38	100
	1972*	18	11	8	3	60	100
9. Children's future	1977	2	3	5	4	86	100
	1972	10	7	5	3	76	100
10. Desire to utilize abilities	1977	28	19	9	5	38	100
	1972	20	13	16	7	45	100
11. Professional training	1977	42	10	10	3	34	100
	1972	18	11	8	3	60	100
12. Spouse's wish	1977	18	4	9	6	63	100
	1972	15	6	6	5	69	100
13. Tax policy	1977	15	4	11	9	62	100
	1972	13	5	11	5	66	100
14. Bureaucracy	1977	26	8	10	8	48	100
	1972	17	7	12	8	56	100
15. Desire to see foreign countries	1977	20	11	26	12	30	100
	1972	8	10	21	9	52	100

*In the 1972 sample, the words "and scholarships" were included in this question.

The data presented in Table I indicate that emigration is motivated in the main by considerations related to personal development, i.e., the desire for higher education, the utilization of talent and knowledge, and professional advancement. Additional factors are the quest for suitable employment, higher income, and a higher standard of living. Personal development is emphasized to a greater extent in the 1977 sample than in the 1972 sample; a remarkably lower percentage of the former group claim to have been influenced by direct material considerations. A desire to see foreign countries also seems to be an increasingly important factor; somewhat more than one in five in the 1977 sample mention this factor, while less than one in ten in the 1972 group do so.

Social Contacts

The study examined various patterns of social interaction which may occur among Israelis who have emigrated to the United States. The following directions were observed: ties may be limited to contact with other Israelis; social relations may be established with the local Jewish community; social contact may be established with non-Jews.

The data in Table II indicate that a larger proportion of the 1977 sample maintain contacts with other Israelis (56 per cent as against only 42 per cent in the 1972 sample). About the same proportion of the 1977 and 1972 samples establish contact with local Jews (53 and 57 per cent, respectively). The extent of contact with non-Jews, however, is strikingly different in the two samples; in 1972, about one in five reported having extensive contact, while one in three report having none; in 1977 one in three report having extensive contact and one in ten report having none. The tendency toward assimilation is also indicated by the growing number of intermarriages between Israelis and non-Jews. While only 2 per cent of the 1972 sample reported having non-Jewish spouses, 8 per cent of the 1977 sample do.

Table II
Extent of Social Contact
(By Percentage)

	Sample	Extent of Social Contact				
		Very Much	Much	Little	None	Total
With Israelis	1972	11	31	51	7	100
	1977	17	39	43	2	100
With local Jews	1972	18	39	38	6	100
	1977	13	40	42	5	100
With non-Jews	1972	2	20	50	29	100
	1977	7	26	57	10	100

Table III provides additional data on the social ties established by Israeli emigrants. A positive relationship exists between social contacts established with other Israelis and with local Jews. Similarly, there is a positive relationship between contact with local Jews and with non-Jews. There is, however, no relationship between ties forged with Israelis and with non-Jews. In terms of the relationship between social contact and the intention to return to Israel, there is a clear negative correlation between ties established with local Jews and non-Jews and the intention to return to Israel. Social contact with Israelis is not significantly related to intention to return to Israel.

Table III
Relation Between Social Contact and Intention to Return to Israel
Coefficients of Weak Monotonicity*
The 1977 Sample, N = 188.
(Decimals Omitted)

	Israelis	Local Jews	Non-Jews	Intention
1. Social contact with Israelis	—	29	01	04
2. Social contact with local Jews	29	—	25	−39
3. Social contact with non-Jews	01	25	—	−36
4. Intention to return to Israel	04	−39	−36	—

*Guttman's weak monotonicity coefficients were used as the measure of correlation. These coefficients vary from +1.00 to −1.00 and indicate the extent to which values of one item increase (decrease) monotonically with increases in another item, without specifying the exact nature of the regression function.

Identity

Emigration to a new country necessitates re-orientation; it involves adjustment to a different language, culture, and way of life. During the initial period of adjustment the emigrant must ask himself: Who am I? How will I present myself to others? With whom shall I associate? In working out answers to these questions, the individual determines his relationship to the new social environment. Future plans will be affected by the identity thus established.

Israelis residing in the United States can assume any of three identities: Israeli, Jewish, American. A set of items dealing with these identities was included in the 1977 study. The data reveal that 99 per cent of the respondents consider themselves to be part of the Jewish people; 96 per cent feel good about their Jewishness; and 92 per cent present themselves to others as Jews. Similarly, 91 per cent of the respondents consider themselves part of Israeli society; 94 per cent feel good about being Israelis; and 81 per cent present themselves as Israelis to others. On the other hand, 35 per cent of the respondents consider themselves to be part of American society; 22 per cent feel good about being American; and 10 per cent present themselves as Americans to others.

Jewish identity is always tied to other ethnic identities. A relatively strong link may be expected to exist between Jewish and Israeli identity, since the past and values of both are virtually the same. Thus, the majority of the subjects whom Simon Herman[12] studied saw their Jewishness and Israeliness as being interrelated. In the present study each identity was dealt with separately. The relation between the various identities could be analyzed, however, by calculating the correlation coefficients. The relations between Jewish, Israeli, and American identity are presented in Table IV. Jewish and Israeli identity are, indeed, positively related to each other, while American identity is negatively related to both Israeli and Jewish identity.[13]

Table IV
Relations Between Jewish, Israeli, and American Identity
Coefficients of Weak Monotonicity*
The 1977 Sample, N=188
(Decimals Omitted)

	American	Jewish	Israeli	Intention to Return
1. American	—			
2. Jewish	−19	—		
3. Israeli	−47	51	—	
4. Intention to return to Israel	−76	35	72	—

*Guttman's weak monotonicity coefficients were used as the measure of correlation. These coefficients vary from +1.00 to −1.00 and indicate the extent to which values of one item increase (decrease) monotonically with increases in another item, without specifying the exact nature of the regression function.

Intention to Return to Israel

What are the intentions of Israelis residing in the U.S. in terms of returning to Israel?

Data in Table V indicate that 84 per cent of the respondents are in favor of returning. Only a small percentage, however, have clear plans of returning to Israel in the near future.

---

[12]S.N. Herman, *Israelis and Jews,* (New York, 1970), p. 44.
[13]This confirms S. N. Herman's finding in *American Students in Israel,* (New York, 1970).

Table V
Intention to Return to Israel
(By Percentage)

	Sample 1977	Sample 1972
Are you thinking of returning to Israel?	(N=184)	(N=372)
Definitely yes	40	37
Probably yes	40	42
Probably no	16	18
Definitely no	4	3
To what extent do you have clear plans about returning to Israel?	(N=183)	(N=362)
Very clear	20	7
Clear	21	15
Not very clear	29	46
Unclear	31	32
If you are thinking of returning to Israel, when do you think this might be?	(N=184)	(N=366)
One year	16	5
2–3 years	18	13
4–5 years	21	5
Hope to return but do not know when	35	56
Not thinking of returning	9	11
Are you for or against returning to Israel?	(N=170)	(N=357)
Very much in favor	33	37
In favor	51	47
Against	13	14
Very much against	3	1

The relation between expressed intention to return to Israel and other variables was examined. One would expect that the considerations involved in the decision to return to Israel after living abroad would be somewhat similar to those involved in the initial decision to leave. The passage of time, however, will have brought about changes: people have grown older; singles may have married (frequently to spouses born in the host country); families may have increased in size; and social and professional ties have probably been established. These factors will have an impact on the decision.

As seen in Table VI, factors which encourage respondents to return to Israel include love for the homeland, the desire to live in a Jewish society, the wish to join other family members, and the children's education and future. The latter two considerations are particularly important for the 1977 sample. Factors deterring the respondents from returning to Israel are bureaucracy, tax policy, and level of income.

Data in Table VII indicate that the perception and presentation of oneself as an Israeli are positively related to the intention to return to Israel. On the other hand, the perception and presentation of oneself as an American are negatively related to the intention to return. The perceived attitudes of referents, especially those of spouses and close friends, have a strong impact on the decision to return. Opportunities for obtaining suitable work in Israel positively influence the decision. Time spent abroad has a negative impact. Use of Hebrew in the home is positively related to the intention to return.

Religious observance is positively (coefficient of 0.24) related to the intention to return to Israel. The majority of *sabras* of Western origin have definite plans to return, while the majority of the other groups do not.

Some scholars maintain that dissatisfaction and frustration are basic determinants of the decision to migrate.[14] Thus it is of interest to compare the attitudes of respondents toward various aspects of life in Israel and in the U.S., and to analyze the relations between satisfaction and the intention to return to Israel.

Table VIII indicates that relatively more respondents are satisfied with their work and general situation in the United States than in Israel. It is their social life in the U.S. which compares unfavorably with that in Israel. Analysis of the relationship between the various aspects of satisfaction shows that satisfaction with the general situation is closely tied to work satisfaction in the U.S. and social satisfaction in Israel.

From Table IX it is clear that the intention to return to Israel is positively related to satisfaction in Israel and dissatisfaction in the United States.

CONCLUSION

The literature on migration stresses the importance of economic factors in the decision to go abroad. The sample of Israelis who were examined in this study, however, placed greater stress on factors related to personal development—opportunities for higher education, professional training,

---

[14]S.N. Eisenstadt, *The Absorption of Immigrants,* (London, 1954).

Table VI
Considerations for Returning to Israel
(By Percentage)

Content	Sample	Extent of Attraction					
		Attracts very much	Attracts	Neither attracts nor deters	Deters	Deters very much	Total
1. Love for homeland	1977	61	25	14	—	—	100
	1972	60	33	6	—	—	100
2. Wish to join the family	1977	50	25	23	—	2	100
	1972	35	32	28	3	2	100
3. Children's education	1977	47	28	21	2	1	100
	1972	31	25	34	7	2	100
4. Desire to live in Jewish society	1977	42	34	22	1	1	100
	1972	46	34	18	1	1	100
5. Children's future	1977	42	25	24	3	5	100
	1972	37	26	31	2	4	100
6. Spouse's wish	1977	14	17	48	9	11	100
	1972	13	21	44	12	10	100
7. Quality of life	1977	10	27	27	17	19	100
	1972	—	—	—	—	—	—
8. Utilize ability and knowledge	1977	10	14	45	16	15	100
	1972	6	13	60	12	9	100
9. Chances for suitable employment	1977	6	15	41	18	19	100
	1972	2	7	46	27	17	100
10. Chances for professional development	1977	5	9	46	20	20	100
	1972	2	8	63	14	14	100
11. Standard of living	1977	2	3	58	24	13	100
	1972	3	4	46	31	16	100
12. Professional training	1977	1	2	56	25	16	100
	1972	1	2	76	13	7	100
13. Level of income	1977	—	1	46	34	19	100
	1972	2	1	41	35	21	100
14. Tax policy	1977	—	—	32	28	39	100
	1972	1	1	40	31	28	100
15. Bureaucracy	1977	—	1	19	29	49	100
	1972	1	—	38	29	32	100

Table VII
Items Related with the Intention to Return to Israel
Coefficients of weak monotonicity*
(Decimals Omitted)

| | Sample | |
	1977	1972
1. *Identity*		
Considers himself part of Israeli society	72	78
Presents himself as Israeli	70	—
Considers himself part of American society	−76	—
Presents himself as American	−79	—
Considers himself part of the Jewish people	35	—
2. *Attitudes of referents*		
Family considers him to be an Israeli	55	—
Colleagues consider him to be an Israeli	65	—
Friends consider him to be an Israeli	71	—
Spouse is in favor of returning to Israel	88	66
3. *Hebrew*		
Speaks Hebrew at home	69	38
Listens to Hebrew broadcasts	52	20
Reads Israeli newspapers	55	43
4. *Considerations related to children and family*		
Future of children attracts to return	72	57
Education of children attracts to return	63	45
Wish of spouse attracts to return	69	64
Wish to join the family attracts to return	60	46
Chances of getting suitable work attracts to return	55	29
Children attending Jewish school	52	—
Spouse non-Jewish	−54	—
5. *Dissatisfaction abroad*		
Not feeling at home	84	50
Dissatisfaction with social life	57	—
Dissatisfaction with general conditions	37	—
6. *Background characteristics*		
Time spent abroad	−67	—
Income	−48	—

*Guttman's weak monotonicity coefficients were used as the measure of correlation. These coefficients vary from +1.00 to −1.00 and indicate the extent to which values of one item increase (decrease) monotonically with increases in another item, without specifying the exact nature of the regression function.

Table VIII
Satisfaction in the US and in Israel
(By Percentage)

Content	Sample	In the US					In Israel				
		Very satisfied	Satisfied	Not so satisfied	Not satisfied	Total	Very satisfied	Satisfied	Not so satisfied	Not satisfied	Total
Work	1977	45	41	9	5	100	27	38	24	12	100
	1972	35	54	9	2	100	18	39	21	22	100
General situation	1977	30	51	18	1	100	22	42	24	13	100
	1972	23	58	15	3	100	14	34	30	21	100
Children's education	1977	28	49	15	8	100	26	52	13	10	100
	1972	35	59	13	3	100	49	40	6	5	100
Social life	1977	16	45	29	9	100	36	48	10	7	100
	1972	10	43	31	16	100	42	49	6	3	100

Table IX

Relations between Satisfaction and Intention to Return to Israel

Coefficients of weak monotonicity*

1977 Sample, N = 188

(Decimals Omitted)

Area of Satisfaction	Satisfaction in the US					Satisfaction in Israel				
	Work	General situation	Children's education	Social life	Intention to return	Work	General situation	Children's education	Social life	Intention to return
1. Work	—					—				
2. General situation	80	—				34	—			
3. Children's education	62	48	—			75	55	—		
4. Social life	37	52	62	—		42	58	25	—	
5. Intention to return	−26	−37	−33	−52	—	40	31	73	29	—

*Guttman's weak monotonicity coefficients were used as the measure of correlation. These coefficients vary from +1.00 to −1.00 and indicate the extent to which values of one item increase (decrease) monotonically with increases in another item, without specifying the exact nature of the regression function.

and the utilization of talent, as well as the desire to experience life in other countries. Thus, the motives of Israelis coming to the United States are more of a pull than a push nature. A number of scholars have argued that if migration is caused by pull factors, the chance of return migration is likely to be high.[15]

In the past, emigration from Israel was stigmatized as unpatriotic and evoked negative responses. Recently, however, Israeli authorities have changed their approach. Having become aware that Israelis residing abroad constitute a potential pool of immigrants, they have employed various means to encourage them to return. Assistance in finding employment and housing, customs reductions, and loans for travel expenses are among the benefits to which returning Israelis are entitled. Judging by the data in this study, it would appear wise for Israeli authorities not to limit their efforts to providing support for those Israelis who have made a decision to return. Israelis residing abroad should be encouraged to maintain their Israeli and Jewish identities—to read Israeli newspapers, listen to Hebrew-language broadcasts, and send their children to Jewish schools. While this cannot guarantee that Israeli emigrants will feel the need to return to Israel, it may considerably increase the chances.

---

[15]Everett S. Lee, "A Theory of Migration," *Demography,* 1966, pp. 47–57, and Samuel, *loc. cit.*

Review
of
the
Year

UNITED STATES
OTHER COUNTRIES

Civic and Political

Intergroup Relations

IN 1978 THERE WAS CONTINUED PRESSURE on Americans, caused by inflation, high taxes, and a general mood of uncertainty. This set the tone for intergroup relations.

Despite relative affluence and broad acceptance, American Jews experienced considerable anxiety as a result of a variety of developments in the intergroup area. Adding to this sense of anxiety were differences between the Jewish community and the Carter administration growing out of efforts to bring about peace in the Middle East, the continued harassment of Jews wishing to leave the Soviet Union, and an increased awareness of such problems as a low Jewish birthrate and sharp rise in intermarriage.

Religion

EVANGELICAL PROTESTANTISM, MISSIONARY ACTIVITIES, AND CULTS

There was a continuation of the growth of evangelical Protestant activities. Four weeks after publication, more than one million copies of the *Holy Bible, New International Version,* a translation by evangelicals for evangelicals, were sold. Religious broadcasting, once relegated to the early morning hours, particularly on Sunday, was becoming what the New York *Times* called "the fourth network"; there were more than 1,000 Christian radio stations and 25 religiously controlled television outlets.

The estimated 50 million evangelical Protestants were emerging from isolation and making their impact felt in the social and political arenas. Attacks continued on pornography, "gay" rights, and sex and violence on television. Two years after the election of Jimmy Carter, a "born again" Christian, to the presidency, *Congressional Quarterly* reported that the evangelical religious movement was becoming a significant factor in American politics. In several instances during the primary contests in 1978, candidates sought to persuade voters to elect "real Christians," or appealed to the public in "the name of Jesus Christ." For the most part, however, evangelical candidates either failed to survive the primaries or lost in the general elections.

Widespread public attention was given to groups like the Unification Church, Hari Krishna, and a wide variety of Hebrew-Christian sects. The spectacular mass suicide and murder in the Guyana jungle by members of Jim Jones's People's Temple highlighted the concern felt by many over these movements. According to one sociologist, some 1,300 new religious cults had sprung up in the United States since 1965.

Of special concern to Jews was the perceived threat of missionary activities. In January the Jewish Community Relations Council of Philadelphia released *The Challenge of the Cults,* which noted that "a distressingly large number of the young people being recruited into so-called cult groups" were Jewish; estimates ran as high as 60 or 70 per cent. In the metropolitan New York area alone there were some 60 such groups whose activities were geared primarily, if not exclusively, to the Jewish community. According to Malcolm Hoenlein, director of the Jewish Community Relations Council of New York, the conversionary techniques of Hebrew-Christian groups included "misrepresentation of biblical scripture; distortion of Jewish symbolism; the use of performing groups to gain entrance to Jewish organizations, synagogues, and institutions; and street corner distribution of cleverly designed humorous pamphlets with titles such as 'Jesus Made Me Kosher.' "

Jewish communal groups in New York, San Francisco, Los Angeles, Philadelphia, Chicago, and other cities mobilized to meet the challenge of the cults and missionaries. On April 5 American Jewish Committee (AJC) staff members met in St. Louis with the leadership of the Lutheran Church-Missouri Synod to express concern about the resolution adopted by the Synod the previous year making Jews a particular target of conversionary appeals. The AJC called for an immediate suspension and total revision of a highly offensive training manual entitled, "Witnessing To Jewish People." Ruth Carter Stapleton, the president's sister and a well-known evangelist, cancelled her appearance as keynote speaker at a Long Island convention of B'nai Yeshua, a Hebrew-Christian group, after she was criticized by officials of AJC and the National Council of Churches. Stapleton indicated in an announcement made on June 2 that she was concerned about the possibility of angering American Jews.

There were other factors besides missionary efforts which adversely affected the attitudes of Jews toward evangelicals. Among these were the Carter administration's policies on Israel; the growing use of the Christian Yellow Pages, which encouraged consumers to deal only with "born again" Christians; and the establishment of Christian physicians', lawyers', and businessmen's groups. The Yellow Pages and Christian groups were particularly resented because they were seen as excluding Jews from the mainstream of American life.

Efforts went forward, however, to improve relations between evangelicals and Jews. One such effort was the publication of *Evangelicals and Jews in Conversation,* edited by Rabbis Marc H. Tanenbaum and A. James Rudin of AJC and Reverend Marvin R. Wilson. The book stressed a "deepened perception" of the values and beliefs of the two groups and illustrated the diversity and pluralism that existed within each. Dr. Wilson noted that Jews had too often been viewed "as trophys to be bagged" by evangelicals. Another indication of rapprochement was the appearance of Billy Graham at the meeting of the national executive council of AJC in Atlanta, Georgia in October. This was Graham's first speech to a major national Jewish organization, and he was given AJC's Interreligious Award. In his remarks the popular evangelist, who had previously made strong statements in support of Israel, called on Christians and Jews to work together for peace in the Middle East and for an end to terrorism. A series of regional dialogues co-sponsored by the Southern Baptist Convention and AJC took place in the fall; more were scheduled for early 1979.

As the year drew to a close, Rabbi Alexander Schindler, president of the Union of American Hebrew Congregations (Reform), called on Jews to mount a "dignified" proselytizing campaign among non-Jews. His proposal, described in a front-page story in the New York *Times,* was unanimously adopted by the UAHC board of trustees. The new policy of the Reform movement precipitated a great deal of discussion in the Jewish community in terms of the impact it would have on Jewish efforts to combat Christian missionary activities and the cults.

CATHOLIC-JEWISH RELATIONS

The year found the Roman Catholic leadership seeking to influence opinion and policy in opposing abortion, the loosening of sexual mores, and other forms of permissiveness in society. At a time of growing uncertainty, the Catholic Church was stepping forward to become the custodian of traditional values and morality. Inevitably, this thrust brought Catholics into harmony with evangelical Protestants on issues like abortion, and conflict with liberal, mainline Protestants and many Jews on a wide range of social and political issues.

As Catholics moved up the economic ladder and pressed their agenda in public life—they were the dominant group in the "pro-life" (anti-abortion) movement and efforts to obtain tax credits for private and parochial schools—they were becoming an increasingly powerful political force. Catholic mayors, often only a generation away from Central and Eastern European backgrounds, governed major cities like Philadelphia, Chicago, and Cleveland, while important state capitals such as those in Connecticut, New York, New Jersey, and California, were presided over by politicians of Irish-Catholic background. The newly formed Right-To-Life party polled enough votes in the gubernatorial election in New York to guarantee it a position on the ballot; it took over fourth place behind the Conservative party, but ahead of the well established Liberal Party. In addition, "right to life" grass roots activity linked to the November elections was an important factor in the defeat of three Democratic senators—Dick Clark of Iowa, Floyd Haskell of Colorado, and Thomas J. McIntyre of New Hampshire—and the election of a number of candidates.

In June *Time* reported that the national Right-To-Life organization claimed up to 11 million members in 1,500 chapters around the nation, and a total budget of $1.3 million. By the time Congress adjourned in October, amendments attached to five different bills had outlawed about 98 per cent of federally-funded abortions, according to an estimate by the Department of Health, Education, and Welfare. As a result of drastic reductions in free abortions for the poor ordered by the federal government and by 33 states since August 1977, federally-funded abortions had been reduced from as many as 350,000 a year to fewer than 900 in the third quarter of 1978.

Catholics had less success in their efforts to obtain tax credits for parents with children in non-public schools. On June 1 the House of Representatives passed such a bill by a close vote. On August 16, however, the Senate eliminated elementary and secondary students from the bill and, in the rush for adjournment, tax credits for college tuition also failed to survive. Opposed to this legislation were a wide variety of groups, including public education officials and most Jewish organizations. In a statement made public on June 11, Carol M. Stix, education chairman of AJC, expressed the organization's opposition to the bill, calling it "an unsound expenditure of public funds" which would "undermine the principle of separation of church and state." She expressed concern that if the principle of partial reimbursement for tuition costs were made legitimate, there would be pressure to grant tax credits for total tuition, leading to increasing abandonment of "inadequately financed public schools."

Despite differences on such issues, the day-to-day relations of Catholics and Jews remained good. Catholics continued to reach out to Jews in order to learn more about the Jewish heritage. On December 10 Bishop Francis J. Mugavero of the Roman Catholic Diocese of Brooklyn issued new guidelines discouraging proselytizing and encouraging the study of Jewish history and tradition. The Diocese was described by Avron I. Brog, chairman of the New York Regional Board of the Anti-Defamation League of B'nai B'rith, as having the most successful Jewish-Catholic dialogue in the country. Similarly, officials in Philadelphia's Catholic parochial schools reported late in the year on a new supplemental curriculum on Judaism being prepared for use in the fall of 1979. The curriculum was geared to heighten awareness of the Jewish roots of Christianity, and of antisemitic attitudes which had led in the past to the persecution of Jews.

Concern was expressed in some Catholic quarters that Jews were not responding in kind to overtures. Returning to a theme that aroused considerable controversy in 1976 when he addressed a meeting of AJC, the priest-sociologist Andrew M. Greeley argued in *An Ugly Little Secret: Anti-Catholicism in North America,* that Jews were turning a blind eye to anti-Catholic sentiments which existed in the Jewish community. The focus of Catholic anger, however, was not so much the Jews *per se,* as the liberal or cosmopolitan society of which Jews were a part. Catholics were stung by such developments as the Supreme Court decision upholding abortion and Congress' unwillingness to approve tax credits for private and parochial schools. In August Senator Daniel Patrick Moynihan (D., N.Y.), co-sponsor of the tax credit legislation, indicated to the American Church hierarchy that the "institutions associated with social progress in American culture are overwhelmingly against us on this issue." He termed the opposition "vindictive" and "vicious," adding that "anti-Catholicism is one form of bigotry which liberalism seems still to tolerate."

The "surge of Catholic anger," as Father Theodore Hesburgh, president of Notre Dame University, dubbed it, was directed at leading institutions and organs of the "cosmopolitan" culture. In *An Ugly Little Secret* and "Anti-Catholicism In The Academy," Greeley charged that prestige colleges and universities had few Catholics on their faculties. In a syndicated column carried in a number of newspapers, Patrick J. Buchanan took Hollywood to task for such films as "Looking For Mr. Goodbar" and "Saturday Night Fever." "To the Hollywood screen writer," he wrote, "the traditional, socially conservative Catholic family, like the racist, Southern sheriff and the corrupt business executive, appears as a stereotypical negative figure." Commenting on "In The Beginning," a half-hour CBS situation comedy featuring a "free-spirited, street-wise nun" and "an uptight, stuffed shirt priest," the *Catholic Standard and Times* of Philadelphia asked, "Is television becoming increasingly anti-Catholic?" The Catholic League for Religious and Civil Rights, modeled after the Anti-Defamation League and AJC, was engaged in countering anti-Catholic bias it allegedly found in the New York *Times, Newsweek, Time* and other national media outlets.

Virgil C. Blum, S.J., president of the Catholic League, noted in the organization's newsletter in November that "the repeated refusals of Congress to lend financial support to parents of independent school children has had the tragic effect of imprisoning our low income minority youth in public schools, which are often wholly inadequate." The following month, in an article "Should Catholics Be Angry?" Blum pointed out that 15 religious and civic organizations endorsed the *amicus curiae* brief submitted by Leo Pfeffer, special counsel to the American Jewish Congress, in the *McRae v. Califano* case in New York, challenging the constitutionality of the Hyde Amendment, which had ended most Medicaid funding of abortions. This, he asserted, was a "most unecumenical challenge of the civil rights of Catholics." "What the Hyde Amendment's opponents have done," *Commonweal,* the liberal Catholic weekly editorialized, "is to inflate the notion of religion, and therefore of establishment and of religious infringement beyond anything relevant to the First Amendment."

In a quite different way Catholic and Jewish intellectuals also seemed to be growing apart. Writing in *National Review* (April 28), Jeffrey Hart noted that "Catholic intellectuals were moving to the left while their Jewish counterparts were going to the right." At the same time that such magazines as *Commentary, The Public Interest* and *The New Republic,* edited by Jews and with large Jewish readerships, were taking strong stands against communism, racial quotas, and welfare schemes, Catholic publications such as *Commonweal, America,* and *The National Catholic Reporter* were embracing "an intellectually jejune and dated leftism."

CHURCH-STATE RELATIONS

With the exception of the tax credit issue, there were few clashes in 1978 over church-state matters. At the close of the year, the American Jewish Congress reported that in the wake of the Supreme Court decisions banning prayer recitation and Bible reading in public schools there had been a steady decline in sectarian holiday observances at Christmas and Easter time. Nonetheless, such observances were still occurring in some parts of the country. In November a suit was filed in Sioux Falls, South Dakota by a group of parents who objected to the use of religious songs and pagents in Christmas programs. In another law suit, a U.S. district judge in Chicago denied a motion by the American Civil Liberties Union asking that the city be required to dismantle a nativity scene in the City Hall courtyard. He ruled, however, that a sign be installed at the scene stating that the display had been donated by private groups and did not represent the official religious outlook of the city. At Marple-Newtown High School in Delaware County, Pennsylvania, a group of Jewish students petitioned the Student Council not to purchase a Christmas tree, but were turned down.

On one matter the religious communities found themselves united. This involved maintenance of the section of the Internal Revenue Code giving a tax exemption to charitable, religious, and educational institutions. The IRS announced that it intended to take away the tax exemption of private schools if they were found by the courts to discriminate or if they failed to show non-discrimination when measured by a number of criteria. One such criterion was the "safe harbor" test; a school would be considered discriminatory if the percentage of minority students enrolled did not equal or exceed 20 per cent of the minority school population in the community served by the school. The IRS's new policy required schools that were "statistically suspect" to take "affirmative action" or risk losing their tax exempt status. The procedure was supported by the Departments of Justice and HEW, as well as the NAACP and ACLU, as a means of putting pressure on the large number of Christian academies that had been founded in the South in an effort to bypass the Supreme Court's school desegregation decisions.

Early in December representatives of Protestant, Roman Catholic, and Jewish groups joined forces at four days of public hearings in Washington to denounce the IRS proposal. Testimony on behalf of the National Jewish Community Relations Advisory Council, the Council of Jewish Federations and Welfare Funds, the Synagogue Council of America, and the American Association for Jewish Education was presented by the American Jewish Congress. The Congress spokesman argued that the proposal would "unfairly burden" the Jewish community: "The absence of Black students [in Jewish schools] can be attributed to facts wholly unconnected to any policy of intentional racial discrimination and is due primarily to the *de minimus* number of minority group students who are Jewish." Because of the intensity of public reaction, the IRS was expected to revise the proposed regulations.

Race Relations

BLACKS AND JEWS

The need of expanding government efforts to meet the tragic plight of the Black underclass ran head-on into efforts of cities and states to cut governmental costs and eliminate corruption from poverty and welfare programs. In New York City, for example, welfare rolls for family and home recipients were down from the peak of 1,002,847 in June 1976 to 884,426 in November 1978. Mayor Koch came into office in New York City following an election campaign in which he attacked "poverty pimps." As Koch mounted a drive seeking to remove ineligibles from the welfare rolls, he and Blanche Bernstein, the head of the City's Human Resources Administration, ran into difficulties with Blacks and Hispanics. In the spring, Representative Charles B. Rangel and State Senator H. Carl McCall filed suit in Federal Court in an attempt to halt Koch's plan to restructure New York's anti-poverty program.

Koch's difficulties with Blacks and other minorities rapidly escalated into a full-blown racial and religious confrontation. Black legislators and other spokesmen for the Black community began to associate his policy decision and personnel changes, which they vehemently opposed, with the fact of his Jewishness. Fred Samuel, a Harlem councilman, observed that as far as Blacks were concerned, Koch was the "Jewish Mayor." (His predecessor, Abraham Beame, had also been a Jew, but according to Samuel, Beame "knew how to reach out to the Black community.") Koch was attacked for appointing "so many Jewish commissioners" and restructuring anti-poverty programs in conformity with "Jewish interests." One Black spokesman publicly declared that the elements which made Blanche Bernstein unfit to head the Human Resources Administration—racism, insensitivity, and lack of charity toward the poor—were attributable to "her Jewish middle-class background."

Behind these charges lay a complex power struggle. Anti-Jewish feelings appeared at a time when Black politicians saw their political power at a low ebb. For the first time in 25 years, the Manhattan borough president's office was held by a white, Andrew J. Stein, following the defeat of Percy E. Sutton in the primary. This was closely related to the loss of Black patronage and control of the City's poverty programs. While Koch did name a Black (Haskell Ward) to head the anti-poverty apparatus, he was a former State Department official with no ties to the New York City political establishment. Koch and Ward promptly cancelled a number of contracts with anti-poverty organizations, including the giant Bedford-Stuyvesant Youth in Action, citing "severe fiscal mismanagement problems." "The Koch Administration has brought anti-Jewish and anti-Black feelings out in the open," stated Horace Morris, director of the New York City Urban League. At the close of the year, Koch attacked his critics, particularly the Black-owned *Amsterdam News,* as racist.

Further exacerbating the situation in New York City were a series of neighborhood conflicts. On June 14, in the Crown Heights section of Brooklyn, a popular Black community leader was killed in a struggle with police who were trying to arrest him. Two nights later, in the same neighborhood, a group of yeshiva students beat into a coma a 16-year-old Black believed to have attacked an elderly hasid. Following the second incident, two young hasidim were arrested, despite protests from other Jews that the men were innocent travelers who happened to be driving through the neighborhood as the police were looking for suspects.

As Dorothy Rabinowitz pointed out in "Blacks, Jews, and New York Politics," (*Commentary,* November), Crown Heights, where approximately 30,000 hasidim and 55,000 Blacks lived, had been the scene of Black-Jewish conflict for a number of years. Blacks charged that because Jews voted in great numbers, they wielded a disproportionate influence in the area. Shortly after the June incident, the *Village Voice* stated that the hasidim ran Crown Heights almost at will. So great was their influence, it was averred by Black leaders, that since 1966 the headquarters of the Lubavitcher rebbe, Rabbi Menachem Schneerson, had been guarded day and night by police patrol cars. The hasidim had organized effective neighborhood patrols to guard against crime and violence.

The two episodes in Crown Heights produced a sharp reaction on the part of Blacks and Jews. A number of protest meetings were organized by Crown Heights Blacks and numerous others from outside the neighborhood. At one such meeting, a Protestant minister was reported to have said, "We're going to get the Jews and the people in the long black coats!" A Black United Front was initiated with some 300 Black men snuffing out candles with their bare fingers and mingling blood in an oath-taking ceremony. In the course of an interview with the New York *Times,* a leader of the Black United Front stated that if Blacks could not stop the City and the hasidim from mistreating them, "maybe it will be time for people like me to step aside and let the people who say that violence is the only answer take over."

The climax of the protests came on July 16, when some 2,000 Blacks gathered at a rally on Eastern Parkway across from the massive Lubavitcher headquarters. The demonstration occurred on the same Sunday that the New York Patrolmen's Benevolent Association chose to schedule a march in Crown Heights to honor the memory of police officers slain in the line of duty. A three-way confrontation took place. One Black speaker, facing the Lubavitcher headquarters, labeled it "the house of oppression." Appeals were made for a boycott of hasidic-owned stores, and the police were urged to stand aside to let the crowd do its work. A group of 24 Black ministers subsequently disassociated themselves from the antisemitism expressed at the rally, but the *Amsterdam News* carried an approving headline, "Blacks Warn Jews."

In commenting on the significance of the events in Crown Heights, Dorothy Rabinowitz noted that "the public expression of antisemitic sentiment, as a means of conveying political antagonism, seems now to have become normal. So much so, that virtually no public notice could be taken of the explicitly anti-Jewish tirades of Crown Heights leaders, the threats to burn down Jewish houses, the enlistments to riot and commit mayhem against Jews." In an effort to head off further racial and religious antagonism, Mayor Koch announced in July the formation of a city-wide Council on Intergroup Relations.

Hardly had the situation in Crown Heights died down when another incident occurred which again exacerbated race relations. On December 2 an elderly hasidic Jew in the Boro Park section of Brooklyn was set upon and killed while on his way home from Sabbath services. A few hours later some 3,000 hasidim, dressed in their traditional black garb, descended on the 66th Police Precinct headquarters to demand greater police protection. Before long, violence broke out; 62 policemen and a number of protesters were injured, the station house door was ripped off, and police records were scattered about.

The Metropolitan Council of the NAACP charged that the failure of the police to make quick arrests in the assault on the police station represented a double standard by the city administration. In January 1979, however, Assemblyman Samuel Hirsch and four other men were arrested on charges growing out of the violent clash in Boro Park.

There were some 50,000 Jews in the Boro Park area, over 95 per cent of them Orthodox and/or hasidic. Most had come to the United States in the aftermath of the Holocaust. Surrounded by other minority groups, the Jews felt that their beards, earlocks, and traditional style of dress made them special targets for cruelty as well as robbery. Ironically, just a few hours before the clash at the station house, the police had arrested three youths who were later charged with killing the hasid. The police reported that the murder had been part of a night-long rampage of stabbings and muggings; other victims had been Haitian, Black, and Hispanic.

The Bakke Case

The serious problems of the Black underclass tended to obscure the fact that, simultaneously, the Black middle class was making significant advances. In a study made public on May 7, the Rand Corporation reported that the wage gap between white and Black workers in the United States had narrowed substantially in recent years, and that with specific reference to Black and white women, the gap had almost completely disappeared. The report indicated, however, that the average salary of Black men was still three-quarters that of white men. The annual report of the National Center For Educational Statistics noted that the number of Black college students had grown from 282,000 in 1966 to 1,062,000 in 1976; the percentage of Blacks among all college students in that period soared from 4.6 per cent to 10.7 per cent. Moreover, as William Julius Wilson, a Black professor of sociology at the University of Chicago, pointed out, almost 80 per cent of current Black collegians were attending predominantly white institutions. More generally, Wilson argued, in a widely discussed book, *The Declining Significance of Race,* that class had become more important than race in determining the life chances of Blacks.

The 1978 edition of the *National Roster of Black Elected Officials*, published by the Joint Center For Political Studies, listed 4,503 Blacks in elective office in 42 states and the District of Columbia. The figure represented a decline in the rate of growth for previous years and, as many Black leaders pointed out, accounted for less than one per cent of the more than 522,000 elected officials in the nation. Black political strength was evident, however, in the number of Black mayors in major cities across the United States, and in the ability of Blacks in Philadelphia to defeat a proposed change in the City Charter that would have permitted Mayor Frank L. Rizzo, widely seen as anti-Black, to run for a third term.

The growth of a Black middle class and its efforts to achieve full equality and advance socially provided the setting for what was probably the single most divisive issue separating Blacks and whites and, more especially, Black and Jews—the Bakke case. On June 28 the Supreme Court handed down its long awaited decision. In a 5–4 split vote, the judgment affirmed the decision of the California Supreme Court to the extent that it held that the special admissions program at the Medical School of the University of California at Davis was unlawful, and that Allen Bakke, who was white, should be admitted. At the same time, the judgment reversed that part of the California Supreme Court ruling which barred the Medical School from giving any consideration to race in its admissions policy. The decision was confusing in that Justice Powell joined with four of his colleagues in affirming the California Supreme Court on one point, and with the four other justices in reversing another point.

In ruling in Bakke's favor, Justice Powell laid great emphasis on the Equal Protection Clause of the 14th Amendment, which was guaranteed to all individuals regardless of race or ethnic origin. At the same time, however, Powell held that race could be taken into account in the admissions process, since diversity was a valid educational objective. The admissions program at Davis, which focused solely on ethnic diversity, hindered rather than furthered attainment of genuine diversity, Powell argued. He then went on to distinguish between diversity and preference: "We have never approved preferential classifications in the absence of proved Constitution or statutory violations."

Speaking for himself and three other colleagues, Justice Stevens argued for the admission of Bakke on narrower grounds. He based his judgment solely on Title VI of the Civil Rights Act of 1964 which prohibited discrimination on the grounds of race, color, or national origin in any program or activity receiving federal funds. The other four justices disagreed with Powell regarding Bakke's admission, and felt that he had not gone nearly far enough in legitimatizing racial considerations in the admissions process. It was constitutionally permissible, they argued, to endorse the explicit use of racial considerations "where there is a sound basis for concluding that minority underrepresentation was substantial and chronic, and that the handicap of past discrimination is impeding access of minorities to the Medical School."

What seemed to emerge from this complex and somewhat ambiguous decision was that affirmative action was permissible, but that the use of racial or ethnic quotas, where there has been no finding of past discrimination on the part of an institution, was not. Predictably, debate swirled about the meaning and implications for the future of the Bakke decision.

Within the Black community the reaction to the Bakke decision was mixed. National Urban League president Vernon Jordan saw it as a "green light to go forward" with affirmative action programs. Others, however, reacted with dismay. A day after the decision the New York *Amsterdam News* headlined the event: "Bakke: We Lose!!" Analyzing the impact of the decision, the newspaper concluded that it had "jeopardized every affirmative action program in the country, not only in colleges and graduate schools, but also in private business and industry." Chicago civil rights leader Jesse Jackson compared the impact of the decision on Blacks to a Nazi march in Skokie or Klan marches in Mississippi. Angry protesters rallied against the decision in San Francisco, Los Angeles, and New York.

The decision exacerbated the already strained relations between Blacks and Jews. The *Amsterdam News* warned that the decision "may further divide Blacks from Jews at the national and local levels." Louis Clayton Jones, a Black columnist, wrote that the "intellectually unstable among us will make common cause with Mr. Bayard Rustin and his friends from B'nai B'rith and the American Jewish Congress who have been vindicated in their opposition to effectively enforceable affirmative action programs by five reactionary members of a nine-man Supreme Court." He warned that overtures would be made encouraging Blacks and Jews to get together to develop new approaches to the enforcement of affirmative action programs. Deriding this, he suggested that such a Black-Jewish coalition be called JEWSAC, an acronym for Jews to Support Affirmative Action Committee.

Most Jewish organizations did, in fact, react favorably to the decision. Harold M. Jacobs, president of the Union of Orthodox Jewish Congregations of America, hailed it as "an historic milestone in the furtherance of equal rights in American society and a reaffirmation of individual rights under law." Bertram Gold, executive vice president of the American Jewish Committee, declared in an article in *Civil Rights Digest* that "both sides won." Noting that his organization had filed a friend-of-the-court brief on behalf of Bakke, Howard M. Squadron, national president of the American Jewish Congress, called on Blacks and Jews to join together in devising "effective affirmative action programs in accordance with the court's ruling."

In the weeks and months that followed the Bakke decision, greater cautiousness developed among Jewish leaders about its long-range implications. The Supreme Court decision had stressed that ethnic diversity was a valid goal in university admissions and that race could be an "important element in the selection process." Writing in *Commentary* in September, William J. Bennett and Terry Eastland warned that universities professing to employ racially nondiscriminatory admissions policies could use them as covers for de facto quota systems. Some also worried that

Justice Powell's approval of the objective of "diversity" would encourage other underrepresented groups in the learned professions, such as Italian-Americans, to seek proportional representation. New York State Senator John Calandra complained in November that Italian-Americans comprised 25 per cent of the City University student body, but only 4 per cent of the faculty. "Every other ethnic group starts yelling about quotas," he said. "I want the Italo-Americans to get what everybody else has. Otherwise I'll fight every budget in Albany."

In January 1979, the NAACP released a report charging that "the plurality of opinions in the Bakke case" had led some educational institutions "to commence tampering with and, in some instances, boldly uprooting special programs aimed at assisting minorities." The report specifically mentioned Rutgers, Yale, and the University of Pennsylvania. A spokesman for Yale Law School responded that Yale had modified some procedures in conformity with the Bakke decision, but that it had not changed its commitment to admit members of minority groups. The NAACP also noted that in the wake of the Bakke decision, lawyers representing white policemen and firemen were seeking to eliminate affirmative action programs that had previously been adopted by such cities as San Francisco, Detroit, Atlanta, and Dayton.

On December 11, the U.S. Supreme Court agreed to review *Weber v. Kaiser Aluminum and Chemical Corp.* in what some termed the "blue collar Bakke case." The case involved a white Louisiana factory worker who charged that a training program designed to increase the number of Blacks in skilled craft jobs illegally discriminated against white workers with greater seniority. At year's end, the Anti-Defamation League of B'nai B'rith prepared to file an *amicus curiae* brief in Weber's behalf. Thus, the stage appeared to be set for yet another intergroup conflict.

Whatever the effect of the Bakke decision on the private sector, it was clear that the federal government was moving ahead with renewed energy in the area of affirmative action. In December the Equal Employment Opportunity Commission issued a new set of guidelines for handling reverse discrimination cases. If an employer made a "reasonable assessment" and found that affirmative action was an "appropriate" remedy, the guidelines indicated, the Commission would not take administrative action against the company on the grounds of reverse discrimination. The guidelines drew criticism from the American Jewish Congress, the American Jewish Committee, and the Anti-Defamation League of B'nai B'rith. In a letter to Eleanor Holmes Norton, chairman of the EEOC, the three organizations reiterated their full support for eliminating discrimination and for special efforts to increase the recruitment and advancement of minorities and women. They expressed concern, however, that the guidelines would give employers the impression that the federal government was demanding that the makeup of the work force be roughly parallel to the makeup of the population, and that employers would feel compelled, despite an absence of any discriminatory practices, to institute a race conscious affirmative action plan. Concerned perhaps by this reaction, Norton, in an interview with the National Catholic News Service, revealed that she planned to investigate and attack "executive suite discrimination" against Catholics and Jews. She said that while "Catholics and Jews have indeed been able to penetrate the workforce ... there are particular industries where there are artificial cutoff points, normally at a fairly low middle management level, for people who are not Anglo-Saxon Protestants."

The year ended, therefore, with considerable uncertainty about affirmative action programs. Black leadership worried about what Vernon E. Jordan, Jr. called "the bitter harvest of a decade of negativism" that featured "indifference to the plight of the poor ... abandonment of affirmative action and letting the cities twist slowly, slowly in the wind." Working class whites and many Jews, on the other hand, feared that their rights and opportunities were being curtailed.

Extremism

ANTISEMITISM

There were manifestations of anti-Jewish prejudice on college campuses. One incident took place at the University of Florida on November 9, the anniversary of "Crystal Night" in Germany. Members of the Sigma Phi Epsilon fraternity who had been feuding with students belonging to the predominantly Jewish Tau Epsilon Phi fraternity, demonstrated in front of the TEP house, uttering antisemitic slogans and obscenities. Other incidents occurred at the University of California, Berkeley, Queens College in New York, the University of Georgia, and the University of North Carolina. On April 30 the New York *Times* reported on increasing clashes at Brooklyn College between militant minority students and Jewish collegians, about half of whom came from Orthodox families. These episodes, however, tended to be isolated, and anti-Jewish hostility remained, in general, at a relatively low level.

SKOKIE

American Jews were greatly concerned about a resurgence of Nazi groups. During the year, Nazis were active in St. Louis, San Francisco, Detroit, Cincinnati, Houston, Kansas City, Milwaukee, and Denver. A predominantly non-Jewish crowd in St. Louis prevented a Nazi group from getting off a truck which brought them to the site of a proposed march and rally. In San Francisco there was an anti-Nazi demonstration involving such groups as the NAACP, Catholic Archdiocese, Protestant Church Council, and Jewish Community Relations Council.

The most important episode involving the Nazis occurred in Skokie, Illinois, where the National Socialist party, under the leadership of Frank Collins, sought to hold a march. Skokie had a population of 70,000, including 40,000 Jews, many of whom were concentration camp survivors. At a meeting of religious and community leaders from Skokie and representatives of the Anti-Defamation League, an initial decision was reached to deal with the threatened march through the classic quarantine method. However, pressure from Nazi survivors who vowed that they were not going to allow anyone to flaunt the swastika forced a revision in this strategy. Three ordinances were enacted by the Skokie officials; one required a permit for any parade or public assembly involving more than 50 persons; a second banned "political organizations" from demonstrating in "military style" uniforms; a third prohibited the display of "symbols offensive to the community" and the distribution of literature that ascribed a "lack of virtue" to racially or ethnically identifiable groups. Concurrently, a small group of Skokie Jews sought an injunction against any Nazi demonstration, because of the injury it would allegedly do to them. These actions raised the issue of freedom of speech, and the American Civil Liberties Union came to the defense of the Nazis. The U.S. District Court and the 7th Circuit Court of Appeals ruled that guarantees of free speech protected even American Nazis.

The proposed march, which was postponed a number of times and finally scheduled for June 25, 1978, quickly became a major media event across the country. Eugene Dubow, Midwest regional director of the American Jewish Committee, pointed out that for many American Jews, particularly those under 35, it was the first time in years that they faced a pointedly antisemitic attack in an area heavily populated by Jews. The Jewish community responded through the Public Affairs Committee of the Jewish United Fund of Metropolitan Chicago, which made plans for a counter-demonstration if all legal appeals failed. Expressions of solidarity were received from various ethnic, religious, and civic groups, and thousands of people from all over the country made ready to gather in Skokie.

The complex series of legal moves finally culminated in a terse, one-sentence order issued by Supreme Court Justice Warren E. Berger on June 12 denying Skokie's request for a temporary stay of the march. Officials in Skokie had hoped that the Supreme Court would hold up the march until the town had a chance to appeal lower Federal Court rulings which had struck down as unconstitutional the three local ordinances designed to prevent the Nazi rally. Having gained a legal victory, the Nazis cancelled their plans to demonstrate in Skokie in favor of a rally in Marquette Park in Chicago. A carefully regulated, but considerably smaller, counter-demonstration by Jewish civic and religious organizations was held nearby. In addition to the usual calls to "burn the Jews" and "warm up the ovens," the Nazis made an effort to cash in on anti-Black feeling in the working-class, white ethnic area by wearing "White Power" T-shirts.

Following this episode debate ensued over the tactics employed in dealing with the Nazis. The veteran head of the Anti-Defamation League in the Midwest, A. Abbot Rosen, argued that the Jewish community had played into the hands of the Nazis by giving them publicity that they would otherwise never have received, given their small numbers and lack of public appeal. Others pointed out, however, that the Nazis came across in the media as pariahs, and that the admittedly high visibility they received did them little good.

The effect on the Jewish community of events in Skokie was considerable. The planned Nazi march was one of a number of occurrences in recent years contributing to a new sense of militancy with regard to Jewish safety and security. It marked, most probably, the end of the quarantine method which Jewish organizations had used for many years to handle gutter bigots and fanatics with little or no political power. It contributed, further, to pushing the Jewish community away from its traditional pro-civil-liberties stance. Some 30,000 members of the ACLU, a significant proportion of them Jews, left the organization in protest against the ACLU's position. There was a drop of 30 per cent in the Illinois membership alone. On May 19 the National Executive Council of the American Jewish Committee adopted by a narrow margin a resolution calling on the organization to take appropriate legal action to halt demonstrations aimed "specifically at highly vulnerable groups such as Jews."

"Holocaust" Television Series

The Skokie case was argued in the Appeals Court a few days before NBC-TV began showing "Holocaust," a four-part, fictionalized drama dealing with the fate of European Jewry during World War II. The nine-and-a-half-hour series marked an important television breakthrough. Nearly 120 million people, including members of the White House staff and cabinet—one of the largest audiences on record for a television special—watched all or part of the series. It was praised by a wide variety of church, communal, and civil rights leaders, including Benjamin Hooks of the NAACP, Vernon Jordan of the National Urban League, and Terry Herndon of the National Education Association. "The lesson of the Holocaust and of the television program by the same name is that it is never too soon for Christians to come to the defense of Jews who are being threatened by any form of antisemitism," Msgr. George Higgins wrote in his widely syndicated column in the Catholic press.

In order to measure the impact of "Holocaust" on viewers, the American Jewish Committee commissioned a survey by Response Analysis. Sixty per cent of the viewers said that watching the program made them better understand Jewish suffering at the hands of the Nazis. Three-quarters of them thought the series accurate, and more than two-thirds felt it was a good idea to present such a program on television. Since 30 per cent of the viewers and almost half of the non-viewers described themselves as poorly informed about the Holocaust, it was significant that almost two-thirds of those surveyed thought it a good idea to teach children about the subject.

"Holocaust" spurred a number of educational efforts. In October some 400 educators from around the world met in Philadelphia at the First International Conference on Teaching the Holocaust. Workshops were also held in a number of other cities. The Anti-Defamation League published *On the Holocaust,* a critique of the treatment of the subject in history textbooks. The American Jewish Committee provided *A Viewer's Guide to Holocaust.*

There was, however, some dissent. NBC reported that one out of four telephone calls it received about the series was unfavorable, as were 13 per cent of the letters that were sent in. In Chicago, where there was a sizeable German-American community, the German-language newspaper the *Abendpost* collected more than 1,500 signatures calling on education officials in Chicago to restrict teaching about the Holocaust. The newspaper argued that such teaching might leave the impression that "a Nazi is a German, a German a Nazi."

"Holocaust" spurred the movement, already underway, to bring to justice alleged Nazi war criminals who were living in the United States. Denaturalization proceedings were held during the year in Chicago, Baltimore, and Fort Lauderdale. When U.S. District Court Judge Norman C. Roettger ruled on July 26 in Fort Lauderdale that Feodor Federenko, a former Nazi concentration camp guard, could keep his American citizenship even though he had lied to obtain it, the American Jewish Congress urged the Department of Justice to appeal the decision. At the close of the year, efforts were underway by survivor groups, and virtually all other Jewish organizations, to get West Germany to extend the statute of limitations that would permit that country to prosecute Nazi war criminals there.

Conclusion

The year's events made it clear that group conflict in the United States could no longer be seen as the product of psychological aberrations which produced prejudice, racism, and antisemitism among some people. Rather, it was rooted in the differing group interests, values, life styles, and even historical memories which existed in a pluralistic society. The deepening sense of Jewish anxiety, highlighted by the revival of Nazism, Black-Jewish friction, and other factors, was promoting a new militancy with regard to the defense of Jewish interests. This militancy was bound to effect the usually liberal social-political posture of American Jews.

MURRAY FRIEDMAN

The United States, Israel, and the Middle East

D URING THE PERIOD UNDER REVIEW, President Jimmy Carter intensified his personal involvement in attempts to settle the Arab-Israel conflict. His efforts were crowned with success in the Camp David accords of September 1978. It took another six months of American pressure and blandishments, however, before the historic Egyptian-Israeli peace treaty could be signed on the White House lawn.

Although the United States had long been involved in Middle East peace efforts, under the Carter administration the American role was transformed from that of catalyst to acknowledged "full partner"—an enhanced role that had been advocated by Egyptian President Anwar Sadat. President Carter conceded that there was an inherent tension between the traditional American role as friend and advocate on behalf of Israel and the U.S. role as honest broker.

In fact, the United States had never been a completely disinterested mediator, since it had its own regional and global interests to protect. There had long been a bipartisan consensus that those fundamental interests included the containment, if not elimination, of Soviet influence; the encouragement of moderate and pro-Western elements; and continued access to and assured supply of Middle East oil to the United States and its West European and Japanese allies.

Israel shared these concerns. But tension became acute when Washington and Jerusalem did not see eye to eye on how American interests in the region might best be preserved, and whether specific Israeli actions harmed these interests.

The Carter administration continued to reaffirm the American commitment to Israel. Marking the anniversary of the Jewish State in the presence of Prime Minister Menachem Begin, President Carter declared on May 1:

> For 30 years we have stood at the side of the proud and independent nation of Israel. I can say without reservation as President of the United States that we will continue to do so not just for another 30 years, but forever . . . The United States will never support any agreement or any action that places Israel's security in jeopardy.

Nevertheless, there was growing concern in Israel and within the American Jewish community that the special relationship between the United States and Israel was being eroded under the impact of new circumstances in the Middle East. The sharpest clash between the administration and Israel's supporters developed in the spring of 1978 over the Carter administration's insistence on portraying Saudi Arabia as a major force for peace and stability in the Middle East. After a bitter fight, the Carter administration won Senate approval for its arms package deal, which tied the sale of previously promised aircraft to Israel not only to congressional

87

acquiescence in the sale of 50 F-5E's to Egypt, but also to the sale of 60 sophisticated F-15's, the most advanced plane in the American arsenal, to Saudi Arabia.

Whatever the long-term effect of the arms sale to Saudi Arabia on the military balance in the region—Israel was to receive 15 F-15's and 75 F-16's—the immediate psychological effect was to enhance the public perception of the power of Arab petro-dollars and to weaken the influence of Israel and its supporters. One administration source reportedly went so far as to crow in private about having "broken the back of the Jewish lobby." Publicly, however, the administration denied any such intention and sought to mend its fences with the Jewish leadership. The controversy over the arms sales package had earlier (in March) led Mark A. Siegel to resign his post as White House liaison to the Jewish community, on the grounds that he was not given accurate information by administration officials about the Saudi arms sale and, more generally, that he was not afforded the opportunity to present the concerns of the Jewish community as he perceived them before administration decisions affecting Israel were reached.

The package deal approach to Middle East arms sales was symptomatic of the linkage between the incipient Egyptian-Israeli treaty and a commitment to work toward resolving the other outstanding issues, notably the future of the West Bank (Judea and Samaria) and Gaza. Prime Minister Begin also gave vocal endorsement to the concept of a comprehensive peace and denied that Israel sought a separate peace with Egypt. But Israel wanted its bilateral treaty with Egypt to stand on its own legally, and Begin strenuously objected to any provisions that would make Sadat's fulfillment of his obligations toward normalization of relations with Israel contingent on progress in negotiations on any other fronts. Since Israel's major concessions to Egypt were tangible and essentially irreversible, Israel was concerned lest Sadat or his successor use lack of progress on the Palestinian issue or absence of negotiations with Syria as an excuse to delay movement toward peaceful relations with Israel.

The United States government, however, was deeply concerned about the negative effect that the appearance of a separate Egyptian-Israeli peace would have on America's relations with other elements in the Arab world. Consequently, the Carter administration took great pains during 1978 and early 1979 to reassure the Saudis, the Jordanians, and the Palestinians that the United States was sympathetic to their interests.

While high-level American diplomatic missions in this direction undertaken by National Security Adviser Zbigniew Brzezinski and Assistant Secretary of State Harold Saunders managed to antagonize Israel and arouse anxiety in the American Jewish community, they failed to win the endorsement of King Hussein of Jordan, or of King Khalid and others in the Saudi royal family. Predictably, the Palestine Liberation Organization (PLO) denounced the American peace initiative. But the open rejection by virtually all Palestinian municipal officials on the West Bank and in Gaza, the exclusion and nearly total isolation of Egypt at Arab League conferences convened in Baghdad in November 1978 and March 1979, and the active part played by Saudi Arabia in imposing political and economic sanctions against Sadat came as a surprise to American policy makers.

Strains in Saudi-U.S. Relations

The increasingly negative role played by the Saudis, despite the friendship the Carter administration had displayed in ramming through Congress the F-15 plane sale, was attributed to a combination of factors. Divisions within the large Saudi royal family became increasingly apparent, with some of the younger members beginning to question the value of Saudi Arabia's traditional reliance upon the United States and demanding that Saudi Arabia diversify its international contacts. The United States had failed to stop Soviet and Cuban influence in South Yemen and the Horn of Africa. Washington had been taken by surprise when Noor Mohammed Taraki overthrew President Mohammed Daud in Afghanistan in April 1978 and greatly increased Moscow's influence in strategic Kabul by signing a 20-year friendship pact with the Soviet Union and bringing some 3,000 Soviet advisers to Afghanistan. These events might have been considered peripheral to American vital interests, but the apparent inability or unwillingness of the United States to prevent the overthrow of Shah Mohammed Reza Pahlevi caused the Saudis to wonder how reliable the United States was as an ally. The U.S., after all, had repeatedly referred to Iran as a bulwark of United States interests in the strategic oil-rich Gulf area. Moreover, the American commitment to Iran had been reflected in the sale of billions of dollars' worth of the most sophisticated arms to the Shah and the presence of tens of thousands of American technicians in the country.

While American policy makers had hoped to convince the Saudis that the loss of Iran made it all the more important for them to give at least tacit support to pro-Western and moderate elements in the Middle East, such as Egypt and Israel, which could serve as a barrier to Soviet penetration, the Saudis sought to buy insurance for themselves by siding with the radical Arab opponents of the Camp David accords, and even allowed rumors to be floated that Riyadh was considering developing ties with Moscow. The Saudis had in the past worked behind the scenes to promote Arab consensus—as in their efforts to overcome Egyptian-Syrian feuding, end the Lebanese civil war, and limit oil price rises—but now the Saudis publicly cast their lot with the Arab majority opposed to the Sadat initiative and also joined the more aggressive of the OPEC members to agree in December 1978 to a 14.5 per cent increase in oil prices.

The Saudi actions proved an embarrassment to the Carter administration. Senator Frank Church (D., Idaho) recalled that the administration had claimed that approving the F-15 sale "would give us much leverage with Saudi Arabia." Following the Baghdad conference and the OPEC action, Senator Church charged that the Saudis "have given us no help of any consequence." The incoming chairman of the Senate Foreign Relations Committee called for a reassessment of American policy toward the Saudis, noting that they "have played a negative role in the Middle East" both with regard to the pursuit of peace and stabilization of oil prices.

The prospect of an impending Egyptian-Israeli peace treaty prompted the rival Ba'ath leaderships in Syria and Iraq temporarily to shelve their long-standing feud and to begin conciliatory moves designed to lead to an eventual union. Similarly, Syria and Jordan continued their steps at gradual coordination and cooperation, and even King Hussein and PLO leader Yasir Arafat, who had been locked in bloody battle in 1970, met to explore ways of countering what they perceived to be the challenge presented to them by the Egyptian-Israeli peace treaty.

Lebanon as PLO Terrorist Base

Whatever the rhetoric about linkage of the Egyptian-Israeli peace treaty to a comprehensive settlement of the Arab-Israel conflict, all sides knew that if Egypt was effectively and permanently removed from the fighting, Israel would be in a far better position to counter any threat mounted from the so-called eastern front—Syria, Lebanon, Jordan, Iraq, and potentially Saudi Arabia. During 1978 the immediate threat to peace in the area came from an escalation of Palestinian terrorist raids launched from Lebanon. The worst outrage occurred in March 1978 when PLO terrorists landed on a beach near Tel Aviv and seized passengers on the highway, killing 37 Israeli citizens and wounding 76 others. The Carter administration quickly condemned this action, but UN Ambassador Andrew Young urged Israel to avoid a "knee-jerk reaction" and to "consider the consequences of violence, even retaliatory violence." More than 400 members of Congress supported strongly worded resolutions condemning PLO terrorism and calling on the president to report to Congress the names of countries supplying arms and other support to the PLO.

After Israel launched a major attack to root out PLO terrorist positions in southern Lebanon, occupying a border area some six miles in depth, the United States undertook intensive behind-the-scenes efforts to prevent a further escalation of violence and to bring about an early Israeli withdrawal. After Israel's punitive raid, administration spokesmen became "even-handed" in their public criticism. Secretary of State Cyrus Vance indicated that both the Palestinian attack and the Israeli response had raised "impediments to the peace process." Department spokesman Hodding Carter III said the U.S. "deplores this new cycle of violence which erupted in the tragic killings in Israel . . . and continued with the military action and tragic loss of innocent civilian lives in Lebanon . . ." He also emphasized that the only real solution lay in a search for "a comprehensive settlement of the Arab-Israeli conflict in all its aspects and for measures which would restore long-term stability in Lebanon."

Although Prime Minister Begin was expected in Washington in a few days—the initial PLO terrorist attack causing his trip to be postponed for a week—the Carter administration rejected Israeli requests to defer action on the Lebanese situation until Begin could discuss it with President Carter. Instead, the United States pressed at the United Nations for the withdrawal of the Israelis and their replacement by a UN peace-keeping force, which was in turn eventually to be replaced by the Lebanese army. While the United States was providing $100 million to equip a new Lebanese army under the control of Lebanese president Elias Sarkis, this was still only a token force of some 3,500. The old Lebanese army had disintegrated during the civil war and the new army was no match for the 30,000 Syrian "peace-keeping" troops, the roughly 10,000 armed Palestinian guerrilla forces, and the various private militias belonging to the different Christian and Muslim factions.

Israel's UN Ambassador Chaim Herzog expressed doubt during the Security Council debate on March 17 that a UN force with sufficient "muscle" to curb the PLO in the border area would be established, especially in view of the Soviet Union's continued supply of arms to the PLO and the $40 million that Saudi Arabia was providing the PLO annually. On March 19 the Security Council adopted an American resolution (by a vote of 12-0, with the Soviet Union and Czechoslovakia abstaining and China not participating) calling for "strict respect for the territorial integrity, sovereignty, and political independence of Lebanon within its internationally recognized boundaries," and calling on Israel "immediately to cease its military action against Lebanese territorial integrity" and to "withdraw forthwith its forces from all Lebanese territory." The Council also decided in accordance with the request of the Lebanese government to create a United Nations interim force for southern Lebanon (UNIFIL) for the purpose of "confirming the withdrawal of Israeli forces, restoring international peace and security, and assisting the government of Lebanon in ensuring the return of its effective authority in the area."

The following day, the Council adopted an additional resolution specifying that UNIFIL was to have a geographically balanced force of 4,000 men (raised in May to an authorized strength of 6,000) drawn from national contingents volunteered by various UN members (France, Norway, Fiji, Ireland, Iran, Nepal, Nigeria, and Senegal). The Israeli delegation charged that the United States had, in private negotiations, yielded to Arab pressure to delete a key phrase in the original draft of the American resolution that would have authorized UNIFIL to control movement in a demilitarized border area, and "to prevent the entry of unauthorized armed persons into the zone," a phrase directed at the PLO. In the resolution text that was adopted this phrase was replaced by wording that authorized the UN force to supervise the cessation of hostilities, insure the peaceful character of the area, control movement, and take measures to restore Lebanese control. The Israelis protested that this wording was too vague and would not have received their approval had they been consulted. American delegates claimed that they had tried to sound out the Israelis, but the latter had been pre-occupied with arrangements to meet Prime Minister Begin.

State Department Criticizes Israel

Israel was also upset by Secretary of State Cyrus R. Vance's report to Congress on April 5 that "a violation" of the 1952 legal agreement under which Israel receives

American arms "may have occurred by reason of the Israeli operations in Lebanon." Vance was responding to inquiries by several members of Congress who contended that Israel's large-scale moves in Lebanon utilizing American-supplied weapons violated a 1976 amendment to the Arms Export Act (prompted by the Turkish intervention in Cyprus) which specified that all U.S. military assistance should be terminated if a recipient country used American arms "in substantial violation" of any agreement. Prime Minister Begin insisted that all Israeli actions were based on "legitimate self-defense" in response to repeated incursions into Israel from bases in Lebanon by Palestinian terrorists. He also reiterated that Israel had no territorial designs against Lebanon. Secretary Vance, in his letter to House Speaker Thomas P. O'Neill, Jr., said that the matter had been discussed with senior Israeli officials and that Israel agreed to comply with the provisions of the Security Council resolution, including Israeli withdrawal. In view of these assurances and because of the "efforts to restore momentum to the vital peace negotiations," he was not recommending to the President any further action against Israel.

According to press reports, earlier State Department drafts of the Vance letter had been tougher in tone and included an implicit warning that American aid might be cut off in the future if the Israeli forces were not soon withdrawn. Representative Benjamin S. Rosenthal (D., N.Y.) reacted angrily to the Vance letter, declaring that it "contradicts prior policy followed consistently by previous administrations that when Israel responded to PLO raids that came out of Lebanon these were legitimate acts of self-defense." He termed the Vance letter "a significant change in American policy, a very disturbing shift."

Israel completed its phased withdrawal in June, but relinquished the last occupied area to a Lebanese Christian militia force headed by Major Saad Haddad, rather than to UNIFIL. Israel defended its action as a move to honor its commitment to protect the Lebanese Christian enclaves which had been cooperating with Israel. An attempt by the Beirut government to move regular Lebanese forces south in August failed when it ran into armed opposition from Haddad's Christian militia, which charged that the force was actually dominated by Syrians. Although the Syrian government had prudently refrained from getting its forces into a direct confrontation with Israel in southern Lebanon in March, the danger of potential conflict increased in October when, for several days, Syrian "peace-keeping" forces shelled Christian areas in Beirut and Israeli gunboats shelled Palestinian bases near the Syrians. President Carter sent a personal message to President Hafez al-Assad, who was then visiting Moscow, asking him to end the bloodshed, and also urged the Soviets and the Saudis to influence Assad. The president had earlier made similar appeals to all the parties involved. Israel Foreign Minister Moshe Dayan, who was on his way to Washington for Egyptian-Israeli peace negotiations following the Camp David agreement, told reporters on October 6 that "the Syrians are acting very negatively, but whether this is meant to torpedo the negotiations, I really can't say."

No full-scale conflict between Syria and Israel occurred during the period under review, but this continued to be a potential danger. That Damascus was not really prepared for total war with Israel was signified by the Syrian government's agreement to the periodic renewal of UNDOF, the UN force that separated Syrian and Israeli forces on the Golan Heights. The Security Council also periodically renewed the mandate of UNIFIL, but when it did so in January 1979 it expressed regret that UNIFIL had not been enabled to complete its tasks, and in particular deplored Israel's "lack of cooperation" and its continued assistance to "irregular armed groups in southern Lebanon." The Israelis were critical of the UN's one-sided approach, arguing that UNIFIL had failed to prevent infiltration by PLO terrorists and that the ultimate mission of UNIFIL, the restoration of Lebanese sovereignty throughout the country, could not be achieved until the Syrian occupation forces withdrew and the Palestinian guerrilla groups were effectively disarmed or removed from the area.

Opposition to U.S. Aid to Syria

In August the House of Representatives adopted by a vote of 280 to 103 an amendment by Representative Edward J. Derwinsky (R., Ill.) to eliminate the $90 million in economic aid to Syria from the Foreign Assistance Appropriations Act for 1979. The main reasons cited for rejecting the aid were Syria's continued military actions against the Christians in Lebanon and Damascus' vehement opposition to the peace process initiated by President Sadat. The Senate had approved the full administration request. A compromise proposal of $60 million, introduced by Representative Silvio O. Conte (R., Mass.) and initially approved, was reversed after intensive lobbying before the conference committee by administration spokesmen— including Secretary Vance, Vice President Walter F. Mondale, Defense Secretary Harold Brown, and National Security Adviser Brzezinski—who pressed for restoration of the full $90 million, arguing that this was a modest but necessary sum to keep the door open to American influence in Syria. The House conferees went along with their Senate colleagues after adoption of an amendment by Matthew McHugh (D., N.Y.) instructing President Carter to allocate the funds "only if the President believes that such aid would serve the process of peace in the Middle East."

The administration was eager not to jeopardize any chance for success of Secretary Vance's post-Camp David summit trip to Damascus. Critics pointed out that the $425 million in economic aid provided by the United States to Syria since 1975 had produced few tangible signs of moderation. Syria's fiery foreign minister, Abdul Halim Khaddam, had repeatedly declared that Sadat should be tried as a criminal and hanged for making peace with Israel; Syria had joined the even more radical states of Libya, Algeria, and South Yemen in breaking relations with Cairo; and within days of the Camp David accords Damascus hosted a summit of the "Steadfastness and Confrontation Front" which reportedly set up a $1-billion fund to undermine the Camp David accords. Vance returned from Syria with little more positive than a sense that while President Assad opposed the terms of Camp David, he did not completely rule out an eventual negotiated settlement on terms favorable to Syria and the Palestinians.

Senator Clifford P. Case (R., N.J.), who opposed the aid to Syria, also decried the American decision to approve the sale of L-100 transport planes to Syria ten days after Camp David. He noted that the Syrians had "reciprocated" these two generous gestures by continuing their onslaught against the accords and by stepping up their "attacks on the Christian community in Lebanon, creating hundreds of casualties."

U.S. Role in Peace Process

Since the details of the Egyptian-Israeli negotiations leading to the signing of the peace treaty in March 1979 are reviewed elsewhere (see Louvish, pp. 253–63), this article will focus primarily on the American role in the process.

The major points of disagreement between the Carter administration and the Begin government during 1978 focused on conflicting interpretations of what Israel was required to do to implement United Nations Security Council Resolution 242 of November 1967 (see AJYB, 1968, Vol. 69, pp. 180–81), the territories occupied by Israel in the 1967 Six Day War, and most crucially the legal status of East Jerusalem, the Gaza Strip, and the West Bank. Begin insisted that the unification of Jerusalem, "Israel's eternal capital," was not negotiable, and that the West Bank be referred to by the biblical names of Judea and Samaria, since, in his view, they were not occupied but had been liberated from the illegal occupation maintained by Jordan between the 1948 and 1967 wars.

The Carter administration tended to follow the general view of previous administrations, first developed under President Johnson after the Six Day War, that although Israel was not required to withdraw to the precise lines of June 5, 1967, which had reflected only the hastily drawn and politically negotiable military armistice lines of 1949, Resolution 242 envisaged substantial Israeli withdrawal on all three fronts—with Egypt, Syria, and Jordan. As for Jerusalem, the U.S. government had acknowledged since the days when Arthur Goldberg was American ambassador to the UN under President Johnson that the city was unique and required special arrangements to assure the interests of the three major monotheistic religions, that the city should be open to all, and that it should not again be physically divided as it had been under Jordanian rule. Nevertheless, the United States refused to recognize any unilateral actions by Israel, such as the extension of Israeli jurisdiction over East Jerusalem or the large-scale new Jewish housing developments therein as having any validity. Since 1969 the U.S. had occasionally voted at the UN to condemn such Israeli actions, but President Carter was the first repeatedly to declare in categorical terms that they were "illegal and an obstacle to peace." He applied the same stigma to Israeli civilian settlements in the West Bank.

This was to result in heated confrontation between Carter and Begin, with the latter insisting that Jewish settlements were not only legal but would be actively encouraged throughout historic *Eretz Yisrael* (the land of Israel). In part, this reflected the ideological differences between Begin's Likud party and the preceding Labor governments. The latter had accepted the principle of returning the densely inhabited portions of the West Bank to Jordan in a peace treaty, and had in general restricted officially approved Jewish settlements to areas that were considered crucial to Israel's security and which were not heavily populated by Arabs. The Begin government also approved, more readily, settlements begun by civilian activists, notably Gush Emunim (the bloc of the faithful) in areas of Jewish biblical and historical significance, such as Shiloh and Elon Moreh, even where they were close to Arab population centers and of debatable security value.

Ironically, the Begin proposal, presented to Sadat at Ismailia on December 25, 1977, to return the *entire* Sinai to Egyptian sovereignty was considerably more generous than what had been widely regarded as the bottom-line Labor party position—adjustment of the international frontier to enable Israel to maintain control of a narrow land corridor along the Gulf of Aqaba from Sharm el Sheikh in the south to El Arish along the Mediterranean. This was regarded as essential to assure free passage for Israeli shipping to the port of Eilat, in view of the history of prior Egyptian blockades that had precipitated the 1956 and 1967 wars. In this regard the Begin government's position was close to that of the United States.

Sinai Settlements Controversy

The fate of the Israeli settlements in Sinai was to become a source of controversy between Egypt and Israel, with the United States tending to back the Egyptian position. The Labor government had on security grounds encouraged their establishment along the Gulf of Aqaba (Eilat) and along the Mediterranean coast in the Rafiah salient, which separated the traditional invasion route in northern Sinai from the densely-populated Gaza Strip. Prime Minister Begin initially had insisted that the Jewish settlements in Sinai would have to remain and be protected by Israeli forces. Begin went so far as to write a letter to the worried settlers of Yamit, pledging that when he retired from office he would settle there.

The fundamental nature of the difference between Sadat and Begin on the settlement issue was apparently not immediately realized when Begin first mentioned his desire to maintain the Jewish settlements during the Ismailia talks. Sadat had brushed the matter aside with a remark to the effect that the question of a few Jewish settlers—there were only some 3,000 in the Rafiah area—should not be allowed to stand in the way of the great vision of peace and reconciliation that he had ushered in with his pilgrimage to Jerusalem. Begin thought that this meant that Sadat's objection to the settlements could be overcome, while the Egyptian leader believed that he had convinced Begin to relinquish the settlements. It was to take another fifteen months of intensive negotiations and vigorous prodding before Begin and the majority of the Israeli Knesset approved the dismantling of the settlements in Sinai, which Sadat had made a non-negotiable precondition for the signing of the peace treaty with Israel.

The controversy had already begun to poison the atmosphere for negotiations in January 1978. At the beginning of the month, angry settlers met with Foreign Minister Dayan and Agriculture Minister Ariel Sharon to protest the turnover of Sinai to Egypt, prompting an Israeli announcement that existing settlements would be expanded. On January 7 Sadat declared that he would not allow "a single Jewish settlement on Egyptian soil" after the completion of the Israel withdrawal. The following day, the Israel Cabinet voted not to establish any new settlements in Sinai, but agreed to extend agricultural lands surrounding the settlements and to encourage additional settlers to help thicken the existing settlements. A few days later Sharon issued orders for bulldozers to clear extensive areas for cultivation in Sinai.

Meanwhile, Gush Emunim members took over a site near ancient Shiloh on the West Bank, planted trees, and laid the cornerstone for a new settlement. They had received government permission for what was ostensibly to be limited to an archaeological dig, although the settlers lacked the proper training, a point that could not have escaped the notice of the Cabinet, which included, as its deputy prime minister, Yigal Yadin, a world-renowned archaeologist.

These Israeli actions infuriated Sadat, and caused anger and dismay in official Washington. National Security Adviser Brzezinski said that the decision to set up additional Sinai settlements reflected "poor judgment" since this "complicated the negotiating process." He expected Israel to show "good judgment and good faith by refraining from such acts." At a press conference on January 12 President Carter said that he and President Sadat viewed the Middle East conflict "about identically." He reiterated his view that Israel had a right under Resolution 242 to obtain "secure" boundaries. The following day, in an interview with editors, Carter said he could not imagine the peace negotiations breaking down over settlements, adding that there might be "some mutual agreements between Jordan, Egypt, and Israel that some of those Israeli settlers could stay on there." But that would depend on whether UN peace-keeping forces were involved, or the responsibility was "Jordan's or Palestine's [sic] or Egypt's." Carter then paused to say that he thought such details should not be discussed in public.

Carter's View of the U.S. Mediating Role

Discussing the American role in the negotiations, President Carter said that it was "an unpleasant thing" for him to be the intermediary for more than nine months between nations who would not even speak to each other. He termed the start of direct negotiations between Egypt and Israel "a very major step forward and a very satisfying thing for me to observe." President Carter said that he privately discussed issues in dispute "without constraint with both Begin and Sadat, and we are very forceful in letting Prime Minister Begin and the Arab leaders know when we disagree with their position." He added that in order to maintain the trust of all parties he was very careful whenever he had an American proposal to put forward as a compromise or as a basis for discussion to do so in writing and to show exactly the same document to all sides, including Jordan and Syria, and to report their reactions to each other. He noted that this was a tedious process and that sometimes the United States took the blame from both sides.

Future of Palestinian Arabs

Other than the settlements, the major differences among Egypt, Israel, and the United States centered on the Palestinian question. Before submitting his 26-point plan for Palestinian self-rule and administrative autonomy to Sadat on December 25, Begin had shown it to President Carter, who had termed it "a realistic negotiating position" offering "a great deal of flexibility." Some State Department officials had counselled Begin not to present the detailed plan to Sadat, since there were many specific points that would arouse Egyptian, Jordanian, and Palestinian objections. They suggested a more general statement of principles that would leave the door open for drawing the others into subsequent negotiations. Begin insisted on presenting the full plan, which predictably upset the Egyptians, and no agreed statement of principles emerged from Ismailia. The only agreement was for joint military and political committees to begin talks in Cairo and Jerusalem, respectively, in January 1978.

Having displeased the Israelis by reference to the "illegality" of the settlements, President Carter proceeded in an interview with television correspondents, on December 28, to discuss the Palestinian issue in a way to "disappoint" Sadat and to make PLO leader Yasir Arafat livid with rage and vow an escalation of "fighting until victory." In response to questions as to what he meant by a Palestinian entity or homeland, Carter replied:

> We do favor a homeland or an entity wherein the Palestinians can live in peace. I think Prime Minister Begin has taken a long step forward in offering President Sadat, and indirectly the Palestinians, self-rule. President Sadat so far is insisting that the so-called Palestinian entity be an independent nation. My own preference is that they not be an independent nation but be tied in some way with the surrounding countries, making a choice, for instance, between Israel and Jordan.

He noted that the Begin autonomy plan offered the Arabs a choice of Jordanian or Israeli citizenship and a chance to run their local affairs. A lot remained to be negotiated, and he added that the United States would go along with any solution deemed acceptable by Israel and the surrounding countries. "But my own personal opinion," the President reiterated, "is that permanent peace can best be maintained if there is not a fairly radical, new, independent nation in the heart of the Middle Eastern area."

At the conclusion of the talks with President Sadat in Aswan on January 4, 1978, President Carter declared that a just and comprehensive peace would require three fundamental principles:

First, true peace must be based on normal relations among the parties to the peace.

Second, there must be withdrawal by Israel from territories occupied in 1967 and agreement on secure and recognized borders for all parties in the context of normal and peaceful relations in accordance with United Nations Resolutions 242 and 338.

Third, there must be a resolution of the Palestinian problem in all its aspects. [This] must recognize the legitimate rights of the Palestinian people and enable the Palestinians to participate in the determination of their future.

The statement went a long way to meeting Sadat's views and stopped just short of speaking of "self-determination" or an independent Palestinian state, although it should be pointed out that the Aswan formula did not explicitly rule out such a possibility. Upon his return home from the Middle East, Carter expressed the hope that agreement by Egypt and Israel on such an agreed set of principles would make it easier for Jordan and eventually Syria to join the negotiations.

Evidence that the course of Egyptian-Israeli negotiations was not to be smooth emerged already in January when the political talks in Jerusalem first were delayed a day until Secretary of State Vance worked out a compromise agenda, and then were broken off on the second day, when Sadat abruptly recalled Foreign Minister Muhammad Ibrahim Kamel. Much was made in the press of the "insult" that Begin had allegedly delivered to Kamel during a dinner toast by referring to him as "a young man" who did not personally remember, as did elder men such as Begin and Vance, how the "great human concept" of self-determination had been misused by the Nazis to bring disaster in Europe. The real reasons for Sadat's decision were more fundamental, since the discussions on the day following the toast seemed to be proceeding well and the Egyptian delegates were as stunned as the Israelis by Sadat's instructions to come home.

It appears that Sadat had only reluctantly and under strong American prodding agreed to the start of the January political talks. Opposition in the Arab world had continued to mount, and even within Egypt some influential advisers were concerned about the symbolism of agreeing to hold the political discussions continually in Jerusalem without any prior indication that Israel would modify its stand on exclusive Israeli political sovereignty over the entire city, including the Arab-inhabited sections. (Significantly, none of the subsequent Egyptian-Israeli negotiations were held in Jerusalem, and Sadat firmly declined Begin's invitation to have the peace treaty ceremonies held there.)

Sadat had hoped to get Begin to agree to a general statement of principles on withdrawal and Palestinian rights at Ismailia, along the lines of the Aswan formula he obtained from Carter, as a means of countering Arab objections to his peace initiative. But in an interview published in the Egyptian magazine *October* on January 14, even *before* the start of the political talks in Jerusalem, Sadat said he now had "absolutely no hope" that a declaration of principles between Egypt and Israel could be reached, adding cryptically that therefore "we will have a different strategy."

In its announcement following the suspension of the talks, the government of Israel expressed its regret and attributed the breakdown to the Egyptian "illusion that Israel would surrender" to unacceptable demands and agree to a declaration of principles in advance of the outcome of the negotiations. Israel, it said, did not set any preconditions but would not accept those dictated by the other side. The Israel government statement recalled that the Egyptian foreign minister had demanded that Israel "transfer the Old City of Jerusalem to foreign rule and further demanded the establishment of a Palestinian state in the territory of Eretz Yisrael in Judea, Samaria, and Gaza. Such a Palestinian state would have extinguished any prospect of peace and would have created a danger to the very existence of the Jewish State." The statement went on to declare that "there has never been, and there will not be, a government in Israel that would agree to such conditions." It concluded by indicating that Egypt could present whatever it wished as a proposal but not a precondition, and that "should the Egyptian government decide to renew the negotiations, Israel will be willing to do so."

Sadat Appeals to American Jews

Seeing that he could not persuade the Israeli leadership itself to meet his terms, Sadat returned to his pre-Jerusalem strategy of attempting to drive a wedge between the United States and Israel. The new tactic in this campaign was an appeal to the American Jewish community to pressure Israel. In an "Open Letter to American Jews," published in the Miami *Herald* on January 29 and reprinted in many other papers around the country, including New York's mass circulation *Daily News,* Sadat called on the Jewish community to assume "a historic responsibility for erecting a formidable edifice for peace," explaining that all people of Jewish faith "shoulder a special responsibility" in reviving the spirit of accommodation and peaceful coexistence. Jews are "most qualified to play a pivotal role in eliminating human suffering and misery," he said, because of their own sad experience of persecution.

Acknowledging that American Jews were "an integral part of the American people," Sadat said that he expected them to refuse to support the "perpetuation of injustice or the suppression of legitimate aspirations." Implicitly attacking Begin's appeals to Jewish solidarity, Sadat said that American Jews "should not be taken for granted by any power, regardless of the merits of its position." He then emphasized that the goal of his peace initiative was to end all war and violence, and eliminate all fears and grievances so that the Israeli would "live side by side with the Egyptian, the Syrian, and the Palestinian in a community of mutual benefit and love."

Sadat stressed that he undertook his historic mission to Jerusalem against all odds, not "to strike a bargain or to reach a compromise," but in order to uproot all "grudges, feuds, and misconceptions" in the area. He proceeded to complain that "the behavior of the Israeli government in the past few weeks has been negative and disappointing," and that his visit to Jerusalem had "not been responded to in a forthcoming manner." Sadat elaborated that he had hoped the spirit prompting his "sacred mission would propel us all to a new plane where we do not spend our time and effort fighting for procedural and peripheral matters." (This was a theme that Sadat returned to frequently. In a meeting in Washington with some American Jewish leaders on the day after the Egyptian-Israeli peace treaty signing in March 1979, Sadat was still complaining of the difficulty he had in dealing with Prime Minister Begin, who, he said, haggled over every detail and insisted that everything, e.g., the Egyptian promise to sell Sinai oil to Israel, be precisely spelled out in legalistic language, instead of trusting in Sadat's good faith now that a new era of peace was being ushered in.)

Sadat said time was of the essence to prove to Arabs and Jews alike that peace could work. He repeated that American Jews had a great responsibility to prevent tragedy by seizing the golden opportunity before the spirit of peace faded away. He then proceeded to ask four pointed questions:

Do you condone the annexation of others' territory by force?

Do you tolerate the suppression of the rights of the Palestinian people to live in peace in their homeland, free from foreign rule and military occupation?

Do you forgive the suppression of human rights of the Palestinians in the West Bank and Gaza and their natural right to liberate their land and emancipate themselves?

Do you agree with those Israeli officials who claim that territorial expansion is more important than the establishment of peace and the normalization of the situation?

Sadat concluded that he was certain that American Jews would "not hesitate to make [their] voices heard in favor of justice and security for all peoples in the Middle East."

Sadat thus placed American Jews in a position they had long sought to avoid. If they joined him in criticizing Begin's policies, they would be undermining a crucial element in Israel's traditional base of domestic support within the United States. If they refused to join in such criticism, Sadat was laying the groundwork for isolating American Jews from the mainstream of the American public, and even opening the door to charges of disloyalty. This potential danger could become actual to the extent that the Carter administration publicly supported the view that the Egyptian position was consistent with the American national interest, while Israeli actions were illegal and constituted obstacles to peace.

The *Daily News* on the same day carried "A Jewish Reply" to Sadat written by Rabbi Alexander M. Schindler, chairman of the Conference of Presidents of Major American Jewish Organizations. After praising Sadat for his "daring" peace initiative and for his recognition of the special Jewish commitment to justice, Schindler disputed Sadat's statement that Israel had not responded to his visit in a forthcoming manner. Schindler argued that "Israel has made far-reaching territorial and political concessions—involving great national risks—in demonstrating its own commitment to peace."

Schindler pointed out that Begin's autonomy plan provided the Palestinian Arabs with more self-rule and self-identity than they enjoyed under Jordanian rule, and that the sincerity of the Israeli people's desire for peace had been demonstrated in the warm welcome they accorded Sadat. The American Jewish leader proceeded to dispute Sadat's evaluation that the Israelis were haggling over procedural and peripheral matters: "Israel's quest for carefully defined security arrangements . . . goes to the heart of the matter." Israel itself needed to be able to guard the peace, not out of a desire for "annexation" or "suppression" of Palestinian rights, but "simply to protect human lives—Arab as well as Jewish—from PLO terrorists still sworn to Israel's destruction, from the danger of Soviet incursion," and from Arab opponents of peace who had denounced Sadat as a traitor.

Schindler went on to point out that Sadat's apparent disdain for the negotiating process and insistence on full acceptance of Egypt's terms ran counter to the American Jewish experience of living in a democracy, which had "persuaded us that there can be no agreement without compromise, no settlement of disputes without mutual concessions." Alluding to Sadat's assertion that American Jews should not be taken for granted by any power, Rabbi Schindler turned aside the implication of possible dual loyalty: "Surely you understand that American Jews support Israel because the Jews are a people, one people . . . because Israel offers a home, a refuge, a place of dignity to every Jew . . . because a strong and free and democratic State of Israel is essential to the security of our own country, America." Rabbi Schindler concluded by suggesting a continuation of the dialogue on Sadat's forthcoming visit to the United States, and a joint call to the Arab rejectionist nations to join the peace process.

American Jews Between Begin and Carter

While Sadat's direct appeal to American Jews was an unusual occurrence, both the Carter administration and the Begin government intensified their ongoing efforts to persuade the American Jewish community to support their respective positions on the contentious issues in the Middle East. In the controversy over the sale of F-15 fighter planes to Saudi Arabia, the organized American Jewish community was vocally supportive of the Israeli opposition to the sale, in keeping with the traditional view prevalent in the American Jewish community that on military matters affecting Israel's vital security, Americans living 6,000 miles away should not attempt to second-guess the decisions of the Israelis, whose lives were on the line.

When a series of "grim" meetings at the White House in March between Prime Minister Begin and President Carter revealed that the two were far apart in their approach to the peace negotiations, American Jews began to be increasingly drawn into the public debate as to who was responsible for the apparent stalemate in the peace process. The debate in the American Jewish community echoed what President Carter on March 9 termed the "very heated debate" in Israel itself on what should be done to bring about peace. (Some suspected that the Carter administration was in fact fanning the fire of controversy.) Particularly at issue were the new civilian settlements being set up in the West Bank with governmental approval, on historic and religious grounds, coupled with repeated declarations by Prime Minister Begin to the effect that Judea and Samaria (the biblical names for the West Bank region) were liberated territory and therefore not subject to the withdrawal provisions of UN Security Council Resolution 242.

On these questions of ideology and tactics there was no unity either within the American or the Israeli Jewish communities. It was the Labor government in Israel in 1967 that had endorsed Resolution 242, and had long accepted the concept of territorial compromise on the West Bank. Justice Arthur Goldberg, a prominent Jewish leader, who, as American ambassador to the United Nations in 1967, was the principal architect of 242, declared in a series of articles and statements in the spring of 1978 that 242 envisaged Israeli withdrawal *on all three* fronts. Heretofore it had only been the extent of withdrawal that had been at issue between the United States and Israel. President Carter warned at his news conference on March 9 that "abandonment" or rejection of the applicability of 242 to the West Bank would be "a very serious blow to the prospects of peace" and a complete reversal of Israeli government policy.

In a Middle East statement adopted at its May annual meeting, the American Jewish Committee coupled its criticism of the Carter administration on the arms sale issue with an endorsement of the view that Resolution 242 "contemplates some territorial adjustments consistent with Israel's legitimate security requirements in all the areas that came under Israeli control" in the 1967 war. The criticism of the Begin position was softened by a reference to recent Israeli government statements which indicated that the Begin government was prepared to negotiate with all its neighbors in this spirit. Begin and Foreign Minister Dayan did in fact reiterate that "everything is negotiable," and that Jordan was entitled to ask for Israeli withdrawal from the West Bank in the negotiations. This was an attempt to move the debate from the level of fundamental ideology to one of negotiating tactics.

The issue of the establishment of new civilian settlements involved both legal and tactical questions. The Carter administration contended that Israeli settlements in the West Bank were inherently illegal under international law and an obstacle to peace. Most American Jews, including the leaders of the American Jewish Committee in their May statement, agreed with Prime Minister Begin that "settlement of

Jews in the Land of Israel is absolutely legal and accords with international law." The issue for the Committee was thus not the legality but the prudence of establishing new settlements while negotiations with Egypt were in progress. The White House, in a March 25 memorandum outlining American-Israeli disagreements following the Carter-Begin talks, said that "Israel would not agree to a policy of stopping the establishment of new settlements, nor the expansion of existing settlements, even if peace negotiations were proceeding." The Committee, in its May statement, urged the Israeli government to consider a "pause" in new settlement activity while negotiations were underway.

Committee of Eight Mission

Concern within the organized American Jewish community over the apparent erosion of Israel's image and the consequent potential decline in support for Israel's policies among the general public in the United States had prompted eight prominent American Jewish leaders to go to Israel in mid-April for private discussions with Prime Minister Begin and other Israeli leaders. The group consisted of the president and chief executive officer of the three major Jewish intergroup relations organizations—the American Jewish Committee, American Jewish Congress, and Anti-Defamation League of B'nai B'rith—and the chairman and executive director of the National Jewish Community Relations Advisory Council. The "committee of eight" presented polling data and other evidence to indicate that support for Israel was softening both in Congress and among the general public. The group agreed in part with Prime Minister Begin's complaint, expressed to the National Press Club in Washington on March 23, that the initial words of praise from the American administration for Begin's peace proposal as a "notable contribution to peace" had unfairly been replaced in recent months by sharp criticism in response to Arab objections and the Carter administration's desire to win Egyptian, Saudi, and Jordanian support. Nevertheless, as the committee of eight pointed out, Israeli statements with regard to Resolution 242, the timing of new settlements, and the emphasis on biblical and historical rights rather than on security considerations in justifying the settlements had unnecessarily confused and alienated even traditional supporters of Israel in America.

Upon their return to the United States, the group met with President Carter and Vice President Walter F. Mondale at the White House. In a statement issued afterwards, the Jewish leaders emphasized that they had made clear to the president and vice president that "the American Jewish community was united and unwavering in its support of Israel's security concerns" and in opposition to the administration's linking of jet sales to Israel with similar sales to Saudi Arabia and Egypt. On the settlement issue, the group said that while "one may legitimately argue about the impact on American public opinion of the timing of new settlements, we continue to challenge the administration's position that settlements are illegal and serve no security function." They termed Begin's peace plan "very imaginative and far-reaching" and deserving of greater support than it had been given by the Carter administration. They concluded by urging the president to call upon President Sadat to return to the negotiating table, and to encourage King Hussein of Jordan to join the talks. The group reported that President Carter had reiterated that "the preeminent commitment of the United States in the Middle East [was] the permanent security of Israel," and that the administration would continue its efforts to bring the parties together to achieve a just and lasting peace.

"Peace Now" versus "Secure Peace"

Whereas the committee of eight had gone to Israel to discuss its concerns quietly with the Israeli government, other American Jews joined the public debate that was reaching unprecedented proportions in Israel. On April 1 an estimated 25,000 to 30,000 persons crowded into Tel Aviv's "Kings of Israel" Square in support of a letter to Prime Minister Begin by some 350 army reservists, mostly combat officers, who had called on the government to give preference to ending the Arab-Israel conflict and "establishing peace and good neighborly relations" over maintaining settlements beyond the Green Line (the 1949 Armistice Line that demarcated Israel from the West Bank and Gaza territories). They favored a territorial compromise, using the slogan "Better a land of peace than a piece of land," and argued that ruling over a million Arabs contradicted the fundamental values of Zionism and democracy. The amorphous group initially had various names but soon came to be known as the "Peace Now" movement.

On April 21 the New York *Times* gave front-page coverage to a letter sent by 36 prominent American Jews expressing their support to the Peace Now leaders in Israel. The group included Nobel Prize laureates Saul Bellow and Kenneth Arrow, other prominent university professors, editors, and authors, as well as individuals long active in Zionist or other Jewish organizational work.

The message, which was initiated by Leonard Fein, professor at Brandeis and editor of *Moment,* stressed that the writers were "lifelong friends of Israel" who were disturbed that the Begin government's response to the Sadat initiative, its reinterpretation of 242, and its expansion of new settlements made their task of maintaining support for Israel "infinitely more difficult." The group welcomed Peace Now's call for greater flexibility in Israel's negotiating position with Egypt. The American Jews also expressed distress at the "dangerous Middle East policies of the American government," and concern at the "apparent readiness of Western nations to abandon Israel." The Americans pledged to continue to work for a secure peace for Israel and greeted with "delight and relief" the emergence of a grass-roots movement in Israel dedicated to safety and peace for Israel.

In response to "Peace Now" a group of supporters of the Begin policies organized under the slogan "Secure Peace" and held a rally on April 16 which they claimed was attended by 40,000 to 50,000 people. They too won vocal support from American Jews, and an *ad hoc* committee of American Jews in support of Begin gathered more than 700 signatures in 48 hours. By July the American supporters of Peace Now had gathered more than 600 names to sign an advertisement in the Jerusalem *Post.* Americans for a Safe Israel placed a full-page ad in the New York *Times* on April 12 showing Holocaust victims under the heading "Six Million Jews Who Were Not Intransigent," and suggested that copies of the ad be sent to President Carter. On May 2 the Zionist Organization of America ran a full-page ad in the *Times* charging that the Carter administration was "selling Israel for petro-dollars" and that "Sadat, not Begin, is the obstacle to peace."

The Labor Zionist Alliance issued a policy statement in New York in May calling upon the Likud government to accept the traditional interpretation of Resolution 242, "namely, peace with defensible borders agreed to in negotiations with all of its neighboring states and including territorial compromises on all fronts, but no return to the 1967 borders." This paralleled the position of the Israel Labor party, which advocated the return of portions of the West Bank to Jordan. While criticizing the Begin position, the Labor Zionist Alliance also assailed the "continued erosion of support" for Israel by the Carter administration, as well as the administration's Saudi-Egyptian-Israeli plane deal package.

Rabbi Arthur Hertzberg, the outgoing president of the American Jewish Congress, pointed out in a New York *Times* interview in April the "terrible dilemma" that had caused American Jews to be very reluctant to criticize Israeli policies. Since they knew that all too often "public dissent in America becomes an anti-Israel weapon," many American Jews regarded it as "the path of safety or wisdom" to keep quiet about their reservations. Presidents' Conference chairman Schindler, who did not personally agree with all elements of Prime Minister Begin's policies, urged that Americans refrain from characterizing Begin's position as "intransigent," pointing out that his tough posture might be simply a good bargaining tactic, especially in view of Begin's assertion that "everything is negotiable." At the same time, Schindler, who had earlier been a supporter of President Carter, said that the president's policies had made him a "question mark" to American Jewry.

Major newspapers, such as the New York *Times* and Washington *Post,* gave considerably more prominent coverage to the critics of Begin than to his supporters. In response to charges that they were thereby aiding the administration's alleged efforts to split the Jewish community and weaken support for Israel, newspaper representatives responded that criticism of Israel by Jews was a "man bites dog" story that naturally aroused more interest and was more newsworthy than the expected traditional posture of Jewish support for Israeli policies.

The Carter administration's Middle East policy continued to raise serious questions and uneasiness in the American Jewish community, despite some extraordinary gestures by the president to win support among the Jewish leadership. Most notable of these was the invitation of more than 1,000 rabbis and other community leaders to the White House lawn for a ceremony marking Israel's 30th anniversary at which the president warmly praised Begin and declared that the United States would continue to stand at the side of Israel "not just for another 30 years but forever." Another gesture was the invitation to 28 American Jewish leaders to accompany Vice President Mondale on a three-day official "goodwill visit" to Israel in early July. Although Mondale had earned a well-deserved reputation in the Jewish community as a friend of Israel and stressed the abiding American-Israeli ties, he too failed to remove the fears within the American Jewish community and in Israel that the administration was preparing to pressure the Begin government to change its policy. In a speech to the Knesset, Mondale again emphasized that although "exact boundaries must be determined through negotiations," Resolution 242 was based on the assumption of a trade-off of withdrawal for peace and recognition. The United States was therefore "convinced that without eventual withdrawal on *all* fronts to boundaries agreed upon in negotiations and safeguarded by effective security arrangements, there can be no lasting peace." (Emphasis added.) He termed the disputes between the United States and Israel over application of the withdrawal provision to the West Bank as "differences between friends," and pledged that American economic and military aid to Israel would "not be held hostage or used as a form of pressure on Israel's negotiating posture." Israeli and American Jewish critics of the administration pointed out that public enunciation of an American position in support of the Arab position was itself a form of pressure, since it weakened Israel's bargaining position.

The Israelis were also disturbed by Mondale's suggestion that Israel's proposed peace treaty with regard to the Sinai—a treaty "in which there would be a negotiated withdrawal and security would be achieved while relinquishing claims to territory" —could be applied to the West Bank as well. When questioned by reporters about this comparison, he acknowledged that there were differences between the two areas, but said he had in mind such measures as demilitarization, electronic sensors, and other arrangements that might enable Israel to relinquish land without loss of security. This had long been National Security Adviser Brzezinski's thesis, but it greatly disturbed the Israelis, who insisted that the security situation in the narrow and heavily populated West Bank and Gaza Strip was fundamentally different from that in the Sinai, with its vast empty spaces. This was in addition to the special historical and ideological attachment of Begin and his supporters to Judea and Samaria.

Disagreement between American and Israeli policy on Jerusalem also surfaced during the vice president's visit when it was initially announced that he would not make an official visit to East Jerusalem, the section of the city controlled by Jordan from 1948 to 1967. After Mayor Teddy Kollek threatened to boycott the Mondale visit, a compromise was worked out whereby the vice president and his wife and daughter made a personal visit to the Western Wall accompanied by Mayor Kollek as their host and guide. The American visitors were greeted by numerous pickets carrying signs critical of United States policy. Rabbi Saul Teplitz, president of the Synagogue Council of America, said, "For the first time in 30 years as an American visitor to Israel, I get the feeling that I am somewhat in an enemy camp," adding that some Israeli friends saw his coming with the Mondale delegation "as an indication that [he] had sold out." To allay that impression some of the American Jewish leaders vigorously expressed their criticisms of current American policy in a private meeting with U.S. Ambassador Samuel Lewis, and in interviews with the Israeli press.

A full-page ad in the Jerusalem *Post* by 33 prominent American Jews in support of the Begin government appeared on July 3, to coincide with the Mondale visit. In addition to Rabbi Schindler, the signatories included two former Presidents' Conference chairmen, Rabbis Herschel Schachter and Israel Miller; prominent industrialists and UJA leaders, such as Max Fisher; Rabbi Joseph Sternstein, president of ZOA, and other leaders of ZOA and Herut in the U. S.; and Gerald S. Strober, chairman of the recently founded Committee of American Jews in Support of Prime Minister Begin. They lauded "the earnest and diligent efforts" Israel was making for peace, and called upon the American government to encourage direct Egyptian-Israeli negotiations "rather than setting unreasonable demands upon one of the parties." The signatories believed they expressed "the sentiments of the overwhelming majority of American Jewry" in supporting the Begin government and commending its "tireless efforts on behalf of peace. . . ."

When Mondale went on to Egypt to meet with President Sadat, the Jewish delegation with him was divided over the wisdom of accompanying him. The problem was resolved when the U.S. government informed the group that their participation would cause "logistical problems." The vice president went to Egypt alone, and American Jews were thus not formally drawn into the negotiating process.

Breakthrough at Camp David

During the summer there were additional trips to the Middle East by special envoy Alfred (Roy) Atherton and Secretary of State Vance, and inconclusive talks among Vance and the Egyptian and Israeli foreign ministers at Leeds Castle, near London, in mid-July. While Egypt and Israel were still far apart on many points, these preliminary discussions had convinced all sides that the two countries were still genuinely eager to reach a peace agreement. Consequently, President Carter sent handwritten notes to President Sadat and Prime Minister Begin asking them to join him in a summit conference at the presidential retreat at Camp David. Both quickly accepted. The conference began on September 5, and after 13 intensive days of extraordinary effort and many crises, President Carter announced that an agreement had been reached. That night the Camp David agreements were signed by the three leaders—Jimmy Carter signing in the capacity of witness—at the White House in a moving ceremony that was televised live around the world (For the main points of the agreements see Louvish, pp. 258–60).

The American Jewish community had been deeply fearful during the conference that Israel would be blamed for the anticipated failure. The community was relieved and overjoyed a the success of the talks and the cordiality that the three leaders expressed to each other. It was a rare moment in which American, Israeli, and Egyptian interests all appeared to converge, and the organized Jewish community was lavish in its praise for Carter, Begin, and Sadat. When the Camp David achievement resulted in a Nobel Peace Prize for both Begin and Sadat, most major American Jewish organizations sent congratulatory telegrams to the Egyptian as well as to the Israeli leader, and Egyptian officials in the United States began to be besieged with invitations to speak at Jewish organizational events.

At the White House signing ceremony, Prime Minister Begin declared that the Camp David summit should be renamed "the Jimmy Carter Conference," a remark that was greeted with laughter and applause. The direct American involvement was indeed crucial to the success of the talks. There were several elements in this. First, there was the president's decision to exclude the press from the deliberations. The president, who had exacerbated the situation by some of his own public statements, had finally come to the realization that even in an open democratic society the process of negotiations had to be insulated from the public. As he explained on the eve of the conference, his hope was that "personal interchange, without the necessity for political posturing or defense of a transient stand or belief, will be constructive." Indeed, there were several issues on which there was a significant evolution from the opening position at the start of the conference to the language agreed upon at the end.

A second factor was the intensive personal involvement of the president, who literally stayed up into the early hours of the morning drafting suggested compromise language and reviewing every aspect of the proposed agreements, departing from the normal practice of leaving details to be worked out by professional aides. Since Sadat and Begin were quite different in personal style and at that point still tended to distrust and dislike each other, President Carter, after a couple of unsuccessful three-way meetings, decided to use his persistence and powers of persuasion to deal with the Egyptian and Israeli leaders separately.

In this effort Carter had another important asset. He had dramatically demonstrated the importance he attached to achieving a peace agreement by taking the unprecedented step of totally devoting himself to the Middle East problem to the exclusion of all other pressing business. Although there was no time limit set at the opening of the conference, it was generally realized that the clock was ticking and that the president of a superpower could not absent himself from other affairs of state for more than a couple of weeks. There was thus implicit pressure to conclude the conference. It could have been ended by announcement of failure, and there was at least one occasion on which Sadat indicated that he was ready to pack up and leave. But he was prevailed upon by Carter to stay.

While the President had no legal power to keep the Egyptians and Israelis at the negotiations, he possessed immense moral and political power stemming from the obvious fact that neither side wanted to be seen as responsible for the failure of the effort. Whatever their differences, the Egyptian and Israeli leaders shared at least one basic goal—maintenance of American support. Both countries were heavily dependent upon American economic and political assistance, and both sought additional military aid as well, which required Congressional approval and ultimately broad support within the American public.

The pressures of time and the desire to achieve a favorable outcome had a number of consequences that were reflected in the Camp David agreements and accompanying documents. On some issues the parties had indeed significantly modified their initial positions. For example, Begin agreed to remove Israeli air bases and to recommend the withdrawal of all civilian settlements from Sinai. He also accepted modifications in the original 26-point autonomy plan for Judea, Samaria (the West Bank), and Gaza to provide detailed arrangements for "full autonomy" and for establishing a "self-governing authority (administrative council)," for elections and for a five-year transition period at the end of which the final status of the area would be determined. This determination would not be made unilaterally by Israel, but in negotiations with Jordan, Egypt, and local Palestinians in such a way as to take into account "the legitimate rights of the Palestinian people and their just requirements." The agreement also outlined the ways in which "the Palestinians will participate in the determination of their own future." While Israel retained a veto power over security matters and the inclusion of individual Palestinians from outside the West Bank, Israel committed itself in effect to allowing duly elected West Bank and Gaza Palestinians to participate, irrespective of their openly anti-Israeli sympathies.

For his part, Sadat modified his earlier demand for an independent Palestinian state, and the Camp David agreements did not use the term "self-determination" or mention the PLO. Although the PLO had officially been recognized as sole legitimate Palestinian representative at the Rabat summit conference, it was anathema to Israel, and not particularly in favor with either Sadat or King Hussein. Sadat also acknowledged Israeli security concerns, and the West Bank-Gaza framework accordingly provided that "all necessary measures will be taken . . . to assure the security of Israel and its neighbors during the transitional period *and beyond.*" (Emphasis added.)

Sadat also agreed to Israel's demand that the detailed "Framework for the Conclusion of a Peace Treaty Between Egypt and Israel" be in a separate document from the more general "Framework for Peace in the Middle East Agreed at Camp David," which dealt only briefly with the Egyptian-Israeli treaty and potential treaties between Israel and its other neighbors, and spelled out in detail the framework for proceeding on the West Bank and Gaza.

There were also differences in the timetables in the two documents. The Egyptian-Israeli framework included an agreement "to negotiate in good faith with a goal of concluding within three months" a peace treaty between Egypt and Israel. (At the Camp David signing ceremony Begin proposed that they try to wrap up the negotiations in two months, an idea to which both Sadat and Carter voiced their assent, but which proved overly optimistic.) Israel agreed to withdraw to an interim line in Sinai within nine months of the treaty signing, and Egypt pledged that "after the interim withdrawal is complete, normal relations will be established between Egypt and Israel . . ." The precise pace of the normalization of relations was not specified at Camp David—the March 1979 peace treaty provided that ambassadors would be exchanged one month after the interim withdrawal—but stated generally that all aspects of the treaty would be implemented within two to three years, including Israel's final withdrawal from Sinai.

The Camp David agreements papered over some issues through the use of ambiguous language subject to conflicting interpretations. For example, while the West Bank-Gaza provisions talked of "full autonomy" and the replacement of the Israeli military government and its civil administration by a freely-elected, "self-governing authority," the new arrangements were to give "due consideration both to the principle of self-government by the inhabitants of these territories and to the legitimate security concerns of the parties involved." It did not say how this would be done when Arab political aspirations and Israeli security requirements clashed, as they were certain to do in the case of Israel's encouragement of the establishment of additional Israeli civilian settlements on "security grounds." The Camp David framework provided that "when the self-governing authority (administrative council) in the West Bank and Gaza is established and inaugurated, the transitional period of five years will begin." But Camp David did not set a deadline for holding the elections, a matter that was to become a subject of heated controversy, with the United States backing Egypt's demand for a target date. Israel had insisted on the parenthetic description of the self-governing authority as an *administrative* council to make it clear that it would have no legislative or judicial authority, but this was to prove a far more restrictive view than that held not only by the Palestinians but by Egyptian and American officials. Although in the Camp David agreement Begin and Sadat pledged that their countries were determined to reach "a just, *comprehensive,* and durable settlement of the Middle East conflict through the conclusion of peace treaties based on Security Council Resolutions 242 and 338 in *all* their parts" (emphasis added), there remained considerable disagreement on what Israel was required to do to implement 242 with regard to the West Bank and Gaza, and to what extent there was linkage between the bilateral Egyptian-Israeli peace treaty and the comprehensive peace. At a background briefing for the press at the conclusion of Camp David, National Security Adviser Brzezinski stated that legally each of the two agreements "stands on its own feet." He pointed out that in the overall political context there was, however, an element of linkage, since progress on one would affect the general climate and the prospects for peace in the Middle East.

In subsequent months Egypt and the United States attempted to tighten the linkage, in order to help Sadat counter the assertion in the Arab world that he had in fact made a separate peace with Israel and thus betrayed the Arab cause. The Israelis were equally vigorous in their insistence that Egyptian fulfillment of its obligations to Israel on such a matter as the normalization of relations be tied only to Israel's fulfillment of its obligations to Egypt, e.g. on withdrawal, and not be linked to progress in the autonomy talks, the entry of Jordan into the negotiating process, or the willingness of West Bank Palestinians to participate. Egypt and Israel also disagreed on how to reconcile the Egyptian-Israeli treaty with obligations Egypt had to other Arab states. Most crucially this involved the problem of Egypt's response if Israel became embroiled in a war with an Arab state with which Egypt had a mutual defense treaty and both Israel and the Arab state claimed that the other was the aggressor.

There were other outstanding issues (most notably involving Jerusalem and the question of existing and new Israeli settlements in the West Bank and Gaza) on which the parties were so far apart that it was finally decided to say nothing explicit on the subjects. In an accompanying exchange of letters, Sadat, Begin, and Carter simply restated their governments' positions on Jerusalem.

The Aftermath of Camp David

While it was the generally accepted view among Middle East specialists that the ultimate resolution of the Jerusalem question had best be deferred until other Arab-Israeli issues had been solved and a spirit of mutual trust and confidence had been achieved, the question of Jerusalem's relationship to the West Bank was immediately brought to the fore by the Camp David framework dealing with Palestinian autonomy. Begin sent President Carter a letter saying that wherever the agreements spoke of "West Bank" the government of Israel understood this to mean "Judea and Samaria." Begin thus put Carter and Sadat on notice that the territory in question was not to be regarded as occupied, and that in any case East Jerusalem was not part of the West Bank. Not surprisingly, among the main questions about the Camp David agreements that King Hussein submitted to President Carter were a number dealing with Jerusalem. The president's answers were transmitted to Hussein by Assistant Secretary of State Harold Saunders, who reaffirmed that the United States regarded East Jerusalem as occupied territory. Saunders indicated that while East Jerusalem would not be included within the boundaries of the proposed autonomous area during the transitional period, the United States was prepared "to support proposals that would permit Arab inhabitants of East Jerusalem who are not Israeli citizens" to vote in the elections leading to self-rule, and that such Jerusalem Arabs might share in the work of the self-governing authority. As for the final status of Jerusalem—that would have to be settled in the Camp David negotiations, to which Hussein had an explicit invitation.

The American response was regarded as "inadequate" by King Hussein, and the Jordanian monarch refused to join in the negotiations. While Saunders was equally unsuccessful in convincing the Saudis to endorse Camp David, he infuriated the Begin government by allegedly implying (in conversations with West Bank personalities) that just as Sadat had obtained a total withdrawal of Israeli personnel from Sinai in exchange for peace, Palestinians who came forward might eventually achieve the power to transform the West Bank-Gaza autonomy plan into the nucleus of a Palestinian state and limit Jewish civilian settlements.

The Saunders mission also precipitated another American-Israeli blowup on the long simmering controversy over Israel's settlement policy. One of the letters accompanying the Camp David agreements was to have dealt with the moratorium on new Israeli settlement construction during the negotiating period. The letters were never completed, because of an apparent "misunderstanding" between Carter and Begin as to what they had agreed upon. Begin understood the moratorium to cover the three-month period specified for completion of the Egyptian-Israeli treaty. Carter assumed it also encompassed the period of the negotiations for election of the West Bank self-governing authority, which might take a year or so. Moreover, since the Palestinian representatives were certain to ask for a limitation on Israeli settlements, the moratorium might well be of an indefinite, if not permanent, length. Carter had agreed that some projected enlargement of existing settlements might take place for purposes of family reunion and natural growth. However, when, in the wake of the Saunders trip, the Israel Cabinet in October announced plans to "thicken" some of the settlements on the West Bank, Secretary of State Vance declared that the United States regarded this as "a very serious matter and [was] deeply disturbed by it." President Carter reportedly sent an even more strongly worded note to Begin. Israeli officials then explained that all they really had in mind was the addition of "several hundred" housing units and construction of a water reservoir and roads.

Despite these irritants, negotiations on the draft of the Egyptian-Israeli peace treaty were completed at Blair House in Washington on November 11, and after some initial objections, the Israel government voted to accept the text on November 21. The Egyptian government insisted, however, on side letters which would have increased the linkage between the treaty and the West Bank autonomy talks, set a target date for the autonomy elections, provided for a review of the Sinai security provisions in the treaty, and left Egypt free to help an Arab state if it was subjected to armed attack by Israel. Israel strenuously objected to linking Egypt's perform- ance of its obligations in such matters as the exchange of ambassadors to progress in the autonomy talks, since these were dependent on the actions of other parties, such as the Palestinians and Jordanians, over whom Israel had no control. Israel also resisted a target date for elections, and insisted that Egypt's commitment to peace with Israel be permanent, and not conditional on outside factors or inconsis- tent commitments Egypt had made to other Arab states in the context of its earlier policy of hostility to Israel. Because of these issues and a few other less serious matters, the target date of December 17 passed without the anticipated signing of an Egyptian-Israeli treaty.

Sadat, who was used to seeing other deadlines pass, was less distressed than President Carter, who openly expressed his impatience. Whether because of the growing crisis in Iran, the impending announcement that the United States was opening diplomatic relations with the People's Republic of China on terms that were seen by many Americans as an abandonment of the U.S. commitment to Taiwan, or simply because the president felt he had spent too much time already on the

Middle East, annoyance with Israel was clearly voiced by the administration. It was also natural that Washington wanted the treaty signed as soon as possible, to forestall the mounting opposition to Sadat in the Arab world.

On December 7 Carter had stated that he "would like to see the accord carried out not grudgingly but enthusiastically." He then went on to declare: "If the Egyptians and the Israelis *violate* the three-month *limit* on negotiating this treaty, it will be a very serious matter." (Emphases added.) This had just the opposite of the desired effect on the Israelis. If what the Camp David agreement called a "goal" of concluding negotiations in three months suddenly turned into an inviolable limit, then what would be the American reaction if Israel accepted a "target date" for West Bank elections and then failed to meet it? The Israelis were also upset when Secretary Vance publicly declared that the proposals Sadat had worked out with him for resolving the points at issue were regarded as "reasonable" by the United States government, and he recommended them as such to Jerusalem. Moreover, on December 14 Carter bluntly stated that it was now up to Israel to accept or reject the treaty.

The brief era of good feeling between Carter and the Jewish community that had been developed in the afterglow of Camp David was quickly dissipated by the president's cold comments in December. The Jewish community was quick to react. "In sharp contrast to his creative efforts at Camp David," the American Jewish Committee declared, "President Carter's repeated expressions of impatience and frustration, either explicitly or implicitly addressed to Israel, have been neither appropriate nor helpful." Rabbi Schindler, now speaking as president of the Union of American Hebrew Congregations, called for a reversal of "the dangerous and failed policy" of the Carter administration "to buy off the Saudis with our weapons and to submit to Egypt's ever harsher conditions for peace with Israel." Such a policy, he said, "is not a prescription for peace; it is an invitation to more war."

On December 19, 33 of the 36 American Jewish leaders who in the spring had sent a letter critical of Begin and supportive of Peace Now, sent a cable to President Carter declaring his position "unacceptable," stating that they believed that Israel's objections to the proposed Egyptian revisions were in fact reasonable, and concluding that the "unfortunate" American posture of blaming Israel for the current impasse did "serious damage to the prospects of peace."

Carter's Role in Achieving an Egyptian-Israeli Treaty

After the arbitrary December 17 deadline had passed without catastrophe and the popular disapproval of the administration's one-sided declarations had sunk in, the United States government resumed its peace-making efforts. The Egyptian and Israeli foreign ministers met with Vance in Brussels in late December, and special envoy Atherton engaged in shuttle diplomacy in January.

An important ingredient was added by Defense Secretary Harold Brown's visit to the area in mid-February. Brown tried to convince Egypt, Saudi Arabia, and

Jordan that the United States remained a dependable ally despite the overthrow of the pro-Western regime of the Shah in Iran. Israeli officials had become increasingly concerned that the Carter administration saw friendship with Saudi Arabia as the keystone of its Middle East policy, and was consequently downgrading the importance of Israel as a positive factor in America's geopolitical and strategic thinking. Brown helped allay these fears when he declared, during his visit to Israel, that he was deeply impressed by the Jewish State's "great value to the United States [as] a strong and stable democratic country." Israeli officials were also "extremely satisfied" with Brown's response to Israel's long-term arms requests.

The conclusion of the treaty required another marathon effort by President Carter. The intangible but significant elements of prestige, personality, and power prevented progress at a second Camp David conference in mid-February. Israel was represented by Foreign Minister Dayan, and Egypt by Prime Minister and Foreign Minister Mustafa Khalil. After five days of inconclusive talks, President Carter invited Prime Minister Begin to come to the United States, but Begin declined when it became known that President Sadat would not come to head the Egyptian delegation. Finally, President Carter decided to go to Cairo and Jerusalem. The president addressed the Egyptian People's Assembly and had intensive discussions with Sadat during March 8–10. He then went to Jerusalem, where he conferred with Begin and his government from March 10 to 13, and addressed the Knesset on March 12. After a brief meeting with Sadat at Cairo airport on March 13, President Carter was finally able to announce that both parties had reached agreement. The treaty was signed in Washington on the White House lawn on March 26.

The president helped bridge the gap between the two countries by adding his personal commitment to the promises of political support and economic assistance that he was making on behalf of the United States. On the crucial question of linkage, President Carter told the Egyptian People's Assembly:

> When two nations conclude a treaty with one another, they have every right to expect that the terms of the treaty will be carried out faithfully and steadfastly. At the same time, there can be little doubt that the two agreements reached at Camp David—negotiated together and signed together—are related, and that a comprehensive peace remains a common objective . . . Both leaders [Sadat and Begin] have reaffirmed that they do not want a separate peace between their two nations. Therefore, our current efforts to complete the treaty negotiations represent not the end of a process, but the beginning of one . . . I pledge to you today that I also remain personally committed to move on to negotiations concerning the West Bank and Gaza Strip and other issues of concern to the Palestinians, and also to future negotiations between Israel and all her neighbors. . . .

Carter went on to urge representative Palestinians to join the negotiations proposed in the Camp David agreements as the only means of fulfilling "the hopes of the Palestinian people for peaceful self-expression."

In his address to the Knesset on March 12, President Carter stressed that the Egyptian-Israeli treaty was the cornerstone of a comprehensive structure of peace, and that he understood "the magnitude of the choices" with which Israel would be faced, even after a peace treaty with Egypt was concluded. He added, "As the time for these choices approaches, remember this pledge that I make to you today: The United States will never support any agreement or any action that places Israel's security in jeopardy." But he made it clear that the United States was determined to push forward: "We must proceed with due caution . . . But we must proceed."

On the question of linkage President Carter told the Israelis:

At Camp David, Prime Minister Begin and President Sadat forged two frameworks for the building of that comprehensive peace. The genius of that accomplishment is that negotiations under these frameworks can go forward independently of each other, without destroying the obvious relationship between them. They are designed to be mutually reinforcing, with the intrinsic flexibility necessary to promote the comprehensive peace that we all desire. . . .

After urging Israel's other Arab neighbors to negotiate directly with Israel as Sadat had done, Carter stressed the importance of keeping the door open "to all the parties in conflict, including the Palestinians, with whom, above all, Israel shares a common interest in living in peace and living with mutual respect."

In an apparent allusion to developments in Iran and the Arabian peninsula, Carter said that peace had become an even more urgent concern in recent weeks because of its influence on Middle East regional security. Israel's own security, he said, would rest not only on how Egyptian-Israeli negotiations "affect the situation on [Israel's] borders, but also on how it affects the forces of stability and moderation beyond [those] borders." An "equitable peace treaty" between Egypt and Israel would greatly help foster a hospitable atmosphere for those positive forces. President Carter then made one of the strongest and most explicit commitments of American support for Israel issued in recent years:

The risks of peace . . . are real. But America is ready to reduce any risks and to balance them within the bounds of our strength and our influence. I came to Israel representing the most powerful country on Earth. And I can assure you that the United States intends to use that power in the pursuit of a stable and peaceful Middle East. We've been centrally involved in this region, and we will stay involved politically, economically, and militarily. We will stand by our friends. We are ready to place our strength at Israel's side when you want it to ensure Israel's security and well-being.

Turning to specifics, President Carter reaffirmed the American commitment to guarantee Israel an adequate oil supply, should its normal sources of supply be interrupted. (The treaty was accompanied by a U.S.-Israeli memorandum of agreement on oil, which extended for a total of 15 years the original five-year American commitment—which Israel had never invoked—contained in the September 1, 1975 agreement. Details were to be worked out within 60 days.) Acknowledging that the peace treaty with Egypt would exacerbate Israel's difficult economic and security problems, President Carter declared: "In the context of peace, we are prepared to see Israel's economic and military relationship with the United States take on new and strong and more meaningful dimensions, even than already exist."

In a separate memorandum of agreement between the United States and Israel, the U. S. reaffirmed all the existing American agreements and assurances, including those accompanying the Sinai II accord of September 1975, with the exception of those provisions that were specifically tied to implementation of that limited agreement and were superseded by the peace treaty. The United States promised to take appropriate measures to promote full observance of the peace, including "diplomatic, economic, and military measures . . . should it be demonstrated to the satisfaction of the United States that there has been a violation or threat of violation of the Treaty of Peace."

Although guarded in its language, the United States was more explicit than in the past regarding the kinds of measures it would undertake:

> The United States will provide support it deems appropriate for proper actions taken by Israel in response to such demonstrated violations of the Treaty of Peace. In particular, if a violation of the Treaty of Peace is deemed to threaten the security of Israel, including, *inter alia,* a blockade of Israel's use of international waterways, a violation of the provisions . . . concerning limitation of forces or an armed attack against Israel, the United States will be prepared to consider, on an urgent basis, such measures as the strengthening of the United States presence in the area, the providing of emergency supplies to Israel, and the exercise of maritime rights in order to put an end to the violation.

In other sections of the memorandum of agreement, the United States also promised to support the parties' overflight and navigation rights, and to oppose any United Nations action or resolution which the U. S. judged as adversely affecting the treaty. The American government also promised to be responsive to Israel's military and economic aid requirements, and said that it would continue to impose restrictions forbidding the unauthorized transfer of American weapons to a third country, and would forbid their use against Israel.

The peace treaty dealt with the problem of a possible conflict between Egypt's prior inter-Arab commitments and its peace treaty with Israel as follows: After stating (article VI, paragraph 4) that "the Parties undertake not to enter into any obligation in conflict with this Treaty," paragraph 5 declared: "Subject to Article 103 of the United Nations Charter, in the event of a conflict between the obligations of the Parties under the present Treaty and any of their other obligations, the obligations under this Treaty will be binding and implemented." (Article 103 provides that the UN Charter take precedence over any treaty provisions inconsistent with the Charter. Thus Egypt could claim that it had not given up its right to aid an Arab state, a fellow member of the UN, if Israel engaged in aggressive action in clear violation of the UN Charter. At the same time Israel could rely on the peaceful settlement requirements of the Charter to prevent Egypt from invoking obligations under mutual assistance defense pacts with other Arab states that antedated and were inconsistent with the peace treaty with Israel.)

Although there was no equally detailed memorandum between the United States and Egypt, similar general assurances that the U. S. would take appropriate action

o prevent violations and achieve compliance with the treaty were contained in
dentic letters sent by President Carter to President Sadat and Prime Minister Begin
on the date of the treaty signing. The United States also confirmed in these letters
that it would itself conduct aerial monitoring, as provided for in the treaty, and
would also "exert its utmost efforts" to have a UN force under the Security Council
be permanently stationed in the limited forces zone. Should the Security Council fail
o act, the president would take the necessary steps "to ensure the establishment of
an acceptable alternative multinational force."

While the text of the Egyptian-Israeli peace treaty did not address itself to the
West Bank-Gaza and Palestinian issues, these questions were dealt with in a joint
letter to President Carter from President Sadat and Prime Minister Begin on March
26, the day of the treaty signing. The two leaders agreed to begin negotiations on
implementing the West Bank-Gaza provisions a month after the treaty's ratifications
were exchanged. If Jordan did not enter the talks, Egypt and Israel would negotiate
themselves for the establishment of the "self-governing authority" in the West Bank
and Gaza, in order to "provide full autonomy to the inhabitants." The parties set
themselves "the goal of completing the negotiations within one year," so that
elections could be held. One month after the self-governing authority was elected,
the clock would begin to run on the five-year transitional period specified in the
Camp David agreements, the Israeli military government and civilian administration would be withdrawn, and the remaining Israeli forces would be redeployed
"into specified security locations." The last paragraph of the joint letter stated: "This
letter also confirms our understanding that the United States government will
participate fully in all stages of negotiations." Thus, while Prime Minister Begin had
succeeded in removing any provisions with regard to negotiations on the Palestinian
autonomy in Judea, Samaria, and Gaza from the text of the Egyptian-Israeli peace
treaty itself, President Sadat had succeeded in getting Israel's agreement that the
United States would be a full participant in the negotiations. This was in line with
Sadat's basic strategy that Egypt's objectives could best be advanced by drawing in
the United States as a full partner.

The Egyptian-Israeli peace treaty was a significant achievement for President
Carter's personal diplomacy. It also marked the recognition by the United States,
in a more explicit and formalized manner than ever before, of its continuing involvement in the peace process in the Middle East.

GEORGE E. GRUEN

American Reaction to the Shcharansky Case

T HE ARREST IN MOSCOW OF ANATOLY SHCHARANSKY on March 15, 1977 on charges of treason and his conviction on July 14, 1978 triggered the most powerful governmental and public response in the United States to the plight of Soviet Jewry since the infamous air-hijacking verdict of December 1970. The 1970 verdict, including two death sentences imposed by a Moscow court, set in motion such strong currents of protest in the United States and the West that, within a very short time, the Kremlin felt compelled to open the "Soviet cage" and allow tens of thousands of Soviet Jews to emigrate. The Shcharansky case exerted a similar effect.

For several years prior to the arrest of Shcharansky, the Soviet Jewish movement in the United States had been at an ebb. The initial burst of activity during 1971–74, involving hundreds of thousands of people in demonstrations, letter writing campaigns, and lobbying, came to an end with the passage in Congress of the Jackson-Vanik Amendment. Approximately 100,000 Soviet Jews emigrated during 1971–74, and the adoption of the Jackson-Vanik Amendment appeared to ensure America's formal commitment to a solution of the Soviet-Jewish problem. Such formal commitment, it was assumed, would result in a continuous flow of Soviet Jewish emigration. Thus, the very success of the protest movement led to a weakening of activism.

The assumption that the situation of Soviet Jewry was bound to improve was incorrect. The Kremlin publicly repudiated its trade agreement with the United States, rejected the application of the Jackson-Vanik Amendment, stepped up harassment and intimidation of Soviet Jews seeking to emigrate, and generally diminished the drive for exodus. The Jewish emigration rate dropped in 1974 and continued to plunge downward during 1975–77 to approximately one-half the 1972–73 level.

In America the organized Soviet Jewry movement faced greater difficulties in mobilizing the necessary resources to respond effectively to the new challenge. Annual "Solidarity Day" demonstrations were characterized by weakened participation and enthusiasm. Various pro-Soviet Jewry activities continued to be carried out by the National Conference on Soviet Jewry and other groups, but the previous excitement and hope were gone. The movement was in the doldrums, with internal debates over strategy sometimes replacing action.

The arrest of Shcharansky radically transformed this situation. The organized American Jewish community was once again galvanized into action, making an impact on the entire voluntary sector in the United States, as well as on Congress and the administration. The case became a *cause célèbre* not unlike the Dreyfus case in France at the turn of the century.

The notoriety of the case and the enormous influence it exerted on various American circles flowed from two factors—concern about détente and concern about Soviet antisemitism. The first concern directly involved the American government, since détente was perceived in the U.S., at least with respect to human rights, as an expression of the Helsinki Final Act. Shcharansky was linked directly, indeed intimately, with Helsinki.

Both the USSR and the United States conceived of the Helsinki Final Act as the consummation of détente. General Secretary (later President) Leonid Brezhnev and President Gerald Ford were present at the signing of the Helsinki Declaration on August 1, 1975. Since 1954, Soviet diplomacy had been oriented toward achieving an agreement with the West that would officially recognize the prevailing territorial arrangements in Eastern Europe and, thus, Kremlin dominance in the area. The West finally acquiesced to this, as expressed in Basket I of the Final Act, when the USSR reciprocated by recognizing the human rights principles incorporated into Basket III, including provisions for the reunion of families. Basket II called for economic, scientific, technological, and cultural exchange.

Détente, at its core, was characterized by linkage; accommodation in one field was to elicit a reciprocal response in another. As applied to the Final Act, linkage meant that progress in Baskets I and II—something greatly desired by the USSR—necessitated a corresponding advance in Basket III. Clearly, then, the human rights principle of the Final Act had the same status as the other principles, and had to be directly or indirectly included in applying any of the other principles. Incorporated in Principle VII of the Final Act was this key phrase: "The right of the individual to know and act upon his rights." This phrase was seen in dissident and democratic circles throughout Eastern Europe as the central element in the entire Helsinki structure. Monitoring lay committees, commonly known as Helsinki watch committees, sprang up everywhere in the area, based precisely on Principle VII. The committees perceived their function as providing information about the fulfillment of the provisions of Helsinki.

Shcharansky's Arrest

On May 12, 1976, the Moscow Watch Committee was established. Shortly thereafter similar committees were set up in Leningrad, Kiev, Vilnius, Tbilisi, and Yerevan. Among the founders of the Moscow group was Anatoly Shcharansky, a young (born in 1948) computer specialist who had been a Jewish activist since being refused an exit visa in 1973. Shcharansky quickly became a leader of the Committee, thus becoming involved with general human rights issues. Because of his impeccable knowledge of English, he became the Committee's translator and interpreter for Western correspondents and high-level visitors, such as American senators and congressmen.

The Kremlin, notwithstanding Helsinki and détente, regarded the watch committees as a fundamental challenge to its authority, even though their total membership was less than 50 persons. Soviet authorities unleashed a barrage of propaganda against the committees; members were harassed and most of them arrested. Pressure on the committees intensified after Jimmy Carter was elected U.S. president, since he symbolized and gave expression to human rights objectives.

It is not surprising that the extremely intelligent and courageous Shcharansky became the KGB's principal target; silencing him would be an object lesson to others, would cut the link to Jewish activists, and would sever the verbal connection with Western contacts. If KGB ingenuity could be utilized to entrap Shcharansky, linking him in some way with espionage, a treason trial could be held that, from the Kremlin viewpoint, would have the effect of destroying the legitimacy and credibility of the Helsinki watch committees, and deterring even the most coura- geous activists. Such a KGB entrapment was attempted through Sanya Lipavsky, a surgeon who undoubtedly had been or became a "plant" of the secret police within the Jewish activist movement. Lipavsky "volunteered" to become an operative of the Central Intelligence Agency. The KGB, after manipulating a situation whereby Lipavsky spent a brief time living with Shcharansky, sprung the trap. Lipavsky "confessed" publicly in an article in *Izvestiia* (March 5, 1977) to being "recruited" by the CIA, and alleged that Shcharansky had been engaged in espionage plans to "undermine the foundations of Soviet power."

The fact of the matter was that Shcharansky had meticulously adhered to Soviet and international law. The specific charges that were brought against him in court in July 1978 could not possibly be considered as involving espionage or treason. "Absurd" was the way Shcharansky described the allegations against him; the term was precise and correct. Moreover, he had no knowledge of Lipavsky's relationship to the CIA.

Protests Over Shcharansky's Arrest

It was the unquestionable innocence of Shcharansky that led President Carter to take the unprecedented step of declaring at a press conference on June 13, 1977 that Shcharansky "has never had any sort of relationship, to our knowledge, with the CIA." Shcharansky's arrest was perceived by the U.S. government as a direct challenge to the Helsinki Final Act and, therefore, as a thrust at détente itself. When the first review conference of the Final Act opened in Belgrade on October 4, 1977. Ambassador Arthur Goldberg, the head of the American delegation, stated: "We are . . . obliged to register vigorous disapproval of repressive measures taken in any country against individuals and private groups whose activities relate solely to promoting the Final Act's goals and promises." The Soviet delegation was put on notice that the arrests of Shcharansky and other members of monitoring watch committees would be an important matter of discussion, since "such repression is contrary to the spirit and letter of our common pledge."

The Shcharansky case was aired, both in private discussions and public sessions throughout the Belgrade meetings, which ran until mid-February, 1978. Ambassa- dor Goldberg and his colleagues repeatedly stressed that interference with the watch committees struck at the very heart of Helsinki. Robert Dole, the senate minority leader, appeared at Belgrade as a delegation member, and warned on November 25, 1977 that "public trials of political dissidents could have a profound impact on pending or subsequent bilateral and multilateral agreements."

For Jews, the arrest of Shcharansky on grounds of treason awakened memories of the Dreyfus case and stirred recollections of the "Doctors' Plot" that had generated a pogrom atmosphere in the USSR in 1953. Anxiety about Soviet antisemitism had been spreading among the American Jewish leadership since the beginning of 1977. The virulent Soviet propaganda campaign directed against Zionism, which but thinly masked anti-Jewish canards, had taken a particularly ugly turn on January 22. On that day, Soviet television carried a prime time, one-hour documentary entitled "Buyers of Souls." Replete with vulgar antisemitic stereotypes, the program listed the names and addresses of several Jewish activists, including Shcharansky. A background voice declared: "These people are all soldiers of Zionism within the Soviet Union, and it is here that they carry out their subversive activity." Following the showing of the documentary, the Soviet media lauded it. The equation of Zionism with subversion in the public mind was strongly reinforced by the publication in *Ogonek* (January 29, 1977), which has a circulation of two million, of a lengthy article entitled "The Espionage Octopus of Zionism."

Soviet Jewish activists warned of the creation of a "pogrom atmosphere" as they described anti-Jewish remarks on buses and in shops. At this point, the *Izvestiia* article detailing the alleged connections between Shcharansky and the CIA appeared. Six days later "Buyers of Souls" was rebroadcast. Four days afterward Shcharansky was arrested. The sequence of events sent a shudder through the American Jewish community.

The National Conference on Soviet Jewry, representing the organized Jewish community, initiated the mobilization of a national campaign on Shcharansky's behalf. Its objective was to sensitize the American public to the issues involved, to encourage official and unofficial efforts for the release of Shcharansky, and, in the event such efforts failed and a trial were held, to activate a vigorous and sustained American response. With the arrival in the United States of Shcharansky's wife Avital in April, the campaign moved into high gear. On April 15, with Mrs. Shcharansky present, Congressman Robert Drinan (D., Mass.), who agreed to serve as American chairman of an "International Committee for the Release of Anatoly Shcharansky," held the first major press conference on the subject in Washington.

While the U.S. government, at various levels, was signalling to Soviet officials that a trial of Shcharansky would prove seriously detrimental to détente, the Jewish community was preoccupied with mounting a major response among critical sectors of American public opinion. A particularly dramatic action by the National Conference on Soviet Jewry was the creation of an Ad Hoc Commission on Justice for Anatoly Shcharansky. Its membership was impressive: William J. McGill, president of Columbia University (who acted as chairman); Senator Frank Church (D., Idaho); Robert McKay, director of the Aspen Institute for Humanistic Studies;

Eleanor Holmes Norton, chairman of the Equal Opportunity Employment Commission; Bayard Rustin, president of the A. Philip Randolph Institute; and Chesterfield Smith, former president of the American Bar Association. The Commission was modelled on the famous John Dewey Commission of the late 30's which had evaluated the Kremlin's trial proceedings against Leon Trotsky. As with the Dewey group, the McGill Commission held public hearings (on October 20, 1977) in the nation's capital. Two of America's most prominent legal specialists on civil liberties acted as co-counsels of the Commission: Alan Dershowitz of Harvard University Law School and Jack Greenberg, director of the NAACP Legal Defense and Education Fund. Aside from drawing public and especially congressional attention to the Shcharansky case—the hearings were held in the Democratic Caucus Room—the Commission sought to gather evidence that would constitute a brief for the Shcharansky defense. A transcript of the proceedings was to be sent to Roman Rudenko, the chief Soviet prosecutor.

To certify the objective judicial character of the hearings, each of the witnesses was sworn in by David L. Bazelon, chief judge of the U.S. Court of Appeals in the District of Columbia. The witnesses included Avital Shcharansky, who flew in specially from Israel; Isaak Elkind, a Soviet attorney who had emigrated to Israel; Jack Minker, professor of computer science at the University of Maryland; Congressman Drinan, and Alfred J. Friendly, Jr., former *Newsweek* correspondent in Moscow, and an official of the U.S. Commission on Security and Cooperation in Europe.

Mrs. Shcharansky's testimony was electrifying. She denounced the charges against her husband as "absurd," noting that it was inconceivable for a Soviet refusenik who was "constantly followed by members of the KGB 24 hours a day" to become a foreign agent. This view was buttressed by the other witnesses, and particularly by documentary material from more than 40 Soviet refuseniks still in the USSR, which was entered into the Commission's records. The statements attested to "the highest moral character" of Shcharansky and to the fact that "all his activities in the Jewish emigration movement were legal under Soviet and international law." Alfred Friendly, who had known Shcharansky extremely well as the translator for Western correspondents of the Helsinki Watch Committee in Moscow, stated: "Shcharansky's only crime was to speak truth and, worst of all, in English."

The American legal profession played a central role in shaping public opinion on the Shcharansky case. At the annual meeting of the Association of American Law Schools held in Atlanta, Georgia on December 27–30, 1977, a quickly assembled and unofficial "human rights" meeting was called into session by Dean Peter Liacouras and Professor Burton Caine, both of Temple University Law School in Philadelphia. The Temple Law School academics had returned on December 22 from a week-long stay in the USSR, where they had met in Moscow with leading Soviet legal and judicial officials, and expressed their concern about the Shcharansky case. Professor Alan Dershowitz of Harvard Law, who had already offered his services as defense counsel to Shcharansky and was rebuffed by Soviet authorities, delivered the principal address outlining the character of the Soviet case. His Harvard Law colleague, Professor Harold Berman, a specialist on Soviet law, described the Soviet legal system. The deans of 72 law schools throughout the U.S., joined by more than 100 law professors, "deplored" the action of the Soviet government in the Shcharansky case as "counter to the rule of law and minimum standards of justice."

The impact on Congress was strong. Particularly significant was the formation of a Congressional Wives Committee for Soviet Jewry, initiated by Marina Wallach, Washington representative of the National Conference on Soviet Jewry. More than 40 wives of key senators and congressmen gathered on January 31, 1978 to greet Avital Shcharansky and to hear a plea on behalf of Soviet Jewish families. Mrs. Shcharansky was so moved by the interest of the group that she burst into tears and found herself unable to complete the speech she was scheduled to deliver. From time to time the Congressional Wives made its influence felt. On March 15, 1978, the first anniversary of Shcharansky's arrest, they gathered in the Capitol Hill office of Senator Harrison Williams (D., N.J.) and petitioned Soviet authorities to allow the Jewish dissenter to "fulfill his dream and rejoin his wife in Israel."

The protest movement, reinforcing continued expressions of concern directed to the Kremlin by the Carter administration, may have helped delay the opening of the Shcharansky trial. Soviet law required that a defendant be brought to trial within nine months after arrest. In December, 1977, however, the Praesidium of the Supreme Soviet, no doubt prompted by high party officials, adopted an *ex post facto* edict, extending the maximum arrest period to 15 months. The Kremlin was probably reluctant to give the American delegation at the Belgrade Conference an opening for drawing world attention to the Shcharansky case.

By March 1978 the Belgrade sessions had come to an end, and the continued incarceration of Shcharansky spurred the American Jewish community to step up its activities. The National Conference on Soviet Jewry called for a variegated action program to mark the anniversary of Shcharansky's arrest. Jewish organizations, and particularly youth and student groups, were asked to participate in a hunger strike. Local leaders were urged to meet with newspaper editors to press for editorials, and to seek from city and state officials the designation of March 15 as "Anatoly Shcharansky Day." Finally, synagogues and congregations were called upon to designate Saturday, March 11 and Saturday, March 18 as special sabbaths, in solidarity with the imprisoned Jewish activist.

The Annual Leadership Conference of the NCSJ, held in Washington on April 9–11, was utilized for the purpose of highlighting the Shcharansky case. On April 9, with the cooperation of the Jewish Community Council of Greater Washington, a public rally involving thousands was held in Lafayette Park opposite the White House. Participants in the Conference also joined on April 10 in a vigil in front of the Soviet embassy.

The Trial and its Aftermath

When the trial of Shcharansky (scheduled for July 10) was finally announced in Moscow on July 8, the U.S. government reacted with vigor. The State Department, clearly anticipating the announcement, had warned the Kremlin the day before that the fate of Shcharansky and Alexander Ginzburg (whose trial was scheduled for the same day) would be "an important indicator of the attitude of the Soviet government both with respect to the Helsinki Accord and to U.S.-Soviet relations." Secretary of State Cyrus Vance now formally declared that the Soviet dissidents were being put on trial "on a number of pretexts" and that they had been merely "asserting fundamental human rights . . . rights guaranteed in international agreements entered into by their [Soviet] government." He noted that his statement reflected "the deepest feelings and values of the American people" and that the trials would "inevitably affect the climate of our relations and impose obstacles to the building of confidence and cooperation between our countries." In keeping with his strong condemnation, Vance announced that, under President Carter's direction, he was cancelling two official trips to the Soviet Union, one by an environmental group headed by Barbara Blum, deputy administrator of the Environmental Protection Agency, and a second led by Dr. Frank Press, the president's science adviser.

If cancellation of high-level visits was designed to signal strong displeasure, the administration was not yet prepared to undertake punitive measures in the economic or political fields. The Shcharansky trial, after all, had not yet begun, and its outcome, in terms of sentencing—a guilty verdict, given the nature of Soviet jurisprudential practices, was certain—was still unknown. The Carter administration specifically rejected any precise linkage between the important strategic arms limitation talks (SALT II) with the USSR and human rights. The talks, part of a continuing long-term process aimed at signing a treaty by the end of 1978, had been scheduled for Geneva on July 13–14. Vance, even while denouncing the planned trials, disclosed that he would meet with Soviet Foreign Minister Andrei Gromyko as scheduled.

Paralleling and interlocking with the U.S. government response was the strong reaction of the organized Jewish community through the National Conference on Soviet Jewry. NCSJ executive director Jerry Goodman appealed for protest actions by local Jewish groups, and called on Congress to reject proposals then circulating that would extend credits for agricultural purposes to the Soviet Union. These proposals, floated in late 1977 and early 1978 and then formalized in a legislative initiative in the House by Representative Paul Findlay (R., Ill.), were supported by farm interests in the Midwest. Their adoption would have circumvented to some extent the Jackson-Vanik Amendment.

The NCSJ action, bolstered by strong public denunciations issued the same day by B'nai B'rith and Hadassah, quickly found expression in a public demonstration. The Greater New York Conference on Soviet Jewry, frequently the standard bearer for local action throughout the country, called for a rally July 10 in New York's garment center to coincide with the opening of the Shcharansky trial. Media coverage was extensive as the chairman of the event, Mervin Riseman, called on Secretary of State Vance to postpone his scheduled meeting with Gromyko and to recall the U.S. ambassador to Moscow for consultations. A spokesman for the New York academic community, Dr. John Sawhill, president of New York University, denounced the Kremlin for holding its Jewish community "hostage." A representative of the legal profession, Orville Schell, past president of the Association of the Bar of the City of New York, stated: "Our obligation is to keep the Russian bear's feet to the fire until he releases Anatoly Shcharansky and other imprisoned persons." Schell revealed that, while on a trip to Moscow the previous March, he had been extended an invitation by the Moscow Collegium of Lawyers to attend the Shcharansky trial as an observer. That promise, he said, had not been kept.

While the rally in New York proceeded, top NCSJ officials and others travelled to Washington to meet with National Security Adviser Zbigniew Brzezinski. Included in the delegation was the chairman of the Conference of Presidents of Major American Jewish Organizations, Theodore R. Mann, who declared that people everywhere "are outraged at the flagrant misuse of a legal process to punish people for claiming rights that in any civilized country would be a matter of course." Another delegation member, Richard Maass, president of the American Jewish Committee, urged the U.S. government to "engage in a total re-evaluation of its attitude toward the Soviet Union and our ability to cooperate with it in the whole spectrum of relationships . . ."

The escalating protest movement exerted a profound impact on Washington. In Congress, a spate of resolutions was introduced. Senator Abraham Ribicoff (D., Conn.) and Representative Robert Drinan (D., Mass.) proposed identical resolutions calling on the USSR to release Shcharansky immediately and permit him to emigrate. Senator Robert Dole (R., Kansas), the former Republican vice-presidential candidate, asked for an indefinite postponement of U.S.-Soviet negotiations on nuclear weapons, pending Soviet compliance with the Helsinki agreement. What finally emerged was a "sense of Congress" bi-partisan resolution, which expressed dismay and deep concern about the Soviet trials. John Rhodes (R., Ariz.), the House minority leader, called the Shcharansky case a "throwback to the days of the pogroms."

The angry congressional reaction was echoed in a specially called hearing of the U.S. Helsinki Commission on Security and Cooperation in Europe, the agency established by Congress to monitor compliance with the Helsinki accord. Representative Dante Fascell (D., Fla.), chairman of the Commission, stated that the trial "raises serious questions about the international integrity of the Soviet government." One witness before the Commission, Senator Robert Packwood (R., Ore.), went as far as urging the U.S. to withdraw unilaterally from the Helsinki accords, a position which found a sympathetic response with several other senators, the AFL-CIO leadership, and some important columnists. A contrary view was taken by Jerry Goodman and by NCJS consultant Dr. William Korey, director of B'nai B'rith

International Policy Research. Both men stated that Helsinki was important as a major international human rights yardstick, and that to reject it would merely play into the hands of the Soviet Union. At the same time, Goodman emphasized that "the Soviet Union has to pay a price for its actions." Korey argued that to the extent that the human rights provisions in Basket III had been reduced by the USSR, the U.S. should reduce application of Basket II provisions dealing with economic and scientific exchanges.

On July 12 President Carter once again stated that the claim that Shcharansky had committed espionage on behalf of the United States was "patently false." In an interview with West European television correspondents, he declared that the Soviets were prosecuting Shcharansky because "he represents an element, a small group in the Soviet Union, who are fighting for the implementation of international agreements which the Soviets themselves have signed." The president stressed that the U.S. would continue "through every legitimate means to let the Soviets know of our displeasure . . ." Among specific steps being considered was the cancellation of sales of advanced technology, such as oil drilling equipment worth $144 million produced by Dresser Industries of Dallas and a large Sperry Rand computer.

On July 13 Alexander Ginzburg was sentenced by a court in Kaluga to eight years in the harshest type of labor camp—"special regime." The next day the Shcharansky trial ended with the imposition of a 13-year sentence, three in prison and ten in a forced labor camp. Shcharansky's powerful and courageous final statement to the Moscow courtroom, printed on front pages of newspapers across the U.S., aroused a massive response. The National Conference on Soviet Jewry and the Conference of Presidents of Major American Jewish Organizations issued a joint statement calling on the administration to "seek an immediate freeze of the export of American technology to the USSR." The statement urged the Jewish community and its supporters to take to the streets in nationwide demonstrations on July 26 "to give personal testimony in solidarity with the agony of Anatoly Shcharansky."

President Carter was in Bonn, West Germany when the Shcharansky verdict was handed down. Condemning the imposed sentence in the strongest possible terms, Carter told a crowd of thousands of West Germans that "we are all sobered by this reminder that, so late in the 20th century, a person can be sent to jail simply for asserting his basic human rights." His words were echoed in the Congress. Senator Jacob K. Javits called the sentencing "an international disgrace and an affront to humankind." His New York colleague, Senator Daniel Patrick Moynihan, called upon the president to cancel the sale of the Sperry Rand Univac computer to Tass, the Soviet news service. Senator Henry Jackson (D., Wash.) and Senator Alan Cranston (D., Calif.) joined in the angry condemnations. On July 23 President Carter formally cancelled the sale of the Sperry Rand computer and held up the sale of oil technology produced by Dresser Industries. The administration announced that in the future it would carefully review all sales of advanced technological equipment to the USSR before final approval.

The United Auto Workers Union cancelled a planned trip of its officials to the USSR in protest against Shcharansky's conviction. On July 17 Vice-President Walter Mondale met with Avital Shcharansky for nearly 30 minutes at the White House. Just prior to the private meeting, he praised Mrs. Shcharansky for her "courage, dignity and strength." Mondale singled out Anatoly Shcharansky's final statement to the Moscow court as one that "will go down in literature as a great statement by an oppressed person." Later that day congressional members of both parties gathered under the sponsorship of the International Committee for the Release of Anatoly Shcharansky to greet Mrs. Shcharansky. The hearing room of the Rayburn House Office Building was jammed as Committee members expressed abhorrence of the Soviet proceedings and called for a U.S. boycott of the 1980 Olympic Games in Moscow, reduction of U.S. trade with the USSR, and suspension of scientific and technological exchanges.

It was a hectic schedule to which Shcharansky's wife subjected herself. In the late afternoon she met with the U.S. Commission on Security and Cooperation in Europe. In the evening she met with the wives of U.S. senators at a reception in the Israel embassy given by the wife of Israel's ambassador to the U.S. Everywhere, Mrs. Shcharansky uttered the same appeal: "In your hands is the fate of the Jewish movement in the Soviet Union and the fate of my husband." Recalling the antisemitism and repression of Stalin, she warned that "unless all those oppressed in the Soviet Union get help, the same catastrophe that happened 40 years ago will be repeated." On July 18 she appeared before the House Science and Technology Committee and repeated the warning that "a catastrophe is emerging [in the USSR] not only for the Soviet people, but a massacre of all human rights advocates." The congressmen responded with expressions of strong support, rejecting quiet diplomacy as leading only to harsher sentences. President Carter's open and vigorous support for Shcharansky was warmly lauded.

Rallies spread across the country as communities heeded the appeal of the NCSJ and the President's Conference. Particularly noteworthy was a rally in Los Angeles on July 24 attended by 2,000 persons, including California Governor Jerry Brown and actor Charlton Heston. Mrs. Shcharansky was the principal speaker, and once again she appealed for help to win freedom for her husband. "I do not have 13 years to wait," she cried. That same day, members of the Los Angeles Bar Association joined with prominent state legal officials and leading law professors to form the Los Angeles Committee of Concerned Lawyers for Soviet Jews. The Committee announced that it would "document individual cases of refuseniks within the Soviet Union and analyze Soviet law as it applies to these cases." A detailed legal critique of the Shcharansky case, in the form of an "open letter to the legal community," appeared in the *New York Law Journal* on July 17. It was signed by Bernard Katzen, chairman of the American section of the International Association of Jewish Lawyers and Jurists and asked lawyers "to help reverse the miscarriage of justice in Moscow" by sending protest letters and telegrams to high legal and judicial officials in the USSR.

In the voluntary sector of society, the strongest reaction to the Shcharansky trial came from the scientific community. Shcharansky, a computer specialist whose graduate thesis had dealt with the application of computers to chess, was from the beginning recognized as a "colleague," a member of the international scientific fraternity. Various organizations, especially the Committee of Concerned Scientists (loosely affiliated with the National Conference on Soviet Jewry) and, to a lesser extent, the Federation of American Scientists, had labored for a number of years to make their colleagues aware of the serious problems confronting Soviet Jewish scientists seeking to emigrate.

Computer specialists were among the first to respond. In the fall of 1977, the 35,000-member Association for Computer Machinery, the largest U.S. computer science group, cut official ties with the USSR in protest against the arrest of Shcharansky. On the day when the Shcharansky trial began, the chairmen of university computer science departments were meeting in conference in Utah. Twenty-seven leading department chairmen sent a cable to the president of the Soviet Academy of Sciences stating that they were "extremely concerned that our fellow computer scientist Anatoly Shcharansky is on trial." The cable warned that "situations of this sort tend to poison the atmosphere and make it increasingly difficult to welcome Soviet scientists to our laboratories and universities."

The question of scientific cooperation with the Soviet Union became a central feature of the protest movement. Thus, 150 scientists and engineers at the Argonne National Laboratory in Illinois sent a letter to the Kremlin warning that "regression to the conditions of 25 years ago [will] inevitably create major new barriers to the cooperation which we have achieved since those times." Similar views were articulated in numerous protest letters and statements, including one signed by 26 Nobel laureates. Especially important was the intervention of the National Academy of Sciences of the United States, which supervises official collaboration with the Soviet Academy of Sciences. Early in 1978, the president of the National Academy, Philip Handler, cabled Leonid Brezhnev that the denial of a fair trial for Shcharansky, including the presence of American legal observers, might imperil U.S.-USSR scientific relations.

The conviction and sentencing of Shcharansky accelerated the protest movement to a point where non-participation by various American scientists in Soviet conferences became standard. An organization called Scientists for Shcharansky, formed by high energy physicists at the Lawrence Berkeley Laboratory, pledged to "withdraw all personal cooperation with the Soviet Union until Anatoly Shcharansky and Yuri Orlov are released from prison." Telegrams carrying this message, signed by 500 scientists, including Nobel laureates, were sent in late July to Soviet officials. The 14th International Congress of Genetics, held in Moscow August 20–31, was boycotted by some 60 American geneticists. Two prominent physicists scheduled to visit the USSR under the intergovernmental physics program administered by the National Academy of Sciences dropped their plans. Nobel laureate Rosalyn S.

Yalow publicly rejected an invitation of the Soviet minister of health to play a central role in a scientific symposium scheduled for October. In early 1979 the protest movement among scientists was still growing. More than 2,400 American scientists signed a "statement of conscience" in which they vowed to withhold all cooperation with the USSR until Orlov and Shcharansky were released. The magnitude of the commitment was unprecedented in scientific circles. The signatories included 13 Nobel laureates, 113 members of the National Academy of Sciences, and the heads of 20 scientific organizations and 18 major laboratories.

Nor would the organized Jewish community of the United States drop its commitment to Shcharansky's release. It remembered vividly the inspired and inspiring words uttered by the young Zionist on the occasion of his sentencing: "Now as I am facing long and hard years of detention, I say, addressing my people and my Avital—'Next year in Jerusalem!' " Even as the Kremlin, during the latter half of 1978 and during 1979, attempted to assuage the anger of the American Jewish community by once again permitting large numbers of Soviet Jews to emigrate (at a rate of approximately 4,000 a month) the outcry on behalf of Shcharansky could not be stilled.

WILLIAM KOREY

Communal

Jewish Education Today

AN EXAMINATION OF DEVELOPMENTS in Jewish education during the last decade discloses that the general contours of the enterprise remain essentially unchanged from the past.[1] Jewish schooling in the United States today, at least from an organizational point of view, is what it has been since the earliest days of Jewish settlement in this country—a voluntary effort of autonomous institutions related to one another more by common aspiration than by ties of formal structure. The vast majority of Jewish schools continue to be linked to synagogues; they are sponsored, maintained, and ultimately controlled by individual congregations. The continued growth of the day school movement at a rate exceeding that predicted by its most ardent supporters has not altered the fact that Jewish education in the main is supplementary schooling which takes place in midweek afternoon and one-day-a-week schools.

This permanence of form and structure in Jewish education serves as background to certain patterns and trends in enrollment, finance, personnel, and curriculum development which carry the stamp of a particular historical moment. What goes on in Jewish schools, as in other schools, tells us as much about the society which supports them as about the schools themselves. Jewish education in the United States cannot be understood in isolation from the interaction of Jews, Judaism, and American life.

The virtual demise of secular Hebrew nationalist and Yiddish schools since the end of World War II has made Jewish education, as we have noted, almost entirely an activity of the synagogue. Even in the case of schools under communal auspices, the support and active participation of local synagogues is essential to their

---

Note: I am indebted to the following people for generously responding to my request for information used in the preparation of this article: Dr. Shimon Frost, acting director, American Association for Jewish Education; Dr. Eli Grad, president, Hebrew College, Boston; Dr. Morton Siegel, director, department of elementary, secondary, and adult education, United Synagogue of America; and Rabbi Daniel Syme, national director of education, Union of American Hebrew Congregations. The manner in which I have chosen to deal with the wealth of material made available to me is entirely my own responsibility.
[1]See Walter Ackerman, "Jewish Education—For What?" *AJYB,* Vol. 70, 1969, pp. 3–36.

functioning. The perception and practice of Jewish education as religious education, both as a faithful representation of Jewish tradition and as a form of minority group identification which is compatible with American mores and norms, has largely determined the character and quality of Jewish schooling in the United States.

American Jews join synagogues and send their children to Jewish schools because they are genuinely desirous of identifying themselves as Jews and want their children to remain Jews. They are able to do so, however, because neither synagogue membership nor school attendance dictate behavior which conflicts with what they perceive as the American way of life. While parents often speak of the school as the guarantor of a Jewish way of life, they are rarely prepared to accept the implications of this position. They shy away from a recognition and acceptance of Judaism as a code of behavior which is central to a definition of self. The discrepancy between the desire of Jews to identify themselves as such and their unwillingness to accept Judaism as a formative factor in their lives has led one perceptive observer to describe their involvement in Jewish education as an exercise in self-deception. A year and more of close study of the workings of an afternoon congregational school led to the conclusion that "... the goals, the values, and the emotions of ... parents seemed tied to a system that appeared little different than that of the non-Jews residing about them. Although these Jews did identify with a Jewish people, history, culture and religion, they did not in their own suburban American lives live according to any Jewish way of life. It wasn't that these Jews didn't want to be living a Jewish way of life, but rather they seemed to find the demands of modern life uncompromising. The Jewish way, as they understood it for their own lives, could not serve as a standard for living that suited the modern circumstances of life in America . . . They have been unable to interpret their Jewish heritage so that it makes sense in their American life . . ."[2]

It is axiomatic that schools function within parameters set by the community which supports them. A close fit between the values of school and society creates that context of mutual support which is a necessary condition for the transmission of culture across generations. Where there is a gap between the two, the aspirations of the school are generally subverted by the more powerful impact of the society. Jewish schools are no exception to this rule, and there can be no constructive understanding of the issues confronting Jewish education without acknowledging the divide that stretches between its aims and the leanings of the population it serves.

Enrollment

The voluntary nature of Jewish education lends particular importance to the statistics of enrollment in Jewish schools. The number of children enrolled, the

---

[2] David Schoem, "Cultural Dilemmas and Self-Deception in an Ethnic Minority School," paper presented at the 77th annual meeting, American Anthropological Association, November, 1978, p. 32.

number of years of attendance, and other relevant data are an index not only of the ability of the schools to attract and hold pupils, but also of their impact. While enrollment in non-governmental schools, i.e., schools which are out of the reach of compulsory education laws, is often affected by factors that have little to do with institutional performance, patterns of recruitment and retention remain important variables in the assessment of educational effectiveness.

The steady rise in Jewish school enrollment which began its ascent immediately after World War II reached a peak in the middle 1960's, and has been declining ever since. During the ten-year interval between 1946 and 1956 the number of children attending Jewish schools of all kinds more than doubled—from 231,028 to 488,432. In the 1957–58 school year, registers counted 553,600 pupils. A decade later (1966–67) the figure stood at 554,468. Data for 1970–71 disclose a decline of 17.5 per cent over the four-year period to a figure of 457,196.[3] A 1974–75 school census reported 391,825 pupils enrolled.[4] Current estimates put the number of children in Jewish schools of all kinds at 360,000. While there is some question about the accuracy of the latest estimate, there is no doubt about the overall direction—Jewish school enrollment has suffered a decline of more than 30 per cent in the period from 1960 to the present.[5] There are no data available which indicate whether or not the downward trend has reached its bottom.

As important as the absolute number of children enrolled in Jewish schools is the percentage of all Jewish children of school age which they represent. A series of school surveys conducted during the 1950's and 1960's revealed that well over 80 per cent of all Jewish children in the United States were receiving some form of Jewish schooling during their elementary school years. There is less certainty about current figures; the available data does not show whether or not the decline in school enrollment has been accompanied by a parallel increase in the number of Jewish children of school age who receive no Jewish education at all.

Various reasons have been offered in explanation of the drop in enrollment—a decline in the Jewish birthrate, population shifts which have taken families with school-age children away from areas served by existing Jewish schools, and dwindling of parental interest. The single published study[6] which bears on the problem, even though conducted in an intermediate-sized community which is not altogether representative of American Jewry, provides some suggestive findings. During the five years between 1966–67 and 1970–71 Jewish school enrollment in Buffalo, New York declined at a mean annual rate of 5.4 per cent. This figure reflects a significant demographic change among Buffalo's Jews: a lower birthrate in younger families

---

[3]Hillel Hochberg, "Trends and Developments in Jewish Education," AJYB, Vol. 73, 1972, p. 199.
[4]American Association for Jewish Education, *Trends in Jewish Enrollment*, 1976, p. 6.
[5]*Ibid.*, p. 8.
[6]George Pollack, "The Buffalo School Population Study," *Jewish Education*, Summer, 1978, pp. 16–22.

and a growing percentage of adults who are beyond child-bearing age. The combination of these two factors has caused a decrease in school registration which has not yet reached a plateau and will continue in a downward direction. In 1975, the year of the study, there were 1,708 children between the ages of 4 and 17 enrolled in Jewish schools—60.7 per cent of the Jewish school-age population. The highest rate of attendance was among children ages 6–13; more than 80 per cent of the children of this age bracket were in school. Those parents who did not send their children to a Jewish school indicated as their primary reason that they were either not interested in providing a Jewish education for their children or that none of the known Jewish schools in the city offered the sort of Jewish education they desired. Neither the cost nor the quality of schooling appear to have been major attractions or deterrents in their decision.

When the statistics of enrollment are broken down by sponsorship and type of school, the following pattern emerges:[7] 35.2 per cent of the students attend schools under Reform auspices; 26.9 per cent are in schools affiliated with the Conservative movement; and 26.5 per cent are enrolled in Orthodox-sponsored schools. One-day-a-week schools account for 30.2 per cent of the total enrollment (a drop from the previous 42.2 per cent); 2 to 5-days-a-week schools enroll 44.4 per cent of the student population; day schools account for 25.4 per cent of all registrations (an increase of 28 per cent over a ten-year period).

Further analysis indicates that Jewish education today, as in the past, is by and large elementary schooling. Despite a reported rise in high school enrollment (programs for youngsters above the age of thirteen which meet at least once a week), the majority of children who attend a Jewish school drop out upon completion of the elementary school level. The high drop-out rate remains one of the most intractable problems confronting Jewish educators. While what they do with a child is surely a factor in the decision to continue or not, a whole complex of factors outside of the school conspires to thwart even the most carefully designed and executed programs. If, as some recent studies seem to suggest, supplementary schooling can be effective if students stay in school long enough, high school programs with the power to attract and hold adolescents are a first-order priority for Jewish education.

One positive factor on the Jewish educational scene today is the noticeable trend toward more intensive Jewish schooling. In Orthodox circles, one-day-a-week schools have practically disappeared; a similar tendency is evident in Conservative schools; and the number of midweek afternoon schools in the Reform movement is on the increase.[8] Overall, the average number of pupil hours per school year in Jewish schools has increased by 35 per cent since 1966–67, from 182 to 248.

The continued expansion of the day school movement, embracing as it does today every sector of organized Jewry, accounts for a significant shift in the direction of more intensive Jewish education. The growth of the Jewish day school is surely one

---

[7]"Trends in Jewish School Enrollment," *loc. cit.,* p. 3.
[8]*Ibid.,* p. 9.

of the hallmarks of American Jewish life in our generation. In 1944 there were 39 day schools in the United States, most of them in New York City; today there are 545. Of that number 86 per cent are under Orthodox auspices; 8 per cent are Conservative-sponsored; 5 per cent designate themselves as communal or independent; and 1 per cent belong to the Reform movement. Over a 15-year period, from 1962 to 1977, day school enrollment has jumped from 60,000 to 92,000 pupils.[9] Approximately one out of every four children in Jewish elementary schools is in a day school.

The day school is, first and foremost, the signal achievement of Orthodox Jewry. Its steadfast adherence to the religious imperative of *talmud-torah* set a standard for Jewish education which has touched both Conservative and Reform Jews. In many instances day school supporters undertook the task of establishing a school in the face of indifference, and even opposition, from official quarters. They were frequently accused of parochialism, ghetto thinking, and, worst of all, un-American behavior. Their persistence accounts in no small measure for the turnabout in the position of Jewish federations, which were once centers of resistance to day schools. In 1971 Max Fischer, then president of the Council of Jewish Federations and Welfare Funds, urged communal leaders "to re-examine their obligations to the day schools . . . for the day school holds one of the very best answers to further Jewish continuity and has earned our most careful consideration of what could be done to help." The growth of the day school movement throughout the United States is a striking index of the maturation of Jewish consciousness in this country. It also tells us what is possible when clearly articulated goals are pursued with sustained and dedicated effort.

The fact that day school growth has passed its peak—actually that point was reached more than 10 years ago—does not mean that new sources of enrollment are not available. Day school registers reflect current Jewish experience in that they include children of new Russian immigrants, Israeli *yordim,* and young couples newly awakened to their Jewish identity.

There is much discussion about the motives which move parents to send their children to day schools. In the case of religiously and otherwise committed families the reasons are obvious. There is also no question that the heightened sensitivity to ethnic identification which has characterized American society in recent years has been a contributing factor. Dissatisfaction with supplementary Jewish schooling and the impact of the alternative school movement, which legitimized withdrawal from the public school, may also be counted as factors. A recent investigation of parental attitudes toward the day school, though based on a small sample, is useful here.[10] The data was collected in a large midwestern city, a setting which is perhaps more

[9]Alvin Schiff, "Jewish Day Schools in America: 1962–1977," *The Pedagogic Reporter,* Fall 1977, pp. 2–7.

[10]Louise Adams, Judith Frankel, and Nancy Newbauer, "Parental Attitudes Toward the Jewish All-Day School," *Jewish Education,* Winter 1972–73, p. 28.

instructive than the traditional centers of Jewish population. Responses to a questionnaire indicate that "the most important considerations for the parents in sending their children to this school seem to be the study of the modern Israeli state, the acquiring of a sense of belonging and pride in being Jewish, participation in the religious aspects of Judaism, and the small number of students per teacher." Another study,[11] conducted in Los Angeles in 1977, indicates that while parents who send their children to a non-Orthodox day school are motivated by specifically Jewish concerns, the primary reason for the decision is the desire for high-level general education.

Parents who are concerned about the Jewish education of their children cannot complain about a lack of opportunities. Today the school, whatever its type, is surrounded by a network of ancillary settings which extend the range of educational activity beyond the limits of formal schooling. Youth groups are well within the reach of every youngster. The largest of the youth organizations are sponsored by national synagogue bodies. Zionist youth groups can be found in every large metropolitan center. The latter work independently of the school and rarely have any contact with it. The synagogue youth organizations are part of the same congregational framework as the school and provide innumerable possibilities for the integration of formal and informal programs.

Summer camps, too, must be reckoned in any assessment of the extent and reach of Jewish education. Hebrew speaking camps, and others as well, have had a profound influence on thousands of youngsters who, long after their days in camp, still carry the stamp of an intensive educational experience. There are many who would claim, and not without justice, that the expansion of educational camping ranks alongside the growth of the day school as a major achievement of Jewish education in the past quarter of a century.

The success of summer camping programs has led many schools to utilize camp settings during the school year. Weekend retreats and camp programs conducted during public school vacations, sponsored by individual schools or organized for a group of schools by bureaus of Jewish education, are now common and considered a necessary part of the school curriculum. In many places monthly weekends in camp combined with guided work at home in-between have replaced the traditional one-day-a-week Sunday School. We do not yet know whether this form of schooling is more effective than conventional programs. There can be no doubt, however, that it is beyond the ability of a formal school setting to duplicate the resonance of a shared experience of study, prayer, and play in a camp environment.

Notice must also be taken of the explosive expansion of Jewish Studies programs in American colleges and universities. Over 300 different institutions of higher learning in this country now offer courses in Jewish Studies; 40 universities offer a

[11]Stuart L. Kelman, *Motivation and Goals: Why Parents Send Their Children to Non-Orthodox Day Schools,* unpublished doctoral dissertation, University of Southern California, 1978.

major in the subject and 27 sponsor graduate programs.[12] This is surely one of the most important developments in Jewish life in the last decade and a half. While little is known about the type of students enrolled in these programs, it is clear that more students than ever before are now involved in college-level Jewish studies.

Goals

Education in its broadest sense is the transmission of a culture across generations. This, of course, is an extremely complex process. The school is but one of a network of agencies and institutions which touch the growing child on his way to responsible maturity. Schools, however, differ from other educating factors in that they alone are capable of developing systematic programs of sequential experiences directed towards a specific goal. Schools, then, provide opportunity for a deliberate weighing of purpose and a careful control of practice. Jewish schools, of course, are no different in this regard.

While statements of aims and objectives in Jewish education generally lack philosophical rigor, and thereby confound attempts to develop logically consistent programs of instruction, their intent is quite clear—to inculcate in pupils the desire and ability to conduct their lives in keeping with the precepts of the Jewish tradition. The latitudinarianism which is a hallmark of modernism, invites a broad spectrum of interpretation of that tradition and its translation into a regimen of daily life. The components of the tradition—God, Torah, and Israel—are variously conceived, and their valence, whether separately or in concert, differentially measured and assessed.

A new generation of Jewish educators has shifted the focus of Jewish schooling from its traditional emphasis on predetermined subject matter to an active concern for the self-expressed needs and interests of the student. The roots of the approach are varied: the writings of radical school reformers; the influence of Piagetian psychology in teacher training programs and graduate schools of education; the ambience of American colleges and universities which give students a voice in governance; the teachings of the "human potential" movement; and the general permissiveness which permeates American society. These young educators are committed to ". . . uncovering the thoughts and feelings of the kids themselves, not on a specific issue but rather in a free-wheeling open-ended way. This should allow the kids to bring in their own experiences with very little intervention on the part of the teacher . . ."[13]

On the high school level this approach involves a high degree of student involvement in all phases of planning and creation, a heightened emphasis on the affective, attention to inter-personal relationships, a readiness to move beyond the framework

---

[12]Will Maslow, *The Structure and Functioning of the American Jewish Community* (New York, 1974).

[13]Burt Jacobson, American Jewish Committee and American Association for Jewish Education, *Report of Work Conference on Current Concerns in Jewish Education,* 1970, pp. 45–46.

of prescribed forms and structures, and an acceptance of the legitimacy of a wide variety of views and patterns of personal expression. The acknowledgement of the centrality of *mitsvot* in Judaism is accompanied by a view of religion as a continued search for self-realization rather than as a closed system of preordained imperatives. Religious practice, as a consequence, becomes a highly personal matter, with the final determinant of the student's religious behavior being his feelings at the moment. The legitimacy of Jewish nationalism finds expression in a commitment to the State of Israel and a recognition of its crucial role in the Jewish future. At the same time, the American Jewish community is also accorded a place of primacy. This conception of learning affords place to traditional modes and methods of study but finds them lacking when used in isolation from broader and more encompassing experiences. The task of the educator then is not simply to direct a school or to inculcate a point of view, but rather to create an environment in which the student is free to experiment in a variety of settings and with an assortment of materials in an encouraged attempt to define a style of Jewishness which suits his needs and tastes.

On the elementary school level this approach has led to experimentation with the "open classroom"[14] and, to a lesser extent, to the establishment of "free" or "alternative" Jewish schools. The open classroom simply seeks to create a better environment for learning; the alternative school, usually found in university centers and conducted by students, constitutes a protest against what is thought to be the lack of Jewish "authenticity" on the part of the organized community.

Much of what we have been discussing here has found expression at the conferences sponsored by the Coalition of Alternatives for Jewish Education, a loosely-knit group of young educators which is an offshoot of the North American Jewish Students Network. The three conferences held so far—one at Brown University in 1976, a second at the University of Rochester in 1977, and a third at the University of California at Irvine in 1978—are a pot-pourri of educational method and technique concocted by imaginative teachers and administrators who insist on "doing their own thing." For the large number of participants the conferences have been "happenings" at which the emphasis is on the "doing" of Jewish education and where the affective component of learning clearly overshadows the purely cognitive.

Attention to the affective and concern for the involvement of students in the development of programs is by no means limited to the Coalition. For almost a decade the Rhea Hirsch School of Education of the Hebrew Union College-Jewish Institute of Religion in Los Angeles has conducted a project in "confluent education." This project is an adaptation, in the setting of the Jewish school, of work done at the Esalen Institute and the University of California at Santa Barbara. As described by one of its major theoreticians, confluent education calls for the "integration or flowing together of the affective and cognitive elements in individual and

---

[14]American Association for Jewish Education, *Opening the Classroom and Individualizing Instruction,* 1972.

group learning . . ."[15] The program in Los Angeles began with the training of teachers on the assumption that changes in the ways students learn could come about only as the result of changes in the behavior of teachers.[16] Teachers who participated in the training program reported that they had gained a great deal. Unfortunately, there has been no published report of a systematic empirical investigation evaluating the impact of confluent education on children in Jewish schools.

On a larger scale we may point to the curriculum development program announced several years ago by the Commission of Jewish Education of the Union of American Hebrew Congregations.[17] The conceptual framework of the undertaking rests on the assumption that ". . . educators must be receptive to the problems and needs of the students and attempt to create a synthesis between the traditional values and present concerns. The focal points of the curriculum are both what the learner wants to learn and what he ought to learn." Student input was achieved through "a national survey . . . conducted to determine the interests, concerns and problems of students on all age levels . . ." Whatever the ultimate form of the curriculum and its effectiveness, there is no question that the approach represents a fundamental commitment to responding to student interests.

Orthodox day schools, whose curricular options are relatively clear-cut, have also explored the significance of the experiential. There is a familiar ring to the observation of a leading day-school spokesman that "too many of our schools are satisfied with formal education conducted in and around the classroom. If our goal of commitment is to be a realistic one we must look for opportunities for students to act out the values and life style we are teaching . . . students will 'learn' more about the plight of Soviet Jewry in two hours devoted to neighborhood campaigning for signatures on a petition . . . than in two weeks of classes on Soviet-Jewish problems . . ."[18] In part, a heightened concern for the affective in day-school education reflects a desire to provide additional support for those students who come from non-Orthodox homes.

A good deal of what we have been describing here may be nothing more than educational gimmickry—harried Jewish educators latching on to another passing fad in general education. A careful reading of the evidence, however, suggests something more significant. The emphasis on the affective may be interpreted as a conclusion drawn from two interacting factors: the failure of most Jewish schools to impart basic knowledge and the belief that the emotive is *the* critical influence in the formation of identity.

---

[15]George I. Brown, *Human Teaching for Human Learning* (New York, 1971), pp. 10–11.
[16]William Cutter and Jack Dauber, Rhea Hirsch School of Education, Hebrew Union College–Jewish Institute of Religion, *Confluent Education in the Jewish Setting,* n.d.
[17]See Jack D. Spiro, "Toward a Conceptual Framework for Reform Jewish Education," *Compass,* Jan.–Feb., 1971.
[18]Haskel Lookstein, "The Jewish Day School: A Symposium," *Tradition,* (Summer 1972), pp. 113–114.

The curricula developed by the Melton Research Center and the United Synagogue Commission on Jewish Education reflect a quite different approach to Jewish education. While certainly not unmindful of the affective aspects of learning, the materials produced by these two agencies of the Conservative movement emphasize subject matter and the development of cognitive skills. The curriculum of the Melton Research Center is ". . . designed to teach information, skills and competencies" and is based on the assumption that "Jewish education must embody the thinking and the wisdom found in Jewish texts—Bible, *Siddur,* Talmud, Midrash and historical documents—and that it [is] desirable to have the students confront those texts directly and extract from them the themes which are basic to Jewish life and religion."[19] Together with a strict definition of subject matter, provided by members of the faculty of the Jewish Theological Seminary, the Melton material mandates a very specific method. The new *Curriculum for the Afternoon Jewish School,* published by the United Synagogue Commission on Jewish Education, is another example of a subject-centered program of study.[20] Though different in structure from the Melton program and more flexible in terms of method, it too rests on the assumption that knowledge is central to the life of the Jew and that what a Jewish child should know is best determined by scholars and educators. Both of these programs reflect a renewed commitment to formal schooling, and a belief in the potential efficacy of the supplementary afternoon school. Whatever the power of other settings, the new curricula of the Conservative movement, like that currently under development in the Reform movement, assume that the great majority of children will receive their Jewish education in the afternoon school. Moreover, they reflect a heightened sense of ideology and stress the religious rather than the nationalist dimension of Jewishness.

The statement of goals of the United Synagogue curriculum is noteworthy from yet another point of view. When it proclaims that ". . . the whole point of studying in the religious school is to learn what makes the Jew different . . . and to make a decision as to why you should be different,"[21] it reveals a shift in the definition of Jewishness and Americanism and the relationship between the two. An earlier generation of Jewish educators stressed the similarities between Judaism and the norms of American democracy. That posture is easily understood when we remember that the perceptions of both teachers and students were in the main shaped by the immigrant experience. A curriculum which consciously teaches the importance of difference is clearly addressing itself to a changed America and to another sort of Jew.

---

[19]Elaine Morris, "The Melton Approach: Accent on the Teacher," *United Synagogue Review,* Winter 1979, p. 6.

[20]United Synagogue Commission on Jewish Education, *A Curriculum for the Afternoon Jewish School,* 1978.

[21]*Ibid.,* p. 505.

The specific content of current curricula, whatever their thrust, is by and large drawn from the time-honored subjects of Jewish study. The literary nature of the Jewish tradition dictates the parameters of subject matter. The individual school, working by itself or guided by outlines prepared by national agencies, chooses the material of instruction and the mode of treatment. Both the time available to the school and its ideological orientation determine the curriculum space allotted any particular subject. As a rule, the more intensive the school the greater the concentration on traditional text or on material drawn from that source. Day schools alone are able to introduce students to the Talmud and cognate Rabbinic literature. There is probably no Jewish school in the country which does not teach Bible and history in some form. Hebrew remains a problematic area for afternoon supplementary schools unless they are willing to devote most of the time at their disposal to language instruction. The new curriculum of the United Synagogue, mindful of the low level of achievement which characterizes most of its affiliated congregational schools, advises that unless there is a commitment to a "concentration" in Hebrew, language instruction should be restricted to a basic phonics program geared to preparing the pupil to follow the synagogue service.

The core subjects of Bible, history, and Hebrew are surrounded by a wide array of courses, reflecting particular educational outlooks. In recent years there has been a decided emphasis on Jewish religious thought. As in the case of other subjects, the more intensive and traditional the school—and the two generally go hand in hand—the greater the reliance on classic texts. Mention should also be made of the near-universal inclusion of Israel and the Holocaust in the curricula of Jewish schools. These two topics, more than any others, pose problems for Jewish educators; when treated as "subject" they are threatened by the heavy hand of trivialization; when viewed as the central events of modern Jewish existence, they call into question many of the assumptions which guide Jewish schools in the United States.

Effectiveness

Discussions of schools and the things they do inevitably lead to questions of their effectiveness. The avowed purpose of schooling is to induce some sort of change in students and it is legitimate to inquire whether or not anything does indeed happen to a child as a result of all those hours spent in a classroom. The information available from research on the effects of schooling is divided. A considerable body of data seems to indicate that schools have very little effect either in terms of cognitive outcomes or in attitude and personality change; other studies argue just as persuasively that schools do make a difference in such matters as political information, "modern" attitudes and behavior, religious behavior and attitudes and general information.

The conventional wisdom of the Jewish community is that Jewish education, especially in its supplementary form, has little impact on students. Indeed there are those who argue that Jewish schools not only fail to achieve their goals, but actually have a negative effect on children in that they confirm the impression that Judaism is irrelevant to their lives.

We have no reliable empirical evidence concerning the effectiveness of Jewish schooling when the criteria are the acquisition of knowledge or the development of skills. Published curricula materials sometimes tell us what schools want to teach. We know little, however, about what teachers actually teach, and even less about what children actually learn. We are similarly ignorant regarding the efficiency of the Jewish school—the relationship between what is learned and the investments involved. While critics are quick to charge that Jewish schools provide their pupils with very little knowledge, it is not clear that they achieve less, all factors considered, than other kinds of schools, public or private. Since the overwhelming majority of children in Jewish schools are of elementary school age, we have no reason to expect that even under the best of circumstances they can acquire anything more than a rudimentary knowledge of Judaism. The rhetoric of both the critics and the defenders of Jewish education is all too often unmindful of the fact that the object of its concern is a child between the ages of seven and twelve. The postulated ineffectiveness of the Jewish school may very well be the ineluctable consequence of the constraints within which it is forced to function.

Several recent studies, marked by a methodological sophistication all too rare in research on Jewish education, report findings which seem to indicate that Jewish schooling does make a difference. One investigator studied adults between the ages of 30 and 45 who had been exposed to Jewish education of varying intensity to determine "what, if any, residual effect Jewish secondary school education in Philadelphia had on the Jewish life style of its graduates."[22] The findings of the study indicate that those respondents who had had an intensive Jewish secondary school education were more involved in Jewish affairs than those who had received a more limited Jewish education. Members of the "intensive" group rated parents and Jewish schooling as the two most important influences on their Jewish identity.

Two other studies suggest that under certain conditions Jewish schooling has an effect which is independent of familial background and other socializing influences.[23] According to Geoffrey Bock, better-schooled Jews are more identified Jewishly. He found that, all other things being equal, there was a positive relationship between time spent in Jewish classrooms during childhood and youth and adult religiosity, involvement in informal Jewish social networks, knowledge of Jewish culture, and support for Israel. When identification is defined as "public Jewishness"—attendance at synagogue services, participation in secular synagogue affairs, support for

---

[22]Sol Ribner, "The Effects of Intensive Jewish Education on Adult Jewish Life Styles," *Jewish Education,* Spring 1978, pp. 6–12.

[23]Geoffrey E. Bock, *The Jewish Schooling of American Jews: A Study of Non-Cognitive Educational Effects,* unpublished doctoral dissertation, Harvard University, 1976, and Harold S. Himmelfarb, "The Non-Linear Impact of Jewish Schooling: Comparing Different Types and Amounts of Jewish Education," *Sociology of Education,* April 1977, pp. 114–129.

Israel, and attitudes about American public issues—Jewish schooling is often as important a factor as Jewish home background. However, approximately 1,000 hours of instruction are necessary before Jewish schooling begins to effect Jewish identification in any significant fashion. The relationship between Jewish identification and schooling appears to reach its peak at about 4,000 hours of attendance in a Jewish school.

Harold Himmelfarb's study attempted to determine the relationship, if any, between adult religious involvement and the "intensity" and "extensity" of Jewish education. He reports that Jewish schooling does not have any statistically significant impact on adult religiosity until there are approximately 3,000 hours of attendance. The discrepancy between the two studies as to the minimum number of hours of instruction required if Jewish schooling is to have any effect may be a function of the criterion measure. The data support the assumption that both identification and religiosity are complex constructs and that the various elements of which they are composed may each require different minimums of instructional hours if schooling is to have any impact. Himmelfarb also found that there is a steady increase in adult religiosity as attendance moves from 3,000 to 4,000 hours; however, beyond 4,000 hours increased schooling does not result in increased religiosity unless reinforced by other factors, particularly the spouse. If such reinforcement occurs there is another significant increase in religiosity when schooling approaches approximately 10,000 hours. Instruction beyond that point appears to have no significant impact on religiosity as defined in this study. These two studies suggest that current curricular changes, no matter how refined and sophisticated, will have little long-range impact on students if they do not inspire attendance at a Jewish school well beyond the elementary level.

Bock's and Himmelfarb's threshold figures place the statistics of Jewish school enrollment in painful perspective. More than 75 per cent of the children who receive a Jewish education attend schools which meet for 2–6 hours a week; the full program of these schools extends over 4–7 years; the overwhelming majority of these children do not continue their studies beyond Bar/Bat Mitzvah or Confirmation; and a large percentage do not get even that far. Even those youngsters who complete the first level of the most intensive kind of supplementary education currently in existence fall short of the minimum number of hours judged essential if schools are to have a long-range impact.

The foregoing supports the long-standing contention of Jewish educators that children do not stay long enough in Jewish schools to permit anything positive to happen. The data suggest that it makes little difference what the schools do, and how they do it, as long as the children leave before a certain point.

Personnel

The critical act of all schooling is the meeting of teacher and pupil, and the quality of that meeting is determined by the personal resources of the teacher, his training, and the climate of the school. Without the painstaking day-to-day work of talented and dedicated teachers there can be no meaningful Jewish education.

The status of the Jewish teacher makes painfully clear the gulf that exists between word and deed in Jewish education. The rhetorical fervor which places education at the center of Jewish life seldom moves to serious consideration of the consequences of the demise of the profession of Jewish teaching. At the present time there are approximately 3,500 teachers employed in day schools and some 5,500 in weekday afternoon schools. Of this number less than one-third may be considered full-time teachers if full-time teaching in day schools is set at 20 hours per week and in afternoon schools at 12 hours per week. We have no exact figures on the number of teachers working in one-day-a-week schools, although it is safe to assume that declining enrollments and school consolidations have reduced this number considerably below the 9,559 reported 20 years ago in the National Study of Jewish Education.[24]

Except in day schools, there are almost no full-time teaching positions available in Jewish education today. During the 1978–79 school year only 15 per cent of 116 teachers appointed to Conservative afternoon schools in the Chicago area were in full-time positions. In the entire Greater Boston area there were only 12 full-time positions available in afternoon schools. Much the same situation obtained in Cleveland.

Salary schedules also contribute to the difficulties of developing a corps of teachers who have made career commitments to Jewish education. A study conducted in the 1975–76 school year by the American Association for Jewish Education found that "teacher salaries in Jewish day and supplementary schools are too low to afford a head of family a decent, comfortable standard of living as the sole wage earner." The analysis of the data gathered from 382 schools in 31 metropolitan areas showed that the median maximum salary of a full-time day school teacher was $13,433 per year, while that of a full-time teacher in a supplementary school was $9,400. The salary figure for day-school teachers was 13.2 per cent below what public school teachers earned. The data reveal a situation which has made it impossible to maintain rigorous standards of certification and professional requirements—the hallmarks of a profession.

There has been no dearth of sensible suggestions for improving the economic situation of teachers: employment by the community rather than by individual schools of limited resources; consolidation of schools in order to increase teaching loads; training teachers so that they would be able to work in both formal and informal settings; and establishing clearly-defined promotion procedures leading to administrative posts. The readiness of the central agencies of the Jewish community to act quickly and tellingly to insure the calling of the Jewish teacher is the ultimate test of their commitment to Jewish education.

---

[24]The data in this section are drawn from George Pollack, *Employment Realities and Career Opportunities in Jewish Education,* paper presented at Hebrew College, Boston, Mass., 1978.

Teachers in the Jewish school system are a varied group: yeshiva graduates who have opted for teaching careers in day schools; graduates of Jewish teacher training institutions; Israelis who are in this country either permanently or temporarily; and those who arrive at a Jewish school through no recognizable route of Jewish learning or training.

Yeshiva graduates are the backbone of the Orthodox day school system. Israeli teachers, both in the day and afternoon schools, pose particular problems. Israelis are the present-day equivalents of the European-born teachers of an earlier period —they are separated from their students by deep cultural differences. While the conscientious teacher from Israel may succeed in bridging the gap, his residence in the United States seriously compromises a curriculum in which Israel is an important element. The penalties of an excess of imports are as severe in education as in economics.

No other institution involved in Jewish education has undergone as much change in the last decade as the Hebrew teachers college—even the name is no longer appropriate. Once the pinnacles of non-rabbinic Jewish learning in this country, these schools today are hard put to maintain their undergraduate programs. Enrollments on the undergraduate level, which require simultaneous attendance at two institutions of higher learning, are considerably below the peak of 1,812 reported in the mid-1960's.[25] The reasons for the decline are many: the growth of Jewish studies programs on college campuses; skyrocketing tuition rates which force many young people to work during the time formerly available for study in these schools; and the decrease in the number of lower-level schools which provide the background necessary for admission. The decline of undergraduate programs has meant a narrowing of opportunities for comprehensive Jewish socialization of young people. Hebrew teachers colleges, also known as colleges of Jewish studies, were more than schools. Attendance at one of these institutions circumscribed the life of the student; it determined his friends, limited his time for non-Jewish activities, and set the boundaries of possible interests.

Several Jewish teacher training schools have developed imaginative new programs. Spertus College in Chicago "supplies" Jewish Studies programs to several colleges in the area. Hebrew College in Boston is developing a program which it hopes will attract students whose backgrounds do not meet formal admission requirements but who are prepared to do make-up work. At the same time the College has invested heavily in adult learning. The various units of Yeshiva University offer a wide variety of pre-professional and professional programs. The Teachers Institute of the Jewish Theological Seminary and its West Coast school, the University of Judaism, as well as the Rhea Hirsch School of Education of the Hebrew Union College–Jewish Institute of Religion in Los Angeles, have successfully launched Master's degree programs for college graduates interested in careers in Jewish

---

[25]Walter I. Ackerman, "A Profile of the Hebrew Teachers College," in Oscar J. Janowsky (ed.), *The Education of American Jewish Teachers* (Boston, 1967), pp. 41–60.

education. Even though the background of the students participating in these programs may be somewhat weaker than was the case of students in the more traditional setting, the fact that they are full-time students attending only one school undoubtedly contributes to a higher level of academic work. It is doubtful, however, that these students will long remain classroom teachers; those who will remain in Jewish education have clearly set their sights on administrative posts.

In contrast to the situation in teaching is that in administration. There are currently some 1,300–1,400 administrative positions in Jewish schools, bureaus of Jewish education, and national agencies.[26] Reform congregations employ 245 full-time principals; the remainder of the 775 Reform schools employ part-time educators, rabbis who perform other duties, or lay administrators. A number of Reform congregations have charged educators with the total responsibility for the congregational educational program, formal and informal, from pre-school through adult education. Conservative congregations employ 350 full-time principals. Day school principalships are generally full-time positions. There is no question that administrators in Jewish schools are as well-qualified as their counterparts in public education. The problem is the lack of qualified personnel to meet the demand; each placement season resembles a game of musical chairs. Salary schedules range from $15,000 per year for principals to as much as $50,000 for directors of central agencies. These salaries, which compare favorably with those paid in similar occupations, have not succeeded in attracting the number of people needed to staff positions currently available.

Finances

While it is difficult to pinpoint the exact relationship between funding and educational effectiveness, it is clear that adequate financial resources are required for schools to initiate and maintain quality programs. Intensive Jewish education is expensive. The recruitment and retention of teachers, curriculum development, and the production of instructional materials—even for the less intensive afternoon and one-day-a-week schools—require large investments of money. Although the current total expenditure for Jewish education in the United States is estimated to be $280,000,000, almost three times the amount expended ten years ago, it is clear that traditional patterns of funding are inadequate to the demands of expanding programs in a period of spiralling inflation.

An analysis of pupil costs by type of school indicates national averages ranging from $2,300 per year in day high schools to $500 for children attending three-day-a-week supplementary schools. Elementary day school expenditures amount to $1,500; communal elementary school expenditures to $750; and communal high school expenditures to $550. Costs for one-day-a-week school pupils are not known.

---

[26]George Pollack, *Employment Realities and Career Opportunities in Jewish Education, loc. cit.*

Varied patterns of record-keeping, coupled with a frequent lack of relevant information, makes it difficult to ascertain the exact amounts contributed by synagogues to the maintenance of their schools. One estimate places the allocation of Reform congregations to educational programs at an average of about 15 to 20 per cent of the total institutional budget. The more intensive the program, of course, the larger will be its share of congregational expenditures. It is reasonable to assume, however, that in a period of decreasing membership and increasing operational costs there will be no significant rise in direct subventions to schools from congregational budgets.

The data on tuition fees for three-day-a-week schools indicate that there is little relationship between charges to parents and the actual costs of maintaining a child in school. Over a 20-year period, from 1951–1952 to 1969–1970, tuition fees rose from $50 a year for members and $65 a year for non-members to $85 and $150, respectively.[27] More recent information indicates little change in the picture; a survey of some 30 Conservative congregational schools shows that tuition fees in 1975–76 averaged $115.[28] Tuition schedules are obviously conditioned by the fear that an increase in fees will result in a decrease in enrollment and perhaps synagogue membership.

Day school tuition is an entirely different matter; here there is a real possibility that ever higher fees will move intensive Jewish education beyond the reach of many Jewish families. Whereas in the 1973–74 school year, day school tuition outside New York City was about $1,000, data for 1978–79 indicate fees of around $1,500. In the New York City area current charges are about $2,000.[29] Tuition, of course, is a major source of day school income; it does not, however, cover the cost of operations, and schools are increasingly forced to look for outside sources of funding.

Federation allocations are a third source of funding for Jewish education. The years since the end of World War II have seen a steady increase in the amount and proportion of federation funds allocated to Jewish education. In 1947 the sums earmarked for Jewish education represented 8.9 per cent of the total funds budgeted for local needs;[30] by 1970 that figure had risen to 13.3 per cent;[31] in 1977 allocations to Jewish education totalled 23.2 per cent of all local disbursements.[32] When expressed in dollar amounts, federation allocations for the period cited (1947–77) rose from $2,215,911 to $27,492,216. A breakdown of the gross figures of federation

---

[27]Hillel Hochberg, "Trends and Developments in Jewish Education," AJYB, Vol. 73, 1972, p. 221.

[28]Seaboard Region, United Synagogue of America, *Survey on Synagogue Finances*, 1975–76.

[29]United Synagogue Commission on Jewish Education, *Tuition Compilation Survey, Solomon Schechter Day Schools,* 1979. Although this study deals only with Conservative schools, fees in Orthodox and Reform day schools are comparable.

[30]Alexander Dushkin and Uriah Engelman, *Jewish Education in the U.S.* (New York, 1959), p. 148.

[31]Hochberg, *loc. cit.,* p. 209.

[32]Council of Jewish Federations and Welfare Funds, *Federation Allocations to Jewish Education,* 1978.

subventions reveals the following pattern of disbursements (expressed as percentages of total allocations to Jewish education):[33]

1. Allocations and subsidies to schools		59.8
a. Day schools	44.0	
b. Congregational schools	2.3	
c. Other schools	13.5	
2. Jewish institutions of higher learning		8.5
3. Services and programs of central agencies		30.8
4. All other		0.9
	Total	100.0

As encouraging as the trends reported here may be, a more refined analysis of the data discloses that federation funds play only a minor role in enabling Jewish schools to function. Total federation allocations in 1977 represented 10 per cent of the costs of Jewish education—an increase of a slight 3 per cent over 1947. While day schools have been the major beneficiaries of federation financing, the sums allocated in recent years cover only about 13 per cent of their budgets. Thus, parents who want intensive Jewish education for their children must, by and large, pay for it themselves.

The never-ending search for additional funds has led some day school supporters to look to the government for funding. They argue that government support falls in the category of aid to children, that it is fully permissible under the equal protection and free exercise clauses of the Constitution, and that the funds made available would be used only for the secular studies component of the day school curriculum. To date, court decisions have approved the use of public tax funds by Jewish day schools only when applied to textbook loans, transportation as a public safety measure, school lunch programs, and certain therapeutic programs.[34] The eligibility of Jewish day schools and other religious elementary and secondary schools for participation in tax-supported school tuition voucher plans remains a moot constitutional issue.

There is a clear need for rethinking the issue of responsibility in the funding of Jewish education. Congregations should review their fiscal procedures to determine what obligations they can sensibly carry. If tuition is primarily the responsibility of the parent, steps must be taken to bring fees into realistic relationship to the costs of instruction in a synagogue setting. The readiness of Jewish parents to shoulder the burden of a high tax rate in support of quality public education must find its counterpart in Jewish education, even if this means a decrease in enrollment. Tuition increases alone, however, cannot solve the financial problems of day schools. Day

---

[33]*Ibid.,* p. 5.

[34]Benson Skeoff, *Tax Funds for Jewish Education: Presentation and Analysis of Various Jewish Views,* 1947–1974, unpublished doctoral dissertation, Washington University, 1975.

school supporters must discover new sources of support.[35] The stance of federations must similarly be subjected to a searching review.

Conclusion

Jewish education in the United States is still largely supplementary schooling which engages children of elementary school age. In the main, these children are second and third generation Americans. This is a fact of considerable consequence for schools charged with the task of developing the Jewish identity of their students. The present enrollment of 360,000 pupils in all kinds of Jewish schools reflects a decline of 30 per cent from the peak of approximately 550,000 reported in the middle of the 1960's. We do not know if this downturn, largely a function of an aging Jewish population and a lower birthrate among young couples, has been accompanied by a parallel decrease in the percentage of children of school age attending Jewish schools. The continued growth of day schools, the decline in the number of one-day-a-week schools, the small but encouraging rise in secondary school programs, and the spread of university-level Jewish studies programs suggest that an increasing number of young people are investing more time over a longer period in Jewish education. That gain, however, is still not large enough to offset the fact that the vast majority of children who enter a Jewish school terminate their studies long before they can be expected to have attained any recognizable or long-lasting skills and competencies. The rate of continuation, surely one of the most critical measures of a school's influence, remains as disturbingly low today as it was ten years ago.

Recent research findings lend empirical support to what Jewish educators have long known and proclaimed: as long as Jewish education remains mainly elementary education which is restricted to 2–5 hours a week of instruction, there is little reason to believe, or even hope, that it can have any long-range impact. The perennial problems of Jewish education—personnel, curriculum, and finances—are in no small measure a function of its limited range. While the schools themselves contribute to drop-out rates, their efforts at self-improvement through the introduction of new curricula and more sophisticated methods and materials are inadequate for the reversal of long-standing attitudes and practice among parents and children alike. The extension of the reach of Jewish schooling into adolescence and beyond demands a concentrated effort which marshals the resources of the entire community. Without a significant shift in the direction of broader participation in secondary school programs, the Jewish school will be forced to forfeit its age-old function as the "treasure house of our people's soul."

WALTER I. ACKERMAN

---

[35]For an imaginative approach to day school financing, see David Hershberg, *Re: Financing the Solomon Schechter Day School,* Solomon Schechter Day School Association of the United Synagogue of America, n.d. See also Alvin Schiff, "Funding Jewish Education—Whose Responsibility?" *Jewish Education,* Summer 1973, pp. 6–12.

Jewish Communal Services:
Programs and Finances

J EWISH FEDERATIONS, through their annual campaigns and endowment funds, provide the major source of contributed support for Jewish overseas and domestic services. Other important sources of income for Jewish services are public funds, service payments, and United Way grants.

The classification of services may be based on geography (local, national, or overseas), may reflect the major program areas of Jewish agencies (community centers, refugee services, welfare and health services, community relations, Jewish education, vocational training, etc.), or may cut across agencies where more than one of them provides aspects of specific services.

The United Jewish Appeal (UJA) provides support for the United Israel Appeal (UIA), the American Jewish Joint Distribution Committee (JDC), and the New York Association for New Americans (NYANA). The Jewish Agency is the operational agency for UIA and Keren Hayesod programs, which include assistance for immigration, agricultural settlement, welfare services, higher education, and youth *aliyah*. JDC programs in various countries, including Israel, are based almost completely on funds raised in the United States. JDC provides subventions to ORT for vocational education, which are supplemented by membership campaigns in the U.S. and by governmental support abroad. NYANA, which resettles refugees in the New York City area, is financed by UJA; parallel programs in other communities are financed directly by local federations.

Among other important overseas agencies are the Hebrew Immigrant Aid Society (HIAS), Hadassah, the National Committee for Labor Israel, the America-Israel Cultural Foundation, and the Jewish National Fund.

Those agencies that specialize in community relations—the American Jewish Committee, Anti-Defamation League, American Jewish Congress, Jewish Labor Committee, Jewish War Veterans, and National Conference on Soviet Jewry—are the main beneficiaries of federation support on the national level. They, and the local community relations councils that exist in more than 100 cities, are joined together in the National Jewish Community Relations Advisory Council.

The national religious agencies include the major seminaries and congregational bodies of the three religious wings. Some Orthodox *yeshivot* in the major cities receive support from local federations.

The Joint Cultural Appeal, administered by the National Foundation for Jewish Culture, encompasses nine agencies. There are also secular institutions of higher learning (Brandeis, Dropsie, and Herzliah), and a number of research and scholarly groups which receive financial assistance from federations. Major national youth groups include Hillel, the B'nai B'rith Youth Organization, and the North American Jewish Students Appeal.

National agencies which serve local programs are the National Jewish Welfare Board (serving community centers), the American Association for Jewish Education, and the National Association of Jewish Vocational Services.

Local programs supported by federations with United Way aid are community centers, family and children's services, hospitals, care for the aged, and (to a nominal extent) vocational services. Federations receive no United Way support for Jewish education, refugee aid, and local community relations.

Amounts Raised

During the 1975–78 period, when the cost of living rose by 21 per cent, the amount raised annually in support of Jewish domestic and overseas needs was between $460 million and $475 million. The sale of Israel Bonds in the United States amounted to $267 million in 1977, and $296 million in 1978. Over $32.3 million in Israel Bonds was turned over to UJA in 1977 in partial payment of federation campaign pledges; in 1978 the figure was over $32.0 million.

Fund Distribution

Federation allocations continued to be directed mainly to UJA—69 per cent in 1976; 66 per cent in 1977; and 64 per cent in 1978. These levels were higher than in most years prior to 1967. Outside of New York City, allocations for refugee aid rose to 2.3 per cent in 1976, and were continuing to rise. Other national and overseas agencies received a relatively stable annual share of about 3 per cent.

Federation allocations for local needs were about 26 per cent in 1976, 28 per cent (estimated) in 1977, and 30 per cent (estimated) in 1978. These levels were higher than those in the preceding decade, but were lower than those in the 1958–66 period.

About one quarter of federation allocations went for Jewish education in the United States. Funds for Jewish education in other countries were provided to the Jewish Agency, mainly through global Keren Hayesod campaigns.

Total allocations by federations for all local services amounted to $112 million in 1977. They were supplemented by $27 million in United Way funds earmarked for those Jewish services eligible for such support.

Five-Year Trend

In the 1972–76 period the greatest increase in aid was in the area of refugee care, which rose ninefold, from $744,000 to $6,704,000 (in 92 communities). During the same period, most other allocations rose from 40 to 50 per cent. Overall allocations by federations rose by 64 per cent, while United Way grants increased by only 18 per cent.

S. P. GOLDBERG

TABLE 1.   AMOUNTS RAISED IN CENTRAL JEWISH COMMUNITY CAMPAIGNS
(Estimates in Millions of Dollars)

Year	Amounts Raised	Consumer Price Index 1975 = 100.0%
1974	$660	—
1975	475	100.0
1976	460	105.8
1977*	465	112.6
1978*	475	121.2

*Estimates based on incomplete reports.

TABLE 2.

SALES OF STATE OF ISRAEL BONDS, 1974–1978

(In Thousands of Dollars)

Year	Total Cash Sales	Sales In U.S.	Sales Abroad
1974	$265,477	$204,257	$61,220
1975	277,311*	226,217	51,094
1976	311,410*	241,690	69,720
1977	331,571*	267,094	64,477
1978	369,801*	295,690	74,111

*Includes sales of five-year and other Israel notes, as listed below.

SALES OF ISRAEL NOTES

(In Thousands of Dollars)

1975(initiation)	$ 20,000	$19,000	$ 1,000
1976	56,500	40,000	16,500
1977	70,500	57,000	13,500
1978	121,280	95,405	25,875

TOTAL SALES AND REDEMPTIONS, 1951–1978

Global sales from 1951 through 1978	$4,220 million
Redemptions 1951 through 1978 . .	1,460 million
Types of Redemptions:	
Tourism	239 million
Jewish Agency	291 million
Other Agencies	225 million
Investments in Israel	190 million
Other	515 million

TABLE 3. DISTRIBUTION OF FUNDS RAISED TO FIELDS OF SERVICE
(Estimates in Thousands of Dollars)

	1976	1975	Total 1974	1973	1972
TOTAL AMOUNT BUDGETED TO BENEFICIARIES[c, d] ...	$385,902	$399,498	$584,530	$332,807	$322,086
%	100.0	100.0	100.0	100.0	100.0
Overseas Agencies	269,257	289,356	485,115	248,577	244,321
%	69.8	72.4	83.0	74.7	75.9
United Jewish Appeal	265,883	286,108	481,737	245,722	240,562
%	68.9	71.6	82.4	73.8	74.7
Other Overseas	3,374	3,248	3,378	2,855	3,759
%	0.9	0.8	0.6	0.9	1.2
Local Refugee Care[f]	7,015	5,595	3,245	1,296	758
%	1.8	1.4	0.6	0.4	0.2
National Agencies	8,083	8,066	8,101	6,886	6,830
%	2.1	2.0	1.4	2.1	2.1
Community Relations	3,918	3,952	4,144	3,245	3,235
%	1.0	1.0	0.7	1.0	1.0
Health & Welfare	20	18	18	18	27
%	#	#	#	#	#
Cultural	1,315	1,370	1,428	1,241	1,167
%	0.3	0.3	0.2	0.4	0.4
Religious	288	303	347	276	374
%	0.1	0.1	0.1	0.1	0.1
Service Agencies	2,542	2,423	2,164	2,106	2,027
%	0.7	0.6	0.4	0.6	0.6
Local Operating Needs	98,313	92,692	84,147	72,966	67,622
%	25.5	23.2	14.4	21.9	21.0
Local Capital Needs	3,234	3,789	3,919	3,079	2,552
%	0.8	0.9	0.7	0.9	0.8

[a] Based upon communities which are currently CJF members and some smaller cities which are not CJF members but which had been included in the base group of communities used in 1948 when this statistical series was started. Minor differences in amounts and percentages due to rounding. United Fund support *excluded* from this table but *included* in Tables 5,6.

[b] Figures for New York include the United Jewish Appeal of Greater New York and Federation of Jewish Philanthropies. Local refugee costs in New York City are borne by NYANA, a direct beneficiary of the UJA nationally. Most overseas and domestic agencies, which are normally included in Welfare Funds in other cities, conduct their own campaigns in New York. The New York UJA included the following beneficiaries (in addition to the National UJA): HIAS and National Jewish Welfare Board. Data for New York UJA are based on estimates of distribution of annual campaign proceeds, regardless of year in which cash is received.

[c] The difference between this amount and "total raised" in Table I represents mainly "shrinkage" allowance for non-payment of pledges, campaign and administrative expenses, elimination of duplicating multiple city gifts and contingency or other reserves.

[d] Includes small undistributed amounts in "total" and "other cities" columns.

[e] Based on data published in CJF Budget Digests.

[f] NYANA is included in UJA totals: ($0.6 million in 1972; $0.9 million in 1973; $2.3 million in 1974; $4.4 million in 1975; $6.1 million in 1976).

Less than .05 of one per cent.

(INCLUDING ISRAEL EMERGENCY FUND) BY JEWISH FEDERATIONS[a]
(Estimates in Thousands of Dollars)

New York City[b]					Other Cities				
1976	*1975*	*1974*	*1973*	*1972*	*1976*	*1975*	*1974*	*1973*	*1972*
$76,754	$80,264	$130,351	$80,725	$79,096	$309,148	$319,234	$454,179	$252,082	$242,990
100.0	100.0	100.0	100.0	100.0	100.0	100.0	100.0	100.0	100.0
50,500	55,000	107,000	58,718	58,638	218,757	234,356	378,115	189,859	185,683
65.8	68.5	82.1	72.7	74.1	70.7	73.4	83.3	75.4	76.4
49,400	54,000	106,000	58,000	58,000	216,483	232,108	375,737	187,722	182,562
64.4	67.3	81.3	71.8	73.3	70.0	72.7	82.7	74.5	75.1
1,100	1,000	1,000	718	638	2,274	2,248	2,378	2,137	3,121
1.4	1.2	0.8	0.9	0.8	0.7	0.7	0.6	0.9	1.3
—	—	—	—	—	7,015	5,595	3,245	1,296	758
—	—	—	—	—	2.3	1.8	0.7	0.5	0.3
1,046[e]	960[e]	726[e]	816[e]	721	7,037	7,016	7,375	6,070	6,109
1.4	1.2	0.5	1.0	0.9	2.3	2.2	1.6	2.4	2.5
—	—	—	—	—	3,918	3,952	4,144	3,245	3,235
—	—	—	—	—	1.3	1.2	0.9	1.3	1.3
—	—	—	—	—	20	18	18	18	27
—	—	—	—	—	#	#	#	#	#
—	—	—	—	—	1,315	1,370	1,428	1,241	1,167
—	—	—	—	—	0.4	0.4	0.3	0.5	0.5
—	—	—	—	—	288	303	347	276	374
—	—	—	—	—	0.1	0.1	0.1	0.1	0.1
1,046[e]	960[e]	726[e]	816[e]	721	1,496	1,463	1,438	1,290	1,306
1.4	1.2	0.5	1.0	0.9	0.5	0.5	0.3	0.5	0.5
25,208	24,304	22,625	21,191	19,737	73,105	68,388	61,522	51,775	47,885
32.8	30.3	17.4	26.3	25.0	23.7	21.4	13.5	20.5	19.7
—	—	—	—	—	3,234	3,789	3,919	3,079	2,552
—	—	—	—	—	1.0	1.2	0.9	1.2	1.1

TABLE 4. DISTRIBUTION OF FEDERATION AND UNITED FUND ALLOCATIONS TO LOCAL JEWISH SERVICES, 1975–1977

(Estimates in Millions of Dollars)

	Total			New York City			Other Cities		
	1975	1976	1977	1975	1976	1977	1975	1976	1977
Fields Receiving United Way Support									
Centers, Camps, Related Programs	$32.6	$35.0	$37.2	$7.7	$8.2	$8.2	$24.9	$26.8	$29.0
Family and Children's Services	24.9	26.3	27.6	6.7	7.0	7.1	18.2	19.3	20.5
Hospitals, Health	11.6	11.5	11.3	5.0	5.0	4.7	6.6	6.5	6.6
Aged	11.8	12.0	12.8	1.8	2.0	2.0	10.0	10.0	10.8
Federation Administration (United Way Funds Only)	0.9	0.9	1.1	0.3	0.3	0.4	0.6	0.6	0.7
Sub-Total	$81.8	$85.7	$90.0	$21.5	$22.5	$22.4	$60.3	$63.2	$ 67.6
Less: Provided by United Funds	25.5	26.6	27.2	2.6	2.7	3.3	22.9	23.9	23.9
Provided by Federations	56.3	59.1	62.8	18.9	19.8	19.1	37.4	39.3	43.7
Fields Receiving Only Federation Support									
Employment Services	4.4	4.6	4.7	1.2	1.1	1.0	3.2	3.5	3.7
Jewish Education	19.0	20.5	22.5	2.3	2.5	2.8	16.7	18.0	19.7
Refugee Aid	5.5a	6.8a	8.0a	(a)	(a)	(a)	5.5	6.8	8.0
Community Relations	3.2b	3.3b	3.5b	(b)	(b)	(b)	3.2	3.3	3.5
Hillel	2.2	2.3	2.4	0.1	0.1	—	2.1	2.2	2.4
Other College Youth	0.6	0.6	0.8	0.1	0.1	0.1	0.5	0.5	0.7
Local Capital	3.8c	3.2c	3.5c	(c)	(c)	(c)	3.8	3.2	3.5
Other	2.9	3.3	3.5	1.4	1.5	1.6	1.5	1.8	1.9
Sub-Total	$41.6	$44.6	$48.9	$5.1	$5.3	$5.5	$36.5	$39.3	$43.4
TOTAL	$123.4	$130.3	$138.9	$26.6	$27.8	$27.9	$96.8	$102.5	$111.0
Provided by Federations*	97.9	103.7	111.7	24.0	25.1	24.6	73.9	78.6	87.1
Provided by United Funds d	25.5	26.6	27.2	2.6	2.7	3.3	22.9	23.9	23.9
TOTAL e	$123.4	$130.3	$138.9	$26.6	$27.8	$27.9	$96.8	$102.5	$111.0

* These totals are based on 110 communities: extrapolations in Table 3 based on all communities yield totals about $4 million higher.

a Funds provided annually by NYANA, financed by UJA: $4.4 million in 1975 and $6.1 million in 1976.

b Provided mainly by national agencies.

c Most capital campaigns are excluded because they are conducted apart from annual campaigns; United Funds in non-federated cities are also excluded.

d Includes in NYC grants by Greater NY Fund and United Hospital Fund to federated agencies.

e Data for other cities in this table are understated from $1–$3 million annually compared with total estimates in Table 3 because functional distributions are not available in all smaller cities.

JEWISH COMMUNAL SERVICES / 157

TABLE 5. DISTRIBUTION OF FEDERATION ALLOCATIONS INCLUDING UNITED WAY FUNDS FOR LOCAL SERVICES IN 110 COMMUNITIES—1975, 1976

(Excluding New York City)

	1976			1975			
	Amount	% of Total	Fed. Alloc.	Amount	% of Total	Fed. Alloc.	% Rise
Family & Children's Service	$19,271,608	19.4		$18,242,625	19.6		5.6
Aged Care	9,952,533	10.0		10,000,609	10.8		(0.5)
Health	6,513,825	6.6		6,561,796	7.1		(0.7)
Centers, Camps, and Related Programs	26,782,479	27.0		24,897,194	26.8		7.6
Local and Regional Hillel	2,238,620	2.3		2,128,495	2.3		5.2
Other College Youth Programs	496,448	.5		506,649	.5		(2.0)
Employment and Guidance	3,476,451	3.5	4.6	3,212,904	3.5	4.6	8.2
Jewish Education	18,018,778	18.1	23.9	16,694,645	17.9	23.8	7.9
Refugee Care	6,809,345	6.9	9.0	5,478,034	5.9	7.8	24.3
Community Relations	3,325,749	3.3	4.4	3,199,860	3.4	4.6	3.9
Other	1,816,802	1.8		1,481,510	1.6		22.6
United Way to Federation for Local Administration	638,285	.6		570,395	.6		11.9
Total	$99,340,923	100.0		$92,974,716	100.0		
Sources of Income							
Federations	$75,469,446	76.0		$70,035,194	75.3		
United Way	23,871,477	24.0		22,939,522	24.7		

TABLE 6. DISTRIBUTION OF FEDERATION ALLOCATIONS* FOR LOCAL SERVICES IN 92 COMMUNITIES—1972, 1976

	1972		1976		Index of Change
	Amount	%	Amount	%	1972=100%
Family Service	$13,839,279	21.5	$18,831,247	19.5	136.1
Aged Care	6,846,895	10.6	9,695,821	10.0	141.6
Health	6,133,299	9.5	6,513,175	6.7	106.2
Centers, Camps, Youth Services	19,765,721	30.6	28,258,034	29.2	143.0
Employment and Guidance	2,365,336	3.7	3,475,451	3.6	146.9
Jewish Education**	11,319,268	17.5	17,709,187	18.3	156.5
		(25.3)		(24.2)	
Refugee Care	744,306	1.1	6,703,953	6.9	900.7
Community Relations	2,032,040	3.2	3,276,058	3.4	161.2
Other	954,013	1.5	1,723,099	1.8	180.6
United Way to Federation for Local Administration #	533,583	0.8	618,289	0.6	115.9
Total	$64,533,740	100.0	$96,804,314	100.0	150.0
Sources of Income					
Federation	$44,704,410	69.3	$73,308,134	75.7	164.0
United Way	19,829,330	30.7	23,496,180	24.3	118.5

* Includes both federations and United Funds; excludes New York City.
** Figures within parentheses are percentages of Jewish Education allocations to total federation allocations.
# Administrative costs of federations are not segregated between local and non-local programs.

Demographic

Jewish Population in the United States, 1979

T HE ESTIMATE of the United States "Jewish Population"* for 1979 is 5,860,900, a modest increase over the previous year's figure of 5,780,960. The South and West comprise 30.2 per cent of the total, as compared to 29.1 in 1978 and 27.8 in 1977. Twenty-three of the 30 states in these regions reported increases in 1979; those reporting significant gains included Arizona, California, Colorado, Florida, Georgia, and Hawaii. The Northeast and Northcentral states represent 69.8 per cent of the total Jewish population, as compared to 70.9 and 72.2 in 1978 and 1977, respectively. Of the 21 states (including the District of Columbia) in these regions, 10 noted population increases. It is important to bear in mind that in situations of shifting population, there is a tendency for growing communities to report changes faster than communities which are experiencing population loss.

Two factors combine to make the total estimate problematic. The extent of the shift to the "sun-belt" states may not yet be fully reported. On the other hand, the New York City area estimate is, in all likelihood, overstated. The figure of 1,228,000 for the city proper is based on the 1970 National Jewish Population Study. Unofficial estimates by the New York Department of City Planning show a 13.5 per cent drop in the city's white population between 1970 and 1977. An extrapolation of this figure to 1979 could reduce the Jewish population figure for New York City to around 1,000,000. The extent to which Jews have shifted their residences to New York City's suburbs and to areas outside Greater New York is unknown. The New York Federation of Jewish Philanthropies is hoping to sponsor a study which will shed light on this manner.

The community estimates listed in Table 3 are provided primarily by local Jewish federations. The estimates cover the fund-raising and service areas of community federations, which generally include the city itself and the more densely populated surrounding areas. This year information on the geographic areas covered by estimates was requested. Several communities previously listed separately are now included in the estimates of nearby larger cities. Details are found in Table 3.

---

*Represents the number of individuals in households in which one or more Jews reside, and therefore includes non-Jews living in such households as a result of intermarriage, etc. For a discussion of this, see AJYB, 1974–75, Vol. 75, pp. 296–297.

159

Estimates for non-federated communities are based on returned questionnaires from local synagogues. An asterisk precedes those cities which submitted estimates in either 1978 or 1979.

National, regional, and state totals are derived by summing the local estimates. The accuracy of these estimates depends on the methods used in obtaining them. Some communities have recently completed population studies, while others employ lists of "known" Jews, taking into consideration the unknown factor. State totals, reported in Table 1, exclude duplicate listings and out-of-state figures where a community extends across state boundaries. Cities with less than 100 Jews (not shown in Table 3) are also included.

ALVIN CHENKIN
MAYNARD MIRAN

APPENDIX

TABLE 1. JEWISH POPULATION IN THE UNITED STATES, 1979

State	Estimated Jewish Population	Total Population*	Estimated Jewish Per Cent Of Total
Alabama	8,805	3,742,000	0.2
Alaska	920	403,000	0.2
Arizona	39,285	2,354,000	1.7
Arkansas	3,395	2,186,000	0.2
California	698,995	22,294,000	3.1
Colorado	41,765	2,670,000	1.6
Connecticut	101,375	3,099,000	3.3
Delaware	10,000	583,000	1.7
District of Columbia	40,000	674,000	5.9
Florida	435,580	8,594,000	5.1
Georgia	33,610	5,084,000	0.7
Hawaii	5,625	897,000	0.6
Idaho	505	878,000	0.1
Illinois	267,525	11,243,000	2.4
Indiana	23,690	5,374,000	0.4
Iowa	8,735	2,896,000	0.3
Kansas	10,755	2,348,000	0.5
Kentucky	11,585	3,498,000	0.3
Louisiana	16,080	3,966,000	0.4
Maine	7,970	1,091,000	0.7
Maryland	185,760	4,143,000	4.5
Massachusetts	250,060	5,774,000	4.3
Michigan	90,195	9,189,000	1.0
Minnesota	33,980	4,008,000	0.8
Mississippi	3,395	2,404,000	0.1
Missouri	73,335	4,860,000	1.5
Montana	645	785,000	0.1
Nebraska	7,905	1,565,000	0.5
Nevada	14,700	660,000	2.2
New Hampshire	5,190	871,000	0.6
New Jersey	440,915	7,327,000	6.0
New Mexico	5,685	1,212,000	0.5
New York	2,141,745	17,748,000	12.1

State	Estimated Jewish Population	Total Population*	Estimated Jewish Per Cent Of Total
North Carolina	13,620	5,577,000	0.2
North Dakota	1,085	652,000	0.2
Ohio	151,870	10,749,000	1.4
Oklahoma	6,040	2,880,000	0.2
Oregon	10,835	2,444,000	0.4
Pennsylvania	421,900	11,750,000	3.6
Rhode Island	22,000	935,000	2.4
South Carolina	8,240	2,918,000	0.3
South Dakota	595	690,000	0.1
Tennessee	17,230	4,357,000	0.4
Texas	71,515	13,014,000	0.5
Utah	2,300	1,307,000	0.2
Vermont	2,465	487,000	0.5
Virginia	58,685	5,148,000	1.1
Washington	18,385	3,774,000	0.5
West Virginia	4,090	1,860,000	0.2
Wisconsin	30,025	4,679,000	0.6
Wyoming	310	424,000	0.1
U.S. TOTAL	5,860,900	218,059,000	2.7

N.B. Details may not add to totals because of rounding.

*July 1, 1978, resident population. Total population, including Armed Forces overseas, was 218,548,000. Total civilian population was 216,432,000. (Sources: U.S. Department of Commerce, Bureau of Census, *Current Population Reports,* Series P.25, No. 799 & No. 809.)

TABLE 2. DISTRIBUTION OF U.S. JEWISH POPULATION BY REGIONS, 1979

Region	Total Population	Per Cent Distribution	Jewish Population	Per Cent Distribution
Northeast:	49,081,000	22.5	3,393,620	57.9
New England	12,256,000	5.6	389,060	6.6
Middle Atlantic	36,825,000	16.9	3,004,560	51.3
North Central:	58,251,000	26.7	699,695	11.9
East North Central	41,233,000	18.9	563,305	9.6
West North Central	17,018,000	7.8	136,390	2.3
South:	70,626,000	32.4	927,630	15.8
South Atlantic	34,579,000	15.9	789,585	13.5
East South Central	14,001,000	6.4	41,015	0.7
West South Central	22,046,000	10.1	97,030	1.7
West:	40,100,000	18.4	839,955	14.3
Mountain	10,289,000	4.7	105,195	1.8
Pacific	29,811,000	13.7	734,760	12.5
TOTALS	218,059,000	100.0	5,860,900	100.0

N.B. Details may not add to totals because of rounding.

TABLE 3. COMMUNITIES WITH JEWISH POPULATIONS OF 100 OR MORE, 1979
(ESTIMATED)

State and City	Jewish Population	State and City	Jewish Population	State and City	Jewish Population
ALABAMA		*Fresno	2,500	Vallejo	400
*Anniston	100	Kern County	850	Ventura County	5,000
*Birmingham	4,000	Lancaster (incl. in Ante-			
*Dothan	205	lope Valley)		**COLORADO**	
*Gadsden	180	*Long Beach	12,500	*Colorado Springs	1,000
Huntsville	650	*Los Angeles Metropolitan		*Denver	40,000
*Mobile	1,200	Area	455,000	Pueblo	375
*Montgomery	1,625	Merced	100		
Selma	210	Modesto	260	**CONNECTICUT**	
Tri-Cities[a]	120	*Monterey	1,500	*Bridgeport	17,000
Tuscaloosa	315	*Oakland (incl. in Alameda		Bristol	250
		& Contra Costa Coun-		Colchester	525
ALASKA		ties)		*Danbury (incl. New Mil-	
*Anchorage	600	Ontario (incl. in Pomona		ford)	3,500
*Fairbanks	210	Valley)		*Greenwich	2,200
		*Orange County	40,000	*Hartford (incl. New Brit-	
ARIZONA		*Palm Springs	4,700	ain)	23,500
*Phoenix	29,000	*Pasadena (also incl. in Los		Lebanon	175
*Tucson	10,000	Angeles Metropolitan		Lower Middlesex	
		Area)	2,000	County[d]	125
ARKANSAS		*Petaluma	800	Manchester (incl. in Hart-	
*Fayetteville	120	*Pomona Valley[c]	3,500	ford)	
*Ft. Smith	160	*Riverside	1,200	*Meriden	1,400
Hot Springs (incl. in Little		*Sacramento	5,700	*Middletown	1,300
Rock)		*Salinas	350	Milford (incl. in New	
*Little Rock	1,820	San Bernardino	1,900	Haven)	
*Pine Bluff	175	*San Diego	26,500	*Moodus	150
Southeast Arkansas[b]	140	*San Francisco	75,000	*New Haven	20,000
Wynne-Forest City	110	*San Jose	14,500	*New London	4,500
		*San Luis Obispo	450	Newtown (incl. in Dan-	
CALIFORNIA		*San Pedro	300	bury)	
*Alameda & Contra Costa		*Santa Barbara	3,800	*Norwalk	4,000
Counties	28,000	*Santa Cruz	1,000	*Norwich	2,500
Antelope Valley	375	*Santa Maria	200	Putnam	110
Bakersfield (incl. in Kern		Santa Monica	8,000	Rockville (incl. in Hart-	
County)		*Santa Rosa	750	ford)	
El Centro	125	Stockton	1,050	*Stamford	12,000
Elsinore	250	*Sun City	800	Torrington	400
*Eureka	250	Tulare and Kings County		*Valley Area[e]	700
Fontana	165	(incl. in Fresno)		Wallingford	440

State and City	Jewish Population	State and City	Jewish Population	State and City	Jewish Population
*Waterbury	3,200	Brunswick	120	INDIANA	
Westport	2,800	*Columbus	1,000	Anderson	105
*Willimantic	400	Dalton	235	Bloomington	300
Winsted	110	Fitzgerald-Cordele	125	*Elkhart	160
		Macon	785	*Evansville	1,200
DELAWARE		*Savannah	2,600	*Ft. Wayne	1,350
*Wilmington (incl. rest of		*Valdosta	145	*Gary (incl. in Northwest	
state)	10,000			Indiana-Calumet	
				Region)	
		HAWAII		*Indianapolis	11,000
DISTRICT OF COLUMBIA		*Hilo	100	Lafayette	600
*Greater Washing-		*Honolulu	5,000	Marion	170
ton [f]	160,000	*Kona	100	Michigan City	400
		*Maui	200	Muncie	175
FLORIDA				*Northwest Indiana-Calu-	
*Brevard County	2,250			met Region [i]	4,500
*Daytona Beach	1,800	IDAHO		*Richmond	110
*Fort Lauderdale	60,000	Boise	120	Shelbyville	140
Fort Myers	300			*South Bend	2,400
Fort Pierce	270	ILLINOIS		*Terre Haute	450
*Gainesville	1,000	Aurora	400		
*Hollywood	55,000	*Bloomington	125	IOWA	
*Jacksonville	6,000	*Champaign-		Cedar Rapids	330
Key West	170	Urbana	1,200	Council Bluffs	245
*Lakeland	800	*Chicago Metropolitan		Davenport (incl. in Quad	
Lehigh Acres	125	Area	253,000	Cities, Ill.)	
*Miami	225,000	Danville	240	*Des Moines	3,500
*Orlando	12,000	Decatur	450	Dubuque	105
*Palm Beach		East St. Louis (incl. in So.		Fort Dodge	115
County	45,000	Ill.)		*Iowa City	750
*Pensacola	725	Elgin	700	Mason City	110
Port Charlotte	150	*Galesburg (incl. in Peoria)		Muscatine	120
*Sarasota	5,800	*Joliet	800	Ottumwa	150
St. Augustine	100	*Kankakee	260	*Sioux City	1,070
*St. Petersburg (incl. Clear-		*Peoria	2,000	Waterloo	435
water)	10,000	Quad Cities [g]	3,000		
*Tallahassee	1,000	Quincy	200	KANSAS	
*Tampa	8,000	Rock Island (incl. in Quad		Topeka	500
		Cities)		*Wichita	1,200
GEORGIA		*Rockford	1,025		
Albany	525	*Southern Illinois [h]	1,200	KENTUCKY	
*Athens	250	*Springfield	1,500	*Lexington	1,400
*Atlanta	25,000	Sterling-Dixon	110		
*Augusta	1,500	*Waukegan	1,200		

State and City	Jewish Population	State and City	Jewish Population	State and City	Jewish Population
*Louisville	9,200	*Fitchburg	300	Grand Rapids	1,500
Paducah	175	*Framingham	16,000	Iron County	160
		*Gardner	100	Iron Mountain	105
LOUISIANA		*Gloucester	400	*Jackson	375
*Alexandria	760	Great Barrington	105	*Kalamazoo	700
*Baton Rouge	1,150	Greenfield	250	*Lansing	1,800
Lafayette	600	*Haverhill	1,600	Marquette County	175
*Lake Charles	250	Holyoke	1,100	Mt. Clemens	420
*Monroe	290	*Hyannis	1,200	Muskegon	525
*New Orleans	10,600	*Lawrence	2,550	*Saginaw	550
*Shreveport	1,600	*Leominster	750	*South Haven	100
		Lowell	2,000		
MAINE		*Lynn (incl.		MINNESOTA	
Augusta	215	Peabody)	19,000	Austin	125
*Bangor	1,500	Medway (incl. in Fra-		*Duluth	1,000
Biddeford-Saco	375	mingham)		Hibbing	155
Calais	135	Milford (incl. in Framing-		*Minneapolis	22,090
*Lewiston-Auburn	1,100	ham)		*Rochester	240
*Portland	3,500	Mills (incl. in Framing-		*St. Paul	9,250
*Waterville	300	ham)		*Virginia	100
		*New Bedford	3,100		
MARYLAND		Newburyport	280	MISSISSIPPI	
*Annapolis	2,000	North Berkshire	675	*Clarksdale	160
*Baltimore	92,000	Northampton	350	*Cleveland	180
*Cumberland	265	*Peabody	2,600	*Greenville	500
Easton Park Area[j]	100	*Pittsfield	1,685	*Greenwood	100
Frederick	400	*Plymouth	500	*Hattiesburg	180
*Hagerstown	275	*Salem	1,150	*Jackson	750
Hartford County	420	Southbridge	105	*Meridian	135
*Montgomery		*Springfield	11,000	Natchez	140
County[f]	70,000	Taunton	1,200	Vicksburg	260
*Prince Georges		Webster	125		
County[f]	20,000	*Worcester	10,000	MISSOURI	
*Salisbury	300			*Columbia	350
				*Joplin	115
MASSACHUSETTS		MICHIGAN		*Kansas City	20,000
*Amherst	750	*Ann Arbor (incl. all		Kennett	110
*Athol	110	Washtenaw		Springfield	230
*Attleboro	200	County)	3,000	*St. Joseph	490
*Beverly	1,000	Battle Creek	245	*St. Louis	60,000
*Boston (incl.		*Bay City	650		
Brockton)	170,000	*Benton Harbor	650	MONTANA	
*Brockton	5,200	*Detroit	75,000	*Billings	160
*Fall River	1,815	*Flint	2,395		

State and City	Jewish Population
NEBRASKA	
*Lincoln	800
*Omaha	6,500
NEVADA	
*Las Vegas	13,500
*Reno	1,200
NEW HAMPSHIRE	
*Claremont	130
*Concord	350
*Dover	425
Keene	105
Laconia	160
*Manchester	2,500
*Nashua	450
*Portsmouth	700
NEW JERSEY	
*Atlantic City (incl. Atlantic County)	11,800
*Bayonne	5,000
*Bergen County[k]	100,000
*Bridgeton	375
*Camden[l]	26,000
*Carteret	300
Elizabeth (incl. in Union County)	
*Englewood (also incl. in Bergen County)	10,000
*Essex County[m]	95,000
Flemington	875
Gloucester County[n]	165
Hoboken	500
*Jersey City	5,200
Metuchen (incl. in North Middlesex County)	
Millville	240
*Monmouth County	32,000
*Morris-Sussex Counties[o]	15,000
Morristown (incl. in Morris County)	
*Mt. Holly	300
Newark (incl. in Essex County)	
New Brunswick (incl. in Raritan Valley)	
North Hudson County[p]	7,000
*North Jersey[q]	33,500
*Northern Middlesex County[r]	19,000
*Ocean County	12,000
*Passaic-Clifton	7,600
Paterson (incl. in North Jersey)	
Perth Amboy (incl. in North Middlesex County)	
Plainfield (incl. in Union County)	
*Princeton	2,600
*Raritan Valley[s]	18,000
Salem	230
*Somerset County[t]	6,000
Somerville (incl. in Somerset County)	
Toms River (incl. in Ocean County)	
*Trenton	8,500
*Union County	39,500
*Vineland[u]	3,335
*Wildwood	425
Willingboro (incl. in Camden)	
NEW MEXICO	
*Albuquerque	5,000
Las Cruces	100
Santa Fe	300
NEW YORK	
*Albany	13,500
Amenia	140
Amsterdam	595
*Auburn	315
*Batavia	165
Beacon	315
*Binghamton (incl. all Broome County)	4,000
Brewster (incl. in Danbury, Ct.)	
*Buffalo	22,000
Canandaigua	135
*Catskill	200
Corning	125
Cortland	440
Dunkirk	200
*Ellenville	1,450
*Elmira	1,400
*Geneva	300
*Glens Falls	360
*Gloversville	535
Herkimer	185
*Highland Falls	105
Hudson	470
*Ithaca	1,000
Jamestown	185
*Kingston	2,400
Liberty	2,100
Loch Sheldrake-Hurleyville	750
Monroe	400
*Monticello	2,400
Mountaindale	150
Greater New York	1,998,000
New York City	1,228,000
Manhattan	171,000
Brooklyn	514,000
Bronx	143,000
Queens	379,000
Staten Island	21,000
Nassau-Suffolk	605,000
Westchester	165,000

State and City	Jewish Population
New Paltz	150
Newark	220
*Newburgh-Middletown	4,900
*Niagara Falls	1,000
Norwich	120
*Olean	140
*Oneonta	175
Oswego	100
Parksville	140
Pawling	105
*Plattsburg	275
Port Jervis	560
*Potsdam	175
*Poughkeepsie	4,900
*Rochester	21,500
Rockland County	25,000
*Rome	205
*Saratoga Springs	500
*Schenectady	5,400
Sharon Springs	165
South Fallsburg	1,100
*Syracuse	11,000
*Troy	1,200
*Utica	2,250
Walden	200
Warwick	100
Watertown	250
White Lake	425
Woodbourne	200
Woodridge	300

NORTH CAROLINA

State and City	Jewish Population
*Asheville	1,000
*Chapel Hill-Durham	1,650
*Charlotte	3,200
*Fayetteville (incl. all Cumberland County)	500
*Gastonia	220
Goldsboro	120
*Greensboro	1,900
High Point	400
*Raleigh	1,375
Rocky Mount	110
Whiteville Zone^v	330
*Wilmington	500
Winston-Salem	440

NORTH DAKOTA

State and City	Jewish Population
*Fargo	500
Grand Forks	100

OHIO

State and City	Jewish Population
*Akron	6,500
Ashtabula	160
*Canton	2,600
*Cincinnati	28,500
*Cleveland	75,000
*Columbus	13,000
*Dayton	6,000
East Liverpool	290
*Elyria	275
Hamilton	560
*Lima	290
Lorain	1,000
*Mansfield	600
*Marion	150
*Middletown	140
New Philadelphia	140
Newark	105
Piqua	120
Portsmouth	120
*Sandusky	150
*Springfield	340
*Steubenville	405
*Toledo	7,500
*Warren	500
*Wooster	200
Youngstown	5,400
Zanesville	350

OKLAHOMA

State and City	Jewish Population
Muskogee	120
*Oklahoma City	2,000
Oklahoma City Zone^w	190
*Tulsa	2,600

OREGON

State and City	Jewish Population
Corvallis	140
*Eugene	1,500
*Portland	8,735
Salem	200

PENNSYLVANIA

State and City	Jewish Population
Aliquippa	400
*Allentown	4,980
*Altoona	1,200
Ambridge	250
Beaver	115
*Beaver Falls	350
Berwick	120
*Bethlehem	960
Braddock	250
*Bradford	150
Brownville	150
*Butler	365
Carbon County	125
*Carnegie	100
Central Bucks County	400
*Chambersburg	340
Chester	2,100
Coatesville	305
Connellsville	110
Donora	100
*Easton	1,300
Ellwood City	110
*Erie	930
Farrell	150
Greensburg	300
*Harrisburg	4,850
*Hazleton	700
Homestead	300
*Indiana	135
*Johnstown	500
Kittanning	175

State and City	Jewish Population
*Lancaster	1,900
*Lebanon	425
Lock Haven	140
*Lower Bucks County[x]	18,000
McKeesport	2,100
Monessen	100
Mt. Carmel	100
Mt. Pleasant	120
New Castle	400
*New Kensington	560
Norristown	2,000
North Penn	200
*Oil City	165
Oxford-Kennett Square	180
*Philadelphia Metropolitan Area	295,000
Phoenixville	300
*Pittsburgh	51,000
*Pottstown	700
Pottsville	500
*Reading	2,800
Sayre	100
*Scranton	4,000
Sharon	470
Shenandoah	230
*State College	450
Stroudsburg	410
Sunbury	160
*Uniontown	290
Upper Beaver	500
*Washington	325
Wayne County	210
West Chester	300
*Wilkes-Barre	4,300
Williamsport	770
*York	1,600

RHODE ISLAND
State and City	Jewish Population
*Providence (incl. rest of state)	22,000

SOUTH CAROLINA
State and City	Jewish Population
*Charleston	3,200
*Columbia	2,300
Florence	370
Greenville	600
Orangeburg County	105
*Spartanburg	295
Sumter	190

SOUTH DAKOTA
State and City	Jewish Population
*Sioux Falls	120

TENNESSEE
State and City	Jewish Population
*Chattanooga	2,250
Johnson City[y]	210
*Knoxville	1,350
*Memphis	9,000
*Nashville	3,700
Oak Ridge	240

TEXAS
State and City	Jewish Population
*Amarillo	300
*Austin	2,100
Baytown	300
*Beaumont	400
Brownsville	160
*Corpus Christi	1,040
*Dallas	20,000
De Witt County[z]	150
*El Paso	5,000
*Ft. Worth	3,000
*Galveston	620
*Houston	27,000
*Laredo	420
*Longview	185
*Lubbock	350
*McAllen	295
*North Texas Zone[aa]	100
Odessa	150
Port Arthur	260
*San Antonio	6,900
Texarkana	100
*Tyler	500
*Waco	750
*Wharton	170

UTAH
State and City	Jewish Population
Ogden	100
*Salt Lake City	2,200

VERMONT
State and City	Jewish Population
Bennington	120
*Burlington	1,800
*Rutland	350
*St. Johnsbury	100

VIRGINIA
State and City	Jewish Population
*Alexandria (incl. Falls Church, Arlington County, and urbanized Fairfax County)[r]	30,000
Arlington (incl. in Alexandria)	
*Danville	180
Fredericksburg	140
Hampton (incl. in Newport News)	
*Harrisonburg	115
Hopewell	140
*Lynchburg	275
Martinsville	135
*Newport News (incl. Hampton)	3,000
*Norfolk (incl. Virginia Beach)	11,000
*Petersburg	600
*Portsmouth (incl. Suffolk)	1,100
*Richmond	10,000
*Roanoke	800
Williamsburg	120
*Winchester	110

WASHINGTON
State and City	Jewish Population
Bellingham	120

State and City	Jewish Population	State and City	Jewish Population	State and City	Jewish Population
Bremerton (incl. in Seattle)		*Parkersburg	155	Manitowoc	175
		Weirton	150	*Milwaukee	23,900
*Seattle	16,000	*Wheeling	650	Oshkosh	120
*Spokane	800			*Racine	405
*Tacoma	750	WISCONSIN		*Sheboygan	200
		*Appleton	270	*Superior	165
WEST VIRGINIA		*Beloit	120	Waukes	135
*Bluefield-Princeton	190	*Eau Claire	120	*Wausau	155
*Charleston	1,150	*Fond du Lac	100		
*Clarksburg	205	Green Bay	440		
Huntington	350	*Kenosha	250	WYOMING	
*Morgantown	200	*Madison	3,000	*Cheyenne	255

*Denotes estimate submitted within two-year period.

ᵃFlorence, Sheffield, Tuscumbia.

ᵇTowns in Chicot, Desha, Drew Counties.

ᶜIncludes Alta Loma, Chino, Claremont, Cucamonga, La Verne, Montclair, Ontario, Pomona, San Dimas, Upland.

ᵈCenterbrook, Chester, Clinton, Deep River, Essex, Killingworth, Old Lyme, Old Saybrook, Seabrook, Westbrook.

ᵉAnsonia, Derby-Shelton, Oxford, Seymour.

ᶠGreater Washington includes urbanized portions of Montgomery and Prince Georges Counties, Maryland, Arlington County, Fairfax County (organized portion); Falls Church, Alexandria, Virginia.

ᵍRock Island, Moline (Illinois); Davenport, Bettendorf (Iowa).

ʰTowns in Alexander, Bond, Clay, Clinton, Crawford, Edwards, Effingham, Fayette, Franklin, Gallatin, Hamilton, Hardin, Jackson, Jasper, Jefferson, Jersey, Johnson, Lawrence, Mascoupin, Madison, Marion, Massac, Montgomery, Perry, Pope, Pulaski, Randolph, Richland, St. Clair, Saline, Union, Wabash, Washington, Wayne, White, Williamson Counties.

ⁱIncludes Crown Point, East Chicago, Gary, Hammond, Munster, Valparaiso, Whiting, and the Greater Calumet region.

ʲTowns in Caroline, Kent, Queen Annes, Talbot Counties.

ᵏAllendale, Elmwood Park, Fair Lawn, Franklin Lakes, Oakland, Midland Park, Rochelle Park, Saddle Brook, Wykoff also included in North Jersey estimate.

ˡIncludes Camden and Burlington Counties.

ᵐIncludes contiguous areas in Hudson, Morris, Somerset, and Union Counties.

ⁿIncludes Clayton, Paulsboro, Woodbury. Excludes Newfield; see Vineland.

ᵒSee footnote (m).

ᵖIncludes Guttenberg, Hudson Heights, North Bergen, North Hudson, Secaucus, Union City, Weehawken, West New York, Woodcliff.

�q Includes Paterson, Wayne, Hawthorne in Passaic County, and nine towns in Bergen County. See footnote (k).

ʳIncludes Perth Amboy, Metuchen, Edison Township (part), Woodbridge.

ˢIncludes in Middlesex County, Cranbury, Dunellen, East Brunswick, Edison Township (part), Jamesburg, Matawan, Middlesex, Monmouth Junction, Old Bridge, Parlin, Piscataway, South River, Spottswood; in Somerset County, Kendall Park, Somerset; in Mercer County, Hightstown.

ᵗExcludes Kendall Park and Somerset, which are included in Raritan Valley.

ᵘIncludes in Cumberland County, Norma, Rosenheim, Vineland; in Salem County, Elmer; in Gloucester County, Clayton, Newfield; in Cape May County, Woodbine.

ᵛBurgaw, Clinton, Dunn, Elizabethtown, Fairmont, Jacksonville, Lumberton, Tabor City, Wallace, Warsaw; and Dillon, Loris, Marion, Mullins, S.C.

ʷTowns in Alfalfa, Beckham, Cadelo, Canadian, Cleveland, Custer, Jackson, Kingfisher, Kiowa, Lincoln, Logan, Oklahoma, Payne, Roger Mills, Tillman, Washita Counties.

ˣBensalem Township, Bristol, Langhorne, Levittown, New Hope, Newtown, Penndel, Warington, Yardley.

ʸIncludes Kingsport and Bristol (including the portion of Bristol in Virginia).

ᶻIncludes communities also in Colorado, Fayette, Gonzales, and La Vaca Counties.

ᵃᵃDenison, Gainesville, Greenville, Paris, Sherman, and Durant (Oklahoma).

Canada

Domestic Affairs

THE POLITICAL UNCERTAINTY GENERATED by the election of a secessionist government led by Premier René Levesque in predominantly French-speaking Quebec was a continuing factor in the country's economic disarray in 1978, with prospective investors holding back expansion capital until the outlook cleared. Undoubtedly, the majority of Québécois sought accommodation of their concerns within the Canadian context. The challenge was to provide them with a sense of lasting security for their culture and identity, and full and equal participation in the responsibilities and opportunities of private and public life.

Prime Minister Pierre Elliott Trudeau was required to call nationwide parliamentary elections in 1979. Given Canada's economic circumstances, that was an unwelcome prospect. The Progressive-Conservative party, led by Joe Clark, a 39-year-old Westerner, vowed, among other things, to reduce government interference in the economy. Whichever party won, the victor would take over a country of squabbling regions with conflicting demands and some serious structural problems. Events in the United States were certain to have a significant impact on developments in Canada, since American companies bought and sold about 70 per cent of Canada's exports and imports and controlled about three-quarters of Canada's large foreign investments.

The gross national product in 1978 grew at the rate of about 3 per cent. This was better than the meager 1.6 per cent registered in 1977, but far below the 5 per cent believed necessary to cut into the nagging unemployment problem. In 1978, despite the fact that 360,000 new jobs were created, the number of unemployed rose to 870,000, and stood at 8.4 per cent of the labor force. The value of the Canadian dollar fell by more than 7 cents. A spate of strikes during the year included that of the postal workers, who were finally ordered back to work by the Canadian Parliament.

Alberta, a former agricultural backwater, was fast emerging as the most assertive of Canada's fractious provinces. Five times the size of New York State, Alberta had almost 85 per cent of Canada's oil and gas, its fastest-growing cities (including two of the country's seven largest), the lowest taxes, the least unemployment, more money than even the politicians knew what to do with, and great confidence in its future. In short, Alberta seemed to have everything—except clout. Of Parliament's 264 seats, Alberta had but 19, fewer than the city of Toronto.

Foreign Relations

Relations between Prime Minister Pierre Trudeau's Liberal government and the Carter administration in the United States became somewhat frayed at the edges.

The maritime boundaries dispute arising from the 1977 adoption of the 200-mile limit proved far harder to settle than anyone had anticipated. An interim agreement on fishing broke down in mid-1978, with each country sending the other's fishermen home. During a visit to Ottawa, U.S. Secretary of State Cyrus Vance agreed with Canadian External Affairs Minister Don Jamieson on special negotiations to decide which fish and boundary issues might be settled.

The Canada-U.S. auto pact, long viewed as a symbol of cooperative action, came under attack in 1978 as Canada's trade deficit with the U.S. remained unacceptably high. As part of an effort to correct the imbalance, the Canadian government entered into a bidding contest that previously had been waged on the state and provincial levels. Canada's offer of multi-million-dollar incentives to both the Ford Motor Company and General Motors angered the U.S. government, which called for an end to the bidding war. At year's end, Canada-U.S. discussions on the pact were continuing, while General Motors was trying to decide whether to follow Ford's example and locate a new plant in Canada.

Most of the handful of U.S. anti-dumping and countervailing duty investigations of Canadian imports were disposed of in Canada's favor, while President Carter resisted efforts by some congressmen to impose protectionist measures on other imports. These developments undoubtedly reflected the fact that the U.S. would be dependent on Canadian support during the multilateral trade negotiations that were scheduled to take place in Geneva in 1979. The likelihood of a new international tariff-cutting agreement contributed in part to some discussion in Canada about the possibility of a free-trade agreement or economic union with the U.S., an idea that would have been unthinkable in the days of the Vietnam war and the Nixon administration.

Tentative discussions took place during the year about a Canadian tax measure the U.S. opposed, and a U.S. tax regulation to which Canada objected; the Canadian regulation prohibited tax deductions for television ads directed at Canadian audiences but placed on U.S. stations; the U.S. tax regulation limited attendance at foreign conventions to two trips a year.

The main bilateral energy issue that was discussed was the construction of the $12-billion pipeline that was to bring Alaskan natural gas through Canada to the energy-hungry lower 48 states. U.S. Secretary of Energy James Schlesinger warned that a number of things had to be done quickly if the project was to be kept alive. One possibility that was broached in government and industry circles was to have the United States abandon the "express route" concept through the north-central United States and instead expand existing gas delivery systems in Canada.

During 1978 two-way trade with China amounted to just over $450 million, with Canadian exports accounting for nearly $370 million. Wheat sales alone came to $310 million. Government officials made a trip to the People's Republic accompanied by senior executives of more than a dozen Canadian companies who were actively pursuing trade there. Progress was made in the negotiations.

JEWISH COMMUNITY

Demography and Immigration

The Jewish population of Canada in 1978 was estimated at 305,000. Leading Jewish centers were Toronto (115,000); Montreal (115,000); Winnipeg (20,000); Vancouver (12,000); and Ottawa (7,500).

There were 13,000 Jews in Toronto living at what was defined as "poverty" level. This figure comprised a solid 13 per cent of Toronto's Jewish population. Jean Lee, supervisor of the financial assistance program at the Jewish Family and Child Service (JFCS), described most of these poor people as invisible in terms of Jewish institutional life. Almost a quarter of the Jewish poor were teenagers in the 15-to-19 age bracket who lived with their families. While many poor Jews were over 65 years of age, just as many were between 50 and 65. Occupationally, many fell into the displaced skills category in millinery, sales, and the fur and textile trades. Some were immigrants, many Sephardic, whose qualifications for employment were inadequate. Included as well were recent emigrants from Montreal.

The need for increased economic aid to meet the future requirements of elderly Jews in Winnipeg was one of the significant findings of a report released by the Commission on Aging of the Winnipeg Jewish Community Council. The report stated that 14.4 per cent of the approximately 3,000 elderly Jews in the city were in financial difficulty, and that 22.7 per cent expected trouble in meeting their future economic needs.

The Jewish Immigrant Aid Services (JIAS) celebrated its 60th anniversary during the year. Bud Cullen, minister of employment and immigration, in an address at the annual meeting of the organization, said that out of the 3,400 refugees who had been admitted to Canada under the Ongoing Refugee Program, approximately one-third were Soviet Jews, and that JIAS had "been instrumental in helping many of these people rebuild their lives in this country." Cullen pointed out that the provisions of the new Immigration Act (1977) allowed Canada to "help persecuted or displaced persons on humanitarian grounds, regardless of whether or not they fall within the United Nations' definition."

Communal Activities

In October Toronto's Temple Sinai made available its facilities for the first Alcoholics Anonymous meeting ever held in a Canadian Jewish synagogue. This step was taken because it was felt that many Jews refused to attend AA meetings that were held in churches. "We are opening our meetings to them with the deliberate intention of creating a more comfortable atmosphere for the Jewish alcoholic," said Rabbi J. Pearlson. He pointed out: "Grandpa's *l'chaim* and compulsory social drinking are significantly different in nature." Rabbi Pearlson said he knew of many Jews with alcohol problems, and hoped that the new AA group would be of assistance to them.

B'nai B'rith District 22, with 75 lodges for men in the five eastern provinces, was close to reaching the 10,000-member mark. Increased interest in smaller communities led to the formation of several new lodges; charters were granted during the year to Moncton, New Brunswick, Bytown in Ottawa, and Bay Cities in the Burlington-Oakville, Ontario region. Moncton, with a population of less than 60 Jewish families, had a lodge membership of 40. B'nai B'rith strove to maintain a sense of identity and a synagogue link for Jews in widely-scattered locations; in one isolated northern Ontario settlement, the organization paid a leader $6,000 annually to make possible the religious education of three children.

Half a million dollars less than in the previous year was allocated to the United Israel Appeal (UIA) in the 1978–79 budget of the Allied Jewish Community Services (AJCS) of Montreal. "There is a shift to a greater recognition of local needs," said Manuel Batshaw, executive vice-president of AJCS. "It is interesting to note that at the board of trustees meeting, not a single question was raised about the fact that more money is going into local needs. This is because there is a desire to maintain a strong, viable Jewish community here." Local agencies received a total of $434,108 more than in the previous year; the allocation to national agencies (Canadian Jewish Congress and JIAS) remained constant.

The 1978–79 budget did not allow for possible additional funds to make up for the drop in government subsidies to day schools. Grades 1 through 4 began receiving their government grants, well into the school year, at a reduced rate of close to 60 per cent. The two francophone schools, Écoles Maimonide and Sepharade, and the French-stream classes in anglophone schools continued to receive 80 per cent subsidies. Grades 5 and up, which were still under associate status with the Protestant School Board, received their grants as usual. AJCS was considering giving $130–150,000 to the École Sepharade so that it could meet the increased demand for Jewish education in French. The anglophone schools agreed to increase their French instruction by one hour per week. The Jewish People's and Peretz Schools undertook a study of children in the first four grades to see if their command of English was being affected by the increased use of French.

A study commissioned by one of Canada's leading women's organizations revealed that there was a great need for Jewish day care in the Toronto community that was not being met. A survey of 571 families by the National Council of Jewish Women (NCJW) found that 81 per cent desired day care with Jewish content and more than half wanted kosher food. Some of the main reasons for the growing desire for Jewish day care reflected an economic situation which resulted in the need for two-income families; an increase in the number of single parent families; a lack of quality care; and an added difficulty in finding appropriate day care for those who wanted their children to be in a Jewish environment with Jewish content. The study had been carried out in 1975 and sent to more than 35 social agencies, including the Toronto Jewish Congress (TJC) and JFCS. Georgina Grossman, coordinator of volunteer services at NCJW, said that the organization was extremely disappointed at the lack of response, especially from Jewish social agencies. "We felt we did our job—to show there's a need in the community. Maybe nobody responded to it because it would have opened up a barrel of worms." Jerry Diamond, executive director of JFCS, stated that the agency "tried eight times to get day care off the ground, but we have never gotten the financial and emotional support of this community." Diamond said he recognized that there was a need for Jewish day care, but argued that it was a middle class need which the community was not willing to support.

A period of retrenchment in the delivery of services to the Jewish community was foreseen by the social planning committee of TJC. Madeleine Epstein, retiring chairman of the committee, stated that while the community was still growing and dispersing throughout metropolitan Toronto, "we will be dealing with reduction rather than growth . . . The sense of buoyancy is gone and new realities must be faced." Irene Fink, reporting for a subcommittee on the aged, indicated that by 1986 the aged population of the Toronto Jewish community would total 18,000, a 61 per cent increase over 1971. To cope with this increase, Fink called for a variety of housing alternatives for senior citizens in private living situations; among them were co-operatives, small group homes, and other integrated forms of housing. Coupled with housing would be supportive social and health services. John Wahl, reporting for the subcommittee on singles, urged the creation of a Jewish dating service under the auspices of the Federation of Jewish Women's Organizations.

About one-third of Jewish foster children were being placed in non-Jewish homes by the Jewish Family Service-Social Service Center (JFS-SSC), due to a critical shortage of Jewish foster parents in Montreal. While refusing to divulge actual figures, JFS-SSC's children's services department described the situation as "urgent," and took a number of steps to bring the matter before the Jewish community. JFS-SSC sought to place all Jewish foster children with Jewish families, but it was just not possible. "We've had a terrible time in getting the community to respond," stated foster home recruitment worker Helena Sonin.

A 1978–79 "hold-the-line" budget of $6,091,178 for national and local Jewish welfare services and the Jewish school system was approved by the executive of TJC. TJC treasurer Murray Segal, who also served as chairman of the Budget and Finance Committee, pointed out that the budget "contemplates continued restraint and recognizes mainly salary and other cost adjustments, with little or no expansion of services." The budget broke down into four major sections: Jewish education—$3,197,449; local services—$1,853,857; national programs—$1,088,172; and special items—$44,700.

Community Relations

Jews in New Brunswick were shocked by the appearance around Passover of *Web of Deceit,* an antisemitic booklet. Its author, Malcolm Ross, also wrote a series of letters to the Moncton *Times* in which he accused "Khazar-Jews" of controlling international banking and of duping "much of Christendom into believing they were God's chosen people . . ." According to Dr. Julius Israeli of Newcastle, "The small Jewish community . . . was shocked and bewildered by these antisemitic activities." *Web of Deceit* was based on material disseminated by the "Canadian Intelligence Service" in Flesherton, Ontario.

On Easter Sunday an act of arson took place in Temple Beth El in Windsor, Ontario. Following a meeting of the local community relations committee, a statement was released to the media: "We do not know who perpetrated the latest outrage at our synagogue, Sunday March 26th, but we know that the people of Windsor and of all of Canada will view with disgust these vandals who perform their perverted work. An attack on any house of God cannot be viewed as a mere prank; it is in fact an attack on the frontline of Canadian society. We are sure that all people in this community support us in deploring this vicious attack on our synagogue."

Jewish community leaders expressed satisfaction with the two-year prison sentence imposed on neo-Nazi leader Donald Andrews. Andrews, a Toronto health inspector, was charged with directing a systematic hate campaign against Jews and Blacks. Andrews' accomplice, Dawyd Zartshansky, got 18 months in a reformatory. Judge Graburn said he was shocked by the offences and agreed with Crown Counsel Edward Geller that they "invited retaliation in a multi-cultural, pluralistic community." The Ontario Election Finances Commission rejected the application of Andrew's Nationalist party of Canada for registration as an official political party in the province. Registration would have meant that the party's name would appear on the ballot, and that it could collect contributions which would be tax exempt.

The Canada-Israel Committee lodged a complaint with the Quebec Press Council over a cover article in the February issue of the magazine *Ici Quebec* attacking Zionism and the State of Israel. The article, "No to Racism of Israel," was written by the magazine's editor-in-chief. The premier of Quebec, René Levesque, commented on the article at a news conference, stating that it was "a lousy article . . . reeking of prejudice." While "it is permissible to criticize Zionism," he noted, "there is a delicate line between anti-Zionism and antisemitism." Levesque insisted that the "Parti Québécois was in no way linked to the magazine." In fact, however, Jean-Marie Cossette, the director of *Ici Quebec,* was elected president of the Montreal branch of the nationalist group.

The Soviet Union, through its assistant press attaché in Ottawa, apologized for having distributed a crudely antisemitic booklet at the Ontario Science Center, but Jewish community leaders refused to accept the apology. Soviet embassy official Igor Lobanov told the *Canadian Jewish News* in two telephone interviews, one of which he initiated, that *The Sword of David,* a 78-page booklet dealing with Zionism and Israel, published by the state-controlled Novosti Press Agency Publishing House, was accidentally distributed at the Soviet spaceship exhibit. "The booklet was meant for the information and education of Soviet embassy personnel, not for the general public," he explained. "We'd like everyone to return the booklet to our embassy." A CJC official stated that *The Sword of David* resembled propaganda disseminated by the Nazis. He termed "a bold-faced lie" Lobanov's claim that the booklet was only for Soviet embassy consumption.

The appearance in Vancouver of the "Yellow Canadian Christian Business Directory 1977–78" was noted with concern by the Pacific Region of CJC.

Following representations to the Department of Justice in Quebec made by CJC, Eastern Region, charges were dropped against a number of small Jewish business establishments in Montreal, which were closed on the Sabbath, for violating the Lord's Day Act. The Department of Justice indicated that it would introduce changes which would permit such businesses to be open on Sundays.

In a letter to Bud Cullen, Alan Rose, executive director of CJC, wrote: "I furnish supporting materials relating to Bishop Valerian Triga's activities as a leading member of the Iron Guard during the war in Rumania. May I reiterate that the Canadian Jewish Congress requests that Bishop Trifa be banned from entry to Canada. We believe that his views and activities are repugnant to all Canadians, and under no circumstances should he be permitted to enter this country. You may be aware that a number of suspected war criminals are resident in Canada. Thus, we are particularly anxious to avoid any possibility of Bishop Trifa visiting Canada, let alone seeking landed immigrant status." In response, Cullen indicated that Canadian officials were "diligently continuing their endeavors to ascertain whether there are statutory prohibitions to Archbishop Trifa's entry into Canada."

"Holocaust," NBC's 9-hour documentary drama, provoked a public debate in the media unprecedented for a television program. Religious leaders in Toronto and Montreal praised the program's moral message, teachers applauded its "sensitizing" effect, and Holocaust survivors called the presentation "timely." At the same time, the series drew critical letters in the press, and a negative reaction from some German, Ukrainian, and Polish viewers.

A motion calling on the Canadian Jewish Congress (CJC) to take an "unequivocal" stand in favor of national unity was resoundingly defeated (84–8) at an executive meeting of the Eastern Region. The majority of those speaking on the motion felt that a firm stand by CJC would be a useless gesture, serving only to antagonize a sector of the Quebec populace against the Jewish community. A minority argued that the CJC leadership should openly express the feelings of the community, and that not to do so was hypocrisy. Walter Roll, CJC Eastern Region secretary, said there was no need to get involved in a political crossfire over Canadian unity. "The only result for us would be getting decimated."

Zionism and Israel

Canadian Jews were deeply concerned whether they were successfully presenting Israel's point of view to the Canadian public. The most recent Gallup Poll showed that some 7 per cent of the population favored the Arab point of view, some 23 per cent favored the Israeli point of view, while 70 per cent indicated that they had no preference.

Israeli Prime Minister Menachem Begin climaxed his official six-day visit to Canada in November by delivering a passionate address to a crowd of 5,000 persons at Toronto's Beth Tzedec synagogue. Amid the tightest security ever mounted for a visiting dignitary, Begin declared that Israel would negotiate with Egypt until a peace treaty was signed, and appealed to the Soviet Union to permit Jewish emigration. To sustained applause, the 65-year-old Israeli leader spoke with deep emotion as he defended Israel's negotiating stance and reaffirmed his government's refusal to withdraw to the pre-1967 armistice lines or to acquiesce to the creation of a PLO-controlled state in Judea and Samaria.

At the United Nations Human Rights Commission meeting in Geneva, Canada voted against a resolution which maintained that Israel had violated a 1949 convention protecting the populations of occupied territories; the resolution was adopted 23 to 2, with 7 abstentions. Canada also voted against another resolution, which affirmed the right of Palestinians to establish an "independent and sovereign state," and called on all nations to support the Palestinians through the Palestine Liberation Organization; this resolution was approved 25 to 3, with 4 abstentions.

Negotiations were successfully concluded for a co-production arrangement between Israeli and Canadian film interests. The pact, covering a three-year period, called for joint financing and planning for feature motion pictures. It was formally signed in Jerusalem.

Arab Boycott

The Canada-Israel Committee (CIC) described as "a positive step forward" the announcement by Ottawa that it intended to introduce legislation requiring all companies and individuals to report boycott requests. The federal government's announcement was made by Secretary of State John Roberts and Defense Minister Barney Danson at a press conference. CIC National Chairman Norman May said the organization saw the proposed changes as a clear indication of the government's goodwill and good faith on the question of combatting the Arab boycott. The legislation was to be introduced in the next session of Parliament.

Roberts and Danson, both of whom represented Toronto ridings, also revealed that "Statements of Fact" in contracts would henceforth require an addition certifying that Canadian companies would comply fully with Canadian government policy. Negative certificates of origin—which stated that goods, services, or components did not originate in a specified nation—would be prohibited as well. Under the terms of the government's 1976 anti-boycott guidelines, which had been criticized by the Jewish community, government services and assistance were denied to companies accepting boycott provisions in contracts. The loophole in the guidelines was that firms not in need of federal aid could flout them and thus acquiesce in the boycott.

Ontario's anti-boycott legislation, Bill 112, was formally signed into law by Lieutenant Governor Pauline McGibbon. CIC issued the following statement: "Bill 112 will greatly contribute towards safeguarding the human rights of all Ontarians, protecting the people of this province from the discriminatory restrictive trade provisions of secondary and tertiary boycotts. This comprehensive legislation constitutes a decisive step in eliminating the intrusion into the Ontario marketplace of the invidious discriminatory practices of the Arab boycott. It is a proud day for Ontarians."

Rabbi Gunther Plaut, president, and Alan Rose, executive vice-president of CJC, sent a telegram to J.C. Thackray, president of Bell Canada Limited, indicating that the Jewish community was disturbed by a report of possible discrimination against Canadian Jews in Bell's contract with Saudi Arabia to provide 500 technicians to modernize the Saudi telephone service. The report alleged that Bell Canada Limited stated in its contract that it had no dealings—investments, subsidiaries, or franchises —in Israel. The president of Bell Canada flatly denied the report. Another telegram was sent to Thackray by Alan Rose, pointing out that guidelines for Bell Canada International employees serving with the Arabian American Oil Company (Aramco) in Saudi Arabia stated: "Obtain proof of religion in the form of baptismal or other certificate." The intent of this requirement was clearly to exclude Jewish applicants.

Soviet Jewry

The House of Commons adopted the following motion in February: "This House asks that Parliament's concern respecting the treatment of Anatoly Shcharansky and other Soviet citizens who have attempted to exercise their rights and freedoms as embodied in the Final Act of the Conference on Security and Co-operation in Europe and agreed to by participating states at Helsinki, be raised at the earliest opportunity at the Belgrade meeting of the CSCE now under way." The minister of state for multiculturalism indicated that Canada's appeals on Shcharansky's behalf, and on behalf of human rights issues in the USSR in general, sparked seven official protests to the Canadian government by the Kremlin. "But we are not backing off the human rights issue. Canada is taking a strong stand," he said.

The Montreal Inter-Faith Task Force for Soviet Jewry arranged a vigil by its Christian members on the first night of Passover in front of the Soviet consulate in

Montreal, to protest the harassment of Josef Mendelevitch, a Jewish prisoner of conscience. The Montreal Committee for Soviet Jewry, the Group of 35, and the Students' Struggle for Soviet Jewry sponsored a demonstration in front of the Soviet consulate in Montreal on April 13 to protest the Kremlin's refusal to permit Vladimir Slepak and his wife to emigrate.

An outdoor rally organized by the Hillel Foundation and the Toronto Student Zionists was held at the University of Toronto in March to mark the anniversary of Anatoly Shcharansky's arrest. The Montreal Students Struggle for Soviet Jewry held a 12-hour fast, at the conclusion of which there was a demonstration in front of the Soviet consulate. The Montreal Group of 35 protested against the harassment of the prisoners of conscience in the Soviet Union at the performance in Montreal of the Moscow Chamber Choir. Members of the Group took their seats for the performance but left in protest minutes before it began. Five remained for the concert wearing prisoners' stripes.

Close to 4,000 people jammed Avenue De La Musée in front of the Soviet consulate in July to protest the harsh sentencing of Soviet activist Anatoly Shcharansky. McGill law professor Irwin Cotler told a large gathering that the undisguised aim of the Soviet government was to crush both the human rights and Jewish activist movements. Cotler, who had power of attorney to act on Shcharansky's behalf, said the Soviets were particularly severe with the 30-year-old computer specialist because he was viewed as the "heart of the movement." Another protest rally took place at the parliament buildings in Toronto, where Premier William Davis urged Canadians to support the Soviet dissidents. Both demonstrations were sponsored by the Montreal and Toronto Committees for Soviet Jewry, with participation from the Group of 35, Student Struggle for Soviet Jewry, and Committee for the Release of Anatoly Shcharansky.

Five hundred people attended a memorial meeting at the Beth Tzedec synagogue for the Jewish writers executed in the Soviet Union on August 12, 1952. The meeting was sponsored by CJC's Toronto Committee for Soviet Jewry and TJC's Committee for Yiddish. Max Shecter, national chairman of the Canadian Committee for Soviet Jewry, presided.

Holocaust Observances

The annual day-long Holocaust symposium was held in Vancouver in May, with more than 700 students and academics in attendance. Introduced into the program was an essay contest on "The Historical Background," sponsored by the religion departments of Capilano College, Langara College, and the University of British Columbia. A standing committee on the Holocaust was formed by the Canadian Council of Christians and Jews and the Pacific Region of the CJC. A community-wide Holocaust remembrance marking Yom Hashoa and the 35th anniversary of the Warsaw Ghetto uprising was held in April in Montreal at the Tifereth Beth David Jerusalem synagogue. The memorial address was given by Rabbi Irving

Greenberg of New York. Another gathering took place in Toronto attended by over 3,000 people. The rally was addressed by Rabbi Gunther Plaut, president of CJC, and Dr. Franklin H. Littell of Temple University, Philadelphia, Pa. Among those participating in the program were the mayor of Toronto, David Crombie; Larry Grossman, MPP, Province of Ontario; and John Roberts, M.P. and secretary of state.

The mayor of Winnipeg, Robert Sheen, proclaimed the period from April 30 to May 6 as Holocaust Remembrance Week, and spoke at the opening ceremony at the YMHA community center. A Winnipeg street was renamed Avenue of the Warsaw Ghetto Heroes for the week. The opening ceremony was followed by a series of seminars attended by about 2,000 people, Jews and non-Jews.

Work was begun on a Holocaust memorial on the lower level of AJCS' Cummings House in Montreal. The $108,000 memorial, designed by architect Saul Berkowitz, was the result of almost two years of research and planning by a committee of young people in their 20's and 30's, chaired by Steven Cummings, working in cooperation with the Association of Survivors of Nazi Oppression. The emphasis of the memorial was to be on education, and every effort would be made through exhibits and programming to attract the interest of children.

Religion

The Canadian Council for Conservative Judaism (CCCJ) was formed to act as the representative organization of the Conservative movement in Canada. CCCJ resulted from a merger of the United Synagogue, the organization of all Conservative synagogues in Canada and the United States, and the Rabbinical Assembly, the rabbinic arm of the movement. Henceforth, CCCJ would be the single voice of Canadian Conservative congregations and their rabbis. In a release issued following its creation, CCCJ declared: "While [we] fully support CJC as the overall representative body of Canadian Jewry, [we] will act for the Conservative movement in inter-religious affairs and, if and when required, will relate on religious issues to the government and people of Canada." There were approximately 30 Conservative synagogues in Canada.

Third-generation Canadian Jews were rapidly abandoning traditional religious observances, but nevertheless maintained a strong sense of Jewish "cultural" identity. This is one of the findings of a survey of 500 Jews in Montreal, Toronto, and Winnipeg undertaken by Paul Bain of the University of British Columbia. The survey showed a startling 63.5 per cent decline in religious practice among third-generation Jews as compared with the second generation. One-third of third-generation Jews never attended a synagogue. On the other hand, cultural identification with being Jewish, as measured in terms of preference for living in a Jewish area, believing that a strong bond unites Jews, and seeing Israel as a cultural center for Jews, was quite strong among the third generation.

In response to a concern expressed by many St. Laurent, Quebec residents, the joint outreach project of AJCS and CJC, Eastern Region attempted to formulate a plan of action to protest the high cost of kosher meat in Montreal.

Delegates taking part in a Jewish-Christian seminar in Ottawa on "The Family Under Attack" identified a number of ways in which religious groups could better help families cope with present-day crises. The seminar was arranged by the Canadian Jewish-Christian Liaison Committee on behalf of the Canadian Conference of Catholic Bishops, Canadian Council of Churches, CJC, and Canadian Council of Christians and Jews.

Jewish Education

The Supreme Court of Ontario turned down a proposal by the North York Board of Education to integrate the Associated Hebrew Schools into the public school system, on the grounds that mandatory religious classes were not within its jurisdiction. In his judgment, Judge John Holland challenged the Board's thesis that options within a school system would surmount the problem of exemption from religious instruction. Although the North York Board of Education approved legal fees to appeal the decision, Jewish spokesmen were divided on the matter. Ben Kayfetz, executive director of the Joint Community Relations Committee, indicated that the Supreme Court judgment meant that "religious courses would be compulsory, an anathema to a Jewish community which has fought to abolish religious instruction in public schools for the past 120 years." Kayfetz drew attention to the fact that there had always been a division of opinion on the issue of subsidies to private schools. He added, "Inflation has made a major difference in the debate."

Reverend John Roberts, chairman of the Educational Program Committee of the North York Board, stated that the Jewish community was being singled out as a "whipping boy" in a controversy relating to Ontario's Heritage Language Program. The controversy centered around the Board of Jewish Education's application to North York to receive partial funding for Hebrew language instruction under a program announced by the Ministry of Education in 1977. "Any group in society has the right to seek funds under that program," said Roberts. He argued that the ministry had reacted "way out of proportion" by claiming that the Board of Jewish Education had violated the intent of the Heritage program. And he added that the Toronto *Star* had completely misinterpreted the issue in charging editorially that the Jewish community was looking for funds to finance private schools.

During the 1977–78 school year, approximately 10,700 Jewish students, representing about half of all eligible youth in the community, were enrolled in the Jewish schools of Toronto; 5,600 were in day schools, of which there were 12; the rest were in supplementary schools offering instruction from one to five days a week. Rabbi Irwin I. Witty, director of the Toronto Jewish Board of Education, stated that low enrollment in Jewish high schools was distressing.

Speaking at the annual convention of the Central Conference of American Rabbis (Reform) held in Toronto, Rabbi Arthur Bielfeld of that city's Temple Emanu-El indicated that the Leo Baeck Day School in Toronto, established five years ago with an enrollment of 180 in nursery through third grade, had taken root and begun to thrive. There were now 250 students and six grades; in 1979 an additional grade was to be added. The school's budget of nearly half a million dollars was supplemented by congregational subsidies, private contributions, and grants from TJC. To enroll a child in Leo Baeck, families had to be members of a recognized synagogue, not necessarily Reform, within the community.

Expansion of government aid to private and parochial day schools in Manitoba was provided for in the 1978–79 school year by amending the shared services provisions of the Public Schools Act. Three Jewish schools, the Winnipeg Hebrew School, Joseph Wolinsky Collegiate, and Ramah Hebrew School, stood to benefit from the new provisions.

Jewish Culture

A play, based in part on the Holocaust research of University of Montreal professor Howard Roiter, had a successful run at Edmonton's Theatre 3. "Yiskor," a dramatic study of five concentration camp inmates, was staged for the first time by the Edmonton Actor's Workshop under the direction of its founder, Martin Fishman, who co-authored the play with Fred Keating. Fishman was initially drawn to the subject matter by Roiter's *Voices From the Holocaust,* which itself had been staged as a play several years ago by Montreal's Saidye Bronfman Centre. A correspondence developed between the two men, with Roiter providing the young Canadian director with complete transcripts of interviews he had conducted with Holocaust survivors.

Norman Cafik, minister of state for multiculturalism, awarded more than $6,000 to CJC's Jewish Historical Society as a grant for its project "Shuls, A Study of Canadian Synagogue Architecture." Another grant of $3,400 went to the National Committee on Yiddish to cover the cost of publishing *A Century of Hebrew and Yiddish Press and Literature in Canada,* by the Yiddish writer H.L. Fuks.

The exhibition "Journey into our Heritage," mounted by the Jewish Historical Society of Western Canada and depicting the history of Jews in the Canadian West, was brought to Toronto for ten days in September. A reception marking the opening of the exhibit was tendered by the Central Region Archives and the Multicultural History Society of Ontario.

CJC's Jewish Music Committee, under the chairmanship of Dr. Sabina Ratner, presented the premiere performance of the commissioned work "Three Songs of the Holocaust," composed by Professor Marvin Duchow of McGill University and performed by Pauline Vaillancourt, noted Quebec soprano, and Jean-Eudes Vaillancourt, pianist, at the Samuel Bronfman House, Montreal. "Three Songs of the Holocaust" is a song cycle inspired by *O the Chimneys,* written by Nobel laureate

Nelly Sachs in 1961. The concert was recorded for broadcast on the CBC in April 1979 as part of the "Arts National Program."

Through the efforts of the Toronto Committee on Yiddish, Yiddish studies at the University of Toronto were now being given on two levels, with full credits to students.

Publications

Dr. Jay Braverman, educational director of United Talmud Torahs, Montreal, published Jerome's *Commentary on Daniel,* under the auspices of the Catholic Biblical Monograph Series. Dr. Braverman's work compares Jerome's commentary with the Apocrypha, Rabbinic literature, and the work of other Jewish and Christian writers, among them Josephus and Origen.

Bronfman Dynasty by Peter C. Newman, editor of *McLeans Magazine,* caused a stir in literary circles. This long-awaited biographical study deals with the Bronfmans, Canada's wealthiest Jewish family.

The Jewish Historical Society of British Columbia published *Pioneers, Pedlars and Prayer Shawls,* which documents the early Jewish settlements in British Columbia and the Yukon.

CJC granted the 1978 H.M. Caiserman Award to Maurice Cohen for *Creation and Destiny of Man.*

Lawrence Freiman's *Don't Fall off the Rocking Horse* is the autobiography of the Ottawa Zionist leader and business tycoon.

A new Hebrew textbook for beginners, written by Professor Moshe Nahir of the Department of Near East and Judaic Studies at the University of Manitoba, was published by the Manitoba Department of Education. It was circulated in the Winnipeg public schools where Hebrew was taught, and made available to local Jewish schools.

Rabbi Gunther Plaut's *Hanging Threads,* a collection of short stories, was well received and widely read.

Genia Silkes, lecturer and writer, was awarded the annual Marilyn Finkler Memorial Award in Literature for "journalistic excellence in furthering awareness of the Holocaust." The Finkler Memorial Fund was established three years ago by Leona and Arnold Finkler and is administered by the Jewish Public Library.

An addition to the growing literature on the Holocaust was Paul Trepman's *Among Men and Beasts.*

Personalia

Allan M. Linden of Toronto, law professor at Osgoode Hall Law School for the past decade, was appointed to the Supreme Court of Ontario. Abraham Mandel of Hamilton was appointed as a county court judge. Marvin Zuker and Harold Rubenstein of Toronto were named judges of the small claims court. Named as members of the Upper Canada Law Society were Clayton Ruby, Joseph B. Pomerant, and Mark Orkin. Herbert S. Levy, former executive vice-president of the B'nai B'rith District No. 22, was named a Toronto citizenship court judge.

Rabbi Harry Joshua Stern, whose lifelong devotion to interfaith causes has earned him the title "The Ecumenical Rabbi," was named the Great Montrealer of the past two decades in the field of religion. A panel of Roman Catholic, Anglican, and Greek Orthodox leaders unanimously chose Stern over three other candidates.

The Adath Israel Congregation of Outremont, Quebec honored Rabbi Charles Bender for 50 years of service to the Jewish community of Montreal, 40 of them with the congregation. A citation was presented to Rabbi Bender by the Canadian government.

Honors accorded to Rabbi Gunther Plaut, president of the CJC, included a Doctor of Laws degree from the University of Toronto, membership in the Order of Canada, and appointment by the government of Ontario to the Ontario Human Rights Commission.

The Order of Canada (replacing the Order of the British Empire) was awarded to Monroe Abbey, Q.C., who was also honored at the annual Jewish National Fund Negev Dinner in Montreal. The Order of Canada was also given to the following: Simon Reisman, formerly deputy minister of finance; Sylvia Ostry, former head of Statistics Canada, former deputy minister of consumer and corporate affairs, and now director of the Economic Council of Canada; Maxwell Commings, well-known Montreal community figure; Sam Cohen, also a Montrealer; Joseph Shoctor, Edmonton, a figure in the world of amateur theater; Ben Wosk of Vancouver; and Edwin Mirvish of Toronto, whose contributions to retailing, the restaurant business, and the professional theater are well known.

Appointed to the Canadian Senate was Jack Marshall, formerly a Progressive Conservative member of the House of Commons from Cornerbrook, Newfoundland. He joined four other Jews in the Senate: David Croll, H. Carl Goldenberg, Sydney Buckwold, and Jack Austin.

Judge Alan B. Gold of Montreal received an honorary degree from the Université de Montreal at a special convocation. Gold had served as chief judge of the Quebec provincial court since 1970. Justice Albert Mayrand of the Quebec court of appeal was also granted an honorary degree at the same ceremony.

Rabbi Shlomo Carlebach, the internationally renowned Hassidic folk singer, settled in Toronto. He planned to divide his time between Toronto, New York City, and Israel.

A team of two students from the Bialik Hebrew Day School in Toronto topped the Diaspora communities at the International Bible Contest in Jerusalem. The two, Rhonda Levin, 15, and Ziv Gamliel, 12, placed second overall behind the Israeli contingent.

Among Canadian personalities who died in 1978 were: Hyman Bessin (68), prominent Ottawa businessman, past president of the Canadian Zionist Organization, and well-known figure in the Orthodox community; Leonard Fine (61), founder of the Toronto post of the Jewish War Veterans and a participant in Israel's War of Independence; Harold Tanenbaum (47), successful Toronto industrialist; Jack Shindman (81), highly regarded in Toronto for his tireless work for JIAS (following World War II he helped in the adjustment of 15,000 displaced Jews who came to Canada); Sophie Wollock (56), founder and general editor of the Montreal Weekly, *The Suburban;* Chaya Surchin, first Canadian national president of Pioneer Women of America, who died at her home in Tel Aviv; Bertha Allen, M.B.E. (79), who was made a member of the British Empire for her work in setting up canteens for servicemen during World War II; Joseph Lunenfeld (60), one of the founders of the United Israel Appeal of Canada and an internationally known Jewish leader; Colonel Edward Churchill (65), dynamic builder of Expo 67 and one of Canada's few Jewish career army officers to gain renown; Haskell B. Masters (82), active in the motion picture business and involved in many Jewish causes; Israel Plattner (75), writer and humorist, and a leader in the Toronto Yiddish-speaking community; and Sam Steinberg of Montreal, businessman and philanthropist, who was an officer of the Order of Canada.

BERNARD BASKIN

Argentina

Domestic Affairs

AT THE END OF 1978 liberal Argentines were greatly concerned about repressive tendencies in the country. While the government denied that there were any political prisoners, there was no gainsaying the fact that many thousands of people were being held without formal charges because they were suspected of being linked to left-wing underground movements. On August 10 the Foreign Ministry expressed indignation over charges by United States officials that the Argentine government was carrying out systematic torture and summary executions. A spokesman described these charges as a "coarse distortion of Argentine reality." Other officials complained that the United States was interfering in the internal affairs of the country. The Permanent Assembly for Human Rights, the Argentine League for the Rights of Man, and the Ecumenical Movement sponsored newspaper advertisements, directed to President Videla and the Supreme Court, requesting information about the thousands of missing Argentines. On December 21 a petition signed by 37,000 people, pleading for information about those missing, was presented to the government.

William Horsey, an economic analyst, stated that the purchasing power of Argentines was cut by 40 per cent during 1978. The official rate of inflation for the eleven-month period from January 1 to November 30 was 147 per cent; most economists insisted that the real figure ran as high as 190 per cent. By the end of 1978 Buenos Aires had become one of the most expensive cities in the world in which to live. In November there was a 48-hour illegal railroad strike that left several million Buenos Aires commuters stranded. Jaime Smart, the government minister of the province of Buenos Aires, declared: "The quality of public health and education is a national disgrace, and the state is busy doing everything except what it should be doing . . . Unfortunately our hospitals are badly run, schools are no more than ranch houses, and there is a lack of internal security because there are not enough policemen."

Antisemitism

While leading military figures stated that they were opposed to antisemitism, lower-eschelon officers and enlisted men in the police and military were notoriously

188

antisemitic. Jewish political prisoners were subjected to particularly cruel torture and questioned about such matters as Israel's plot to take over Argentina and Jewish plans to subvert Christianity. Prisoners reported that in many places of detention there were swastikas and portraits of Hitler. At the end of the year, a pamphlet was distributed within one of the unions which indicated in diagram form that Zionism was the main root leading to the tree of subversive activity. Approximately 800 Jews have disappeared in the last few years.

The most significant antisemitic incident continued to be the Timerman affair. Human rights advocates around the world were shocked by the way the Argentine government treated this Jewish journalist. Timerman was still under house arrest at the end of the year, despite the fact that a military tribunal had failed to come up with any charges against him, and the Supreme Court had stated that there was absolutely no reason for him to be held. Most liberal Argentines took it for granted that Timerman's continued arrest was attributable to antisemitism, and that the whole case started because *La Opinion,* the newspaper which he published, was regarded as too important to be in the hands of a Jew and at the service of the Jewish community.

In January the University of Buenos Aires reconfirmed the notorious antisemite Walter Bevaraggi Allende in his post as a professor on the law faculty. *Cabildo* was published monthly throughout the year and continued its attacks on the Jewish community. In March a powerful bomb exploded at the main entrance of the Sociedad Hebraica Argentina, causing considerable damage. The bomb was detonated prior to a planned meeting protesting a PLO terrorist raid on the Tel-Aviv-Haifa highway. The meeting was never held because the government denied permission, stating that such a public manifestation required ten days notice under the laws of the state of siege.

In February the executive branch of the government reviewed a plan to establish a register of non-catholic religious organizations; this had originally been proposed during Juan Peron's first presidency. Many meetings were held during the year between government representatives and Protestant and Jewish leaders to iron out possible difficulties relating to the register. At the end of the year it had not yet been established.

Relations with Israel

Ties between Argentina and Israel were strengthened as a result of the latter's sale of planes and armaments to the former, and an increase in commercial traffic between the two countries. Israel ambassador Ram Nirgad was very much in the public eye, appearing on television and radio. He played an active role in Argentine Jewish life and maintained very privileged relations with leading figures in the Argentine military and political establishment.

There were numerous important Israeli visitors to Argentina during 1978: Generals Hod and Gur, Finance Minister Simcha Erlich, Hebrew University president

Avraham Harman, Minister of Industry, Commerce and Tourism Yigal Hurvitz, M.K.'s Zina Harman and Abraham Katz, as well as Faye Schenk, Raphael Kotlowicz, Zvi Adar, Yitzhak Korn, and Haim Finkelsztein. During a six-day official visit to Argentina in March, Hurvitz stated that Israel had imported 45 million dollars worth of Argentine goods in 1977, while Argentina had purchased only 5 million dollars of Israeli goods. Hurvitz indicated his desire to strengthen commercial ties between the two nations.

Bishop Hilarion Capuchi, who was freed by the Israeli government upon direct intercession by Pope Paul VI after serving three years of a 12-year sentence for complicity with Arab terrorism, arrived in Argentina in April. Capuchi celebrated a mass in Buenos Aires' metropolitan cathedral in the presence of the ambassadors of Syria, Saudi Arabia, Egypt, and Algeria, the chargés d'affaires of Iran and Libya, and the director of the local office of the Arab League. In his public declarations Capuchi spoke with respect about Judaism as a religion while attacking Israel. The Argentine Zionist Organization (OSA) published a statement identifying Capuchi as an agent of the PLO.

The 30th anniversary of the State of Israel was celebrated in May. More than 20,000 people were present for a four-hour program held in Luna Park, Buenos Aires' largest indoor auditorium. It was the first time in many years that the Argentine Jewish community had expressed its solidarity with Israel on a massive scale. The main speaker was the former commander-in-chief of the Israeli Defense Forces, General Haim Laskov. Celebrations were organized by every important Jewish organization throughout the country. The final celebration took place in the beginning of November, when over 13,000 people attended a multi-media show in the Gran Rex Theater in the center of Buenos Aires.

The Argentine *aliyah* figure for 1978 was about 2,000; approximately 37,000 Argentine Jews had made *aliyah* since the founding of the State of Israel.

JEWISH COMMUNITY

Demography

The Jewish population of Argentina in 1978 was approximately 300,000. Some 225,000 Jews were living in Buenos Aires, while the leading communities in the interior were (the figures are for estimated numbers of families): Rosario, 2,500; Córdoba, 1,600; Santa Fé, 1,200; Mendoza, 800; Bahía Blanca, 800; Tucumán, 700; Mar del Plata, 600; Paraná, 550; Rivera, 400; Resistencia, 320; Corrientes, 300; Concordia, 250; and San Juan, 250.

Communal Activities

The Asociación Mutual Israelita Argentina (AMIA), a 37,500-member Ash-kenazi group, was the largest Jewish organization in the country. Well over 90 per cent of its budget came from the four Ashkenazi cemeteries in greater Buenos Aires that it owned and administered. AMIA held elections in May; 8,866 votes were cast. Abraham Grunberg was elected president. The composition of the board of directors reflected the percentage of votes received by the various slates: Labor, 41; Likud, 13; Movimiento Sionista Apartidario (General Zionists), 9; Agudat Israel, 8: Mizrachi, 8; Movimiento Sionista Renovador (Shinui), 6; and Freie Shtime, 5. AMIA was the principal source of social assistance to Argentine Jews, handling over 500 cases monthly. It was noted that the number of indigency cases was on the rise.

In March Dr. Nehemías Resnizky was reelected president of the Delegación de Asociaciones Israelitas Argentinas (DAIA), which officially represented the Jewish community on political matters before the Argentine government. In April Resnizky denounced the existence of pogrom forces in the country, stating that DAIA was keeping a close watch on them. He also spoke of the danger of "internal disintegration" as a result of assimilation.

Marcos Korenhendler was named president of the Organización Sionista Argentina (OSA), which had some 23,000 members throughout the country.

Of Argentina's 300,000 Jews, 70,000 were thought to be Sephardi. Jews of Syrian and Lebanese origin belonged to the Asociación Israelita Sefaradí Argentina (AISA); those of Moroccan origin to the Congregación Israelita Latina; and those of Turkish and Balkan origin to the Asociación Comunidad Israelita Sefaradí de Buenos Aires (ACIS). Each of these groups had its own cemetery. The Entidad Coordinadora Sefaradí Argentina (ECSA) continued its efforts to centralize Sephardi communal affairs. Three hundred students took courses during the year at the Centro de Investigación y Difusión de la Cultura Sefaradí (Center for the Investigation and Diffusion of Sephardic Culture).

Despite repeated calls by communal leaders to unite the Sephardi and Ashkenazi communities, nothing was done in 1978 to bring this goal any closer. The two groups maintained separate cemeteries, philanthropic agencies, campaigns in support of Israel, and, with the exception of the Comunidad Bet El, synagogues.

The Organización Sionista Femenina Argentina (OFSA), with over 30,000 members, was the most important women's organization. The Federación Argentina de Centros Comunitarios Macabeos (FACCMA) united the four leading Jewish sports clubs of Buenos Aires, the largest of which was the Sociedad Hebraica Argentina (SHA), with some 22,000 members. SHA, which is similar to the YM-YWHAs in the United States, offered a wide range of sport, social, and cultural activities. SHA maintained the Escuela de Instructores y Tecnicos en Trabajo Institucional (EDITTI: School for Institutional Leadership Training) in cooperation with the Jewish Agency. Club Nautico Hacoach claimed some 11,000 members and had two major facilities—an 11-story building in the center of Buenos Aires, as well as a large area for open-air activities in the famed Tigre region. Macabi also had a large building in Buenos Aires, as well as a camping area in the suburbs; it claimed a membership of 10,000. The fourth group that made up FACCMA was the Club Atletico Sefaradí Argentino (CASA) with some 10,000 members. CASA was the only club that offered kosher dining facilities and which observed *shabbat*. CASA added significantly to its physical plant during the year.

Active on the Jewish scene were YIVO (Yiddish Institute for Scientific Research), which completed 50 years of work in Argentina, offering courses in Yiddish (including one in the Catholic El Salvador University directed by Prof. I. Niborsky) and maintaining a library and museum; B'nai B'rith, which sponsored a visit by William Korey, director of international policy research for B'nai B'rith International, at the end of October; the Latin American office of the Joint Distribution Committee, which was headed by Alfredo Berlfein; the Hogar Israelita Argentina para Ancianos y Niños, a home for hundreds of adolescents and aged people; the Consejo Argentino de Mujeres Israelitas (CAMI: Argentine Council of Jewish Women), which sponsored a golden-age club and occupational therapy services; the Asociación Filantrópica Israelita (AFI), which maintained a model old-age home in San Miguel; and the local office of HIAS, which was directed by Alex Rubin. Prof. Manuel Tenenbaum of Uruguay became the new director of the Latin American section of the World Jewish Congress in January, succeeding the veteran Mark Turkow. The South American office of the American Jewish Committee was moved to New York, where it was headed by Jacob Kovadloff, who had been forced to leave Argentina in 1977 after repeated threats against his life. Sheerit Ha-pleita was the organization uniting survivors of the concentration camps; HORIM was the parent-teacher association of the Jewish school system. Keren Hayesod was reorganized under the leadership of Jacobo Fitterman. Keren Kayemet Le'Yisrael continued its work.

In January Zalman Wassertsug, the well-known Yiddish writer and journalist, left his post on the *Wa-ad Hakehilot* after 25 years of dedicated work. During the same month *Die Presse,* the only Yiddish daily in South America, celebrated the 60th year of its founding. June marked the completion of the first year of publication of *Nueva Presencia,* the Spanish-language supplement to *Die Presse. Nueva Presencia* was well-received by the Argentine Jewish community and quickly built up a sizeable readership. It had a most cordial dialogue with the Arabic periodical *Assalam* during January with respect to the necessary conditions for peace in the Middle East. In February Héctor Caram and Hermann Schiller, the editors of *Assalam* and *Nueva Presencia,* respectively, published a joint communiqué expressing their mutual desire for peace, and congratulating Argentine Arabs and Jews on their fraternal relationship. *Assalam* was attacked for its pro-Israel stand in February by the Arab-Spanish bilingual publication *Bandera Arabe* (The Arab Flag).

Dr. Asher Mibashan was given a testimonial dinner in February by the World Jewish Congress in honor of his *aliyah.* Mibashan had been for many years the Buenos Aires correspondent of the JTA and owner-publisher (after his famed father's demise) of the Editorial Candelabro, one of the few publishing houses specializing in Spanish-language books of Jewish interest.

At the beginning of April, the B'nai B'rith executive committee of District 20 (South America) met in Buenos Aires, and local Jewish organizations and the Latin American branch of the World Jewish Congress participated in the discussions. During one of the meetings, DAIA president Resnizky stated that "Jewish life in Argentina was normal in all aspects: religious, educational, sports, and cultural." Terrorism, he argued, had been almost completely contained. A number of observers felt that DAIA's position was too cautious with regard to exposing the dangers of right-wing terrorism and the failure of the government to halt antisemitic activities in the prisons.

The 35th anniversary of the Warsaw Ghetto uprising was marked at a large gathering which was addressed by Israeli ambassador Ram Nirgad. In June a DAIA delegation met with Henry Kissinger during his brief stay in Argentina during the World Cup Football Championship. During the same month OFSA held its 15th colloquium and elected Amalia Polack as president. Also in June, at the convention of the International Council of Jewish Women, a special Latin American committee was established, headed by Sara Breitman of Buenos Aires. The 55th anniversary of the weekly *Avoda Mundo Israelita* was observed in the same month.

The Latin American Jewish Congress held its second colloquium on cultural pluralism at the beginning of December in Teatro San Martin. It was attended by government officials and leading Argentine intellectuals. The colloquium was followed by the 26th plenary session of the Latin American section of the World Jewish Congress, with representation from the entire continent.

DAIA, as well as the World Jewish Congress, issued statements to the national press on the occasion of the 40th anniversary of Crystal Night. AMIA sponsored its annual Jewish Book Month following the High Holy Days. Approximately 2,700 people purchased books, while some 25,000 people visited the exposition. In November, Nissim Gaon, president of the World Sephardi Association and vice-president of the World Jewish Congress, visited Buenos Aires and spoke at a large number of gatherings. In September the Jewish community of Santa Fé celebrated its 75th anniversary with festive ceremonies. During a visit to Buenos Aires at the end of September, President Abraham Harman of the Hebrew University announced the inauguration of the San Martin Chair of Latin American studies, under the auspices of the Argentine Friends of the Hebrew University.

Jewish Education

Jaime Barylko continued as director of AMIA's *Wa-ad Ha-hinnukh,* which was the community's central board of Jewish education. It served some 30 primary schools in the city of Buenos Aires and some 15 in the suburbs, with a total student enrollment of 7,500. There were 35 schools in the provinces with about 2,000 students. There were some 5,500 children in the nation's kindergartens; the high school and post high school student population was estimated at 3,500. Approximately 900 teachers worked in the Jewish school system. AMIA treasurer Luis Perelmuter, in a press conference in March, stated that AMIA would give its largest subsidies to schools charging the least tuition. Some schools received subsidies of up to 50 per cent. Perelmuter said that almost half of the 7-million-dollar AMIA budget was set aside for education.

The Iosef Draznin Teachers Seminary celebrated its 30th anniversary in February. The school, which was located in the historic agricultural community of Moisésville, had graduated 22 teachers in the past two years; all of them worked in the provinces. Eighty teachers from the interior took part in a summer retreat in Necochea in January, under the auspices of AMIA. In April AMIA's cultural department opened the Instituto de Estudios Judios Superiores for young adults. ORT, directed by Eva Kamenszain, increased its student body to over 550 young people. The Centro de Estudios Judaicos, sponsored by the Jewish Agency and the University of Tel-Aviv, completed its third year under the direction of Yaacov Rubel.

The Seminario Rabinico Latinoamericano (Conservative), under Rabbi Marshall T. Meyer, opened Abarbanel, a teacher training institute. The Seminario's departments included the Instituto Franz Rosenzweig, devoted to adult education; two secondary schools, Solomon Schechter and Bet Hillel; the Rabbinical Department which in July ordained Mario Ablin, who became rabbi of the B'nei Yisroel community in Santiago, Chile; and the Instituto para Estudios Religiosos Superiores (Institute for Higher Religious Studies), which brought together Catholic, Protestant, and Jewish scholars.

Religion

The declining importance of religious observance among Argentine Jews was evident in the small number of Jews present in the 50-odd synagogues in Greater Buenos Aires during the high holidays. There were no more than 10,000 Jews in all of the synagogues during Rosh Hashanah. Even on Yom Kippur the number probably did not rise above 20,000. A growing number of Jews attended non-orthodox services.

Rabbi Shlomoh Ben Hamu (Orthodox) served as the head of the rabbinate of AMIA, which remained non-pluralistic despite statements to the contrary. At the same time, only non-orthodox rabbis were active in the struggle for human rights in Argentina, and were responsible for practically all significant ecumenical activity. Agudat Yisrael's Seminario Rabínico Marcos Guertzenstein had seven rabbis on its teaching staff; several graduates of the school were pursuing advanced studies in Israel. The Orthodox movement sponsored several other schools, including one for female students.

Roberto Graetz was rabbi of Emanuel, the only Reform synagogue in Argentina; he served also as the Latin American director of the World Union of Progressive

Judaism. Marshall T. Meyer continued to serve as rabbi of the Conservative Comunidad Bet El and as director for Latin America of the World Council of Synagogues. The Seminario Rabínico Latinoamericano arranged for Rabbi Seymour Siegel of the Jewish Theological Seminary of America to conduct Yom Kippur services at the World Cancer Congress in Buenos Aires.

Publications

Mundo Israelita was the weekly Spanish-language organ of the Avodah political party. Other periodicals included the German-language weekly *Judisches Wochenblatt;* the Yiddish *Davka,* the Mapam fortnightly *Nueva Sion;* the Spanish fortnightly *La Luz;* the DAIA bi-monthly *Informativo;* and *Majshavot,* the Spanish quarterly journal published by the Seminario Rabínico Latinoamericano and the World Council of Synagogues.

In January the Argentine-Jewish author Bernardo Verbitsky won the Ricardo Rojas Biennial Literary Competition for his work *Critica y Ensayo.* He also received the Carlos D. Liorente Fiction Prize for *Hermana y Sombra.* Also in January, Editors Pelagia published Lazaro Schallman's *Pela Szechter: The Singer who Survived the Holocaust.* Yehudah & Co. continued the publication of a Pentateuch containing a Spanish translation of Rashi's commentary by Jaime Barylko. Acerbo Cultural put out additional volumes of a bilingual edition of the Babylonian Talmud; Abraham Weiss served as director of the project. Simcha Sne, the Yiddish and Spanish writer, received the Honor Badge of the Argentine Writers Association, SADE, for *The Peace and the Blood.* Cesar Tiempo received several awards for *Capturas Recomendadas.* Boleslao Lewin and Jaime Barylko received Fernando Jeno prizes in Mexico, the former for his studies of Crypto-Jews in colonial America, the latter for his book *Introdución al Judaismo.* The Seminario Rabínico Latinoamericano, in collaboration with the Editorial Paidos, published a Spanish-language version of Martin Buber's *Hassidic Tales* in four volumes.

Personalia

Moisés Winograd, philanthropist and former vice-president of the Hogar Israelita Argentina para Ancianos y Niños, died in Buenos Aires in February, aged 76. Gregorio Joison, former president of the Banco Israelita and an important philanthropist who had donated the children's ward to the Hospital Israelita, died in Buenos Aires in March at the age of 83. Luis Kardúner, well-known journalist and Zionist leader, who was awarded first prize by the Argentine-Jewish Institute of Culture and Information in 1950 for his study *Alejandro Aguado,* died in Buenos Aires in June, aged 71. Lázaro Schallman, journalist, publisher, and educator, died in Buenos Aires in July, aged 73. Gregorio Verbitsky, who had been press-attaché at the Israel embassy in Buenos Aires, ambassador to the Dominican Republic, as well as a member of the Israeli diplomatic mission to the UN, died in Buenos Aires in August, aged 68. Jacobo Ficher, leading Argentine composer and musicologist, died in Buenos Aires in September, aged 82. Isaac Mizrach, who was active in the agrarian cooperative movement and Zionist affairs, died in Buenos Aires in October, aged 74. Simón Mirelman, a leading communal figure, past president of SHA and Hospital Israelita, and the founder, with the American Jewish Committee, of the Instituto Judio-Argentino de Cultura e Información, died in Buenos Aires in October, aged 84. Jose Aisenson, architect, who designed several Jewish institutions, died in October, aged 65. Jaime Goldenstein, president of the *Wa-ad Ha-hinnukh,* who developed innovative educational programs, died in Buenos Aires in December, aged 49.

NAOMI F. MEYER

Western Europe

Great Britain

Domestic Affairs

THE YEAR 1978 OPENED AMID OPTIMISTIC EXPECTATIONS that North Sea oil would flow in abundance and help the country overcome its balance of payments problems. There also seemed to be good prospects for industrial growth. By spring, however, it became clear that this scenario would not materialize, and that the government was unsuccessfully trying to reconcile a relatively tight monetary stance with an expansionary fiscal policy. On the favorable side, inflation was kept in single figures, unemployment fell slightly from 6 to 5½ per cent, and the gross national product rose by 3–3½ per cent.

The government survived, but it was widely believed that Prime Minister James Callaghan's surprise decision in autumn to postpone elections was attributable to a lack of confidence in the result. The minority Labor government retained the confidence of the House of Commons by a narrow margin, but it was defeated on a number of issues.

Nationwide opposition to racism was affirmed in February by a Conservative party decision to nominate a representative to the all-party Joint Committee Against Racialism (AJYB, 1978, Vol. 78, p. 217), which already included members from the Labor and Liberal parties, the British Youth Council, the National Union of Students, as well as ethnic and religious groups, including the Board of Deputies of British Jews. The Committee campaign, launched in April, culminated in September in a rally attended by 2,000 people; in July two leaflets were issued to "alert the people against the dangers which racialist organizations such as the National Front [NF] pose to Britain's democratic traditions."

The Jewish community's fight against the Front, strengthened in February by Zionist Federation (ZF) support for its campaign, was marred by controversy surrounding the Anti-Nazi League (ANL), which had strong links to the anti-Zionist extreme left. However, year-end meetings between the Board of Deputies, ZF, and ANL representatives gave hope of reconciliation.

A survey conducted by *New Society* magazine in May showed one in four young white people interviewed in South Hackney and Shoreditch (both underprivileged urban areas of London often described as NF strongholds) supporting or prepared to support the Front. Yet, while NF fielded 900 candidates in local government elections in May, none was returned to any of the 32 borough councils in Greater London or the 80 English metropolitan and district councils outside it. In the Greater London Council area, NF put forward 602 candidates (as against 91 in 1977) but won a reduced share of the poll in many places where it had previously done well, and failed to achieve its declared aim of replacing the liberals as the electorate's third choice. Voting figures in parliamentary by-elections provided further evidence of NF's electoral decline.

The formation in August of a new all-party Parliamentary Deposit Reform Group to promote reform of the system whereby anyone could deposit £150 and stand for Parliament, followed the failure in May of Greville Janner, MP's Representation of the People (Deposit and Nominations) Bill to obtain a second reading. The Bill, introduced in March, was designed to make it more difficult for NF to use the parliamentary electoral process to disseminate its doctrines at the public's expense.

Relations with Israel

The British government, as the Queen put it in her speech marking the opening of Parliament, supported "all endeavors to ensure a just and lasting peace in the Middle East." In February, following talks with President Sadat, Prime Minister Callaghan stated the government's view that "Israel should show flexibility in negotiations, but that Israel's security is paramount." In March Foreign Secretary David Owen reiterated that Britain regarded Israeli settlements in occupied territory as illegal. In July Minister of State for Foreign Affairs Frank Judd argued that it was in the interest of Israel to face up to the implications of United Nations Resolution 242 and accept the need for withdrawal from the occupied territories. In September Great Britain urged its Common Market partners to back U.S. diplomatic efforts to gain Arab approval for the Camp David agreements.

The official British view was that no role in the negotiating process was possible for the PLO until it recognized Israel's right to exist. However, requests for the closure of the PLO office in London, following an attack on a bus in Israel in April and the killing of an El Al hostess in London in August, brought no change in the government policy of tolerating the presence of PLO representatives. "There is no legal bar to the operation of a PLO office here while its activities remain within the law," said Judd. A request that El Al security guards be allowed to retain weapons outside the Heathrow airport area was turned down, but the British Airport Authority announced that El Al check-in desks at Heathrow would be protected by bullet-proof screens. In July 11 Iraqi diplomats and embassy employees were expelled from Britain in connection with Arab terrorist activities in London.

There were 354 pro-Israel and 68 pro-Arab MP's, according to a survey carried out for ZF. Of 95 MP's who held ministerial posts, 39 (including 7 Cabinet ministers) were pro-Israel; the 19 members of the Tory Shadow Cabinet included 8 pro-Israelis.

The resignation in November of Secretary of State for Trade Edmund Dell reduced the number of Jews in the Cabinet to three and the overall total of Jewish ministers to ten. In May Malcolm Rifkind, MP reported that there were nine Jewish Conservative MP's compared with two in 1970. The Conservative Friends of Israel, with 117 members (out of a total of 280 Conservative MP's), was the largest political lobby in Parliament.

Ian Mikardo's defeat in Labor party executive elections in October left only two Jewish members, but in the party's Socialist co-operative section, prominent pro-Arab John Cartwright, MP was replaced by pro-Israeli Leslie Huckfield. For the first time an Arab representative was officially invited as a delegate to the Labor party conference.

In February the National Organization of Labor Students voted to affiliate with the pro-Arab Labor Council for the Middle East. In April the National Union of Students conference reintroduced the "no platform for racists and fascists" policy which had been the basis for earlier anti-Zionist campaigns at universities and colleges.

The launching of a new campaign on behalf of Syrian Jewry resulted in over 90 MP's signing a motion in the Commons in July, and a petition to UN Secretary General Waldheim in September.

In April *Al Sabah,* an ultra-nationalist Arab-language newspaper that had been suspended by the Jordanian government in 1975, began publication in London. In October the Press Council rejected a complaint by Eric Moonman, MP against the *Sunday Times,* for its "Insight" team's investigation into allegations of torture of Arab prisoners in Israel. In December *Middle East International,* the monthly organ of the pro-Arab lobby, became fortnightly.

Arab Boycott

While British exports to Israel showed a modest increase (from £237 million to £274 million) between 1975 and 1977, exports to Arab countries doubled (from £1,386 million to £2,702 million). There was no way to measure the impact of the boycott.

The nine-man Select Committee under Lord Redcliffe-Maud which the House of Lords had established after Lord Byer's Foreign Boycotts Bill (see AJYB, 1979, Vol. 79, p. 220) had secured a second reading in February, decided in August not to recommend its reintroduction for a third. The Committee was persuaded by government and business community spokesmen that anti-boycott legislation would damage British interests in the Arab world. The Committee felt, however, that the government should take a close look at cases where public funds were used to support boycott-related transactions. In addition, it argued that government departments and embassies should cease authenticating signatures on "negative certificates of origin"; should take all diplomatic opportunities informally to reduce the incidence of secondary and tertiary boycotts; and should undertake an initiative within the European Economic Community (EEC) to develop a common European policy toward the boycott, and in support of EEC's fundamental principle of nondiscrimination.

In May suspicions were voiced that the Post Office's £4 million telecommunication contract with Libya (its third in two years, bringing the total order to £11 million) contained a boycott clause. In June an Anti-Boycott Coordinating Committee spokesman pointed out that the reported refusal by Delta-T Devices, a British firm, to deal with Israeli companies which refused to denounce Israel's actions in Lebanon was the first case in which commercial dealings had been openly linked to expressions of political opinion.

British Secretary of State for Trade Edmund Dell voiced concern that the "extraterritorial" aspects of the U.S. Export Administration Act infringed on Great Britain's jurisdiction and could harm British trade and employment. The matter came up in relation to British Petroleum Trading Ltd., a subsidiary of British Petroleum, which was half-owned by the British government, and had government-nominated directors on its board. The company cooperated with the Arab boycott.

JEWISH COMMUNITY

Demography

The Jewish population of Great Britain was estimated to be 410,000. Leading Jewish population centers were London (280,000), Manchester (35,000), Leeds (18,000), and Glasgow (13,000).

Synagogue marriages fell slightly in 1977, to 1,378 (19 less than in 1976 and 180 below the 1973-7 average), the Board of Deputies research unit reported in June. Although the largest losses, said unit director Barry Kosmin, occurred in the Reform synagogue movement, which appeared to have reached its peak in the early 1970's (184 marriages in 1977, as against 203 in 1976 and an average of 217 in 1973-7), in overall percentage terms there was hardly any movement among the three main religious groupings. The right-wing Orthodox segment of the community, however, continued to grow. In Greater Manchester there was a marriage boom which accounted for 195 of a total 422 provincial marriages; Manchester was the only provincial center in which marriages exceeded burials. More typically, in Wales only 16 people married, while 59 died; in Scotland 90 married, while 157 died. Burials and cremations under Jewish auspices totalled 4,749, which was 319 fewer than in 1976 and 111 below the 1973-7 average. Following the national trend, the proportion of cremations increased.

Increased Jewish marital problems caused the Jewish Marriage Education Council to establish a special divorce counselling department in February. In July Asher

Fishman expressed concern at the United Synagogue Council about the large number of Jews divorcing in civil courts, without application for a religious *get.* In 1977 the London Beth Din received 226 applications for *gittim,* and wrote 145.

Communal Activities

Concern about the needs of the elderly was voiced by Jewish Welfare Board (JWB) executive director Melvyn Carlowe in April. Six organizations had waiting lists totalling 614 people, many of whom had applied to more than one agency. The organizations were the Jewish Home and Hospital at Tottenham, the Jewish Blind Society, the Association of Jewish Refugees, Hammerson House, Nightingale House (which was being renovated at a cost of £1½ million), and JWB itself, which in December announced a £2.7 million residential project in Redbridge, to be completed in two to three years.

The B'nai B'rith Housing Society announced a new departure in April, providing flatlets in North-West London not only for 95 elderly Jews, but also for single people. In May the Duke of Gloucester opened the Westlon Housing Association's first venture, the Annette White Lodge, which was to provide sheltered housing for the elderly in London's East Finchley. In April the Abbeyfield Camden (Jewish) Society opened the first Jewish Abbeyfield House, a communal living scheme for the elderly.

In February, after 90 years' service to Jewish migrants, the Jews' Temporary Shelter amended its constitution to become the JTS Housing Fund, which made available interest-free loans for immigrant housing. In April the 40-year-old Central British Fund for Jewish Relief and Rehabilitation changed its name to World Jewish Relief. In October the Linath Hazadak Aid Society closed after 50 years of helping London's East End Jewish poor.

In March the Ranulf Association was formed to provide housing for the mentally handicapped. In May the Jewish Autistic Society was established to work with local authorities in the area of residential and day centers for autistic and similarly handicapped Jewish children, and to provide counselling. In July Norwood Homes for Jewish Children expanded its program to include the deaf and autistic, making it the leading welfare organization for Jewish children in Britain. In October the Haven Foundation's home for mentally handicapped adults, administered by JWB in London's Crouch End, was officially opened.

In January the first national Jewish youth solidarity conference established a standing committee to promote greater coordination between the various youth movements and the establishment of local youth councils. In May work began on a £250,000 youth center adjoining London's Western Synagogue and on a £300,000 Oxford and St. George North London Jewish Center. In July the Association of Jewish Youth (AJY), which operated four centers, announced that it was looking for additional full-time staff. In September work began on a £700,000 Brady-Maccabi youth and community center at Edgware, Middlesex. In October a new extension to the Barkingside Jewish Youth Center (an amalgamation of the Cambridge and Hackney Clubs and the Stepney Jewish Lads' Club) was dedicated.

In October Pierre Gildesgame instituted an annual £1,000 Jewish Youth Leader-of-the-Year award to focus communal attention on the area of youth work.

Zionism

In May some 80,000 people attended "Twelve Hours for Israel" in London's Earl's Court. It was the biggest single gathering in the history of Anglo-Jewry and included a speech by Israel Foreign Minister Moshe Dayan and a 7,500-strong youth cavalcade from all over England.

ZF, which in February formed a Committee for Youth Affairs comprising representatives of Jewish and Zionist youth organizations, grew in strength. After leaving Mizrachi in June, the Federation of Synagogues returned to ZF. In December the Progressive Religious Organization of Zionists, established by the Reform and Liberal synagogues in July, also affiliated with ZF. At year's end, ZF and Mizrachi had yet to agree on the terms of a merger that was required by the World Zionist Organization (WZO) as part of a reorganization plan.

In April the Joint Israel Appeal (JIA) set up a new National Leadership, Development and Recruitment Committee designed to build up a total of 5,000 active campaigners over a three-year period to canvas the estimated 100,000 Jewish families in Britain. JIA currently received 15,000 to 18,000 donations annually, said Committee chairman Monty Sumray, which meant that only 15 per cent of the population was being reached.

Britain's *aliyah* figure for 1977 of nearly 1,000 was the best since 1972, according to WZO. The 1977 level was 4 per cent above that of 1976, but was still much below the 1969 peak of over 1,700.

Soviet Jewry

British concern over Soviet Jewry found expression in May when the Foreign Office described the trial of Yuri Orlov as "very disturbing." A Labor party statement in July condemned the trial of Soviet dissidents, but the party's International Committee rejected a Liberal party invitation in September to join a campaign against Moscow as the venue for the 1980 Olympic Games.

The British Soviet Jewry movement rejected the advice of Foreign Secretary David Owen that it broaden the focus of its concern. Jewish organizations throughout the country continued their activities, which included marches, e.g., in Manchester in March, with ex-refusnik Silva Zalmanson as guest of honor; demonstrations, e.g., in London in April, to mark the opening of a world campaign on behalf of Vladimir Slepak, organized by the National Council for Soviet Jewry; petition campaigns, e.g., in London in July, in support of Ida Nudel and Maria Slepak, under the aegis of the 35's; and lobbying, e.g., in Glasgow in December, where the soviet deputy minister of culture was staying.

In September the Liverpool City Council voted to end its "twinning" link with Odessa, and requested the Association of Municipal Authorities to call on other local governments to take similar action.

Religion

In July Jews' College principal Rabbi Dr. N.L. Rabinovitch criticized the United Synagogue's (US) belt-tightening plan, which called for the shifting of synagogue personnel to those places where they could be of greatest use, without reducing the availability of religious services. Rabinovitch contended that lay leaders should not have the authority to cut synagogue budgets or eliminate religious functionaries. What was required, he maintained, were more rabbis and more synagogues.

An editorial in the *Jewish Chronicle* pointed out that there were four vacant ministerial posts in London alone, and that between 1971 and 1978 only two rabbinic graduates had emerged from Jews' College. There was also a shortage of cantors.

In July the US Council decided to impose levies on members to help meet the building costs of two fledgling congregations at Belmont and Pinner. Plans were completed for a new US *mikva* at Kingsbury Green, London.

Despite the chief rabbi's proposal that women be given a place on synagogue boards, in June the US Council approved a clause of the Scheme of the United Synagogue Act excluding women from office.

With the admission of a 28th member, the Hampstead Reform synagogue, the Association of Reform Synagogues of Great Britain (RSGB) grew to four times its original size. According to chairman Jeffery Rose, it was the fastest growing religious organization in Britain. In October the RSGB assembly of rabbis adopted proposals requiring ritual immersion for converts and a traditional form of *get* for divorce.

Although agreement in January between the chief rabbi, haham, and London Beth Din *dayanim* seemed to clear the way for a merger of London's three separate kashrut authorities, it emerged that this was conditional upon the new body's coming under the Shechita Board's administration, which was unacceptable to the kashrut authorities. In August London Board for Shechita treasurer H. Cansino reported a decline in the drift from kashrut observance. Throughout the year, the National Council of Shechita Boards expressed concern about imports of Empire Kosher Poultry Products from the United States.

In October the massacre of the Jews of York in 1190 was commemorated with a plaque at Clifford's Tower, York Castle, unveiled by the Archbishop of York and Jewish religious authorities, including the chief rabbi.

Jewish Education

Among all sectors of the Jewish community concern was expressed that the growth in Jewish education was not being matched by the availability of qualified teachers. Edward Conway, administrative director of the chief rabbi's Jewish Education Development Trust (JEDT) committee on teacher training, wrote in the *Jewish Chronicle* in March that the number of Jewish day schools had grown from 23 in 1954 to 57 in 1977, and the number of pupils attending them from 4,460 to 12,780. There was a critical shortage of teachers to serve these students. ZF education director Shoshana Eytan highlighted a similar problem at ZF Trust's 13 schools (8 in the provinces and 5 in London), which were attended by some 5,000 pupils. A report by JEDT in September indicated a number of steps that had been taken to deal with the shortage of teachers; several educators had been invited to make recommendations on ways of better recruiting and training teachers; the Trust had extended financial support to the Hebrew University and Bar Ilan University to enable teachers to attend training courses at the two institutions (40 participated in 1978); and the London Board for Jewish Religious Education, with the support of JEDT, had sent six students to Israel for a one-year foundation course prior to three years of teacher training in Britain. In April the Council for National Academic Awards authorized Jews' College and the North London Polytechnic to offer a joint Jewish studies program for prospective Jewish day school teachers, leading to a B. Ed. degree. This program replaced the Trent Park scheme, which over a six-year period had provided some 20 teachers for Jewish schools.

JEDT gave £100,000 and £1.8 million to help cover the construction costs of new Jewish primary schools in Leeds and Kingsbury (London), respectively. A. Brown, the director of the London Board for Jewish Religious Education, indicated that his group had under its jurisdiction 7,000 talmud torah pupils, 2,500 day school pupils, and 1,500 pupils in non-Jewish schools who received some religious education. In July, for the first time in 12 years, delegates from the Federation of Synagogues attended a Board meeting.

In December the Hillel Foundation reported a healthy increase in the number of students attending educational and social activities under its auspices. US was contributing toward the cost of maintaining a full-time councillor for Jewish students at universities in London.

In August the Yakar Educational Foundation acquired premises in Stanmore (London) for residential seminars, weekly courses, and special lectures covering a wide range of Jewish topics.

In May a fellowship in Holocaust studies was endowed at the Oxford Center for Post-Graduate Hebrew Studies.

Publications

The *Jewish Chronicle*-Harold H. Wingate Literary Awards went to Dan Jacobson for his novel *Confessions of Josef Baisz,* and to Lionel Kochan for his study *The Jew and his History.*

Other historical works published during the year included *The World's Greatest Story: The Epic of the Jewish People in Biblical Times* by Joan Comay; *Diamonds and Coral: Anglo-Dutch Jews and Eighteenth Century Trade* by Gedalia Yogev; *Karl Marx and the Radical Critique of Judaism* by Julius Carlebach; *Jewish Socialist Movements 1871–1917* by Nora Levin; and *The Jewish Intelligentsia and Russian Marxism* by Robert J. Brym.

Zionist history was represented by *The Zionist Revolution* by Harold Fisch; *Two Rothschilds and the Land of Israel* by Simon Schama; *Exile and Return: The Emergence of Jewish Statehood* by Martin Gilbert; *Palestine: Retreat from the Mandate* by Michael J. Cohen; *The Economic War Against the Jews* by Terence Prittie and Walter Henry Nelson; *The Jewish Paradox* by Nahum Goldmann; *Education, Employment and Migration: Israel in Comparative Perspective* by Paul Ritterband; and *The Plumbat Affair* by Elaine Davenport, Paul Eddy, and Peter Gillman.

Religious publications included *Judaism for Today: An Ancient Faith with a Modern Message* by Liberal Rabbi John D. Rayner and Bernard Hooker; *The Mannah Machine* by George Sassoon and Rodney Dale; *The Day that God Laughed* by Hyam Maccoby; *Hadar Ha-Karmel* by Rav Mayer Lerner, edited by J.D. Feld; and *Donum Gentillicium: New Testament Studies in Honour of David Daube,* edited by C.K. Barrett, E. Bammel, and W.D. Davies.

Volumes of essays were *Janus: A Summing Up* by Arthur Koestler; and *Russian Thinkers* by Isaiah Berlin, edited by Henry Hardy and Aileen Kelly.

Among notable works of fiction were *The Shadow Master* by Elaine Feinstein; *Now Newman was Old* by Chaim Bermant; *Mother Russia* by Robert Littell; *Family Business* by Anthony Blond; *A Five Year Sentence* by Bernice Rubens; *The Chelsea Murders* by Lionel Davidson; *The Face of Terror* by Emanuel Litvinoff; *Said the Old Man to the Young Man* by Arnold Wesker; and *On Margate Sands* by Bernard Kops.

Two further volumes (XXII and XXIII) of the *Leo Baeck Year Book,* edited by Robert Weltsch, also appeared.

Personalia

British Jews who received honors in 1978 included Gerald Bernard Kaufman, minister of state for the Department of Industry, who was made a privy counsellor, and Vivian David Lipman, director of ancient monuments and historic buildings, Department of the Environment, who was made a commander of the Royal Victorian Order. Knighthoods were conferred on Hans Lee Kornberg, Sir William Dunn

Professor of Biochemistry, Cambridge University; Peter Wendel Seligman, business-man; and Andrew Shonfield, director of the Royal Institute for International Affairs. Victor Mishcon, who received a life peerage, became Baron Mishcon of Lambeth in Greater London.

British Jews who died in 1978 included Rudy Sternberg, Lord Plurenden, busi-nessman, in January, aged 60; Michael Fenton, founding member of the Royal College of General Practitioners, in January, aged 77; Harold Abrahams, British and international athletics champion, in January, aged 78; Lord Lyons of Brighton, Labor party publicity adviser, in January, aged 59; Harold Poster, philanthropist and Zionist, in January, aged 66; Leo Genn, actor and lawyer, in January, aged 72; Marcus Lipton, Labor MP and Zionist, in February, aged 77; Jacob Halevy, Zionist leader, in February, aged 79; Lionel Jacobson, businessman and philanthropist, in February, aged 72; Ephraim Rosenberg, celebrated cantor, in February, in Netanya, aged 61; Joseph Wainstein, Yiddishist, in February, aged 88; Eli Munk, rabbi, in March, in Jerusalem, aged 77; Ronnie Waldman, top BBC executive, in March, aged 63; Itzhak Nathani, leader of British Mapam, in March, aged 74; Arthur Sigismund Diamond, eminent jurist, in March, aged 80; Charles Landstone, *Jewish Chronicle* theater critic, in April, aged 87; Julain Braunsweg, founder of London's Festival Ballet, in April, aged 80; Robert Vas, Hungarian-born British film-maker, in April, aged 47; Rowland Benson, professor of mechanical engineering, Manchester Uni-versity, in April, aged 53; Alfred Diamond, businessman and communal worker, in April, aged 76; Jack Hart, boxing referee, in May, aged 78; Andrew Kampfner, rabbi and educator, in May, aged 59; Bruno Jablonsky, aeronautical engineer, in May, aged 85; Serge Krish, musician, in May, aged 91; Joseph Rosenwasser, British Library assistant keeper of oriental manuscripts and printed books, in June, aged 69; Roy Cowan, Jewish humorist, in June, in Australia; Sascha Lasserson, violinist, in July, aged 88; Kopel Kahana, eminent talmudist, in July, aged 83; Moses Dryan, Glasgow rabbi, in July; Mavis Ronson, photographer, in August, aged 42; Lucjan Blit, Polish socialist journalist and academic, in September, aged 73; Cecil Arono-witz, violinist, in September, aged 62; Jack Emanuel Winocour, barrister, journalist and writer, in September, aged 65; Helen Kapp, painter, in October, aged 76; Edmond Kapp, caricaturist, in October, aged 87; David Glass, professor of demog-raphy, London School of Economics, in October, aged 67; Edwin Herbert, 2nd Viscount Samuel, administrator, in Jerusalem, in November, aged 80; Professor Aron Holzel, pediatrician, in November, aged 69; Hans Liebeschuetz, medieval historian, in November, aged 85; Arthur Lehman Goodhart, historian, in Novem-ber, aged 87; Katerina Wilcynski, artist, in November; Lou Praeger, dance band leader, in November, in Majorca, aged 70; Julius Unsdorfer, rabbi, in December, aged 59; Sir Julius Salmon, director of the J. Lyons restaurant chain, in December, aged 75; and Edgar Lustgarten, author and broadcaster, in December, aged 71.

LIONEL AND MIRIAM KOCHAN

France

Domestic Affairs

THE DIN AND TURMOIL of the national legislative election campaign dominated events in the early months of 1978. Constant quarreling between the Socialists and Communists, the partners in the left coalition, kept changing the prognosis for the outcome of the election. As the quarreling increased, nothing seemed less likely than harmony between the two groups, if the left did come to power. The Communists, fearing large Socialist party gains, tried to maneuver Socialist leaders, most notably François Mitterrand, into embarrassing positions. They spread rumors that the Socialists had little desire to change the system in France and wanted only to replace their rightist rivals. At the same time, professionally conducted polls showed the left retaining, even increasing, its following. Thus, despite the deep schism between the Communists and Socialists over the Common Program to which both sides had been so strongly committed, hopes for a left victory, i.e., a left coalition with a virtual majority, were not abandoned.

In Jewish circles there were debates over how best to deploy the Jewish vote, which, although not a determining factor, was not entirely without weight in the large cities, especially in the Paris region. The official position of Jewry remained what it had always been: the Jewish community was a religious, not a political, entity and would therefore not issue directives or otherwise try to influence Jewish voters. This formal call for "confessional" non-intervention in politics, however, begged the question that was troubling most Jews: how would the outcome of the elections affect Franco-Israeli relations? The Communists' pro-Arab bias should have moved many Jews with leftist views to choose government majority candidates, many of whom ostentatiously called attention to their pro-Israel sympathies. But the old conditioned reflex was still there—the fear of antisemitism on the right. While there are no statistics on this matter, there is reason to believe that the majority of French Jews voted for the left, even if without enthusiasm. Many leftist Jewish groups in France, Zionists included, campaigned for Jewish support of the Common Program on the assumption that the socialists would dominate the left coalition and thus determine foreign policy.

In the first round of the parliamentary elections, held on March 12, the left coalition won 48.95 per cent of the vote; the government coalition won 46.8 per cent, with the remainder going to various small groups. (A clear majority was needed to govern.) This result did not meet the expectations of the left, which had been counting on 52 per cent in this round. Neither did the returns altogether dissolve fears in the governing majority, which was not yet prepared to claim a victory, despite the probability that it would win more votes in the second round. During the next week, the Socialists, Communists and Left Radicals quickly ratified an agreement on the Common Program, notwithstanding many months of bitter disagreement over the matter. The second round of elections on March 19 was a victory for the governing majority, giving it 290 seats in Parliament, against 201 for the opposition.

The defeat of the left sounded the death knell of the Common Program. The Communists blamed the Socialists for the failure at the polls, charging them with having sabotaged the Program. The Socialists counter-attacked with charges that the Communists had deliberately undermined the coalition out of fear that the Socialists would dominate it. In the Communist party, several groups of dissident intellectuals called party policy and leadership into question. In the Socialist party as well, internal conflicts broke out, and by early 1979 the rivalry between François Mitterrand and Michel Rocard (former leader of the leftist Unified Socialist party whose position was now to the right of Mitterrand's) came out into the open.

Among the dissidents in the French Communist party—self-defined as "Communist critics"—were several Jews. One of them, Jean Elleinstein, the historian, had considerable influence among Communist students. Elleinstein advanced the idea that a new theory of socialism was needed, and that none of the principals of Marxist-Leninism could be taken for granted. Thus he, though personally a dejudaized Jew, was not prepared to challenge the nationalist conception of Jewishness. During a debate on the subject at the Jewish community center in Paris, he said it was appropriate to refer to Soviet Jews as "prisoners of Zion." This attitude sharply differed from that of other influential Jewish Communists who clung to the old ways and preached assimilation. For example, André Wurmser, one of the leading writers for *L'Humanité,* continued to defend Soviet policy on the Jews and, in the face of all the evidence, denied the existence of Soviet antisemitism.

Guy Konopnicki, the Jewish leader of a Communist student group, went even further than Elleinstein. He demonstrated with Zionist students against Soviet antisemitism in front of the USSR offices, wearing a conspicuous Jewish insignia on his arm. Konopnicki gave literary expression to his views in a satirical book, *Long Live the 100-Year Anniversary of the French Communist Party.*

Foreign Affairs

The issue that enlivened foreign policy debates was European unity. Fear of a supranational European community, dominated by West Germany and directed by the United States, became the propaganda cry of both orthodox Gaullists and Communists. On this issue the division was not between left and right; there was far greater agreement between former council president Michel Debré, a fanatical Gaullist, and Communist party Secretary General Georges Marchais, than between Marchais and Mitterrand, the Socialist leader.

There was no significant change in the French attitude toward the Middle East conflict. Israel was still condemned, either explicitly or in broad hints, because it refused to accept the Palestinian state extolled by the PLO. France's resentment against her omission from all talks dealing with the Middle East peace treaty was reflected in sour comments about the Camp David agreement and the awarding of the Nobel Peace Prize to Begin and Sadat. The pre-Six Day War friendship between France and Israel appeared to be finished, with no probability of renewal in the foreseeable future.

Antisemitism

The offices of MRAP (the communist-inspired Movement Against Racism and Antisemitism and for Peace) in and around Paris were attacked several times. In March 1978 the Paris office of Betar, the right-wing Zionist youth group, was dynamited; the explosion happened at night, so that no one was injured, although there was heavy damage. On July 14, Bastille Day, explosives placed at the apartment of Jean Dutourd, a contributor to the afternoon daily *France-Soir,* destroyed his home completely. A group belonging to the "Franco-Arab Rejectionist Front" claimed responsibility for the terrorist act against this non-Jewish writer, who was accused of being at the service of Jewry, and whose paper was charged with being an organ of Jewish interests. On May 20 three armed Palestinian terrorists managed to enter the El Al waiting room at Orly airport, where passengers were gathering before boarding a plane; the attempted attack failed, and all three terrorists were killed, as was a French security officer.

In April 1978 the synagogue in Drancy, a Paris suburb, was destroyed by fire. Drancy was the point of departure for tens of thousands of Jews sent in boxcars to Auschwitz during the German occupation. The immediate suspicion was that the fire was the work of terrorists, but after a police investigation it was judged to be accidental.

Heated discussions of the Darquier de Pellepoix affair ran for weeks in the Paris press. De Pellepoix, a virulent antisemite long before the war, had been commissioner of Jewish affairs in the Petain government, and had collaborated closely with Gestapo specialists in Jewish deportation. After the liberation, he found refuge in Spain, but was condemned to death *in absentia.* A reporter for the widely circulated liberal weekly *L'Express* went to Madrid to interview de Pellepoix, who was ill and intellectually deteriorated. When asked about his anti-Jewish activities, he declared that his antisemitism was well justified. De Pellepoix categorically denied the reality of the Holocaust, stating that at Auschwitz "they gassed only lice." The interview stirred up a storm of protest, with some people accusing the magazine's editors— among them a number of Jews, including the eminent Raymond Aron—of having given scandalous publicity to the obsessive, maniacal Jew-hatred of a war criminal. Others praised the editors for focusing on the barbarity of the Nazis and their French collaborators. The affair made the younger generation aware of an episode in French history they knew little about; the subject, after all, received scant attention in the history books used in primary and secondary schools.

On the heels of the de Pellepoix affair came the case of Robert Faurisson, a professor of literature at the University of Lyon whose political position was unclear, but who had not been considered an extreme rightist. Launching into research far removed from his own specialty—the history of Hitler's concentration camps—he arrived at the conclusion that the gas chambers had never existed, that they were a pure invention whose purpose was to serve not truth, but tourism. "Gas Chambers and Crematories as a Tourist Attraction" was the title under which he lectured on the events of World War II. After he became the target of hostile student demonstrations, Faurisson suspended his lectures. MRAP and LICA (the International League Against Antisemitism) brought suit against him.

JEWISH COMMUNITY

Demography

The Jewish population of France was estimated to be 650,000. Paris was the leading Jewish center, with a population of 300,000. Other important Jewish communities were Marseilles (65,000), Nice (20,000), Lyons (20,000), and Toulouse (18,000).

Communal Activities

The decline in contributions to the Fonds Social Juif Unifié (FSJU, United Jewish Philanthropic Fund), which began more than two years ago, continued through 1978, causing concern among leaders of Jewish social service agencies. FSJU concentrated on assisting business enterprises and cultural organizations.

Full-time Jewish schools, in Paris as well as the larger provincial cities, were badly hurt by a lack of funds. In the most important secondary schools—Yavneh and Maimonides in Paris, Sarcelles in the Paris suburbs, Akiba in Strasbourg, and others in Lyons and Marseilles—many scholarship requests were denied. There was also a shortage of teachers. As a partial remedy, an investment fund for Jewish schools was created with some help from the Israel government, which was deeply concerned about Jewish education in the Diaspora as an indispensable means of promoting Zionist ideology and encouraging *aliyah*. (The *aliyah* figure for 1978 was estimated to be around 1,000, and was made up primarily of intellectuals, religious Jews, and retired individuals.)

In May Israel's 30th anniversary was celebrated with great fanfare, not only in the big cities with large Jewish communities, but also in towns with few Jews. In many cases, municipal officials other than Communists participated.

Due to a lack of funds, the *Centre d'Information Pour le Moyen-Orient* (CIPM, Middle East Information Center), a documentation and liaison agency whose purpose was to counteract Arab propaganda, was closed down. Its demise caused great concern in Jewish circles.

One serious problem facing religious French Jews, particularly of the Consistory, was a severe shortage of rabbis. There were many reasons for this shortage, but one of them certainly was the meager salary paid French rabbis (except in Alsace and Lorraine, where a concordat provided for remuneration by the state). Another factor was that many of the most committed and best-educated rabbis were precisely those who gave up on the idea of living in France and went to Israel.

The central Consistory (still formally "of Israelites in France and Algeria"), as well as the Paris Consistory, were badly handicapped by the economic crisis and a lack of power. Nevertheless, in the Paris region, Consistory president Jean-Paul Elkanan and other leaders made a strong effort to promote religious observance. In Paris and its suburbs there were 62 Jewish community groups, 82 talmud torahs, and scattered post-bar mitzvah classes; the majority were subvented by FSJU. The Consistory organized *Tikavatenu,* a youth group whose purpose was to encourage the observance of Judaism.

Culture

There was a revival of interest in Yiddish language and culture, reflecting in part the growth of regionalism and ethnic autonomism in France. The award of the 1978 Nobel Prize for literature to Isaac Bashevis Singer greatly strengthened this trend, particularly among children of East European immigrants to France who were seeking "roots." This somewhat romantic neo-Yiddishism even attracted some Sephardic Jews of North African origin. A very active organization, the *Societé pour la culture et la langue yiddish* (Society for Yiddish Culture and Language) was formed.

At the annual arts festival in Avignon, young actors presented a series of theater performances, *"Le Chant juif profond"* ("Deep Jewish Song"), which featured examples of Yiddish, Spanish-Jewish, and Arab-Jewish folklore.

Publications

Ce que je crois ("What I Believe," Grasset), by André Chouraqui, is the spiritual biography of a Jewish religious liberal. Brought up in a small Algerian town, Chouraqui from high school onward followed the pattern of most educated, middle class Jews in the country, taking the royal road to full integration into French culture, hence assimilation. As a student in Paris during the critical period of the late 1930's, he experienced a spiritual crisis which led him to return to the religion of his childhood. The process of return was intensified and broadened during his war years in the underground resistance. Chouraqui became a Zionist, serving as a lawyer for the *Alliance Israelite Universelle* before moving to Jerusalem, where he pursued political and literary careers.

Another Algerian Jew, Shmuel Trigano, wrote a book a few years ago that demonstrated an original approach to Jewish spiritual life. His second book, *La Nouvelle Question Juive* ("The New Jewish Question," Gallimard), a penetrating view of the present crisis in Jewish civilization, concludes with a categorical condemnation of what Trigano calls "Jewish modernity."

Jacques Givet's *Le genocide inachevé* ("The Unfinished Genocide," Plon) is a sharp attack on leftist intellectuals who support the Palestinians and scorn Israel. Givet considers the anti-Zionism of these intellectuals to be a continuation of the eternal anti-Judaism that, on the one hand, denies Jewish existence and, on the other, blames Jews for existing.

The publication in French of a collection of essays *Fidelité et Utopie* ("Loyalty and Utopia," Calmann-Levy), by Professor Gershom Scholem, awakened the interest of the educated public, Jewish and non-Jewish, in the work and personality of this historian of Jewish mysticism.

Since Isaac Bashevis Singer won the Nobel Prize, almost all of his works have been published in French. The most recent was *Shosha* (Stock), a novel.

L'Amant ("The Lover," Calmann-Levy), an Israeli best-selling novel about the 1973 Yom Kippur War by Avraham B. Yehoshua, appeared in a French translation.

Vivre à Gurs ("Living at Gurs," Maspero), by Hanna Schramm and Barbara Vormeier, deals with one of the largest camps in the south of France under the Petain regime. There were thousands of German Jews at Gurs, but the two former inmates who wrote this account were non-Jewish anti-Nazis.

Les Juifs et l'ideologie ("The Jews and Ideology," Julliard), by Henri Arvon, is a penetrating study of socialist antisemitism.

Nous autres Juifs ("We Other Jews," Hachette), by Arnold Mandel, is a panoramic view of Jewish existence on several levels.

The 1978 WIZO Literary Prize was awarded to Leon Poliakov for *Europe Suicidaire* ("Suicidal Europe," Calmann-Levy).

ARNOLD MANDEL

Central Europe

Federal Republic of Germany

Domestic Affairs

$\mathbf{F}$OR THE FEDERAL REPUBLIC OF GERMANY 1978 brought stabilization on the domestic political front and a perceptible, though slight, economic upturn. In an address at the end of the year, Chancellor Helmut Schmidt said he felt gratified, because "peace has been preserved, and freedom and internal order in our country have been strengthened further." He looked confidently to the future, since "the soil has been prepared for favorable political and economic development."

The economic situation of West Germany's citizens improved during 1978. While the inflation rate rose by an average 2.6 per cent, the gross income of employed persons increased by about 5.5 per cent. The gross national product grew by 3.4 per cent, as against 2.6 per cent the year before. Average unemployment for the year was down to 4.3 per cent, from 4.5 per cent in 1977.

On March 5 communal elections took place in Bavaria and Schleswig-Holstein. The radical right National Democratic party (NDP) lost five of its seven seats and retained representation in only two communal bodies. On June 4 Lower Saxony elected a new state legislature. Also on June 4 the city-state of Hamburg voted for its Assembly (city parliament). On October 15 new state legislatures were elected in Hesse and Bavaria.

In August the prime minister of the state of Baden-Württemberg, Hans Filbinger, resigned his office after considerable public discussion of his activities during the Nazi era. Filbinger had been a judge in the Navy during the Nazi years and in this capacity had meted out several death sentences. He defended himself with lawsuits and claims of having actively resisted the Nazis. However, as the facts of the case came to the fore, his situation became untenable and he was persuaded by his party, the Christian Democratic Union (CDU), to resign.

Extremism

At the end of 1978 the Federal Ministry of the Interior stated that neither left-wing nor right-wing extremist organizations endangered the fundamental democratic character of the Federal Republic.

213

Neo-Nazi splinter groups and, in some instances, NPD maintained contact with like-minded groups abroad, particularly in Austria, Belgium, Brazil, Denmark, France, Great Britain, Switzerland, Spain, and the United States. The NSDAP Foreign Organization, headed by Gary Lauck, an American, supplied Nazi and antisemitic propaganda material for the right-radical scene in the Federal Republic. From other countries, too, plentiful materials arrived in Germany: from Italy, medals commemorating Hitler; from Japan and England, toys with Nazi symbols; from Spain, offset reprints of Hitler's *Mein Kampf;* from Great Britain, T-shirts with swastikas.

Some of the most active neo-Nazi groups during 1978 were the Deutsche Bürgerinitiative (German Citizens' Initiative), led by Manfred Roeder, who early in the year fled to South America to escape the German courts; the Reichsleitung der NSDAP (Leadership Corps of the NSDAP), headed by Wilhelm Wübbels, which published several pamphlets and held pro-Nazi meetings; and the Bürger- und Bauerninitiative (Citizens' and Farmers' Initiative) under Thies Christophersen, which disseminated Nazi ideas through literature and at various events. Erwin Schönborn's Kampfbund Deutscher Soldaten (German Soldiers' Combat League) campaigned against further prosecution of Nazi criminals, and denounced war crime "legends", particularly the "gas chamber lie"; in November Schönborn was fined DM 1,200 for libeling a Bundeswehr general. Henry Beier's Kampfgruppe Grossdeutschland (Greater Germany Combat Group) disseminated Nazi propaganda. The Aktionsfront Nationaler Sozialisten (National Socialists' Action Front), led by a former Bundeswehr lieutenant, 23-year-old Michael Kühnen, was involved in acts of violence; during November Kühnen was sentenced to six months' detention for engaging in pro-Nazi propaganda. Werner Braun's Deutsch-Völkische Gemeinschaft (German Racial Community) distributed pro-Nazi pamphlets; in October Braun, who had called for the "extermination of Zionism," was sentenced to a year's detention and fined DM 14,000.

Also in the public eye were the Deutsche Volksunion (German People's Union) and the National-Freiheitliche Rechte (National Liberal Right Wing), both headed by Dr. Gerhard Frey, an ultra-rightist publisher in Munich, who owned the weekly *Deutsche National-Zeitung,* the largest right-radical publication. Through his organizations, Frey had thousands of activists at his disposal; through his various newspapers he won a following in the hundreds of thousands. The *Deutsche National-Zeitung* claimed that Jews in the Federal Republic were treated "like a class with superior rights." Offenses by Jews were not prosecuted by the German courts, the paper asserted, whereas the German people were kept "foreyer in debt servitude." The German taxpayer was said to "serve as a milk cow for the Jewish State, to be milked at will." The newspaper also scored what it described as the continued tormenting of "so-called Nazi culprits" in "mammoth trials."

All of the neo-Nazi groups glorified Nazism, whitewashed or denied Nazi crimes, and fomented anti-Jewish sentiment; their aim was to restore a Nazi dictatorship in Germany. The report of the Office for the Defense of the Federal Constitution for 1977 had emphasized that, to a far greater extent than in earlier years, neo-Nazi groups and individuals had gained attention through swastika daubings, desecration of Jewish cemeteries, and the distribution of propaganda. These tendencies continued during 1978. At the end of the year, a report by the German security agencies voiced concern that the arms and explosives found in the possession of radical rightists might signal a new readiness to resort to armed force on the model of ultra-left terrorism. Juveniles were said to predominate among the militant elements. At the end of the year, the Pressedienst Demokratische Initiative (Press Service of the Democratic Initiative), a federation of writers and journalists, warned against trivializing the significance of neo-Nazi youth organizations. While such groups often were small in numbers, they displayed increasing aggressiveness toward Jews and Israel. Government agencies were accused of negligence and excessive tolerance in combatting this development.

The government repeatedly underscored its determination to use the most stringent legal means against militant ultra-right groups. In this connection the government also voiced disapproval of the "commercialization of the Hitler era" through books, recordings, and toys, with the explicit exception of publications seeking seriously to come to grips with the Nazi period. Between January 1975 and July 1978, some 750 criminal proceedings and investigations were conducted in the Federal Republic relating to the dissemination of neo-Nazi propaganda and Nazi symbols. The courts, however, imposed prison sentences in only 16 cases, and in only two of these did the defendants serve their full sentences—15 months each. Fines were imposed in 18 instances.

Neo-Nazi activities, particularly daubings and sticker campaigns, were reported in many locations during 1978. At Fürth in Franconia a citizens' committee was formed to curb the distribution of neo-Nazi publications, to provide young people with better information about the Nazi period, and to activate the public against ultra-right tendencies. At Münster in Westphalia, following numerous neo-Nazi and antisemitic daubing incidents, 146 Protestant churchmen declared their solidarity with the Jewish community. The minister of culture, education, and religious affairs in the state of Lower Saxony, Werner Remmers, suspended Karl-Heinz Kausch, a high-school principal in Hannoversch-Münden, for disseminating pro-Nazi and anti-Jewish ideas among students and others. Disciplinary measures were also ordered against two teachers at the school.

In Hamburg during July Wolf-Dieter Eckart, an editor of ultra-rightist publications, was sentenced to two years in prison for spreading pro-Nazi and antisemitic propaganda. In November in Lüneburg four German members of the NSDAP Foreign Organization, Oliver Schreiber, Volker Heidel, Joachim Nowald, and Andreas Kirchmann, were convicted of racial incitement and dissemination of Nazi propaganda and given prison sentences ranging from two days to 21 months. In Koblenz during July Gunnar Pahl, a member of the same group, was sentenced to six months. In Brunswick a bomb was found in the home of a member of the NSDAP Foreign Organization. Toward the end of the year a court in Celle was preparing to try six neo-Nazis accused of several robberies to obtain arms and money for planned terrorist actions; they were Michael Kühnen, Uwe Rohwer, Manfred Böm, Lothar-Harald Schulte, Lutz Wegener and Klaus Dieter Puls.

The activities of NPD posed considerable problems for police and security agencies. While a decision handed down by the administrative court of the state of Baden-Württemberg in April 1978 ruled that NPD was not to be regarded as subversive of the constitution, the federal government did view it as that. The Nazi regime was persistently glorified in the group's pronouncements. In several cities NPD demonstrations led to bloody clashes between police and counter-demonstrators, mainly leftists. In most such episodes the police figured as the protectors of the officially permitted NPD events.

Evidence of radical para-fascist thinking among segments of the younger generation was not limited to the adherents of neo-Nazi youth organizations or other ultra-rightist groups. For many young people the Nazi era had lost both its horror and its meaning for the present and future—either because the young people were uninformed or because they did not want to be informed, preferring to concern themselves with their own present-day problems. Though basically apolitical, young people became receptive to certain peculiar features of the Nazi past, which could serve as signs of rebellion against the authority of adults or the state. The swastika, Nazi uniforms, and even the idea of a "strong man" in the mold of Hitler, fascinated a good many young people, and held a symbolic meaning for them that was far removed from historical reality but helped satisfy their formless urge toward what was new and different. In this para-fascist thinking there also was room for Nazi-like defamation of, and threats against, Jews.

Left-wing extremism, like that of the right, did not represent a serious threat to the country, the federal government emphasized—adding, however, that ultra-leftist tendencies and activities called for careful watching and effective counteraction. The largest left-wing radical organization, the German Communist party (DKP), had 42,000 members in 1977, according to the Office for the Defense of the Federal Constitution. The New Left, which did not follow the Moscow line, continued to be represented primarily by the Communist League of West Germany (KBW), which reportedly had about 2,500 members in 1977. Late that year 2,281 left-wing extremists were reported to be employed in the civil service. During 1977 ultra-left terrorist acts had accounted for nine deaths in West Germany; in 1978 the number of such acts decreased. During the first half of the year 19 persons suspected of terrorist activities were arrested; 37 others remained on the "wanted" list.

Several German ultra-leftist terrorists were convicted by German or foreign courts during 1978. In September in Düsseldorf Willy Peter Stoll, a terrorist, was shot to death by police, as was a presumed terrorist, Michael Knoll, in Dortmund during the same month. In November two unidentified German terrorists shot and killed two Dutch border guards. In May Yugoslav authorities arrested four Germans suspected of being terrorists, who were released at the end of the year.

According to the Office for the Defense of the Federal Constitution, 187 foreign extremist organizations, leftist and rightist, existed in the Federal Republic during 1977, with about 57,800 members in all. Ultra-leftists were in the majority: 53 of the groups were orthodox Communist in orientation, and 99 belonged to the New Left. Twenty-four of all the groups worked underground and were committed to the use of force as a means of achieving their political aims. In June 1978 the federal administrative court in Berlin reaffirmed the bans on the General Union of Palestinian Students and the General Union of Palestinian Workers, originally decreed by the Ministry of the Interior in 1972, on the grounds that the organizations endangered the internal security of the Federal Republic. According to the court, proven aspects of their activities justified the assumption that, given certain opportunities, they would actively aid or abet the perpetrators of terrorist plots.

Antisemitism

As in previous years, antisemitic incidents in West Germany were linked, in most cases, to neo-Nazi episodes and developments. The culprits were usually members of ultra-right groups or Nazi-minded loners. Groups like Gary Lauck's NSDAP Foreign Organization and Erwin Schönborn's German Soldiers' Combat League played a prominent role in such events. Other groups, such as those associated with Gerhard Frey, also engaged in anti-Jewish and anti-Israel agitation, and made their influence felt among a following much larger than that of other ultra-rightist splinter groups.

Members of the NSDAP Foreign Organization were responsible for the daubing of antisemitic slogans at the Bergen-Belsen concentration camp memorial during May. In November a 17-year-old student affiliated with the youth organization of NPD confessed having defaced the synagogue in Osnabrück with swastikas, the Star of David, and the words "Death to the Jews." In connection with the commemorations of the Crystal Night pogrom of 1938, in November, antisemitic daubings appeared in a number of places. In the course of the year Jewish cemeteries were desecrated in Hagenbach, Willmars-Neustädles, Karlstadt, Frankfurt, and Neckarsulm. In October unidentified persons bombed the offices of the West Berlin Jewish community as well as an Israeli-owned store there. One of the bombs was defused in time; the other caused property damage.

Foreign Relations

The Federal Republic continued to play a major role among free Western nations during 1978. It sought to contribute constructively to the political and economic consolidation of the European countries, particularly within the framework of the European Economic Community, but also within the Western alliance. In July the heads of state of seven important industrial nations—Canada, France, Great Britain, Italy, Japan, the United States, and West Germany—met in Bonn to work out measures for stimulating economic growth and curbing inflation. President Carter combined his stay in Bonn with a four-day official visit to the Federal Republic. Earlier, in May, the Soviet party chief Leonid I. Brezhnev and Queen Elizabeth II of Great Britain had visited the country.

In September the Syrian head of state, Hafez al-Assad, came to Bonn. On this occasion German political figures stressed their unconditional support for the peace initiative of the president of Egypt, Anwar al-Sadat, and for Egypt's and Israel's efforts to secure a peace treaty. At a reception for President Assad, West German President Walter Scheel expressly distanced himself from the views of his guest, noting that Syria played a key role in the Middle East conflict and bore great responsibility for peace. The president stated:

We Germans and Europeans, having an immediate interest in Middle East peace, seek to support any efforts which, in our opinion, might make a peaceful solution possible or might make it easier to attain . . . The attitude of the Nine [EEC] toward the efforts to resolve the Middle East conflict justly and durably through negotiations is well-known. This attitude is based on the principles of the declaration of June 29, 1977. Furthermore, we are convinced that these principles, which rest on Resolution 242 of the United Nations Security Council, afford a basis for peace in the Middle East—that the Arabs' territorial rights and Israel's need for security can be reconciled.

Like President Scheel, other German political leaders made it clear that Bonn was not seeking to steer a course of its own in Middle East affairs, but meant to pursue a common Middle East policy with the other member states of EEC. Stress was laid on Bonn's principle of evenhandedness toward Israel and the Arab states. However, critical comments directed toward Jerusalem were repeatedly heard in Bonn in regard to Israel's settlement policy and Israeli military intervention in Lebanon. In March SPD politicians described the Israeli incursion into Lebanon, in the wake of Palestinian terrorist acts, as a "disproportionate action" and as "unrestrained aggression." Klaus Thüsing, an SPD deputy in the Bundestag, declared that with actions like that in Lebanon, Israeli policy was maneuvering itself "into a corner in which it can hardly escape the reproach of having taken over the law of the jungle from the other side."

The West German mass media, too, became increasingly critical of Israel during the year, charging it with insufficient readiness to compromise. The sympathy of the press clearly lay with the Egyptian president and his policies. When the Nobel Peace Prize was awarded to President Sadat and Prime Minister Begin, the award to the latter was criticized, with commentators maintaining that the Israeli head of government had yet to prove himself worthy of this distinction.

In June, when Fahd ibn Abdel Aziz, the Saudi Arabian Crown Prince, visited Bonn, Chancellor Helmut Schmidt emphasized that the posture of his government was determined by the UN's Resolution 242 and EEC's declaration of June 1977. The West German position, he said, affirmed Israel's right to exist within secure boundaries, but also recognized the right of the Palestinians to self-determination and their right to organize their own state. Later in the year the federal government stressed that it welcomed the results of the Camp David summit talks, and in this context voiced particular appreciation for the efforts of the U.S. government in achieving progress on the road toward a Middle East peace.

During a visit by the Sudanese president, Gaafar al-Numeiry, in October, Chancellor Schmidt voiced the hope that after Camp David the other parties to the conflict would also find themselves able to take part in the negotiating process, so as to bring the goal of a comprehensive peace settlement within reach. On the occasion of a state visit by King Hussein of Jordan, in November, President Scheel expressed the opinion that the peace talks based on the Camp David summit were a step in the right direction. In this process, he said, the decisive issue would be how to reconcile Israel's right to exist with the legitimate rights of the Palestinians—including, in Bonn's view, the right to self-determination.

In August the federal government stressed its firm determination to continue its policy of rejecting racism and race discrimination, in concert with its partners in the European Economic Community. As to the UN's World Conference to Combat Racism and Racial Discrimination, held in Geneva, the government regretted that the meeting had developed in a way that forbade the members of EEC to continue as participants; they could not be party to a final declaration accusing Israel of racial discrimination. The same accusation had prompted the federal government, in 1975, to vote against a General Assembly resolution equating Zionism and racism.

Relations with Israel

Despite criticism of Israel's foreign policy by West German political figures, and especially by the mass media, German-Israeli relationships in various areas, such as business, culture, tourism, and sports, continued to develop and consolidate during the year. Some 132,000 German tourists, a record number, visited Israel. Among tourists from European countries, West Germans for the first time constituted the largest number. Within two years the number of German visitors to Israel had more than doubled.

In April the Israeli ambassador in Bonn, Yohanan Meroz, took issue with news reports claiming that German-Israeli relations were being impaired by the allegedly anti-German attitude of the Israeli head of government. The ambassador acknowledged that Prime Minister Begin, having lost his entire family in the German extermination camps of Eastern Europe, carried a heritage of dreadful memories with him. He stated, however, that the formal, official relations between the Federal Republic and Israel were not affected by this in any way.

In July the Institute for Public Opinion Research in Allensbach published the results of a poll concerning Israel. Asked about their personal sympathies, 44 per cent of the respondents said they favored Israel (in 1970 the figure had been 46 per cent, in 1974, 50 per cent); 7 per cent sided with the Arabs; the rest were undecided. Forty per cent thought Israel would be able to hold her own vis-à-vis the Arabs over the long term; 20 per cent thought the Arabs would prove stronger, and 40 per cent gave no concrete answer. Late in 1974 only 26 per cent of respondents had thought Israel had a chance of surviving.

In May on the 30th anniversary of the founding of Israel, Chancellor Schmidt said in a telegram to Prime Minister Begin: "I am sure we will jointly succeed in extending and strengthening the relations between our two states further, on the basis of what has already been achieved." On the same occasion, Foreign Minister Genscher wrote to Israeli Foreign Minister Moshe Dayan: "The public in the Federal Republic of Germany has been observing with admiration the constructive accomplishments of the people of Israel since the founding of the State. I am happy that we have jointly succeeded in shaping a close and mutually trusting relationship between our nations and governments. Against the background of a tragic past, we have determinedly directed our gaze to the future."

Noted public figures attended a commemorative meeting held in Cologne by the Deutsch-Israelische Gesellschaft (German-Israeli Society) to mark the 30th anniversary of Israel. The speakers were Ambassador Meroz; the mayor of Jerusalem, Teddy Kollek; and Klaus von Dohnanyi, deputy minister in the West German Foreign Ministry. The latter said the federal government's chief objective in the Middle East was to promote developments that would reduce the distrust between Israel and her Arab neighbors and would help foster lasting peaceful relations between them. Bonn, he said, could not let itself be forced to accept the proposition that championship of Israel's existence was incompatible with friendly relations with the Arab countries. History, he stated, had once more given the Germans an opportunity to work for peace with the people of Israel.

In August Chancellor Schmidt, congratulating Prime Minister Begin on his 65th birthday, voiced the hope that Begin's efforts toward a solution of the Middle East conflict would succeed in bringing the hoped-for peace and with it a secure, happy future to the Israeli people and its neighbors. On Rosh Ha-shanah 5739 Schmidt stated in a telegram to Begin: "You may look back with pride and satisfaction on what you have accomplished in the year now ending. For the first time in more than 30 years, peace in the Middle East has come closer. I hope with you that it will prove possible to remove the remaining obstacles and to bring the desired just and durable peace to Israel and her neighboring nations." Apropos of the awarding of the Nobel Peace Prize, Schmidt wired Begin: "The courageous policy initiated by you and President Sadat thus obtains the recognition it deserves . . . We all hope in our hearts that there will be no new obstacles to the negotiations. May I assure you of my support." On Golda Meir's death in December, Schmidt telegraphed to Begin: "Golda Meir won influence and significance for your country throughout the world. Her political effectiveness radiated far beyond the borders of Israel. No one will forget the first visit of a German Chancellor to Israel, in June 1973, when Mrs. Meir was host to Willy Brandt. That encounter has had a fruitful effect on the relations between Germany and Israel—a matter of high significance for the Federal Republic."

In February the Israeli opposition leader, Shimon Peres, conferred with Social Democratic politicians in Bonn. In June Moshe Meron, vice president of the Knesset, was received in Bonn. Also in June Foreign Minister Genscher visited Jerusalem. The first member of a West German government to be received by Prime Minister Begin, he conferred with Israeli political leaders and paid a visit to Yad Vashem. In August Israel's minister of finance, Simcha Ehrlich, came to Bonn for discussions. During October an SPD delegation headed by Herbert Wehner visited Israel. Many other representatives of governing and opposition parties, as well as communal officials and labor leaders from the two nations, also met for discussions in West Germany and Israel.

One major topic of discussion between Israeli and German representatives was the problem of the German statute of limitations for Nazi crimes. Israeli spokesmen repeatedly called on the Bundestag to suspend the statute of limitations and asked that proceedings against Nazi culprits, such as the Majdanek trial in Düsseldorf, be expedited as much as possible.

In May CDU Bundestag deputy Erik Blumenfeld, speaking as president of the German-Israeli Society, asked that the federal government take all possible measures to render harmless the Arab terrorist groups in the country and to curb their sympathizers. Among the latter he counted some 300 demonstrators who during the Israel Independence Day celebrations held in Berlin in May had agitated against the Jewish State and demanded recognition of the PLO by the Bonn government. In December a statement adopted by the German-Israeli Society declared: "Resolutions frequently passed by United Nations and UNESCO bodies in condemnation of Israel are destructive and a hindrance to peace. The task of the United Nations and its affiliated organizations is to serve human rights and peace among nations, not to perpetuate hatred and discrimination."

The chairman of Israel's Council for Youth Exchanges, Adi Amorai, noted on a visit to Bonn in August that youth exchanges between Germany and Israel had increased considerably in the past two years. Some 2,000 young Israelis were now visiting the Federal Republic each year, he said, while twice that many young Germans were going to Israel. As in previous years, a number of young Germans volunteered to serve in various social projects in Israel under the auspices of a German church organization, Aktion Sühnezeichen/Friedensdienste (Operation Atonement/Services for Peace). In 1978 the organization marked its 20th year. During April two members of the group were killed in the course of an attack by Palestinian terrorists in Nablus; several others were wounded. Operation Atonement declared that, despite the attack, it would continue to serve the causes of reconciliation with Israel and of better Jewish-Arab relations.

Yad Vashem again awarded the honorific title "Righteous Among the Peoples" to several Germans who during the Nazi years had aided persecuted Jews: Gertrude

Kochanowski, Dorothee Heuer, Albert Heuer, Erika Patzschke, Herbert Patzschke, Elizabeth Auer, Grete Daene, and Wilhelm Daene.

In February the city of Munich presented the Hebrew University in Jerusalem with a donation of DM 50,000 toward the establishment of professorships in German language and literature. In April the Volkswagenwerk Foundation of Hanover provided approximately DM 900,000 toward the creation and financing of a department of German studies at the Hebrew University. In December the European Committee of the Weizmann Institute of Science at Rehovoth met in Bonn. The Institute has for many years cooperated closely with German scientists and scientific institutions and has received financial support from the latter.

Restitution

Discussions about a final settlement of restitution payments for Nazi injustices, primarily to satisfy claims in hardship cases, still failed to lead to a tangible result during 1978. However, in November the SPD delegation in the Bundestag unanimously adopted a resolution calling for a "Restitution Foundation." It should be set up by the federal government, the resolution stated, to satisfy justified claims which could not be dealt with in the framework of existing laws. "All past efforts notwithstanding, we still are duty-bound to do whatever is possible," the SPD parliamentarians stressed.

Nazi Trials

The approach of the effective date of the statute of limitations on Nazi crimes, set by law for the end of 1979, triggered vigorous public discussion during 1978, particularly in the mass media and within the political parties. Opinions on whether the statute should take effect as scheduled remained divided, with the parties and the public about evenly split. But whereas early in the year efforts to suspend the statute seemed to have no chance of success in the Bundestag, events took a turn during the late fall, when SPD decided to introduce a bill providing for a general suspension with respect to all kinds of murder. The initiative came from the leader of the SPD group in the Bundestag, Herbert Wehner, himself a victim of Nazi persecution. Toward the end of the year some members of the CDU opposition in the Bundestag also announced that they would vote for the proposed suspension. However, a majority of the CDU and CSU deputies—including their leader, Helmut Kohl—persisted in the view that the statute of limitations should be retained and that prosecution of Nazi crimes should be finally concluded. Similarly, a majority of FDP, whose members belonged to the governing coalition, maintained their opposition to extending or suspending the statute; this was also the position of the party leader, Foreign Minister Genscher. However, by the end of the year, even some FDP deputies indicated a possible change of mind. There appeared to be a real chance of a parliamentary majority favoring suspension of the statute with respect to murder. Numerous democratic organizations, as well as the Jewish community, publicly and emphatically endorsed suspension of the statute.

The head of the Central Office for the Investigation of Nazi Crimes in Ludwigsburg, Dr. Adalbert Rückerl, stated in December that, regardless of the discussions about the statute of limitations and the final settlement of this matter, there was a real possibility of suspects still being convicted after 1980. Whether or not the statute took effect, there would be no visible change in the way Nazi trials were conducted after 1979, he said; proceedings concerning thousands of suspects had been interrupted, so that it remained possible to prosecute them beyond 1980. In this connection, however, Rückerl again pointed out the difficulties of conducting prosecutions more than 30 years after the end of the Third Reich. Almost all the material received by the Central Office during the past six years concerned only crimes with relatively few victims and correspondingly few participants and witnesses, he stated; and in such cases, fact-finding was particularly difficult. Given the most favorable circumstances today, four or five years elapsed from the time a suspect became known to the Central Office until a verdict was handed down.

As of the end of the year, proceedings against nearly 4,000 Nazi suspects were still pending before West German courts. In general the duration of pre-trial investigations and trials had greatly increased, while the percentage of convictions had markedly declined. The overall duration of such proceedings averaged 16.8 years by 1977, up from 3.6 years in 1962. Pre-trial investigations of Nazi crimes, which around 1969 lasted no more than five years in a given case, had been taking up to 13 years in cases coming before the courts since 1975. Between 1945 and 1964, 9.9 per cent of defendants in Nazi trials were convicted; in the years from 1965 to 1976, the rate was only 1.5 per cent. At the end of 1978 the Central Office in Ludwigsburg was still engaged in about 190 preliminary investigations, involving an unknown number of suspects.

By January 1, 1978 a total of 84,403 individuals had been investigated in connection with Nazi crimes, the government stated. Up to that date, 6,432 had been convicted and sentenced—14 of them to death, 164 to life imprisonment. (All of these figures refer to the territory of the present Federal Republic.) Because of such factors as death, acquittal, or quashing of the proceedings, 74,263 persons remained unpunished. The government had no precise information about convictions of Germans for Nazi crimes by foreign courts. According to estimates, the Soviet Union convicted about 24,000 Germans; Poland, 16,000; Austria, 13,000; the German Democratic Republic, 12,000; France, 1,000; other Western powers, 5,000.

The prosecutor's office in Munich reported in December that it still had 32 investigations of Nazi crimes pending. However, the office said, the difficulties of establishing proof had increased so much between 1973 and 1977 that not a single indictment could be brought during that period. In 1978 there had been two indictments. The agency further stated that new charges of Nazi crimes kept arriving from Eastern bloc countries. Of late, the Soviet Union and Poland had also forwarded actual testimony, some of it recorded as much as ten years earlier by authorities in those countries.

Heinz Eyrich, the minister of justice in the state of Baden-Württemberg, stated in December that the chances of putting a newly discovered Nazi criminal in the dock and convicting him were constantly growing slimmer. Difficulties in conducting investigations and establishing proof contributed to this problem, the minister said, and so did the age of the accused. In Baden-Württemberg, he noted, only a single indictment could be brought during the past five years, and this proceeding had to be abandoned, because the 73-year-old defendant's state of health made him unfit for trial.

Saarbrücken: In July Friedrich Wilhelm Heinen, a former *SS* member, was sentenced to lifetime detention for the murder of Jews.

Karlsruhe: In March Wilhelm Eickhoff, a former sergeant in the *SS,* was sentenced on appeal to lifetime imprisonment for murdering Jews in White Ruthenia.

Limburg: In May Richard Hospodarsch, a one-time chief sergeant in the *SS,* was sentenced to seven years' detention for aiding in the murder of Jews in Poland.

Hanover: In April a former *SS* chief sergeant, Friedrich Rathje, was sentenced to two years' imprisonment, subject to probation, for aiding in the murder of 900 Jews in Poland. In September a one-time inmate and *kapo* in the Majdanek concentration camp, Karl Johann Galka, was put on trial on charges of murder. The trial of Heinrich Niemeier, a former *SS* member accused of murdering inmates in Auschwitz, began in October.

Stuttgart: In October a retrial was begun in the case of Richard Pal, a former *SS* member accused of murdering Jews in Poland.

Bielefeld: In September Wilhelm Westerheide and Johanne Zelle were put on trial for murdering Jews in western Russia.

Bochum: In September Theodor Börsch, Ernst Abraham, Johann Förster, Josef Lengl, Georg Hasenkamp, and one other former member of the Security Police went on trial for mass murder of Jews in White Ruthenia. By the end of the year proceedings against three of the defendants had been abandoned on the grounds that they were unfit to stand trial.

Cologne: In July the prosecutor's office indicted Kurt Lischka, formerly an *SS* lieutenant-colonel, for aiding in the murder of thousands of French Jews. In September Walter Knop, a former *SS* master sergeant, went on trial for murdering concentration camp inmates. In November court proceedings were begun against two former first lieutenants in the *SS,* Martin Patz and Karl Misling, for murdering prison inmates in Warsaw.

Düsseldorf: The trial of 14 former *SS* guards at the Majdanek death camp entered its fourth year in November. During December proceedings against one of the defendants, August Wilhelm Reinartz, were abandoned because of his unfitness to stand trial. In September the treatment of Jewish witnesses at the trial drew criticism from Professor Hans Maier, the president of the Zentralkomitee der Deutschen Katholiken (Central Committee of German Catholics). He found it appalling that witnesses who had suffered in concentration camps were sometimes examined in a way which placed a heavy psychological burden on them and exceeded the limits of decency. He voiced regret that witnesses had been insulted, that the suffering and death of camp inmates had been minimized, and that the defendants and their attorneys had tried again and again to represent as pure fiction the facts about the Nazi annihilation policy—facts proven a thousand times over.

Lübeck: In September Arvids Bajars, a former member of the Latvian police, was put on trial for shooting Jews and Latvians. After six days, the proceedings were indefinitely suspended on the grounds that the defendant was not fit to stand trial.

Dortmund: In December the prosecutor's office indicted a Dutchman, Siert Bruins, also known as Siegfried Bruns, for murdering Jews in the Netherlands. He had been found and arrested during July in Hagen, where he had lived incognito. Before long, he was released on bail, and extradition to the Netherlands was denied.

Stade: In December Erich Scharfetter, a former medical orderly in the Waffen-*SS,* went on trial for murdering Jewish concentration camp inmates.

Aschaffenburg: The trial of former *SS* members Hans Olejak and Ewald Pansegrau for murder of Jews in a sub-camp at Auschwitz, begun in September 1977, continued. In October 1978 the prosecutor's office reported that Jewish witnesses had been pressured, probably by ultra-rightists, to give false testimony exculpating the defendants.

JEWISH COMMUNITY

Demography

On January 1, 1978 the 66 Jewish communities in the Federal Republic and in West Berlin had 27,316 registered members: 13,031 females and 14,285 males. Their average age was 44.4 years. Jews in the Federal Republic and West Berlin who were not members of a community were estimated to number 10,000 to 15,000. As of January 1, 1979, the number of registered members was 27,295: 13,063 women and 14,232 men, with an average age of 44.5 years. During 1978, 704 immigrants and 354 emigrants were recorded, as were 93 births and 435 deaths; there were 50 converts to Judaism.

Communal Activities

In April representatives of the Zentralrat der Juden in Deutschland (Central Council of Jews in Germany) met in Bonn with SPD leaders, chiefly to discuss ways of dealing with the Nazi past in school curricula, with neo-Nazi and antisemitic manifestations in West Germany, and with political radicalism of the right and left. Both sides stressed their determination to help insure that the schools place greater emphasis on the Third Reich and its historical significance. The same point was made at a meeting held in Karlsruhe during April between Central Council representatives and a delegation from the Union of Teachers and Scholars, which represents most of the teachers in West Germany. A joint declaration emphasized that informing youth about the events of the Nazi era, particularly the persecution and killing of Jews, was essential to the future of German democracy. The Union and the Central Council agreed to request the ministers of culture, education, and religious affairs in the various states to develop a comprehensive curriculum about the evils of the Third Reich, so as to motivate young people to confront the events of the past.

In February the chairman of the Central Council's board, Werner Nachmann, called on West Germany's responsible political forces to proceed more sharply against neo-Nazi tendencies. While it was a mistake to overestimate the significance of right-wing extremism, he said, it had to be fought and eliminated where it appeared. In April Nachmann was a member of a delegation of the World Jewish Congress that visited Poland on the occasion of the 35th anniversary of the Warsaw ghetto uprising and the opening of a Jewish museum in Auschwitz. In September he was elected a vice president of WJC's European section. In June he accompanied Foreign Minister Genscher on a visit to Israel. In the same month he protested to the German Football League about the hospitality that had been extended to the former Nazi Luftwaffe colonel and neo-Nazi propagandist Hans-Ulrich Rudel during the world championship games in Argentina.

In February the president of the Bundestag, Dr. Karl Carstens, attended a meeting of the Central Council's board of directors held at Karlsruhe, and visited the Jewish community in that city. In September West German President Walter Scheel paid a visit to the Berlin community. He stated in an address that there were few other cities where, over the centuries, Jews had contributed so much to European culture. In November representatives of the SPD faction in the Bundestag visited the Berlin Jewish community. In June the community's president, Heinz Galinski, scored "the German Democratic Republic's wholly one-sided, hostile attitude toward Israel." Commenting on an East Berlin visit by Yasir Arafat, the leader of the Palestine Liberation Organization, Galinski noted that East German arms shipments to the PLO were discussed for the first time on this occasion—a move he characterized as morally reprehensible. As an Auschwitz survivor he felt duty-bound, he said, to ask the East German government whether it did not realize that the Democratic Republic, being a German state, had the same moral obligations toward Israel as did the Federal Republic.

All Jewish communities held special commemorative gatherings and services to mark the 35th anniversary of the Warsaw ghetto uprising, as well as the 40th anniversary of the Crystal Night in November.

A new Jewish community was founded during September in Giessen, in the state of Hesse. A new synagogue was consecrated during March in the old-age center of the Frankfurt Jewish community. In October the Würzburg community joined with the Rabbinerkonferenz in der Bundesrepublik (Conference of Rabbis in the Federal

Republic) in a celebration of the 100th anniversary of the death of Seligmann Baer Bamberger, the famous "Würzburg *Rav,*" who in 1864 founded the Jewish teachers' training college in that city. In June the Zionistische Organisation in Deutschland (Zionist Organization in Germany) elected Ernst Simons as its new president, and bade farewell to Shmuel Ras, who returned to Israel after three years as the organization's secretary general. Among the many events scheduled by B'nai B'rith, the outstanding one was a meeting with the Egyptian ambassador in Bonn, Omar Sirry, who explained Egypt's peace initiative.

Youth

On May 14 at Sobernheim the Bund Jüdischer Jugend (League of Jewish Youth) was created as the new top-level organization of all committed young Jews in West Germany between the ages of 16 and 35; Benno Reicher was elected chairman. The aim of the League was to promote Jewish awareness and activism. Later in the year the group organized seminars on current Jewish problems, and social gatherings.

A youth conclave focusing on "The Third Reich, the Present Day and Ourselves" was convened by the Central Council of Jews in Germany during November, in Dortmund. About one hundred young Jews attended. Noted German politicians and representatives of the three youth organizations affiliated with political parties in the Bundestag served as speakers and discussion partners, together with rabbis, German and foreign scholars, and leaders of Jewish organizations in the country.

The Bundesverband Jüdischer Studenten in Deutschland (Federal Association of Jewish Students in Germany) cooperated with the National Union of Israel Students in organizing a seminar, held in Jerusalem during September. The purpose of the seminar was to broaden the participants' knowledge of Israel and the Middle East, mainly in view of the fact that Jewish students in Germany were becoming increasingly involved in discussions with Palestinians and with leftist or anti-Jewish students. Thirty Jewish students from West Germany and West Berlin participated. The Association also organized seminars in West Germany and in collaboration with foreign Jewish student groups, in London and Vienna. Among the topics discussed were the Middle East, religious questions, neo-Nazi and antisemitic tendencies, and youth problems. At a delegates' conference in Munich during December, it was noted that the organization had intensified its contacts with the Central Council of Jews in Germany and other Jewish organizations, and had established ties with the Conference of Rabbis. Contacts were also made with the major non-Jewish student organizations in the country. In all, about 500 Jewish students took part in the Association's activities.

With all local affiliates participating, Makkabi Deutschland (Maccabiah Germany), the umbrella organization of all Jewish sports groups in the country, held its general convention in Frankfurt during June; Harry Schartenberg of Düsseldorf was elected president. Maccabiah's European championship soccer games took place in Duisburg during June. Players from five countries—Belgium, Denmark,

Great Britain, Israel, and West Germany—took part; Israel was the winner. In November in Frankfurt, Maccabiah Germany hosted a convention of the European Maccabiah Confederation, marking the 80th year of the Jewish sports movement in Germany and the 30th year of the State of Israel. Participants included representatives of the Maccabi World Union, headquartered in Israel, and of the European Maccabiah movement.

Christian-Jewish Cooperation

The 40th anniversary of Crystal Night was the central focus of attention in terms of Christian-Jewish relations. Commemorative gatherings, silent marches, radio and television programs, as well as religious services, were the ways in which the West German population marked the event. A declaration by President Walter Scheel stated:

> After November 9, 1938, few Germans had the courage to face the consequences of the pogrom. But we today, being able to see the larger contexts, must not evade the truth, even where it is distressing and shameful. The wrong we did to others fell dreadfully back on us: the outrage of 1938 ended in the defeat of 1945. Our country is committed to justice and peace, and so, for the sake of our own future, we must not forget the November days of 1938. This we owe the Jewish people; we owe it to the world and we owe it to ourselves.

The president of the Bundestag, Karl Carstens, pleaded before that body that the events of 1938 not be erased from memory and that the coming generation be informed about them. "Our Jewish fellow citizens," he said, "must be able to count on us to curb any revival of antisemitism in Germany, decisively and without exception." In Munich the Bavarian CSU asserted that the Federal Republic in the years after the war had sought "with heart and hand" to atone for the Nazi crimes, insofar as it was possible to do so. Erhard Eppler, a leader of SPD, emphasized that the happenings of those days stood as a warning for the living. He added that a primitive kind of antisemitism still existed and that it had to be dealt with rigorously. Similar views were expressed by the Council of the Protestant Church in Germany, the German Conference of Bishops, the Alliance of Christian Churches, and other religious bodies.

The Conference of State Ministers of Culture, Education and Religious Affairs, the top education agency in the Federal Republic, called on all school principals to see that the Nazi crimes, as well as Nazi ideology and its sources, were appropriately presented to pupils of all age groups. This measure took into account the complaints of Jewish and democratic groups that German youth lacked adequate knowledge of Nazism. The Conference of State Ministers stressed that schools today must "actively counteract the uncritical acceptance of portrayals that whitewash or actually glorify the Third Reich and its representatives, characterized as it was by dictatorship, genocide and inhumanity."

In a number of places, stones and tablets commemorating the persecution of Jews were unveiled on November 9. Several cities took the anniversary of the Nazi pogrom as an occasion to strike the names of Adolf Hitler and other leading Nazis from their lists of honorary citizens. The city of Hamelin declined to take this step, on the grounds that honorary citizenship granted during the Third Reich could not be withdrawn. A spokesman for the city added that the need for such "purging" appeared dubious anyway, in view of the fact that Hamelin was "in the company of another 180 German cities" in which Hitler remained registered as an honorary citizen.

For its activities in 1978 the Coordinating Council of the Societies for Christian-Jewish Cooperation chose the theme "Martin Buber: Dialogue Today." Brotherhood Week, in early March, was conducted under the same motto. The Coordinating Council's Buber-Rosenzweig Medal for 1978 went to Grete Schaeder and Albrecht Goes, authors of several publications about Buber. On the occasion of Buber's 100th birthday, on February 8, the post office issued a commemorative stamp. In July a comprehensive Buber exhibition was opened in Worms, jointly sponsored by the Coordinating Council, the Rhineland-Palatinate state government, and the Hebrew University. Smaller Buber exhibitions were held in several other cities. In the course of the year, the Lambert Schneider publishing house in Heidelberg reissued 18 books by and about Buber, some of which had been out of print for decades. The Karl Hermann Flach Foundation awarded its Martin Buber Prize to Walter Hesselbach, a Frankfurt banker and labor leader, for his efforts "in behalf of better understanding between Germans and Jews." The citation, by Heinz-Herbert Karry, minister of economics of the state of Hesse, emphasized Hesselbach's role in the building of the State of Israel.

The village council of Oberammergau in Bavaria decided that the passion play scheduled for May 1980 would once more feature the traditional version by Alois Daisenberger, which had been criticized as anti-Jewish. A revised version, based on a text by Ferdinand Rosner, which had already been welcomed in Jewish quarters, would not be performed. However, the new producer, Hans Maier, stated that he would stage the play in the spirit of reconciliation and eliminate any elements of hatred. He indicated that he would comply with the wish of Joseph Cardinal Ratzinger, Archbishop of Munich, that the text be made to conform with the guidelines of the Second Vatican Council, and would also take the suggestions and wishes of Jewish organizations into account as much as possible. However, there would be no falsification of the Bible. The prologue, Maier elaborated, would emphasize that there was no such thing as Jewish collective guilt in the death of Jesus. During July in Paris the Conference of European Rabbis voiced profound misgivings about the refusal of the organizing committee for the Oberammergau passion play to perform the reformed text. During July the passion play was the subject of a Jewish-Catholic dialogue in Munich, attended by representatives of the German Catholic Church and by a delegation of the American Jewish Committee, led by Rabbi Marc H. Tanenbaum.

During November in Munich the local Jewish community and the United Lutheran Church of Germany expressed concern that radio and television paid little attention to Jews and Judaism. The airing of the American TV series *Holocaust,* scheduled for January 1979, was described as an important event, of equal concern to Jews and Christians in Germany. To deepen the understanding of the *Holocaust* series, the national network decided to present two documentaries, on the history of antisemitism and on the "final solution." Following each installment of *Holocaust,* live broadcasts were to be aired in which historians, psychologists, and eyewitnesses would discuss the various aspects of Nazism. The government-sponsored centers for political education in Bonn and Düsseldorf, as well as other educational institutions, compiled background materials for *Holocaust* for distribution to students in all types of educational programs.

In 1978, as in previous years, the president awarded the Service Cross of the Federal Order of Merit to several German citizens who had aided persecuted Jews during the Nazi period. Those receiving the medal were Hertha Brockschmidt, Elisabeth Weeg, Katharina Overath, and Walter Händeler.

In memory of the Jewish physician, writer, and educator Janusz Korczak of Poland, whose 100th birthday occurred in July, a memorial plaque was unveiled in the university clinic in Würzburg. In October the Leo Baeck Institute in New York presented the Leo Baeck Gold Medal to the German publisher Axel Springer, in recognition of his efforts on behalf of German-Jewish reconciliation. In June CDU party chairman Helmut Kohl visited the Leo Baeck Institute in New York and addressed a gathering of Jews from Germany.

Publications

Publications on Jewish and Israeli themes were amply represented in the offerings of German-language book publishers.

In the field of Jewish history the following titles appeared: Monika Richarz, *Jüdisches Leben in Deutschland: Selbstzeugnisse zur Sozialgeschichte im Kaiserreich* ("Jewish Life in Germany: Original Documents on the Social History of the Empire"; Deutsche Verlagsanstalt, Stuttgart); Jürgen Thorwald, *Das Gewürz: Die Saga der Juden in Amerika* ("The Condiment: The Saga of the Jews in America"; Droemer, Munich); Stefi Jersch-Wenzel, *Juden und Franzosen in der Wirtschaft des Raumes Berlin-Brandenburg zur Zeit des Merkantilismus* ("Jews and French in the Economy of the Berlin-Brandenburg Region During the Era of Mercantilism"; Colloquium, Berlin); Haim Hillel Ben-Sasson, editor, *Geschichte des jüdischen Volkes* ("History of the Jewish People," 3 vols.; C.H. Beck, Munich); Henriette Hannah Bodenheimer, *Der Durchbruch des politischen Zionismus in Köln 1890–1900: Eine Dokumentation* ("The Breakthrough of Political Zionism in Cologne, 1890–1900: A Documentation"; Bund, Cologne); Nahum Goldmann, *Das jüdische Paradox: Zionismus und Judentum nach Hitler* ("The Jewish Paradox: Zionism and Jewry After Hitler"; Europäische Verlagsanstalt, Cologne); Heinz-Dietrich Löwe,

Antisemitismus und reaktionäre Utopie: Russischer Konservatismus im Kampf gegen den Wandel von Staat und Gesellschaft ("Anti-Semitism and Reactionary Utopianism: Russian Conservatism in the Struggle against Political and Social Change"; Hoffmann und Campe, Hamburg); Birgitta Mogge, *Rhetorik des Hasses: Eugen Dühring und die Genese seines anti-semitischen Wortschatzes* ("Rhetoric of Hate: Eugen Dühring and the Genesis of His Anti-Semitic Vocabulary"; Gesellschaft für Buchdruckerei, Neuss); *Das jüdische Prag: Eine Sammelschrift* ("Jewish Prague: An Anthology"; with texts by Max Brod, Franz Kafka, Else Lasker-Schüler, Isidor Pollak, Robert Weltsch, Franz Werfel; Jüdischer Verlag, Königstein); Inge Fleischhauer and Hillel Klein, *Über die jüdische Identität: Eine psychohistorische Studie* ("On Jewish Identity: A Psychohistorical Study"; Jüdischer Verlag, Königstein); Werner Schochow, *Deutsch-jüdische Geschichtswissenschaft: Eine Geschichte ihrer Organisationsformen* ("German-Jewish Historiography: A History of Its Organizational Forms"; Colloquium, Berlin); Guido Kisch, *Judentaufen: Eine historisch-biographisch-psychologisch-soziologische Studie* ("Baptism of Jews: A Study in History, Biography, Psychology, and Sociology"; Colloquium, Berlin); Günther Stemberger, *Geschichte der jüdischen Literatur: Eine Einführung* ("History of Jewish Literature: An Introduction"; C.H. Beck, Munich); Helmut Dinse and Sol Liptzin: *Einführung in die jiddische Literatur* ("Introduction to Yiddish Literature"; Metzler, Stuttgart).

Israel and Middle East problems were the subjects of the following books: Herbert Fasching, Ferdinand Staudinger and Ferdinand Dexinger, *Gelobtes Land: Begegnung mit Israel* ("Promised Land: Encounter With Israel"; Tyrolia, Würzburg); Avraham Negev, *Funde und Schätze im Land der Bibel* ("Finds and Treasures in the Land of the Bible"; Calwer, Stuttgart); Gustav Stein, editor, *Menschenrechte in Israel und Deutschland: Ein Symposium der Gesellschaft zur Förderung der wissenschaftlichen Zusammenarbeit mit der Universität Tel Aviv* ("Human Rights in Israel and Germany: A Symposium of the Society for the Advancement of Scholarly Collaboration with Tel Aviv University"; Verlag Wissenschaft und Politik, Cologne); Günther and Leslie Petzold, *Shavei Zion: Blüte in Israel aus schwäbischer Wurzel* ("Shavei Zion: A Blossom in Israel from a Swabian Root"; Bleicher, Gerlingen); Alfred Salomon, *David und Jerusalem: Ein Reiseführer, den die Bibel schrieb* ("David and Jerusalem: A Travel Guide Written in the Bible"; Aussaat, Wuppertal); Hilla and Max Jacoby, *Shalom: Impressionen aus dem Heiligen Land* ("Shalom: Impressions from the Holy Land"; Hoffmann und Campe, Hamburg); Herbert Haag, *Das Land der Bibel: Gestalt, Geschichte, Erforschung* ("The Land of the Bible: Aspects, History, Exploration"; Pattloch, Aschaffenburg); Franz Ansprenger, *Juden und Araber in einem Land: Die politischen Beziehungen der beiden Völker im Mandatsgebiet Palästina und im Staat Israel* ("Jews and Arabs in One Country: The Political Relationships of the Two Peoples Under the Palestinian Mandate and in the State of Israel"; Mathias Grünewald, Mainz); *Wir wollen Frieden: Bilder und Gedichte von jüdischen und arabischen Kindern aus Israel* (We Want Peace: Pictures and Poems by Jewish and Arab Children in Israel"; Herder,

Freiburg); Rusia Lampel, . . . *als ob wir im Frieden lebten: Das Mädchen Lo-lo will ein Buch schreiben, durchstreift Jerusalem und findet sich selbst* (". . . As If We Lived in Peace: Lo-lo Means to Write a Book, Roams Jerusalem and Finds Herself"; Herder, Freiburg).

The Nazi era and related topics were dealt with in the following books: Dieter Bossmann, editor, *Was ich über Adolf Hitler gehört habe: Folgen eines Tabus— Auszüge aus Schüler-Aufsätzen von heute* ("What I Know About Adolf Hitler: Consequences of a Taboo—Excerpts from Present-Day School Themes"; Fischer-Taschenbuch, Frankfurt); Fred Hahn, *Lieber Stürmer: Leserbriefe an das NS-Kampfblatt 1924 bis 1945* ("Dear Stürmer: Readers' Letters to the Nazi Propaganda Paper, 1924 to 1945"; Seewald, Stuttgart); Falk Pingel, *Häftlinge unter SS-Herr-schaft: Widerstand, Selbstbehauptung und Vernichtung im Konzentrationslager* ("Prisoners under *SS* Rule: Resistance, Self-preservation and Annihilation in the Concentration Camps"; Hoffmann und Campe, Hamburg); Fritz Bringmann, *Kin-dermord am Bullenhuserdamm: SS-Verbrechen in Hamburg—Menschenversuche an Kindern* ("Child Murder on Bullenhuserdamm: *SS* Crimes in Hamburg—Experi-ments on Children"; Röderberg, Frankfurt); Kazimierz Moczarski, *Gespräche mit dem Henker: Das Leben des SS-Gruppenführers und Generalleutnants der Polizei Jürgen Stroop aufgezeichnet im Mokotow-Gefängnis zu Warschau* ("Conversations With the Hangman: The Life of *SS* and Police Lieutenant General Jürgen Stroop, Recorded in the Mokotow Prison in Warsaw"; from the Polish; Droste, Düsseldorf); Max Oppenheimer, Horst Stuckmann and Rudi Schneider, *Als die Synagogen brannten: Zur Funktion des Antisemitismus gestern und heute* ("When the Syna-gogues Blazed: On the Function of Anti-semitism, Yesterday and Today"; Röder-berg, Frankfurt); Hartmut Metzger, *Kristallnacht: Dokumente von gestern zum Gedenken heute* ("Crystal Night: Documents of Yesterday for Remembrance Today"; Calwer, Stuttgart); Jürgen Pomorin and Reinhard Junge, *Die Neonazis und wie man sie bekämpfen kann* ("The Neo-Nazis and How to Fight Them"; Weltkreis, Dortmund).

On questions of religion and faith the following were published: Ulrich Gerhardt, *Jüdisches Leben im jüdischen Ritual: Studien und Beobachtungen 1902–1933* ("Jew-ish Life in Jewish Ritual: Studies and Observations, 1902–1933"; Schneider, Heidel-berg); Shemaryahu and Gregor Siefer, editors, *Religion und Politik in der Gesell-schaft des 20. Jahrhunderts: Ein Symposium mit israelischen und deutschen Wissenschaftlern* ("Religion and Politics in 20th Century Society: A Symposium of Israeli and German Scholars"; Keil, Bonn); Hermann Cohen, *Religion der Vernunft aus den Quellen des Judentums: Eine jüdische Religionsphilosophie* ("Religion of Reason Out of the Sources of Judaism: A Jewish Philosophy of Religion"; Fourier, Wiesbaden); Hellmut Gollwitzer and Rolf Rendtorff, *Thema: Juden-Christen—Ein Gespräch* ("Topic: Jews and Christians—A Dialogue"; Radius, Stuttgart); Werner M.T. Keuck, *Maria und die Bibel Israels* ("Mary and the Bible of Israel"; Kanisius, Freiburg); Magnus Magnusson, *Auf den Spuren der Bibel: Die berühmten Über-lieferungen des Alten Testaments, von der Archäologie neu entdeckt* ("On the Track of the Bible: The Famous Traditions of the Old Testament, Rediscovered by Archaeology"; Bertelsmann, Munich); Pinchas Lapide, Franz Mussner and Ulrich Wilckens, *Was Juden und Christen voneinander denken* ("What Jews and Christians Think of Each Other"; Herder, Freiburg); Walter Strolz, editor, *Jüdische Hoffnungskraft und christlicher Glaube* ("Jewish Hope and Christian Faith"; Herder, Freiburg); Roland Gradwohl, *Die Worte aus dem Feuer: Wie die Gebote das Leben erfüllen* ("The Words From the Fire: How the Commandments Give Fulfillment to Life"; Herder, Freiburg); Michael Brocke and Walter Strolz, editors, *Das Vaterunser: Vom Gemeinsamen im Beten der Juden und Christen* ("The Lord's Prayer: Common Features in Jewish and Christian Praying"; Herder, Freiburg); Pnina Navè, editor, *Du, unser Vater: Jüdische Gebete für Christen* ("Thou, Our Father: Jewish Prayers for Christians"; Herder, Freiburg); Thomas and G. Sartory, editors, *Weisung in Freude: Aus der jüdischen Überlieferung* ("Joyous Instruction: From Jewish Tradition"; Herder, Freiburg); Martin Levi Bass, *Jesus für Israel: Leben und Botschaft eines Judenmissionars—Rabbinerschüler in Hamburg, Emigration nach Argentinien, Taufe, Theologie* ("Jesus for Israel: The Life and Message of a Missionary to the Jews—Rabbinical Student in Hamburg, Emigration to Argentina, Baptism, Theology"; Verlag der Evangelisch-lutherischen Mission, Erlangen); Pinchas E. Lapide, *Hebräisch in den Kirchen: Forschungen zum jüdisch-christlichen Dialog* ("Hebrew in the Churches: Explorations Concerning Jewish-Christian Dialogue," Vol. 1; Neukirchener, Neukirchen).

Biographical subjects included the following: Ernst Simon, *Martin Bubers lebendiges Erbe* ("Martin Buber's Living Heritage"; Schneider, Heidelberg); Roger Mosre, *Gotteserfahrung bei Martin Buber: Eine theologische Untersuchung* ("The Experience of God in Martin Buber: A Theological Inquiry"; Schneider, Heidelberg); Hugo S. Bergmann, *Die dialogische Philosophie von Kierkegaard bis Buber* ("The Philosophy of Dialogue from Kierkegaard to Buber"; Schneider, Heidelberg); Sigrid Bauschinger, *Else Lasker-Schüler: Ihr Werk und ihre Zeit* ("Else Lasker-Schüler: Her Work and Times"; Schneider, Heidelberg); Schalom Ben-Chorin, *Zwiesprache mit Martin Buber* ("Dialogue With Martin Buber"; Bleicher, Gerlingen); Paul B. Mendes-Flohr, *Von der Mystik zum Dialog: Martin Bubers geistige Entwicklung bis hin zu "Ich und Du"* ("From Mysticism to Dialogue: Martin Buber's Spiritual Development up to 'I and Thou' "; Jüdischer Verlag, Königstein); Wolfram Köhler, *Der Chef-Redakteur: Theodor Wolff—Ein Leben in Europa 1868–1943* ("The Editor in Chief: Theodor Wolff—A Life in Europe, 1868–1943"; Droste, Düsseldorf); Janusz Korczak, *Verteidigt die Kinder! Erzählende Pädagogik* ("Defend the Children! Narrative Pedagogy"; Gütersloh, Gütersloh); Teddy Kollek and Amos Kollek, *Ein Leben für Jerusalem* ("A Life for Jerusalem"; Hoffmann und Campe, Hamburg); Christoph Stölzl, *Kafkas böses Böhmen: Zur Sozialgeschichte eines Prager Juden* ("Kafka's Evil Bohemia: Concerning the Social History of a Prague Jew"; Edition Text und Kritik, Munich); Inge Deutschkron, *Ich trug den gelben Stern* ("I Wore the Yellow Star"; Wissenschaft und Politik, Cologne); Jürgen Schultz, editor, *Mein Judentum: Jüdische Autoren schildern ihr Selbstverständnis*

("My Judaism: Jewish Authors Describe Their Self-understanding"; Kreuz, Stuttgart).

In the field of literature, the following books were issued: Gertrud Kolmar, *Eine jüdische Mutter* ("A Jewish Mother"; Kösel, Munich); Edgar Hilsenrath, *Nacht: Roman aus dem Konzentrationslager* ("Night: A Novel of the Concentration Camp"; Literarischer Verlag Braun, Cologne); Ephraim Kishon, *Salomons Urteil zweite Instanz* ("Solomon's Judgment, On Appeal"; Ullstein, Berlin); Ephraim Kishon, *Kishon für Kenner: ABC der Heiterkeit* ("Kishon for Connoisseurs: An ABC of Humor"; Langen-Müller, Munich); Ephraim Kishon, *Das grosse Kishon-Karussell: Gesammelte Satiren 1968–1976* ("The Great Kishon Carousel: Collected Satires, 1968–1976"; Langen-Müller, Munich); Leoni Ossowski, *Sterne ohne Himmel: Roman eines jüdischen Jungen im Dritten Reich* ("Stars Without Sky: A Novel of a Jewish Boy in the Third Reich"; Beltz, Weinheim); Salcia Landmann, editor, *Scholem Alejchem: Neue Anatevka-Geschichten* ("Sholom Aleichem: New Stories of Anatevka"; Limes, Munich); Berndt W. Wessling, *Die Töchter Zions: Roman* ("The Daughters of Zion: A Novel"; Hoffmann und Campe, Hamburg); Jean Amery, *Charles Bovary, Landarzt: Porträt eines einfachen Mannes* ("Charles Bovary, Country Doctor: Portrait of a Plain Man"; Klett, Stuttgart).

Personalia

Werner Nachmann, chairman of the board of the Central Council of Jews in Germany and president of the Senior Council of Jews in Baden, was awarded the Medal of Merit of the state of Baden-Württemberg. Kurt Neuwald, president of the Jewish community in Gelsenkirchen, received the Great Cross of the Order of Merit of the Federal Republic of Germany for his services on behalf of West Germany's Jewish citizens.

Dr. Leo Adlerstein, chairman of the board of the Jewish community in Düsseldorf and a board member of the Federation of Societies of Friends of the Hebrew University in West Germany, received the title of Honorary Fellow of the Hebrew University. The Cultural Circle of the Federal Association of German Industry presented its literary award for the year to the poet Rose Ausländer. A street in Düsseldorf was named after the late Dr. Josef Neuberger, one-time minister of justice in the state of North Rhine-Westphalia and chairman of the board of the Jewish community in Düsseldorf.

Dr. Alexander Besser, publicist and attorney, died in Frankfurt on July 8, aged 78. Dr. Paul Arnsberg, journalist, historian, and for many years a representative of the Jewish community, died in Frankfurt on December 10, aged 79.

FRIEDO SACHSER

German Democratic Republic

In its Rosh ha-Shanah message for 5739, the Verband der jüdischen Gemeinden der DDR (Federation of Jewish Communities in the German Democratic Republic) stated: "On balance, we may be satisfied with what many of our fellow religionists, both men and women, have accomplished here. Our communities, small as they have unfortunately become, have gained a good reputation beyond the borders of our country, and, thanks to the efforts of outstanding individuals, our Federation has won worldwide recognition, as is shown by our cooperation in international as well as national bodies."

The eight communities affiliated with the Federation had fewer than 800 members in 1978. In East Berlin there were about 360 Jews; only 120 of them were under 60 years old. The president of the Federation, Helmut Aris, was 70 years old in May; he had held his office since 1962.

On the 40th anniversary of Crystal Night in November, Erich Honecker, secretary general of the SED (Socialist Unity party) and chairman of the Council of State of the German Democratic Republic, sent Helmut Aris a message stating, among other things:

> It is my desire to assure you and all members of the Jewish communities in the German Democratic Republic of our vigilant remembrance of the victims and their measureless sufferings. In doing so, I am mindful of the fact that our socialist state of workers and peasants has forever cut the ground from under any reactionary forces. As a secure home of humanitarianism and progress, our state guarantees all citizens equal participation in the life of the society . . . By building socialism, our nation, as master of its fate, shapes its new life. In this process, citizens of the Jewish faith have an active share. They have equal rights in the German Democratic Republic, and enjoy equal respect. As they practice their religion and cultivate their tradition, they may continue to count on the full understanding of our state and our society.

Aris thanked Honecker for his words, which, he said, "we view as renewed confirmation of the great solicitude the German Democratic Republic bestows on the work of the Jewish communities." The message, he stated, gave Jewish citizens "an incentive and an obligation to continue working for the well-being of our socialist homeland, for peace and for understanding among nations."

The East German population marked Crystal Night with commemorations and the laying of wreaths in many places, including Dresden and Leipzig, at the former Sachsenhausen concentration camp, and St. Sophia's Church, the Weissensee Jewish cemetery, and the newly restored Rykestrasse synagogue in East Berlin. The events were attended by representatives of the state, the church, and the various Jewish communities in Eastern Europe. The Lutheran Church of East Germany,

235

in a message marking the Crystal Night anniversary, recalled the guilt Christians shared in the persecution of the Jews. A Crystal Night study group of the Lutheran Church published an informative brochure, *Als die Synagogen brannten: Kristall-nacht und Kirche* ("When the Synagogues Blazed: The Crystal Night and the Church"). The introduction noted that the majority of Germans and Christians witnessed the persecution of Jews passively, "with arms folded." The brochure stated that its aim was to help restore names and faces to the six million murdered Jews.

In September Bishop Albrecht Schönherr, chairman of the Bund der evangeli-schen Kirchen in der DDR (Federation of Lutheran Churches in the German Democratic Republic) expressed deep misgivings over the influence of the still unmastered Nazi past on present-day youth in East Germany. Despite the efforts of the state to extirpate the dire legacy of Nazism, an appalling amount of fascist thinking was still to be found among young people, he asserted. The head of the secretariat of the Federation of Lutheran Churches, Manfred Stolpe, commented that his organization was aware of several cases of antisemitic utterances and actions by young people in East Germany, but warned against exaggerating the significance of these incidents. It would be a mistake to speak of anything like a Hitler cult in East Germany, he said. The East Berlin weekly *Weltbühne* also rejected the allega-tion that the country was antisemitic. East Germany had repeatedly spoken out against the policies of the Israeli government, it was explained, "but never against Israel or against the Jews." Opposition to Zionism could not be equated with antisemitism, *Weltbühne* maintained.

Since 1945, 12,681 Nazi criminals have been sentenced in the territory of East Germany; 1,578 persons have been acquitted. Proceedings were abandoned, for various reasons, in 2,187 cases. The judgments included 118 death sentences and 240 sentences to life imprisonment. Since 1964, 54 judgments against Nazi criminals have been handed down; a number of investigations are still under way. At the end of 1978, 42 Nazi criminals were in prison in East Germany, 24 of them for life. The office of the Prosecutor General did not rule out the possibility that additional Nazi criminals might be tracked down. In August an East Berlin court pronounced a life sentence on Herbert Paland, 63, a former member of the Nazi secret field police, for war crimes.

The East German government kept up its consistently pro-Arab and anti-Israel policy during the year. It was one of the severest critics of the Egyptian-Israeli peace negotiations. East German Foreign Minister Oskar Fischer stated during the fall, before the UN General Assembly, that attempts to create sham solutions through separate agreements amounted to "playing with fire." In the opinion of *Neues Deutschland,* the official organ of SED, the Middle East debate in the UN made it clear that "Arab suffering" in the territories occupied by Israel would not end until "the aggressor totally withdraws its troops." In November the newspaper also accused the Jewish State of "continual mistreatment of prisoners" and "constant violation of human rights." In the territories occupied by Israel, "deportation, robbery and terror" were said to prevail. These crimes were described as "part of a policy of de-Arabization and Zionist settlement," in an effort by Israel to create a *fait accompli* on the Golan Heights, in the Gaza Strip, and on the West Bank.

The Communist regime's anti-Israel posture received support in Jewish circles. Thus, in October Franz Loeser wrote in *Weltbühne:*

> The dreams of a home where Jews might live free from antisemitism, in peace with each other and their neighbors, was destroyed by the rulers in Tel Aviv. Zionism has not done away with antisemitism; on the contrary, it has added fuel to it through its aggressive and chauvinistic policies. Zionism has not brought the Jews peace but has driven the citizens of Israel from one war into another since the state was born. To rob the Palestinians of their land and property, the Zionists not only stand ready to perpetrate brutal racism and dreadful murder upon the Palestinians; evidently they do not even shrink from dragging humankind into a world war in order to put through their Zionist dream.

In East Berlin during March, PLO chief Yasir Arafat signed an agreement providing for cooperation between SED and the PLO. On this occasion, East German politicians stressed their determination to increase support for the PLO and the Arab nations. East Germany's solidarity "with the Arab nations fighting the Israeli aggressors and their backers" required renewed and greater efforts, said Kurt Seibt, a top functionary of SED and president of the East German Solidarity Committee. Similarly, SED Secretary General Erich Honecker assured Arafat of "the continued unqualified solidarity of the people of the German Democratic Republic with the struggle of the Arab people of Palestine for the realization of its national rights, under the PLO's leadership." In June Arafat took part in a "Week of Solidarity with the Struggle of Middle Eastern Anti-imperialist Forces for Peace and Social Progress," held in East Berlin.

In June the Libyan chief of state, Muammar al-Qaddafi, paid a state visit to East Berlin. In October Syrian President Hafez al-Assad was received there. He and SED Secretary General Honecker signed a declaration in which they advocated a "comprehensive, just and durable settlement in the Middle East." Such a settlement, the declaration stated, could be attained only "through Israeli withdrawal from all Arab territories occupied in 1967 and through realization of the Palestinian people's inalienable rights."

FRIEDO SACHSER

Eastern Europe

Soviet Union

Domestic Affairs

THERE WAS ONLY ONE CHANGE in the top Soviet leadership during the period under review (1977–78). In 1977 Nikolaii Podgorny was ousted from his position as chairman of the Supreme Soviet and from his membership in the ruling Politburo. Since then the 76-year-old former leader has been relegated to the status of a non-person; his name has gradually disappeared from books and encyclopedias, and cities named for him have been renamed. Leonid Brezhnev, now head of both party and state (chairman of the Supreme Soviet), was the undisputed leader of the USSR. At 73, and obviously ill, he was not always up to the demands of his job. Brezhnev continued to be the object of a cult of personality, receiving countless honors, medals, and even a literary prize for his memoirs.

The question of a successor to Brezhnev was, of course, not discussed in the Soviet press. In October 1977 two of Brezhnev's close collaborators, Konstantin Chernenko and Vasily Kuznetzov, were elected candidate members of the Politburo. Feodor Kulakov, one of the youngest members of the Politburo, and considered a possible successor to Brezhnev, passed away in July 1978, at the age of 60.

The problem of succession was complicated by deep differences in the top ruling circle between leaders (Kosygin, Kirilenko, Ustinov) in charge of the day-to-day management of state affairs and ideologists (Suslov, Ponomarev) who followed the dogmatic principles of Stalinism. Both groups were aware that the Soviet Union's economic base was limited and that additional resources, including imports from abroad, were needed to implement successive five-year plans. They were split, however, over the methods to be applied to obtain these resources. More generally, they differed over how to deal with the internal situation, and over the conduct of foreign affairs.

While Brezhnev adhered to a policy of internal "moderation," holding police repression to certain limits, rigid controls and censorship were maintained in all areas of Soviet life. The Soviet Union remained a conservative society unwilling to tolerate dissent. Nevertheless, fear of the police and other state authorities substantially decreased, and in some sectors of Soviet society persons not seeking emigration or otherwise joining dissident groups openly disagreed with the official line. In 1978 a group of writers prepared an uncensored volume of literary essays and submitted it for publication. Although the authorities refused to publish the volume, one of its authors, the poet Andrei Voznesenski, was permitted to go to the United States for a lecture tour.

According to reliable reports, the ruling body of the Communist party rejected pleas for the rehabilitation of Nikolai Bukharin, the erstwhile party theoretician executed by Stalin in 1938. This was a significant decision, indicating the considerable power held in the party by the Stalinist wing. At the same time, there was evident a growing trend, reflected in Soviet literary and journalistic writings (see *Molodaia Gvardiia,* No. 11, 1977), toward a return to "national" or "historic" Russia. Current poetry was replete with references to the old Russian holy places, monasteries, and the like, and it became fashionable among sophisticates to use crosses as decorations. There was also an interest in Russian Christian philosophy; books by Berdiaev, Fedotov, Frank, and Bulgakov were much sought after on the black market. The mood was also reflected in some of the writings appearing in *Samizdat.* Sixty-two years after the October revolution, it appeared that the era of revolutionary dreamers was at an end in Russia, which was gradually returning to its historical past.

The new constitution adopted in 1977 replaced the one promulgated under Stalin in 1936; while acknowledging all manner of "rights" and "freedoms," it did not fundamentally change the established totalitarian regime. Three thousand copies of a Yiddish text of the new constitution appeared in Khabarovsk, and were made available to the inhabitants of Birobidzhan.

Dissidence

While the Soviet Union was a party to the Helsinki agreement on human rights signed by 35 countries in 1975, it viewed the accord in a way very different from that of the Western nations. At the follow-up conference to Helsinki in Belgrade in June 1977, the Soviet delegate Iulii Vorontsev made it clear that the Soviets would not accept criticism of their behavior or permit case-by-case examination of complaints.

Soviet authorities were unable to liquidate dissidence. Indeed, for the first time in the Soviet Union since the early 1920's, there was, unacknowledged by the government, open and vocal opposition. There were many instances of repression by the authorities, including trials and commitments to mental institutions *(psikhushka).* Andreii Sakharov, the prominent academician and leader of the human rights movement, not only openly protested illegal acts of the authorities, but attended trials of arrested dissidents to monitor the proceedings. This was a significant development, perhaps indicating reluctance, or even weakness, on the part of the authorities in their fight against dissent. Among the prominent dissenters arrested by the authorities were Iurii Orlov, a scientist and a leader of the Moscow

Helsinki Watch Committee, who was charged in June 1977 with anti-Soviet activity and later sentenced to seven years of prison, and five years of exile; Aleksandr Ginzburg, a representative of the Fund for Assistance of Political Prisoners, an organization created abroad by Aleksandr Solzhenitsyn, who was sentenced to eight years of labor camp and three years of exile; and Anatoly Shcharansky, an activist in both general and Jewish dissidence, who was accused of being a foreign spy, and received an unusually harsh sentence of 13 years imprisonment.[1]

As of mid-1978 some 20 members of various groups monitoring the Helsinki agreement had been arrested, but this did not put a stop to their activities. In their fight against dissent, Soviet authorities tried to neutralize the activities of known oppositionists by imposing additional camp or prison terms on them when they completed earlier terms. Thus, Anatolii Marchenko, one of the founders of the Moscow Helsinki Watch Committee, went on trial for additional criminal acts just before he completed 11 years of prison and exile in September 1978. Lev Lukianenko, a member of the Ukrainian Helsinki Watch Committee, who had served 15 years in labor camps, was sentenced, in June 1978, to an additional 10-year term. Reports from Moscow indicated that Georgii Vodimov, Lev Kopelev, and Vladimir Kornilov, all well-known writers, were threatened with arrest for their participation in the human rights movement.

While general dissidence in the Soviet Union mainly involved intellectuals and scientists, factory workers also joined in the effort. In December 1977 a small group of workers complained to American correspondents that the authorities were dealing harshly with workers protesting poor labor conditions and corrupt acts; such workers were placed under arrest or confined in mental institutions (New York *Times,* Dec. 2, 1977). The press conference was organized by a miner, Vladimir Klebanov. Andreii Amalrik, the dissident writer, who was granted an exit visa, stated in Paris that resistance among Soviet workers had reached significant proportions, and that there were cases of strikes directed by underground workers' committees (*Novoye Russkoye Slovo,* New York, January 5, 1978).

In March 1978 Soviet authorities revoked the citizenship of the well-known cellist and conductor Mstislav Rostropovich and his wife, the singer Galina Vishnevskaia. They took up residence in the United States.

Nationalities

There was growing unrest among various national minorities. National committees monitoring compliance with the Helsinki agreement insisted not only on respect for individual rights, but also on guarantees relating to specific national concerns. Ethnic movements in the Ukraine, Georgia, Lithuania, and among the Crimean Tatars presented demands relating to language, education, and other matters. While

---

[1]In 1979 two Soviet spies held in the United States were exchanged for Ginzburg and Valentin Moroz, a Ukrainian oppositionist.

it was difficult to gauge the present status of these demands, it appeared that the Soviet Union had not remained immune to the global phenomenon of increased ethnic affirmation.

At the beginning of 1978, students and workers took to the streets of Tbilisi in Georgia to protest a plan to drop Georgian as the official language of the republic. Soviet authorities, seeking to further a policy of unification, had tried to downgrade the use of the language, hoping that this would prove acceptable to the population. Following the protests, the plan was withdrawn, as were similar plans for neighboring Armenia and Azerbaizhan. All three Soviet Republics are in the border region adjoining Iran and Turkey, and the language issue there has been a very sensitive problem.

According to official figures, there were 200 mosques in Central Asia, which had a population of some 20,000,000 Moslems. Soviet authorities maintained their refusal to permit the Crimean Tatars to return to their native Crimea, from which they had been expelled in May 1944. Mustapha Dzemilev, the fighter for Tatar national rights, was again exiled for four years to Yakut ASSR, and his parents and his sister's family were expelled from the Crimea. A large number of Crimean Tatars were being absorbed into Uzbekistan in Central Asia, where Soviet authorities were encouraging them to intermarry with the Moslem Uzbeks. The Tatars were discouraged from preserving their national heritage through song, dance, or folklore.

There was unrest in the Baltic countries, where the Soviet policy of assimilation ran into opposition from those seeking to preserve local languages and religious traditions.

Economic Affairs

Toward the end of 1977, Kremlin leaders announced a reduction in the production goals of the five-year plan. It was obvious that the Soviet Union was experiencing a declining rate of economic growth. Available statistics indicated that the output of coal, steel, cement, and meat would fall below the levels anticipated for the end of the 1976–1980 plan. Although grain output was somewhat better in 1978, purchases abroad continued. At the same time, Nikolaii Baibakov, the chief economic planner, announced a substantial increase in consumer goods for 1979. Soviet planners were clearly worried not only about reduced industrial output, but also about the lack of improvement in labor productivity.

Work continued on a 2,000-mile railroad across Siberia to the Pacific. The completion of the railroad would facilitate the settlement of European population groups in an area containing rich deposits of minerals and timber.

Foreign Affairs

The rift with China continued. An improvement in Chinese-U.S. relations did not please the Soviets, and the Moscow press attacked the Chinese "revisionists" who had discarded the "correct" Marxist line in favor of good relations with capitalist countries. In June 1978 Brezhnev accused the Carter administration of playing "the Chinese card." While there was no significant change in conditions at the Chinese-Soviet frontier, there were occasional reports of border clashes, illegal crossings, and the like. Leonid Ilichev, the Soviet deputy foreign minister, went to Peking in April 1978 to discuss border disputes. The disputed areas, it should be noted, included territory in the area of the Ussuri and Amur rivers, where the Jewish Autonomous Region of Birobidzhan was located. Chinese sources reported that one million Soviet soldiers were stationed along the 4,000-mile frontier.

Kremlin leaders went out of their way to assure the countries of Western Europe of their dedication to peace. In June 1977 Brezhnev visited Paris, where he met with French President Giscard d'Estaing. At the beginning of 1978 Brezhnev sent letters to the NATO countries warning them against the introduction of neutron bombs. Soviet-U.S. talks continued on an arms limitation treaty (SALT II) with the expectation that a treaty might be concluded in 1979.

Kremlin authorities refused to permit Santiago Carillo, the Spanish Communist leader, to deliver a speech at the celebration of the 60th anniversary of the October revolution in Moscow in November 1977. Carillo was ostracized because of the Spanish party's stand rejecting the idea of a dictatorship of the proletariat. Official Soviet publications repeatedly attacked "Euro-Communists" for adopting an anti-Soviet line.

Relations with Israel

Throughout the period under review the Kremlin maintained its rigid pro-Arab policy and engaged in anti-Israel and anti-Zionist propaganda. It supported the idea of a Middle East peace conference to be held in Geneva. When, in 1977, Egypt invited the Soviet Union to participate in a preliminary meeting in Cairo, it refused, viewing the proposal as a cover for a separate deal between Egypt and Israel. Following a meeting between Brezhnev and Syrian Foreign Minister Abdul Halim Khadaam, Moscow called for an overall settlement of the Middle East conflict. The Soviets were unhappy about President Sadat's visit to Jerusalem. They repeatedly expressed their support of the PLO. Several Arab states received large supplies of Soviet arms. At the same time, frankly anti-Jewish films were included in indoctrination courses of the Red Army.

An Israeli parliamentary delegation visited the Soviet Union in November 1978. The invited delegates, Yossi Sarid (Labor), Naftali Feder (Mapam), Avraham Melamed (National Religious party), Toufik Toubi (Rakah CP), Z. Burshtein (CP) and A. Zakhruni (Shelli) were criticized by the Israeli press for accepting the Soviet invitation. Upon their return, the delegates stated that they believed that the Kremlin leaders were beginning to rethink their harshly negative policy toward Israel.

JEWISH COMMUNITY

Demography

A national census, which might shed new light on the Jewish population of the Soviet Union, was expected to be taken in January 1979. The best current estimate, taking into account the continued emigration of Jews, was 2,666,000. *Sovetish Heimland* (No. 10, Oct. 1978) carried an item from the 1977 AMERICAN JEWISH YEAR BOOK on world Jewish population which gave figures for the larger Jewish communities. In contrast to previous practice, the figure for the USSR was altered to conform to the official Soviet Jewish population estimate of 2,150,000.

Communal and Religious Life

There were no Jewish communal organizations in the USSR. Jewish religious life was represented by a small number of Jewish congregations *(dvadtsatkas)* and synagogues. The exact number of synagogues was not known, but Soviet authorities spoke in terms of dozens of synagogues and hundreds of *minyonim.* Synagogues were functioning in a state of isolation, since any kind of coordination of Jewish activities was discouraged.

Iakov Fishman and Iakov Mikelberg were rabbi and president, respectively, of the Moscow Jewish congregation. The Moscow Yeshiva Kol Iakov continued to function, but it had few students and was not able to train desperately needed rabbinical personnel. The production of religious articles (e.g., prayer shawls, prayerbooks, phylacteries, *mezuzot*) was discouraged, and importation from abroad was forbidden. (Rabbi Pinhas Teitz of Elizabeth, New Jersey did succeed in shipping *esrogim* and *lulavim* to the Soviet Union.) In 1978 a sufficient quantity of flour (some 264 tons) for Passover *matzot* was allocated in Moscow, Kiev, Leningrad, and Tbilisi. The situation in the provincial towns was less satisfactory, with Jews being dependent on the good will of local officials to obtain *matzot.* In an interesting development, Rosh Ha-shanah greetings from the rabbi and president of the Moscow congregation and Ilya Zhidovetski of the Kiev congregation were received by Rabbi Teitz and Atlanta Mayor Maynard Jackson. (Jackson had visited the Kiev synagogue.)

While there were no *chedorim,* and steps were taken against religious instruction, there were increasing signs of interest in Jewish religious observance. This was probably related to the heightened national consciousness among Jews, and the increased religiosity of the Russian Greek Orthodox population. (*Molodezh Moldavii* [Oct. 17, 1978], a Moldavian newspaper, reported that many members of the

Komsomol [Communist youth organization] in both the cities and villages were secretly baptizing their newborn babies in the Greek Orthodox Church.) As had been the case for a number of years, during Simhat Torah large numbers of Jews, mostly youths, came to the Moscow synagogue on Archipova Street in an expression of Jewish solidarity. At the same time, it was noted that among recent Soviet emigrés to the West were a number of individuals who had converted to Greek Orthodoxy, and who, in their life abroad, took no interest in the problems connected with Jewish life.

Antisemitism and Discrimination

Anti-Jewish sentiments pervaded Soviet society. To a significant degree, the spread of such feelings was related to the increasingly militant nationalistic mood of the Russian population. The Soviet pro-Arab stand provided an additional channel for anti-Jewish bias, creating a situation in which it was difficult to determine where anti-Zionism ended and antisemitism began.

The press, cinema, radio, and television were all involved in the anti-Jewish campaign. On March 12, 1977 the widely-read Soviet magazine *Ogonek* lauded T.S. Solodar's *Wild Wormwood,* a book containing a crude attack on the Jewish religion and pointing to the spiritual kinship between the "followers of Hitler and Herzl." On November 16, 1977 *Krasnaia Zvezda,* a Red Army newspaper, informed its readers that of 165 "death corporations" (meaning the arms industry), 158 were controlled by pro-Zionist capitalists. The same paper claimed on May 11, 1978 that the aim of the Israeli government was the "physical destruction of the Arab people of Palestine." In attacking Jews and Zionists indiscriminately, the Soviet Jew-baiter L. Korneev ominously referred to them as "cosmopolitans," a contemptuous term used during the anti-Jewish campaign conducted by Stalin during the 1940's. On September 18, 1978, *Komsomolskaia Pravda* published a piece by V. Polezhaev repeating the familiar antisemitic charge of a Jewish Masonic conspiracy.

De facto anti-Jewish quotas had been re-established in the Soviet Union. Jewish applicants experienced great difficulties in gaining admission to the major universities in Moscow, Leningrad, and Kiev. In addition, they were not eligible for admission to some specialized schools, such as foreign service, journalism, and others. The authoritative Soviet statistical annual of education, science, and culture (*Narodnoe Obrazovanie, Nauka i Kultura V.S.S.S.R. 1977*) indicated that in 1976 the number of Jewish students attending universities was 66,900 (1.3 per cent of the total university population). In 1972 the figure had stood at 88,500 (1.9 per cent). (For further comparisons, see AJYB, 1979, Vol. 79, p. 94). Nevertheless, in 1975 there were 385,000 Soviet Jewish functionaries with specialized higher education, and 180,000 with specialized secondary degrees. The number of Jewish scientific workers rose from 64,393 in 1970 to 69,374 in 1975, but the percentage of Jews among all scientific workers fell from 6.9 to 6.1 per cent. The academic councils of Soviet universities placed all manner of obstacles in the way of Jews seeking candidate degrees (the equivalent of the European doctorate); dissertations were either rejected, or it took an inordinately long time to defend them.

There were almost no Jews in top positions of the party, state, or armed forces. Veniamin Dymshitz, the veteran deputy premier, was still on the job, but his post was administrative in nature; he was also one of very few Jewish members of the Central Committee of the party.

Jewish Resistance

Jewish dissidents and "refusniks" openly demonstrated against Soviet anti-Jewish policy and the obstacles placed in the way of would-be emigrants. In October 1977, 20 Jews were held under house arrest during the session of the Supreme Soviet in Moscow, in order to keep them from holding a demonstration. In late 1977 more than 100 Soviet Jewish activists, in an open letter to the delegates attending the Belgrade Conference, presented a detailed list of Soviet violations of the Helsinki accord with regard to Jewish culture and Jewish emigration. In December 1978 Soviet police raided the homes of Jewish dissidents in Moscow, Leningrad, and Riga, confiscating, among other things, Jewish books and publications.

While dissent centered around the problems of emigration, some Jewish groups and individuals sought to improve the condition of Jewish life in the USSR. In Moscow there were some 25 underground Hebrew teachers with about 250 students; in Leningrad, 12 teachers and some 120 students. Jewish *Samizdat* publications continued to appear despite the repressive measures taken by the authorities. Among the unofficial publications were *Jews in the Modern World* and *Jewish Thought.* From time to time, seminars on Jewish and general subjects were held in private apartments. At the end of 1978 a questionnaire dealing with Jewish identity and the possibilities of Jewish life in the Soviet Union was distributed by Jewish activists.

According to available figures, a total 29,000 Jews left the Soviet Union in 1978, as compared with 16,000 in 1977. The total Jewish emigration figure for the 1968–78 period was 175,000. More than 60 per cent of the emigrants went to countries other than Israel; only an insignificant number sought to return to Russia. (Maria Davidovich, who emigrated to Israel after her husband, Colonel Davidovich, died in Minsk, later returned to the USSR.) In November 1978, six years after he applied for an exit visa, Valentin Levich, probably the most prominent scientist among the Jewish "refusniks," was granted a visa, and left for Israel.

It was not clear why the Soviets permitted an increased number of Jews to emigrate in 1978. Some saw the action as connected with the continuing negotiations on a SALT agreement. Others thought it reflected a Soviet desire to meet the conditions of the Jackson-Vanik amendment, and thus open the way for increased trade with the United States.

Among recent emigrants from the Soviet Union there were a substantial number of Russians, including many intellectuals and some 40,000 Volga Germans; 1,100

Armenians left in 1978. Some 3,000 members of the Russian Pentacostal Christian sect have appealed to the Belgrade Conference for assistance in their emigration project.

Culture

There were no Jewish schools in the Soviet Union, and the authorities discouraged activities conducted in Yiddish. The only Jewish periodical, the Yiddish-language *Sovetish Heimland*, carried a page on Yiddish grammar and summary translations in Russian and English. In 1978 the Khabarovsk party school issued a brochure, *For Those Who Study Yiddish*, intended for individuals preparing for work in the Yiddish press.

Despite the negative attitude of the authorities, certain forms of Jewish cultural life were maintained, particularly the theater and the arts. Theater groups conducted by amateurs with some professional help functioned in many cities of the USSR. The Kaunas Yiddish Folk Theater, with its drama and vocal ensembles, presented many concerts in Lithuania and other parts of the Soviet Union. The Birobidzhaner Folk Theater offered a new version of *Tevie der Milchiger* under the direction of Berta Shtilman. The Vilna Yiddish Folk Theater, under the direction of Iudl Kaz, presented a number of plays and variety performances. The Moscow Dramatic Ensemble, under a new director, Joseph Rivlin, performed in many cities of the Ukraine and Moldavia. Rivlin replaced Beniamin Schwarzer, the veteran director, who died in February 1978. The various theater groups in Chernovits, Kiev, and Leningrad maintained their activities despite the loss of members through emigration.

A new professional Yiddish Chamber Theater attached to the Jewish Autonomous Region of Birobidzhan began to function in 1978 under the direction of Iuri Sherling. This was the first legitimate Yiddish theater to emerge in Russia since World War II, and its initial presentations in Moscow were attended by overflow audiences.

Since 1972 the official Soviet statistical publication has failed to include a listing of Yiddish books published in the USSR. As far as could be ascertained, the following new books appeared during the period under review: Mendel Lifshitz, *A Zun mit a Regn* (A Sun and a Rain); Shmuel Halkin, *Fir Piesen* (Four Plays); Haim Malamed, *Varem Ash* (Warm Ashes); Note Lurie, *Yam un Himl* (Sun and Sky); and Ben Halpern, *Mein Yiches* (My Origins). Between 1946 and 1978 only 65 books in Yiddish appeared in the Soviet Union.

Despite the scarcity of published Yiddish books, *Sovetish Heimland* reported that there were 100 Yiddish writers in the USSR. A memorial meeting in honor of Leib Kvitko, one of the Yiddish poets killed by Stalin in 1952, was held in Moscow early in 1978. Sophia Saitan, the Yiddish actress, read Kvitko's poetry in the original, and a Russian writer, Lev Ozerov, presented Kvitko's work in Russian translation.

In the summer of 1978 the strongly nationalistic Soviet magazine *Oktiabr* (October) published, in three successive issues, *Tiazhelyi Pesok* (Heavy Sand), a novel by

Anatolii Rybakov. Rybakov, a Jew and an accepted Soviet writer, dealt in a sympathetic way with the fate of several generations of a Jewish family. The publication of the novel in *Oktiabr* reflected a clear attempt by the authorities to counter the persistent anti-Jewish bias in Soviet writing.

Commemoration of the Holocaust

While the authorities continued to discourage memorial meetings devoted to the Holocaust, from time to time small gatherings were organized by local groups. The 50-foot-high monument erected at Babi Iar, scene of the German massacre in Kiev, depicted 11 dead and dying victims falling into the Babi Iar ravine. The inscription, however, made no reference to Jews. It read: "Here, in 1941-43, German fascist occupiers murdered more than 100,000 citizens and prisoners of war."

Personalia

Chaim Dobin, a Soviet writer, son of the well-known Jewish writer and scholar Shimon Dobin, died at the age of 76, in Leningrad. Israel Serebrianyi, a Soviet Yiddish literary critic, who also wrote in Russian, died at the age of 78. Gersh Budker, a leading Soviet nuclear physicist and member of the Soviet Academy of Sciences, died at the age of 69. Aleksandr Luria, a Moscow University psychologist and a foreign member of the National Academy of Sciences of the United States, died at the age of 75.

LEON SHAPIRO

Poland

THERE WERE NO SIGNIFICANT POLITICAL CHANGES in Poland during 1978. Looking to its powerful neighbor on the east, Poland conformed to Moscow's dictates while trying to enlarge the limited independence it was able to muster in national affairs. Because of the economic difficulties facing the country—insufficient food and consumer goods—the government, in an effort to obtain foreign loans, agreed to permit Western banks to monitor its economic policies.

Dissidence was increasing among both the intelligentsia and the workers. The oldest of the dissident groups was the Workers Defense Committees (KOR), which came to the aid of those punished for participation in demonstrations against the high cost of food (see AJYB, 1978, Vol. 78, p. 457). The Committees published an information bulletin that had a substantial circulation. Another dissident group was the Movement for the Defense of Human Rights, which demanded radical changes in official policy. The Movement's views were presented to the public in a monthly, *Opinion*. There was also the so-called "Flying University," through which dissident scholars and writers presented unorthodox views to Polish audiences. While they continued their activities, all dissident groups were aware that the geographic position of Poland made it difficult, if not impossible, to effect any revolutionary change in the country without provoking the immediate intervention of the Soviet Union.

The Catholic Church maintained its strong position not only in the religious area, but also in calling the attention of the government to such matters as the housing crisis, the rising cost of food, and religious education of the young. The election in 1978 of a Polish Pope, the former Cardinal Karol Vojtyla, further complicated the strained relations between church and state. The Communist leadership of Poland hailed the election, but was not happy about the new Pope's expressed desire to visit his native country.

Edvard Gierek continued in his post as secretary of the PPZR (Polish Communist party). Piotr Jaroszewicz was prime minister; the head of state (with limited powers) was Henryk Jablonski. Gierek strictly followed the Soviet line in both the Warsaw Pact and Council for Mutual Economic Assistance, and adhered to the Soviet's rigid anti-Israel policy.

Boleslaw Piasecki died at the age of 64. A pre-World War II fascist and antisemitic propagandist, he created, after the liberation, a fellow-traveling Catholic group, the Pax. A supporter of the Communist regime, he was a member of the 16-man Council of the State and a deputy in the parliament. His writings had been banned by the Vatican (see AJYB, 1965, Vol. 66, p. 432).

JEWISH COMMUNITY

The Jewish population of Poland was approximately 6,000. Some local informants believed that there were, in addition, a considerable number of Jews who had changed their names and been totally integrated into Polish society.

There was a Union of Religious Congregations, but its activities were very limited, due to the total absence of rabbinic personnel and religious education for children. However, it did provide religious burials and *matzot* for Passover. Religious services were conducted by knowledgeable older men. The well-known Warsaw Nozyk Synagogue had a Hebrew sign indicating its affiliation with the Union. For the high holidays, it invited a cantor from Budapest to lead services which were attended by 100 people. There was a *shochet* in Warsaw who also served the city of Lodz. In Krakow only two synagogues were functioning. The Union operated a Jewish communal kitchen in Warsaw that provided kosher meals. Moses Findelsztein was chairman of the Religious Union.

The Jewish Cultural and Social Union, the central secular organization of Polish Jews, had a membership of about 1,500, with 17 local affiliates; Ruta Gutkowska was the executive head. The Union was active in, among other cities, Warsaw, Wroclaw, Walbrzych, Lodz, Krakow, Dzierzionow, Szczecin, and Katowice. Its activities, under strict Communist control, were limited to lectures, theatrical productions, and customary party tasks. Its newspaper, *Folksztyme,* also appeared in a Polish edition, in an effort to reach the younger generation.

The Jewish Historical Institute in Warsaw maintained its research activities in accordance with the official line of the party.

The Yiddish State Theater, under the direction of Szymon Szurmej, continued to stage impressive productions. The theater had its own well-equipped building, seating 1,400, in Warsaw, and performed three times weekly. It also performed in Wroclaw, which was the center for experimentation in the theater. Audiences were provided with Polish translations of the plays. Among the performers were non-Jews who had learned Yiddish.

Yiddish as a language was slowly disappearing. All Yiddish schools had been closed in the 1960's, when the government conducted its campaign against "Zionism."

LEON SHAPIRO

Rumania

Rumania, one of the largest countries of the "socialist bloc," and with vulnerable borders, broke away several years ago from the imposed tutelage of Moscow and maintained its own foreign policy, including correct relations with China. Unlike other Communist countries, it refused to condemn the peace negotiations between Israel and Egypt. Nicolae Ceausescu, head of the Party and president of Rumania, was committed to a totally independent "road to socialism." In 1978 he objected to Soviet demands for an increased military budget, and refused to accept overall Soviet command of the armies of the seven countries of the Warsaw Pact, of which Rumania remained a member. This courageous act of resistance to Soviet supremacy was followed by Rumania's condemnation of the Soviet-supported Vietnamese intervention in Cambodia. While the Ceausescu regime maintained absolute internal control over the population, the independent stance taken by Ceausescu with respect to Moscow could not but affect the climate in the country. Foreign films were permitted, and books by Western writers were readily available.

The Ceausescu regime maintained foreign trade with the Soviet Union and the West. Joint corporations with Western partners were created. High U.S. officials visited Rumania at the end of 1978 to confer on issues of interest to both countries. At the same time, Rumania remained a part of the Council for Mutual Economic Assistance, which largely determined the economic relationships among the countries within the Soviet sphere.

JEWISH COMMUNITY

The Jewish population of Rumania was estimated to be about 45,000, including Jews who were not identified with either the religious or secular sector of the community. This figure, which is somewhat lower than previous estimates, might reflect the continued flow of Jewish emigration. The matter of Jewish emigration was important to the Rumanian government because its position as a most-favored nation in terms of trade with the United States depended on the status of human rights and the free flow of emigration. While there were reports that of late it had become difficult to obtain exit visas, Jewish circles were hopeful that there would be no drastic change of policy.

Although Rumanian Jews enjoyed all religious and social rights accorded other national minorities, Jewish life, because of the general restrictions imposed by the regime, continued to decline both in the religious and secular sectors.

250

Jewish activities were coordinated by the Federation of Jewish Communities, an officially-recognized agency covering some 68 local communities and over 130 synagogues. Some of the synagogues did not have a daily *minyan,* but all conducted Sabbath and holiday services. Bucharest, the capital city, had a *mikva.* More than 20 talmud torahs provided Jewish instruction to the young, and special classes in Jewish studies and Hebrew language were functioning in many cities. The Federation's semi-monthly *Revista Culturui Mosaic,* issued in Yiddish, Hebrew, and Rumanian, with a circulation of about 10,000 and covering matters of general Jewish interest, rabbinic material, and Hebrew and Yiddish literature, was the only such periodical in Eastern Europe. The Federation also published a Jewish calendar *(luah)* containing information on Jewish life. It maintained a library and a museum. In 1978, in connection with commemoration of the Holocaust, a special exhibit was presented at the museum. The museum also housed a comprehensive exhibit on the history of Rumanian Jewry, prepared with the help of Prof. Alexander Visnu of the University of Bucharest.

The Federation financed its own activities, including supervision of *kashrut,* but received state funds, as did other religious bodies, for the salaries of rabbinic and administrative personnel. The Memorial Foundation for Jewish Culture financed some of the cultural activities of the Federation.

Chief Rabbi Moses Rosen continued as president of the Federation and was, in fact, the organizer and promoter of all Jewish religious and cultural activities. He was also a member of the Rumanian parliament, which gave him added status.

In the summer of 1978 the Federation celebrated the 30th anniversary of Rabbi Rosen's service as chief rabbi. Among the guests attending the ceremonies were Shlomo Goren, chief rabbi of Israel; Joseph Burg, Israeli minister of the interior; Jacob Kaplan, chief rabbi of France; Gerhard Rigner of the World Jewish Congress; Rabbi Abraham Shneour of New York; and Laszlo Shalga, the Orthodox chief rabbi of Hungary. The celebration was a memorable Jewish event, particularly important in a country within the Soviet sphere of influence.

With the approval of the authorities, the Federation, in the person of Rabbi Rosen, maintained close contact with Jewish organizations abroad, including the World Jewish Congress, JDC, B'nai B'rith, the Memorial Foundation for Jewish Culture, and organizations in Israel.

The secular Jewish sector outside the Federation included a highly-regarded, state-supported Yiddish theater with its own 300-seat building. The state also supported the publication of Yiddish books. Among recent titles were Chaim Goldenstein's *Zvei Novelen* (Two Novels), *Bucharester Shriftn* (Bucharest Writings), and Israel Bercovici's *Hundert Yor Yiddisher Theater in Rumanie, 1876–1976* (A Hundred Years of Yiddish Theater in Rumania).

The Federation conducted a comprehensive welfare program in Bucharest, where the majority of the Jewish population resided, as well as in the provincial cities. It operated 11 kosher restaurants in Bucharest, Arad, Iassy, Dorohoi, Bacau, Galatzi, Cluj-Napoca, Oradei, Timosara, Botosani, and Brazov. About 2,000 meals were served daily, most of them provided free of charge to persons in need. Kosher meals were delivered to the homes of sick people and invalids. During Passover, the Federation conducted *sedorim* and distributed *matzot* in Bucharest and in the provincial cities. Public celebrations were arranged during Purim and Hanukkah. The aged and sick received free medical care through the Federation's clinics. There were nine old-age homes and hostels, and cash grants were made to individuals in need and unable to work. The social welfare activities were subvented by JDC, with some expenses covered by the Federation from its own funds.

In the course of its activities, the Federation expressed full support for the policies enunciated by President Ceausescu.

LEON SHAPIRO

Israel

A NEW ERA IN ISRAEL–ARAB RELATIONS opened on March 26, 1979 with the signing of a peace treaty with Egypt, the first to be concluded between Israel and an Arab state. In the negotiations, which had taken place with many ups and downs throughout 1978 and the first quarter of 1979, the United States played an active role, with President Jimmy Carter making dramatic personal interventions at Camp David in September 1978 and in Cairo and Jerusalem in March 1979.

Prime Minister Menachem Begin met with fierce criticism from the Gush Emunim religious activist group and some of his own followers, but the Labor and left-wing opposition backed the treaty, while criticizing Begin's conduct of the negotiations and his autonomy scheme for Judea and Samaria (the "West Bank") and the Gaza Strip.

Palestinian terrorist activities continued throughout 1978, culminating in the hijacking of a bus near Tel Aviv in mid-March, which left 36 people dead and 76 wounded. Immediately afterward, Israel mounted a large-scale military operation to clear southern Lebanon of terrorists, and a United Nations force was sent in to keep order.

The Begin government ran into many difficulties on the domestic front: there was discord between ministers; inflation reached an almost record level; and there was considerable labor trouble, with the Histadrut adopting a growingly hostile attitude toward Finance Minister Simcha Ehrlich's policies.

The Peace Negotiations

According to unconfirmed press reports, the groundwork for Egyptian President Sadat's historic visit to Jerusalem in November 1977 (see AJYB 1979, Vol. 79, pp. 271–2) had been laid by Prime Minister Begin during his visit to Rumania in August. At that time, Begin held talks with President Ceausescu, who met with Sadat shortly thereafter. Foreign Minister Moshe Dayan was reported to have had a secret meeting with Egyptian Deputy Prime Minister Muhammed Hassan al-Tohami on September 17 in Morocco, during an ostensible stopover in Paris on his way to the United States, and was said to have offered to hand back the whole of Sinai to Egyptian rule.

The atmosphere after the meeting between President Sadat and Prime Minister Begin at Ismailia was not promising. Virulent attacks on Begin appeared in the

Egyptian press. Mustafa Amin, a well-known journalist, denounced Begin in the Cairo weekly *Akhbar al-Yom* as a "Shylock" who was determined to get his pound of flesh from the Egyptians.

After a meeting at Aswan on January 4, President Carter and President Sadat issued a joint statement of principles, which set a pattern of American–Egyptian agreement on the main lines of a peace settlement. It read:

> First, true peace must be based on normal relations among the parties to the peace. Peace means more than just an end to belligerency. Second, there must be withdrawal by Israel from territories occupied in 1967 and agreement on secure and recognized borders for all parties in the context of normal and peaceful relations in accordance with United Nations Resolutions 242 and 338. And third, there must be a resolution of the Palestinian problem in all its aspects. This must recognize the legitimate rights of the Palestinian people and enable the Palestinians to participate in the determination of their future.

Prime Minister Begin told a Herut party meeting on January 8 that the Israel Defense Forces would not evacuate Judea, Samaria and the Gaza Strip under his autonomy plan, and Israel would not recognize Jordanian sovereignty over the areas. The offer to give back the entire Sinai Peninsula might be rescinded if Egypt did not permit the Israeli settlements in the Rafa area to remain there, he declared. He told visiting U.S. congressmen on the 15th that he would rather resign than give up the settlements. Sadat, on the other hand, complained in an interview with the Jerusalem *Post* on January 12 that "the new spirit" engendered by his peace initiative had not affected Israeli policy-making. "It lives with me only," he declared. To a Cairo weekly he said, "Begin gave me nothing. It was I that gave him everything. I gave him security and legitimacy, and I got nothing in return."

Local Arab leaders in Judea, Samaria, and the Gaza Strip rejected the Israeli plan for limited self-rule. Mayor Elias Freij of Bethlehem declared: "We cannot accept the Israeli military presence"; Mayor Fahd Kawasmi of Hebron insisted on an independent Palestinian state; Mayor Karim Khalaf of Ramallah proclaimed allegiance to the Palestine Liberation Organization as the only representative of the Palestinians.

The two committees agreed upon at Ismailiya met, but their deliberations were broken off a few days after they started. The Israeli delegation to the Military Committee, headed by Defense Minister Ezer Weizman and Chief of Staff Mordecai Gur, arrived in Cairo on January 11 and was reported to be making good progress after two days' talk with the Egyptians, who were led by Defense Minister Mohammed Abd al-Ghani Gamasy. The political committee assembled in Jerusalem on the 17th under the chairmanship of Foreign Minister Moshe Dayan, the American delegation being headed by Secretary of State Cyrus Vance and the Egyptian delegation by Foreign Minister Mohammed Ibrahim Kamel. At the political committee meeting on January 18, the American delegation submitted a draft statement of principles based on the Carter–Sadat statement of January 4. The committee started to discuss the draft and was reported to be making good progress, when, the next day, the Egyptian delegation was recalled by President Sadat. Among the reasons given by commentators for the breakdown in the negotiations were the establishment in the southern Gaza Strip and the Rafa-el-Arish area of four new settlements and 20 "footholds" consisting of fiberglass houses and watertanks, and a sharp exchange between Begin and Kamel at a dinner for the Egyptian delegation given in Jerusalem on January 17.

On January 18 the Israeli cabinet declared that the suspension of the negotiations "proved once more that the Egyptian government was under the illusion that Israel would surrender to unacceptable demands," including withdrawal from Sinai, Golan, Judea, Samaria, and Gaza, the transfer of the Old City of Jerusalem to "foreign rule," and the establishment of a Palestinian state. The statement accused the Egyptian government of "astonishing intransigence," but declared that Israel was willing to renew the negotiations if the Egyptians so decided. Begin told a French UJA mission on January 19 that, despite the suspension of negotiations, "peace is inevitable." He reiterated, however, that no government could dismantle the Jewish settlements in northern Sinai. On January 22 the cabinet announced that, in view of the campaign of vilification in the Egyptian press, the return of the civilian members of the Israeli delegation to the military committee in Cairo would be deferred. The military representatives, headed by Major General Abraham Tamir, remained in Egypt. At the end of January, Defense Minister Ezer Weizman returned to Cairo for a few days to continue the talks, which were adjourned pending President Sadat's discussions with President Carter in the U.S. on February 9.

During the next nine months, there were ups and downs in the negotiations, which continued, on various levels and in various centers, between Egypt and Israel and between the two countries and the United States. U.S. Assistant Secretary of State Alfred Atherton shuttled back and forth between Jerusalem and Cairo in January and February in an attempt to obtain agreement on a joint statement of principles as a basis for the renewal of the talks.

The cabinet officially protested on February 12 against Secretary of State Vance's statement two days before that Israel's Sinai settlements "should not exist." This, it was said, was "in complete contradiction" to President Carter's sympathetic reaction to the Israeli peace plan in December. On February 21 the cabinet rejected Vance's proposal that "there should be a homeland for the Palestinians" (linked to Jordan) on the grounds that it would inevitably lead to the establishment of a "Palestinian state ruled by the terrorist organizations." Serious disquiet was expressed by Israeli spokesmen about a U.S. proposal to link arms supplies to Israel with the supply of war planes and other military equipment to Egypt and Saudi Arabia. In particular, the proposed sale of F-15 fighters to Saudi Arabia, it was argued, would open a new front and force Israel to reconsider its views with respect to defensible borders. Other points of friction between the U.S. and Israel were the Israeli claim that Resolution 242 (of 1967) did not necessarily imply withdrawal from the West Bank, and American calls for the suspension of further Israeli settlement in the West Bank.

On March 5 Defense Minister Weizman went to the U.S. for talks to prepare for a visit by Prime Minister Begin. The differences between Israel and the United States came to a head during Begin's talks in Washington on March 21–22, which Begin described as "the most difficult in my life." President Carter spelled out six points of disagreement between America and Israel, declaring that Israel must reconsider its position if there was to be any hope of reviving the peace negotiations. While Foreign Minister Dayan said that the crisis in Israel–American relations was not the worst on record, Weizman called for the establishment of a "national peace government" to include Labor and other parties. The Labor party demanded Begin's resignation because of his "failure" in Washington. Begin told the Knesset on March 29 that he believed an agreement could be reached on a joint declaration of principles, provided Egypt withdrew demands for total withdrawal to the 1967 borders and the establishment of a Palestinian state. Labor leader Shimon Peres condemned the government for establishing new settlements during the negotiations and for misinterpreting Resolution 242. He declared that a majority in the Knesset favored the Labor Alignment's policy of territorial compromise. The House endorsed Begin's statement by a majority of 64 to 32, with nine abstentions, including seven members of the Democratic Movement for Change (DMC). Begin sent a letter to President Sadat urging him to present an Egyptian peace plan which could be discussed in renewed direct negotiations.

Large-scale demonstrations were held by the Peace Now Movement (later renamed the Peace Movement), founded by a group of young army reserve officers, whose main slogan was "Better Peace than a Greater Israel." Counter-demonstrations in favor of government policy were held by the Movement for a Secure Peace. Abie Nathan, who had run a one-man peace movement for several years, held a 45-day hunger strike for peace, which he ended only after an appeal by Begin and other ministers, backed by the Knesset in an all-party resolution. In mid-April the government adopted a more positive approach to Resolution 242, regarding it as a basis for negotiations with all neighboring Arab states, including Jordan, and promising that any Arab counter-proposals to Israel's autonomy scheme would be discussed on their merits.

A crucial question was whether the autonomy regime was to be regarded as permanent or transitional, and the United States asked Israel to agree that the final status of the West Bank and Gaza would be determined at the end of the five-year period. After prolonged discussions, the cabinet resolved on June 18 that five years after the autonomy had come into force upon the establishment of peace, "the nature of the future relations between the parties will be discussed and agreed upon, if any of the parties should so demand." The DMC ministers and Ezer Weizman, as well as the Labor opposition, regarded the reply as inadequate. Some of the DMC leaders called for the party to leave the coalition, and Weizman, reportedly, decided to wash his hands of the peace negotiations and concentrate on the work of his ministry. Foreign Minister Dayan told the Knesset on June 19 that the government regarded the proposal for administrative autonomy as the permanent framework for the future of Judea, Samaria, and Gaza. The Knesset approved the government's policy by 69 votes to 37, with 10 abstentions, including most of the DMC members; Weizman absented himself from the vote. On June 25 the cabinet categorically rejected a reported Egyptian proposal that Judea and Samaria be handed over to Jordan and Gaza to Egypt as a precondition for negotiations.

On July 9 President Carter expressed his disappointment at Israel's reply to American queries and voiced his anxiety at the stalemate in the negotiations. During a visit to Israel on June 30–July 3, U.S. Vice-President Mondale declared that peace would be achieved only by fulfilling the "implicit bargain" of Resolution 242—peace in exchange for Israeli withdrawal on all fronts to secure boundaries negotiated between the parties. At the same time, he promised continuing economic and military aid to Israel. Such aid, he added, would not be used as a form of pressure.

After a visit by Mondale to Cairo, the Egyptians issued a six-point plan providing that Israel should withdraw its forces, military government, and settlements from the West Bank, including Jerusalem and the Gaza Strip, at the outset of the transitional period, and that the administration of the two areas should be supervised by Jordan and Egypt, respectively, in cooperation with Palestinian representatives. At the end of the five-year transitional period, according to the plan, "the Palestinian people will be able to determine their own future." On July 9 the cabinet turned down the Egyptian proposals, but agreed to send Foreign Minister Dayan to London for talks with Egyptian Foreign Minister Kamel and Secretary of State Vance.

On the same day Labor party chairman Shimon Peres met with President Sadat in Vienna, and the two men unofficially endorsed a draft statement issued on behalf of the Socialist International by its chairman, Willy Brandt, and Austrian Chancellor Bruno Kreisky. The statement backed the Aswan formula of January 4, recognizing the right of the Palestinians "to participate in the determination of their own future," but called for negotiations to determine the exact location of the peace boundaries, and approved "Israeli security measures," thus implicitly endorsing the principle of border modifications and the idea of an Israeli military presence in the West Bank after peace. Peres stressed that he was not negotiating on behalf of Israel.

On June 13 Defense Minister Weizman, in response to a personal invitation, went to Salzburg for talks with Sadat. He told the cabinet on the 16th that Sadat had considerably softened the proposals made in his six-point plan, and sought, in return, a "territorial gesture" (understood to mean the return of El-Arish and Mt. Sinai) from Israel before the reopening of peace negotiations. The cabinet announced, however, that "the government and its authorized representatives" had "the exclusive authority to negotiate with Egypt." Sadat said, in an interview published the same day, that he could speak "the same language" with Weizman and Peres, but not with Begin. "I think I have really cleared my conscience when I made these talks with Mr. Peres . . . and Mr. Weizman," he declared.

There were angry exchanges in the Knesset on the 19th between Begin and the Labor opposition over Peres' meeting with Sadat. Begin revealed that Peres had also met with King Hassan of Morocco, and that he himself had refused to agree to a meeting between the Labor leader and King Hussein of Jordan. The Labor party expressed "profound shock" over the prime minister's "irresponsible and reckless statement," while the cabinet, on the 23rd, condemned "personal attacks by Labor party leaders" on the prime minister. Begin declared that he viewed his Labor party critics with "cold contempt."

After the talks between the three foreign ministers, held at Leeds Castle, near London, on July 17–20, Dayan reported that Kamel had rejected any possibility of territorial compromise and reaffirmed the Egyptian hard line. Dayan stated, however, that he was convinced that Egypt sincerely wanted peace. On July 23 the cabinet rejected the proposal to hand over El-Arish and Mount Sinai. "You don't get something for nothing," Begin declared. "Not a single grain of desert sand" would be handed over without something in exchange. Nevertheless, Begin sent Sadat a message proposing that the two governments appoint representatives to negotiate gestures on a reciprocal basis. Dayan announced in the Knesset on the 24th that Israel would be prepared to discuss sovereignty over Judea, Samaria, and Gaza after the end of the five-year transitional period and would consider territorial compromise if this was proposed by the Arabs.

The negotiations had reached a critical phase. The Egyptians told the remaining members of the Israeli military delegation to leave Cairo. President Sadat rejected Begin's call for mutual concessions, describing Israel as a thief demanding payment for stolen goods, and declared that there would be no further talks unless Israel agreed to give up every inch of the "occupied land." Begin reacted calmly to Sadat's attacks and suggested the possibility of a "permanent partial settlement" if full-scale peace was impracticable at the moment.

After a further round of talks by U.S. special envoy Alfred Atherton, the deadlock was broken by Secretary of State Vance, who met Israeli leaders in Jerusalem on August 5–7 and announced on the eighth, after a meeting with President Sadat in Alexandria, that the two leaders had agreed to attend a tripartite summit conference at Camp David. Begin was accompanied to Camp David by Foreign Minister Moshe Dayan, Defense Minister Ezer Weizman, and legal advisers. The discussions were held under conditions of complete secrecy between September 5 and 16. President Carter, assisted by Vance, played an active part in the negotiations. Complete agreement was announced by the three leaders in Washington, and Carter said the results exceeded all expectations. Two documents were signed: "A Framework for Peace in the Middle East" and "A Framework for the Conclusion of a Peace Treaty Between Israel and Egypt." Carter signed the documents as a "witness" on behalf of the United States.

In "A Framework for Peace in the Middle East" the parties declared that they were "determined to reach a just, comprehensive, and durable settlement of the Middle East conflict through the conclusion of peace treaties based on Security Council Resolutions 242 and 338 in all their parts." The framework was intended "to constitute a basis for peace not only between Egypt and Israel but also between Israel and each of its neighbors." Egypt, Israel, Jordan and "the representatives of the Palestinians" were to negotiate a "resolution of the Palestinian problem in all its aspects." The document went on: "In order to ensure a peaceful and orderly transfer of authority, and taking into account the security concerns of all parties, there should be transitional arrangements for the West Bank and Gaza for a period not exceeding five years. In order to provide full autonomy to the inhabitants . . . the Israeli military government and its civilian administration will be withdrawn as soon as a self-governing authority has been freely elected by the inhabitants of these areas to replace the existing military government." Jordan was invited to join the negotiations, as were Palestinians from the West Bank and Gaza or "other Palestinians as mutually agreed." There was to be "a strong local police force," and Israeli and Jordanian forces were to organize joint patrols and control posts.

The five-year transitional period was to begin after the inauguration of the "self-governing authority (administrative council)." Not later than the third year after its inception, negotiations were to take place between Egypt, Jordan, Israel, and the elected representatives of the inhabitants "to determine the final status of the West Bank and Gaza." At the same time, representatives of Israel and Jordan, together with representatives of the inhabitants, were to negotiate a peace treaty between Israel and Jordan. The agreed solution had to take account of the "legitimate rights of the Palestinian people and their just requirements." The Palestinians were to "participate in the determination of their own future" through negotiations and the submission of an agreement to "a vote by the elected representatives of the inhabitants of the West Bank and Gaza."

In "A Framework for the Conclusion of a Peace Treaty Between Israel and Egypt" the two nations set a target date of three months for reaching a final agreement, and invited "the other parties to the conflict to conclude similar peace treaties with a view to achieving a comprehensive peace in the area." The framework called for the "full exercise of Egyptian sovereignty" in the whole of Sinai, and the withdrawal of Israeli armed forces; the right of free passage by Israeli ships through the Gulf of Suez and the Suez Canal; the stationing of not more than one Egyptian division within an area lying approximately 50 km. east of the Gulf of Suez and the Suez Canal; the presence of only UN forces and civil police within an area 20–40 km. west of the international border; the limiting of Israeli forces in an area 3 km. east of the international border (i.e., inside Israeli territory); and the stationing of UN forces which could not be removed without approval by the Security Council, including all five permanent members, in the Sharm el-Sheikh area. Within nine months of the signing of the peace treaty, Israeli forces were to withdraw east of the line from El-Arish to Ras Mohammed. After this interim withdrawal, full normal relations were to be established between Egypt and Israel.

In a letter accompanying the agreement, President Sadat wrote that "all Israeli settlers must be withdrawn from Sinai, failing which the 'framework' shall be void and invalid." Prime Minister Begin undertook to submit this demand to a free vote of the Knesset. In another letter, President Sadat declared that "Arab Jerusalem is an integral part of the West Bank" and should be "under Arab sovereignty." Begin noted, in a letter to President Carter, that the government of Israel had decreed in July 1967 that "Jerusalem is one city indivisible, the capital of the State of Israel." Carter, in a letter to Sadat, reaffirmed the previous U.S. position, which was close to Egypt's.

There was widespread uneasiness in Israel about the proposal to remove the Sinai settlements. The cabinet approved the Camp David agreement by an 11–2 vote. (Yigal Hurvitz and Eliezer Shostak of La'am opposed the treaty, while Hayim Landau of Herut abstained; Yitzhak Modai (Liberal) and the three NRP ministers did not take part in the vote.) The agreements were presented to the Knesset on September 27 as a package, in spite of some demands for a separate vote on the removal of the settlements. Most parties allowed their members to follow their consciences in voting. Prime Minister Begin declared that peace negotiations would not even begin unless the Knesset authorized the government to withdraw the Israeli settlers from Sinai. Labor leader Peres criticized the government's conduct of the negotiations, especially the decision to yield the whole of Sinai at the beginning of the talks, the autonomy plan, and the removal of the settlements. He stated, however, that Labor as a responsible opposition group, would support the agreements. In his summing up, Begin said that, in effect, over 90 per cent of the peace treaty with Egypt had already been agreed upon. A Labor motion calling on the government to make another attempt to avert the withdrawal of the settlements was rejected, and the agreements were approved by 84 votes, with 19 against (4 Herut, 3 La'am, 3 NRP, 4 Labor, 4 Communists, and 1 Poalei Agudat Israel) and 17 abstentions (5 Herut, 4 La'am, 4 NRP, 2 Labor, and 2 others). Hurvitz resigned from the cabinet after the vote. Also prominent among the coalition supporters who openly opposed the Camp David agreements were Moshe Arens, chairman of the Knesset Defense and Foreign Affairs Committee, Geula Cohen of Herut, Moshe Shamir of La'am, and Rabbi Hayim Druckman of the NRP and Gush Emunim.

The talks opened in Washington on October 12, with Secretary Vance leading the American delegation, Foreign Minister Dayan and Defense Minister Weizman representing Israel, and Defense Minister Kamal Hassan Ali and acting Foreign Minister Butrus Ghali representing Egypt. The Israeli delegation was kept on a tight rein and had to report back frequently to the Cabinet Defense Committee. From time to time, knotty points were referred to the full cabinet. President Carter intervened actively in the negotiations when difficulties arose.

Considerable dissatisfaction was expressed in Israel over statements made by U.S. Assistant Secretary of State Harold Saunders interpreting the Camp David agreements, in visits to several Arab states and particularly in his talks with King Hussein and West Bank leaders. Prime Minister Begin told Saunders in Jerusalem on October 20 that the U.S. was apparently taking sides, thus prejudicing future negotiations and undermining its own role as an honest broker. Begin also wrote to President Carter about the matter.

Among the points of disagreement during the Washington negotiations were the question of continued Israeli settlement in the West Bank during the talks; Egyptian demands for a target date for the implementation of the autonomy plan and a definite linkage between the plan and the treaty with Egypt; the Israeli demand that the treaty with Egypt have precedence over all other commitments, especially Egypt's mutual defense treaties with other Arab countries; the extent to which the treaty with Egypt would be a precedent for agreements with other Arab countries; the date for the exchange of ambassadors; the continued supply of oil to Israel from the Alma wells in western Sinai after their transfer to Egypt; and the American commitment to help Israel bear the heavy financial and economic burdens involved in the redeployment of its forces in the Negev and the building of new military airfields to replace those in Sinai.

On November 11 agreement was reached between the negotiating teams on the text of a treaty, but when Dayan and Weizman reported back, the Israeli cabinet objected to some of the wording, and the Egyptians came up with objections on their side. On the 21st the Israeli government withdrew its reservations and announced its readiness to sign the treaty as agreed at Blair House. The Israelis now hoped that the treaty could be signed before December 17, the end of the three-month period since Camp David. Begin proposed that the signing take place at Oslo on December 10, when he and President Sadat were due to receive the Nobel Peace Prize. The Egyptians insisted, however, on side-letters to modify the clauses referring to the priority of the treaty obligations over other commitments, the question of linkage, and a number of additional points. Sadat sent a representative to Oslo to receive the prize in his name, while Secretary of State Vance went to Cairo to discuss the Egyptian demands.

A critical situation arose in U.S.-Israel relations when Vance brought the Egyptian proposals to Jerusalem and strongly urged the government to accept them. The cabinet declared that these were "new demands . . . inconsistent with the Camp David framework or . . . not included in it," and it rejected them as "unacceptable." Anger was expressed at American statements blaming Israel for the deadlock. The Jerusalem *Post* (December 15) accused the U.S. of "partisanship." "Throughout the negotiations," the paper said, "Sadat has always upped the ante. Agreement at one stage has inevitably led to new conditions at the next. And the U.S. has also consistently then placed itself with Sadat."

During the next three months, further attempts were made to re-start the negotiations. Dayan met Egyptian Prime Minister Mustapha Khalil and Secretary Vance in Brussels on December 23, and the cabinet expressed willingness to continue the talks. Alfred Atherton shuttled back and forth between Cairo and Jerusalem in the second half of January 1978 in an unsuccessful attempt to disentangle the legal problems involved in the disputed clauses. U.S. Secretary of Defense Harold Brown visited Israel, Egypt, Saudi Arabia, and Jordan in mid-February to discuss Israel's defense needs and the strategic situation in the area, particularly in view of the fall of the Shah of Iran. Brown said he was deeply impressed by his visit and Israel's "great value to the U.S. as a strong and stable democratic country." Israeli officials said they were "extremely satisfied" with Brown's response to Israel's long-term arms requests.

Brown's visit was followed by a second Camp David conference, at which Israel was represented by Foreign Minister Dayan and Egypt by Premier and Foreign Minister Mustapha Khalil. On February 25, after five days of discussion, President Carter invited Prime Minister Begin to come to Washington for talks with Khalil and himself. The cabinet decided, however, with Dayan and Weizman dissenting, to decline the invitation because the Camp David talks had produced "no progress." Indeed, it was noted that Khalil had presented new proposals which "in fact nullify the idea of a peace treaty" and had rejected all Israeli counterproposals. Begin also objected to meeting with Khalil instead of Sadat, who was head of government as well as head of state, and who alone had the authority to make important decisions. At the same time, the cabinet statement added: "The prime minister is prepared at any time convenient to President Carter to leave for the U.S. to meet the president." The same evening, Carter telephoned Begin and invited him to come to Washington. The talks, from March 1–4, were difficult, but on the last evening Carter presented important new proposals, which the cabinet accepted by nine votes to three, with four abstentions.

On March 9 Carter set out on a decisive visit to Cairo and Jerusalem, which at last led to agreement on the terms of the treaty. After a day in Cairo, the president arrived in Israel accompanied by Secretary Vance, National Security Adviser Zbigniew Brzezinski and Defense Secretary Harold Brown. He addressed the cabinet Defense Committee, the full cabinet, the Knesset, and the Knesset Defense and Foreign Affairs Committee. An all-night meeting of the cabinet did not produce agreement, but on the 13th, at a meeting with Begin, the differences were narrowed down, and on the same day, after a meeting with President Sadat, Carter was able to announce that the final major points at issue had been settled. The Israeli cabinet approved the compromise on the 14th and formally confirmed the text of the whole treaty, with its annexes, on the 19th. The Knesset approved the treaty on the 22nd by 95 votes to 18, with 2 abstentions and 3 not participating in the vote, after 108 of the 120 members had spoken in the two-day debate. Dayan, Weizman, and Energy Minister Yitzhak Moda went to Washington to settle the matters of American aid, a U.S.-Israel memorandum of agreement providing United States backing for the treaty and Israeli oil supplies from the Sinai wells.

The treaty was signed in Washington on March 26 by Carter, Sadat, and Begin. It consisted of nine articles, with a military annex, an annex on relations between the parties, agreed minutes interpreting key articles of the treaty, and an exchange of letters between the three signatories. Among the main provisions dealing with controversial issues were an interpretation of Article VI stipulating the binding character of the obligations under the treaty; the completion of Israeli withdrawal from Sinai within three years; the evacuation of El-Arish, together with an area linking it with Egypt, within two months, and the evacuation of the rest of western Sinai, up to the El-Arish–Ras-Muhammad line, in specified stages, within nine months; the exchange of ambassadors one month after the conclusion of this interim withdrawal; security arrangements to be reviewed at the request of either party, but altered only by agreement; consultation by the United States with the parties in the event of an actual or threatened violation of the treaty; the beginning of negotiations on the autonomy plan within a month, with the goal of completing them within one year. In the U.S.-Israel memorandum of agreement, the United States undertook to support "proper actions taken by Israel" in response to demonstrated violations of the treaty; to oppose and, if necessary, vote against (i.e., veto) any action in the UN adversely affecting the treaty; and, subject to congressional authorization, to be responsive to Israel's military and economic requirements.

Lebanon

Israel kept a close watch over developments in Lebanon during the year, helping the Christian militias in the south to strengthen their hold on the area and resist the Palestinian terrorists.

On March 14, three days after the terrorist outrage north of Tel Aviv (see below), Israeli forces advanced into southern Lebanon and landed on the country's Mediterranean coast to attack Palestinian terrorist bases. The Israeli forces had the cooperation of the Christian militias and some of the Shi'ite Muslim villagers. By the 19th, they were in control of almost the entire area between the border and the Litani River. Israel sent in supplies, opened clinics for the population, and helped to repair war damage to encourage the villagers to return. Eighteen Israeli soldiers were killed in the operation, which was known as "Operation Litani." Israeli forces were withdrawn by stages after a United Nations Interim Force in Lebanon (UNIFIL) was sent into the area; the withdrawal was completed by mid-June. Concern was repeatedly expressed about the infiltration of Palestinian irregulars into the areas held by UNIFIL.

On July 2 the cabinet expressed deep concern over massive Syrian bombardment of Christian areas in Lebanon. Syria was repeatedly warned to end what Major General Shlomo Gazit, chief of Military Intelligence, called the systematic destruction of the Christian community in Lebanon. Israel demanded that any Lebanese forces sent into southern Lebanon include no Syrian advisers or officers, and recognize the leadership of Major Sa'ad Haddad and Major Sami Shidiak, the commanders of the Christian militias. No Lebanese troops were sent south during the year.

On October 5, after the interception of a Palestinian terrorist bomb ship in the Gulf of Eilat (see below) and the dispatch by the Syrians of two brigades of the Palestinian Liberation Army into the Beirut area, Israeli missile boats shelled PLO and Syrian targets west of Beirut.

Terrorism

Palestinian terrorist attacks against the civilian population continued throughout the year. The public was called upon to notify the police immediately of any suspicious objects, and a number of explosive charges were discovered and dismantled. Several people, however, were killed and injured in markets, buses, and other public places. Katyusha rockets were fired by Palestinians in south Lebanon at towns and villages in the north of Israel.

Thirty-six people were killed and 76 injured on March 11 in one of the worst terrorist outrages on record. Eleven terrorists landed in two rubber boats on the coast south of Haifa. As they made their way inland, they killed six people whom they encountered and commandeered a car. One group drove south in the car, fired on a bus on its way north, boarded it, and forced its driver to turn around toward Tel Aviv. Meanwhile, the other group attacked and halted a second north-bound bus and forced it, too, to turn around. The passengers from the first bus were herded into the second, which now held about 70 people, most of them women and children, and the terrorists began firing at passing vehicles. Determined to prevent the bus from entering Tel Aviv, the police blocked the road near the Country Club just north of the city and succeeded in halting the vehicle. A fierce battle took place between the police and terrorists, and the bus caught fire, apparently from a terrorist grenade or bazooka shell. A curfew—the first since 1968—was imposed over the populous area between north Tel Aviv and Natanya, while thousands of troops, police, and civil guards searched for terrorists thought to be still at large. The curfew was called off the following evening, when it became clear that none had escaped. Nine terrorists involved in the raid were killed and two captured.

A disaster was averted when a bomb-laden freighter, manned by seven al-Fatah terrorists, was sunk by an Israel navy patrol boat off the coast of Sinai, about 100km. south of Eilat, on September 30. The ship, which had been fitted with a rocket launcher in a Syrian port and then loaded with ammunition and 5–6 tons of explosives in Lebanon, had been under surveillance for some time. Flying a Cypriot flag, the ship sailed through the Suez Canal and the Gulf of Suez to the place where it was sunk. The terrorists had intended to fire 42 rockets simultaneously at the port of Eilat and then ram the boat onto the packed beach.

Population and Immigration

The population at the beginning of 1979 stood at 3,730,000: 3,135,000 Jews and 595,000 (16 per cent) non-Jews. The Jewish population increased by 58,000 (1.9 per cent) during the year: 46,000 due to natural increase and 12,000 to the excess of immigrants *(olim)* over emigrants *(yordim)*. The number of non-Jews grew by 3.3 per cent.

About 26,000 persons—16,400 *olim* and 9,800 potential *olim*—came to settle in Israel during the year (28 per cent more than in 1977). Some 11,700 of the newcomers came from the Soviet Union and about 3,000 from the United States (2,600 of the latter, potential *olim*)—41 per cent and 51 per cent more than in the previous year, respectively. Two thousand came from Argentina, somewhat fewer than in 1977. The upward trend continued in the early months of 1979, owing mainly to increased departures from the Soviet Union and Iran.

Election of President

Yitzhak Navon, who had been an unsuccessful candidate for the Labor nomination to the presidency in 1973, became Israel's fifth president on May 29, in succession to Professor Ephraim Katzir. He was the first Sephardi and the first sabra to hold the post.

When Katzir announced, toward the end of 1977, that he did not intend to stand for a second term, a Navon-for-President committee was launched. Another name mentioned was that of Dr. Eliezer Rimalt, former leader of the Liberal party, but it was reported that Prime Minister Begin wanted to ensure the election of a Sephardi. In March he announced the candidacy of Dr. Yitzhak Chavet, an Egyptian-born research scientist, but there was considerable opposition to this nomination, even among government supporters, on the grounds that Chavet was almost unknown in public life, and he withdrew from the contest toward the end of the month. After the National Religious party decided to support Navon, Rimalt also withdrew, and Navon was elected on April 19, as the only candidate, by 86 votes, with 23 abstentions.

Yitzhak Navon, born in 1921, scion of a Sephardi family which settled in Jerusalem in the 17th century, started his career as a teacher, and from 1944-48 was active in the Arab department of the Haganah. From 1949 to 1952 he served in the Foreign Ministry, and from 1952 to 1963 was head of Prime Minister David Ben-Gurion's office. After two years as director of the Cultural Division of the Ministry of Education and Culture, he was elected to the Knesset in 1965 as a member of the Rafi list, officiating as deputy speaker, chairman of the Defense and Foreign Affairs Committee, and chairman of the Zionist General Council. He wrote two popular musical shows based on Sephardi folk lore.

Political Affairs

Unrest in the Herut wing of the Likud over Prime Minister Begin's peace proposals was reflected in a January 9 vote on the nomination to the post of minister-without-portfolio. Haim Landau, Begin's nominee, was elected by the central committee, with 306 votes, but Shmuel Katz, who had resigned as the prime minister's adviser on information in protest against the proposals, received 207 votes. Geula Cohen (Herut) and Moshe Shamir (Likud-La'am) bitterly attacked Begin, especially after the Camp David agreements, as did the Gush Emunim religious activist movement and Rabbi Hayim Druckman of the National Religious party. In June it was reported that Defense Minister Ezer Weizman (Herut) had criticized Begin and Foreign Minister Dayan for their inflexibility in the peace negotiations, and pressure for his resignation was reported from Herut and La'am circles. The matter soon blew over, however.

Yigael Hurvitz (Likud-La'am), minister of industry, commerce, and tourism, resigned towards the end of July in protest against over-spending by the government, but withdrew his resignation (see Economic Affairs, below). He resigned again at the end of September in protest against the Camp David agreements, after abstaining in the Knesset vote approving them. The other La'am minister, Eliezer Shostak (Health), voted for the accord. This disagreement aggravated dissension within the movement on other matters, and on November 17 La'am split into two factions, with four Knesset members each.

There was also disquiet in the Liberal wing of Likud over Finance Minister Simcha Ehrlich's economic policy, which was openly criticized by Energy Minister Yitzhak Moda'i. Moda'i also resented the transfer of the Industry, Commerce and Tourism portfolio to Gideon Patt (Liberal), who was succeeded as minister of housing by David Levi (Herut) in January 1979. (Levi retained the Immigrant Absorption portfolio.) Moda'i was placated by the addition to his responsibilities of the Communications portfolio.

From the beginning of the year, there was friction within the Democratic Movement for Change between the group headed by its leader, Professor Yigael Yadin, and Justice Minister Shmuel Tamir, and a more radical group led by Professor Amnon Rubinstein. Meir Zorea resigned from the Knesset in February in protest against the activities of the Rubinstein group, which had criticized his hawkish proclivities. The disagreements erupted again in May and June, when the DMC doves favored leaving the cabinet in protest against the government's conduct of the peace negotiations, and came to a head during the election, on June 28, of the party's council. Three lists competed, led by Yadin, Rubinstein, and Transport Minister Meir Amit, respectively (the latter consisting mainly of former Labor supporters). The party split at the end of August, with the Yadin group retaining the name Democratic and the Rubinstein and Amit factions joining forces to form Change and Initiative. Seven Knesset members supported Yadin; seven, including Amit, who resigned his cabinet post, joined Shay; one became independent. Toward the end of the year, NRP demanded the dismissal of one of the Democratic Movement's ministers, claiming that DM was now over-represented. However, when Begin indicated that DM would leave the coalition if this demand was met, thus endangering his majority, the crisis died down.

The Labor party began to recover from the 1977 debacle under the leadership of its chairman, Shimon Peres, with the assistance of Haim Bar-Lev as secretary. Its shattered finances were improved by a levy among the members and cuts in staff. While there was criticism of the re-election of many of the "old-guard" to the party's governing bodies, a number of academics, who had organized to support the party and press for internal reforms, were co-opted onto the council, and former Chief of Staff Mordecai Gur, former UN Ambassador Hayim Herzog, and Ya'akov Levenson, chairman of Bank Hapo'alim, were elected to the leadership bureau. Despite differences between hawks and doves, the party presented a fairly united front in the debates over the government's peace policy. Relations between Peres and former Prime Minister Yitzhak Rabin remained chilly.

Cabinet Changes
(see table in AJYB 1979, Vol. 79, p. 268)

	Incumbent	New Appointment (w.e.f. January 15, 1979)
Construction & Housing	Gideon Patt (Likud-Liberal)	David Levi (Likud-Herut)[1]
Industry, Commerce, & Tourism	Yigael Hurvitz (Likud-La'am)[2]	Gideon Patt (Likud-Liberal)
Transport	Meir Amit (DMC)[3]	Haim Landau (Likud-Herut)
Communications	Meir Amit (DMC)[3]	Yitzhak Moda'i (Likud-Liberal)[4]

[1]In addition to Immigrant Absorption
[2]Resigned September 13
[3]Resigned October 1
[4]In addition to Energy and Infrastructure

Separate local elections were held in November, under a new system of direct voting for mayors and local council chairmen. Incumbents Teddy Kollek (Labor) in Jerusalem, Shlomo Lahat (Likud) in Tel Aviv, and Eliahu Nawi (Independent Labor) in Beersheba were re-elected by large majorities, while Arye Gurel retained the mayoralty for Labor in Haifa. The Likud won control of ten smaller localities from the Alignment, but the latter improved its total vote over the 1973 figure because of its better showing in the large cities. A noteworthy feature was the low voter turn-out—55 per cent, compared with 72 per cent in 1973. There was a higher turn-out in the Arab sector, where Labor registered gains over Rakah (Communists). Tewfik Ziad (Communist) retained the mayoralty of Nazareth, but with a reduced majority. There was a second round of voting in 30 localities, where no candidate had received the required 40 per cent of the total vote.

A television straw poll conducted in 11 cities indicated that, if the electorate had been voting for the Knesset, the Alignment would have emerged as the largest party, with 48 seats (compared with 32 in May 1977), as against 46 for the Likud. The

Alignment's gains would have come mainly at the expense of the Democratic Movement for Change. Although the poll was criticized as unrepresentative and unscientific, the results gave a fillip to the morale of the Labor party.

Economic Affairs

Economic developments in 1978 were dominated by renewed growth in private and public consumption, continuing inflationary pressures which stimulated industrial unrest, and an effort to contain inflation by restraining government spending. The consumer price index rose by 50 per cent in the course of the year. There was an increase in the gross national product and in foreign investment.

Finance Minister Simcha Ehrlich's budget for 1978–79, totalling IL 182 billion (about $11.7 billion) was based on the assumption of 30 per cent inflation during the year. It was severely criticized as inflationary when it was presented on January 7, not only by the opposition, but also by Bank of Israel governor Arnon Gafny and some Likud supporters. The cabinet thereupon decided to cut the expenditure side by IL 3 billion.

At the beginning of the year, Histadrut Secretary-General Yeruham Meshel proposed that the government freeze taxes, subsidies, and the price of government services for six months, in return for a partial wage freeze. Finance Minister Ehrlich was prepared only to limit tax and price increases, and demanded a total wage freeze in the public sphere. The Histadrut rejected these proposals. In April the Histadrut and the Manufacturers' Association agreed on a 20-per-cent increase in the cost-of-living allowance, but as it was liable to income tax and compensated for only 70 per cent of the past rise in prices, the Histadrut demanded, in addition, a general wage increase of 15 per cent.

To compensate for the unexpectedly high rate of inflation, Ehrlich introduced a supplementary budget of IL 28 billion in mid-July, but agreed, after Industry, Commerce and Tourism Minister Hurvitz resigned in protest, that it should be cut by IL 3 billion. Increases in the cost of fuel by 18-25 per cent and of electricity by 14 per cent in October, and cuts in subsidies on essential foodstuffs in November, produced another wave of price rises, which stimulated further labor unrest. The government at first resisted the Histadrut's demand for a 15-per-cent wage increase, but ultimately accepted it, as well as additional increases for special groups. In October there was another 12.9 per cent increase in the cost-of-living allowance, and in January 1979 an 8.3 per cent advance was paid on the increase due in April.

Throughout the year there were numerous strikes for wage increases to compensate for rising prices. Among the groups involved were seamen, teachers, postmen, airline staffs, journalists, engineers, technicians, nurses and physicians in public employ, and civil servants in administrative posts. There were increases in salaries for judges, Knesset members, and cabinet ministers.

After stagnation in 1976 and 1977, the gross national product rose by five per cent in 1978. Private consumption grew by eight per cent, compared with an increase of only two per cent in each of the two preceding years. Public consumption grew by four per cent, owing mainly to higher defense expenditure, after drops of 19 per cent in 1976 and 13 per cent in 1977. Industrial output went up by 5.7 per cent, somewhat less than in 1977.

The currency was devaluated during the year by 23 per cent—from IL 15 per U.S. dollar to IL 19—but as this was less than half the rise in prices, the profitability of exports was affected. Imports (goods and services) grew by 10 per cent, mainly owing to higher defense procurements and increased foreign investments, after a drop in the previous year, while exports, in real terms, were up by only 3 per cent, after increases of 16 and 12 per cent, respectively, in 1976 and 1977. Consequently, the deficit in the balance of payments ($3.4 billion) was $800,000 higher, and the total foreign-currency debt of the economy rose by $2.6 billion, to $16.5 billion. Of the total resources at the disposal of the economy (domestic production plus imports), 39 per cent went to private consumption, 24–25 per cent to exports, 15 per cent to defense, 14–15 per cent to investment, and 6–7 per cent to civilian public consumption.

Other Domestic Matters

Early in January the Knesset passed a law providing that Israeli citizens should not be extradited for crimes committed abroad, but it did not apply to persons acquiring Israeli citizenship after the commission of an offence. Pressure for the passing of the law was connected with the French demand for the extradition of Samuel Flatto-Sharon (see AJYB 1978, Vol. 78, p. 472).

There was bitter parliamentary and public controversy over a bill, presented in accordance with the coalition agreement with the religious parties, changing the conditions under which young religious women could be exempted from army service. The bill abolished the committees before which applicants for exemption had to prove good faith, and provided that any young woman testifying before a civil or rabbinic judge that she was religiously observant should be automatically exempt, while laying down penalties for false statements. The law was passed in July against the opposition of the Labor-Mapam Alignment, the left-wing parties and DMC, who charged that it would facilitate wholesale evasion and would be unfair to young women who had to, or chose to, serve. An Alignment bill to obligate young women exempted on religious grounds to do national civilian service passed its first reading, but was blocked in committee. A number of young women called up for service in the reserves refused to comply, as a demonstration of protest against the law, on the grounds that, as a result of the larger number of exemptions expected, they would have to serve more frequently or for longer periods.

The government rejected a proposal for a general amnesty to celebrate the 30th anniversary of Israel's independence and decided instead to appoint several commit- tees, each headed by a retired Supreme Court justice, to examine the files individu- ally and make recommendations for clemency, through the minister of justice, to the president. The great majority of their recommendations were adopted, but the proposal to reduce the 15-year sentence of Michael Tsour, former manager of the Israel Corporation (see AJYB 1976 Vol. 76, p. 413) and the five-year sentence of Asher Yadlin, former chairman of Kupat Holim (see AJYB 1978, Vol. 78, p. 476), were rejected. Justice Minister Shmuel Tamir explained that he refused to recommend clemency in these cases, owing to the need to stamp out corruption.

In April the Knesset passed a law, proposed by Education and Culture Minister Zevulun Hammer, providing free, but not compulsory, secondary education. The cost was to be met by a small increase (0.3 per cent of wages from employees and 0.1 per cent from employers) in national insurance contributions. The law was unopposed, but it was criticized as benefiting mainly the middle class, since the children of lower-paid workers, if they continued beyond the compulsory education age, were already exempt from payment under the existing graded fee system.

A committee headed by Erwin Shimron, appointed toward the end of 1977 to recommend measures to combat crime (see AJYB 1979, Vol. 79, p. 280), reported on February 19 that "organized crime Israeli style" (but not "American style") existed in the country. Although "crime in Israel has not reached the dimensions known in many western countries," the report stated, "crime and disrespect for the law have seriously affected the quality of our life, our national economy and, most seriously of all, the inner fiber of our society." The government announced the appointment of a special cabinet committee of three to follow up on the Shimron committee's recommendations and a "general staff," headed by the attorney general, the inspector general of the police, and the director general of the treasury, to coordinate measures to fight crime.

For the first time, a member of the Knesset was sent to prison. Shmuel Rechtman (Likud-Liberal), mayor of Rehovot, was charged with taking a bribe from a building contractor, and his parliamentary immunity was withdrawn, with his consent, by a vote of the House. Early in January, he was sentenced to three-and-a-half years' imprisonment, but appealed to the Supreme Court and continued to take part in the Knesset's proceedings until his appeal was dismissed, when he resigned.

Resentment and indignation were expressed by settlers in the Rafa Approaches (Pit'hat Rafiah) in northern Sinai, in eastern Sinai, and in Ophira (Sharm al-Sheikh) at their impending evacuation under the terms of the peace treaty with Egypt, which would be the first voluntary abandonment of Jewish settlements in Zionist history. The Jewish Agency announced plans for the relocation of the settlements in a new area in the western Negev, to be called Pit'hat Shalom ("Opening to Peace" or "Peace District"), but the settlers' representatives declared that they would refuse to move.

The elections to the Chief Rabbinate were scheduled for July, having already been postponed for nine months. In May Rabbi Shaul Yisraeli announced his candidacy for the post of Ashkenazi chief rabbi in opposition to the incumbent, Rabbi Shlomo Goren. He was supported by Sephardi Chief Rabbi Ovadia Yosef, whose relations with Rabbi Goren had been tense for some time, but was opposed by NRP and other circles. The results of the election by local religious councils and the rabbinate of their representatives to the electoral college indicated that Rabbi Yisraeli might be successful, but at the end of June a private members' bill postponing the elections for another year was rushed through by members of the Likud, the Alignment, and NRP. David Glass (NRP), chairman of the Knesset's Law Committee, promised that, in the interim, comprehensive reforms would be made in the constitution of the Chief Rabbinate. The main reform envisaged was the election of one chief rabbi and one president of the rabbinic supreme court (instead of two chief rabbis), with one of the two offices being held by an Ashkenazi and the other by a Sephardi.

Israel and World Jewry

The Likud's rise to power (see AJYB 1979, Vol. 79, pp. 260–8) was reflected in the composition of the 29th Zionist Congress, which was held in Jerusalem from February 20 to March 1. The Likud, which registered gains in the election of delegates from Diaspora countries, as well as those representing Israeli parties in proportion to their Knesset strengths, was now the largest party, with 174 delegates (111 at the 28th Congress, in 1972). The Confederation of United Zionists (including Hadassah) also increased its strength, with 113 delegates (78 in 1972), while Labor (including Poale Zion) dropped from 157 to 93. In addition, there were 77 Mizrachi delegates (84 in 1972), 27 from Mapam (31 in 1972), 26 from DMC, which was represented for the first time, 75 from international Jewish organizations, 10 from the Israel Zionist Council, and 40 others. All parties were represented in the executive. Arye Dulzin (Likud) was elected chairman, and the Likud took over from Labor the Aliyah, Youth and Pioneering, and Education and Culture departments, as well as sharing control of Agricultural Settlement; a Labor representative was elected treasurer.

The Congress passed, against bitter opposition from Mizrachi and Herut delegates, a resolution affirming that all World Zionist departments and programs in Israel should be administered in accordance with the principle of equal treatment for all religious trends in Judaism. It approved a budget totaling $50.7 million, the largest items being $20.7 million for immigration from the free countries, $7.7 million for youth and pioneering efforts, and $5.9 million for education and culture.

Toward the end of June, the Jewish Agency Assembly approved a budget of $350 million for the 1978–79 fiscal year, the largest items being $66.5 million for immigration and absorption and $37.9 million for youth *aliyah*. In addition, $48 million was allocated for the first stage of "Project Renewal" for slum clearance and rehabilitation, which had been proposed by Prime Minister Begin. It was designed to facilitate a planned and comprehensive effort to provide housing, education, and social services for 160 development towns and disadvantaged neighborhoods over a five-year period.

Israeli Arabs

There were signs of growing extremism among some sections of the Israeli Arab population, particularly university students, under the influence of PLO supporters in the administered areas. The Ibn al-Balad ("Sons of the Village") association, which boycotted the Knesset elections, and other even more extreme groups, denied the legitimacy of "the Zionist entity," i.e., the State of Israel, and denounced the "compromising attitude" of Rakah, the Israeli Communist party, which called for the establishment of a Palestinian Arab state side by side with Israel.

Apprehension was expressed in Jewish circles at the growing proportion of Arabs in Galilee and the lack of progress in Jewish settlement in the area. Out of a total population of 560,000 in the Northern District at the beginning of 1978, there were 291,000 Jews (52 per cent). However, in the two largest sub-districts, those of Jezreel and Acre, there were only 190,000 Jews (43 per cent) out of a total population of 442,000. A plan was initiated to establish a score of "lookout posts," each manned by a few families, to prevent illegal building on state or agricultural land in Galilee.

Special problems were presented by the Bedouin, especially in the Negev. With growing prosperity, their flocks had been expanding beyond the grazing capacity of the area. To prevent their encroachment on land in the south and center of the country and to keep the number of sheep and goats down to authorized limits, the Ministry of Agriculture established the "Green Patrol," whose activities came under some criticism after complaints from Bedouin about rough handling by members of the Patrol. Other difficulties arose over Bedouin claims to ownership of large areas on which they had grazed for many years. This question became acute in view of the impending need to relocate airfields and other military installations in the Negev after the evacuation of Sinai under the terms of the peace treaty with Egypt.

In December a subcommittee of the Knesset Defense and Foreign Affairs Committee recommended the replacement of the prime minister's advisor on Arab affairs by a cabinet minister who would take responsibility for matters concerning the Arab sector. In response to a Knesset motion on December 6, Minister-Without-Portfolio Moshe Nissim pointed to recent progress among the Arab population and noted that, for the first time, Israeli Arabs had been permitted to go on the *haj* (pilgrimage) to Mecca. He promised more intensive efforts in the areas of town and country planning, housing, education, and economic development. He declared that "the majority of Israel's Arab citizens are unreservedly and unconditionally loyal to the State," and promised that the government would show goodwill in dealing with "a sector which has its own way of life, its own conditions and its own problems." He added, however, that the government would not tolerate anti-Israel manifestations.

Personalia

Lieut.-Gen. David Ivri was appointed O.C. Israel Air Force on October 28, 1977; Shmuel Katz resigned as the prime minister's advisor on external information on

January 4 and was succeeded by Harry Hurvitz on May 21. Shmuel Lahis and Harry Rosen were appointed director-general and secretary-general, respectively, of the Jewish Agency, on February 1. Hayim Zohar was appointed secretary-general of the World Zionist Organization on April 14. Maj.-Gen. Dan Shomron (who was in charge of the Entebbe operation in 1976) was appointed O.C. Southern Command on February 3. Maj.-Gen. Yekutiel Adam was appointed deputy chief of staff and O.C. operations on March 15. Lieut.-Gen. Rafael Eitan was appointed chief of staff of the Israel Defense Forces on April 1, in succession to Lieut.-Gen. Mordecai Gur. Brig.-Gen. Binyamin Ben-Eliezer was appointed O.C. Judea and Samaria on May 3. Prof. Yitzhak Zamir, dean of the Hebrew University Law School, was appointed attorney-general on August 1. Yosef Ciechanover was appointed director-general of the Foreign Ministry on September 1. Professor Yehuda Blum was appointed Israel ambassador to the UN in succession to Hayim Herzog on September 5. Ephraim Evron was appointed Israel ambassador in Washington, in succession to Simha Dinitz, on December 15.

Aharon Propes, organizer of the Israel Festival, died in Tel Aviv, January 5, at the age of 73. Professor Yosef Heineman, associate professor of Hebrew literature at the Hebrew University, died in Jerusalem, January 9, at the age of 62. Mindru Katz, Israeli musician, died in Istanbul, January 29, at the age of 52. Mordecai Makleff, former IDF chief of staff, manager of the Dead Sea works, died in Germany, February 22, at the age of 58. Amihai Paglin, the prime minister's advisor on anti-terrorist activities, died in Tel Aviv, February 25, at the age of 55. Pinhas Rosen, former minister of justice and leader of the Independent Liberal party, died in Kfar Saba, May 3, at the age of 91. Ludwig Mayer, veteran Jerusalem bookseller, died in Jerusalem, July 2, at the age of 99. Max Nurock, veteran diplomat, died in Jerusalem, July 22, at the age of 85. Zivia Lubetkin-Cukierman, Warsaw Ghetto revolt leader, died in Nahariya, August 11, at the age of 64. Arye Dissentshik, editor of *Maariv* (evening paper), died in Ramat Gan, August 14, at the age of 70. Dr. Helena Kagan, medical pioneer, died in Jerusalem, August 22, at the age of 89. Shaul Avigur, Haganah pioneer, died in Tel Aviv, August 29, at the age of 79. Irma Lindheim, former national president of Hadassah, died in Mishmar Ha'emek, October 4, at the age of 91. Arthur Lourie, veteran Zionist and Israeli diplomat, died in Jerusalem, October 5, at the age of 75. Edwin, second Viscount Samuel, died in Jerusalem, November, at the age of 80. Golda Meir, former prime minister, died in Jerusalem, December 8, at the age of 80.

MISHA LOUVISH

South Africa

Domestic Affairs

DISCLOSURES IN 1978 about the abuse of funds in the South African Department of Information led to the greatest political scandal in the country's history. The department was abolished and its secretary, Dr. Eschel Rhoodie, was retired prematurely. After a judicial investigation, recommendations were made that criminal charges be brought against Rhoodie and others. Two commissions, led by judges Anton Mostert and Rudolf Erasmus, revealed, among other things, that state funds had been used to finance *The Citizen,* a party political newspaper. The scandal led to the resignation of Dr. Connie Mulder, the cabinet minister responsible for the department who had run a close second to Pieter W. Botha in the election to succeed Balthazar John Vorster as prime minister. Vorster had been elected state president when Dr. Nicolaas Diederichs died in August.

Another major issue confronting the country was the resolution of the question concerning the independence of South West Africa. Lengthy negotiations with Britain, the United States, Canada, France, and West Germany led to a formula by which the former German territory, mandated to South Africa by the League of Nations, would gain its independence. Problems arose, however, in implementing the agreement. At year's end the territory remained under the leadership of Marthinus T. Steyn, administrator-general appointed by South Africa. An election was held in the territory, but this was recognized only by South Africa. A second election, approved by the United Nations, was scheduled for 1979.

The guerilla war on the border between South West Africa and Angola continued as the South West African People's Organization (SWAPO), under the leadership of Sam Nujoma, sought to assume control over the area. In February the country was horrified by the assassination of Toiva Shiyagaya, minister of health and welfare of Ovambo, by a SWAPO member, while he was addressing a political meeting at Okahau. In March Chief Clemens Kapuuo, veteran Herero leader and president of the Democratic Turnhalle Alliance, was killed by an assassin outside his store in Katutura township near Windhoek, the capital city of Namibia. Dr. Robert Sobukwe, leader of the Pan Africanist Congress, who had long been detained in prison for his political activities, died in February 1978. At his funeral several Black leaders, including Chief Gatsha Buthelezi, chief minister of KwaZulu, were forcibly expelled by the mourners.

In April diplomatic relations between South Africa and Transkei, the first independent Black homeland, were severed by the Transkei prime minister, Paramount Chief Kaizer Matanzima, as a result of his dissatisfaction at the incorporation of the territory of East Griqualand into the South African province of Natal.

In June the National party celebrated the 30th year of its accession to power.

The country's economic situation was not markedly improved by the measures adopted to contain inflation and restore a more favorable balance of payments. However, as the world's major producer of gold, South Africa benefited from its price rise to over $200 an ounce.

Relations with Israel

The various agreements entered into between Israel and South Africa during the February visit to South Africa of Israel Finance Minister Simcha Ehrlich were widely thought to herald a drive by Israel to increase trade with South Africa. It was also rumored that Israel sought to serve as a bridgehead for South Africa in the export of industrial goods to both the EEC and the United States. Ehrlich, however, denied this, stressing that an increase in raw materials imported from South Africa was intended exclusively for use in Israeli industry. Ehrlich stated that he expected R40-million worth of trade to result from his visit. Other matters discussed included Israeli fishing rights in South African waters, the improvement of air services between the two countries, and the establishment and expansion of joint industrial ventures.

During 1978 South Africa's exports to Israel increased by 50 per cent, from R29.3 million to R43.7 million. During the same period, South African exports to Israel increased from R13.39 million to R21.57 million. South African exports consisted mainly of steel, while Israel's exports were largely phosphates and other chemicals. A new dimension was added to Israel-South Africa trade relations by the signing in January 1979 of a contract whereby South Africa agreed to export substantial amounts of steam coal to Israel.

In March a dispute arose between El Al Israel Airlines and South African Airways during which El Al stated that unless agreement was reached about new services which it required between the two countries, it would withdraw its services altogether. There were no political connotations to the dispute. A compromise was subsequently reached, resulting in the start of the first South African Airways flights to Israel.

Public and official reaction to the celebration of Israel's 30th anniversary was widespread and congratulatory. Most newspapers featured articles on the occasion, and a number included special supplements devoted to Israel. When Golda Meir died in December 1978, many thousands of messages of sympathy were received by the Israel embassy and Jewish organizations.

In January 1979, Yitzhak Ofek, chairman of the Israel Olympic Committee, announced a decision to sever all links between his committee and South Africa, a decision which did not find favor with either the Israel Foreign Ministry or the Jews of South Africa. At a plenary session of the committee the decision was reversed.

In June 1978 the Israel ambassador, Itzhak Unna, refused an invitation to be guest of honor at the premier of the play *Golda* in Pretoria's Breytenbach Theater, because the theater was closed to Blacks. He later attended the play at a Johannesburg theater which was open to all races. Unna's example was followed by many other envoys, and his attitude was enthusiastically endorsed by a very broad section of the public and the press, both English and Afrikaans. Appeals to the authorities to open the theater to all races were organized on a large scale, but to no avail. However, a campaign to boycott the theater did have a marked effect. The South African Jewish Board of Deputies (SAJBD) unequivocally endorsed the ambassador's stand in accordance with its resolve to do everything possible to eliminate all forms of discrimination based on race, creed, or color. It was highly significant that the overwhelming support which Unna received was forthcoming against a background of stern official reaction to what was described by certain government ministers as improper interference by a foreign diplomat.

Antisemitism

Attempts by various racist groups to organize themselves into movements were of some concern. Two groups in particular, the Afrikanerweerstandsbeweging (AWB—Afrikaner Resistance Movement) and the National Front (NF) gained much publicity. NF, made up mainly of disgruntled British immigrants, began distributing anti-Zionist and racist literature in an area of Johannesburg largely populated by Jews. SAJBD issued frequent warnings that this material was provocative to the Jewish community. In January 1979 NF held a public rally which was picketed by some 500 young Jews who prevented the meeting from starting. Shortly thereafter, NF disintegrated when its leaders fled the country one by one. The first to leave was NF founder Jack Noble, who averred that he was returning to Britain to contest a seat in the British general elections as an NF candidate. Some NF members who had been charged with fraud and theft fled the country while charges against them were pending.

Die Afrikaner, official organ of the ultra-right Herstigte Nationale party (HNP), continued to play on the theme of an international Jewish conspiracy and to propagate calumnies about the Holocaust, denying that it ever took place. It conducted a vituperative campaign against SAJBD for its stand against racial discrimination and intolerance, and accused it of having organized the demonstration against NF, and of preventing John Tyndall, chairman of the British NF, from visiting South Africa.

An organization calling itself "Boerenasie" launched an appeal for membership, announcing its intention to take power and expel all Jews from South Africa. Its publications *Sonop/Sunup* and *Facts/Feite* were banned, and the state initiated legal proceedings against its leaders. S.E.D. Brown, in his publication the *SA Observer*, continued to promulgate virulently anti-Jewish views, with particular emphasis on the Holocaust and Israel. A number of editions were banned.

Holocaust, the television film, was not shown on the national television service of the S.A. Broadcasting Corporation (SABC), but was exhibited privately and received wide and generally favorable reviews. Embittered attacks on the film were made in the extremist press. SABC continued to deny Jewish clergymen the opportunity of conducting either the daily Bible reading or Epilogue on TV, notwithstanding requests in this regard, and numerous press articles about the matter. The head of SABC English religious broadcasts, Bill Chalmers, continued to hold his post despite many protests over his advocacy of the theory of an evil international conspiracy involving Jews and others. While accepting the fact that SABC ascribed to Christian national principles, misgivings were expressed in Jewish circles about the attitudes of SABC toward the South African Jewish community.

JEWISH COMMUNITY

Communal Activities

The major event of the year was the 30th national congress of SAJBD, in May, which coincided with the celebration of the 75th anniversary of the organization. The keynote address at the congress was delivered by Philip Klutznick; also participating was Sidney Vincent, director of the Jewish Community Federation of Cleveland, Ohio. The congress dealt with the major issues confronting the community, in particular with the problem of maintaining Jewish identity in a community having little trained manpower and suffering severe financial difficulties. Vincent had been invited to study the structure of the community and to recommend changes which would make for more effective use of human and material resources. Vincent's report, which was presented after the congress, was far-reaching in its suggestions, and led to a detailed memorandum on the subject by SAJBD executive director Denis Diamond. An ongoing commission was appointed to implement Vincent's suggestions and monitor progress.

Another area of concern that received a great deal of attention at the congress was the question of participation by the Jewish community in attempts to improve intergroup relations in South Africa. Chief Gatsha Buthelezi and Professor Piet Cillie, a leading Afrikaner thinker, were invited to contribute major papers before the congress on the subject. A publication, *Towards a Responsible Community,* containing the major addresses delivered over a period of some 20 years by Arthur Suzman, Q.C., chairman of the Public Relations Committee of SAJBD, was issued to coincide with his retirement from that position. Suzman's valedictory address, in its unequivocal condemnation of racial prejudice and call for the defense of freedom of thought and conscience, well reflected the attitude of the delegates, who overwhelmingly passed a resolution that was widely publicized locally and abroad, and which had far-reaching implications for SAJBD policies. It read:

> Congress urges all Jewish organizations and all individual members of our community to associate themselves with, and actively support, by peaceful and legitimate means, the elimination of unjust discrimination based on race, creed or color. Congress commends the Executive Council for the steps taken to promote harmony and understanding between all sections of the community and urges the Executive to intensify its efforts to extend knowledge of the Jewish people, their history and culture amongst all fellow-citizens.

At a banquet to celebrate the Board's 75th anniversary attended by the late Dr. Nicolaas Diederichs, the state president, the matter of intergroup relations again received attention in an address by SAJBD president D.K. Mann. He called on individual Jews to lend exemplary support to efforts being undertaken to alleviate the tensions and problems of a racially divided society.

David K. Mann and Dr. Israel Abramowitz were re-elected as president and chairman of SAJBD, respectively. Denis Diamond, SAJBD executive director, announced his intention to retire from office prior to his emigration to Israel.

Dr. Arthur Hertzberg of the United States launched the United Communal Fund (UCF) campaign in February 1978. UCF, under the chairmanship of Mendel Kaplan, sought to meet the needs of South African Jewish institutions that were being adversely effected by increased emigration and a deteriorating financial climate.

Zionism

Aliyah was the central theme of the 35th South African Zionist Federation (SAZF) conference held in September, which was launched by Dr. Abraham Avi-Hai, chairman of Keren Hayesod. It was once again decided not to hold Zionist elections, but to retain the present key by which the various parties were allocated representation on the SAZF Executive Council. Itz Kalmanowitz and Julius Weinstein were elected chairman and president of SAZF, respectively. Leib Frank, for many years chief executive of the SAZF Israel office in Tel Aviv, retired at the end of 1978 and was succeeded by It Stein.

Considerable public interest was shown in remarks made at the conference by Ambassador Unna of Israel. He stated that the frequent claim that Israel and South Africa were in the same boat was not true. South Africa was under attack because its "internal political, economic and social structure contained built-in elements of discrimination against the non-white population groups," whereas Israel was under attack simply because it existed. Despite Israel's deep objection to South African race policies, Unna added, it steadfastly refused to indulge in blanket condemnation of South Africa. Thus, there were positive and mutually beneficial relations between the two countries.

In March 1978 the Women's biennial Zionist campaign was launched by Mk. Moshe Shamir and Judge Hadassa Ben Itto.

Religion

Rabbi Zalman Posner of the United States was the main speaker at the conference of the South African Federation of Synagogues (SAFOS). The conference heard Dr. Allie Dubb discuss the demographic survey of the South African Jewish community which he had conducted on behalf of SAJBD; the results were being published by the Hebrew University in Jerusalem. Ivan H. Sackheim was elected chairman of SAFOS.

Education

Dr. Eliezer Shmueli, director-general of the Israel Ministry of Education, was the main speaker at the 18th national conference of the South African Board of Jewish Education (SABJE). Isaac Joffee was elected chairman in succession to Ivan Greenstein. The conference focused its attention on the problem of maintaining the high standards of the ten Jewish day schools in the major cities in the face of higher costs and the likelihood of restricted income from UCF.

Jewish Culture

SAJBD arranged a function to launch *A Cloud and a Way,* a volume of Yiddish poetry by David Wolpe, 250 copies of which were purchased by the South African Jewish Trust (SAJT) for distribution to Jewish libraries throughout the world. The internationally renowned Yiddish poet David Fram was honored at a function organized by SAJBD, SAJT, and the South African Yiddish Cultural Federation (SAYCF) to celebrate his 75th birthday.

Significant books written by Jews included *The Early Cape Muslims,* by Dr. Frank Bradlow and Margaret Cairns; *Sarah Gertrude Millin, a South African Life,* by Martin Rubin; and *Oorwintering in die Vreemde,* a collection of Afrikaans poetry by Olga Kirsch, who has lived in Israel since 1948.

Lionel Abrahams was one of the winners of the prestigious Pringle Award for creative writing published in South Africa.

An exhibition of paintings on the theme of the Holocaust by Frank Startz was well received. The artist presented one of his works to SAJBD. Graphic works were commissioned by SAJBD and UCF from Aileen Lipkin, who held a prestigious exhibition at the Johannesburg Art Gallery. Professor Lippy Lipshitz, sculptor and former head of the University of Cape Town Michaelis Art School, received the Association of Arts Medal prior to his *aliyah* to Israel, in recognition of his services to art in South Africa.

Collections of memorabilia were acquired from various persons for inclusion in the Harry and Friedel Abt Museum of SAJBD. One such collection was the papers of Sallie Kussel, reflecting a lifetime of service to South African Jewry, and most particularly to the Union of Jewish Women. A collection of valuable stamps and messages of remembrance from Israeli leaders to the parents of the late Alex Buchen, who fell in the Israel War of Independence, was presented to SAJBD by Alex's uncle, Leo Buchen.

Visitors from abroad who delivered lectures included: Dr. Beryl Frymer of the United States; Professor Michael Davies of Hebrew University; Dr. Eliezer Oren of Ben Gurion University; Rabbi Louis I. Rabinowitz, former Johannesburg Chief Rabbi, now of Jerusalem; Eliyahu Honig of Hebrew University; Chaim Bermant of London; and Max I. Dimont of the United States.

To much public acclaim, SAJBD organized the second Johannesburg Film Festival. Together with the French embassy, SAJBD sponsored a French Film Festival. Both festivals included a number of films of Jewish interest.

Much valuable ongoing cultural and educational work throughout the country was done by the Union of Jewish Women, the Women's Zionist Council, SAZF, SAYCF, and SAJBD.

Personalia

Justice C.S. Margo and Wolf Isaacs were appointed honorary colonels of the 24th and 2nd squadrons of the South African Air Force, respectively. David Friedman, S.C. was appointed a judge. Hans Adler was awarded an honorary doctorate by the University of the Witwatersrand.

Helen Suzman, for many years the only representative in Parliament of the opposition Progressive party and champion of Black rights, was awarded the United Nations Award for Human Rights.

Dr. Leah Bronner was appointed associate professor of Hebrew studies, and Dr. Max B. Feldman, professor of psychological medicine, at the University of the Witwatersrand. Sandra Fredman was awarded a Rhodes Scholarship. Dr. Solly Morris, ex-city engineer of Cape Town, received a gold medal from the Institute of Municipal Engineers of Great Britain in recognition of his contribution to South Africa's advanced urban transport system. David Lazarus was elected mayor of East London for the 20th successive year. Ted Mauerberger and Louis Kreiner were re-elected mayor and deputy mayor of Cape Town, respectively. Neville Cohen was reappointed mayor of Port Elizabeth. Reeva Forman was elected as the first woman president of the Johannesburg chapter of Jaycees. Gerald Leissner was named Jaycees International "senator of the year" from among 26,000 candidates. Ellen Colley received the UJW "woman of the year" award.

People appointed to important Jewish offices included: L.D. Sandler, rabbi, Randburg Hebrew Congregation; Mervyn Danker, principal, Theodor Herzl School, Port Elizabeth; Harry Hurwitz, adviser on external information to the prime minister of

Israel; Inez Jacobson, chairman, Transvaal Jewish Welfare Council; Meish Zimmerman, deputy director, SABJE; Jack Rubenchick, governor, Haifa University; Dr. Herman Davidson, chairman, Natal Zionist Council; Harold Levy, S.C., chairman, SAJBD Cape Committee, upon the *aliyah* of Dr. Aubrey Zabow; and Josh Goldberg, community director, Council of Natal Jewry.

Among prominent Jews who died during the year were: Alf Blumberg, president, S.A. Maccabi, in February; Norman Lourie, founder, Balfour Park Sports Club and S.A. Habonim, in March; Leon Gluckman, actor-producer, in March; Jack Rubik, editor of *Barkai,* in April; Israel Pinshaw, secretary, SAJBD Cape Council, in May; Rae Greenblatt, secretary, Women's Zionist Council, in May; Taiby Segal, prolific Yiddish writer, in May; Dave Epstein, member, Transvaal Provincial Council, in May; Esther Plen, community worker, in June; Esther Lipworth, devoted Zionist, in June; and Sophie Bellville Stern, who died a few months short of her 107th birthday, in August.

DENIS DIAMOND

World Jewish Population

T HERE ARE NO PRECISE DATA on Jewish population in the various countries. The figures presented below represent the best possible estimates for 1978. They are based on local censuses, communal registration figures, and data obtained from a special inquiry conducted in 1977 (See AJYB, 1978, Vol. 78, p. 517). Some figures were obtained from local informants, mostly people involved in Jewish communal affairs. The figures are of varying degrees of accuracy and are subject to substantial margins of error. Where students of Jewish population differ significantly as to the estimated number of Jews in a particular country, this is so indicated. The figures will be revised when more accurate data become available.

DISTRIBUTION BY CONTINENTS

The estimated world Jewish population at the end of 1978 was 14,396,000. Of the total number, about 6,783,000 (47 per cent) lived in the Americas, some 4,142,000 (29 per cent) in Europe, including the Asian parts of Turkey and the USSR, and over 3,221,000 (22 per cent) in Asia. Only some 174,000 (1.5 per cent) remained in Africa, and 75,000 (0.5 per cent) in Australia and New Zealand.

TABLE 1. DISTRIBUTION OF JEWISH POPULATION BY CONTINENTS, 1978

Continent	Number	Per Cent
Europe (including Asiatic USSR and Turkey)	4,142,450	29.0
America (North, Central, and South)	6,783,220	47.0
Asia	3,221,010	22.0
Africa	174,320	1.5
Australia and New Zealand	75,000	0.5
TOTAL	14,396,000*	100.0

*Because sources and dates were not always identical, there may be discrepancies between figures given in the tables below and those in other sections of this volume.

Various estimates have been put forward for the Jewish populations of the Soviet Union, the United States, Argentina, and France. If the lower estimate were accepted in each case, the total world Jewish population would be smaller by about one million than the estimate offered here.

Europe

Of the approximately 4,142,000 Jews in Europe, over 2,800,000 were in the Communist area, including 2,666,000 in the Soviet Union, 80,000 in Hungary, some 45,000 in Rumania, and about 6,000 in Poland. There was a continuing debate about the number of Jews in the USSR. Some Israeli scholars accepted the official Soviet figure, and suggested that, with continuing Jewish emigration, the number of Soviet Jews was below 2,000,000. Without going into details, it seems that a figure of about 2,600,000 is nearer to the actual situation (See "Soviet Jewry Since the Death of Stalin," AJYB, 1979, Vol. 79, pp. 79–80).

Over 1,300,000 Jews lived in non-Communist countries. France had about 650,000, making it the largest Jewish community in Western Europe. (Other sources estimated the French Jewish population as being 550,000). Great Britain had 410,000, Belgium 41,000, Italy 41,000, and Germany (including both East and West Germany) 38,000.

TABLE 2. ESTIMATED JEWISH POPULATION IN EUROPE, BY COUNTRIES, 1978

Country	Total Population[a]	Jewish Population
Albania	2,620,000	300
Austria	7,520,000	13,000[x]
Belgium	9,830,000	41,000
Bulgaria	8,800,000	7,000
Czechoslovakia	15,030,000	13,000
Denmark	5,090,000	7,500[x]
Finland	4,740,000	1,350
France	53,080,000	650,000
Germany	79,210,000	38,000[b]
Gibraltar	30,000	650[x]
Great Britain	55,850,000	410,000
Greece	9,280,000	6,000
Hungary	10,650,000	80,000
Ireland	3,190,000	4,000
Italy	56,450,000	41,000
Luxembourg	360,000	1,000
Malta	330,000	50
Netherlands	13,850,000	30,000[x]
Norway	4,040,000	1,000
Poland	34,700,000	6,000
Portugal	9,730,000	600
Rumania	21,660,000	45,000
Spain	36,670,000	10,000
Sweden	8,260,000	16,000[x]
Switzerland	6,330,000	21,000
Turkey	42,130,000	27,000[xc]

USSR	258,930,000	2,666,000
Yugoslavia	21,910,000	6,000
TOTAL		4,142,450

[a]United Nations Statistical Office, *Monthly Bulletin of Statistics,* and other sources, including local publications.

[b]Includes West Germany, East Germany, and both sectors of Berlin.

[c]Includes Asian regions of the USSR and Turkey.

[x]Reply to 1977 inquiry.

North, Central, and South America

The number of Jews in the United States, including all persons living in Jewish households, was estimated at about 5,860,900 (see the article "Jewish Population in the United States, 1979" in this volume.) Some Israeli demographers disagreed with this figure and suggested an estimate one quarter million smaller. Canada had an estimated 305,000 Jews, and Central and South America about 580,000. The Jewish population figure for Argentina was 300,000. While this estimate was accepted by some local informants, it was contested by others.

TABLE 3. ESTIMATED JEWISH POPULATION IN NORTH, CENTRAL, AND SOUTH AMERICA AND THE WEST INDIES, BY COUNTRIES, 1978

Country	Total Population[a]	Jewish Population
Canada	23,280,000	305,000[x]
Mexico	64,590,000	37,500
United States	216,820,000	5,860,900
Total North America		6,203,400
Barbados	250,000	70[x]
Costa Rica	2,060,000	2,500[x]
Cuba	9,600,000	1,500
Curacao	150,000	700
Dominican Republic	4,980,000	250
El Salvador	4,260,000	350[x]
Guatemala	6,440,000	2,000
Haiti	4,750,000	150
Honduras	2,830,000	200
Jamaica	2,090,000	500
Nicaragua	2,310,000	200
Panama	1,770,000	2,000
Trinidad	1,100,000	500
Total Central America and West Indies		10,920
Argentina	26,060,000	300,000
Bolivia	5,950,000	2,000
Brazil	112,240,000	150,000[x]

Chile	10,660,000	28,000
Colombia	25,050,000	14,000
Ecuador	7,560,000	1,000
Paraguay	2,800,000	1,200
Peru	16,360,000	5,200[x]
Surinam	450,000	500
Uruguay	2,850,000	50,000
Venezuela	12,740,000	17,000
Total South America		568,900
TOTAL		6,783,220

[a]See Table 2, note[a].
[x]See Table 2, note[x].

Asia, Australia, and New Zealand

The Jewish population of Asia was 3,221,410. Of this figure, 3,135,000, or approximately 97 per cent, were in Israel, the second largest Jewish population center in the world. There were 70,000 Jews in Iran and 8,000 in India. It was difficult to ascertain if events in Lebanon had any impact on the number of Jews in Lebanon and Syria.

The Jewish population of Australia was estimated at about 70,000, and that of New Zealand at 5,000.

TABLE 4. ESTIMATED JEWISH POPULATION IN ASIA, BY COUNTRIES, 1978

Country	Total Population[a]	Jewish Population
Afghanistan	17,450,000	200
Burma	31,510,000	200
China	865,680,000	30
Cyprus	640,000	30
Hong Kong	4,510,000	250
India	625,820,000	8,000[x]
Indonesia	143,280,000	100
Iran	34,270,000	70,000
Iraq	11,910,000	450
Israel	3,730,000	3,135,000
Japan	113,860,000	400[x]
Lebanon	3,060,000	400
Pakistan	75,280,000	250
Philippines	54,030,000	200
Singapore	2,310,000	500
Syria	7,840,000	4,500
Yemen	7,080,000	500
TOTAL		3,221,010

[a]See Table 2, note[a].
[x]See Table 2, note[x].

TABLE 5. ESTIMATED JEWISH POPULATION IN AUSTRALIA AND NEW ZEALAND, 1978

Country	Total Population[a]	Jewish Population
Australia	14,070,000	70,000[x]
New Zealand	3,111,000	5,000
TOTAL		75,000

[a]See Table 2, note[a].
[x]See Table 2, note[x].

Africa

The Jewish population of Africa stood at about 175,770, including some 118,000 in South Africa. It was not clear whether events in Rhodesia had a substantial impact on the number of Jews there. An estimated 22,000 were in Ethiopia. The Jewish communities of the Maghreb were very small—some 22,000 in Morocco, 7,000 in Tunisia, and about 1,000 in Algeria. Egypt had 400 Jews and Libya 20.

TABLE 6. ESTIMATED JEWISH POPULATION IN AFRICA, BY COUNTRIES, 1978

Country	Total Population[a]	Jewish Population
Algeria	17,300,000	1,000
Egypt	38,070,000	400
Ethiopia	28,680,000	22,000
Kenya	13,850,000	300
Libya	2,440,000	20
Morocco	17,830,000	22,000
Republic of South Africa	26,130,000	118,000[x]
Rhodesia	6,530,000	3,000
Tunisia	5,740,000	7,000
Zaire	25,630,000	200
Zambia	5,140,000	400
TOTAL		174,320

[a]See Table 2, note[a].
[x]See Table 2, note[x].

COMMUNITIES WITH LARGEST JEWISH POPULATION

The largest Jewish community was in the United States, followed by Israel and the Soviet Union. Together they accounted for some 81 per cent of the world Jewish population. France, Great Britain, Canada, and Argentina had Jewish communities of 300,000 or over. Brazil had a Jewish population of 150,000, while that of South Africa stood at 118,000. The balance of the countries had Jewish communities of less than 100,000 each.

TABLE 7. COUNTRIES WITH LARGEST JEWISH POPULATION

Country	Jewish Population
United States	5,860,900
Israel	3,135,000
Soviet Union	2,666,000
France	650,000
Great Britain	410,000
Canada	305,000
Argentina	300,000

TABLE 8. ESTIMATED JEWISH POPULATION, SELECTED CITIES*

City	Jewish Population
Adelaide	1,600[x]
Amsterdam	20,000[x]
Ankara	550[x]
Antwerp	13,000
Athens	2,800
Auckland	1,500
Basel	2,300
Belgrade	1,500
Berlin (both sectors)	6,000
Bern	800
Bogota	5,500
Bombay (and district)	6,970[x]
Bordeaux	7,500
Brisbane	1,500[x]
Brussels	24,500
Bucharest	40,000
Budapest	65,000
Calcutta	300[x]

Cape Town	25,650[x]
Cochin	500
Copenhagen	7,000[x]
Durban	5,990[x]
Florence	1,400
Geneva	3,250
Glasgow	13,000[x]
Goteborg	4,000[x]
Grenoble	8,000
Guatemala City	1,500
Haifa	210,000
Helsinki	1,000
Istanbul	23,000[x]
Izmir	2,500[x]
Jerusalem	272,000
Johannesburg	57,500
Kharkov	80,000
Kiev	170,000
Kobe	80[x]
Leeds	18,000[x]
Leningrad	165,000
Lima	5,000[x]
Lisbon	550
Liverpool	6,500[x]
London (greater)	280,000[x]
Luxembourg	850
Lyons	20,000
Madrid	3,000
Malmo	4,000[x]
Manchester (greater)	35,000[x]
Manila	300
Marseille	65,000
Melbourne	34,000
Mexico, D.F.	32,500
Milan	9,000
Montevideo	48,000
Montreal	115,000[x]
Moscow	285,000
Nice	20,000
Odessa	120,000
Oslo	750
Ottawa	7,500[x]
Paris	300,000

Perth	3,200[x]
Plovdiv	1,000
Porto Alegre	12,000[x]
Prague	3,000
Rabat	2,500
Recife	3,000[x]
Rio de Janeiro	55,000[x]
Rome	12,000
Salisbury	2,000[x]
Salonika	1,300
San Jose	2,500[x]
Sao Paulo	75,000[x]
Sarajevo	1,100
Sofia	4,000
Stockholm	8,000[x]
Strasbourg	12,000
Subotica	250
Sverdlovsk	40,000
Sydney	28,500[x]
Teheran	50,000
Tel Aviv-Jaffa	394,000
Tokyo	320[x]
Toronto	115,000[x]
Toulouse	18,000
Trieste	1,200
Vancouver	12,000[x]
Valparaiso	4,000
Vienna	10,000
Wellington	1,500
Warsaw	4,500
Winnipeg	20,000[x]
Zagreb	1,200
Zhitomir	20,000
Zurich	6,150

*For cities in the United States, see Table 3 of the article "Jewish Population in the United States" in this volume.

[x]See Table 2, note[x].

LEON SHAPIRO

Directories

Lists

Necrology

National Jewish Organizations[1]

UNITED STATES

Organizations are listed according to functions as follows:

Religious, Educational	302
Cultural	297
Community Relations	293
Overseas Aid	300
Social Welfare	321
Social, Mutual Benefit	319
Zionist and Pro-Israel	324

Note also cross-references under these headings:

Professional Associations	331
Women's Organizations	332
Youth and Student Organizations	332

COMMUNITY RELATIONS

AMERICAN COUNCIL FOR JUDAISM (1943). 307 Fifth Ave., Suite 1006, N.Y.C., 10016. (212)889-1313. Pres. Clarence L. Coleman, Jr.; Sec. Alan V. Stone. Seeks to advance the universal principles of a Judaism free of nationalism, and the national, civic, cultural, and social integration into American institutions of Americans of Jewish faith. *Brief: Special Interest Report.*

AMERICAN JEWISH ALTERNATIVES TO ZIONISM, INC. (1968). 133 E. 73 St., N.Y.C., 10021. Pres. Elmer Berger; V.

Pres. Mrs. Arthur Gutman. Applies Jewish values of justice and humanity to the Arab-Israel conflict in the Middle East; rejects nationality attachment of Jews, particularly American Jews, to the State of Israel as self-segregating, inconsistent with American constitutional concepts of individual citizenship and separation of church and state, and as being a principal obstacle to Middle East peace. *Report.*

AMERICAN JEWISH COMMITTEE (1906). Institute of Human Relations, 165 E. 56 St., N.Y.C., 10022. (212)751-4000. Pres.

[1]Information in this directory is based upon replies to questionnaires circulated by the editors. Inclusion in this list does not necessarily imply approval of the organizations by the publishers, nor can they assume responsibility for the accuracy of the data. An asterisk (*) indicates that no reply was received and that the information, which includes title of organization, year of founding, and address, is reprinted from AJYB, 1979, Vol. 79.

Richard Maass; Exec. V. Pres. Bertram H. Gold. Seeks to prevent infraction of civil and religious rights of Jews in any part of the world; to advance the cause of human rights for people of all races, creeds, and nationalities; to interpret the position of Israel to the American public; and to help American Jews maintain and enrich their Jewish identity and, at the same time, achieve full integration in American life; includes Jacob and Hilda Blaustein Center for Human Relations, William E. Wiener Oral History Library, Leonard and Rose Sperry International Center for the Resolution of Group Conflict. AMERICAN JEWISH YEAR BOOK (with Jewish Publication Society of America); *Commentary; Present Tense; What's Doing at the Committee.*

AMERICAN JEWISH CONGRESS (1918). Stephen Wise Congress House, 15 E. 84 St., N.Y.C., 10028. (212)879-4500. Pres. Howard M. Squadron; Exec. Dir. Henry Siegman. Works to foster the creative religious and cultural survival of the Jewish people; to help Israel develop in peace, freedom, and security; to eliminate all forms of racial and religious bigotry; to advance civil rights, protect civil liberties, defend religious freedom, and safeguard the separation of church and state. *Congress Monthly; Judaism.*

———, WOMEN'S DIVISION OF (1933). Stephen Wise Congress House, 15 E. 84 St., N.Y.C., 10028. (212)879-4500. Pres. Leona Chanin; Exec. Dir. Esther H. Kolatch. Committed to the achievement of social justice through its international and domestic programs; works for a free and secure Israel, world peace, human dignity, and the creative continuity of the Jewish people; supports Louise Waterman Wise Youth Hostel in Jerusalem.

ANTI-DEFAMATION LEAGUE OF B'NAI B'RITH (1913). 823 United Nations Plaza, N.Y.C., 10017. Nat. Chmn. Maxwell E. Greenberg; Nat. Dir. Nathan Perlmutter. Seeks to combat antisemitism and to secure justice and fair treatment for all citizens through law, education and community relations. *ADL Bulletin: Face to Face; Fact Finding Report; Israel Backgrounder; Law Notes; Rights.*

ASSOCIATION OF JEWISH CENTER WORKERS (1918). 15 E. 26 St., N.Y.C., 10010. (212)532-4949. Pres. William Budd; Exec. Dir. Debbie Schwartz. Seeks to enhance and improve the standards, techniques, practices, scope, and public understanding of Jewish community center and kindred work. *The Kesher; Viewpoints.*

ASSOCIATION OF JEWISH COMMUNITY RELATIONS WORKERS (1950). 55 W. 42 St., Suite 1530, N.Y.C., 10036. (212)564-3450. Pres. Joel Ollander. Aims to stimulate higher standards of professional practice in Jewish community relations; encourages research and training toward that end; conducts educational programs and seminars; aims to encourage cooperation between community relations workers and those working in other areas of Jewish communal service.

COMMISSION ON SOCIAL ACTION OF REFORM JUDAISM (1953) (under the auspices of the Union of American Hebrew Congregations). 838 Fifth Ave., N.Y.C., 10021. (212)249-0100. Chmn. Alex Ross; Dir. Albert Vorspan; Assoc. Dir. David Saperstein. Develops materials to assist Reform synagogues in setting up social-action programs relating the principles of Judaism to contemporary social problems; assists congregations in studying the moral and religious implications in social issues such as civil rights, civil liberties, church-state relations; guides congregational social-action committees. *Issues of Conscience; Newsletter.*

CONFERENCE OF PRESIDENTS OF MAJOR AMERICAN JEWISH ORGANIZATIONS (1955). 515 Park Ave., N.Y.C., 10022. (212)752-1616. Chmn. Theodore R. Mann; Exec. Dir. Yehuda Hellman. Coordinates the activities of 32 major American Jewish organizations as they relate to American-Israeli affairs, and problems affecting Jews in other lands. *Annual Report; Middle East Memo.*

CONSULTATIVE COUNCIL OF JEWISH ORGANIZATIONS-CCJO (1946). 61 Broadway, N.Y.C., 10006. (212)425-5170. Co-Chmn. Jules Braunschvig (Alliance Israélite Universelle), Harry Batshaw (Canadian Friends of Alliance Israélite Universelle), Basil Bard; V. Chmn. Marcel Franco (American Friends of Alliance Israélite Universelle); Sec.-Gen. Moses Moskowitz. A nongovernmental organization in consultative status with the UN, UNESCO, International Labor Organization, UNICEF, and the Council of Europe; cooperates and consults with, advises and renders assistance to the Economic and Social Council of the United Nations on all problems relating to human rights and economic, social, cultural, educational, and related matters pertaining to Jews.

COORDINATING BOARD OF JEWISH ORGANIZATIONS (1947). 1640 Rhode Island Ave., N.W., Washington, D.C., 20036. (202)857-6600. Pres. Jack J. Spitzer (B'nai B'rith), Lord Fisher of Camden (Board of Deputies of British Jews), Maurice Porter (South African Jewish Board of Deputies); Exec. V. Pres. Daniel Thursz (U.S.). As an organization in consultative status with the Economic and Social Council of the United Nations, represents the three constituents (B'nai B'rith, the Board of Deputies of British Jews, and the South African Jewish Board of Deputies) in the appropriate United Nations bodies for the purpose of promoting human rights, with special attention to combatting persecution or discrimination on grounds of race, religion, or origin.

COUNCIL OF JEWISH ORGANIZATIONS IN CIVIL SERVICE, INC. (1948). 45 E. 33 St., N.Y.C., 10016. (212)689-2015. Pres. Louis Weiser; Sec. Robert H. Gottlieb. Supports merit system; combats discrimination; promotes all Jewish interest projects; sponsors scholarships; is member of Greater N.Y. Conference on Soviet Jewry, Jewish Labor Committee, America-Israel Friendship League. *CJO Digest.*

INSTITUTE FOR JEWISH POLICY PLANNING AND RESEARCH (see Synagogue Council of America, p. 312).

INTERNATIONAL CONFERENCE OF JEWISH COMMUNAL SERVICE (1966). 15 E. 26 St., N.Y.C., 10010. (212)683-8056. Pres. Herbert Millman; Sec.-Gen. Miriam R. Ephraim. Established by Jewish communal workers to strengthen their understanding of each other's programs and to communicate with colleagues in order to enrich quality of their work. Conducts quadrennial international conferences in Jerusalem and periodic regional meetings. *Proceedings of International Conferences; Newsletter.*

JEWISH LABOR COMMITTEE (1934). Atran Center for Jewish Culture, 25 E. 78 St., N.Y.C., 10021. (212)535-3700. Pres. Jacob Sheinkman; Exec. Dir. Emanuel Muravchik. Serves as a link between the Jewish community and the trade union movement; works with the AFL-CIO and other unions to combat all forms of racial and religious discrimination in the United States and abroad; furthers labor support for Israel's security and Soviet Jewry, and Jewish communal support for labor, social, and economic change; supports Yiddish cultural institutions. *JLC News.*

————, NATIONAL TRADE UNION COUNCIL FOR HUMAN RIGHTS (1956). Atran Center for Jewish Culture, 25 E. 78 St., N.Y.C., 10021. (212)535-3700. Chmn. Wilbur Daniels; Exec. Sec. Betty Kaye Taylor. Works with trade unions on programs and issues affecting labor and the Jewish community.

————, WOMEN'S DIVISION OF (1947). Atran Center for Jewish Culture, 25 E. 78 St., N.Y.C., 10021. (212)535-3700. Nat. Chmn. Eleanor Schachner. Supports the general activities of the Jewish Labor Committee; provides secondary school and college scholarships for needy Israeli students; participates in educational and cultural activities.

————, WORKMEN'S CIRCLE DIVISION OF (1939). Atran Center for Jewish Culture, 25 E. 78 St., N.Y.C., 10021. (212)535-3700. Chmn. Saul Charrow; Co-Chmn. Samuel Perel. Promotes aims of, and raises funds for, the Jewish Labor Committee among the Workmen's Circle branches; conducts Yiddish educational and cultural activities.

JEWISH WAR VETERANS OF THE UNITED STATES OF AMERICA (1896). 1712 New Hampshire Ave., N. W., Washington, D.C., 20009. (202)265-6280. Nat. Comdr. Nathan M. Goldberg; Nat. Exec. Dir. Irwin R. Ziff. Seeks to foster true allegiance to the United States; to combat bigotry and prevent defamation of Jews; to encourage the doctrine of universal liberty, equal rights, and full justice to all men; to cooperate with and support existing educational institutions and establish new ones; to foster the education of ex-servicemen, ex-servicewomen, and members in the ideals and principles of Americanism. *Jewish Veteran.*

————: NATIONAL MEMORIAL, INC; NATIONAL SHRINE TO THE JEWISH WAR DEAD (1958). 1712 New Hampshire Ave., N.W., Washington, D.C., 20009. (202)

265-6280. Pres. Meyer J. Abgott; Treas. Cherie Siegel. Administers shrine in Washington, D.C., a repository for medals and honors won by Jewish men and women for valor from Revolutionary War to present; maintains *Golden Book* of names of the war dead.

NATIONAL CONFERENCE ON SOVIET JEWRY (formerly AMERICAN JEWISH CONFERENCE ON SOVIET JEWRY) (1964; reorg. 1971). 10 E. 40 St., Suite 907, N.Y.C., 10016. (212)679-6122. Chmn. Eugene Gold; Exec. Dir. Jerry Goodman. Coordinating agency for major national Jewish organizations and local community groups in the U.S., acting on behalf of Soviet Jewry through public education and social action; stimulates all segments of the community to maintain an interest in the problems of Soviet Jews by publishing reports and special pamphlets, sponsoring special programs and projects, organizing public meetings and forums. *News Bulletin, Leadership Wrap-Up Series; Activities Report.*

————: SOVIET JEWRY RESEARCH BUREAU. Chmn. Charlotte Jacobson. Organized by NCSJ to monitor emigration trends. Primary task is the accumulation, evaluation, and processing of information regarding Soviet Jews, especially those who apply for emigration.

NATIONAL JEWISH COMMISSION ON LAW AND PUBLIC AFFAIRS (COLPA) (1965). 919 3rd Ave., N.Y.C., 10022. (212)755-2180. Pres. Howard Zuckerman; Exec. Dir. Dennis Rapps. Voluntary association of attorneys whose purpose is to represent the Orthodox Jewish community on legal matters and matters of public affairs.

NATIONAL JEWISH COMMUNITY RELATIONS ADVISORY COUNCIL (1944). 55 West 42 St., N.Y.C., 10036. (212)564-3450. Chmn. Theodore R. Mann; Exec. V. Chmn. Albert D. Chernin; Sec. Raymond Epstein. Consultative, advisory, and coordinating council of 11 national Jewish organizations and 106 local Jewish councils that seeks cooperatively the promotion of understanding of Israel and the Middle East; freedom for Jews in the Soviet Union; equal status and opportunity for all groups, including Jews, with full expression of distinctive group values and full participation in the general society. Through the processes of the Council, its constituent organizations seek agreement on policies, strategies, and programs for most effective utilization of their collective resources for common ends. *Guide to Program Planning for Jewish Community Relations.*

NORTH AMERICAN JEWISH YOUTH COUNCIL (1965). 515 Park Ave., N.Y.C., 10022. (212)751-6070. Co-Chmn. Lynn Goldstein, Michael Horowitz. Provides a framework for coordination and exchange of programs and information among national Jewish youth organizations to help them deepen the concern of American Jewish youth for world Jewry; represents Jewish youth in the Conference of Presidents, United States Youth Council, etc.

STUDENT STRUGGLE FOR SOVIET JEWRY, INC. (1964). 200 W. 72 St., N.Y.C., 10023. (212)799-8900. Nat. Dir. Jacob Birnbaum; Nat. Coord. Glenn Richter. Provides information and action guidance to adult and student organizations, communities and schools throughout U.S. and Canada; assists individual Soviet Jews financially and by publicity campaigns; helps Russian Jews in the U.S.; aids Rumanian Jews seeking emigration; maintains speakers bureau. *Soviet Jewry Action Newsletter.*

UNION OF COUNCILS FOR SOVIET JEWS (1969). 680 Main St., Suite 302, Waltham, Mass., 02154. (617)893-4780. Pres. Robert Gordon; Exec. Dir. Diana Appelbaum. A confederation of 28 grass-roots organizations established in support of Soviet Jewry. Acts as a clearinghouse for information; organizes demonstrations in support of Soviet Jews. *Alert.*

WORLD JEWISH CONGRESS (1936; org. in U.S. 1939). 1 Park Ave., Suite 418, N.Y.C., 10016. (212)679-0600. Pres. Philip M. Klutznick; Chmn. Gov. Bd. Lord Fisher of Camden; Chmn. Amer. Sect. Jacob Katzman; Chmn. No. Amer. Sect. Edgar N. Bronfman; Sec. Gen. Gerhart M. Reigner (Geneva); Dir. No. Amer. Branch, Exec. Dir. Amer. Sect. Israel Singer. Seeks to intensify bonds of world Jewry with Israel as central force in Jewish life; to strengthen solidarity among Jews everywhere and secure their rights, status, and interests as individuals and communities; to encourage development of Jewish social, religious, and cultural life throughout the world and coordinate efforts by Jewish communities and organizations to cope with any Jewish problem; to work for human rights generally. Represents its affiliated organizations

—most representative bodies of Jewish communities in more than 60 countries and 18 national organizations in Amer. section—at UN, OAS, UNESCO, Council of Europe, ILO, UNICEF and other governmental, intergovernmental, and international authorities. Publications (including those by Institute of Jewish Affairs, London): *Christian Attitudes on Jews and Judaism; Compendium of Current Jewish Research; Folk, Velt un Medinah; Gesher; Jewish Journal of Sociology; Patterns of Prejudice; Soviet Jewish Affairs.*

CULTURAL

AMERICAN ACADEMY FOR JEWISH RESEARCH (1920). 3080 Broadway, N.Y.C., 10027. Pres. Salo W. Baron; Sec. Isaac E. Barzilay. Encourages research by aiding scholars in need and by giving grants for the publication of scholarly works. *Proceedings, American Academy for Jewish Research.*

AMERICAN BIBLICAL ENCYCLOPEDIA SOCIETY (1930). 24 West Maple Ave., Monsey, N.Y., 10952. (914)356-0046. Pres. Leo Jung; Exec. V. Pres. Bernard Greenbaum; Author-Ed. Menachem M. Kasher. Fosters biblical-talmudical research; sponsors and publishes *Torah Shelemah* (the Encyclopedia of Biblical Interpretation) and related publications; disseminates the teachings and values of the Bible. *Noam.*

AMERICAN HISTADRUT CULTURAL EXCHANGE INSTITUTE (1962) 33 E. 67 St., N.Y.C., 10021. (212)628-1000. Nat. Chmn. Herbert Levine; Coordinator, Karen Chaikin. Serves as a vehicle for promoting better understanding of the efforts to create in Israel a society based on social justice. Provides a forum for the joint exploration of the urgent social problems of our times by American and Israeli labor, academic and community leaders. Publishes pamphlets and books on various Israeli and Middle East topics.

AMERICAN JEWISH HISTORICAL SOCIETY (1892). 2 Thornton Rd., Waltham, Mass., 02154. (617)891-8110. Pres. Saul Viener; Dir. Bernard Wax. Collects, catalogues, publishes and displays material on the history of the Jews in America; serves as an information center for inquiries on American Jewish history; maintains archives of original source material on American Jewish history; sponsors lectures and exhibitions; makes available historic Yiddish films and audio/visual material. *American Jewish History; Newsletter.*

AMERICAN JEWISH PRESS ASSOCIATION (formerly AMERICAN ASSOCIATION OF ENGLISH JEWISH NEWSPAPERS) (1943) c/o Jewish Exponent, 226 S. 16 St., Philadelphia, Pa. 19102. (212)893-5740. Pres. Frank F. Wundohl; V. Pres. Milton Firestone. Sec. Doris Sky. Seeks the advancement of Jewish journalism, the attainment of the highest editorial and business standards for members, and the maintenance of strong Jewish press in the U.S. and Canada. *AJPA Bulletin.*

AMERICAN SOCIETY FOR JEWISH MUSIC (1974). 155 Fifth Ave., N.Y.C. 10010. (212)533-2601. Pres. Albert Weisser; V. Pres.-Treas. Paul Kavon; Sec. Hadássah B. Markson. Seeks to raise standards of composition and performance in Jewish liturgical and secular music; encourages research in all areas of Jewish music; publishes scholarly journal; presents programs and sponsors performances of new and rarely heard works and encourages their recording; commissions new works of Jewish interest. *Musica Judaica.*

ASSOCIATED AMERICAN JEWISH MUSEUMS, INC. (1971). 303 LeRoi Road, Pittsburgh, Pa., 15208. Pres. Walter Jacob; V. Pres. William Rosenthall; Sec. Robert H. Lehman; Treas. Jason Z. Edelstein. Maintains regional collections of Jewish art, historical and ritual objects, as well as a central catalogue of such objects in the collections of Jewish museums throughout the U.S.; helps Jewish museums acquire, identify and classify objects; arranges exchanges of collections, exhibits, and individual objects among Jewish museums; encourages the creation of Jewish art, ceremonial and ritual objects.

ASSOCIATION FOR THE SOCIOLOGICAL STUDY OF JEWRY (1971). (201)932-7720. Dept. of Sociology, University College, Rutgers University, New Brunswick, N.J. 08903. Pres. Celia S. Heller; Sec.-Treas. Chaim I. Waxman. Arranges academic sessions among social scientists studying Jewry; facilitates communication among social scientists studying Jewry through meetings, newsletter, and related materials. *Contemporary Jewry: A Journal of Sociological Inquiry.*

298 / AMERICAN JEWISH YEAR BOOK, 1980

ASSOCIATION OF JEWISH LIBRARIES (1966).
c/o National Foundation for Jewish Culture, 408 Chanin Bldg., 122 E. 42 St., N.Y.C., 10017. (212)490-2280. Pres. Harvey P. Horowitz; Sec. Stephanie M. Stern. Seeks to promote and improve services and professional standards in Jewish libraries; serves as a center for the dissemination of Jewish library information and guidance; promotes publication of literature in the field; encourages the establishment of Jewish libraries and collections of Judaica and the choice of Jewish librarianship as a vocation. *AJL Bulletin; Proceedings.*

ASSOCIATION OF JEWISH PUBLISHERS (1962). 838 Fifth Ave., N.Y.C., 10021. Pres. Jacob Steinberg. As a nonprofit group, provides a forum for discussion of mutual problems by publishers, authors, and other individuals and institutions concerned with books of Jewish interest.

CENTER FOR HOLOCAUST STUDIES, INC. (1974). 1605 Ave. J., Bklyn, N.Y., 11230. Dir. Yaffa Eliach; Chmn. Adv. Bd. Allen J. Bodner. Collects and preserves documents and memorabilia, oral histories and literary works on the Holocaust period for purpose of documentation and research; arranges lectures and exhibits; maintains speakers bureau and audio-visual department. *Newsletter.*

CENTRAL YIDDISH CULTURE ORGANIZATION (CYCO), INC. (1943). 25 E. 78 St., N.Y.C., 10021. Pres. Noah Singman; Sec. Jona Gutkowicz. Promotes and publishes Yiddish books; distributes books from other Yiddish publishing houses throughout the world; publishes annual bibliographical and statistical register of Yiddish books, and catalogues of new publications. *Zukunft.*

CONFERENCE ON JEWISH SOCIAL STUDIES, INC. (formerly CONFERENCE ON JEWISH RELATIONS, INC.) (1939). 250 W. 57 St., N.Y.C., 10019. Pres. Jeannette M. Baron; Hon. Pres. Salo W. Baron; V. Pres. Joseph L. Blau, J. M. Kaplan. Publishes scientific studies on the Jews in the modern world, dealing with such aspects as antisemitism, demography, economic stratification, history, philosophy, and political developments. *Jewish Social Studies.*

CONGRESS FOR JEWISH CULTURE, INC. (1948). 25 E. 78 St., N.Y.C., 10021. (212) 879-2232. Pres. Joseph Landis; Exec. Dir.

Hyman B. Bass. Seeks to centralize and promote Jewish culture and cultural activities throughout the world, and to unify fund raising for these activities. *Bulletin fun Kultur Kongres; Zukunft; Leksikon fun der Nayer Yiddisher Literature; Pinkos far der Forshung fun der Yiddisher Literature un Presse; World of Yiddish.*

HEBREW ARTS SCHOOL FOR MUSIC AND DANCE (1952). 129 W. 67 St., N.Y.C., 10023. (212)362-8060. Bd. Chmn. and Pres. Abraham Goodman; Dir. Tzipora H. Jochsberger; Sec. Benjamin W. Mehlman. Chartered by the Board of Regents, University of the State of New York. Provides children with training in music, dance, and art, combining instruction in Western culture with the cultural heritage of the Jewish people; adult division offers instrumental, vocal, dance, and art classes, music workshops for teachers, ensemble workshops, and classes of special interest covering many areas of music-making, dance, and art; has Jewish Music Teacher Training Institute, a parttime program for professional musicians or music majors; sponsors Hebrew Arts Chamber Players, Hebrew Arts String Quartet, Quadro Barocco, Jewish Young People's concerts in schools, and other concert series.

HEBREW CULTURE FOUNDATION (1955). 515 Park Ave., N.Y.C., 10022. (212)752-0600. Chmn. Milton R. Konvitz; Sec. Moshe Avital. Sponsors the introduction of the study of Hebrew language and literature in institutions of higher learning in the United States.

HISTADRUTH IVRITH OF AMERICA (1916; reorg. 1922). 1841 Broadway, N.Y.C., 10023. (212)581-5151. Pres. Myron Fenster; Exec. Dir. Shlomo Shamir. Emphasizes the primacy of Hebrew in Jewish life, culture, and education; aims to disseminate knowledge of written and spoken Hebrew in the Diaspora, thus building a cultural bridge between State of Israel and Jewish communities throughout the world. *Hadoar; Lamishpaha.*

JEWISH ACADEMY OF ARTS AND SCIENCES, INC. (1925). c/o Sec'y, 123 Gregory Ave., West Orange, N.J., 07052. (201)731-1137. Headquarters: Dropsie University, Philadelphia, Pa. 19132. Pres. Jewish Center, N.Y.C. Leo Jung; Pres. Emeritus Dropsie Univ. Abraham I. Katsh. Scholarship, contributions, accomplishments of Jews in the arts and sciences; recognition by election to membership and/or fellowship; publishes papers delivered at annual convocations. *Annals.*

JEWISH BOOK COUNCIL OF JWB (1925). 15 E. 26 St., N.Y.C., 10010. (212)532-4949. Pres. Sidney B. Hoenig; Dir. Sharon Strassfeld. Promotes knowledge of Jewish books through dissemination of booklists, program materials; stimulates observance of Jewish Book Month; presents literary awards and library citations; cooperates with publishers of Jewish books, and gives advice on general Jewish literature. *Jewish Book Annual; Books in Review.*

JEWISH INFORMATION BUREAU, INC. (1932). 250 W. 57 St., N.Y.C., 10019. (212)582-5318. Chmn. Judah A. Richards; V. Chmn. Eleazar Lipsky. Serves as clearinghouse of information for inquiries regarding Jews, Judaism, Israel, and Jewish affairs; refers inquiries to communal agencies. *Index.*

JEWISH MUSEUM (1904) (under auspices of Jewish Theological Seminary of America). 1109 Fifth Ave., N.Y.C., 10028. (212)860-1888. Dir. Joy Ungerleider-Meyerson; Admin. Ruth Dolkart. Main repository in U.S. of Jewish ceremonial objects. Collection ranges from Biblical archaeology to contemporary Judaica. Offers changing exhibitions of paintings, sculpture and photography, in addition to films, lectures, and children's programs. Dedicated to exploring richness and diversity of past and present Jewish life; publishes catalogues of exhibitions.

JEWISH MUSIC COUNCIL OF JWB (1944). 15 E. 26 St., N.Y.C., 10010. (212)532-4949. Chmn. Leonard Kaplan; Dir. Irene Heskes. Promotes Jewish music activities nationally, annually sponsors and promotes the Jewish Music Festival, and encourages participation on a community basis. *Jewish Music Notes* and numerous music resource publications for national distribution.

JEWISH PUBLICATION SOCIETY OF AMERICA (1888). 117 S. 17th St., Philadelphia, Pa., 19103. (215)564-5925. Pres. Edward B. Shils; Ed. Maier Deshell; Exec. V. Pres. Bernard I. Levinson. Publishes and disseminates books of Jewish interest on history, religion, and literature for the purpose of helping to preserve the Jewish heritage and culture. AMERICAN JEWISH YEAR BOOK (with American Jewish Committee).

JUDAH L. MAGNES MEMORIAL MUSEUM— JEWISH MUSEUM OF THE WEST (1962). 2911 Russell St., Berkeley, Calif., 94705. (415)849-2710. Pres. Marvin Weinreb; V. Pres. Alfred Fromm; Dir. Seymour Fromer. Serves both as museum and library, combining historical and literary materials illustrating Jewish life in the Bay Area, the Western States, and around the world; provides archives of world Jewish history and Jewish art; repository of historical documents intended for scholarly use; changing exhibits, facilities open to the general public.

LEO BAECK INSTITUTE, INC. (1955). 129 E. 73 St., N.Y.C., 10021. Pres. Max Gruenewald; Sec. Fred Grubel (212)744-6400. Engages in historical research, the presentation and publication of the history of German-speaking Jewry, and in the collection of books, manuscripts and documents in this field; publishes monographs. *LBI Bulletin; LBI News; LBI Year Book; LBI Library and Archives News.*

MEMORIAL FOUNDATION FOR JEWISH CULTURE, INC. (1964). 15 E. 26 St., N.Y.C., 10010. (212)679-4074. Pres. Nahum Goldmann; Exec. Dir. Norman E. Frimer. Supports Jewish cultural and educational programs all over the world, in cooperation with universities and established scholarly organizations; conducts annual scholarship and fellowship program. *Annual Report.*

NATIONAL FOUNDATION FOR JEWISH CULTURE (1960). 1512 Chanin Bldg., 122 E. 42 St., N.Y.C., 10017. (212)490-2280. Pres. Amos Comay; Exec. Dir. Harry I. Barron. Provides consultation, guidance, and support to Jewish communities, organizations, educational and other institutions, and individuals for activities in the field of Jewish culture; awards fellowships and other grants to students preparing for careers in Jewish scholarship and to established scholars; makes awards for creative efforts in Jewish cultural arts and for Jewish programming in small and intermediate communities; encourages teaching of Jewish studies in colleges and universities; serves as clearinghouse of information on American Jewish culture; administers Joint Cultural Appeal among local Jewish welfare funds in behalf of 9 national cultural organizations, and administers Council for Archives and Research Libraries in Jewish Studies. *Jewish Cultural News.*

NATIONAL HEBREW CULTURE COUNCIL (1952). 1776 Broadway, N.Y.C., 10019. (212)247-0741. Pres. Frances K. Thau; Exec. Dir. Judah Lapson. Cultivates the study of Hebrew as a modern language in American public high schools and colleges, providing guidance to community groups and public educational authorities; annually administers National Voluntary Examination in Hebrew Culture and Knowledge of Israel in the public high schools, and conducts summer seminar and tour of Israel for teachers and other educational personnel of the public school system, in cooperation with Hebrew University and WZO. *Hebrew in Colleges and Universities.*

RESEARCH FOUNDATION FOR JEWISH IMMIGRATION, INC. (1971). 570 Seventh Ave., N.Y.C., 10018. (212)869-8610. Pres. Curt C. Silberman; Sec. Herbert A. Strauss. Studies and records the history of the migration and acculturation of Jewish Nazi persecutees in the various resettlement countries; is in process of preparing worldwide biographical handbook of outstanding emigrés, in partnership with the Institut für Zeitgeschichte, Munich, Germany.

SOCIETY FOR THE HISTORY OF CZECHOSLOVAK JEWS, INC. (1961). 87–08 Santiago St., Holliswood, N.Y., 11423. Pres. Lewis Weiner; Sec. Joseph Abeles. Studies the history of the Czechoslovak Jews, collects material and disseminates information through the publication of books and pamphlets. *The Jews of Czechoslovakia* book series, Vol. I (1968), Vol. II (1971); Vol. III in prep. Annual reports and pamphlets.

YESHIVA UNIVERSITY MUSEUM (1973). 2520 Amsterdam Ave., N.Y.C., 10033. (212)960-5390. Curator Dalia Tawil. Dir. of Admin. Sylvia A. Hershkowitz. Collects, preserves, interprets, and displays ceremonial objects, rare books and scrolls, models, paintings, and other works of art expressing the Jewish religious experience historically, to the present.

YIDDISHER KULTUR FARBAND—YKUF (1937). 853 Broadway, Suite 2121, N.Y.C., 10003. (212)228-1955. Pres. Itche Goldberg. Publishes a monthly magazine and books by contemporary and classical Jewish writers; conducts cultural forums and exhibits works by contemporary Jewish artists and materials of Jewish historical value. *Yiddishe Kultur.*

YIVO INSTITUTE FOR JEWISH RESEARCH, INC. (1925). 1048 Fifth Ave., N.Y.C., 10028. (212)535-6700. Chmn. Morris Laub. Engages in Jewish social and humanistic research; maintains library and archives of material pertaining to Jewish life; serves as information center for organizations, local institutions, information media, and individual scholars and laymen; publishes books. *Yedies fun Yivo— News of the Yivo; Yidishe Shprakh; Yivo Annual of Jewish Social Science; Yivo Bleter.*

————: MAX WEINREICH CENTER FOR ADVANCED JEWISH STUDIES (1968). 1048 Fifth Ave., N.Y.C., 10028. (212)535-6700. Pres. Nathan Reich; Act. Dean Marvin I. Herzog. Trains scholars in the fields of Eastern European Jewish life and culture; the Holocaust; the mass settlement of Jews in the U.S. and other countries; Yiddish language, literature, and folklore through inter-university courses and seminars and its panel of consultants. *Annual Bulletin.*

OVERSEAS AID

AMERICAN COUNCIL FOR JUDAISM PHILANTHROPIC FUND (1955). 386 Park Ave. S., 10th fl., N.Y.C., 10016. (212)684-1525. Pres. Charles J. Tanenbaum; Exec. Dir. Anna Walling Matson. Through offices in Austria, France, West Germany, Italy and the United States, maintains programs offering freedom of choice and resettlement assistance in Western Europe and the United States to Jewish refugees from the Soviet Union, Eastern Europe and Arab countries.

AMERICAN FRIENDS OF THE ALLIANCE ISRAÉLITE UNIVERSELLE, INC. (1946). 61 Broadway, N.Y.C., 10006. (212)425-5170. Pres. Marcel Franco; Exec. Dir. Saadiah Cherniak. Helps networks of Jewish schools in Europe, Asia, and Africa. *Alliance Review.*

AMERICAN JEWISH JOINT DISTRIBUTION COMMITTEE, INC.—JDC (1914). 60 E. 42 St., N.Y.C., 10017. (212)687-6200. Pres. Donald M. Robinson; Exec. V. Pres. Ralph I. Goldman. Organizes and finances rescue, relief, and rehabilitation programs for imperiled and needy Jews overseas; conducts wide range of health, welfare, rehabilitation, education programs and aid to cultural and religious institutions, programs benefiting 430,000 Jews in 25 countries overseas. Major areas of operation are Israel, North Africa, Iran and Europe. *Guidelines for Services Needed for the Aged; Helping the Blind in Israel; JDC Annual Report; JDC in Israel; JDC Overseas Guide; JDC World.*

AMERICAN ORT FEDERATION, INC.—ORGANIZATION FOR REHABILITATION THROUGH TRAINING (1924). 817 Broadway, N.Y.C., 10003. (212)677-4400. Pres. Harold Friedman; Exec. Dir. Paul Bernick. Teaches vocational skills in 24 countries around the world, particularly in Israel, to over 100,000 persons annually, with the largest program of 50,000 trainees in Israel. The teaching staff numbers about 3,400. Annual cost of program is about $80 million. *ORT Bulletin; ORT Yearbook.*

————: AMERICAN AND EUROPEAN FRIENDS OF ORT (1941). 817 Broadway, N.Y.C., 10003. (212)677-4400. Pres. Simon Jaglom; Chmn. Exec. Com. Jacques Zwibak. Promotes the ORT idea among Americans of European extraction; supports the Litton ORT Auto-Mechanics School in Jerusalem.

————: AMERICAN LABOR ORT (1937). 817 Broadway., N.Y.C., 10003. (212)677-4400. Chmn. Shelley Appleton; Exec. Sec. Samuel Milman. Promotes ORT program of vocational training among Jews.

————: BUSINESS AND PROFESSIONAL ORT (formerly YOUNG MEN'S AND WOMEN'S ORT) (1937). 817 Broadway, N.Y.C., 10003. (212)677-4400. Pres. Rose Seidel Kalich; Exec. Sec. Helen S. Kreisler. Promotes work of American ORT Federation.

————: NATIONAL ORT LEAGUE (1914). 817 Broadway, N.Y.C., 10003. (212)677-4400. Pres. Bruce B. Teicholz; Chmn. Exec. Bd. Jack Weinstein; Exec. V. Pres. and Sec. Jacob Zonis. Promotes ORT idea among Jewish fraternal *landsmanshaften,* national and local organizations, congregations; helps to equip ORT installations and Jewish artisans abroad, especially in Israel. *ORT Bulletin.*

————: WOMEN'S AMERICAN ORT (1927). 1250 Broadway, N.Y.C., 10001. (212)594-8500. Pres. Ruth Eisenberg; Exec. V. Pres.

Nathan Gould. Represents and advances the program and philosophy of ORT among the women of the American Jewish community through membership and educational activities; supports materially the vocational training operations of World ORT; contributes to the American Jewish community through participation in its authorized campaigns and through general education to help raise the level of Jewish consciousness among American Jewish women; through its American Affairs program, cooperates in efforts to improve quality of education and vocational training in U.S. *Facts and Findings; Highlights; Insights; The Merchandiser; Women's American ORT Reporter.*

A.R.I.F.—ASSOCIATION POUR LE RÉTABLISSEMENT DES INSTITUTIONS ET OEUVRES ISRAÉLITES EN FRANCE, INC. (1944). 119 E. 95 St., N.Y.C., 10028. (212)-876-1448. Pres. Baroness Robert de Gunzburg; Sec.-Treas. Simon Langer. Helps Jewish religious and cultural institutions in France.

CONFERENCE ON JEWISH MATERIAL CLAIMS AGAINST GERMANY, INC. (1951). 15 E. 26 St., N.Y.C., 10010. (212)679-4074. Pres. Nahum Goldmann; Sec. Norman E. Frimer. Utilizes balance of funds received from the German Federal Republic under Luxembourg agreement for relief to needy Jewish victims of Nazi persecution and needy non-Jews who risked their lives to help such victims. *Annual Report.*

FREELAND LEAGUE (1935). 200 W. 72 St., N.Y.C., 10023. (212)787-6675. Pres. Nathan Turak; Exec. Sec. Mordkhe Schaechter. Promotes the development and use of Yiddish as a living language. *Afn Shvel.*

HIAS, INC. (1884; reorg. 1954). 200 Park Ave. S., N.Y.C., 10003. (212)674-6800. Pres. Edwin Shapiro; Exec. V. Pres. Gaynor I. Jacobson. Worldwide Jewish migration agency with offices, affiliates, committees in United States, Europe, North Africa, Latin America, Canada, Australia, Israel, and New Zealand. Assists migrants and refugees from Eastern Europe, the Middle East, North Africa, and Latin America to find new homes in the United States and other countries. Responsible for premigration planning, visa documentation, consular representation and intervention, transportation, reception, initial adjustment and reunion of families; carries on adjustment of status and naturalization programs; provides protective service for aliens and naturalized citizens; works in the United States through local community agencies for the integration of immigrants; conducts a planned program of resettlement for Jewish immigrants in Latin America; has worldwide location service to assist in locating missing friends and relatives; conducts educational campaigns on opportunities for migration and resettlement, with particular emphasis on family reunion. *F.Y.I.; HIAS Annual Report; HIAS Bulletin; Statistical Abstract.*

JEWISH RESTITUTION SUCCESSOR ORGANIZATION (1948). 15–19 E. 26 St., N.Y.C., 10010. (212)679-4074. Pres. Maurice M. Bookstein; Sec. Saul Kagan. Acts to discover, claim, receive, and assist in the recovery of Jewish heirless or unclaimed property; to utilize such assets or to provide for their utilization for the relief, rehabilitation, and resettlement of surviving victims of Nazi persecution.

UNITED JEWISH APPEAL, INC. (1939). 1290 Ave. of the Americas, N.Y.C., 10019. (212)757-1500. Gen. Chmn. Irwin S. Field; Pres. Frank R. Lautenberg; Exec. V. Chmn. Irving Bernstein. Channels funds for overseas humanitarian aid, supporting immigration and settlement in Israel, rehabilitation and relief in 30 nations, and refugee assistance in U.S. through Joint Distribution Committee, United Israel Appeal, United HIAS Service and New York Association for New Americans.

———, FACULTY ADVISORY CABINET (1975). 1290 Ave. of the Americas. (212)-757-1500. Chmn. Michael Walzer; Dir. Melvin L. Libman. To promote faculty leadership support for local and national UJA campaigns through educational and personal commitment; to make use of faculty resources and expertise on behalf of UJA and Israel.

———, RABBINIC CABINET (1972). 1290 Ave. of the Americas, N.Y.C., 10019. (212)757-1500. Chmn. Stanley S. Rabinowitz; Dir. Melvin L. Libman. To promote rabbinic leadership support for local and national UJA campaigns through education and personal commitment; to make use of rabbinic resources on behalf of UJA and Israel.

———, UNIVERSITY PROGRAMS DEPT. (1970). 1290 Ave. of the Americas, N.Y.C., 10019. (212)757-1500. Student Advisory Board. To crystallize Jewish commitment on the campus through an educational fund-raising campaign involving various programs, leadership training, and opportunities for participation in community functions.

———, WOMEN'S DIVISION OF (1946). 1290 Ave. of the Americas, N.Y.C., 10019. (212)757-1500. Pres. Peggy Steine; Nat. Chmn. Bernice Waldman; Dir. Nan Goldberg. *Ideas That Click; Right Now; Women's Division Record.*

———, YOUNG LEADERSHIP CABINET (1977). 1290 Ave. of the Americas, N.Y.C., 10019. (212)757-1500. Exec. Dir. Laurence H. Rubinstein; Chmn. Stanley D. Frankel. Committed to the creative survival of Jews, Judaism, and Israel through dialogues with leading scholars and writers, and through peer exchanges at retreats, conferences, missions to Israel, and special programs. *Cabinet Communiqués.*

———, YOUNG WOMEN'S LEADERSHIP CABINET (1977). 1290 Ave. of the Americas, N.Y.C., 10019. (212)757-1500. Nat. Chmn. Jane Sherman; Dir. Barbara P. Faske. Encourages young Jewish women to become involved with the organized Jewish community. *Cabinet Update.*

WOMEN'S SOCIAL SERVICE FOR ISRAEL, INC. (1937). 240 W. 98 St., N.Y.C., 10025. (212)666-7880. Pres. Rosi Michael; Sec. Dory Gordon. Maintains in Israel apartments for the aged, old age homes, nursing home, hospital for incurable diseases, rehabilitation department, department for bone injuries, soup kitchen. *Annual Journal; Newsletter.*

RELIGIOUS AND EDUCATIONAL

AGUDAS ISRAEL WORLD ORGANIZATION (1912). 471 West End Ave., N.Y.C., 10024. (212) 874-7979. Chmn. Central Com. Am. Sect. Isaac Lewin. Represents the interests of Orthodox Jewry on the national and international scenes.

AGUDATH ISRAEL OF AMERICA (1912). 5 Beekman St., N.Y.C., 10038. (212)964-1620. Exec. Pres. Morris Sherer; Exec. Dir. Boruch B. Borchardt. Mobilizes Orthodox Jews to cope with Jewish problems in the spirit of the Torah; sponsors a broad range of constructive projects in fields of religion, education, children's welfare, protection of Jewish religious rights and social services. *Jewish Observer; Dos Yiddishe Vort.*

——, CHILDREN'S DIVISION—PIRCHEI AGUDATH ISRAEL (1925). 5 Beekman St., N.Y.C., 10038 (212)964-1620. Pres. Avrohom Portowitz; Nat. Dir. Joshua Silbermintz. Educates Orthodox Jewish children in Torah; encourages sense of communal responsibility; communal celebrations, learning groups, and welfare projects. *Darkeinu; Leaders Guide.*

——, GIRLS' DIVISION—BNOS AGUDATH ISRAEL (1921). 5 Beekman St., N.Y.C., 10038. (212)964-1620. Natl. Coordinator Shanie Meyer. Educates Jewish girls to the historic nature of the Jewish people; encourages greater devotion to and understanding of the Torah. *Kol Bnos.*

——, WOMEN'S DIVISION—N'SHEI AGUDATH ISRAEL OF AMERICA (1940). 5 Beekman St., N.Y.C., 10038. (212)964-1620. Pres. Esther Bohensky, Josephine Reichel. Organizes Jewish women for philanthropic work in the U.S. and Israel and for intense Torah education, seeking to train Torah-guided Jewish mothers.

——, YOUTH DIVISION—ZEIREI AGUDATH ISRAEL (1921). 5 Beekman St., N.Y.C., 10038. (212)964-1620. Pres. Joseph Ashkenazi; Exec. Dir. David Pitterman. Educates Jewish youth to realize the historic nature of the Jewish people as the people of the Torah and to seek solutions to all the problems of the Jewish people in Israel in the spirit of the Torah. *The Zeirei Forum; Am Hatorah, Daf Chizuk, Yom Tov Publications.*

AMERICAN ASSOCIATION FOR JEWISH EDUCATION (1939). 114 Fifth Ave., N.Y.C., 10011. (212)675-5656. Pres. Arthur Brody; Dir. Shimon Frost. Coordinates, promotes, and services Jewish education nationally through 18 constituent national organizations and 51 affiliated bureaus of Jewish education; conducts and administers exchange program for Israeli teachers; offers fellowships in Jewish educational leadership; sponsors and supports the National Curriculum Research Institute, including the Dept. of Methods & Materials, the National Board of License, and the Commission on Teaching About Israel. Engages in statistical and other educational research; provides community consultations; and conducts community studies. *Information; Research Bulletins; Jewish Education News; Jewish Education Directory; Pedagogic Reporter; Curriculum Newsletter; Roundup.*

ASSOCIATION FOR JEWISH STUDIES (1969). Widener Library M., Harvard University, Cambridge, Mass., 02138. (617)495-2985. Pres. Michael A. Meyer; Exec. Sec. Charles Berlin. Seeks to promote, maintain, and improve the teaching of Jewish studies in American colleges and universities by sponsoring meetings and conferences, publishing a newsletter and other scholarly materials, setting standards for programs in Jewish studies, aiding in the placement of teachers, coordinating research and cooperating with other scholarly organizations. *AJS Review; Newsletter.*

ASSOCIATION OF JEWISH CHAPLAINS OF THE ARMED FORCES (1946). 15 E. 26 St., N.Y.C., 10010. (212)532-4949. Pres. Joseph J. Weiss; Sec. Norman Twersky. An organization of former and current chaplains of the armed forces of the U.S. which seeks to enhance the religious program of Jewish chaplains in the armed forces of the U.S. and in Veterans' Administration hospitals.

ASSOCIATION OF ORTHODOX JEWISH SCIENTISTS (1947). 116 E. 27 St., N.Y.C., 10016. (212)889-1364. Pres. Reuben Rudman; Bd. Chmn. Herbert Goldstein. Seeks to contribute to the development of science within the framework of Orthodox Jewish tradition; to obtain and disseminate information relating to the interaction between the Jewish traditional way of life and scientific developments—on both an ideological and practical level; to assist in the solution of problems pertaining to Orthodox Jews engaged in scientific teaching or research. *Intercom; Proceedings.*

BETH MEDROSH ELYON (ACADEMY OF HIGHER LEARNING AND RESEARCH) (1943). 73 Main St., Monsey, N.Y., 10952. V. Pres. Ira Miller; Chmn. of Bd. Arthur Sternfield. Provides postgraduate courses and research work in higher Jewish studies; offers scholarships and fellowships. *Annual Journal.*

B'NAI B'RITH HILLEL FOUNDATIONS, INC. (1923). 1640 Rhode Island Ave., N.W., Washington, D.C., 20036. (202)857-6600. Chmn. B'nai B'rith Hillel Com. Albert A. Spiegel; Internat. Dir. Oscar Groner; Chmn. Exec. Com. Seymour Martin Lipset. Provides a program of cultural, religious, educational, social, and counseling content to Jewish college and university students on 350 campuses in the United States, Australia, Canada, England, Israel, the Netherlands, South Africa, Switzerland, Italy, Colombia, Brazil, Venezuela and Sweden. *Clearing House; Campus;* Hillel "Little Book" series; *Inside Hillel.*

B'NAI B'RITH YOUTH ORGANIZATION (1924). 1640 Rhode Island Ave., N.W., Washington, D.C., 20036. (202)857-6600. Chmn. Youth Com. Horace Stern; Internat. Dir. Sidney Clearfield. To help Jewish teenagers achieve self-fulfillment and to make a maximum contribution to the Jewish community and their country's culture; to help the members acquire a greater knowledge and appreciation of Jewish religion and culture. *BBYO Advisor; Monday Morning; Shofar.*

BRANDEIS-BARDIN INSTITUTE (1941). 1101 Peppertree Lane, Simi Valley, Calif., 93064. (805)526-1131. Chmn. of Bd. Willard Chotiner; V. Chmn. Richard Gunther; Dir. Dennis Prager; Pres. Ira Weiner. Maintains Brandeis Camp Institute (BCI) for college students as a leadership training institute; Camp Alonim for children 8–16; and House of the Book Association weekend institutes for married adults, in an effort to instill an appreciation of Jewish cultural and spiritual heritage and to create a desire for active participation in the American Jewish community. *Brandeis-Bardin News.*

CANTORS ASSEMBLY (1947). 150 Fifth Ave., N.Y.C., 10011. (212)691-8020. Pres. Kurt Silbermann; Exec. V. Pres. Samuel Rosenbaum. Seeks to unite all cantors who are adherents to traditional Judaism and who serve as full-time cantors in bona fide congregations, to conserve and promote the musical traditions of the Jews, and to elevate the status of the cantorial profession. *Annual Proceedings; Journal of Synagogue Music.*

CENTRAL CONFERENCE OF AMERICAN RABBIS (1889). 790 Madison Ave., N.Y.C., 10021. (212)734-7166. Pres. Rabbi Jerome R. Malino; Exec. V. Pres. Rabbi Joseph B. Glaser. Seeks to conserve and promote Judaism and to disseminate its teachings in a liberal spirit. *Journal of Reform Judaism; CCAR Yearbook.*

CENTRAL YESHIVA BETH JOSEPH RABBINICAL SEMINARY (in Europe 1891; in U.S. 1941). 1427 49 St., Brooklyn, N.Y. 11219. Pres. and Dean Jacob Jofen. Maintains a school for teaching Orthodox rabbis and teachers, and promoting the cause of higher Torah learning.

CLEVELAND COLLEGE OF JEWISH STUDIES (1964). 26500 Shaker Blvd., Beachwood, Ohio, 44122. (216)464-4050. Dir. Meir Ben-Horin; Bd. Chmn. Maurice Terkel; V. Chmn. Eli Reshotko. Trains Hebrew- and religious-school teachers; serves as the department of Hebraic and Judaic studies for Cleveland-area colleges and universities; offers intensive Ulpan and Judaic studies for community; serves as Jewish information center through its library; grants teachers diplomas and degrees of Bachelor of Hebrew Literature, Bachelor of Judaic Studies, Bachelor of Religious Education, Master of Science in Religious Education, and Master of Hebrew Literature.

DROPSIE UNIVERSITY (1907). Broad and York Sts., Philadelphia, Pa., 19132 (215)-229-1566. Pres. Leon J. Perelman; Sec. Joseph B. Saltz. The only nonsectarian and nontheological graduate institution in America completely dedicated to Hebrew, Biblical and Middle Eastern studies; offers graduate programs in these areas. Course study includes the cultures and languages of Arabic, Aramaic, Ugaritic, Akkadian, and ancient Egyptian peoples; offers Ph.D. degree. *Jewish Quarterly Review.*

———, ALUMNI ASSOCIATION OF (1925). Broad and York Sts., Philadelphia, Pa. 19132. (215)229-1566. Pres. Sidney B. Hoenig; Sec. Hanoch Guy. Enhances the relationship of the alumni to the University. *Newsletter.*

GRATZ COLLEGE (1895). 10 St. and Tabor Rd., Philadelphia, Pa., 19141. Chmn. Bd. of Overseers Daniel C. Cohen; Pres. Daniel Isaacman; Dean Saul P. Wachs. Prepares teachers for Jewish schools and teachers of Hebrew for public high schools; grants Master of Hebrew Literature, Bachelor of Hebrew Literature and Bachelor of Arts in Jewish Studies degrees; is accredited by the

Middle States Association of Colleges and Secondary Schools and the Association of Hebrew Colleges; provides studies in Judaica and Hebraica, maintains a Hebrew high school, two college preparatory departments for cadet teachers, and a school of observation and practice; provides Jewish studies for adults; community-service division (central agency for Jewish education) coordinates Jewish education in the city and provides consultation services to Jewish schools of all leanings. *Alumni Newspaper; College Bulletin; DCS Bulletin; Gratz Chats; GC Annual of Jewish Studies; 75th Anniversary Volume; Kinnereth; Telem Yearbook; What's New.*

HEBREW COLLEGE (1921). 43 Hawes St., Brookline, Mass., 02146. (617)232-8710. Pres. Eli Grad; Assoc. Dean Michael Libenson. Provides intensive programs of study in all areas of Jewish culture from the high-school through college and graduate-school levels, also at branch in Hartford; maintains ongoing programs with most major local universities; offers the degrees of Bachelor and Master of Hebrew Literature, and Bachelor and Master of Jewish Education, with teaching certification; trains men and women to teach, conduct and supervise Jewish schools; offers extensive Ulpan program; offers courses designed to deepen the community's awareness of the Jewish heritage. *Hebrew College Bulletin.*

HEBREW THEOLOGICAL COLLEGE (1921). 7135 N. Carpenter Rd., Skokie, Ill., 60077. (312)267-9800. Pres. Irving J. Rosenbaum; Exec. Bd. Chmn. Paul Rosenberg; Sec. Joseph R. Friedman. An institution of higher Jewish learning which includes a division of advanced Hebrew studies, a school of liberal arts and sciences, a rabbinic ordination program, and a graduate school in Judaic studies. Trains rabbis, teachers, educational administrators, communal workers, and knowledgeable lay leaders for the Jewish community. *News; Annual Journal.*

HEBREW UNION COLLEGE—JEWISH INSTITUTE OF RELIGION (1875). 3101 Clifton Ave., Cincinnati, Ohio, 45220. (513)221-1875; Pres. Alfred Gottschalk; Exec. V. Pres. Uri D. Herscher. Chmn. Bd. of Govs. Jules Backman. Academic centers: 3101 Clifton Ave., Cincinnati, Ohio, 45220 (1875), Eugene Mihaly, Exec. Dean; One W. 4 St., N.Y.C., 10012 (1922), Paul M.

Steinberg, Dean; 3077 University Ave., Los Angeles, Ca., 90007 (1954), Uri D. Herscher, Chief Adm. Officer; 13 King David St., Jerusalem, Israel (1963), Ezra Spicehandler, Dean. Prepares students for rabbinate, cantorate, religious-school teaching and administration, community service, academic careers; promotes Jewish studies; maintains libraries and a museum; offers bachelor's, master's and doctoral degrees; engages in archaeological excavations; publishes scholarly works through Hebrew Union College Press. *American Jewish Archives; Bibliographica Judaica; HUC—JIR Catalogue; Hebrew Union College Annual; Studies in Bibliography and Booklore; The Chronicle.*

———: AMERICAN JEWISH ARCHIVES (1947). Cincinnati. Dir. Jacob R. Marcus; Assoc. Dir. Abraham Peck. Maintained for the preservation and study of North and South American Jewish historical records. *American Jewish Archives.*

———: AMERICAN JEWISH PERIODICAL CENTER (1957). Cincinnati. Dir. Jacob R. Marcus; Exec. Dir. Herbert C. Zafren. Maintains microfilms of all American Jewish periodicals, 1823–1925; selected periodicals, since 1925. *Jewish Periodicals and Newspapers on Microfilm (1957); First Supplement (1960).*

———: JEROME H. LOUCHHEIM SCHOOL OF JUDAIC STUDIES (1969). Los Angeles. Acting Dir. Frida Kerner Furman. Offers programs leading to M.A., B.S., B.A. and Associate in Arts degrees; offers courses as part of the undergraduate program of the University of Southern California.

———: EDGAR F. MAGNIN SCHOOL OF GRADUATE STUDIES (1956). Los Angeles. Dir. Stanley Chyet. Offers programs leading to Ph.D., D.H.S., and M.A. degrees; offers program for rabbinic graduates of the college leading to the D.H.L. degree; participates in cooperative doctoral programs with the University of Southern California.

———: NELSON GLUECK SCHOOL OF BIBLICAL ARCHAEOLOGY (1963). Jerusalem. Dir. Avraham Biran. Offers graduate-level programs in Bible, archaeology and Judaica. Summer excavations are carried out by scholars and students. University credit may be earned by participants in excavations. Consortium of colleges, universities and seminaries is affiliated with the school.

_____: RHEA HIRSCH SCHOOL OF EDUCATION (1967). Los Angeles. Dir. William Cutter. Offers B.S. degree and M.A. program in Jewish and Hebrew education; conducts summer institutes and joint programs with University of Southern California; conducts certificate programs for teachers and librarians.

_____: SCHOOL OF EDUCATION (1947). 1 W. 4 St., N.Y.C., 10012. (212)873-0200. Pres. Alfred Gottschalk; Dean Paul M. Steinberg. Trains and certifies teachers and principals for Reform religious schools; offers M.A. degree with specialization in religious education; offers extension programs in various suburban centers.

_____: SCHOOL OF GRADUATE STUDIES (1949). Cincinnati. Dean Herbert H. Paper. Offers programs leading to M.A. and Ph.D. degrees; offers program leading to D.H.L. degree for rabbinic graduates of the college.

_____: SCHOOL OF JEWISH COMMUNAL SERVICE (1968). 3077 University Ave., Los Angeles, Calif., 90007. Dir. Gerald B. Bubis. Offers certificate and master's degree to those employed in Jewish communal services, or preparing for such work; offers joint M.A. in Jewish education and communal service with Rhea Hirsch School; offers M.A. and M.S.W. in conjunction with the University of Southern California School of Social Work and with the George Warren Brown School of Social Work of Washington University.

_____: SCHOOL OF JEWISH STUDIES (1963). Jerusalem. Dean Ezra Spicehandler. Offers M.A. program leading to ordination for Israeli students; offers an academic, work-study year for undergraduate students from American colleges and universities; offers a one-year program in cooperation with Hebrew University for advanced students, and a one-year program for all first-year rabbinic students of the college and for master's degree candidates of the Rhea Hirsch School of Education.

_____: SCHOOL OF SACRED MUSIC (1947). 1 W. 4 St., N.Y.C., 10012. (212)873-0200. Dean Paul M. Steinberg. Trains cantors and music personnel for congregations; offers B.S.M., M.A., and Ph.D. degrees. *Sacred Music Press.*

_____: SKIRBALL MUSEUM (1913; 1972 in Calif.). 3077 University Mall, Los Angeles, Calif., 90007. Dir. Nancy Berman. Collects, preserves, researches and exhibits art and artifacts made by or for Jews, or otherwise associated with Jews and Judaism. Provides opportunity to faculty and students to do research in the field of Jewish art.

HERZLIAH-JEWISH TEACHERS SEMINARY (1967). 69 Bank St., N.Y.C., 10014. Pres. Eli Goldstein; Exec. Dir. Aviva Barzel; V. Pres. for Academic Affairs Meir Ben-Horin. Offers undergraduate and graduate programs in Jewish studies; continuing education courses for teachers in Hebrew and Yiddish schools; academic and professional programs in major disciplines of Judaism, historic and contemporary, with emphasis on Hebrew language and literature; Yiddish language and literature, Jewish education, history, philosophy, and sociology.

_____: GRADUATE DIVISION (1965). Dean Meir Ben-Horin. Offers programs leading to degree of Doctor of Jewish Literature in Hebrew language and literature, Yiddish language and literature, Jewish education, history, philosophy, and sociology. Admits men and women who have bachelor's degree and background in Hebrew, Yiddish, and Jewish studies. Annual Horace M. Kallen lecture by major Jewish scholars.

_____: HERZLIAH HEBREW TEACHERS INSTITUTE, INC. (1921). V. Pres. for Academic Affairs Meir Ben-Horin. Offers four-year, college-level programs in Hebrew and Jewish subjects, nationally recognized Hebrew teachers diploma, preparatory courses, and Yiddish courses.

_____: JEWISH TEACHERS SEMINARY AND PEOPLE'S UNIVERSITY, INC. (1918). V. Pres. for Academic Affairs Meir Ben-Horin. Offers four-year, college-level programs leading to Yiddish teachers diploma and Bachelor of Jewish Literature; offers preparatory courses and Hebrew courses.

_____: MUSIC DIVISION (1964). Performing Arts Div. Dir. Cantor Marvin Antosofsky. Offers studies in traditional and contemporary music, religious, Yiddish, secular and Hebraic; offers certificate and degree programs in Jewish music education and cantorial art, and artist diploma.

INTERNATIONAL ASSOCIATION OF HILLEL DIRECTORS (1949). Hofstra University, Hempstead, N.Y. 11550. (516)560-3270. Pres. Frank A. Fischer; V. Pres. Richard Marker. Seeks to promote professional relationships and exchanges of experience, develop personnel standards and qualifications, safeguard integrity of Hillel profession; represents and advocates before National Hillel Staff, National Hillel Commission, B'nai B'rith Supreme Lodge, Jewish Federations and Welfare Funds.

JEWISH CHAUTAUQUA SOCIETY, INC. (sponsored by NATIONAL FEDERATION OF TEMPLE BROTHERHOODS) (1893). 838 Fifth Ave. N.Y.C., 10021. (212)249-0100. Pres. Lawrence M. Halperin; Exec. Dir. Av Bondarin. Disseminates authoritative knowledge about Jews and Judaism; assigns rabbis to lecture at colleges; endows courses in Judaism for college credit at universities; donates Jewish reference books to college libraries; sends rabbis to serve as counselor-teachers at Christian Church summer camps and as chaplains at Boy Scout camps; sponsors institutes on Judaism for Christian clergy; produces motion pictures for public service television and group showings. *Brotherhood.*

JEWISH MINISTERS CANTORS ASSOCIATION OF AMERICA, INC. (1900). 3 W. 16 St., N.Y.C., 10011. (212)675-6601. Pres. Sidney Mandel; V. Pres. David Rosenzweig. To further and propagate traditional liturgy; to place cantors in synagogues throughout the U.S. and Canada; to develop the cantors of the future. *Kol Lakol.*

JEWISH RECONSTRUCTIONIST FOUNDATION (1940). 432 Park Ave. S., N.Y.C., 10016. (212)889-9080. Pres. Ira Eisenstein; Exec. V. Pres. Ludwig Nadelmann; Chmn. of Bd. Benjamin Wm. Mehlman. Dedicated to the advancement of Judaism as the evolving religious civilization of the Jewish people. Coordinates all Reconstructionist activities and sponsors the Reconstructionist Rabbinical College, Reconstructionist Press, Reconstructionist Federation (congregations and *havurot*), Reconstructionist Rabbinical Assn., a women's organization, and university fellowship. *Reconstructionist.*

————: RECONSTRUCTIONIST FEDERATION OF CONGREGATIONS AND FELLOWSHIPS (1954). 432 Park Ave. S., N.Y.C., 10016. (212)889-9080. Pres. Herbert Winer; Exec.

Dir. Ira Eisenstein; Assoc. Dir. Ludwig Nadelman. Services affiliated congregations and *havurot* educationally and administratively; fosters the establishment of new Reconstructionist congregations and fellowship groups. *Newsletter.*

————: RECONSTRUCTIONIST RABBINICAL ASSOCIATION (1975). 432 Park Ave. So., N.Y.C., 10016. (212)889-9080. Pres. Rabbi Dennis Sasso; Secs. Rabbis Ilene Schneider, Neal Weinberg. Advances the principles of Reconstructionist Judaism; provides forum for fellowship and exchange of ideas for Reconstructionist rabbis; cooperates with Reconstructionist Rabbinical College, and Reconstructionist Federation of Congregations and Havurot. *RRA Newsletter.*

JEWISH TEACHERS ASSOCIATION—MORIM (1926). 45 E. 33 St., N.Y.C., 10016. (212)-684-0556. Pres. Michael Leinwand; Sec. Dorothy G. Posner. Promotes the religious, social, and moral welfare of children; provides a program of professional, cultural, and social activities for its members; cooperates with other organizations for the promotion of goodwill and understanding. *JTA Bulletin.*

JEWISH THEOLOGICAL SEMINARY OF AMERICA (1886; reorg. 1902). 3080 Broadway, N.Y.C., 10027. (212)749-8000. Chancellor Gerson D. Cohen; Chmn. Bd. of Dir. Sol. M. Linowitz. Organized for the perpetuation of the tenets of the Jewish religion, cultivation of Hebrew literature, pursuit of biblical and archaeological research, advancement of Jewish scholarship; maintains a library with extensive collections of Hebraica and Judaica, a department for the training of rabbis, a pastoral psychiatry center, the Jewish Museum, and such youth programs as the Ramah Camps and the Leaders Training Fellowship. *Conservative Judaism.*

————: AMERICAN STUDENT CENTER IN JERUSALEM (1962). P.O. Box 196, Jerusalem, Israel. Dean Shamma Friedman; Dir. Reuven Hammer. Offers programs for Rabbinical students, classes in Judaica for qualified Israelis and Americans, and an intensive program of Jewish studies for undergraduates.

————: CANTORS INSTITUTE AND SEMINARY COLLEGE OF JEWISH MUSIC (1952). 3080 Broadway, N.Y.C., 10027.

(212)749-8000. Dir. Dean Morton J. Waldman. Trains cantors, music teachers, and choral directors for congregations. Offers programs leading to degrees of B.S.M., M.S.M., and D.S.M., and diploma of *Hazzan*.

———: DEPARTMENT OF RADIO AND TELEVISION (1944). 3080 Broadway, N.Y.C., 10027. Exec. Prod. Milton E. Krents. Produces radio and TV programs expressing the Jewish tradition in its broadest sense, with emphasis on the universal human situation: "Eternal Light," a weekly radio program; 7 "Eternal Light" TV programs, produced in cooperation with NBC; and 12 "Directions" telecasts with ABC; distributes program scripts and related reading lists.

———: FANNIE AND MAXWELL ABBEL RESEARCH INSTITUTE IN RABBINICS (1951). 3080 Broadway, N.Y.C., 10027. (212)749-8000. Co-Dirs. Louis Finkelstein, Saul Lieberman. Fosters research in Rabbinics; prepares scientific editions of early Rabbinic works.

———: INSTITUTE FOR ADVANCED STUDY IN THE HUMANITIES (1968). 3080 Broadway, N.Y.C., 10027. (212)749-8000. Dean Ismar Schorsch. A graduate program leading to M.A. degree in all aspects of Jewish studies and Ph.D. in Bible, Jewish education, history, literature, philosophy, or rabbinics.

———: INSTITUTE FOR RELIGIOUS AND SOCIAL STUDIES (N.Y.C. 1938; Chicago 1944; Boston 1945). 3080 Broadway, N.Y.C., 10027. (212)749-8000. Pres. Gerson D. Cohen; Dir. Jessica Feingold. Serves as a scholarly and scientific fellowship of clergymen and other religious teachers who desire authoritative information regarding some of the basic issues now confronting spiritually-minded men.

———: MELTON RESEARCH CENTER (1960). 3080 Broadway, N.Y.C., 10027. (212)749-8000. Exec. Dir. Elaine Morris. Devises new curricula and materials for Jewish education; has intensive program for training curriculum writers; recruits, trains and retrains educators through seminars and in-service programs; maintains consultant and supervisory relationships with a limited number of pilot schools. *Melton Newsletter*.

———: SCHOCKEN INSTITUTE FOR JEWISH RESEARCH (1961). 6 Balfour St., Jerusalem, Israel. Librarian Yaakov Katzenstein. Incorporates Schocken library and its related research institutes in medieval Hebrew poetry and Jewish mysticism. *Schocken Institute Yearbook (P'raqim)*.

———: SEMINARY COLLEGE OF JEWISH STUDIES-TEACHERS INSTITUTE (1909). 3080 Broadway, N.Y.C., 10027. (212)749-8000. Dean Ivan G. Marcus. Offers complete college program in Judaica leading to B.H.L. degree; conducts joint program with Columbia University, enabling students to receive B.A. from Columbia and B.H.L. from the Seminary, after four years.

———: UNIVERSITY OF JUDAISM (1947). 15600 Mulholland Dr., Los Angeles, Calif., 90024. (213)476-9777. Pres. David L. Lieber; V. Pres. Max Vorspan, David Gordis. West Coast school of JTS. Serves as center of undergraduate and graduate study of Judaica; offers pre-professional and professional programs in Jewish education and allied fields, including a pre-rabbinic program and joint program enabling students to receive B.A. from UCLA and B.H.L. from U. of J. after 4 years, as well as a broad range of adult education and Jewish activities.

MACHNE ISRAEL, INC. (1940). 770 Eastern Parkway, Bklyn., N.Y., 11213. (212)493-9250. Pres. Menachem M. Schneerson (Lubavitcher Rebbe); Dir., Treas. M.A. Hodakov; Sec. Nissan Mindel. The Lubavitcher movement's organ dedicated to the social, spiritual, and material welfare of Jews throughout the world.

MERKOS L'INYONEI CHINUCH, INC. (THE CENTRAL ORGANIZATION FOR JEWISH EDUCATION) (1940). 770 Eastern Parkway, Bklyn., N.Y., 11213. (212)493-9250. Pres. Menachem M. Schneerson (the Lubavitcher Rebbe); Dir. Treas. M.A. Hodakov; Sec. Nissan Mindel. The educational arm of the Lubavitcher movement. Seeks to promote Jewish education among Jews, regardless of their background, in the spirit of Torah-true Judaism; to establish contact with alienated Jewish youth, to stimulate concern and active interest in Jewish education on all levels, and to promote religious observance as a daily experience among all Jews; maintains worldwide network of regional offices, schools, summer camps and Chabad-Lubavitch Houses; publishes Jewish educational literature in numerous languages and monthly journal in five languages: *Conversaciones con la juventud; Conversations avec les jeunes; Schmuessen mit kinder un yugent; Sihot la No-ar; Talks and Tales.*

MESIVTA YESHIVA RABBI CHAIM BERLIN RABBINICAL ACADEMY (1905). 1593 Coney Island Ave., Bklyn., N.Y., 11230. Pres. Pincus Iseson; Exec. V. Pres. Rabbi Bezalel Reifman. Maintains elementary division in the Hebrew and English departments, lower Hebrew division and Mesivta high school, rabbinical academy, and postgraduate school for advanced studies in Talmud and other branches of rabbinic scholarship; maintains Camp Morris, a summer study camp. *Igud News Letter; Kol Torah; Kuntrasim; Merchav; Shofar.*

MIRRER YESHIVA CENTRAL INSTITUTE (in Poland 1817; in U.S. 1947). 1791-5 Ocean Parkway, Brooklyn, N.Y., 11223. Pres. and Dean Rabbi Shrage Moshe Kalmanowitz; Exec. Dir. and Sec. Manfred Handelsman. Maintains rabbinical college, postgraduate school for Talmudic research, accredited high school, and Kollel and Sephardic divisions; dedicated to the dissemination of Torah scholarship in the community and abroad; engages in rescue and rehabilitation of scholars overseas.

NATIONAL COMMITTEE FOR FURTHERANCE OF JEWISH EDUCATION (1951). 824 Eastern Parkway, Brooklyn, N.Y., 11213. (212)735-0200. Exec. V. Pres. Jacob J. Hecht; Sec. Morris Drucker. Seeks to disseminate the ideals of Torah-true education among the youth of America; aids poor, sick and needy in U.S. and Israel; maintains camp for underprivileged children; sponsors Hadar Ha Torah and Machon Chana, seeking to win back college youth and others to the fold of Judaism; maintains schools and dormitory facilities; sponsors Heroes Fund to aid widows and orphans of heroes fallen in recent Israeli wars. *Panorama; Passover Handbook; Seder Guide; Spiritual Suicide; Focus.*

NATIONAL COUNCIL FOR JEWISH EDUCATION (1926). 114 Fifth Ave., N.Y.C., 10011. (212)675-5656. Pres. Leivy Smolar; Exec. Sec. Jack M. Horden. Fellowship of Jewish education profession, comprising administrators and supervisors of national and local Jewish educational institutions and agencies, and teachers in Hebrew high schools and Jewish teachers colleges, of all ideological groupings; conducts annual national and regional conferences in all areas of Jewish education; represents the Jewish education profession before the Jewish community; co-sponsors, with American Association for Jewish Education, a personnel committee and other projects; cooperates with Jewish Agency department of education and culture in promoting Hebrew culture and studies; conducts lectureship at Hebrew University. *Jewish Education; Sheviley Hahinuch.*

NATIONAL COUNCIL OF BETH JACOB SCHOOLS, INC. (1945). 1415 E. 7 St., Bklyn, N.Y., 11230. (212)979-7400. Pres. Israel M. Zaks; Chmn. of Bd. Shimon Newhouse; Sec. David Rosenberg. Operates Orthodox all-day schools from kindergarten through high school for girls, a residence high school in Ferndale, N.Y., a national institute for master instructors, and a summer camp for girls. *Baís Yaakov Digest; Pnimia Call.*

NATIONAL COUNCIL OF YOUNG ISRAEL (1912). 3 W. 16 St., N.Y.C., 10011. (212)-929-1525. Nat. Pres. Nathaniel Saperstein; Exec. V. Pres. Ephraim H. Sturm. Maintains a program of spiritual, cultural, social and communal activity towards the advancement and perpetuation of traditional, Torah-true Judaism; seeks to instill in American youth an understanding and appreciation of the ethical and spiritual values of Judaism. Sponsors kosher dining clubs and fraternity houses and an Israel program. *Viewpoint; Hashkofa Series; Massorah Newspaper.*

———, AMERICAN FRIENDS OF YOUNG ISRAEL SYNAGOGUES IN ISRAEL (1926). 3 W. 16 St., N.Y.C., 10011. (212)929-1525. Chmn. Marvin Luban; Exec. V. Pres. Ephraim H. Sturm. Promotes Young Israel synagogues and youth work in synagogues in Israel.

———, ARMED FORCES BUREAU (1912). 3 W. 16 St., N.Y.C., 10011. (212)929-1525. Dir. Stanley W. Schlessel; Assoc. Dir. Sidney Weg. Advises and guides the inductees into the armed forces with regard to Sabbath observance, *kashrut,* and Orthodox behavior. *Guide for the Orthodox Serviceman.*

_____, EMPLOYMENT BUREAU (1912). 3 W. 16 St., N.Y.C., 10011. (212)929-1525. Exec. V. Pres. Ephraim H. Sturm; Employment Dir. Dorothy Stein. Operates an on-the-job training program under federal contract; helps secure employment, particularly for Sabbath observers and Russian immigrants; offers vocational guidance. *Viewpoint.*

_____: INSTITUTE FOR JEWISH STUDIES (1947). 3 W. 16 St., N.Y.C., 10011. (212)-929-1525. Pres. Nathaniel Saperstein; Exec. V. Pres. Rabbi Ephraim H. Sturm. Introduces students to Jewish learning and knowledge; helps form adult branch schools; aids Young Israel synagogues in their adult education programs. *Bulletin.*

_____: INTERCOLLEGIATE COUNCIL AND YOUNG SINGLE ADULTS (formerly MASSORAH INTERCOLLEGIATES OF YOUNG ISRAEL; 1951). 3 W. 16 St., N.Y.C., 10011. (212)929-1525. Pres. Sidney Weg; Dir. Stanley W. Schlessel. Organizes and operates kosher dining clubs on college and university campuses; provides information and counseling on *kashrut* observance at college; gives college-age youth understanding and appreciation of Judaism and information on issues important to Jewish community; arranges seminars and meetings; publishes pamphlets and monographs. *Hashkafa.*

_____: YISRAEL HATZAIR (reorg. 1968). 3 W. 16 St., N.Y.C., 10011. (212)929-1525. Pres. Jackie Goldstein; Nat. Dir. Arnold Grant. Fosters a program of spiritual, cultural, social, and communal activities for the advancement and perpetuation of traditional Torah-true Judaism; strives to instill an understanding and appreciation of the high ethical and spiritual values and to demonstrate compatibility of ancient faith of Israel with good Americanism.

NATIONAL FEDERATION OF JEWISH MEN'S CLUBS, INC. (1929). 475 Riverside Dr., Suite 244, N.Y.C., 10027. (212)749-8100. Pres. Samuel G. Berlin; Exec. Dir. David L. Blumenfeld. Promotes principles and objectives of Conservative Judaism by organizing, sponsoring, and developing men's clubs or brotherhoods; supports Leaders' Training Fellowship national youth organization; sponsors Hebrew Literacy Adult Education Program; presents awards for service to American Jewry. *Torchlight.*

NATIONAL JEWISH CONFERENCE CENTER (1974). 250 W. 57 St., N.Y.C., 10019. (212)582-6116. Chmn. Neil Norry; Dir. Irving Greenberg; Exec. Dir. Jeffrey Heilpern. Devoted to leadership education and policy guidance for the American Jewish community. Conducts weekend retreats and community gatherings, as well as conferences on various topics. *Newsletter.*

_____, ZACHOR: THE HOLOCAUST RESOURCE CENTER (1978). 250 W. 57 St., N.Y.C., 10019. (212)582-6116. Chmn. Irv Frank. Assoc. Dir. Michael Berenbaum. Disseminates information on the Holocaust to the American Jewish community; develops Holocaust memorial projects; advises communities and organizations on curricula and special projects; sponsors a Faculty Seminar on the Holocaust and a Task Force on Holocaust Liturgy. *Shoah: A Review of Holocaust Studies and Commemorations.*

NATIONAL JEWISH HOSPITALITY COMMITTEE (1973). 201 S. 18 St., Rm. 1519, Philadelphia, Pa., 19103. (215)546-8293. Pres. Allen S. Maller; Exec. Dir. Steven S. Jacobs. Assists converts and prospective converts to Judaism, persons involved in intermarriages, and the parents of Jewish youth under the influence of cults and missionaries, as well as the youths themselves. *Our Choice.*

NATIONAL JEWISH INFORMATION SERVICE FOR THE PROPAGATION OF JUDAISM, INC. (1960). 5174 W. 8th St., Los Angeles, Calif., 90036. (213)936-6033. Pres. Moshe M. Maggal; V. Pres. Lawrence J. Epstein; Corr. Sec. Rachel D. Maggal. Seeks to convert non-Jews to Judaism and revert Jews to Judaism; maintains College for Jewish Ambassadors for the training of Jewish missionaries and the Correspondence Academy of Judaism for instruction on Judaism through the mail. *Voice of Judaism.*

NER ISRAEL RABBINICAL COLLEGE (1933). 400 Mt. Wilson Lane, Baltimore, Md., 21208. (301)484-7200. Pres. Rabbi Jacob I. Ruderman; V. Pres. Rabbi Herman N. Neuberger. Trains rabbis and educators for Jewish communities in America and worldwide. Offers bachelors, masters and doctoral degrees in talmudic law as well as Teachers Diploma. College has four divisions: Mechina High School, Rabbinical College, Teachers Training Institute, Graduate School. Maintains an active community service division. Operates special program for Iranian Jewish students. *Ner Israel Bulletin; Alumni Bulletin; Ohr Hanair Talmudic Journal.*

OZAR HATORAH, INC. (1946). 411 Fifth Ave., N.Y.C., 10016. (212)684-4733. Pres. Joseph Shalom; Intl. Pres. S.D. Sassoon; V. Pres. Moshe Milstein. Establishes and maintains elementary, secondary and boarding schools, combining a program of religious and secular education for Jewish youth in Morocco, Iran, Syria and France. *Bulletin.*

P'EYLIM—AMERICAN YESHIVA STUDENT UNION (1951). 3 W. 16 St., N.Y.C., 10011. (212)989-2500. Pres. Nisson Alpert; Dir. Avraham Hirsch. Aids and sponsors pioneer work by American graduate teachers and rabbis in new villages and towns in Israel; does religious, organizational, and educational work and counseling among new immigrant youth; maintains summer camps for poor immigrant youth in Israel; belongs to worldwide P'eylim movement which has groups in Argentina, Brazil, Canada, England, Belgium, the Netherlands, Switzerland, France, and Israel; engages in relief and educational work among North African immigrants in France and Canada, assisting them to relocate and reestablish a strong Jewish community life. *P'eylim Reporter; N'she P'eylim News.*

*RABBINICAL ALLIANCE OF AMERICA (IGUD HARABONIM) (1944). 156 Fifth Ave., Suite 807, N.Y.C., 10010. Pres. Rabbi Abraham B. Hecht. Seeks to promulgate the cause of Torah-true Judaism through an organized rabbinate that is consistently Orthodox; seeks to elevate the position of Orthodox rabbis nationally, and to defend the welfare of Jews the world over. Also has Beth Din Rabbinical Court. *Perspective.*

RABBINICAL ASSEMBLY (1900). 3080 Broadway, N.Y.C., 10027. (212)749-8000. Pres. Rabbi Saul I. Teplitz; Exec. V. Pres. Rabbi Wolfe Kelman. Seeks to promote Conservative Judaism, and to foster the spirit of fellowship and cooperation among rabbis and other Jewish scholars; cooperates with the Jewish Theological Seminary of America and the United Synagogue of America. *Beineinu; Conservative Judaism; Proceedings of the Rabbinical Assembly.*

RABBINICAL COLLEGE OF TELSHE, INC. (1941). 28400 Euclid Ave., Wickliffe, Ohio, 44092. (216)943-5300. Pres. Rabbi Mordecai Gifter; V. Pres. Rabbi Abba Zalka Gewirtz. College for higher Jewish learning specializing in talmudic studies and rabbinics; maintains a preparatory academy including secular high school, a postgraduate department, a teachers training school, and a teachers seminary for women. *Pri Etz Chaim; Peer Mordechai; Alumni Bulletin.*

RABBINICAL COUNCIL OF AMERICA, INC. (1923; reorg. 1936). 1250 Broadway, Suite 802, N.Y.C., 10001. Pres. Bernard Rosensweig; Exec. V. Pres. Israel Klavan. Promotes Orthodox Judaism in the community; supports institutions for study of Torah; stimulates creation of new traditional agencies. *Hadorom; Record; Sermon Manual; Tradition.*

RECONSTRUCTIONIST RABBINICAL COLLEGE (1968). 2308 N. Broad St., Philadelphia, Pa., 19132. (215)223-8121. Pres. Ira Eisenstein. Trains rabbis for all areas of Jewish communal life: synagogues, academic and educational positions, Hillel centers, Federation agencies; requires students to pursue outside graduate studies in religion and related subjects; confers title of rabbi and grants degree of Doctor of Hebrew Letters. *Jewish Civilization: Essays and Studies.*

RESEARCH INSTITUTE OF RELIGIOUS JEWRY, INC. (1941; reorg. 1954). 471 West End Ave., N.Y.C., 10024. (212)874-7979. Chmn. Isaac Strahl; Sec. Marcus Levine. Engages in research and publishes studies concerning the situation of religious Jewry and its problems all over the world.

SHOLEM ALEICHEM FOLK INSTITUTE, INC. (1918). 3301 Bainbridge Ave., Bronx, N.Y., 10467. Pres. Burt Levey; Sec. Noah Zingman. Aims to imbue children with Jewish values through teaching Yiddish language and literature, Hebrew and the Bible, Jewish history, the significance of Jewish holidays, folk and choral singing, and facts about Jewish life in America and Israel. *Kinder Journal* (Yiddish).

SOCIETY OF FRIENDS OF THE TOURO SYNAGOGUE, NATIONAL HISTORIC SHRINE, INC. (1948). 85 Touro St., Newport, R.I., 02840. (401)847-4794. Pres. Seebert J. Goldowsky; Sec. Theodore Lewis. Assists in the maintenance of the Touro Synagogue as a national historic site.

SPERTUS COLLEGE OF JUDAICA (1925). 618 S. Michigan Ave., Chicago, Ill., 60605. Pres. David Weinstein; Bd. Chmn. Philip Spertus. Educates teachers of Hebraica and Judaica for elementary and secondary Jewish schools; certifies Hebrew teachers for public and private Illinois schools; provides Chicago area colleges and universities with specialized undergraduate and graduate programs in Judaica and serves as a Department of Judaic Studies to these colleges and universities; serves as Midwest Jewish information center through its Asher Library and Maurice Spertus Museum of Judaica; grants degrees of Master of Arts in Jewish Education and in Jewish Communal Service, Bachelor of Arts, and Bachelor of Judaic Studies. *Journal of Jewish Art.*

SYNAGOGUE COUNCIL OF AMERICA (1926). 432 Park Ave. S., N.Y.C., 10016. (212)-686-8670. Pres. Rabbi Saul I. Teplitz; Exec. V. Pres. Rabbi Bernard Mandelbaum. Serves as spokesman for, and coordinates policies of, national rabbinical and lay synagogal organizations of Conservative, Orthodox, and Reform branches of American Judaism. Sponsors Institute for Jewish Policy Planning and Research. *SCA Report; Analysis.*

——: INSTITUTE FOR JEWISH POLICY PLANNING AND RESEARCH OF (1972). 1776 Massachusetts Ave., N.W., Washington, D.C., 20036. (202)872-1337. Chmn. Max M. Kampelman. Seeks to strengthen American Jewry by conducting and promoting systematic study of major issues confronting its future vitality, for which it enlists informed academic and lay people; sponsors research and analysis on the subject and disseminates findings to synagogues and other Jewish organizations. *Analysis of Jewish Policy Issues; Background.*

TORAH UMESORAH—NATIONAL SOCIETY FOR HEBREW DAY SCHOOLS (1944). 229 Park Ave. S., N.Y.C., 10003. (212)674-6700. Nat. Pres. Samuel C. Feuerstein; Nat. Dir. Joseph Kaminetsky. Establishes Hebrew day schools throughout U.S. and Canada and services them in all areas including placement and curriculum guidance; conducts teacher training institutes, a special fellowship program, seminars,

and workshops for in-service training of teachers; publishes textbooks and supplementary reading material; conducts education research and has established Fryer Fdn. for research in ethics and character education; supervises federal aid programs for Hebrew day schools throughout the U.S. *Olomeinu—Our World; Tempo; Torah Umesorah Report; Machberet Hamenahel.*

——: INSTITUTE FOR PROFESSIONAL ENRICHMENT (1973). 22 E. 28 St., N.Y.C., 10016. (212)683-3216. Dir. Bernard Dov Milians. Provides enriched training and upgraded credentials for administrative, guidance, and classroom personnel of Hebrew day schools and for Torah-community leaders; offers graduate and undergraduate programs, in affiliation with accredited universities which award full degrees: M.A. in geriatric counseling, early childhood and elementary education, applied human relations (adult, family, alcoholism counseling), health, nutrition; M.B.A. in management; M.S. in special education, reading; B.S. in education; B.A. in liberal arts, social sciences, business, gerontology. *Professional Enrichment News (PEN).*

——: NATIONAL ASSOCIATION OF HEBREW DAY SCHOOL ADMINISTRATORS (1960). 229 Park Ave. S., N.Y.C., 10003. (212)674-6700. Pres. David H. Schwartz; Bd. Chmn. Rabbi Saul Wolf; Exec. Coord. Bernard Dov Milians. Coordinates the work of the fiscal directors of Hebrew day schools throughout the country. *NAHDSA Review.*

——: NATIONAL ASSOCIATION OF HEBREW DAY SCHOOL PARENT-TEACHER ASSOCIATIONS (1948). 229 Park Ave. S., N.Y.C., 10003. (212)674-6700. Nat. Pres. Mrs. Henry C. Rhein; Exec. Secy. Mrs. Samuel Brand; Chmn. of Bd. Mrs. Clarence Horwitz. Acts as a clearinghouse and service agency to PTAs of Hebrew day schools; organizes parent education courses and sets up programs for individual PTAs. *National Program Notes; PTA Bulletin; Fundraising With a Flair; PTA With a Purpose for the Hebrew Day School.*

——: NATIONAL CONFERENCE OF YESHIVA PRINCIPALS (1956). 229 Park Ave. S., N.Y.C., 10003. (212)674-6700. Pres. Rabbi Chaim Feuerman; Exec. V. Pres. Rabbi Joshua Fishman; Bd. Chmn. David

Mykoff. A professional organization of primary and secondary yeshiva day-school principals which seeks to make yeshiva day-school education more effective. *Machberet Hamenahel.*

_____: NATIONAL YESHIVA TEACHERS BOARD OF LICENSE (1953). 229 Park Ave. S., N.Y.C., 10003. (212) 674-6700. Bd. Chmn. Elias Schwartz; Ex. Consult. Zvi H. Shurin. Issues licenses to qualified instructors for all grades of the Hebrew day school and the general field of Torah education.

_____: SAMUEL A. FRYER EDUCATIONAL RESEARCH FOUNDATION (1966). 229 Park Ave. S., N.Y.C., 10003. (212)674-6700. Chmn. Bd. of Trustees Jack Sable; Dir. Louis Nulman. Strengthens the ethics programs of Hebrew day, afternoon, and Sunday schools, summer camps, and Jewish centers through moral sensitivity-training program; provides extensive teacher-training program; publishes monographs, newsletter, and teachers' bulletin. *Fryer Foundation Newsletter.*

TOURO COLLEGE (1970). 30 W. 44 St., N.Y.C., 10036. (212)575-0190. Pres. Bernard Lander. Chartered by the N.Y. State Board of Regents to operate and maintain nonprofit, four-year college with liberal arts programs leading to B.A. and B.S. degrees, with an emphasis on the relevance of the Jewish heritage to the general culture of Western civilization. *Annual Bulletin.*

UNION OF AMERICAN HEBREW CONGREGATIONS (1873). 838 Fifth Ave., N.Y.C., 10021. (212)249-0100. Pres. Rabbi Alexander M. Schindler; Bd. Chmn. Matthew H. Ross. Serves as the central congregational body of Reform Judaism in the Western Hemisphere; serves its approximately 740 affiliated temples and membership with religious, educational, cultural, and administrative programs. *Keeping Posted; Reform Judaism.*

_____: AMERICAN CONFERENCE OF CANTORS OF (1956). 838 Fifth Ave., N.Y.C., 10021. (212)249-0100. Pres. Ramon Gilbert; Exec. Dir. Raymond Smolover. Members receive investiture and commissioning as cantors at ordination-investiture ceremonies at Hebrew Union College-Jewish Institute of Religion-Sacred School of Music. Through Joint Placement Commission, serves congregations seeking cantors and music directors. Dedicated to creative Judaism, preserving the best of the past, and encouraging new and vital approaches to religious ritual, music and ceremonies.

_____: COMMISSION ON SOCIAL ACTION OF REFORM JUDAISM (see p. 294).

_____: NATIONAL ASSOCIATION OF TEMPLE ADMINISTRATORS OF (1941). 838 Fifth Ave., N.Y.C., 10021. (212)249-0100. Pres. Walter C. Baron; Adm. Sec. Harold Press. Fosters Reform Judaism; prepares and disseminates administrative information and procedures to member synagogues of UAHC; provides and encourages proper and adequate training of professional synagogue executives; formulates and establishes professional ideals and standards for the synagogue executive. *NATA Journal.*

_____: NATIONAL ASSOCIATION OF TEMPLE EDUCATORS (1955). 838 Fifth Ave., N.Y.C., 10021. (212)249-0100. Pres. Fred W. Marcus; V. Pres. Richard M. Morin. Represents the temple educator within the general body of Reform Judaism; fosters the full-time profession of the temple educator; encourages the growth and development of Jewish religious education consistent with the aims of Reform Judaism; stimulates communal interest in and responsibility for Jewish religious education. *NATE News; Compass Magazine.*

_____: NATIONAL FEDERATION OF TEMPLE BROTHERHOODS (1923). 838 Fifth Ave., N.Y.C., 10021. (212)249-0100. Pres. Lawrence M. Halperin; Exec. Dir. Av Bondarin. Promotes Jewish education among its members, along with participation in temple, brotherhood, and interfaith activities; sponsors the Jewish Chautauqua Society. *Brotherhood.*

_____: NATIONAL FEDERATION OF TEMPLE SISTERHOODS (1913). 838 Fifth Ave., N.Y.C., 10021. (212)249-0100. Pres. Lillian Maltzer; Exec. Dir. Eleanor R. Schwartz. Serves more than 600 sisterhoods of Reform Judaism; inter-religious understanding and social justice; scholarships and grants to rabbinic students; braille and large type Judaic materials for Jewish blind; projects for Israel, Soviet Jewry and the aging; is an affiliate of UAHC and is the women's agency of Reform Judaism; works on behalf of the

Hebrew Union College-Jewish Institute of Religion; cooperates with World Union for Progressive Judaism. *Notes for Now.*

_____: NORTH AMERICAN FEDERATION OF TEMPLE YOUTH (NFTY; formerly NATIONAL FEDERATION OF TEMPLE YOUTH; 1939). 838 Fifth Ave., N.Y.C., 10021. (212)249-0100. Dirs. Stephen Schafer; Leonard Troupp; Daniel Freelander; Pres. Paul Andy Hodes. Seeks to train Reform Jewish youth in the values of the synagogue and their application to daily life through service to the community and congregation; runs department of summer camps and national leadership training institutes; arranges overseas academic tours and work programs, international student exchange programs, college student programs in the U.S. and Israel, including an accredited study program in Israel. *Visions; NFTY News.*

_____, AND CENTRAL CONFERENCE OF AMERICAN RABBIS: COMMISSION ON JEWISH EDUCATION OF (1923). 838 Fifth Ave., N.Y.C., 10021. (212)249-0100. Chmn. Martin S. Rozenberg; Dir. Rabbi Daniel B. Syme. Develops curricula and teachers' manuals; conducts pilot projects and offers educational guidance and consultation at all age levels to member congregations and affiliates and associate bodies. *What's Happening; Compass; E³.*

_____, AND CENTRAL CONFERENCE OF AMERICAN RABBIS: JOINT COMMISSION ON SYNAGOGUE ADMINISTRATION (1962). 838 Fifth Ave., N.Y.C., 10021. (212)249-0100. Chmn. Lillian Maltzer; Dir. Myron E. Schoen. Assists congregations in management, finance, building maintenance, design, construction, and art aspects of synagogues; maintains the Synagogue Architectural Library consisting of photos, slides, and plans of contemporary and older synagogue buildings. *Synagogue Service.*

UNION OF ORTHODOX JEWISH CONGREGATIONS OF AMERICA (1898). 116 E. 27 St., N.Y.C., 10016. Pres. Julius Berman; Exec. V. Pres. Pinchas Stolper. Serves as the national central body of Orthodox synagogues; provides educational, religious, and organizational guidance to groups, and men's clubs; represents the Orthodox Jewish community in relationship to governmental and civic bodies, and the general Jewish community; conducts the national

authoritative U Kashruth certification service. *Jewish Action; Jewish Life; Keeping Posted; U News Reporter.*

_____: NATIONAL CONFERENCE OF SYNAGOGUE YOUTH (1954). 116 E. 27 St., N.Y.C., 10016. Pres. Amy Sholiton; Nat. Dir. Baruch Taub. Serves as central body for youth groups of traditional congregations; provides such national activities and services as educational guidance, Torah study groups, Chavrusa-community service, programs consultation, Torah library, Torah fund scholarships, Ben Zakkai Honor Society, Friends of NCSY; conducts national and regional events including week-long seminars, summer Torah tours in over 200 communities, Israel summer seminar for teens and collegiates, Camp NCSY in Israel for preteens. Divisions include Senior NCSY in 18 regions and 465 chapters; Junior NCSY for preteens, CYT-College Youth for Torah; B'nai Torah Day School and NCSY in Israel. *Keeping Posted With NCSY; Advisors' Newsletter; Mitsvos Ma'asiyos; Holiday Series; Jewish Thought Series; Leadership Manual Series; Texts for Teen Study.*

_____: WOMEN'S BRANCH (1923). 84 Fifth Ave., N.Y.C., 10011. (212)929-8857. Pres. Mrs. Samuel A. Turk; Exec. Dir. Judy Paikin. Seeks to spread knowledge for the understanding and practice of Orthodox Judaism, and to unite all Orthodox women and their synagogal organizations, services affiliates with educational and programming materials, leadership and organizational guidance and has an NGO representative at UN. *Hachodesh; Hakol.*

UNION OF ORTHODOX RABBIS OF THE UNITED STATES AND CANADA (1900). 235 E. Broadway, N.Y.C., 10002. Pres. Rabbi Moshe Feinstein; Chmn. Rabbi Symcha Elberg, Dir. Rabbi Hersh M. Ginsberg. Seeks to foster and promote Torah-true Judaism in U.S. and Canada; assists in the establishment and maintenance of *yeshivot* in the United States; maintains committee on marriage and divorce and aids individuals with marital difficulties; disseminates knowledge of traditional Jewish rites and practices and publishes regulations on synagogal structure; maintains rabbinical court for resolving individual and communal conflicts. *Hapardes.*

UNION OF SEPHARDIC CONGREGATIONS, INC. (1929). 8 W. 70 St., N.Y.C., 10023. (212)873-0300. Pres. The Haham, Solomon Gaon; Sec. Joseph Tarica; Bd. Chmn. Victor Tarry. Promotes the religious interests of Sephardic Jews; prepares and distributes Sephardic prayer books and provides religious leaders for Sephardic congregations.

UNITED LUBAVITCHER YESHIVOTH (1940). 841-853 Ocean Parkway, Brooklyn, N.Y., 11230. (212)859-7600. Pres. Eli N. Sklar; Chmn. Exec. Com. Rabbi S. Gourary. Supports and organizes Jewish day schools and rabbinical seminaries in the U.S.A. and abroad.

UNITED ORTHODOX SERVICES, INC. (1971). 1311-49 St., Brooklyn, N.Y., 11219. Coordinator Rabbi Zev Perl; Adm. Dir. Ira Axelrod; Exec. Sec. Lillian Deutsch. Centralized religious administrative umbrella organization, with 35 affiliates worldwide; acts as liaison between various religious groups with specialized functions and the Jewish community; initiates projects of its own.

UNITED SYNAGOGUE OF AMERICA (1913). 155 Fifth Ave., N.Y.C. 10010. (212)533-7800. Pres. Simon Schwartz; Exec. V. Pres. Rabbi Benjamin Z. Kreitman. National organization of Conservative Jewish congregations. Maintains 12 departments and 20 regional offices to assist its affiliated congregations with religious, educational, youth, community, and administrative programming and guidance; aims to enhance the cause of Conservative Judaism, further religious observance, encourage establishment of Jewish religious schools; embraces all elements essentially loyal to traditional Judaism. *Program Suggestions; United Synagogue Review; Yearbook Directory and Buyers' Guide.*

———, ATID, COLLEGE AGE ORGANIZATION OF (1960). 155 Fifth Ave., N.Y.C., 10010. (212)533-7800. Dir. Paul Freedman. Student Advisory Board. Seeks to develop a program for strengthening identification with Judaism, based on the personality development, needs and interests of the collegian. *ATID Curricula Judaica; ATID Bibliography. ATID Bookmobile Project.*

———: COMMISSION ON JEWISH EDUCATION (1930). 155 Fifth Ave., N.Y.C., 10010. (212)533-7800. Chmn. Rabbi Joel H. Zaiman; Dir. Morton Siegel. Promotes higher educational standards in Conservative congregational schools and Solomon Schechter Day Schools and publishes material for the advancement of their educational program. *Briefs; Impact; In Your Hands; Your Child.*

———, JEWISH EDUCATORS ASSEMBLY OF (1951). 155 Fifth Ave., N.Y.C., 10010. (212)533-7800. Pres. Solomon Goldman; Admin. Herbert L. Tepper. Promotes, extends, and strengthens the program of Jewish education on all levels in the community in consonance with the philosophy of the Conservative movement. *Annual Yearbook; Newsletters.*

———: JOINT COMMISSION ON SOCIAL ACTION (1958). 155 Fifth Ave., N.Y.C. 10010. (212)533-7800. Co-chmn. Jerry Wagner, Dolly Moser; Dir. Muriel Bermar. Consists of representatives of United Synagogue of America, Women's League for Conservative Judaism, Rabbinical Assembly, and National Federation of Jewish Men's Clubs; reviews public issues and cooperates with civic and Jewish community organizations to achieve social action goals. *Judaism in Social Action.*

———, KADIMA OF (formerly PRE-USY; reorg. 1968). 155 Fifth Ave., N.Y.C., 10010. (212)533-7800. Int. Co-ordinator Carol Chapnick Silk; Dir. Kathy Garon-Wolf. Involves Jewish pre-teens in a meaningful religious, educational, and social environment; fosters a sense of identity and commitment to the Jewish community and Conservative Movement; conducts synagogue-based chapter programs and regional Kadima days and weekends. *KADIMA; Mitzvah of the Month; Kadima Kesher; Advisors Aid Series; Chagim; Games.*

———, NATIONAL ACADEMY FOR ADULT JEWISH STUDIES OF (1940). 155 Fifth Ave., N.Y.C., 10010. (212)533-7800. Chmn. Martin D. Cohn; Dir. Morton Siegel. Provides guidance and information on resources, courses, and other projects in adult Jewish education; prepares and publishes pamphlets, study guides, tracts, and texts for use in adult-education programs; publishes the Jewish Tract series and distributes El-Am edition of *Talmud.* Distributes black-and-white and color films of "Eternal Light" TV programs on

Jewish subjects, produced by Jewish Theological Seminary in cooperation with NBC. *Bulletin.*

———, NATIONAL ASSOCIATION OF SYNAGOGUE ADMINISTRATORS OF (1948). 155 Fifth Ave., N.Y.C. 10010. (212)533-7800. Pres. Stanley I. Minch. Aids congregations affiliated with the United Synagogue of America to further aims of Conservative Judaism through more effective administration; advances professional standards and promotes new methods in administration; cooperates in United Synagogue placement services and administrative surveys. *NASA Newsletter; NASA Journal.*

———, UNITED SYNAGOGUE YOUTH OF (1951). 155 Fifth Ave., N.Y.C., 10010. (212)533-7800. Pres. Jeremy Fingerman; Exec. Dir. Paul Freedman. Seeks to develop a program for strengthening identification with Conservative Judaism, based on the personality development, needs, and interests of the adolescent. *Achshav; Advisors Newsletter; Tikun Olam; USY Alumni Assn. Newsletter.*

———, WOMEN'S LEAGUE FOR CONSERVATIVE JUDAISM (formerly NATIONAL WOMEN'S LEAGUE) (1918). 48 E. 74 St., N.Y.C., 10021. (212)628-1600. Pres. Goldie Kweller. Constitutes parent body of Conservative women's groups in U.S., Canada, Puerto Rico, Mexico, and Israel; provides them with programs in religion, education, social action, leadership training, Israel affairs, and community affairs; publishes books of Jewish interest; contributes to support of Jewish Theological Seminary and Mathilde Schechter Residence Hall. *Women's League Outlook.*

WEST COAST TALMUDICAL SEMINARY (Yeshiva Ohr Elchonon) (1953). 851 No. Kings Rd., Los Angeles, Calif., 90069. (213)651-1820. Headmaster, Robert Jones; Dean, Rabbi Ezra Schochet; Exec. Dir. Rabbi Levi Bukiet. Provides facilities for intensive Torah education as well as Orthodox rabbinical training on the West Coast; conducts an accredited college preparatory high school combined with a full program of Torah-Talmudic training and a graduate Talmudical division on college level.

WORLD COUNCIL OF SYNAGOGUES (1957). 155 Fifth Ave., N.Y.C., 10010. (212)533-7800. Pres. David Zucker; Dir. Muriel M. Bermar; Exec. Dir. in Israel, Pesach Schindler. International representative of Conservative organizations and congregations (Hatenuah Hamasoratit); promotes the growth and development of the Conservative movement in Israel and throughout the world; supports new congregations and educational institutions overseas; holds biennial international convention; represents the world Conservative movement in the World Zionist Organization.

WORLD UNION FOR PROGRESSIVE JUDAISM, LTD. (1926). 838 Fifth Ave., N.Y.C., 10021. (212)249-0100. Pres. David H. Wice; Exec. Dir. Richard G. Hirsch; Sec. Jane Evans; N.A. Bd. Dir. Ira S. Youdovin. Promotes and coordinates efforts of Reform, Liberal, and Progressive congregations throughout the world; supports new congregations; assigns and employs rabbis overseas; sponsors seminaries and schools; organizes international conferences of Liberal Jews. *International Conference Reports; News and Views; Shalhevet* (Israel); *Teshuva* (Argentina).

YAVNE HEBREW THEOLOGICAL SEMINARY (1924). 510 Dahill Road, Brooklyn, N.Y., 11218. (212)436-5610. Pres. Nathan Shapiro; Exec. Dir. Solomon K. Shapiro. School for higher Jewish learning; trains rabbis and teachers as Jewish leaders for American Jewish communities; maintains branch in Jerusalem for higher Jewish education-Machon Maharshal and for an exchange student program. *Yavne Newsletter.*

YAVNEH, NATIONAL RELIGIOUS JEWISH STUDENTS ASSOCIATION (1960). 25 W. 26 St., N.Y.C., 10010. (212)679-4574. Pres. Joseph Offenbacher; Exec. Dir. Mory Korenblit. Seeks to promote religious Jewish and Zionist education on the college campus, to facilitate full observance of halakhic Judaism, to integrate the insights gained in college studies, and to become a force for the dissemination of Torah Judaism in the Jewish community; initiated *kiruv* programs aimed at drawing into the established Jewish community alienated and assimilated Jewish students; publishes occasional monographs in *Yavneh Studies Series;* conducts summer tours to Israel and Western Europe and an Eastern Europe holocaust study tour. *Kol Yavneh, Parshat Hashavua Series; Yavneh Shiron, Guide to Jewish Life on the College Campus; Yavneh Dispatch.*

YESHIVA UNIVERSITY (1886). 500 W. 185 St., N.Y.C., 10033. (212)960-5400. Pres. Norman Lamm; Chmn. Bd. of Trustees Herbert Tenzer. The nation's oldest and largest private university founded under Jewish auspices, with a broad range of undergraduate, graduate, and professional schools, a network of affiliates, publications, a widespread program of research, community service agencies, and a museum. Curricula lead to bachelor's, master's, doctoral, and professional degrees. Undergraduate schools provide general studies curricula supplemented by courses in Jewish learning; graduate schools prepare for careers in medicine, law, mathematics, physics, social work, education, psychology, Semitic languages, literatures, and cultures, and other fields. It has five undergraduate schools, eight graduate schools, and three affiliates, with its four main centers located in Manhattan and the Bronx. *Inside Yeshiva University; Yeshiva University Report.*

Undergraduate schools for men at Main Center: Yeshiva College (Dean Daniel C. Kurtzer) provides liberal arts and sciences curricula; grants B.A. degree. Erna Michael College of Hebraic Studies (Dean Jacob M. Rabinowitz) awards Hebraic Studies and Hebrew Teacher's diplomas, B.A., and B.S. James Striar School of General Jewish Studies (Dir. Morris J. Besdin) grants Associate in Arts degree.

Undergraduate schools for women at Midtown Center, 245 Lexington Ave., N.Y.C., 10016; Stern College for Women (Dean Karen Bacon) offers liberal arts and sciences curricula supplemented by Jewish studies courses; awards B.A., Jewish Studies certificate, Hebrew Teacher's diploma. Teachers Institute for Women (Dir. Baruch N. Faivelson) trains professionals for education and community agency work; awards Hebrew Teacher's diploma and B.S. in Education.

Sponsors two high schools for boys and two for girls (Manhattan and Brooklyn).

Auxiliary services include: Stone-Saperstein Center for Jewish Education, Sephardic Studies Program, Brookdale Foundation Programs for the Aged, Maxwell R. Maybaum Institute of Material Sciences and Quantum Electronics.

———, ALBERT EINSTEIN COLLEGE OF MEDICINE (1955). Eastchester Rd. and Morris Pk. Ave., Bronx, N.Y., 10461. Dean Ephraim Friedman. Prepares physicians and conducts research in the health sciences; awards M.D. degree; includes Sue Golding Graduate Division of Medical Sciences (Dir. Jonathan R. Warner), which grants Ph.D. degree. Einstein College's clinical facilities and affiliates encompass five Bronx hospitals, including Bronx Municipal Hospital, Montefiore Hospital and Medical Center, and the Rose F. Kennedy Center for Research in Mental Retardation and Human Development. *AECOM News; AECOM Newsletter.*

———, ALUMNI OFFICE, 500 West 185th Street, N.Y.C., 10033. Dir. Richard M. Joel. Seeks to foster a close allegiance of alumni to their alma mater by maintaining ties with all alumni and servicing the following associations: Yeshiva College Alumni (Pres. Sam Bloom); Erna Michael College of Hebraic Studies Alumni; James Striar School of General Jewish Studies Alumni; Stern College Alumnae (Pres. Doina L. Bryskin, Marga Marx); Teachers Institute for Women Alumnae (Pres. Rivka Brass Finkelstein); Albert Einstein College of Medicine Alumni (Pres. Robert M. Chaflin); Ferkauf Graduate School of Humanities and Social Sciences Alumni (Pres. Alvin I. Schiff); Wurzweiler School of Social Work Alumni (Pres. Neva Rephun, Norman Winkler); Bernard Revel Graduate School—Harry Fischel School Alumni (Pres. Bernard Rosensweig); Rabbinic Alumni (Pres. Max N. Schreier); Alumni Council (Chmn. Abraham S. Guterman) offers guidance to Pres. and Bd. of Trustees on university's academic development and service activities. *Alumni Review; AECOM Alumni News; Jewish Social Work Forum; Stern College Alumnae Newsletter; Wurzweiler School of Social Work Alumni Association Newsletter; Yeshiva College Alumni Bulletin.*

———, BELFER GRADUATE SCHOOL OF SCIENCE (1958). 500 W. 185 St., N.Y.C., 10033. Dir. Dr. David Finkelstein. Offers programs in mathematics and physics, including college teaching in those areas; conducts advanced research projects; confers M.A. and Ph.D. degrees.

———, BELFER INSTITUTE FOR ADVANCED BIOMEDICAL STUDIES (1978). Eastchester Rd. and Morris Pk. Ave., Bronx, N.Y. 10461. Dir. Ernst R. Jaffe. Offers post-doctoral program that coordinates projects for research fellows and associates, and the development of new training programs; awards certificate at term's completion.

_____, BENJAMIN N. CARDOZO SCHOOL OF LAW (1976). 55 Fifth Ave., N.Y.C., 10003. Dean Monrad G. Paulsen. Prepares students for the professional practice of law or other activities in which legal training is useful; grants L.L.D. degree.

_____, BERNARD REVEL GRADUATE SCHOOL (1937). 500 W. 185 St., N.Y.C., 10033. Dean Sid Z. Leiman. Offers graduate work in Judaic studies and Semitic languages, literatures, and cultures; confers M.S., M.A., and Ph.D. degrees.

_____, FERKAUF GRADUATE SCHOOL OF HUMANITIES AND SOCIAL SCIENCES (1957). 55 Fifth Ave., N.Y.C., 10003. Dean Morton Berger. Offers graduate programs in education, psychology, Jewish education, and special education; grants M.S., M.A., Specialist's Certificate, Doctor of Education, and Ph.D. degrees.

_____, HARRY FISCHEL SCHOOL FOR HIGHER JEWISH STUDIES (1945). 500 W. 185 St., N.Y.C., 10033. Dean Sid Z. Leiman. Offers summer graduate work in Judaic studies and Semitic languages, literatures, and cultures; confers M.S., M.A., and Ph.D. degrees.

_____, (affiliate) RABBI ISAAC ELCHANAN THEOLOGICAL SEMINARY (1896). 2540 Amsterdam Ave., N.Y.C., 10033. Chmn. Bd. of Trustees Charles H. Bendheim; Dir. Rabbi Zevulun Charlop. Offers comprehensive training in higher Jewish studies; grants *semikha* (ordination) and the degrees of Master of Religious Education, Master of Hebrew Literature, Doctor of Religious Education, and Doctor of Hebrew Literature; includes Kollel (Institute for Advanced Research in Rabbinics; Dir. Rabbi Hershel Schachter) and auxiliaries. Cantorial Training Institute (Dir. Macy Nulman) provides professional training of cantors and other musical personnel for the Jewish community; awards Associate Cantor's certificate and cantorial diploma. Sephardic Community Activities Program (Dir. Rabbi Herbert C. Dobrinsky): serves the specific needs of 70 Sephardi synagogues in the U.S. and Canada; holds such events as annual Sephardic Cultural Festival; maintains Sephardic Home Study Group program. *American Sephardi.* Community Service Division (Dir. Victor B. Geller) makes educational, organizational, programming, consultative, and placement resources available to

congregations, schools, organizations, and communities in the U.S. and Canada, through its youth bureau, department of adult education, lecture bureau, placement bureau, and rabbinic alumni. National Commission on Torah Education (Dir. Robert S. Hirt); Camp Morasha (Dir. Zvi Reich) offers Jewish study program; Educators Council of America (Dir. Robert S. Hirt) formulates uniform educational standards, provides guidance to professional staffs, rabbis, lay leaders with regard to curriculum, and promotes Jewish education.

_____, SOCIETY OF THE FOUNDERS OF THE ALBERT EINSTEIN COLLEGE OF MEDICINE (1953). 55 Fifth Ave., N.Y.C., 10003. Exec. Dir. Edwin Cohen. Seeks to further community support of Einstein College.

_____, WOMEN'S ORGANIZATION (1928). 55 Fifth Ave., N.Y.C., 10003. Pres. Mrs. Stanley Schwartz; Exec. Dir. Malkah Isseroff. Supports Yeshiva University's national scholarship program for students training in education, community service, law, medicine, and other professions, and its development program. *YUWO News Briefs.*

_____, WURZWEILER SCHOOL OF SOCIAL WORK (1957). 55 Fifth Ave., N.Y.C., 10003. Dean Lloyd Setleis. Offers graduate programs in social casework, social group work, community social work; grants Master of Social Work and Doctor of Social Welfare degrees.

_____, YESHIVA UNIVERSITY GERONTOLOGICAL INSTITUTE.

_____, (affiliate) YESHIVA UNIVERSITY OF LOS ANGELES (1977). 9760 West Pico Blvd., Los Angeles, Calif., 90035. (213)-553-4478. Bd. Chmn. Samuel Belzberg; Co-chmn. Roland E. Arnall; Dean of Admin. Rabbi Marvin Hier. Offers Jewish studies program for college-age men with limited Hebrew background, Yeshiva program for day-school and yeshiva high-school graduates, and Bet Medrash program of Torah scholarship; students encouraged to pursue B.A. or B.S. degree at college of their choice; completion of YULA program leads to additional degree or diploma; sponsors high school serving girls (grades 9-12) and boys (grades 9-11). *Response.*

YESHIVATH TORAH VODAATH AND MESIVTA RABBINICAL SEMINARY (1918). 425 E. 9 St., Brooklyn, N.Y., 11218. (212)-941-8000. Pres. Henry Hirsch; Chmn. of Bd. Fred F. Weiss; Sec. Earl H. Spero. Offers Hebrew and secular education from elementary level through rabbinical ordination and post-graduate work; maintains a teachers institute and community-service bureau; maintains a dormitory and a nonprofit camp program for boys. *Chronicle; Mesivta Vanguard; Thought of the Week; Torah Vodaath News.*

———, ALUMNI ASSOCIATION (1941). 425 E. 9 St., Brooklyn, N.Y., 11218. (212)941-8000. Pres. Marcus Saffer; Chmn. of Bd. Seymour Pluchenik. Promotes social and cultural ties between the alumni and the schools through fund raising; offers vocational guidance to students; operates Camp Torah Vodaath; sponsors research fellowship program for boys. *Annual Journal; Hamesivta Torah Periodical.*

SOCIAL, MUTUAL BENEFIT

AMERICAN ASSOCIATION FOR ETHIOPIAN JEWS (1969). 304 Robin Hood Lane, Costa Mesa, Ca. 92627. Pres. Howard M. Lenhoff. Provides educational material and support for Ethiopian Jews in Africa and in Israel.

AMERICAN FEDERATION OF JEWISH FIGHTERS, CAMP INMATES AND NAZI VICTIMS, INC. (1971). 623 United Nations Plaza, N.Y.C., 10017. (212)689-7400. Pres. Solomon Zynstein; Exec. Dir. Elliot Welles. Seeks to perpetuate memory of victims of the Holocaust and make Jewish and non-Jewish youth aware of the Holocaust and resistance period. *Martyrdom and Resistance.*

AMERICAN FEDERATION OF JEWS FROM CENTRAL EUROPE, INC. (1942). 570 Seventh Ave., N.Y.C., 10018. (212)869-8610. Pres. Curt C. Silberman; Exec. V. Pres. Herbert A. Strauss. Seeks to safeguard the rights and interests of American Jews of Central European descent, especially in reference to restitution and indemnification; through its Research Foundation for Jewish Immigration sponsors research and publications on the history of Central European Jewry and the history of their immigration and acculturation in the U.S.; sponsors a social program for needy Nazi victims in the U.S. in cooperation with

United Help, Inc. and other specialized social agencies. Undertakes cultural activities, annual conferences, publication, and lecture programs. Member, Council of Jews from Germany.

AMERICAN SEPHARDI FEDERATION (1972). 521 Fifth Ave., N.Y.C., 10017. (212)697-1845. Pres. Liliane L. Winn; Exec. Dir. Gary Schaer; Chmn. Bd. Dirs. Morrie Yohai. Seeks to preserve the Sephardi heritage in the United States, Israel, and throughout the world by fostering and supporting religious and cultural activities of Sephardi congregations, organizations and communities, and uniting them in one overall organization; supports Jewish institutions of higher learning and those for the training of Sephardi lay and religious leaders to serve their communities everywhere; assists Sephardi charitable, cultural, religious and educational institutions everywhere; disseminates information by the publication, or assistance in the publication, of books and other literature dealing with Sephardi culture and tradition in the United States; supports efforts of the World Sephardi Federation to alleviate social disparities in Israel. *Sephardi World.*

AMERICAN VETERANS OF ISRAEL (1949). c/o Samuel E. Alexander, 548 E. Walnut St., Long Beach, N.Y., 11561. (516)431-8316. Pres. Harry Eisner; Sec. Samuel E. Alexander. Maintains contact with American and Canadian volunteers who served in Aliyah Bet and/or Israel's War of Independence; promotes Israel's welfare; holds memorial services at grave of Col. David Marcus; is affiliated with World Mahal. *Newsletter.*

ASSOCIATION OF YUGOSLAV JEWS IN THE UNITED STATES, INC. (1940). 247 W. 99 St., N.Y.C., 10025. (212)865-2211. Pres. Sal Musafia; Sec. Mile Weiss. Assists members and Jews and Jewish organizations in Yugoslavia; cooperates with organization of former Yugoslav Jews in Israel and elsewhere. *Bulletin.*

BNAI ZION—THE AMERICAN FRATERNAL ZIONIST ORGANIZATION (1908). 136 E. 39 St., N.Y.C., 10016. (212)725-1211. Pres. Paul Safro; Exec. V. Pres. Herman Z. Quittman. Fosters principles of Americanism, fraternalism, and Zionism; fosters Hebrew culture; offers life insurance, Blue Cross hospitalization, and other benefits to its members; sponsors settlements, youth centers, medical clinics, and Bnai Zion Home for Retardates in Rosh Ha'ayin, Israel. Program is dedicated to furtherance of America-Israel friendship. *Bnai Zion Foundation Newsletter; Bnai Zion Voice.*

BRITH ABRAHAM (1887). 853 Broadway, N.Y.C., 10003. Grand Master Samuel F. Schwab. Protects Jewish rights and combats antisemitism; supports Israel and major Jewish organizations; maintains foundation in support of Soviet Jewry; aids Jewish education and Camp Loyaltown for Retarded. *Beacon.*

BRITH SHOLOM (1905). Adelphia House, 1235 Chestnut St., Philadelphia, Pa., 19107. (215)568-4225. Nat. Pres. Bennett Goldstein; Nat. Exec. Dir. Albert Liss. Fraternal organization devoted to community welfare, protection of rights of Jewish people and activities which foster Jewish identity and provide support for Israel; sponsors Brith Sholom House for senior citizens in Philadelphia and Brith Sholom Beit Halochem under construction in Haifa, a rehabilitation center for Israel's permanently war-wounded. *Community Relations Digest; Brith Sholom News.*

CENTRAL SEPHARDIC JEWISH COMMUNITY OF AMERICA (1940). 8 W. 70 St., N.Y.C., 10023. Pres. Solomon Altchek; Sec. Isaac Molho. Seeks to foster Sephardic culture, education and communal institutions. Sponsors wide range of activities; raises funds for Sephardic causes in U.S. and Israel.

FREE SONS OF ISRAEL (1849). 932 Broadway, N.Y.C., 10010. (212)260-4222. Grand Master Louis J. Seide; Grand Sec. Murray Birnback. Promotes fraternalism; supports State of Israel, UJA, Soviet Jewry, Israel Bonds, and other Jewish charities; fights antisemitism; awards scholarships. Local lodges have own publications.

JEWISH LABOR BUND (Directed by WORLD COORDINATING COMMITTEE OF THE BUND) (1897; reorg. 1947). 25 E. 78 St., N.Y.C., 10021. (212)535-0850. Exec. Sec. Jacob S. Hertz. Coordinates activities of the Bund organizations throughout the world and represents them in the Socialist International; spreads the ideas of Socialism as formulated by the Jewish Labor Bund; publishes pamphlets and periodicals on world problems, Jewish life, socialist theory and policy, and on the history, activities, and ideology of the Jewish Labor Bund. *Unser Tsait* (U.S.); *Foroys* (Mexico); *Lebns-Fragn* (Israel); *Unser Gedank* (Australia); *Unser Shtimme* (France).

JEWISH PEACE FELLOWSHIP (1941). Box 271, Nyack, N.Y., 10960. (914)358-4601. Pres. Naomi Goodman; Hon. Chmn. Isidor B. Hoffman. Unites those who believe that Jewish ideals and experience provide inspiration for a nonviolent philosophy and way of life; offers draft counseling, especially for conscientious objection based on Jewish "religious training and belief"; encourages Jewish community to become more knowledgeable, concerned, and active in regard to the war/peace problem. *JPF Newsletter.*

JEWISH SOCIALIST VERBAND OF AMERICA (1921). 45 E. 33 St., N.Y.C., 10016. (212)686-1536. Pres. Morris Bagno; Nat. Sec. Maurice Petrushka. Promotes ideals of democratic socialism and Yiddish culture; affiliated with Social Democrats, USA. *Der Wecker.*

SEPHARDIC JEWISH BROTHERHOOD OF AMERICA, INC. (1915). 97–29 64th Rd., Rego Park, N.Y., 11374. (212)459-1600. Pres. Bernard Ouziel; Sec. Jack Ezratty. Promotes the industrial, social, educational, and religious welfare of its members, offers funeral and burial benefits, scholarships and aid to needy. *Sephardic Brother.*

UNITED ORDER TRUE SISTERS, INC. (1846). 150 W. 85 St., N.Y.C., 10024. (212)362-2502. Nat. Pres. Mrs. Bernard S. Weinberg; Nat. Sec. Mrs. Martin Sporn. Philanthropic, fraternal, community service; nat. projects; cancer service; aids handicapped children, deaf, blind, etc. *Echo.*

WORKMEN'S CIRCLE (1900). 45 E. 33 St., N.Y.C., 10016. (212)889-6800. Pres. Bernard Backer; Exec. Dir. William Stern. Provides fraternal benefits and activities, Jewish educational programs, secularist Yiddish schools for children, community activities, both in Jewish life and on the American scene, cooperation with the labor movement. *The Call; Inner Circle; Kinder Zeitung; Kultur un Lebn.*

———, DIVISION OF JEWISH LABOR COMMITTEE (see p. 295).

SOCIAL WELFARE

AMERICAN JEWISH CORRECTIONAL CHAP-
LAINS ASSOCIATION, INC. (formerly NA-
TIONAL COUNCIL OF JEWISH PRISON
CHAPLAINS) (1937). 10 E. 73 St., N.Y.C.,
10021. (212)879-8415. (Cooperating with
the New York Board of Rabbis and Jewish
Family Service.) Pres. Irving Koslowe;
Exec. Dir. Paul L. Hait. Provides religious
services and guidance to Jewish men and
women in penal and correctional institutions; serves as a liaison between inmates
and their families; upgrades the quality of
correctional ministrations through conferences, professional workshops, and conventions. *Bulletin.*

AMERICAN JEWISH SOCIETY FOR SERVICE,
INC., (1949). 15 E. 26 St., Rm. 1302,
N.Y.C., 10010. (212)683-6178. Pres. E.
Kenneth Marx; Exec. Dir. Elly Saltzman.
Conducts four voluntary work service
camps each summer to enable young peo-
ple to live their faith by serving other peo-
ple. *Newsletter.*

AMC CANCER RESEARCH CENTER AND
HOSPITAL (formerly Jewish CONSUMP-
TIVES' RELIEF SOCIETY, 1904; incorporated as AMERICAN MEDICAL CENTER AT
DENVER, 1954). 6401 West Colfax Ave.,
Lakewood, Colo., 80214. (303)233-6501.
Manfred L. Minzer, Jr.; Chmn. Bd. of
Trustees, Bishop George R. Evans. A national cancer hospital that provides the
finest specialized treatment available to patients, regardless of ability to pay; pursues,
as a progressive science research center,
promising leads in the prevention, detec-
tion, and control of cancer.

———: NATIONAL COUNCIL OF AUXILIAR-
IES (1904; reorg. 1936). 6401 W. Colfax,
Lakewood, Colo., 80214. (303)233-6501.
Pres. Sue Snyder. Provides support for the
AMC Cancer Research Center and Hospital program by disseminating information,
fund-raising, and acting as admissions
officers for patients from chapter cities
throughout the country. *Bulletin.*

ASSOCIATION OF JEWISH FAMILY AND
CHILDREN'S AGENCIES (1972). 200 Park
Ave. S., N.Y.C., 10003. (212)674-6800.
Pres. Oscar Respitz; Exec. Dir. Martin
Greenberg. The national service organiza-
tion for Jewish family and children's agen-
cies in Canada and the United States. Rein-

forces member agencies in their efforts to
sustain and enhance the quality of Jewish
family and communal life. *Newsletter.*

BARON DE HIRSCH FUND (1891). 386 Park
Ave. S., N.Y.C., 10016. (212)532-7088.
Pres. Ezra Pascal Mager; Mng. Dir. Theodore Norman. Aids Jewish immigrants and
their children in the U.S., Israel, and elsewhere by giving grants to agencies active in
educational and vocational fields; has limited program for study tours in U.S. by
Israeli agriculturists.

B'NAI B'RITH INTERNATIONAL (1943). 1640
Rhode Island Ave., N.W., Washington,
D.C., 20036. (202)857-6600. Pres. Jack J.
Spitzer; Exec. V. Pres. Daniel Thursz. International Jewish organization, with affiliates in 42 countries. Programs include
communal service, social action, and public affairs, with emphasis on preserving Judaism through projects in and for Israel
and for Soviet Jewry; teen and college-age
movements; adult Jewish education. *The
National Jewish Monthly; Shofar.*

———, ANTI-DEFAMATION LEAGUE OF
(see p. 294).

———, CAREER AND COUNSELING SER-
VICES (1938). 1640 Rhode Island Ave.,
N.W., Washington, D.C., 20036. (202)857-
6600. Chmn. Stanley M. Kaufman; Nat.
Dir. S. Norman Feingold. Conducts educational and occupational research and engages in a broad publications program;
provides direct group and individual guidance services for youths and adults
through professionally staffed regional
offices in many population centers. *B'nai
B'rith Career and Counseling Services
Newsletter; Catalogue of Publications;
Counselors Information Service; College
Guide for Jewish Youth.*

———. HILLEL FOUNDATIONS, INC. (see p.
304).

———: INTERNATIONAL ASSOCIATION OF
HILLEL DIRECTORS (see p. 307).

———, WOMEN (1897). 1640 Rhode Island
Ave., N.W., Washington, D.C., 20036.
(202)857-6689. Pres. Evelyn Wasserstrom;
Exec. Dir. Edna J. Wolf. Participates in
contemporary Jewish life through youth
and adult Jewish education programs,
human rights endeavors, and community-
service activities; supports a variety of services to Israel; conducts community ser-

vice programs for the disadvantaged and the handicapped, and public affairs programs. *Women's World.*

——, YOUTH ORGANIZATION (see p. 304).

CITY OF HOPE—A NATIONAL MEDICAL CENTER UNDER JEWISH AUSPICES (1913). 208 W. 8 St., Los Angeles, Calif., 90014. (213)626-4611. Pres. M. E. Hersch; Exec. Dir. Ben Horowitz. Admits on completely free, nonsectarian basis patients from all parts of the nation suffering from cancer and leukemia, blood, heart, and respiratory ailments, and certain maladies of heredity and metabolism including diabetes; makes available its consultation service to doctors and hospitals throughout the nation, concerning diagnosis and treatment of their patients; as a unique pilot medical center, seeks improvements in the quality, quantity, economy, and efficiency of health care. Thousands of original findings have emerged from its staff who are conducting clinical and basic research in the catastrophic maladies, lupus erythematosus, Huntington's disease, genetics, and the neurosciences. *Pilot; President's Newsletter; City of Hope Quarterly.*

CONFERENCE OF JEWISH COMMUNAL SERVICE (1899). 15 E. 26 St., N.Y.C., 10010. (212)683-8056. Pres. Bernard Olshansky; Exec. Dir. Matthew Penn. Serves as forum for all professional philosophies in community service, for testing new experiences, proposing new ideas, and questioning or reaffirming old concepts. Concerned with advancement of professional personnel practices and standards. *Concurrents; Journal of Jewish Communal Service.*

COUNCIL OF JEWISH FEDERATIONS AND WELFARE FUNDS, INC. (1932). 575 Lexington Ave., N.Y.C., 10022. (212)751-1311. Pres. Morton L. Mandel; Exec. V. Pres. Philip Bernstein. Provides national and regional services to more than 190 associated federations embracing 800 communities in the United States and Canada, aiding in fund raising, community organization, health and welfare planning, personnel recruitment, and public relations. *Directory of Jewish Federations, Welfare Funds and Community Councils; Directory of Jewish Health and Welfare Agencies* (triennial); *Jewish Communal Services: Programs and Finances; Yearbook of Jewish Social Services; Annual Report.*

HOPE CENTER FOR THE RETARDED (1965). 3601 E. 32 Ave., Denver, Colo., 80205. (303)388-4801. Pres. Al Perington; Exec. Dir. George E. Brantley; Sec. Lorraine Faulstich. Provides services to developmentally disabled of community: preschool training, day training and work activities center, speech and language pathology, occupational arts and crafts, and recreational therapy, social services.

INTERNATIONAL COUNCIL ON JEWISH SOCIAL AND WELFARE SERVICES (1961). 200 Park Ave. S., N.Y.C., 10003. (N.Y. liaison office with UN headquarters.) Chmn. Donald M. Robinson; V. Chmn. William Haber; The Rt. Hon. Lord Nathan; Exec. Sec. Leonard Seidenman; Dep. Exec. Sec. Theodore D. Feder. Provides for exchange of views and information among member agencies on problems of Jewish social and welfare services, including medical care, old age, welfare, child care, rehabilitation, technical assistance, vocational training, agricultural, and other resettlement, economic assistance, refugees, migration, integration and related problems, representation of views to governments and international organizations. Members: six national and international organizations.

JEWISH BRAILLE INSTITUTE OF AMERICA, INC. (1931). 110 E. 30 St., N.Y.C., 10016. (212)889-2525. Pres. Mrs. David M. Levitt; Exec. Dir. Gerald M. Kass. Seeks to serve the religious and cultural needs of the Jewish blind by publishing braille prayer books in Hebrew and English; provides Yiddish, Hebrew, and English records for Jewish blind throughout the world who cannot read braille; maintains worldwide free braille lending library. *Jewish Braille Review; JBI Voice.*

JEWISH CONCILIATION BOARD OF AMERICA, INC. (1922). 120 W. 57 St., N.Y.C., 10019. (212)582-3577. Pres. Lewis Bart Stone. Evaluates and attempts to resolve conflicts within families, organizations, and businesses to avoid litigation; offers, without charge, mediation, arbitration, and counseling services by rabbis, attorneys, and social workers; refers cases to other agencies, where indicated.

JWB (NATL. JEWISH WELFARE BOARD) (1917). 15 E. 26 St., N.Y.C. 10010. Pres. Robert L. Adler; Exec. V. Pres. Arthur Rotman. Major service agency for Jewish community centers and camps serving more than a million Jews in the U.S. and Canada; U.S. Government accredited agency for providing services and programs to Jewish military families and hospitalized veterans; promotes Jewish culture through its Book and Music Councils, JWB lecture bureau, and Jewish educational, cultural and Israel-related projects. *JWB Circle; Jewish Community Center Program Aids; Books in Review; Jewish Music Notes; Running the Center; Contact; JWB Facts; Public Relations Idea Exchange; JWB Personnel Reporter; Sherut; The Jewish Chaplain; Jewish Lay Leader; Mail Call.*

————: COMMISSION ON JEWISH CHAPLAINCY (1940). 15 E. 26 St., N.Y.C., 10010. Chmn. Rabbi Judah Nadich; Dir. Rabbi Gilbert Kollin. Recruits, endorses, and serves Jewish military and Veterans Administration chaplains on behalf of the American Jewish community and the three major rabbinic bodies; trains and assists Jewish lay leaders where there are no chaplains, for service to Jewish military personnel, their families, and hospitalized veterans. *Jewish Chaplain; Jewish Lay Leader.*

————, JEWISH BOOK COUNCIL (see p. 299).

————, JEWISH MUSIC COUNCIL (see p. 299).

LEO N. LEVI MEMORIAL NATIONAL ARTHRITIS HOSPITAL (sponsored by B'nai B'rith) (1914). 300 Prospect Ave., Hot Springs, Ark., 71901. (501)624-1281. Pres. Mrs. Leonard A. Bagen; Adm. D. E. Wagoner. Maintains a nonprofit nonsectarian hospital for treatment of sufferers from arthritis and related diseases.

NATIONAL ASSOCIATION OF JEWISH FAMILY, CHILDREN'S AND HEALTH PROFESSIONALS (1965). 1175 S. College Ave., Columbus, Ohio 43209. (614)231-1890. Pres. Peter M. Glick; V. Pres. Ruth Cohen, Simon Krakow. Brings together Jewish caseworkers and related professionals in Jewish family, children, and health services. Seeks to improve personnel standards, further Jewish continuity and identity, and strengthen Jewish family life; provides forums for professional discussion at national conference of Jewish communal service and regional meetings; takes action on social policy issues; provides a vehicle for representation of Jewish caseworkers and others in various national associations and activities. *Newsletter.*

NATIONAL ASSOCIATION OF JEWISH HOMES FOR THE AGED (1960). 2525 Centerville Road, Dallas, Texas, 75228. (214)327-4503. Pres. Sidney Friedman; Exec. V. Pres. Herbert Shore; Pres. Elect, Howard Bram. Serves as a national representative of voluntary Jewish homes for the aged. Conducts annual meetings, conferences, workshops and institutes. Provides for sharing information, studies and clearinghouse functions. *Directory; Progress Report.*

NATIONAL ASSOCIATION OF JEWISH VOCATIONAL SERVICES (formerly Jewish Occupational Council) (1940). 600 Pennsylvania Ave., S.E., Washington, D.C. 20036. (202)466-2678. Pres. Robert E. Greenstein; Exec. Dir. Mark J. Ugoretz. Acts as coordinating body for all Jewish agencies having programs in educational vocational guidance, job placement, vocational rehabilitation, skills-training, sheltered workshops, and occupational research. *Newsletter;* Information bulletins.

NATIONAL COUNCIL OF JEWISH PRISON CHAPLAINS, INC. (see AMERICAN JEWISH CORRECTIONAL CHAPLAINS ASSOCIATION, INC.).

NATIONAL COUNCIL OF JEWISH WOMEN (1893). 15 E. 26 St., N.Y.C., 10010. (212)-532-1740. Nat. Pres. Esther R. Landa; Exec. Dir. Marjorie M. Cohen. Operates programs in education, social and legislative action, and community service for children and youth, the aging, the disadvantaged in Jewish and general communities; concerns include juvenile justice system as basis for legislative reform and community projects; deeply involved in women's issues; promotes education in Israel through NCJW Research Institute for Innovation in Education at Hebrew University, Jerusalem. *NCJW Journal; Washington Newsletter; Children Without Justice; Manual for Action; Symposium on Status Offenders Proceedings; Windows on Day Care; Innocent Victims.*

NATIONAL JEWISH COMMITTEE ON SCOUTING (1926). Boy Scouts of America. North Brunswick, N.J., 08902. (201)249-6000. Chmn. Melvin B. Neisner; Exec. Dir. Harry Lasker. Seeks to stimulate Boy Scout activity among Jewish boys. *Ner*

Tamid for Boy Scouts and Explorers; Scouting in Synagogues and Centers.

NATIONAL JEWISH HOSPITAL AND RE-SEARCH CENTER (1899). 3800 E. Colfax Ave., Denver, Colo., 80206. (303)388-4461. Pres. Richard N. Bluestein; Natl. Chmn. Andrew Goodman. Offers nation-wide, nonsectarian care for adults and chil-dren suffering from tuberculosis, asthma, emphysema, chronic bronchitis, cystic fibrosis, and other immunological and pul-monary disorders. *NJH Report.*

_____: THE NATIONAL ASTHMA CENTER (1907). 1999 Julian St., Denver, Colo., 80204. (303)458-1999. Bd. Pres. Richard N. Bluestein; Exec. V. Pres. Jack Gersh-tenson. Administers care and treatment to children from the ages of 5–16 suffering from chronic, intractable asthma; per-forms outpatient services for people of all ages; research and dissemination of infor-mation. *National Asthma Center News.*

WORLD CONFEDERATION OF JEWISH COM-MUNITY CENTERS (1947). 15 E. 26 St., N.Y.C., 10010. (212)532-4949. Pres. Mor-ton L. Mandell; Exec. Dir. Herbert Mill-man. Serves as a council of national and continental federations of Jewish commu-nity centers; fosters development of the JCC movement worldwide; provides a forum for exchange of information among centers. *Newsletter.*

ZIONIST AND PRO-ISRAEL

AMERICA-ISRAEL FRIENDSHIP LEAGUE (1971). 134 E. 39 St., N.Y.C., 10016. (212)-679-4822. Pres. Herbert Tenzer; Exec. Dir. Ilana Artman. Seeks to further the existing goodwill between the two nations on a peo-ple-to-people basis.

AMERICAN ASSOCIATES OF BEN-GURION UNIVERSITY OF THE NEGEV. (1973). 342 Madison Ave., Room 1923, N.Y.C., 10017. (212)687-7721. Pres. Aron Chile-wich; Chmn. Exec. Com. Bobbie Abrams; Exec. V. Pres. David N. Adler. Serves as the University's publicity and fund-raising link to the United States. The Associates are committed to publicizing University activities and curriculum, securing student scholarships, transferring contributions, and encouraging American interest in the University. *The Messenger.*

AMERICAN COMMITTEE FOR SHAARE ZEDEK HOSPITAL IN JERUSALEM, INC. (1949). 49 W. 45 St., N.Y.C., 10036. (212)-354-8801. Pres. Charles Bendheim; Bd. Chmn. Max Stern; Sec. Isaac Strahl; Treas. Norbert Strauss. Raises funds for the vari-ous needs of the Shaare Zedek Hospital, Jerusalem, such as equipment and medical supplies, a nurses training school, research, and construction of the new Shaare Zedek Medical Center. *Shaare Zedek News Quar-terly.*

AMERICAN COMMITTEE FOR THE WEIZ-MANN INSTITUTE OF SCIENCE, INC. (1944). 515 Park Ave., N.Y.C., 10022. (212)752-1300. Pres. Stephen L. Stulman; Chmn. of Bd. Morris L. Levinson; Exec. Dir. Harold Hill. Secures support for basic and applied scientific research. *Interface; Rehovot; Research.*

AMERICAN FRIENDS OF HAIFA UNIVERSITY (1969). 60 E. 42 St., N.Y.C., 10017. Hon. Pres. Charles J. Bensley; V. Pres. Sigmund Strochlitz. Supports the development and maintenance of the various programs of the University of Haifa, among them the Arab Jewish center, Yiddish department, Bridging the Gap project, department of management, school of education, kibbutz movement, and fine arts department; ar-ranges overseas academic programs for American and Canadian students. *Newslet-ter.*

AMERICAN FRIENDS OF RELIGIOUS FREE-DOM IN ISRAEL (1963). P.O. Box. 5888, Washington, D.C., 20014. (301)530-1737. Exec. Dir. Alex Hershaft. Calls for com-plete religious freedom and separation of church and state in Israel; publicizes viola-tions of religious freedom to bring the in-fluence of the benevolent opinion of the American Jewish community to bear on solution of this problem; assists other groups and individuals working toward these goals.

AMERICAN FRIENDS OF THE HEBREW UNI-VERSITY (1925; Inc. 1931). 11 E. 69 St., N.Y.C., 10021. (212)472-9829. Pres. Stan-ley M. Bogen; Exec. V. Pres. Seymour Fishman; Chmn. of Bd. Max M. Kampel-man; Chmn. Exec. Comm. Julian B. Ve-nezky. Fosters the growth, development, and maintenance of the Hebrew University of Jerusalem; collects funds and conducts programs of information throughout the United States interpreting the work of the

Hebrew University and its significance; administers American student programs and arranges exchange professorships in the United States and Israel. Created, and recruits support for, Truman Research Institute. *American Friends Bulletin; News from the Hebrew University of Jerusalem; Scopus Magazine.*

AMERICAN FRIENDS OF THE ISRAEL MUSEUM (1968). 10 E. 40 St., N.Y.C., 10016. (212)683-5190. Pres. Norbert Schimmel; Exec. Dir. Michele Cohn Tocci. Raises funds for special projects of the Israel Museum in Jerusalem; solicits contributions of works of art for exhibition and educational purposes. *Newsletter.*

AMERICAN FRIENDS OF THE JERUSALEM MENTAL HEALTH CENTER—EZRATH NASHIM, INC. (1895). 10 E. 40 St., N.Y.C., 10016. (212)725-8175. Pres. Joel Finkle; Exec. Dir. S. Alvin Schwartz; Bd. Chmn. Irwin S. Meltzer. Supports the growth, development, and maintenance of the Jerusalem Mental Health Center, which includes a 250-bed hospital, comprehensive outpatient clinic, drug abuse clinic, and the Jacob Herzog Psychiatric Research Center; Israel's only non-profit, voluntary psychiatric hospital; is used as a teaching facility by Israel's major medical schools. *Progress Reports; Ezrah.*

AMERICAN FRIENDS OF THE TEL AVIV UNIVERSITY, INC. (1955). 342 Madison Ave., N.Y.C., 10017. (212)687-5651. Pres. M. Robert Hecht; V. Pres. Yona Ettinger, Malcolm Rosenberg; Exec. V. Pres. Zvi Almog. Supports development and maintenance of the Tel Aviv University. Sponsors exchange student programs and exchange professorships in U.S. and Israel. *Tel Aviv University Report.*

AMERICAN-ISRAEL CULTURAL FOUNDATION, INC. (1939). 485 Madison Ave., N.Y.C., 10022. (212)751-2700. Bd. Chmn. Isaac Stern; Pres. William Mazer; Exec. Dir. Stanley Grayson. Membership organization supporting Israeli cultural institutions, such as Israel Philharmonic and Israel Chamber Orchestra, Tel Aviv Museum, Rubin Academies, Bat Sheva Dance Co.; sponsors cultural exchange between U.S. and Israel; awards scholarships in all arts to young Israelis for study in Israel and abroad. *Hadashot; Tarbut.*

AMERICAN ISRAEL PUBLIC AFFAIRS COMMITTEE (1954). 444 North Capitol St., N.W., Suite 412, Washington, D.C., 20001. (202)638-2256. Pres. Lawrence Weinberg; Exec. Dir. Morris J. Amitay. Registered to lobby on behalf of legislation affecting Israel, Soviet Jewry, and arms sales to Middle East; represents Americans who believe support for a secure Israel is in U.S. interest.

AMERICAN-ISRAELI LIGHTHOUSE, INC. (1928; reorg. 1955). 30 E. 60 St., N.Y.C., 10022. (212)838-5322. Nat. Pres. Mrs. Leonard F. Dank; Nat. Sec. Mrs. L.T. Rosenbaum. Provides education and rehabilitation for the blind and physically handicapped in Israel to effect their social and vocational integration into the seeing community; built and maintains Rehabilitation Center for the Blind (Migdal Or) in Haifa. *Tower.*

AMERICAN JEWISH LEAGUE FOR ISRAEL (1957). 595 Madison Ave., N.Y.C., 10022. (212)371-1583. Hon. Pres. Seymour R. Levine; Chmn. Exec. Com. Eleazar Lipsky; Chmn. of Bd. Samuel Rothberg. Seeks to unite all those who, notwithstanding differing philosophies of Jewish life, are committed to the historical ideals of Zionism; works, independently of class or party, for the welfare of Israel as a whole. Not identified with any political parties in Israel. *Bulletin of the American Jewish League for Israel.*

AMERICAN MIZRACHI WOMEN (formerly MIZRACHI WOMEN'S ORGANIZATION OF AMERICA) (1925). 817 Broadway, N.Y.C., 10003. (212)477-4720. Nat. Pres. Sarah P. Shane; Exec. Dir. Marvin Leff. Conducts social service, child care, and vocational-educational programs in Israel in an environment of traditional Judaism; promotes cultural activities for the purpose of disseminating Zionist ideals and strengthening traditional Judaism in America. *The American Mizrachi Woman.*

AMERICAN PHYSICIANS FELLOWSHIP, INC. FOR MEDICINE IN ISRAEL (1950). 2001 Beacon St., Brookline, Mass., 02146. (617)232-5382. Pres. Arkadi M. Rywlin; Sec. Manuel M. Glazier. Helps Israel become a major world medical center; secures fellowships for selected Israeli physicians and arranges lectureships in Israel by prominent American physicians; supports Jerusalem Academy of Medicine;

supervises U.S. and Canadian medical and paramedical emergency volunteers in Israel; maintains Israel Institute of the History of Medicine; contributes medical books, periodicals, instruments, and drugs. *APF News.*

AMERICAN RED MAGEN DAVID FOR ISRAEL, INC. (1941). 888 7th Ave., N.Y.C., 10019. (212)757-1627. Nat. Pres. Joseph Handleman;Nat. Chmn. Emanuel Celler; Nat. Exec. V. Pres. Benjamin Saxe. An authorized tax exempt organization; the sole support arm in the United States of Magen David Adom in Israel with a national membership and chapter program. Educates and involves its members in activities of Magen David Adom, Israel's Red Cross Service; raises funds for MDA's emergency medical services, including collection and distribution of blood and blood products for Israel's military and civilian population; supplies ambulances, bloodmobiles, and mobile cardiac rescue units serving all hospitals and communities throughout Israel; supports MDA's 73 emergency medical clinics and helps provide training and equipment for volunteer emergency paramedical corps. *Chapter Highlights; Lifeline.*

AMERICAN TECHNION SOCIETY. (1940). 271 Madison Ave., N.Y.C., 10016. (212)889-2050. Pres. Alexander Hassan; Exec. V. Pres. Louis E. Levitan. Supports the work of the Technion-Israel Institute of Technology, Haifa, which trains nearly 10,000 students in 20 departments and a medical school, and conducts research across a broad spectrum of science and technology. *ATS Newsletter; ATS Women's Division Newsletter; Technion Magazine.*

AMERICAN ZIONIST FEDERATION (1939; reorg. 1949 and 1970). 515 Park Ave., N.Y.C., 10022. (212)371-7750. Pres. Joseph P. Sternstein; Exec. Dir. Carmella Carr. Consolidates the efforts of the existing Zionist constituency in such areas as public and communal affairs, education, youth and aliyah, and invites the affiliation and participation of like-minded individuals and organizations in the community-at-large. Seeks to conduct a Zionist program designed to create a greater appreciation of Jewish culture within the American Jewish community in furtherance of the continuity of Jewish life and the spiritual centrality of Israel as the Jewish homeland. Composed of 15 National Zionist organizations; 10

Zionist youth movements; individual members-at-large; corporate affiliates. Maintains regional offices in Pittsburgh, Denver, Los Angeles, Chicago, Boston, Cleveland, Detroit, and New York. *News & Views.*

AMERICAN ZIONIST YOUTH FOUNDATION, INC. (1973). 515 Park Ave., N.Y.C., 10022. (212)751-6070. Bd. Chmn. David Sidorsky; Exec. Dir. Donald Adelman. Sponsors educational programs and services for American Jewish youth including tours to Israel, programs of volunteer service or study in leading institutions of science, scholarship and arts; sponsors field workers who promote Jewish and Zionist programming on campus; prepares and provides specialists who present and interpret the Israeli experience for community centers and federations throughout the country. *Activist Newsletter.*

————: AMERICAN ZIONIST YOUTH COUNCIL (1951). 515 Park Ave., N.Y.C., 10022. (212)751-6070. Chmn. Tom Gutherz. Acts as spokesman and representative of Zionist youth in interpreting Israel to the youth of America; represents, coordinates, and implements activities of the Zionist youth movements in the U.S.

AMPAL—AMERICAN ISRAEL CORPORATION (1942). 10 Rockefeller Plaza, N.Y.C., 10020. (212)586-3232. Pres. Ralph Cohen; V. Pres. Shimon Topor. Finances and invests in Israel economic enterprises; mobilizes finance and investment capital in the U.S. through sale of own debenture issues and utilization of bank credit lines. *Annual Report; Prospectuses.*

BAR-ILAN UNIVERSITY IN ISRAEL (1955). 641 Lexington Ave., N.Y.C., 10022. (212)-751-6366. Chancellor Joseph H. Lookstein; Pres. Emanuel Rackman; Chmn. Bd. of Trustees, Phillip Stollman; Pres. Amer. Bd. of Overseers, Mrs. Jerome L. Stern; Exec. V. Chmn. Internat. Bd. of Overseers, Rabbi Karpol Bender. A liberal arts and sciences institution, located in Ramat-Gan, Israel, and chartered by Board of Regents of State of New York. *Bar-Ilan News; Academic Research; Philosophia.*

BRIT TRUMPELDOR BETAR OF AMERICA, INC. (1935). 85-40 149 St., Briarwood, N.Y., 11435. Pres. Gary Segal; V. Pres. Shari Olenberg. Teaches Jewish youth love of the Jewish people and prepares them for aliyah; emphasizes learning Hebrew; keeps its members ready for mobilization in times of crisis; stresses Jewish pride and self-respect; seeks to aid and protect Jewish communities everywhere. *Herut.*

DROR—YOUNG ZIONIST ORGANIZATION, INC. (1948). 215 Park Ave. S., N.Y.C., 10003. Pres. Robby Regev; V. Pres. Hagai Aizenberg; Sec. Mark Cohen. Fosters Zionist program for youth with emphasis on aliyah to the Kibbutz Ha'meuchad; stresses Jewish and labor education; maintains leadership seminar and work-study programs in Israel, summer camps in the U.S. and Canada. Sponsors two *garinim* in Israel. *Alon Dror; Igeret Dror.*

_____: GARIN YARDEN, THE YOUNG KIBBUTZ MOVEMENT. (1976). Pres. Eva Rubenstein; Sec. Rachel Weisman; Exec. Off. Danny Siegal. Aids those interested in making *aliyah* to an Israeli kibbutz; affiliated with Kibbutz Hameuchad. *Newsletter.*

EMUNAH (formerly HAPOEL HAMIZRACHI WOMEN'S ORGANIZATION) (1948). 370 Seventh Ave., N.Y.C., 10001. (212)564-9045. Nat. Pres. Mrs. Toby Willig; Exec. Dir. Shirley Singer. Maintains and supports religious nurseries, day care centers, and teacher training schools for the underprivileged in Israel. *The Emunah Woman.*

FEDERATED COUNCIL OF ISRAEL INSTITUTIONS—FCII (1940). 38 Park Row, N.Y.C., 10038. (212)227-3152. Chmn. Bd. Z. Shapiro; Exec. V. Pres. Julius Novack. Central fund-raising organization for 104 affiliated institutions; handles and executes estates, wills, and bequests for the traditional institutions in Israel; clearinghouse for information on budget, size, functions, etc. of traditional educational, welfare, and philanthropic institutions in Israel, working cooperatively with the Israel government and the overseas department of the Council of Jewish Federations and Welfare Funds, New York. *Annual Financial Reports and Statistics on Affiliates.*

FUND FOR HIGHER EDUCATION (IN ISRAEL) (1970). 1500 Broadway, Suite 1900, N.Y.C., 10036. (212)354-4660. Chmn. Louis Warschaw; Pres. Amnon Barness; Sec. Richard Segal; V. Pres., Nat. Campaign Dir. Joel R. Erenberg. Supports, on a project-by-project basis, institutions of higher learning in Israel and the U.S.

HADASSAH, THE WOMEN'S ZIONIST ORGANIZATION OF AMERICA, INC. (1912). 50 W. 58 St., N.Y.C., 10019. (212)355-7900. Pres. Bernice S. Tannenbaum; Exec. Dir. Aline Kaplan. In America helps interpret Israel to the American people; provides basic Jewish education as a background for intelligent and creative Jewish living in America; sponsors Hashachar, largest Zionist youth movement in U.S., which has four divisions: Young Judaea, Intermediate Judaea, Senior Judaea, and Hamagshimim; operates eight Zionist youth camps in this country; supports summer and all-year courses in Israel. Maintains in Israel Hadassah-Hebrew University Medical Center for healing, teaching, and research; Hadassah Community College; Seligsberg/Brandeis Comprehensive High School; and Hadassah Vocational Guidance Institute. Is largest organizational contributor to Youth Aliyah and to Jewish National Fund for land purchase and reclamation. *Hadassah Headlines; Hadassah Magazine.*

_____. HASHACHAR (formerly YOUNG JUDEA and JUNIOR HADASSAH; org. 1909, reorg. 1967). 817 Broadway, N.Y.C., 10003. Nat. Pres. of Senior Judaea (high school level) Danny Spinack; Nat. Coordinator of Hamagshimim (college level) David Lehrer; Nat. Dir. Irv Widaen. Seeks to educate Jewish youth from the ages of 10–25 toward Jewish and Zionist values, active commitment to and participation in the American and Israeli Jewish communities, with *aliyah* as a prime goal; maintains summer camps and summer and year programs in Israel. *Hamagshimim Journal; Kol Hat'una; The Young Judaean; Daf L'Madrichim.*

HASHOMER HATZAIR, INC. 150 Fifth Ave., Suite 1002, N.Y.C., 10011. (212)929-4955.

_____: AMERICANS FOR PROGRESSIVE ISRAEL (1951). (212)255-8760. Nat. Chmn. Bernard Harkavy; Exec. Dir. Linda Rubin. Affiliated with Kibbutz Artzi. Believes Zionism is the National Liberation Movement of the Jewish people; educates members towards an understanding of their Jewishness and progressive values; dignity of labor, social justice, and the brotherhood of nations. *Background Bulletin; Progressive Israel; Israel Horizons.*

_____: SOCIALIST ZIONIST YOUTH MOVEMENT (1923). Nat. Sec. Tuvia Liberman; Dir. Shlomo Margolit. Seeks to educate

Jewish youth to an understanding of Zionism as the national liberation movement of the Jewish people. Promotes *aliyah* to kibbutzim. Espouses socialist ideals of peace, justice, democracy, industry, and brotherhood. *Youth and Nation; Young Guard; La Madrich; Hayasad; Layidiatcha.*

HEBREW UNIVERSITY-TECHNION JOINT MAINTENANCE APPEAL (1954). 11 E. 69 St., N.Y.C., 10021. (212)988-8418. Chmn. Daniel G. Ross; Dir. Clifford B. Surloff. Conducts maintenance campaigns formerly conducted by the American Friends of the Hebrew University and the American Technion Society; participates in community campaigns throughout the U.S., excluding New York City.

HERUT-U.S.A. (formerly UNITED ZIONIST-REVISIONISTS OF AMERICA) (1925). 41 E. 42 St., N.Y.C., 10017. Chmn. Harry S. Taubenfeld; Exec. Dir. Steven Leibowitz. Supports Herut policy in Israel and seeks Jabotinskean solutions of problems facing American, Russian, and world Jewry; assists in the fostering of private enterprises and developments in Israel; fosters maximalist Zionism among Jews in America. Subsidiaries: Betar Zionist Youth, Young Herut Concerned Jewish Youth, Tel-Hai Fund, and For the Children of Israel. *Igeret Betar; Herut Magazine.*

THEODOR HERZL FOUNDATION (1954). 515 Park Ave., N.Y.C., 10022. (212)752-0600. Chmn. Kalman Sultanik; Sec. Isadore Hamlin. Cultural activities, lectures, conferences, courses in modern Hebrew and Jewish subjects, Israel, Zionism and Jewish history. *Midstream.*

———: THEODOR HERZL INSTITUTE. Chmn. Jacques Torczyner. Program geared to review of contemporary problems on Jewish scene here and abroad; presentation of Jewish heritage values in light of Zionist experience of the ages; study of modern Israel; and Jewish social research with particular consideration of history and impact of Zionism. *Herzl Institute Bulletin.*

———: HERZL PRESS. Chmn. Kalman Sultanik. Publishes books and pamphlets on Israel, Zionism, and general Jewish subjects.

ICHUD HABONIM LABOR ZIONIST YOUTH (1935). 575 Sixth Ave., N.Y.C., 10011. (212)255-1796. Sec. Gen. Tom Gutherz; Dir. Florence Litton. Fosters identification with pioneering in Israel; stimulates study of Jewish life, history, and culture; sponsors community action projects, seven summer camps in North America, programs in Israel, and Garinei Aliyah to Kibbutz Grofit and Kibbutz Gezer. *Bagolah; Haboneh; Hamaapil; Iggeret L'Chaverim.*

ISRAEL MUSIC FOUNDATION (1948). 109 Cedarhurst Ave., Cedarhurst, N.Y., 11516. (516)569-1541. Pres. Oscar Regen; Sec. Oliver Sabin. Supports and stimulates the growth of music in Israel, and disseminates recorded Israeli music in the U.S. and throughout the world.

JEWISH NATIONAL FUND OF AMERICA (1901). 42 E. 69 St., N.Y.C., 10021. (212)-879-9300. Pres. William Berkowitz; Exec. V. Pres. Samuel I. Cohen. Exclusive fundraising agency of the world Zionist movement for the afforestation, reclamation, and development of the land of Israel, including the construction of roads and preparation of sites for new settlements; helps emphasize the importance of Israel in schools and synagogues throughout the world. *JNF Almanac; Land and Life.*

KEREN OR, INC. (1956). 1133 Broadway, N.Y.C., 10010. (212)255-1180. Pres. Ira Guilden; V. Pres. and Sec. Samuel I. Hendler; Exec. Dir. Jacob Igra. Funds the Keren-Or Center for Multi-Handicapped Blind Children; participates in the program for such children at the Rothschild Hospital in Haifa; funds entire professional staff and special programs at the Jewish Institute for the Blind (established 1902) that houses, clothes, feeds, educates and trains blind from childhood into adulthood. *Newsletter.*

LABOR ZIONIST ALLIANCE reorg. (formerly FARBAND LABOR ZIONIST ORDER, now uniting membership and branches of POALE ZION—UNITED LABOR ZIONIST ORGANIZATION OF AMERICA AND AMERICAN HABONIM ASSOCIATION) (1913). 575 Sixth Ave., N.Y.C., 10011. (212)989-0300. Pres. Allen Pollack; Exec. V. Pres. Bernard M. Weisberg. Seeks to enhance Jewish life, culture, and education in U.S. and Canada; aids in building State of Israel as a cooperative commonwealth, and its Labor movement organized in the

Histadrut; supports efforts toward a more democratic society throughout the world; furthers the democratization of the Jewish community in America and the welfare of Jews everywhere; works with labor and liberal forces in America. *Alliance Newsletter.*

LEAGUE FOR LABOR ISRAEL (1938; reorg. 1961). 575 Sixth Ave., N.Y.C., 10011. (212)989-0300. Pres. Allen Pollack; Sec. Bernard M. Weisberg. Conducts labor Zionist educational, youth, and cultural activities in the American Jewish community and promotes educational travel to Israel.

NATIONAL COMMITTEE FOR LABOR ISRAEL —ISRAEL HISTADRUT CAMPAIGN (1923). 33 E. 67 St., N.Y.C., 10021. (212)628-1000. Pres. Judah J. Shapiro; Exec. V. Pres. Bernard B. Jacobson. Provides funds for the social welfare, vocational, health, and cultural institutions and other services of Histadrut to benefit workers and immigrants and to assist in the integration of newcomers as productive citizens in Israel; promotes an understanding of the aims and achievements of Israel labor among Jews and non-Jews in America. Fund-raising arms are: Israel Histadrut Campaign, Israel Histadrut Foundation.

———: AMERICAN TRADE UNION COUNCIL FOR HISTADRUT (1947). 33 E. 67 St., N.Y.C., 10021. (212)628-1000. Chmn. Matthew Schoenwald. Nat. Consultant, Gregory J. Bardacke. Carries on educational activities among American and Canadian trade unions for health, educational, and welfare activities of the Histadrut in Israel. *Shalom.*

PEC ISRAEL ECONOMIC CORPORATION (formerly PALESTINE ECONOMIC CORPORATION) (1926). 511 Fifth Ave., N.Y.C., 10017. (212)687-2400. Pres. Stephen Shalom; Sec.-Asst. Treas. William Gold. Investments and loans in Israel. *Annual Report.*

PEF ISRAEL ENDOWMENT FUNDS, INC. (1922). 511 Fifth Ave., N.Y.C., 10017. (212)687-2400. Pres. Sidney Musher; Sec. Burt Allen Solomon. Uses funds for Israeli educational and philanthropic institutions and for constructive relief, modern education, and scientific research in Israel. *Annual Report.*

PIONEER WOMEN, THE WOMEN'S LABOR ZIONIST ORGANIZATION OF AMERICA, INC. (1925). 200 Madison Ave., N.Y.C.,

10016. (212)725-8010. Pres. Frieda Leemon; Exec. Dir. Shoshonna Ebstein. Supports, in cooperation with Na'amat, a widespread network of educational, vocational, and social services for women, children, and youth in Israel. Provides counseling and legal aid services for women, particularly war widows. Authorized agency of Youth Aliyah. Foremost in women's rights efforts. In America, supports Jewish educational, youth, cultural programs; participates in civic affairs. *Pioneer Woman.*

POALE AGUDATH ISRAEL OF AMERICA, INC. (1948). 156 Fifth Ave., N.Y.C., 10010. (212)924-9475. Pres. David B. Hollander; Presidium: Alexander Herman, Anshel Wainhaus. Aims to educate American Jews to the values of Orthodoxy, *aliyah,* and *halutziut;* supports kibbutzim, trade schools, *yeshivot,* teachers' college, civic and health centers, children's homes in Israel. *Achdut; PAI Views; PAI Bulletin.*

———: WOMEN'S DIVISION OF (1948). Presidium: Ethel Blasbalg, Sarah Iwanisky, Bertha Rittenberg. Assists Poale Agudath Israel to build and support children's homes, kindergartens, and trade schools in Israel. *Yediot PAI.*

RASSCO ISRAEL CORPORATION AND RASSCO FINANCIAL CORPORATION (1950). 535 Madison Ave., N.Y.C., 10022. Pres. Shmuel Lavi; Bd. Chmn. Igal Weinstein. Maintains ties with Western Hemisphere investments.

RELIGIOUS ZIONISTS OF AMERICA. 25 W. 26 St., N.Y.C., 10010.

———: BNEI AKIVA OF NORTH AMERICA (1934). 25 W. 26 St., N.Y.C., 10010. Pres. Dov A. Bloom; Sec. Rafi Neeman. Seeks to interest youth in *aliyah* to Israel and social justice through pioneering *(halutziut)* as an integral part of their religious observance; sponsors five summer camps, a leadership training camp for eleventh graders, a work-study program on a religious kibbutz for high school graduates, summer tours to Israel; establishes nuclei of college students for kibbutz or other settlement. *Arivon; Hamvoser; Pinkas Lamadrich; Z'raim.*

———: MIZRACHI-HAPOEL HAMIZRACHI (1909; merged 1957). 25 W. 26 St., N.Y.C., 10010. Pres. Louis Bernstein; Exec. V. Pres. Israel Friedman. Dedicated to building the Jewish State based on principles of Torah; conducts cultural work, educational program, public relations; sponsors NOAM and Bnei Akiva; raises funds for religious educational institutions in Israel. *Horizon; Kolenu; Mizrachi News Bulletin.*

———: MIZRACHI PALESTINE FUND (1928). 25 W. 26 St., N.Y.C., 10010. Chmn. Joseph Wilon; Sec. Israel Friedman. Fund-raising arm of Mizrachi movement.

———: NATIONAL COUNCIL FOR TORAH EDUCATION OF MIZRACHI-HAPOEL HAMIZRACHI (1939). 25 W. 26 St., N.Y.C., 10010. Pres. Israel Shaw; Dir. Meyer Golombek. Organizes and supervises *yeshivot* and Talmud Torahs; prepares and trains teachers; publishes textbooks and educational materials; conducts a placement agency for Hebrew schools; organizes summer seminars for Hebrew educators in cooperation with Torah department of Jewish Agency; conducts *Ulpan.*

———: NOAM-HAMISHMERET HATZEIRA (1970). 25 W. 26 St., N.Y.C., 10010. Chmn. Sarah J. Sanders; Exec. Dir. David Stahl. Sponsors three core groups to settle in Israel; conducts summer and year volunteer and study programs to Israel; organizes educational programs for young adults in the U.S., through weekly meetings, Shabbatonim, leadership seminars, etc. *Bechol Zot.*

SOCIETY OF ISRAEL PHILATELISTS (1948). 40–67 61 St., Woodside, N.Y., 11377. (212)458-9759. Pres. Joseph Schwartz; Exec. Sec. Irvin Girer. Promotes interest in, and knowledge of, all phases of Israel philately through sponsorship of chapters and research groups, maintenance of a philatelic library, and support of public and private exhibitions. *Israel Philatelist.*

STATE OF ISRAEL BONDS (1951). 215 Park Ave. S., N.Y.C., 10003. (212)677-9650. Pres. Michael Arnon; Gen. Chmn. Sam Rothberg; Exec. V. Pres. Morris Sipser. Seeks to provide large-scale investment funds for the economic development of the State of Israel through the sale of State of Israel bonds in the U.S., Canada, Western Europe and other parts of the free world.

UNITED CHARITY INSTITUTIONS OF JERUSALEM, INC. (1903). 1141 Broadway, N.Y.C., 10001. Pres. Zevulun Charlop;

Exec. Dir. S. Gabel. Raises funds for the maintenance of schools, kitchens, clinics, and dispensaries in Israel; free loan foundations in Israel.

UNITED ISRAEL APPEAL, INC. (1925). 515 Park Ave., N.Y.C., 10022. (212)688-0800. Chmn. Jerold C. Hoffberger; Exec. V. Chmn. Irving Kessler. As principal beneficiary of the United Jewish Appeal, serves as link between American Jewish community and Jewish Agency in Israel, its operating agent; assists in resettlement and absorption of refugees in Israel, and supervises flow and expenditures for this purpose. *Briefings.*

UNITED STATES COMMITTEE—SPORTS FOR ISRAEL, INC. (1948). 130 E. 59 St., N.Y.C., 10022. (212)752-1740. Pres. Nat Holman; Exec. Dir. Leonard K. Straus. Sponsors U.S. participation in, and fields and selects U.S. team for, World Maccabiah Games in Israel every four years; promotes physical education and sports program in Israel and total fitness of Israeli and American Jewish youths; provides funds, technical and material assistance to Wingate Institute for Physical Education and Sport in Israel; sponsors U.S. coaches for training programs in Israel and provides advanced training and competition in U.S. for Israel's national sports teams, athletes and coaches; offers scholarships at U.S. colleges to Israeli physical education students; elects members of the Jewish Sports Hall of Fame, Wingate Institute, Natanya, Israel. *Report;* Journal of the U.S. team in Israel's Maccabiah Games.

WOMEN'S LEAGUE FOR ISRAEL, INC. (1928). 1860 Broadway, N.Y.C., 10023. (212)245-8742. Pres. Violet Wiles; Exec. Dir. Regina Wermiel. Promotes the welfare of young people in Israel, especially young women immigrants; built and maintains Y-style homes in Jerusalem, Haifa, Tel Aviv and Natanya for young women; in cooperation with Ministry of Labor and Social Betterment operates live-in vocational training center for girls, including handicapped, in Natanya, and weaving workshop for blind. *Bulletin; Israel News Digest.*

WORLD CONFEDERATION OF UNITED ZIONISTS (1946; reorg. 1958). 595 Madison Ave., N.Y.C., 10022. (212)371-1452. Co-Presidents Charlotte Jacobson, Kalman Sultanik, Melech Topiol. The largest diaspora-centered Zionist grouping in the world, distinguished from all other groups in the Zionist movement in that it has no association or affiliation with any political party in Israel, but derives its inspiration and strength from the whole spectrum of Zionist, Jewish, and Israeli life; supports projects identified with Israel; sponsors non-party halutzic youth movements in diaspora; promotes Zionist education and strives for an Israel-oriented creative Jewish survival in the diaspora. *Zionist Information Views.*

WORLD ZIONIST ORGANIZATION-AMERICAN SECTION (1971). 515 Park Ave., N.Y.C., 10022. (212)752-0600. Chmn. Charlotte Jacobson; Exec. V. Chmn. Isadore Hamlin. As the American section of the overall Zionist body throughout the world, it operates primarily in the field of aliyah from the free countries, education in the diaspora, youth and hechalutz, organization and information, cultural institutions, publications, and handling activities of Jewish National Fund; conducts a worldwide Hebrew cultural program including special seminars and pedagogic manuals; disperses information and assists in research projects concerning Israel; promotes, publishes, and distributes books, periodicals, and pamphlets concerning developments in Israel, Zionism, and Jewish history; sponsors "Panoramas de Israel" radio program in the Latin American countries. *Israel Digest; Israel y America Latina.*

_____, NORTH AMERICAN ALIYAH MOVEMENT (1968). 515 Park Ave., N.Y.C., 10022. (212)752-0600. Pres. Rabbi Moshe Berliner. Promotes and facilitates *aliyah* and *klitah* from the U.S. and Canada to Israel; serves as a social framework for North American immigrants to Israel. *Aliyon; NAAM Letter; Coming Home.*

_____, ZIONIST ARCHIVES AND LIBRARY OF THE (1939). 515 Park Ave., N.Y.C., 10022. (212)752-0600. Dir. and Librarian Sylvia Landress. Serves as an archives and information service for material on Israel, Palestine, the Middle East, Zionism, and all aspects of Jewish life.

ZIONIST ORGANIZATION OF AMERICA (1897). ZOA House, 4 E. 34 St., N.Y.C., 10016. (212)481-1500. Pres. Ivan J. Novick; Nat. Exec. Dir. Paul Flacks. Seeks to safeguard the integrity and independence of Israel by means consistent with the laws of the U.S., to assist in the economic development of Israel, and to foster the unity of the Jewish people and the centrality of Israel in Jewish life in the spirit of General Zionism. *American Zionist; Public Affairs Memorandum; ZINS Weekly News Bulletin; ZOA in Review.*

PROFESSIONAL ASSOCIATIONS*

AMERICAN CONFERENCE OF CANTORS (Religious, Educational)

AMERICAN JEWISH CORRECTIONAL CHAPLAINS ASSOCIATION, INC. (Social Welfare)

AMERICAN JEWISH PRESS ASSOCIATION (Cultural)

AMERICAN JEWISH PUBLIC RELATIONS SOCIETY (1957). 21–41 34th Ave., Astoria, N.Y. 11106. (212)876-3050. Pres. Riki Englander Kosut; Treas. Hyman Brickman. Advances professional status of workers in the public-relations field in Jewish communal service; upholds a professional code of ethics and standards; serves as a clearinghouse for employment opportunities; exchanges professional information and ideas; presents awards for excellence in professional attainments, including the "Maggid Award" for outstanding literary or artistic achievement which enhances Jewish life. *The Handout.*

ASSOCIATION OF JEWISH CENTER WORKERS (Community Relations)

ASSOCIATION OF JEWISH CHAPLAINS OF THE ARMED FORCES (Religious, Educational)

ASSOCIATION OF JEWISH COMMUNITY RELATIONS WORKERS (Community Relations)

CANTORS ASSEMBLY OF AMERICA (Religious, Educational)

COUNCIL OF JEWISH ORGANIZATIONS IN CIVIL SERVICE (Community Relations)

EDUCATORS ASSEMBLY OF THE UNITED SYNAGOGUE OF AMERICA (Religious, Educational)

INTERNATIONAL ASSOCIATION OF HILLEL DIRECTORS (Religious, Educational)

*For fuller listing see under categories in parentheses.

INTERNATIONAL CONFERENCE OF JEWISH COMMUNAL SERVICE (Community Relations)

JEWISH MINISTERS CANTORS ASSOCIATION OF AMERICA, INC. (Religious, Educational)

JEWISH TEACHERS ASSOCIATION—MORIM (Religious, Educational)

NATIONAL ASSOCIATION OF JEWISH CENTER WORKERS (Community Relations)

NATIONAL ASSOCIATION OF SYNAGOGUE ADMINISTRATORS, UNITED SYNAGOGUE OF AMERICA (Religious, Educational)

NATIONAL ASSOCIATION OF TEMPLE ADMINISTRATORS, UNION OF AMERICAN HEBREW CONGREGATIONS (Religious, Educational)

NATIONAL ASSOCIATION OF TEMPLE EDUCATORS, UNION OF AMERICAN HEBREW CONGREGATIONS (Religious, Educational)

NATIONAL CONFERENCE OF JEWISH COMMUNAL SERVICE (Social Welfare)

NATIONAL CONFERENCE OF YESHIVA PRINCIPALS (Religious, Educational)

NATIONAL JEWISH WELFARE BOARD COMMISSION ON JEWISH CHAPLAINCY (Social Welfare)

WOMEN'S ORGANIZATIONS*

AMERICAN MIZRACHI WOMEN (Zionist and Pro-Israel)

B'NAI B'RITH WOMEN (Social Welfare)

BRANDEIS UNIVERSITY NATIONAL WOMEN'S COMMITTEE (1948). Brandeis University, Waltham, Mass., 02154. (617)-647-2194. Natl. Pres. Esther Schwartz; Exec. Dir. Harriette L. Chandler. Responsible for support and maintenance of Brandeis University libraries; sponsors University on Wheels and, through its chapters, study-group programs based on faculty-prepared syllabi, volunteer work in educational services, and a program of New Books for Old Sales; constitutes largest "Friends of a Library" group in U.S.

HADASSAH, THE WOMEN'S ZIONIST ORGANIZATION OF AMERICA, INC. (Zionist and Pro-Israel)

NATIONAL COUNCIL OF JEWISH WOMEN (Social Welfare)

NATIONAL FEDERATION OF TEMPLE SISTERHOODS, UNION OF AMERICAN HEBREW CONGREGATIONS (Religious, Educational)

PIONEER WOMEN, THE WOMEN'S LABOR ZIONIST ORGANIZATION OF AMERICA (Zionist and Pro-Israel)

UNITED ORDER OF TRUE SISTERS (Social, Mutual Benefit)

WOMEN'S AMERICAN ORT, FEDERATION (Overseas Aid)

WOMEN'S BRANCH OF THE UNION OF ORTHODOX JEWISH CONGREGATIONS OF AMERICA (Religious, Educational)

WOMEN'S DIVISION OF POALE AGUDATH OF AMERICA (Zionist and Pro-Israel)

WOMEN'S DIVISION OF THE AMERICAN JEWISH CONGRESS (Community Relations)

WOMEN'S DIVISION OF THE JEWISH LABOR COMMITTEE (Community Relations)

WOMEN'S DIVISION OF THE UNITED JEWISH APPEAL (Overseas Aid)

WOMEN'S LEAGUE FOR ISRAEL, INC. (Zionist and Pro-Israel)

WOMEN'S ORGANIZATION OF HAPOEL HAMIZRACHI (Zionist and Pro-Israel)

YESHIVA UNIVERSITY WOMEN'S ORGANIZATION (Religious, Educational)

YOUTH AND STUDENT ORGANIZATIONS*

AMERICAN ZIONIST YOUTH FOUNDATION, INC. (Zionist and Pro-Israel)

———: AMERICAN ZIONIST YOUTH COUNCIL

---

*For fuller listing see under categories in parentheses.

ATID, COLLEGE AGE ORGANIZATION, UNITED SYNAGOGUE OF AMERICA (Religious, Educational)

B'NAI B'RITH HILLEL FOUNDATIONS, INC. (Religious, Educational)

B'NAI B'RITH YOUTH ORGANIZATION (Religious, Educational)

B'NEI AKIVA OF NORTH AMERICA, RELIGIOUS ZIONISTS OF AMERICA (Zionist and Pro-Israel)

BNOS AGUDATH ISRAEL, AGUDATH ISRAEL OF AMERICA (Religious, Educational)

DROR YOUNG ZIONIST ORGANIZATION (Zionist and Pro-Israel)

HASHACHAR—WOMEN'S ZIONIST ORGANIZATION OF AMERICA (Zionist and Pro-Israel)

HASHOMER HATZAIR, ZIONIST YOUTH MOVEMENT (Zionist and Pro-Israel)

ICHUD HABONIM LABOR ZIONIST YOUTH (Zionist and Pro-Israel)

JEWISH STUDENT PRESS-SERVICE (1970)— JEWISH STUDENT EDITORIAL PROJECTS, INC. 15 East 26th St., Suite 1350, N.Y.C., 10010. (212)679-1411. Ed.-in-Chief Susan Grossman; Admin. Dir. Leslie Schnur. Serves all Jewish student and young adult publications, as well as many Anglo-Jewish newspapers, in North America, through monthly feature packets of articles and graphics. Holds annual national and local editors' conference for member publications. Provides technical and editorial assistance; keeps complete file of member publications since 1970; maintains Israel Bureau. *Jewish Press Features.*

KADIMA (Religious, Educational)

MASSORAH INTERCOLLEGIATES OF YOUNG ISRAEL, NATIONAL COUNCIL OF YOUNG ISRAEL (Religious, Educational)

NATIONAL CONFERENCE OF SYNAGOGUE YOUTH, UNION OF ORTHODOX JEWISH CONGREGATIONS OF AMERICA (Religious, Educational)

NATIONAL FEDERATION OF TEMPLE YOUTH, UNION OF AMERICAN HEBREW CONGREGATIONS (Religious, Educational)

NOAR MIZRACHI-HAMISHMERET (NOAM) —RELIGIOUS ZIONISTS OF AMERICA (Zionist and Pro-Israel)

NORTH AMERICAN JEWISH STUDENTS APPEAL (1971). 15 E. 26 St., N.Y.C. 10010. (212)679-2293. Pres. Steven M. Cohen; Exec. Dir. Roberta Shiffman. Serves as central fund-raising mechanism for national, independent, Jewish student organizations; insures accountability of public Jewish communal funds used by these agencies; assists Jewish students undertaking projects of concern to Jewish communities; advises and assists Jewish organizations in determining student project feasibility and impact; fosters development of Jewish student leadership in the Jewish community. Beneficiaries include local and regional Jewish student projects on campuses throughout North America; founding constituents include Jewish Student Press Service, North American Jewish Students Network, Student Struggle for Soviet Jewry, *Response,* and Yugntruf; beneficiaries include Harvard Law School Jewish Students Assn., Bay Area Jewish Women's Conference, and State Univ. of N.Y. Jewish Student Union.

NORTH AMERICAN JEWISH STUDENTS' NETWORK (1969). 15 E. 26 St., N.Y.C., 10010. (212)689-0790. Chmn. Simcha Jacobovici; Exec. Dir. Steven Bauman. Coordinates information and programs among all Jewish student organizations in North America; promotes development of student-controlled Jewish student organizations; maintains contacts and coordinates programs with Jewish students throughout the world through the World Union of Jewish Students; runs the Jewish Student Speakers Bureau; sponsors regional conferences, National Jewish Women's Conference, first Pan American Jewish Students Conference, North American Jewish Students' Congress on Israel, and Conference on Alternatives in Jewish Education. *Guide to Jewish Student Groups in North America; Network.*

NORTH AMERICAN JEWISH YOUTH COUNCIL (Community Relations)

STUDENT STRUGGLE FOR SOVIET JEWRY, INC. (Community Relations)

UNITED SYNAGOGUE YOUTH, UNITED SYNAGOGUE OF AMERICA (Religious, Educational)

WOMEN'S LEAGUE FOR CONSERVATIVE JU-
DAISM (Religious, Educational)

YAVNEH, NATIONAL RELIGIOUS JEWISH
STUDENTS ASSOCIATION (Religious, Educational)

YUGNTRUF YOUTH FOR YIDDISH (1966).
3328 Bainbridge Ave., Bronx, N.Y., 10467.
(212)654-8540. Pres. Paula Teitelbaum;
Exec. Dir. David Neal Miller. A worldwide, non-political organization for high
school and college students with a knowledge of, or interest in, Yiddish. Organizes
artistic and social activities. Offers services
of full-time field worker to assist in forming
Yiddish courses and clubs throughout the
USA. *Fum Khaver Tsu Khaver; Yugntruf.*

ZEIREI AGUDATH ISRAEL, AGUDATH IS-
RAEL OF AMERICA (Religious, Educational)

CANADA

CANADA-ISRAEL SECURITIES, LTD., STATE
OF ISRAEL BONDS (1953). 1255 University
St., Montreal, PQ, H3B 3W7. Pres. Allan
Bronfman; Sec. Max Wolofsky. Sale of
State of Israel Bonds in Canada. *Israel
Bond News.*

CANADIAN ASSOCIATION FOR LABOR IS-
RAEL (HISTADRUT) (1944). 4770 Kent
Ave., Rm. 301, Montreal, PQ, H3W 1H2.
Nat. Pres. Bernard M. Bloomfield; Nat.
Exec. Dir. Bernard Morris. Raises funds
for Histadrut institutions in Israel, sup-
porting their rehabilitation tasks. *Hista-
drut Foto News; Histadrut Review.*

CANADIAN FOUNDATION FOR JEWISH CUL-
TURE (1965). 150 Beverley St., Toronto,
M5T 1Y6. (416)869-3811. Pres. Joseph L.
Kronick; Exec. Sec. Edmond Y. Lipsitz.
Promotes Jewish studies at university level
and encourages original research and
scholarship in Jewish subjects; awards annual scholarships and grants-in-aid to
scholars in Canada.

CANADIAN FRIENDS OF THE ALLIANCE
ISRAÉLITE UNIVERSELLE (1958). 5711
Edgemore Ave., Montreal, PQ, H4W 1V8.
(514)487-1243. Pres. Harry Batshaw;
Exec. Sec. Marlene Salomon. Supports the
educational work of the Alliance.

CANADIAN FRIENDS OF THE HEBREW UNI-
VERSITY (1944). 1506 McGregor Ave.,
Montreal, PQ, H3G 1B9. (514)932-2133.
Nat. Pres. Ralph Halbert; Nat. Hon. Sec.

Samuel R. Risk; Exec. Dir. Jonathan
Livny. Represents and publicizes the Hebrew University in Canada; serves as fund-
raising arm for the University in Canada;
processes Canadians for study at the university. *Scopus.*

CANADIAN JEWISH CONGRESS (1919; reorg.
1934). 1590 Ave. Docteur Penfield, Montreal, PQ, H3G 1C5. (514)931-7531. Pres.
W. Gunther Plaut; Exec. V. Pres. Alan
Rose. The official voice of Canadian Jewry
at home and abroad. Acts on all matters
affecting the status, rights and welfare of
Canadian Jews. *I.O.I.; Cercle Juif.*

CANADIAN ORT ORGANIZATION (Organization of Rehabilitation Through Training) (1940). 5165 Sherbrooke St. W., Suite
208, Montreal, PQ, H4A 1T6. (514)481-
2787. Pres. J.A. Lyone Heppner; Exec.
Dir. Max E. Levy. Carries on fund-raising
projects in support of the worldwide voca-
tional-training school network of ORT.
Canadian ORT Reporter.

———: WOMEN'S CANADIAN ORT (1940).
3101 Bathurst St., Toronto, Ont., M6A
2A6. (416)787-0339. Pres. Dorothy Shoi-
chet; Exec. Dir. Diane Uslaner. *Focus.*

CANADIAN SEPHARDIC FEDERATION
(1973). 1310 Greene Ave., Montreal PQ,
H3Z 2B2. (514)934-0804. Pres. Charles
Chocron; Exec. Dir. Avi Shlush. Preserves
and promotes Sephardic identity, particularly among youth; works for the unity of
the Jewish people; emphasizes relations between Sephardi communities all over the
world; seeks better situation for Sephardim
in Israel; supports Israel by all means. *Horizon Sephardi.*

CANADIAN YOUNG JUDEA (1917). 788 Marlee Ave., Toronto, Ont., M6B 3K1. (416)-
787-5350. Nat. Pres. Richard Freedman;
Exec. Dir. Tina Ornstein. Strives to attract
Jewish youth to Zionism, with goal of
aliyah; operates nine summer camps in
Canada and Israel; is sponsored by Canadian Hadassah-WIZO and Zionist Organization of Canada, and affiliated with Ha-
noar Hatzioni in Israel. *Yedion; Judaean;
Ekronot; Mini-Mag.*

CANADIAN ZIONIST FEDERATION (1967).
1310 Greene Ave., Westmount, Montreal
PQ, H3Z 2B2. (514)934-0804. Pres. Philip
Givens; Exec. V. Pres. Leon Kronitz. Umbrella organization of all Zionist- and Israel-oriented groups in Canada; carries on

major activities in all areas of Jewish life through its departments of education and culture, *aliyah*, youth and students, public affairs, and fund-raising for the purpose of strengthening the State of Israel and the Canadian Jewish community. *Canadian Zionist; The Reporter.*

———: BUREAU OF EDUCATION AND CULTURE (1972). Pres. Philip Givens; Exec. V. Pres. and Dir. of Educ. Leon Kronitz. Provides counseling by pedagogic experts, inservice teacher training courses and seminars in Canada and Israel; operates teacher placement bureau, national pedagogic council and research center; publishes and distributes educational material and teaching aids; conducts annual Bible contests and Hebrew language courses for adults. *Al Mitzpe Hahinuch.*

HADASSAH—WIZO ORGANIZATION OF CANADA (1916). 1310 Greene Ave., 9th fl., Montreal, PQ, H3Z 2B2. (514)937-9431. Nat. Pres. Mrs. Charles Balinsky; Nat. Exec. V. Pres. Lily Frank. Assists needy Israelis by sponsoring health, education, and social welfare services; seeks to strengthen and perpetuate Jewish identity; encourages Jewish and Hebrew culture in promoting Canadian ideals of democracy and pursuit of peace. *Orah.*

JEWISH COLONIZATION ASSOCIATION OF CANADA (1907). 5151 Cote St. Catherine Rd., Montreal, PQ, H3W 1M6. Pres. Lazarus Phillips; Sec. Morley M. Cohen; Mgr. M.J. Lister. Promotes Jewish land settlement in Canada through loans to established farmers; helps new immigrant farmers to purchase farms, or settles them on farms owned by the Association; provides agricultural advice and supervision; contributes funds to Canadian Jewish Loan Cassa for loans to small businessmen and artisans.

JEWISH IMMIGRANT AID SERVICES OF CANADA (JIAS) (1919). 5151 Cote Ste. Catherine Rd., Montreal, PQ, H3W 1M6. (514)-342-9351. Nat. Pres. Charles Kent; Nat. Exec. V. Pres. Joseph Kage. Serves as a national agency for immigration and immigrant welfare. *JIAS Bulletin; JIAS News; Studies and Documents on Immigration and Integration in Canada.*

JEWISH NATIONAL FUND OF CANADA (KEREN KAYEMETH LE ISRAEL, INC.) (1902). 1980 Sherbrooke St. W., Suite 250,

Montreal, PQ, H3H, 2M7. Nat. Pres. Nathan Scott; Exec. V. Pres. Harris D. Gulko. Seeks to create, provide, enlarge, and administer a fund to be made up of voluntary contributions from the Jewish community and others, to be used for charitable purposes. *JNF Bulletin.*

LABOR ZIONIST MOVEMENT OF CANADA (1939). 4770 Kent Ave., Montreal, PQ, H3W 1H2. Nat. Pres. Sydney L. Wax; Nat. Exec. Dir. Leo J. Moss. Disseminates information and publications on Israel and Jewish life; arranges special events, lectures, and seminars; coordinates communal and political activities of its constituent bodies (Pioneer Women, Na'amat, Labor Zionist Alliance, Poale Zion party, Habonim-Dror Youth, Israel Histadrut, affiliated Hebrew elementary and high schools in Montreal and Toronto). *Canadian Jewish Quarterly; Viewpoints; Briefacts; Insight.*

MIZRACHI-HAPOEL HAMIZRACHI ORGANIZATION OF CANADA (1941). 5497A Victoria Ave., Suite 101, Montreal, PQ, H3W 2R1. (514)739-4748. Nat. Pres. Kurt Rothschild; Nat. Exec. Dir. Rabbi Sender Shizgal; Sec. Seymour Mishkin. Promotes religious Zionism, aimed at making Israel a state based on Torah; maintains Bnei Akiva, a summer camp, adult education program, and touring department; supports Mizrachi-Hapoel Hamizrachi and other religious Zionist institutions in Israel which strengthen traditional Judaism. *Mizrachi Newsletter.*

NATIONAL COUNCIL OF JEWISH WOMEN OF CANADA (1947). 300A Wilson Ave., Suite 2, Downsview, Ont., M3H 1S8. Nat. Pres. Marjorie Blankstein; Exec. Sec. Florence Greenberg. Dedicated to furthering human welfare in Jewish and non-Jewish communities, locally, nationally, and internationally; provides essential services and stimulates and educates the individual and the community through an integrated program of education, service, and social action. *Keeping You Posted.*

NATIONAL JOINT COMMUNITY RELATIONS COMMITTEE OF CANADIAN JEWISH CONGRESS AND B'NAI B'RITH IN CANADA (1936). 150 Beverley St., Toronto, Ont., M5T 1Y6. 869-3811. Chmn. Rabbi Jordan Pearlson; Nat. Exec. Dir. Ben G. Kayfetz. Seeks to safeguard the status, rights, and welfare of Jews in Canada; to combat antisemitism and promote understanding and goodwill among all ethnic and religious groups.

UNITED JEWISH TEACHERS' SEMINARY (1946). 5237 Clanranald Ave., Montreal, PQ, H3X, 2S5. (514)489-4401. Dir. A. Aisenbach. Trains teachers for Yiddish and Hebrew schools under auspices of Canadian Jewish Congress. *Yitonenu*.

ZIONIST ORGANIZATION OF CANADA (1892; reorg. 1919). 788 Marlee Ave., Toronto, Ont., M6B 3K1. (416)781-3571. Nat. Pres. David Monson; Exec. V. Pres. George Liban. Furthers general Zionist aims by operating six youth camps in Canada and one in Israel; maintains Zionist book club; arranges programs, lectures; sponsors Young Judea, Youth Centre Project in Jerusalem Forest, Israel.

Jewish Federations, Welfare Funds, Community Councils

THIS directory is one of a series compiled annually by the Council of Jewish Federations and Welfare Funds. Virtually all of these community organizations are affiliated with the Council as their national association for sharing of common services, interchange of experience, and joint consultation and action.

These communities comprise at least 95 per cent of the Jewish population of the United States and about 90 per cent of the Jewish population of Canada. Listed for each community is the local central agency—federation, welfare fund, or community council—with its address, telephone number, and the names of the president and executive officer.

The names "federation," "welfare fund," and "Jewish community council" are not definitive, and their structures and functions vary from city to city. What is called a federa-

tion in one city, for example, may be called a community council in another. In the main, these central agencies have responsibility for some or all of the following functions: (a) raising of funds for local, national, and overseas services; (b) allocation and distribution of funds for these purposes; (c) coordination and central planning of local services, such as family welfare, child care, health, recreation, community relations within the Jewish community and with the general community, Jewish education, care of the aged, and vocational guidance; to strengthen these services, eliminate duplication, and fill gaps; (d) in small and some intermediate cities, direct administration of local social services.

In the directory, (*) preceding a listing identifies an organization *not* affiliated with the Council of Jewish Federations and Welfare Funds.

UNITED STATES

ALABAMA

BIRMINGHAM

BIRMINGHAM JEWISH FEDERATION (1935; reorg. 1971); P.O. Box 9157 (35213); (205)-879-0416. Pres. Mrs. Solomon P. Kimerling; Exec. Dir. Seymour Marcus.

JEWISH COMMUNITY COUNCIL (1962); P.O. Box 7377, 3960 Montclair Rd. (35223); (205)879-0411. Pres. Mayer U. Newfield; Exec. Dir. Harold E. Katz.

MOBILE

MOBILE JEWISH WELFARE FUND, INC. (Inc. 1966); 404 C One Office Park (36609); (205)-343-7197. Pres. Mark H. Berkin.

MONTGOMERY

JEWISH FEDERATION OF MONTGOMERY, INC. (1930); P.O. Box 1150 (36102); (205)-263-7674. Pres. Perry Mendel; Sec. Jeanette C. Waldo.

TRI-CITIES

*TRI-CITIES JEWISH FEDERATION CHARITIES, INC. (1933; Inc. 1956); Route 7, Florence (35632); Pres. Mrs. M. F. Shipper.

ARIZONA

PHOENIX

GREATER PHOENIX JEWISH FEDERATION (incl. surrounding communities) (1940); 1718 W. Maryland Ave. (85015); (602)249-1845. Pres. Neal Kurn; Exec. Dir. Herman Markowitz.

TUCSON

JEWISH COMMUNITY COUNCIL (1942); 102 N. Plumer (85719); (602)884-8921. Pres. S. Leonard Scheff; Exec. Dir. Charles Plotkin.

ARKANSAS

LITTLE ROCK

JEWISH FEDERATION OF LITTLE ROCK (1911); 221 Donaghey Bldg; Main at 7th (72201); (501)372-3571. Pres. Allan B. Mendel; Exec. Sec. Nanci Goldman.

CALIFORNIA

LONG BEACH

JEWISH COMMUNITY FEDERATION (1937); (sponsors UNITED JEWISH WELFARE FUND); 3801 E. Willow Ave. (90815); (213)-426-7601. Pres. Arthur Miller; Exec. Dir. Harold Benowitz.

LOS ANGELES

JEWISH FEDERATION—COUNCIL OF GREATER LOS ANGELES (1912; reorg. 1959) (sponsors UNITED JEWISH WELFARE FUND); 6505 Wilshire Blvd. (90048); (213)-852-1234. Pres. Irwin H. Goldenberg; Exec. V. Pres. Alvin Bronstein.

OAKLAND

JEWISH WELFARE FEDERATION OF THE GREATER EAST BAY (1918); 3245 Sheffield Ave. (94602); (415)533-7462. Pres. Marshall Cornblum; Exec. V. Pres. Ernest Siegel.

ORANGE COUNTY

JEWISH FEDERATION-COUNCIL OF ORANGE COUNTY (1964; Inc. 1965); (sponsors UNITED JEWISH WELFARE FUND); 3303 Harbor Blvd., Costa Mesa (92626); (714)754-1944. Pres. Marvin Neban; Exec. Dir. Mortimer Greenberg. Costa Mesa (92626); (714)-754-1944. Pres. Marvin Neban; Exec. Dir. Mortimer Greenberg.

PALM SPRINGS

JEWISH WELFARE FEDERATION OF PALM SPRINGS-DESERT AREA (1971); 216 E. Arenas Rd. (92262); (714)325-7281. Pres. Zachary Pitts; Exec. Dir. Samuel J. Rosenthal.

SACRAMENTO

JEWISH FEDERATION OF SACRAMENTO (1948). 2351 Wyda Way (95825); (916)486-0906. Pres. Alan Brodovsky; Exec. Dir. Ephraim Spivek.

SAN BERNARDINO

SAN BERNARDINO UNITED JEWISH WELFARE FUND, INC. (1936; Inc. 1957); Congregation Emanu-el, 3512 No. "E" St. (92405). Pres. William Russler.

SAN DIEGO

UNITED JEWISH FEDERATION OF GREATER SAN DIEGO (1935); 5511 El Cajon Blvd. (92115); (714)582-2483. Pres. Arthur Levinson; Exec. Dir. Donald L. Gartner.

SAN FRANCISCO

JEWISH WELFARE FEDERATION OF SAN FRANCISCO, MARIN COUNTY AND THE PENINSULA (1910; reorg. 1955); 254 Sutter St. (94108); (415)781-3082. Pres. Jerome I. Braun; Exec. Dir. Brian Lurie.

SAN JOSE

JEWISH FEDERATION OF GREATER SAN JOSE (incl. Santa Clara County except Palo Alto and Los Altos) (1930; reorg. 1950); 1777 Hamilton Ave., Suite 201 (95125); (408)267-2770. Pres. Mrs. Harry Goldman; Exec. Dir. Nat Bent.

SANTA BARBARA

*SANTA BARBARA JEWISH FEDERATION, P.O. Box 3314 (93105); (805)962-0770. Pres. M. Howard Goldman.

STOCKTON

*STOCKTON JEWISH WELFARE FUND (1972); 5105 N. El Dorado St. (95207); (209)-477-9306. Pres. Joel M. Senderov; Treas. Harry Green.

VENTURA

*VENTURA COUNTY JEWISH COUNCIL—TEMPLE BETH TORAH (1938); 7620 Foothill Rd. (93003); (805)647-4181. Pres. Paul Karlsberg.

COLORADO

DENVER

ALLIED JEWISH FEDERATION OF DENVER (1936); (sponsors ALLIED JEWISH CAMPAIGN); 300 S. Dahlia St. (80222); (303)321-3399. Pres. Jack Grazi; Exec. Dir. Harold Cohen.

CONNECTICUT

BRIDGEPORT

UNITED JEWISH COUNCIL OF GREATER BRIDGEPORT, INC. (1936); (sponsors UNITED JEWISH CAMPAIGN); 4200 Park Ave. (06604); (203)372-6504. Pres. Helen B. Wasserman; Exec. Dir. Michael P. Shapiro.

DANBURY

JEWISH FEDERATION OF GREATER DANBURY (1945); 8 West St. (06810); (203)792-6353. Pres. Albert Kohn; Exec. Dir. Jonathan H. Spinner.

HARTFORD

GREATER HARTFORD JEWISH FEDERATION (1945); 333 Bloomfield Ave., W. Hartford (06117); (203)236-3278. Pres. Bernard B. Kaplan; Exec. Dir. Don Cooper.

MERIDEN

*MERIDEN JEWISH WELFARE FUND, INC. (1944); 127 E. Main St. (06450); (203)235-2581. Pres. Joseph Barker; Sec. Harold Rosen.

NEW HAVEN

NEW HAVEN JEWISH FEDERATION (1928); (sponsors COMBINED JEWISH APPEAL) (1969); 1162 Chapel St. (06511); (203)562-2137. Pres. Josef Adler; Exec. Dir. Arthur Spiegel.

NEW LONDON

JEWISH COMMUNITY COUNCIL OF GREATER NEW LONDON, INC. (1950; Inc. 1970); 302 State St. (06320); (203)442-8062. Pres. Jerry Winter; Exec. Dir. Eugene F. Elander.

NORWALK

JEWISH FEDERATION OF GREATER NORWALK (1946; reorg. 1964); Shorehaven Rd., East Norwalk (06855); (203)853-3440. Pres. Norman J. Weinberger; Exec. Dir. Roy Stuppler.

STAMFORD

UNITED JEWISH FEDERATION (Reincorp. 1973); 1035 Newfield Ave. (06905); (203)322-6935. Pres. Bernard Samers; Exec. Dir. Donald H. Klein.

WATERBURY

JEWISH FEDERATION OF WATERBURY, INC. (1938); 1020 Country Club Rd. (06720); (203)758-2441. Pres. Donald Liebeskind; Exec. Dir. Robert Kessler.

DELAWARE

WILMINGTON

JEWISH FEDERATION OF DELAWARE, INC. (1935); 101 Garden of Eden Rd. (19803); (302)478-6200. Pres. Nisson A. Finkelstein; Exec. Dir. Mike Ruvel.

DISTRICT OF COLUMBIA

WASHINGTON

UNITED JEWISH APPEAL—FEDERATION OF GREATER WASHINGTON, INC. (1935); 4701 Willard Ave., Chevy Chase, Md. (20015); (301)652-6480. Pres. Jerome J. Dick; Exec. V. Pres. Elton J. Kerness.

FLORIDA

FT. LAUDERDALE

JEWISH FEDERATION OF GREATER FT. LAUDERDALE (1967); 2999 N.W. 33rd Ave. (33311); (305)484-8200. Pres. Leo Goodman; Exec. Dir. Leslie Gottlieb.

HOLLYWOOD

JEWISH FEDERATION OF SOUTH BROWARD, INC. (1943); 2719 Hollywood Blvd. (33020); (305)921-8810. Pres. Mrs. Theodore Newman; Exec. Dir. Sumner Kaye.

JACKSONVILLE

JACKSONVILLE JEWISH COMMUNITY COUNCIL (1935); 5846 Mt. Carmel Terr. (32216); (904)733-7613. Pres. E. Theodore Cohn; Exec. Dir. Gerald L. Goldsmith.

MIAMI

GREATER MIAMI JEWISH FEDERATION, INC. (1938); 4200 Biscayne Blvd. (33137); (305)576-4000. Pres. L. Jules Arkin; Exec. V. Pres. Myron J. Brodie.

ORLANDO

JEWISH FEDERATION OF GREATER ORLANDO (1949); 851 No. Maitland Ave., P.O.

Box 1508, Maitland (32751); (305)645-5933. Pres. Sy Israel; Exec. Dir. Paul Jeser.

PALM BEACH COUNTY

JEWISH FEDERATION OF PALM BEACH COUNTY, INC. (1938); 2415 Okeechobee Blvd., West Palm Beach (33409); (305)689-5900. Pres. Alan L. Shulman; Exec. Dir. Norman J. Schimelman.

PENSACOLA

*PENSACOLA FEDERATED JEWISH CHARITIES (1942); 1320 E. Lee St. (32503); (904)-438-1464. Pres. Gene Rosenbaum; Sec. Mrs. Harry Saffer.

PINELLAS COUNTY (incl. Clearwater and St. Petersburg)

JEWISH FEDERATION OF PINELLAS COUNTY, INC. (1950; reincorp. 1974); 8167 Elbow Lane, North, St. Petersburg (33710); (813)344-5795. Pres. Reva Kent; Exec. Dir. Ron Weisinger.

SARASOTA

SARASOTA JEWISH COMMUNITY COUNCIL, INC. (1959); 1900 Main Bldg., Suite 300 (33577); (813)955-6275. Pres. Sol Levites; Exec. Dir. Florence S. Sinclair.

TAMPA

TAMPA JEWISH FEDERATION (1941); 2808 Horatio (33609); (813)872-4451. Pres. Ben Greenbaum; Exec. Dir. Gary S. Alter.

GEORGIA

ATLANTA

ATLANTA JEWISH FEDERATION, INC. (1905; reorg. 1967); 1753 Peachtree Rd., N.E. (30309); (404)873-1661. Pres. Max Rittenbaum; Exec. Dir. David I. Sarnat.

AUGUSTA

FEDERATION OF JEWISH CHARITIES (1937); P.O. Box 3251, Hill Station (30909) c/o Hillel Silver, Treas; Pres. Morton Wittenberg; Exec. Dir. Sheldon Sklar.

COLUMBUS

JEWISH WELFARE FEDERATION OF COLUMBUS, INC. (1941); P.O. Box 1303 (31902); (404)561-3953. Pres. Bernard Witt; Sec. David Helman.

SAVANNAH

SAVANNAH JEWISH COUNCIL (1943); (sponsors UJA-FEDERATION CAMPAIGN); P.O. Box 6546, 5111 Abercorn St. (31405); (912)-355-8111. Pres. Aaron Levy; Exec. Dir. Stan Ramati.

IDAHO

BOISE

*SOUTHERN IDAHO JEWISH WELFARE FUND (1947); 1776 Commerce Ave. (83705); (208)344-3574. Pres. Kal Sarlat; Treas. Martin Heuman.

ILLINOIS

CHAMPAIGN-URBANA

FEDERATED JEWISH CHARITIES (1929); (member Central Illinois Jewish Federation); 1707 Parkhaven Dr., Champaign (61820); (217)356-3373. Co-Chmn. Stanley Levy, Zelda Derber; Exec. Sec. Mrs. Donald Ginsberg.

CHICAGO

JEWISH FEDERATION OF METROPOLITAN CHICAGO (1900); 1 S. Franklin St. (60606); (312)346-6700. Pres. David Smerling; Exec. V. Pres. Steven Nasatir.

JEWISH UNITED FUND OF METROPOLITAN CHICAGO (1968); 1 S. Franklin St. (60606); (312)346-6700. Pres. David Smerling; Exec. V. Pres. James P. Rice.

DECATUR

JEWISH FEDERATION (member Central Illinois Jewish Federation) (1942); 78 Montgomery Pl. (62522); Pres. Don Champion.

ELGIN

ELGIN AREA JEWISH WELFARE CHEST (1938); 330 Division St. (60120); (312)741-5656. Pres. Gerald Levine; Treas. Harry Seigle.

JOLIET

JOLIET JEWISH WELFARE CHEST (1938); 250 N. Midland Ave. (60435); (815)725-7078. Pres. Robert S. Krockey; Sec. Rabbi Morris M. Hershman.

PEORIA

CENTRAL ILLINOIS JEWISH FEDERATION (1969); 3100 N. Knoxville, Suite 17 (61603); (309)686-0611. Pres. Ted Century; Exec. Dir. Peretz Katz.

JEWISH FEDERATION OF PEORIA (member CENTRAL ILLINOIS JEWISH FEDERATION) (1933; Inc. 1947); 3100 N. Knoxville, Suite 17 (61603); (309)686-0611. Pres. Joseph Settler; Exec. Dir. Peretz A. Katz.

ROCK ISLAND—MOLINE—DAVENPORT—BETTENDORF

UNITED JEWISH CHARITIES OF QUAD CITIES (1938; comb. 1973); 1804 7th Ave., Rock Island (61201); (309)786-7775. Pres. Morton Kaplan; Sec. Jay Gellerman.

ROCKFORD

ROCKFORD JEWISH COMMUNITY COUNCIL (1937); 1500 Parkview Ave. (61107); (815)-399-5497. Pres. Toby Toback; Exec. Dir. Daniel Tannenbaum.

SOUTHERN ILLINOIS

JEWISH FEDERATION OF SOUTHERN ILLINOIS (incl. all of Illinois south of Carlinville and Paducah, Ky.) (1941); (618)398-6100. 6464 W. Main, Suite 7A, Belleville (62223); Pres. Mrs. Frank Altman; Exec. Dir. Bruce J. Samborn.

SPRINGFIELD

SPRINGFIELD JEWISH FEDERATION (member CENTRAL ILLINOIS JEWISH FEDERATION) (1941); 730 E. Vine St. (62703); (217)-528-3446. Pres. Edith M. Myers; Exec. Sec. Lenore Loeb.

INDIANA

EVANSVILLE

EVANSVILLE JEWISH COMMUNITY COUNCIL, INC. (1936; Inc. 1964); P.O. Box 5026 (47715); (812)476-1571. Pres. Mrs. Sadelle Berger.

FORT WAYNE

FORT WAYNE JEWISH FEDERATION (1921); 227 E. Washington Blvd. (46802); (219)422-4776. Pres. Janet H. Latz; Exec. Dir. Benjamin Eisbart.

INDIANAPOLIS

JEWISH WELFARE FEDERATION, INC. (1905); 615 N. Alabama St. (46204); (317)-637-2473. Pres. Philip D. Pecar; Exec. V. Pres. Frank H. Newman.

LAFAYETTE

FEDERATED JEWISH CHARITIES (1924); P.O. Box 676 (47902); (317)742-9081. Pres. Leslie Feld; Fin. Sec. Louis Pearlman, Jr.

MICHIGAN CITY

MICHIGAN CITY UNITED JEWISH WELFARE FUND; 2800 Franklin St. (46360); (219)874-4477. Pres. Irving Loeber; Treas. Harold Leinwand.

MUNCIE

*MUNCIE JEWISH WELFARE FUND (1945); c/o Beth El Temple; P.O. Box 2792 (47302); (317)284-1497. Chmn. Edward J. Dobrow; Treas. Robert Koor.

NORTHWEST INDIANA

THE JEWISH FEDERATION, INC. (1941; reorg. 1959); 2939 Jewett St., Highland (46322); (219)887-0541. Pres. Alan Hurst; Exec. Dir. Barnett Labowitz.

SOUTH BEND

JEWISH FEDERATION OF ST. JOSEPH VALLEY (1946); 804 Sherland Bldg. (46601); (219)233-1164. Pres. Ronald Cohen; Exec. V. Pres. Bernard Natkow.

IOWA

CEDAR RAPIDS

*JEWISH WELFARE FUND OF LINN COUNTY (1941); 115 7 St. S.E. (52401); (319) 366-3553. Chmn. Norman Lipsky; Treas. Jay Beecher.

DES MOINES

JEWISH FEDERATION OF GREATER DES MOINES (1914); 910 Polk Blvd. (50312); (515)277-6321. Pres. Fred Lorber; Exec. Dir. Jay Yoskowitz.

SIOUX CITY

JEWISH FEDERATION (1921); 525 14 St. (51105); (712)258-0618. Pres. A. Frank Baron; Exec. Dir. Joseph Bluestein.

WATERLOO

WATERLOO JEWISH FEDERATION (1941); c/o Congregation Sons of Jacob, 411 Mitchell Ave. (50702); Pres. Irving Uze.

KANSAS

TOPEKA

*TOPEKA-LAWRENCE JEWISH FEDERATION (1939); 101 Redbud Lane (66607); Pres. William Rudnick.

WICHITA

MID-KANSAS JEWISH WELFARE FEDERATION, INC. (1935); 400 N. Woodlawn, Suite 28 (67206); (316)686-4741. Pres. Joan Beren.

KENTUCKY

LOUISVILLE

JEWISH COMMUNITY FEDERATION OF LOUISVILLE, INC. (1934); (sponsors UNITED JEWISH CAMPAIGN); 702 Marion E. Taylor Bldg. (40202); (502)587-6891. Frank Lipschutz; Exec. Dir. Norbert Fruehauf.

LOUISIANA

ALEXANDRIA

THE JEWISH WELFARE FEDERATION AND COMMUNITY COUNCIL OF CENTRAL LOUISIANA (1938); 1261 Heyman Lane (71301); (318)442-1264. Pres. Harold Katz; Sec.-Treas. Mrs. George Kuplesky.

BATON ROUGE

JEWISH FEDERATION OF GREATER BATON ROUGE (1971); P.O. Box 15123 (70895); (504)275-9335. Pres. Felix R. Weill; Exec. Dir. Ian Heller.

MONROE

UNITED JEWISH CHARITIES OF NORTHEAST LOUISIANA (1938); 2400 Orrel Pl. (71201); (318)388-2859. Pres. Sol Rosenberg; Sec.-Treas. Herman E. Hirsch.

NEW ORLEANS

JEWISH FEDERATION OF GREATER NEW ORLEANS (1913; reorg. 1977); 211 Camp St. (70130); (504)525-0673. Pres. Marvin L. Jacobs; Exec. Dir. Gerald C. Lasensky.

SHREVEPORT

SHREVEPORT JEWISH FEDERATION (1941; Inc. 1967); 2030 Line Ave. (71104); (318)-221-4129. Pres. David Greenberg; Exec. Dir. K. Bernard Klein.

MAINE

BANGOR

*JEWISH COMMUNITY COUNCIL (1949); 28 Somerset St. (04401); (207)945-5631. Pres. Sam Nyer; Exec. Dir. Alan Coren.

LEWISTON-AUBURN

JEWISH FEDERATION (1947); (sponsors UNITED JEWISH APPEAL); 134 College St., Lewiston (04240); (207)782-8062. Pres. Bertha Allen; Exec. Dir. Howard G. Joress.

PORTLAND

JEWISH FEDERATION COMMUNITY COUNCIL OF SOUTHERN MAINE (1942); (sponsors UNITED JEWISH APPEAL); 341 Cumberland

Ave. (04101); (207)773-7254. Pres. David N. Lewis; Exec. Dir. Sanford Cutler.

MARYLAND

ANNAPOLIS

*ANNAPOLIS JEWISH WELFARE FUND (1946); 601 Ridgley Ave. (21401); Pres. Anton Grobani.

BALTIMORE

ASSOCIATED JEWISH CHARITIES & WELFARE FUND, INC. (a merger of the Associated Jewish Charities & Jewish Welfare Fund) (1920; reorg. 1969); 319 W. Monument St. (21201); (301)727-4828. Pres. Bernard Manekin; Exec. V. Pres. Robert I. Hiller.

MASSACHUSETTS

BOSTON

COMBINED JEWISH PHILANTHROPIES OF GREATER BOSTON, INC. (1895; reorg. 1961); 72 Franklin St. (02110); (617)542-8080. Pres. Leo Dunn; Exec. Dir. Bernard Olshansky.

FITCHBURG

*JEWISH FEDERATION OF FITCHBURG (1939); 40 Boutelle St. (01420); (617)342-2227. Pres. Elliot L. Zide; Treas. Allen I. Rome.

FRAMINGHAM

GREATER FRAMINGHAM JEWISH FEDERATION (1968; Inc. 1969); 1000 Worchester Road, Framingham Centre (01701); (617)-879-3301. Pres. Harvey Stone; Exec. Dir. Howard Kummer.

HAVERHILL

*HAVERHILL UNITED JEWISH APPEAL, INC., 514 Main St. (01830); (617)373-3861. Pres. Norman Birenbaum; Exec. Dir. Joseph H. Elgart.

HOLYOKE

COMBINED JEWISH APPEAL OF HOLYOKE (1939); 378 Maple St. (01040); (413)534-3369. Pres. Herbert Goldberg; Exec. Dir. Dov Sussman.

LAWRENCE

*JEWISH COMMUNITY COUNCIL OF GREATER LAWRENCE (1906); 580 Haverhill St. (01841); (617)686-4157. Pres. Michael Baker; Exec. Dir. Irving Linn.

LEOMINSTER

LEOMINSTER JEWISH COMMUNITY COUNCIL, INC. (1939); 30 Grove Ave. (01453);

(617)537-7906. Pres. Marc Levine; Sec.-Treas. Edith Chatkis.

NEW BEDFORD

JEWISH FEDERATION OF GREATER NEW BEDFORD, INC. (1938; Inc. 1954); 467 Hawthorn St., North Dartmouth (02747); (617)-997-7471. Pres. Robert J. Greene; Exec. Dir. Gerald A. Kleinman.

NORTH SHORE

JEWISH FEDERATION OF THE NORTH SHORE, INC. (1938); 4 Community Rd., Marblehead (01945); (617)598-1810. Pres. Norman S. Rosenfield; Exec. Dir. Gerald S. Ferman.

PITTSFIELD

*JEWISH COMMUNITY COUNCIL (1940); 235 E. St. (01201); (413)442-4360. Pres. Howard Kaufman; Exec. Dir. Sanford Lubin.

SPRINGFIELD

SPRINGFIELD JEWISH FEDERATION, INC. (1938); (sponsors UNITED JEWISH WELFARE FUND); 1160 Dickinson (01108); (413)737-4313. Pres. Harold Rosen; Exec. Dir. Eli Asher.

WORCESTER

WORCESTER JEWISH FEDERATION, INC. (1947; Inc. 1957); (sponsors JEWISH WELFARE FUND, 1939); 633 Salisbury St. (01609); (617)756-1543. Pres. Morton H. Sigel; Exec. Dir. Melvin S. Cohen.

MICHIGAN

BAY CITY

*NORTHEASTERN MICHIGAN JEWISH WELFARE FEDERATION (1940); 1100 Center Ave., Apt. 305 (48706); (517)892-2338. Sec. Hanna Hertzenberg.

DETROIT

JEWISH WELFARE FEDERATION OF DETROIT (1899); (sponsors ALLIED JEWISH CAMPAIGN); Fred M. Butzel Memorial Bldg., 163 Madison (48226); (313)965-3939. Pres. George M. Zeltzer; Exec. Dir. Sol Drachler.

FLINT

JEWISH COMMUNITY COUNCIL (1936); 120 W. Kearsley St. (48502); (313)767-5922; Pres. Ira B. Marder; Exec. Dir. Arnold S. Feder.

GRAND RAPIDS

JEWISH COMMUNITY FUND OF GRAND RAPIDS (1930); 1121 Keneberry Way S.E. (49506); (616)949-5238. Pres. Joseph N. Schwartz; Sec. Mrs. William Deutsch.

KALAMAZOO

KALAMAZOO JEWISH FEDERATION (1949); c/o Congregation of Moses, 2501 Stadium Dr. (49008); (616)349-8396. Pres. Martin Gall.

LANSING

GREATER LANSING JEWISH WELFARE FEDERATION (1939); 319 Hillcrest (48823); (517)351-3197. Pres. Isaac Green; Exec. Dir. Henry Jurkewicz.

SAGINAW

SAGINAW JEWISH WELFARE FEDERATION (1939); 1424 S. Washington Ave. (48607); (517)753-5230. Pres. Norman Rotenberg; Fin. Sec. Mrs. Henry Feldman.

MINNESOTA

DULUTH

JEWISH FEDERATION & COMMUNITY COUNCIL (1937); 1602 E. 2nd St. (55812); (218)-724-8857. Pres. R. L. Solon; Exec. Dir. Mrs. Arnold Nides.

MINNEAPOLIS

MINNEAPOLIS FEDERATION FOR JEWISH SERVICES (1929; Inc. 1930); 811 La Salle Ave. (55402); (612)339-7491. Pres. Theresa Berman; Exec. Dir. Franklin Fogelson.

ST. PAUL

UNITED JEWISH FUND AND COUNCIL (1935); 790 S. Cleveland (55116); (612)690-1707. Pres. Annette Newman; Exec. Dir. David Tenenbaum.

MISSISSIPPI

JACKSON

*JEWISH WELFARE FUND (1945); 4135 N. Honeysuckle Lane (39211); (601)956-6215. Drive Chmn. Emanuel Crystal.

VICKSBURG

*JEWISH WELFARE FEDERATION (1936); 1210 Washington St. (39180); (601)636-7531. Pres. Richard Marcus.

MISSOURI

KANSAS CITY

JEWISH FEDERATION OF GREATER KANSAS CITY (1933); 25 E. 12 St. (64106); (816)421-5808. Pres. Donald H. Tranin; Exec. Dir. Sol Koenigsberg.

ST. JOSEPH

UNITED JEWISH FUND OF ST. JOSEPH (1915); 2903 Sherman Ave. (64506); (816)-279-3436. Pres. Robert Meyer; Exec. Sec. Ann Saferstein.

ST. LOUIS

JEWISH FEDERATION OF ST. LOUIS (incl. St. Louis County) (1901); 611 Olive St., Suite 1520 (63101); (314)621-8120. Pres. Harry Epstein; V. Pres. David Rabinovitz.

NEBRASKA

LINCOLN

LINCOLN JEWISH WELFARE FEDERATION, INC. (1931; Inc. 1961); P.O. Box 80014 (68501); (402)435-0230. Pres. Yale Gotsdiner; Exec. Dir. Louis B. Finkelstein.

OMAHA

JEWISH FEDERATION OF OMAHA (1903); 333 S. 132 St. (68154); (402)334-8200. Pres. Mrs. Morris Fellman; Exec. Dir. Louis B. Solomon.

NEVADA

LAS VEGAS

LAS VEGAS COMBINED JEWISH APPEAL (1973); 846 E. Sahara Ave. #4 (89104); (702)732-0556. Pres. Lloyd Katz; Exec. Dir. Jerry Countess.

NEW HAMPSHIRE

MANCHESTER

JEWISH COMMUNITY COUNCIL OF GREATER MANCHESTER (1913); 698 Beech St. (03104); (603)627-7679. Pres. Irving Singer; Exec. Dir. Joseph Peimer.

NEW JERSEY

ATLANTIC CITY

FEDERATION OF JEWISH AGENCIES OF ATLANTIC COUNTY (1924); 5321 Atlantic Ave., Ventnor City (08406); Pres. (609)822-7122. Esther G. Mitnick; Exec. Dir. Murray Schneier.

BERGEN COUNTY

UNITED JEWISH FEDERATION OF BERGEN COUNTY (1953, Inc. 1978); 111 Kinderkamack Rd., River Edge (07661); (201)488-6800. Pres. Sidney Silverstein; Exec. V. Pres. James P. Young.

CENTRAL NEW JERSEY

JEWISH FEDERATION OF CENTRAL NEW JERSEY (sponsors UNITED JEWISH CAMPAIGN); (1940; expanded 1973 to include Westfield and Plainfield); Green Lane, Union (07083); (201)351-5060. Pres. Alan Goldstein; Exec. V. Pres. Burton Lazarow.

ENGLEWOOD

UNITED JEWISH FUND OF ENGLEWOOD AND SURROUNDING COMMUNITIES (1952); 153 Tenafly Rd. (07631); (201)569-1070. Pres. Sam Lieben; Exec. Dir. George Hantgan.

JERSEY CITY

UNITED JEWISH APPEAL (1939); 604 Bergen Ave. (07304); (201)332-6644. Chmn. Bernard Kaye; Exec. Dir. Abraham Mintz.

METROPOLITAN NEW JERSEY

JEWISH COMMUNITY FEDERATION (sponsors UNITED JEWISH APPEAL) (1923); 60 Glenwood Ave., East Orange (07017); (201)-673-6800. Pres. Horace Bier; Exec. V. Pres. Carmi Schwartz.

MONMOUTH COUNTY

JEWISH FEDERATION OF GREATER MONMOUTH COUNTY (Formerly Shore Area) (1971); 100 Grant Ave. (07723); (201)531-6200. Pres. Samuel Jaffe; Exec. Dir. Clifford R. Josephson.

MORRIS COUNTY

UNITED JEWISH FEDERATION OF MORRIS-SUSSEX; 500 Route 10, Ledgewood (07852); (201)584-1850. Pres. Daniel Drench; Exec. Dir. Elliot Cohan.

NORTH JERSEY

JEWISH FEDERATION OF NORTH JERSEY (formerly Jewish Community Council) (1933); (sponsors UNITED JEWISH APPEAL DRIVE); 1 Pike Dr., Wayne (07470); (201)-595-0555. Pres. Norman Zelnick; Exec. Dir. Richard Krieger.

NORTHERN MIDDLESEX COUNTY

JEWISH FEDERATION OF NORTHERN MIDDLESEX COUNTY (sponsors UNITED JEWISH

APPEAL) (1975); Lord St., Avenel (07001); (201)636-8660. Pres. Ted Simkin; Exec. Dir. Arthur Eisenstein.

OCEAN COUNTY

OCEAN COUNTY JEWISH FEDERATION; 120 Madison Ave., Lakewood (08701); (201)363-0530. Pres. Herbert Wishnick; Exec. Dir. Marvin Relkin.

PASSAIC-CLIFTON

JEWISH COMMUNITY COUNCIL OF PASSAIC-CLIFTON AND VICINITY (1933); (sponsors UNITED JEWISH CAMPAIGN); 199 Scoles Ave. (07012). (201)777-7031. Pres. Benjamin Geller; Exec. Dir. Marden Prau.

RARITAN VALLEY

JEWISH FEDERATION OF RARITAN VALLEY (1948); 2 South Adelaide Ave., Highland Park (08904); (201)246-1905. Pres. Jacob Krishner; Exec. Dir. Howard Kieval.

SOMERSET COUNTY

JEWISH FEDERATION OF SOMERSET COUNTY (1960); 11 Park Ave., P.O. Box 874, Somerville (08876); (201)725-2231. Pres. Kenneth Strausfield; Exec. Dir. Burt Shimanovsky.

SOUTHERN NEW JERSEY

JEWISH FEDERATION OF SOUTHERN NEW JERSEY (incl. Camden and Burlington Counties) (1922); (sponsors ALLIED JEWISH APPEAL); 2393 W. Marlton Pike, Cherry Hill (08002); (609)665-6100. Pres. Alan Wechsler; Exec. V. Pres. Bernard Dubin.

TRENTON

JEWISH FEDERATION OF GREATER TRENTON (1929); 999 Lower Ferry Rd., P.O. Box 7249 (08628); (609)883-9110. Pres. David Kravitz; Exec. Dir. Mark M. Edell.

VINELAND

JEWISH COMMUNITY COUNCIL OF GREATER VINELAND, INC. (1971); (sponsors ALLIED JEWISH APPEAL); 629 Wood St. (08360); (609)696-4445. Pres. Sheldon Goldberg; Exec. Dir. Melvin May.

NEW MEXICO

ALBUQUERQUE

JEWISH COMMUNITY COUNCIL OF ALBUQUERQUE, INC. (1938); 600 Louisiana Blvd., S.E. (87108); (505)266-5641. Pres. Harry Epstein; Exec. Dir. Charles Vogel.

NEW YORK

ALBANY

GREATER ALBANY JEWISH FEDERATION (1938); (sponsors JEWISH WELFARE FUND); 19 Colvin Ave. (12206); (518)459-8000. Pres. Marvin A. Freedman; Exec. Dir. Steven F. Windmueller.

BROOME COUNTY

THE JEWISH FEDERATION OF BROOME COUNTY (1937; Inc. 1958); 500 Clubhouse Rd., Binghamton (13903); (607)724-2332. Pres. Gerald Ansell; Exec. Dir. Stanley Bard.

BUFFALO

UNITED JEWISH FEDERATION OF BUFFALO, INC. (1903); sponsors UNITED JEWISH FUND CAMPAIGN); 787 Delaware Ave. (14209); (716)886-7750. Pres. Leonard Rochwarger; Exec. Dir. Morris Rombro.

ELMIRA

ELMIRA JEWISH WELFARE FUND, INC. (1942); P.O. Box 3087, Grandview Rd. (14905); (607)734-8122. Pres. Irving Etkind; Exec. Dir. Ernest G. Budwig.

GLENS FALLS

*GLENS FALLS JEWISH WELFARE FUND (1939); 6 Arbor Dr. (12801); (518)792-3287. Chmn. Orel Friedman.

HUDSON

*JEWISH WELFARE FUND OF HUDSON, N.Y., INC. (1947); Joslen Blvd. (12534); (518)828-6848. Pres. Albert Rapport.

KINGSTON

JEWISH FEDERATION OF GREATER KINGSTON, INC. (1951); 159 Green St. (12401); (914)338-8131. Pres. Joseph Cohen; Admn. Lucy Cohen.

NEW YORK CITY

FEDERATION OF JEWISH PHILANTHROPIES OF NEW YORK (incl. Greater New York, Nassau, Suffolk, and Westchester Counties) (1917); 130 E. 59th St. (10022); (212)751-1000. Pres. Harry R. Mancher; Exec. V. Pres. Sanford Solender.

UNITED JEWISH APPEAL—FEDERATION OF JEWISH PHILANTHROPIES—JOINT CAMPAIGN (1974); 220 W. 58 St. (10019); (212)-265-2000. Pres. William Rosenwald; Exec. V. Pres. Sanford Solender; Bd. Chmn. Laurence A. Tisch.

UNITED JEWISH APPEAL OF GREATER NEW YORK, INC. (incl. Greater New York, Nassau, Suffolk, and Westchester Counties) (1939); 220 W. 58th St. (10019); (212)265-2200. Pres. Stephen Shalom; Exec. V. Pres. Ernest W. Michel.

NEWBURGH-MIDDLETOWN

JEWISH FEDERATION OF NEWBURGH AND MIDDLETOWN, INC. (1925); 360 Powell Ave. (12550); (914)562-7860. Pres. Florence Levine; Exec. Dir. Carol Rosengart.

NIAGARA FALLS

JEWISH FEDERATION OF NIAGARA FALLS, N.Y., INC. (1935); 209 United Office Bldg. (14303); (716)284-4575. Pres. Robert D. Wisbaum; Exec. Dir. Miriam Schaffer.

POUGHKEEPSIE

*JEWISH WELFARE FUND-DUTCHESS CTY. (1941); 110 Grand Ave. (12603); (914)471-9811. Pres. Arthur Levinsohn; Exec. Dir. Mark Baron.

ROCHESTER

JEWISH COMMUNITY FEDERATION OF ROCHESTER, N.Y., INC. (1937); 440 Main St. E. (14604); (716)325-3393. Pres. Irving Ruderman; Exec. Dir. Darrell D. Friedman.

SCHENECTADY

JEWISH COMMUNITY COUNCIL (incl. surrounding communities) (1938); (sponsors SCHENECTADY UJA AND FEDERATED WELFARE FUND); 2565 Balltown Rd., P.O. Box 2649 (12309); (518)393-1136. Pres. Philip Ziffer; Exec. Dir. Haim Morag.

SYRACUSE

SYRACUSE JEWISH FEDERATION, INC. (1918); P.O. Box 5004, 201 E. Jefferson St. (13201); (315)422-4104. Pres. Leonard S. Goldberg; Exec. Dir. Gilbert D. Orlik.

TROY

TROY JEWISH COMMUNITY COUNCIL, INC. (1936); 2500 21 St. (12180); (518)274-0700. Pres. Elliot Schwebel.

UTICA

JEWISH COMMUNITY COUNCIL OF UTICA, N.Y., INC. (1933, Inc. 1950); (sponsors UNITED JEWISH APPEAL OF UTICA); 2310 Oneida St. (13501); (315)733-2343. Pres. Helen Sperling; Exec. Dir. Irving Epstein.

NORTH CAROLINA

ASHEVILLE

FEDERATED JEWISH CHARITIES OF ASHEVILLE, INC., 236 Charlotte St. (28801); (704)-253-0701. Pres. Robert Carr; Exec. Dir. Ronald Cahn.

CHARLOTTE

CHARLOTTE JEWISH FEDERATION (1940); P.O. Box 220188 (28222); (704)366-0358. Pres. Harry Lemer; Exec. Dir. Marvin Bienstock.

GREENSBORO

GREENSBORO JEWISH FEDERATION (1940); 414 Church St., Suite 11, Greensboro (27401); Pres. Robert Lavites; Exec. Dir. Sherman Harris.

HIGH POINT

HIGH POINT JEWISH FEDERATION; 1308 Long Creek, High Point (27260); (919)431-7101. Campaign Chmn. Harry Samet.

WINSTON-SALEM

WINSTON-SALEM JEWISH COMMUNITY COUNCIL; 710 Lichfield Rd., Winston Salem (27104); (919)725-7576; Pres. Alan Andler.

OHIO

AKRON

AKRON JEWISH COMMUNITY FEDERATION (1935); 750 White Pond Dr. (44320); (216)-867-7850. Pres. David Locksin; Exec. Dir. Steven Drysdale.

CANTON

JEWISH COMMUNITY FEDERATION OF CANTON (1935; reorg. 1955); 2631 Harvard Ave., N.W. (44709); (216)453-0133. Pres. Stanford L. Sirak; Exec. Dir. Revella R. Kopstein.

CINCINNATI

JEWISH FEDERATION OF CINCINNATI AND VICINITY (merger of the Associated Jewish Agencies and Jewish Welfare Fund) (1896; reorg. 1967); 200 West 4th St. (45202); (513)-381-5800. Pres. Lee S. Rosenberg; Exec. V. Pres. Harold Goldberg.

CLEVELAND

JEWISH COMMUNITY FEDERATION OF CLEVELAND (1903); 1750 Euclid Ave. (44115); (216)566-9200. Pres. Albert B. Ratner; Exec. Dir. Stanley B. Horowitz.

COLUMBUS

COLUMBUS JEWISH FEDERATION (1926); 1175 College Ave. (43209); (614)237-7686. Pres. Ernest Stern; Exec. V. Pres. Ben M. Mandelkorn.

DAYTON

JEWISH COMMUNITY COUNCIL OF DAYTON (1943); 4501 Denlinger Rd. (45426); (513)-854-4150. Pres. Irvin Zipperstein; Exec. V. Pres. Peter Wells.

LIMA

FEDERATED JEWISH CHARITIES OF LIMA DISTRICT (1935); 2417 West Market St. (45805); (419)224-8941. Pres. Morris Goldberg.

STEUBENVILLE

JEWISH COMMUNITY COUNCIL (1938); P.O. Box 472 (43952); (614)282-9031. Pres. Morris Denmark; Exec. Sec. Mrs. Joseph Freedman.

TOLEDO

JEWISH WELFARE FEDERATION OF TOLEDO, INC. (1907; reorg. 1960); 5151 Monroe St., Suite 226 West (43623); (419)-885-4461. Pres. David Katz; Exec. Dir. Alvin S. Levinson.

WARREN

JEWISH FEDERATION (1938); 3893 E. Market St. (44483); Pres. William Lippy.

YOUNGSTOWN

JEWISH FEDERATION OF YOUNGSTOWN, OHIO, INC. (1935); P.O. Box 449 (44501); (216)746-3251. Pres. Bert Tamarkin; Exec. Dir. Stanley Engel.

OKLAHOMA

ARDMORE

*JEWISH FEDERATION (1934); 23 "B" St., S.W. (73401); Chmn. Ike Fishman.

OKLAHOMA CITY

JEWISH COMMUNITY COUNCIL (1941); 3923 N. Pennsylvania, Suite 101 (73112); (405)-524-4324. Pres. Marvin Weiss; Exec. Dir. Jay B. Bachrach.

TULSA

TULSA JEWISH COMMUNITY COUNCIL (1938); (sponsors TULSA UNITED JEWISH CAMPAIGN); 3314 E. 51 St., Suite T (74135); (918)749-4427. Pres. Donald Newman; Exec. Dir. Nathan Loshak.

OREGON

PORTLAND

JEWISH FEDERATION OF PORTLAND (incl. State of Oregon and adjacent Washington communities) (1920; reorg. 1956); P.O. Box 19407, 6651 S. W. Capitol Highway (97219); Pres. Stanley G. Marcus; Exec. Dir. David Roberts.

PENNSYLVANIA

ALLENTOWN

JEWISH FEDERATION OF ALLENTOWN, INC. (1938; Inc. 1948); P.O. Box 236, 22nd and Tilghman Sts. (18105); (215)435-3571. Pres. Arnan Finkelstein.

ALTOONA

FEDERATION OF JEWISH PHILANTHROPIES (1920; reorg. 1940); 1308 17th St. (16601); (814)944-4072. Pres. Neil Port.

BUTLER

BUTLER JEWISH WELFARE FUND (incl. Butler County) (1938); P.O. Box 992 (16001); (412)283-4500. Pres. Julius Bernstein; Sec. Maurice Horwitz.

EASTON

JEWISH COMMUNITY COUNCIL OF EASTON, PA. AND VICINITY (1939); (sponsors ALLIED WELFARE APPEAL); 660 Ferry St. (18042); (215)253-4235. Pres. Eugene Goldman.

ERIE

JEWISH COMMUNITY COUNCIL OF ERIE (1946); 32 W. 8th St., Suite 512 (16501); (814)455-4474. Pres. Sidney Wexler.

HARRISBURG

UNITED JEWISH COMMUNITY OF GREATER HARRISBURG (1933); 100 Vaughn St. (17110); (717)236-9555. Pres. Jay Maisel; Exec. Dir. Albert Hursh.

HAZELTON

JEWISH COMMUNITY COUNCIL (1960); Laurel & Hemlock Sts. (18201); (717)454-3528. Pres. David Rosen; Exec. Dir. Steven Wendell.

JOHNSTOWN

UNITED JEWISH FEDERATION OF JOHNSTOWN (1938); 1334 Luzerne St. (15905); (814)255-1447. Pres. Isadore Glasser.

LANCASTER

UNITED JEWISH COMMUNITY COUNCIL OF LANCASTER, PA., INC. (1928); 2120 Oregon

Pike (17601); (717)569-7352. Pres. Jay S. Poser; Exec. Dir. Lawrence Pallas.

LEVITTOWN

JEWISH FEDERATION OF LOWER BUCKS COUNTY (1956; Inc. 1957); 15 Stonybrook Dr. E. (19055); (215)547-1400. Pres. Arthur M. Abramsohn; Exec. Dir. Elliot Gershenson.

NEW CASTLE

UNITED JEWISH APPEAL OF NEW CASTLE, PA. (1967); 3218 Plank Rd. (16105); (412)-654-7438. Chmn. Dale Pearlman.

NORRISTOWN

JEWISH COMMUNITY CENTER (serving Central Montgomery County) (1936); Brown and Powell Sts. (19401); (215)275-8797. Pres. Norman Kutner; Exec. Dir. Harold M. Kamsler.

PHILADELPHIA

FEDERATION OF JEWISH AGENCIES OF GREATER PHILADELPHIA (1901; reorg. 1956); 226 South 16 St. (19102); (215)893-5600. Pres. Ronald Rubin; Exec. Dir. Robert Forman.

PITTSBURGH

UNITED JEWISH FEDERATION OF GREATER PITTSBURGH (1912; reorg. 1955); 234 McKee Pl. (15213); (412)681-8000. Pres. Sidney N. Busis; Exec. V. Pres. William Kahn.

POTTSVILLE

UNITED JEWISH CHARITIES (1935); 2300 Mahantongo St. (17901); (717)622-5890. Chmn. Henry Gilbert; Exec. Sec. Gertrude Perkins.

READING

JEWISH FEDERATION OF READING, PA., INC. (1935); (sponsors UNITED JEWISH CAMPAIGN); 1700 City Line St. (19604); (215)921-2766. Pres. Benjamin J. Cutler; Exec. Dir. David Morris.

SCRANTON

SCRANTON-LACKAWANNA JEWISH COUNCIL (incl. Lackawanna County) (1945); 601 Jefferson Ave. (18510); (717)961-2300. Pres. Mrs. Seymour Bachman; Exec. Dir. Seymour Brotman.

SHARON

SHENANGO VALLEY JEWISH FEDERATION (1940); 840 Highland Rd. (16146); (412)346-4754. Pres. Leon Bolotin; Treas. Irwin Yanowitz.

UNIONTOWN

UNITED JEWISH FEDERATION (1939); 406 W. Main St. (15401), c/o Jewish Community Center; (412)438-4681. Pres. Harold Cohen; Sec. Morris H. Samuels.

WILKES-BARRE

THE WYOMING VALLEY JEWISH COMMITTEE (1935); (sponsors UNITED JEWISH APPEAL); 60 S. River St. (18701); (717)824-4646. Pres. William Smulowitz; Exec. Dir. Monty Pomm.

YORK

YORK COUNCIL OF JEWISH CHARITIES, INC.; 120 E. Market St. (17401); (717)843-0918. Pres. Robert Erdos; Exec. Dir. Alan Dameshek.

RHODE ISLAND

PROVIDENCE

JEWISH FEDERATION OF RHODE ISLAND (1945); 130 Sessions St. (02906); (401)421-4111. Pres. Marvin S. Holland; Exec. Dir. Sanford Lupovitz.

SOUTH CAROLINA

CHARLESTON

JEWISH WELFARE FUND (1949); 1645 Millbrook Dr. (29407); P.O. Box 31298; (803)-571-6565. Pres. Melvin Solomon; Exec. Dir. Nathan Shulman.

COLUMBIA

JEWISH WELFARE FEDERATION OF COLUMBIA (1960); 4540 Trenholm Rd. (29206); (803)787-2023. Pres. Melton Kligman; Exec. Dir. Jack Weintraub.

SOUTH DAKOTA

SIOUX FALLS

JEWISH WELFARE FUND (1938); National Reserve Bldg. (57102); (605)336-2880. Pres. Richard M. Light; Exec. Sec. Louis R. Hurwitz.

TENNESSEE

CHATTANOOGA

CHATTANOOGA JEWISH WELFARE FEDERATION (1931); 5326 Lynnland Terrace (37411); (615)894-1317. Pres. Paul Lefkoff; Exec. Dir. Alan J. Hersh.

KNOXVILLE

JEWISH WELFARE FUND, INC. (1939); 6800 Deane Hill Dr., P.O. Box 10882 (37919);

(615)690-6343. Pres. Gordon Brown; Exec. Dir. Mike Pousman.

MEMPHIS

JEWISH SERVICE AGENCY (incl. Shelby County) (1864; Inc. 1906); 6560 Poplar Ave., P. O. Box 38268 (38138); (901)767-5161. Pres. Jerrold Graber; Exec. Dir. Jack Lieberman.

MEMPHIS JEWISH FEDERATION (incl. Shelby County) (1934); 6560 Poplar Ave., P. O. Box 38268 (38138); (901)767-5161. Pres. Samuel Weintraub; Exec. Dir. Howard Weisband.

NASHVILLE

JEWISH FEDERATION OF NASHVILLE & MIDDLE TENNESSEE (1936); 3500 West End Ave. (37205); (615)297-3588. Pres. Herman Kaplan; Exec. Arthur Landa.

TEXAS

AUSTIN

JEWISH COMMUNITY COUNCIL OF AUSTIN (1939; reorg. 1956); 8301 Balcones Dr., Suite 308–1 (78759); (512)345-6940. Pres. Richard Karotkin; Exec. Dir. Charles P. Epstein.

BEAUMONT

BEAUMONT JEWISH FEDERATION OF TEXAS, INC. (Org. and Inc. 1967); P. O. Box 1981 (77704); (713)833-5427. Pres. Edwin Gale; Dir. Isadore Harris.

CORPUS CHRISTI

CORPUS CHRISTI JEWISH COMMUNITY COUNCIL (1953); 750 Everhart Rd. (78411); (512)855-6239. Pres. Madelyn Loeb; Exec. Dir. Lillian Racusin.

COMBINED JEWISH APPEAL OF CORPUS CHRISTI (1962); 750 Everhart Rd. (78411); (512)855-6239. Pres. Jule Pels; Exec. Dir. Lillian Racusin.

DALLAS

JEWISH FEDERATION OF GREATER DALLAS (1911); 7800 Northaven Rd., Suite A (75230); (214)369-3313. Pres. Morris P. Newberger; Exec. Dir. Morris A. Stein.

EL PASO

JEWISH FEDERATION OF EL PASO, INC. (incl. surrounding communities) (1939); 405 Mardi Gras, P. O. Box 12097 (79912); (915)-584-4438. Pres. Mrs. Robert E. Goodman; Exec. Dir. Howard Burnham.

FORT WORTH

JEWISH FEDERATION OF FORT WORTH (1936); 6801 Granbury Rd. (76133); (817)-292-3081. Pres. Hortense Deifik; Exec. Dir. Norman A. Mogul.

GALVESTON

GALVESTON COUNTY JEWISH COMMUNITY COUNCIL & WELFARE ASSOCIATION (1936); P. O. Box 146 (77553); (713)938-7143. Pres. Sidney Kay; Sec. Mrs. Charles Rosenbloom.

HOUSTON

JEWISH FEDERATION OF GREATER HOUSTON, INC. (incl. neighboring communities) (1937); (sponsors UNITED JEWISH CAMPAIGN); 5601 S. Braeswood Blvd. (77096); (713)729-7000. Pres. Joel Spira; Exec. Dir. Hans Mayer.

SAN ANTONIO

JEWISH FEDERATION OF SAN ANTONIO (incl. Bexar County) (1922); 8434 Ahern Dr. (78216); (512)341-8234. Pres. Richard Goldsmith; Exec. Dir. Saul Silverman.

TYLER

*FEDERATION OF JEWISH WELFARE FUNDS (1938); P. O. Box 934 (75710); Pres. Ralph Davis.

WACO

JEWISH WELFARE COUNCIL OF WACO (1949); P. O. Box 8031 (76710); (817)776-3740. Pres. Eli Berkman.

UTAH

SALT LAKE CITY

UNITED JEWISH COUNCIL AND SALT LAKE JEWISH WELFARE FUND (1936); 2416 E. 1700 South (84108); (801)581-0098. Pres. Ralph Tannenbaum; Exec. Dir. Bernard Solomon.

VIRGINIA

NEWPORT NEWS

JEWISH FEDERATION OF NEWPORT NEWS —HAMPTON, INC. (1942); 2700 Spring Rd. (23606); P. O. Box 6680; (804)595-5544. Pres. Joe Frank; Exec. Dir. Jay Rostov.

NORFOLK

UNITED JEWISH FEDERATION, INC. OF NORFOLK AND VIRGINIA BEACH, VA. (1937); 7300 Newport Ave., P. O. Box 9776

(23505); (804)489-8040. Pres. Marvin Simon; Exec. Dir. Michael D. Fischer.

PORTSMOUTH

PORTSMOUTH JEWISH COMMUNITY COUNCIL (1919); Rm. 430, Dominion Nat'l Bank Bldg. (23704); (804)393-2557. Pres. Mrs. Joseph Ginsburg; Exec. Dir. Jeremy S. Neimand.

RICHMOND

JEWISH COMMUNITY FEDERATION OF RICHMOND, INC. (1935); 5403 Monument Ave., P. O. Box 8237 (23226); (804)288-0045. Pres. J.Y. Plotkin; Exec. Dir. Stephen M. Abramson.

ROANOKE

JEWISH COMMUNITY COUNCIL; 2728 Colonial Ave., S.W. (24015); (703)982-2300. Chmn. Arnold P. Masinter.

WASHINGTON

SEATTLE

JEWISH FEDERATION OF GREATER SEATTLE (incl. King County, Everett and Bremerton) (1926); Suite 525, Securities Bldg. (98101); (206)622-8211. Pres. Charles Kaplan; Exec. Dir. Murray Shiff.

SPOKANE

*JEWISH COMMUNITY COUNCIL OF SPOKANE (incl. Spokane County) (1927); (sponsors UNITED JEWISH FUND) (1936); 401 Paulsen Bldg. (99021); (509)838-2949. Pres. Samuel Huppin; Sec. Robert N. Arick.

WEST VIRGINIA

CHARLESTON

FEDERATED JEWISH CHARITIES OF CHARLESTON, INC. (1937); P. O. Box 1613 (25326); (304)342-6459. Pres. Robert Levine; Exec. Sec. Charles Cohen.

HUNTINGTON

FEDERATED JEWISH CHARITIES (1939); P. O. Box 947 (25713); (304)523-9326. Pres. William H. Glick; Sec. Andrew Katz.

WHEELING

UNITED JEWISH FEDERATION OF OHIO VALLEY, INC. (1933); 20 Hawthorne Court (26003); Pres. Dr. Harold Saferstein.

WISCONSIN

APPLETON

UNITED JEWISH CHARITIES OF APPLETON (1963); 3131 N. Meade St. (54911); (414)-733-1848. Co-Chmn. Arnold Cohodas and Dov Edelstein; Treas. Mrs. Harold Rusky.

GREEN BAY

GREEN BAY JEWISH WELFARE FUND; P. O. Box 335 (54305); Pres. Stuart Milson; Treas. Herman J. Robitshek.

KENOSHA

KENOSHA JEWISH WELFARE FUND (1938); 6537–7th Ave. (53140); (414)658-8635. Pres. Charles Selsberg; Sec.-Treas. Mrs. S. M. Lapp.

MADISON

MADISON JEWISH COMMUNITY COUNCIL, INC. (1940); 310 N. Midvale Blvd., Suite 325 (53705); Pres. Harvey Malofsky; Exec. Dir. Robert Gast.

MILWAUKEE

MILWAUKEE JEWISH FEDERATION, INC. (1938); 1360 N. Prospect Ave. (53202); (414)-271-8338. Pres. Esther Leah Ritz; Exec. V. Pres. Melvin S. Zaret.

RACINE

RACINE JEWISH WELFARE BOARD (1946); 944 Main St. (53403); (414)633-7093. Pres. Jess Levin; Exec. Sec. Betty Goldberg.

SHEBOYGAN

JEWISH WELFARE COUNCIL OF SHEBOYGAN (1927); 1404 North Ave. (53081); Sec. Mrs. Abe Alpert.

CANADA

ALBERTA

CALGARY

CALGARY JEWISH COMMUNITY COUNCIL (1962); 102-18th Ave., S.E. (T2G 1K8); (403)263-5650. Pres. S. Bruce Green; Exec. Dir. Harry S. Shatz.

EDMONTON

EDMONTON JEWISH COMMUNITY COUNCIL, INC. (1954; Inc. 1965); 7200–156 St. (T5R 1X3); (403)487-5120. Pres. David Grossman; Exec. Dir. Gerald Rubin.

BRITISH COLUMBIA

VANCOUVER

*JEWISH COMMUNITY FUND & COUNCIL OF VANCOUVER (1932); 950 W. 41 Ave. (V5Z 2N7); (604)261-8101. Pres. Irvine E. Epstein; Exec. Dir. Morris Saltzman.

MANITOBA

WINNIPEG

WINNIPEG JEWISH COMMUNITY COUNCIL (incl. Combined Jewish Appeal of Winnipeg) (org. 1938, reorg. 1973); 370 Hargrave St., (R3B 2K1); (204)943-0406. Pres. Al Omson; Exec. Dir. Izzy Peltz.

ONTARIO

HAMILTON

HAMILTON JEWISH FEDERATION (incl. United Jewish Welfare Fund) (org. 1934, merged 1971); 57 Delaware Ave. (L8M 1T6); (416)528-8570. Pres. Bernard Greenbaum; Exec. Dir. Samuel Soifer.

LONDON

*LONDON JEWISH COMMUNITY COUNCIL (1932); 532 Huron St. (24), (N5Y 4J5); (519)-433-2201. Pres. Gerald Klein; Exec. Dir. Lily Feldman.

OTTAWA

JEWISH COMMUNITY COUNCIL OF OTTAWA (1934); 151 Chapel St. (K1N 7Y2); (613)-232-7306. Pres. Gilbert Greenberg; Exec. V. Pres. Hy Hochberg.

ST. CATHARINES

*UNITED JEWISH WELFARE FUND OF ST. CATHARINES; c/o Jewish Community Centre, Church St.; Pres. Jack Silverstein; Sec. Syd Goldford.

TORONTO

TORONTO JEWISH CONGRESS (1937); 150 Beverley St. (M5T 1Y6); (416)869-3811. Pres. Rose Wolfe; Exec. V. Pres. Irwin Gold.

WINDSOR

JEWISH COMMUNITY COUNCIL (1938); 1641 Ouellette Ave. (N8X 1K9); (519)254-7558. Pres. Bernard Putterman; Exec. Dir. Joseph Eisenberg.

QUEBEC

MONTREAL

ALLIED JEWISH COMMUNITY SERVICES (merger of FEDERATION OF JEWISH COMMUNITY SERVICES AND COMBINED JEWISH APPEAL) (1965); 5151 Cote St. Catherine Rd. (H3W 1M6); (514)735-3541. Pres. Hillel B. Becker; Exec. V. Pres. Manuel G. Batshaw.

Jewish Periodicals[1]

UNITED STATES

ALABAMA

CONTEMPORARY JEWRY (1974 under the name Jewish Sociology and Social Research). Dept. of Sociology, Univ. of Alabama, Birmingham, 35294. Murray B. Binderman. Semi-annually. Assn. for the Sociological Study of Jewry.

JEWISH MONITOR (1948). P. O. Box 396, Sheffield, 35660. (205)764-5085. Stanley Goldstein. Monthly.

ARIZONA

ARIZONA POST (1946). 102 N. Plumer Ave., Tucson, 85719. (602)884-8921. Martha K. Rothman. Bi-monthly. Tucson Jewish Community Council.

PHOENIX JEWISH NEWS (1947). 1530 West Thomas Rd., Phoenix, 85015. (602)264-0536. Pearl R. Newmark. Biweekly.

CALIFORNIA

B'NAI B'RITH MESSENGER (1897). 2510 W. 7 St., Los Angeles, 90057. (213)380-5000. Joseph J. Cummins. Weekly.

HERITAGE-SOUTHWEST JEWISH PRESS (1954). 2130 S. Vermont Ave., Los Angeles, 90007. Weekly. Herb Brin. (Also SAN DIEGO JEWISH PRESS-HERITAGE, San Diego [weekly]; CENTRAL CALIFORNIA JEWISH HERITAGE, Sacramento and Fresno area [monthly]; ORANGE COUNTY JEWISH HERITAGE, Orange County area [weekly].)

ISRAEL TODAY (1973). 10340½ Reseda Blvd., Northridge, 91326. (213)786-4000. Phil Blazer. Bi-weekly.

JEWISH OBSERVER OF THE EAST BAY (1967). 3245 Sheffield Ave., Oakland, 94602. (415)533-7462. Julie Simon Glenn. Fortnighty. Jewish Federation of the Greater East Bay.

JEWISH SPECTATOR (1935). P.O. Box 2016, Santa Monica, 90406. (213)829-2484. Trude Weiss-Rosmarin. Quarterly.

JEWISH STAR (1956). 693 Mission St. #305, San Francisco, 94105. (415)421-4874. Alfred Berger. Monthly.

SAN FRANCISCO JEWISH BULLETIN (1943). 870 Market St., San Francisco, 94102. Geoffrey Fisher. Weekly. San Francisco Jewish Community Publications.

WESTERN STATES JEWISH HISTORICAL QUARTERLY (1968). 2429 23rd St., Santa Monica, 90405. (213)399-3585. Dr.

[1]Information in this directory is based upon answers furnished by the publications themselves, and the publishers of the YEAR BOOK assume no responsibility for the accuracy of the data presented; nor does inclusion in this list necessarily imply approval or endorsement of the periodicals. The information provided here includes the year of organization and the name of the editor, managing editor, or publisher; unless otherwise stated, the language used by the periodical is English. An asterisk (*) indicates that no reply was received and that the information, including name of publication, date of founding, address, and telephone number, is reprinted from AJYB, 1979, Vol. 79. For organizational bulletins, consult organizational listings.

Norton B. Stern. Quarterly. Southern California Jewish Historical Society.

COLORADO

INTERMOUNTAIN JEWISH NEWS (1913). 1275 Sherman St., Denver, 80203. (303)-861-2234. Mrs. Max Goldberg. Weekly.

CONNECTICUT

CONNECTICUT JEWISH LEDGER (1929). P.O. Box 1923, Hartford, 06101. Berthold Gaster. Weekly.

JEWISH DIGEST (1955). 1363 Fairfield Ave., Bridgeport, 06605. (203)384-2284. Bernard Postal. Monthly.

DELAWARE

JEWISH VOICE (1967). 701 Shipley St., Wilmington, 19801. Ruth J. Kaplan. Bimonthly. Jewish Federation of Delaware.

DISTRICT OF COLUMBIA

AMERICAN JEWISH JOURNAL (1944). 894 National Press Bldg., Washington, 20910. (301)585-1756. David Mondzac. Quarterly.

JEWISH VETERAN (1896). 1712 New Hampshire Ave., N.W., Washington, 20009. (202)265-6280. Judy Sternberg. Bi-weekly. Jewish War Veterans of the U.S.A.

NATIONAL JEWISH MONTHLY (1886 under the name Menorah). 1640 Rhode Island Ave., N.W., Washington, 20036. (202)857-6645. Charles Fenyvesi. Monthly. B'nai B'rith.

NEAR EAST REPORT (1957). 444 North Capitol St., N.W., Washington, 20001. (202)-638-1225. Alan M. Tigay. Weekly. Near East Research, Inc.

FLORIDA

JEWISH FLORIDIAN (1927). P.O. Box 012973, Miami, 33137. (305)373-4605. Fred K. Shochet. Weekly.

SOUTHERN JEWISH WEEKLY (1924). P.O. Box 3297, Jacksonville, 32206. (904)355-3459. Isadore Moscovitz. Weekly.

GEORGIA

SOUTHERN ISRAELITE (1925). P.O. Box 77388, 188–15 St. N.W., Atlanta, 30357. (404)876-8248. Vida Goldgar. Weekly.

ILLINOIS

CHICAGO JEWISH POST AND OPINION (1953). 6350 N. Albany, Chicago, 60659. Weekly.

JEWISH COMMUNITY NEWS (1945). 6464 West Main, Suite 7A, Belleville, 62223. (618)398-6100. Joshua Samborn. Monthly. Jewish Federation of Southern Illinois.

SENTINEL (1911). 323 S. Franklin St., Chicago, 60606. 663-1101. J. I. Fishbein. Weekly.

INDIANA

INDIANA JEWISH POST AND OPINION (1935). 611 N. Park Ave., Indianapolis, 46204. (317)634-1307. Jo Ann Pinkowitz. Weekly.

JEWISH POST AND OPINION. 611 N. Park Ave., Indianapolis, 46204. (317)634-1307. Gabriel Cohen.

KENTUCKY

KENTUCKY JEWISH POST AND OPINION (1931). 1551 Bardstown Rd., Louisville, 40205. (502)459-1914. Matthew J. Hott. Weekly.

LOUISIANA

THE JEWISH CIVIC PRESS (1965). P.O. Box 15500, New Orleans, 70175. Abner Tritt. Monthly.

JEWISH TIMES (1974). 211 Camp St., Suite 500, New Orleans, 70130. (504)524-3147. Mollie Braverman. Biweekly.

MARYLAND

BALTIMORE JEWISH TIMES (1919). 2104 N. Charles St., Baltimore, 21093. (301)752-3504. Gary Rosenblatt. Weekly.

JEWISH WEEK (1965). 8630 Fenton St., Suite 611, Silver Spring, 20910. (301)565-9336. Joseph M. Hochstein. Weekly.

MASSACHUSETTS

AMERICAN JEWISH HISTORY (1893). 2 Thornton Road, Waltham, 02154. (617)-891-8110. Nathan M. Kaganoff. Quarterly. American Jewish Historical Society.

JEWISH ADVOCATE (1902). 251 Causeway St., Boston, 02114. (617)227-5130. Joseph G. Weisberg, Alexander Brin. Weekly.

JEWISH CHRONICLE (1976). 340 Main St., Suite 551, Worcester, 01608. (617)752-2512. Regina Arsenault. Monthly.

JEWISH CIVIC LEADER (1926). 11 Harvard St., Worcester, 01609. (617)791-0953. Phyllis Goldstein. Weekly.

JEWISH REPORTER (1970). 1000 Worcester Road, Framingham, 01701. (617)879-3300. Deanne Stone, Jehudah H. Leftin. Monthly. Greater Framingham Jewish Federation.

JEWISH TIMES (1945). 118 Cypress St., Brookline, 02146. (617)566-7710. Ann Kostant. Weekly.

JEWISH WEEKLY NEWS (1945). P.O. Box 1569, Springfield, 01101. (413)739-4771. Leslie B. Kahn. Weekly.

THE JOURNAL. 140 Washington St., Salem, 01970. (617)744-5675. Ellen Bob. Bi-weekly.

MOMENT (1975). 462 Boylston St., Boston, 02116. (617)536-6252. Leonard Fein. Monthly except Jan.-Feb., July-August.

MICHIGAN

JEWISH NEWS (1942). 17515 W. 9 Mile Rd., Suite 865, Southfield, 48075. (313)424-8833. Philip Slomovitz. Weekly.

MICHIGAN JEWISH HISTORY (1960). 163 Madison, Detroit, 48237. (313)548-9176. Phillip Applebaum. Semi-annual. Jewish Historical Society of Michigan.

MINNESOTA

AMERICAN JEWISH WORLD (1912). 9 N. 4th St., Minneapolis, 55401. (612)332-6318. Norman Gold. Weekly.

MISSOURI

KANSAS CITY JEWISH CHRONICLE (1920). P.O. Box 8709, Kansas City, 64114. (816)-648-4620. Milton Firestone. Weekly.

MISSOURI JEWISH POST AND OPINION (1948). 8235 Olive St., St. Louis, 63132. (314)993-2842. Kathie Sutin. Weekly.

ST. LOUIS JEWISH LIGHT (1947). 611 Olive St., Room 1541, St. Louis, 63101. (314)-241-4943. Robert A. Cohn. Biweekly. Jewish Federation of St. Louis.

NEBRASKA

JEWISH PRESS (1921). 333 S. 132 St., Omaha, 68154. (402)334-8200. Morris Maline. Weekly. Jewish Federation of Omaha.

NEVADA

JEWISH REPORTER (1976). 1030 E. Twain Ave., Las Vegas, 89109. (702)732-0556. Jerry Countess. Monthly. Las Vegas Combined Jewish Appeal.

LAS VEGAS ISRAELITE (1965). P.O. Box 14096, Las Vegas, 89114. Jack Tell. Weekly.

NEW JERSEY

JEWISH COMMUNITY NEWS (1963). Green Lane, Union, 07083. (201)351-5060. Fran Gold. Daily. Jewish Federation of Central N.J.

JEWISH COMMUNITY VOICE (1941). 2393 W. Marlton Pike, Cherry Hill, 08002. (609)-665-6100. Alex B. Einbinder. Biweekly. Jewish Federation of Southern N.J.

JEWISH JOURNAL (1956). 2 S. Adelaide Ave., Highland Park, 08904. Clifford B. Ross. Biweekly. Jewish Federation of Raritan Valley.

JEWISH NEWS (1947). 60 Glenwood Ave., East Orange, 07017. (201)678-4955. Harry Weingast. Weekly. Jewish Community Federation of Metropolitan New Jersey.

JEWISH RECORD (1939). 1537 Atlantic Ave., Atlantic City, 08401. (609)344-5119. Martin Korik. Weekly.

JEWISH STANDARD (1931). 40 Journal Sq., Jersey City, 07306. (201)653-6330. Morris J. Janoff. Weekly.

JEWISH VOICE (1975). Lord St., Avenel, 07001. (201)636-8660. Herbert Rosen. Biweekly. Northern Middlesex County Jewish Federation.

MORRIS/SUSSEX JEWISH NEWS (1972). 500 Route 10, Ledgewood, 07852, (201)584-1850. Rhoda Hasson. Monthly. United Jewish Federation of Morris/Sussex.

NEW YORK

ALBANY JEWISH WORLD (1965). 416 Smith St., Schenectady, 12305. (518)370-5483. Sam S. Clevenson. Weekly.

BUFFALO JEWISH REVIEW (1918). 15 E. Mohawk St., Buffalo, 14203. (716)854-2192. Steve Lipman. Weekly. Kahaal Nahalot Israel.

JEWISH AMERICAN RECORD (1973). P.O. Box 1100, 275 Cadman Plaza East, Brooklyn, 11202. (212)646-5184. Alex Novitsky. Monthly.

JEWISH CURRENT EVENTS (1959). 430 Keller Ave., Elmont, L.I., 11003. Samuel Deutsch. Biweekly.

JEWISH LEDGER (1924). 721 Monroe Ave., Rochester, 14607. (716)275-9090. Donald Wolin. Weekly.

JEWISH WORLD OF LONG ISLAND (1971). 1029 Brighton Beach Ave., Brooklyn, 11235. (212)769-2000. Jerome W. Lippman. Biweekly.

MODERN JEWISH STUDIES ANNUAL (1977). Acad. 1309, Queens College, 65-30 Kissena Blvd., Flushing, 11367. (212)520-7067. Joseph C. Landis, Daniel Walden. Annual. English-Yiddish.

REPORTER. 500 Clubhouse Rd., Binghamton, 13903. (607)724-2360. Shelley Prober. Weekly. Jewish Federation of Broome County.

SH'MA (1970). Box 567, Port Washington, N.Y., 11050. (516)944-9791. Eugene B. Borowitz. Biweekly (except June, July, Aug.).

YUGNTRUF (1964). 3328 Bainbridge Ave., Bx., 10467. (212)654-8540. Gitl Schaechter. Quarterly. Yiddish. Yugntruf Youth for Yiddish.

NEW YORK CITY

AFN SHVEL (1941). 200 W. 72 St., 10023. (212)787-6675. Editorial board. Quarterly. Yiddish. Freeland League.

ALGEMEINER JOURNAL (1972). 404 Park Ave., So., 10016. (212)689-3390. Gershon Jacobson. Weekly. Yiddish.

AMERICAN JEWISH YEAR BOOK (1899). 165 E. 56 St., 10022. (212)751-4000. Morris Fine, Milton Himmelfarb. Annual. American Jewish Committee and Jewish Publication Society.

AMERICAN MIZRACHI WOMAN (1925). 817 Broadway, 10003. (212)477-4720. Agatha Leifer. Irregular. American Mizrachi Women.

AMERICAN ZIONIST (1910). 4 E. 34 St., 10016. (212)481-1481. Elias Cooper. Bimonthly. Zionist Organization of America.

AUFBAU (1934). 2121 Broadway, 10023. (212)873-7400. Hans Steinitz. Weekly. English-German. New World Club, Inc.

BITZARON (1939). P.O. Box 798, Cooper Station, 10003. (212)598-3209. Hayim Leaf. Bimonthly. Hebrew. Hebrew Literature Foundation.

B'NAI YIDDISH (1968). 41 Union Sq., 10003. (212)989-3162. Itzik Kozlovsky. Bimonthly. English-Yiddish.

THE CALL (1932). 45 E. 33 St., 10016. (212)-889-6800. William Stern. Quarterly. Workmen's Circle.

COMMENTARY (1945). 165 E. 56 St., 10022. Norman Podhoretz. Monthly. American Jewish Committee.

CONGRESS MONTHLY (1934). 15 E. 84 St., 10028. Herbert Poster. Monthly (except July and August). American Jewish Congress.

CONSERVATIVE JUDAISM (1945). 3080 Broadway, 10027. Malka Rabinowitz. Quarterly. Rabbinical Assembly and Jewish Theological Seminary of America.

ECONOMIC HORIZONS (1953). 500 Fifth Ave., 10036. (212)354-6510. Phil Opher. Quarterly. American-Israel Chamber of Commerce and Industry, Inc.

HADAROM (1957). 1250 Broadway, 10001. Charles B. Chavel. Semiannual. Hebrew. Rabbinical Council of America, Inc.

HADASSAH MAGAZINE (formerly HADASSAH NEWSLETTER; 1921). (212)355-7900. 50 W. 58 St., 10019. Jesse Zel Lurie. Monthly (except for combined issues of June-July and Aug.-Sept.). Hadassah, Women's Zionist Organization of America.

HADOAR (1921). 1841 Broadway, 10023. (212)581-5151. Itzhak Ivry. Weekly. Hebrew. Histadruth Ivrith of America.

IMPACT (1942 under the name of SYNAGOGUE SCHOOL). 155 Fifth Ave., 10010. Morton Siegel. Quarterly. English-

Hebrew. United Synagogue Commission on Jewish Education.

U INSTITUTIONAL AND INDUSTRIAL KO-SHER PRODUCTS DIRECTORY (1967). 116 E. 27 St., 10016. (212)725-3415. Yaakov Lipschutz. Irregular. Union of Orthodox Jewish Congregations of America.

ISRAEL HORIZONS (1952). 150 Fifth Ave., 10011. (212)679-9498. Richard Yaffe. Monthly (except July-August). Americans for Progressive Israel.

ISRAEL QUALITY (1976). 500 Fifth Ave., 10036. (212)354-6510. Irene Ribner. Quarterly. American-Israel Chamber of Commerce and Government of Israel Trade Center.

JEWISH ACTION (1950). 116 East 27 St., 10016. (212)725-3400. Yaakov Kornreich. Bimonthly. Union of Orthodox Jewish Congregations of America.

JEWISH BOOK ANNUAL (1942). 15 East 26th St., 10010. Jacob Kabakoff. Annual. English-Hebrew-Yiddish. JWB Jewish Book Council.

JEWISH BOOKS IN REVIEW (1945). 15 E. 26 St., 10010. Bimonthly. JWB Jewish Book Council.

JEWISH BRAILLE REVIEW (1931). 110 E. 30 St., 10016. (212)889-2525. Jacob Freid. Monthly. English-Braille. Jewish Braille Institute of America, Inc.

JEWISH CURRENTS (1946). 22 E. 17 St., Suite 601, 10003. (212)924-5740. Morris U. Schappes. Monthly.

JEWISH DAILY FORWARD (1897). 45 E. 33 St., 10016. (212)889-8200. Simon Weber. Daily. Yiddish. Forward Association, Inc.

JEWISH EDUCATION (1928). 114 Fifth Ave., 10011. (212)675-5656. Alvin I. Schiff. Quarterly. National Council for Jewish Education.

JEWISH EDUCATION DIRECTORY (1951). 114 Fifth Ave., 10011. (212)675-5656. Triannual. American Association for Jewish Education.

JEWISH EDUCATION NEWS (1939), 114 Fifth Ave., 10011. (212)675-5656. Gary Gobetz. Irregular. American Assn. for Jewish Education.

JEWISH FRONTIER (1934). 575 6th Ave., 10011. (212)989-0300. Mitchell Cohen. Monthly. Labor Zionist Letters, Inc.

JEWISH GUARDIAN (1974). G.P.O. Box 2143, Brooklyn, 11202. (212)384-4541. Pinchus David. Quarterly. Neturei Karta of U.S.A.

JEWISH JOURNAL (1970). 16 Court St., Brooklyn, 11241. (212)624-7991. Sylvia Adelman. Weekly.

JEWISH LIFE (1946). 116 E. 27 St., 10016. (212)725-3400. Yaakov Jacobs. Quarterly. Union of Orthodox Jewish Congregations of America.

JEWISH MUSIC NOTES (1945). 15 E. 26 St., 10010. Irene Heskes. Semiannual. JWB Jewish Music Council.

JEWISH OBSERVER (1963). 5 Beekman St., 10038. Nisson Wolpin. (212)964-1620. Monthly (except July and August). Agudath Israel of America.

JEWISH POST OF NEW YORK (1974). 101 Fifth Ave., 10003. Charles Roth. Weekly.

JEWISH PRESS (1950). 338 3rd Ave., Brooklyn, 11215. Sholom Klass. Weekly.

JEWISH SOCIAL STUDIES (1939). 250 W. 57 St., 10019. Tobey B. Gitelle. Quarterly. Conference on Jewish Social Studies, Inc.

JEWISH TELEGRAPHIC AGENCY COMMUNITY NEWS REPORTER (1962). 165 W. 46 St., Rm. 511, 10036. (212)575-9370. Murray Zuckoff. Weekly.

JEWISH TELEGRAPHIC AGENCY DAILY NEWS BULLETIN (1917). 165 W. 46 St., Rm. 511, 10036. (212)575-9370. Murray Zuckoff. Daily.

JEWISH TELEGRAPHIC AGENCY WEEKLY NEWS DIGEST (1933). 165 W. 46 St., Rm. 511, 10036. (212)575-9370. Murray Zuckoff. Weekly.

JEWISH WEEK (1876, reorg. 1970). 1 Park Ave., 10016. (212)686-2320. Philip Hochstein. Weekly.

JWB CIRCLE (1946). 15 E. 26 St., 10010. (212)532-4949. Lionel Koppman. Bimonthly. JWB.

JOURNAL OF JEWISH COMMUNAL SERVICE (1899). 15 E. 26 St., 10010. (212)683-8056.

Sanford N. Sherman. Quarterly. The Conference of Jewish Communal Service.

JOURNAL OF REFORM JUDAISM. 790 Madison Ave., 10021. (212)734-7166. Bernard Martin. Quarterly. Central Conference of American Rabbis.

JUDAISM (1952). 15 E. 84 St., 10028. (212)-879-4500. Robert Gordis. Quarterly. American Jewish Congress, World Jewish Congress.

KINDER JOURNAL (1920). 3301 Bainbridge Ave., Bronx, N.Y., 10467. (212)881-3588. Bella Gottesman. Quarterly. Yiddish. Sholem Aleichem Folk Institute, Inc.

KINDER ZEITUNG (1930). 45 E. 33 St., 10016. (212)889-6800. Joseph Mlotek, Jack Noskowitz. Saul Maltz, Mates Olitzky. Bimonthly. English-Yiddish. Workmen's Circle.

KOL YAVNEH (1960). 25 W. 26 St., 10010. (212)679-4574. Roslyn M. Sherman. Bimonthly. Yavneh, National Religious Jewish Students Association.

U KOSHER PRODUCTS DIRECTORY (1925). 116 E. 27 St., 10016. (212)725-3415. Yaakov Lipschutz. Irregular. Union of Orthodox Jewish Congregations of America—Kashruth Div.

KULTUR UN LEBN—CULTURE AND LIFE (1967). 45 E. 33 St., 10016. Joseph Mlotek. Quarterly. Yiddish. Workmen's Circle.

LILITH–THE JEWISH FEMINIST MAGAZINE (1976). 250 W. 57 St., 10019. (212)757-0818. Susan Weidman Schneider. Quarterly.

LONG ISLAND JEWISH PRESS (1942). 95-20 63 Rd., Rego Park, 11374. Abraham B. Shoulson. Monthly.

MIDSTREAM (1955). 515 Park Ave., 10022. Joel Carmichael. (212)752-0600. Monthly (bi-monthly June–Sept.). Theodor Herzl Foundation.

MORNING FREIHEIT (1922). 22 W. 21 St., 10010. (212)255-7661. Paul Novick. Three times a week. Yiddish-English.

U NEWS REPORTER (1956). 116 E. 27 St., 10016. (212)725-3415. Yaakov Lipschutz.

Irregular. Union of Orthodox Jewish Congregations of America—Kashruth Div.

OLOMEINU—OUR WORLD (1945). 229 Park Ave. S., 10003. (212)674-6700. Nosson Scherman, Yaakov Fruchter. Monthly. English-Hebrew. Torah Umesorah National Society for Hebrew Day Schools.

U PASSOVER PRODUCTS DIRECTORY (1923). 116 E. 27 St., 10016. (212)725-3415. Yaakov Lipschutz. Annual. Union of Orthodox Jewish Congregations of America—Kashruth Div.

PEDAGOGIC REPORTER (1949). 114 Fifth Ave., 10011. (212)675-5656. Mordecai H. Lewittes. Three times yearly. American Association for Jewish Education.

PIONEER WOMAN (1926). 315 Fifth Ave., 10016. (212)725-8010. David C. Gross, Judith A. Sokoloff. Bimonthly. English-Yiddish-Hebrew. Pioneer Women, Women's Labor Zionist Organization of America.

PRESENT TENSE (1973). 165 E. 56 St., 10022. (212)751-4000. Murray Polner. Quarterly. American Jewish Committee.

PROCEEDINGS OF THE AMERICAN ACADEMY FOR JEWISH RESEARCH (1920). 3080 Broadway, 10027. Isaac E. Barzilay. Annual. Hebrew, Arabic and English. American Academy for Jewish Research.

RABBINICAL COUNCIL RECORD (1953). 1250 Broadway, 10001. Louis Bernstein. Quarterly. Rabbinical Council of America.

RECONSTRUCTIONIST (1935). 432 Park Ave. South, 10016. (212)889-9080. Ira Eisenstein. Monthly (Sept.–June). Jewish Reconstructionist Foundation, Inc.

REFORM JUDAISM (1972; formerly Dimensions in American Judaism). 838 Fifth Ave., 10021. (212)249-0100. Aron Hirt-Manheimer. Monthly (Sept.-May, except Dec.). Union of American Hebrew Congregations.

RESPONSE (1967). 523 W. 113 St., 10025. (212)850-4902. Steven M. Cohen. Quarterly. Jewish Educational Ventures, Inc.

SEVEN ARTS FEATURE SYNDICATE. See *News Syndicates.* p. (360).

SHEVILEY HAHINUCH (1939). 114 Fifth Ave., 10011. (212)675-5656. Matthew Mosinkis. Quarterly. Hebrew. National Council for Jewish Education.

SHMUESSEN MIT KINDER UN YUGENT (1942). 770 Eastern Parkway, Brooklyn, 11213. (212)493-9250. Nissan Mindel. Monthly. Yiddish. Merkos L'Inyonei Chinuch, Inc.

SHOAH (1978). 250 W. 57 St., 10019. (212)-582-6116. Jane Gerber. Quarterly. National Jewish Conference Center.

SYNAGOGUE LIGHT (1933). 47 Beekman St., 10038. (212)227-7800. Meyer Hager. Bimonthly. Union of Chassidic Rabbis.

TALKS AND TALES (1942). 770 Eastern Parkway, Brooklyn, 11213. (212)493-9250. Nissan Mindel. Monthly (also Hebrew, French and Spanish editions). Merkos L'Inyonei Chinuch, Inc.

TRADITION (1958). 1250 Broadway, Suite 802, 10001. Walter S. Wurzburger. Quarterly. Rabbinical Council of America.

UNITED SYNAGOGUE REVIEW (1943). 155 Fifth Ave., 10010. (212)533-7800. Marvin S. Wiener. Quarterly. United Synagogue of America.

UNSER TSAIT (1941). 25 E. 78 St., 10021. (212)535-0850. Jacob S. Hertz. Monthly. Yiddish. World Jewish Labor Bund.

DER WECKER (1921). 45 E. 33 St., 10016. (212)686-1536. Elias Schulman. Bimonthly. Yiddish. Jewish Socialist Verband of America.

WESTCHESTER JEWISH TRIBUNE (1942). 95-20 63 Rd., Rego Park, 11374. Abraham B. Shoulson. Monthly.

WOMEN'S AMERICAN ORT REPORTER (1966). 1250 Broadway, 10001. (212)594-8500. Elie Faust-Lévy. Bimonthly. Women's American ORT.

WOMEN'S LEAGUE OUTLOOK (1930). 48 E. 74 St., 10021. (212)628-1600. Mrs. Harry I. Kiesler. Quarterly. Women's League for Conservative Judaism.

WORLD OVER (1940). 426 W. 58 St., 10019. (212)245-8200. Stephen Schaffzin, Linda K. Schaffzin. Bi-monthly. Board of Jewish Education, Inc.

YAVNEH REVIEW (1963). 25 W. 26 St., 10010. (212)679-4574. Shalom Carmy. Annual. Yavneh, National Religious Jewish Students Association.

YEARBOOK OF THE CENTRAL CONFERENCE OF AMERICAN RABBIS (1890). 790 Madison Ave., 10021. (212)734-7166. Elliot L. Stevens. Annual. Central Conference of American Rabbis.

YIDDISH (1973). Queens College, Acad. 1309, 65-30 Kissena Blvd., Flushing, N.Y., 11367. (212)520-7067. Joseph C. Landis. Quarterly. Queens College Press.

DI YIDDISHE HEIM (1958). 770 Eastern Parkway, Bklyn., 11213. (212)493-9250. Rachel Altein, Tema Gurary. Quarterly. English-Yiddish. Agudas Nshei Ub'nos Chabad.

YIDDISHE KULTUR (1938). 853 Broadway. 10003. (212)228-1955. Itche Goldberg. Monthly (except June-July, Aug.-Sept.). Yiddish. Yiddisher Kultur Farband, Inc. —YKUF.

YIDISHE SHPRAKH (1941). 1048 Fifth Ave., 10028. (212)231-7905. Mordkhe Schaechter. Three times a year. Yiddish. Yivo Institute for Jewish Research, Inc.

DOS YIDDISHE VORT (1953). 5 Beekman St., 10038. (212)964-1620. Joseph Friedenson. Monthly. Yiddish. Agudath Israel of America.

YIDDISHER KEMFER (1906). 575 Sixth Ave., 10011. (212)741-2404. Mordechai Strigler. Weekly. Yiddish. Labor Zionist Letters, Inc.

YIVO ANNUAL OF JEWISH SOCIAL SCIENCE (1946). 1048 Fifth Ave., 10028. (212)535-6700. David Roskies. Biannually. Yivo Institute for Jewish Research, Inc.

YIVO BLETER (1931). 1048 Fifth Ave., 10027. (212)535-6700. Editorial board. Irregular. Yiddish. Yivo Institute for Jewish Research, Inc.

YOUNG ISRAEL VIEWPOINT (1952). 3 W. 16 St., 10011. C.H. Rosen. Monthly (except July, August). National Council of Young Israel.

YOUNG JUDAEAN (1912). 817 Broadway, 10003. (212)260-4700. Barbara Gingold.

Monthly (Nov.-June). Hadassah Zionist Youth Commission.

YOUTH AND NATION (1934). 150 Fifth Ave., 10011. (212)929-4955. Reuven Belfort. Quarterly. Hashomer Hatzair Zionist Youth Movement.

ZUKUNFT (1892). 25 E. 78 St., 10021. Hyman Bass, Moshe Crystal, I. Hirshaut. Monthly (bimonthly May–Aug.). Yiddish. Congress for Jewish Culture and CYCO.

NORTH CAROLINA

AMERICAN JEWISH TIMES—OUTLOOK (1934; reorg. 1950). P.O. Box 33218, Charlotte, 28233. (704)372-3296. Ronald Unger. Monthly.

OHIO

THE AMERICAN ISRAELITE (1954). 906 Main St., Cincinnati, 45202. (513)621-3145. Henry C. Segal. Weekly.

AMERICAN JEWISH ARCHIVES (1947). 3101 Clifton Ave., Cincinnati, 45220. (513)221-1875. Jacob R. Marcus, Abraham J. Peck. Semiannually. American Jewish Archives of Hebrew Union College-Jewish Institute of Religion.

CLEVELAND JEWISH NEWS (1964). 13910 Cedar Road., Cleveland, 44118. (216)371-0800. Jerry D. Barach. Weekly.

DAYTON JEWISH CHRONICLE (1961). 118 Salem Ave., Dayton, 45406. 222-0783. Anne M. Hammerman. Weekly.

INDEX TO JEWISH PERIODICALS (1963). P.O. Box 18570, Cleveland Hts., 44118. (216)321-7296. Jean H. Foxman, Miriam Leikind, Bess Rosenfeld. Semiannually.

OHIO JEWISH CHRONICLE (1921). 2831 E. Main St., Columbus, 43209. Milton J. Pinsky. Weekly.

STARK JEWISH NEWS (1920). P.O. Box 9112, Canton, 44711. (216)494-7792. David F. Leopold. Elaine M. Garfinkle. Monthly.

STUDIES IN BIBLIOGRAPHY AND BOOKLORE (1953). 3101 Clifton Ave., Cincinnati, 45220. (513)221-1875. Herbert C. Zafren. Irregular. English-Hebrew-German. Library of Hebrew Union College—Jewish Institute of Religion.

TOLEDO JEWISH NEWS (1951). 2506 Evergreen St., Toledo, 43606. Burt Silverman. Monthly. Jewish Welfare Federation.

YOUNGSTOWN JEWISH TIMES (1935). P.O. Box 777, Youngstown, 44501. (216)746-6192. Harry Alter. Fortnightly.

OKLAHOMA

SOUTHWEST JEWISH CHRONICLE (1929). 324 N. Robinson St., Rm. 313, Oklahoma City, 73102. (405)236-4226. E. F. Friedman. Quarterly.

*TULSA JEWISH REVIEW (1930). 2205 E. 51 St., Tulsa, 74105. Ann R. Fellows. Monthly. Tulsa Section, National Council of Jewish Women.

PENNSYLVANIA

JEWISH CHRONICLE (1962). 315 S. Bellefield Ave., Pittsburgh, 15213. (412)687-1000. Albert W. Bloom. Weekly. Pittsburgh Jewish Publication and Education Foundation.

JEWISH EXPONENT (1887). 226 S. 16 St., Philadelphia, 19102. (215)893-5700. Frank F. Wundohl. Weekly. Federation of Jewish Agencies of Greater Philadelphia.

JEWISH QUARTERLY REVIEW (1910). Broad and York Sts., Philadelphia, 19132. (215)-229-0110. Abraham I. Katsh. Quarterly. Dropsie University.

*JEWISH TIMES OF THE GREATER NORTHEAST. (1925). 2417 Welsh Road, Philadelphia, 19114. (215)464-3900. Leon E. Brown. Weekly.

RHODE ISLAND

RHODE ISLAND JEWISH HISTORICAL NOTES (1954). 130 Sessions St., Providence, 02906. Albert Salzberg. Annual. Rhode Island Jewish Historical Assn.

TENNESSEE

HEBREW WATCHMAN (1925). 227 Jefferson Ave., Memphis, 38103. (901)526-2215. Herman I. Goldberger. Weekly.

OBSERVER (1934). P.O. Box 15431, Nashville, 37215. (615)292-9861. Jana Bart.

TEXAS

JEWISH CIVIC PRESS (1971). P.O. Box 35656, Houston, 77035. Abner Tritt. Monthly.

360 / AMERICAN JEWISH YEAR BOOK, 1980

JEWISH HERALD-VOICE (1908). P.O. Box 153, Houston, 77001. (713)661-3116. Joseph W. Samuels. Weekly.

TEXAS JEWISH POST (1947). P.O. Box 742, Fort Worth, 76101. 11333 N. Central Expressway, Dallas, 75243. (214)692-7283. Jimmy Wisch. Weekly.

VIRGINIA

UJF NEWS (1946). P.O. Box 9776, Norfolk, 23505. (804)489-8040. Reba Karp. Weekly. United Jewish Federation of Norfolk and Virginia Beach.

WASHINGTON

JEWISH TRANSCRIPT (1924). Securities Building, Rm. 929, Seattle, 98101. (206)-624-0136. Philip R. Scheier. Bimonthly. Jewish Federation of Greater Seattle.

WISCONSIN

WISCONSIN JEWISH CHRONICLE (1921). 1360 N. Prospect Ave., Milwaukee, 53202. (414)271-2992. Lawrence Hankin. Weekly.-Wisc. Jewish Publications Foundation.

NEWS SYNDICATES

JEWISH PRESS FEATURES (1970). 15 E. 26 St., Suite 1350, N.Y.C. 10010. (212)679-1411. Susan Grossman. Monthly. Jewish Student Press Service.

JEWISH TELEGRAPHIC AGENCY, INC. (1917). 165 W. 46 St., Rm. 511, N.Y.C., 10036. (212)575-9370. Murray Zuckoff. Daily.

SEVEN ARTS FEATURE SYNDICATE AND WORLD WIDE NEWS SERVICE (1923). 165 W. 46 St., Rm. 511, N.Y.C., 10036. (212)-247-3595. John Kayston. Semi-weekly.

CANADA

BULLETIN DU CERCLE JUIF DE LANGUE FRANÇAISE DU CONGRES JUIF CANADIEN (1952). 1590 Avenue Docteur Penfield, Montreal, P.Q., H3G 1C5. (514)931-7531. M. Charles Dadoun. Bimonthly. French. Canadian Jewish Congress.

CANADIAN JEWISH HERALD (1977). 17 Anselme Lavigne Blvd., Dollard des Ormeaux, P.Q., H9A 1N3. (514)684-7667. Dan Nimrod. Quarterly.

CANADIAN JEWISH NEWS (1960). 562 Eglinton Ave. E., Ste. 401, Toronto, Ont., M4P 1P1. 481-6434. Ralph Hyman. Weekly.

CANADIAN JEWISH OUTLOOK (1963). P.O. Box 65, Station B, Toronto, Ont., M5T 2T2. 364-3711. Editorial Board. Monthly.

CANADIAN JEWISH WEEKLY (VOCHENBLATT; formerly DER KAMPF, reorg. 1941). 430 King St. W., #209, Toronto, Ont., MV5 IL5. (416)364-3711. Joshua Gershman. Biweekly. Yiddish.

CANADIAN ZIONIST (1934). 1310 Greene Ave., Montreal, P.Q., H3Z 2B2. (514)934-0804. Dr. Leon Kronitz. Bi-monthly (except July–Aug.). Canadian Zionist Federation.

CHRONICLE REVIEW (1914). 4781 Van Horne, Montreal, P.Q., H3W 1J1. Arnold Ages. Monthly.

JEWISH POST (1925). P.O. Box 3777, St. B, Winnipeg, Man., R2W 3R6. (204)633-5575. Martin Levin. Weekly.

JEWISH STANDARD (1929). Suite 507, 8 Colborne St., Toronto, Ont. M5E 1E1. (416)-363-3289. Julius Hayman. Semi-monthly.

JEWISH WESTERN BULLETIN (1930). 3268 Heather St., Vancouver, B.C. V5Z 3K5. Samuel Kaplan. Weekly.

KANADER ADLER-JEWISH EAGLE (1907); 4180 De Courtrai, Suite 218, Montreal, P.Q., H3S 1C3. (514)735-6577. Mordco Husid. Weekly. Yiddish. Combined Jewish Organizations of Montreal.

OTTAWA JEWISH BULLETIN & REVIEW (1946). 151 Chapel St., Ottawa, Ont., K1N 7Y2. 232-7306. Nancy Zalman. Biweekly. Jewish Community Council of Ottawa.

UNDZER VEG (1925). 272 Codsell Ave., Downsview, Ont., M3H 3R2. 636-4021. Joseph Kligman. Quarterly. Yiddish-English. Achdut HaAvoda-Poale Zion of Canada.

VIEWPOINTS (1966). 1590 Ave. Docteur Penfield, Montreal, P.Q., H3G 1C5. (514)931-7531. Borys Wajsman. Quarterly. Canadian Jewish Congress.

WESTERN JEWISH NEWS (1925). P.O. Box 87, 400–259 Portage Ave., Winnipeg, Man., R3C 2G6. 942-6361. Pauline Essers. Weekly.

WINDSOR JEWISH COMMUNITY COUNCIL BULLETIN (1938). 1641 Ouellette Ave., Windsor, Ont., N8X 1K9. (519)254-7558. Joseph Eisenberg. Monthly. Windsor Jewish Community Council.

Necrology: United States[1]

ALCALAY, ISSAC A., rabbi, communal leader; b. Sofia, Bulgaria, (?), 1882; d. Brooklyn, N.Y., Dec. 29, 1978; in U.S. since 1942; chief rabbi of Serbia, 1909; rep. of Serbian government, 1915–18; founder, first pres. Rabbinical Fed. of Yugoslavia, 1923; founder, rabbinical school, Belgrade; chief rabbi of Yugoslavia, 1924; planned and attended first Sephardic Congress, Vienna, 1925; first Jewish senator, Yugoslav Parliament, 1930–38; v. pres. World Sephardic Fed.; chief rabbi, Central Sephardic Jewish Community of America, 1943–68; bd. mem. Amer. Jewish Joint Distribution Comm.; chief rabbi, Assn. of Yugoslav Jews in the U.S.; author of a study on travels of Jews through the Balkans at the end of the 18th and beginning of the 19th centuries (1928).

ALLIGER, JOSEPH K., business exec., communal leader; b. Ukraine, Russia, Feb. 22, 1896; d. Miami, Fla., June 15, 1978; in U.S. since 1898; founder, bd. chmn. Sterling Investing Corp.; past pres. Long Island Region, Zionist Org. of America; mem.bd. dirs.: Hebrew Immigrant Aid Soc.; Jewish Natl. Fund; Zionist Org. of America; Jewish Info. Bureau; Natl. Conf. Christians and Jews; chmn.: Great Neck, N.Y. UJA; State of Israel Bonds; was instrumental in getting thousands of Jews out of Germany in the pre-Nazi and early Nazi eras; awarded personal citations by Levi Eshkol for work done for Israel and by Eleanor Roosevelt for humanitarian work.

BELDOCH, ALBERT I., manufacturer, philanthropist; b. Brooklyn, N.Y., Apr. 15, 1901; d. Great Neck, N.Y., Nov. 6, 1978; founder, bd. chmn. Beldoch Industries; commissioner, Hewlitt Bay Fire Dept., 1945–63; active in: United Cerebral Palsy, 1958–78; Boy Scouts of America; Police Boys Club; dir. New Nautilus Hotel; founder, dir. Natl. Knitted Outerwear Assn.; a founder, chmn., hon. chmn. Knitgoods and Yarn Div., ADL; United Hebrew Community: mem. since 1933; v. pres.; chmn. exec. bd.; pres. 1958–78; mem. Fed. of Jewish Philanthropies; chmn. UJA; chmn. ADL, 1963–78; honored by: Cerebral Palsy, 1974; ADL, 1976; UJA-Fed. of Jewish Philanthropies, 1977.

BELFER, MAURICE, business exec., philanthropist; b. (?); d. (?), March (?), 1978; bd. mem. Knickerbocker Feather Co.; master builder, science fellow, Yeshiva U.; benefactor: Hebrew U.; Yeshiva Dov Revel; Queens Jewish Center; ADL; active: UJA-Fed. of Jewish Philanthropies; Greater N.Y. Comm. for State of Israel Bonds.

BRESLAU, ISADORE, rabbi, communal leader; b. Kabilnik, Russia, Jan. 19, 1897; d. Washington, D.C., Nov. 18, 1978; in U.S. since 1906; founded Mill End Shops; U.S. Navy, WWI; U.S. Army chaplain, WWII; Zionist Org. of America: past natl. sec.; natl. exec. v. pres.; co-founder, past pres. Louis D. Brandeis District; delegate to World Zionist Cong., 1939; a founder,

---

[1]Including Jewish residents of the United States who died between January 1 and December 31, 1978.

NECROLOGY / 363

Jewish Community Council of Greater Washington; Washington UJA: founder, gen. chmn., pres.; gen. chmn. State of Israel Bonds; co-founder, Natl. UJA; natl. pres. Amer. Assn. for Jewish Ed.; benefactor, Weizmann Inst.; honored by: Jewish Natl. Fund; UJA; Histadrut; Technion Inst.

BUCHOLTZ, SAMUEL H., psychologist, communal worker; b. N.Y.C., (?), 1909; d. Los Angeles, Ca., May (?), 1978; exec. dir. Temple Israel, L.A., 1952–68; social worker, Jewish Bd. of Guardians; chmn. L.A. chapter, Amer. Jewish Com.

CAPLAN, LOUIS, attorney, philanthropist, communal leader; b. Oil City, Pa., Sept. 15, 1886; d. Pittsburgh, Pa., Dec. 17, 1978; private law practice since 1912; first lieutenant, U.S. Army, 1918–19; mem. firm Sachs & Caplan, 1919–45; sr. counsel, Thorp, Reed, & Armstrong; mem. bd. dirs.: May, Stern, & Co.; Keystone Bank; Webster Hall Hotel Corp.; Alien Enemy Hearing Officer, WW II; mem. Amer. and Pa. Bar Assns.; pres. Allegheny County Bar Assn.; dir. Action Housing, Pittsburgh, since 1957; mem.: Amer. Law Inst.; Judicial Conf., U.S. Third Judicial Circuit; trustee: Maurice & Laura Falk Found.; Leon Falk Family Trust; Lehman-Epstine Trust; Halpern Found.; Rodef Shalom Congregation, Pittsburgh; mem. bd. govs. Hebrew Union Coll.-Jewish Inst. of Religion, 1949–69; pres. Pittsburgh United Jewish Fed., 1956–58; Amer. Jewish Com.: mem. since 1939; mem. bd. dirs.; past natl. v. pres.; chmn. exec. bd.; pres. 1961–62; hon. pres. since 1962; past. pres. Louis J. & Mary E. Horowitz Found.; recipient: award, Natl. Council Christians and Jews, 1953; Man-of-Year award, Jewish War Veterans, Pittsburgh, 1961; established in his honor: Louis Caplan Lectures in Law, U. of Pittsburgh Law School, 1962; Louis Caplan Human Relations Award, Pittsburgh chapter, Amer. Jewish Com.; hon. LLD, U. of Pittsburgh, 1966; Louis Caplan Center for Community Services and Louis Caplan Center of Group Identity and Mental Health, 1977.

CHERNOW, MICHAEL, business exec., philanthropist; b. (?); d. (?), July 1, 1978; co-founder, Monet Jewelers; benefactor: Dept. of Dermatology, NYU School of Medicine; Dialysis Center of the Palm Beaches; Arnold & Marie Schwarz Coll. of Pharmacy & Health Sciences; Dept. of

Urology (Michael & Stella Chernow Urological Suite), Brookdale Hosp. Medical Center; Chemotherapy Found.; Albert Einstein Coll. of Medicine; Natl. Jewish Hosp. and Research Center at Denver; Hebrew Hosp. for the Chronic Sick; Jewish Memorial Hosp.; Sinai Fraternal Order; Emunal-Hapoel Hamizrachi Women; Congregation Adereth El; Beth Israel Medical Center; mem. Congregation Rodeph Sholom; active, UJA-Fed. of Jewish Philanthropies, Fund for Higher Ed. in Israel.

CHURGIN, GERSHON A., educator, author; b. Pohost, Russia, Dec. 3, 1903; d. N.Y.C., Apr. 11, 1978; in U.S. since 1932; principal, W. Talmud Torah, Baltimore, 1930–39; Yeshiva U.: instructor, 1939–50; prof. Jewish philosophy and Hebrew literature, 1950–72; instructor: Herzlia Hebrew Teachers Inst., N.Y.; Touro Coll.; Vassar Coll.; mem. Hebrew PEN; contributor: *Sefer Hashanah,* Vol. VII (1944); *Bitzaron* (1944); *Hatekufah,* Vol. 34–35 (1949); *Talpioth* (1953); *SURA,* Israel-Amer. Annual (1953–54, 1956); *Zeramin* (1959); co-editor, *Bitzaron;* author: *Currents in Modern Philosophy* (1959); *Horizons of Thought; Studies in Jewish and General Philosophy* (1968).

DAVID, MORRIS, business exec., philanthropist; b. Jania, Greece, (?), 1904; d. N.Y.C., March 16, 1978; in U.S. since 1908; founder, first pres. Crown-Tex Corp.; benefactor: Congregation Sherith Israel, N.Y.; Kehila Kedosha of Jannina; Gilrod Found.; founder: David Biological Laboratory, Belfer School of Science, Yeshiva U.; Congregation Emeth Ve Shalom, Cedarhurst, L.I.; Sephardic Home for the Aged, Brooklyn: founder; chmn. Finance Com.; chmn. bd. dirs.; co-chmn. Dinner Com.; co-sponsored publication of third edition of *Kaddish* by David de Sola Pool; science fellow, Yeshiva U.

DAVIDSON, PHILIP, business exec., philanthropist; b. (?); d. (?), June 3, 1978; mem.: Gen. Contractors Assn. of N.Y.; Plumbing & Heating Wholesalers Assn.; benefactor, League School; bd. mem.: Hampshire House; Hosp. for Joint Diseases and Medical Center, 1973–78; Woodmere Academy: trustee, 1948–55; treas. 1953–55; UJA-Fed. of Jewish Philanthropies: bd. mem., past chmn. Plumbing, Heating, and Piping Div.; supporter, Israel Ed. Fund; mem.

Metropolitan Synagogue of N.Y.; benefactor, Metropolitan Jewish Geriatric Center.

EMIOT, ISRAEL, author; b. (?), Poland, Jan. 15, 1909; d. Rochester, N.Y., March 6, 1978; coordinator, Yiddish cultural events, Jewish Center of Rochester; author: four books of poetry; six books of poetry and short stories; contributor of poems and short stories to the Yiddish press in Poland, the *Jewish Daily Forward,* and other Yiddish newspapers and magazines in the U.S.; recipient: prize for best book of poetry, Jewish Book Council of America, 1962; Kessel Prize, Mexico; World Cong. for Jewish Culture Award.

ENGEL, IRVING M., attorney, communal leader; b. Birmingham, Ala., Oct. 19, 1891; d. N.Y.C., Dec. 4, 1978; sr. mem. firm of Engel & Judge; pres. Jewish Found. for Ed. of Women, 1944–50; natl. pres. Amer. Jewish Com., 1954–59; mem.: Temple Emanu-El, N.Y.; bd. trustees, Amer. Friends of Hebrew U.; French Legion of Honor; Tunisian Legion of Honor; established in his honor: Irving M. Engel Fellowship for Research in the Field of Human Rights, Yale Law School, 1963; Irving M. Engel Fund for Social Justice, Amer. Jewish Com., 1971.

FORMAN, PHILLIP, judge, communal leader; b. N.Y.C., (?), 1895; d. Trenton, N.J., Aug. 17, 1978; mem. Bar, since 1917; appointed assistant U.S. attorney for southern district of N.J., 1923; appointed district attorney for same area, 1928; district court judge, 1932; chief judge, 1951; mem. U.S. Court of Appeals for the Third Circuit; a founder, Jewish Fed. of Trenton; active in: Amer. Jewish Joint Distribution Com.; Jewish Welfare Bd.; Amer. Jewish Com.

FRYDMAN, SZAJKO (Zosa Szajkowski), historian, author; b. Zareby, Poland, Jan. 10, 1911; d. N.Y.C., Sept. 26, 1978; in U.S. since 1941; served in: French Foreign Legion; U.S. Army, WW II; research associate, Yivo Inst.; mem. Amer. Academy for Jewish Research; author: *Studies of History of Jewish Immigration in France Until 1914; History of Jewish Labor Unions in France Until 1914; Antisemitism in the French Labor Movement Until the End of the Dreyfus Affair* (1948); *The Attitude of American Jews to East European Jewish Immigration, 1881–1893* (1951); *Jewish Emigration Policy in the Period of the Rumanian "Exodus", 1899–1903* (1951);

Agricultural Credit and Napoleon's Anti-Jewish Decrees (1953); *The Economic Status of the Jews of Alsace, Metz and Lorraine, 1648–1789* (1954); *Poverty and Social Welfare Among French Jews, 1800–1880* (1954); *Jews and the 1871 Decree of Paris; The Sephardic Jews of France During the Revolution of 1789* (1955); *The Emancipation of Jews During the French Revolution* (1959); *The French Central Jewish Consistory During the Second World War* (1959); *Autonomy and Communal Jewish Debts During the French Revolution of 1789* (1959); *Franco Judaica, Analytical Bibliography, 1500–1789* (1962); *The Struggle for Yiddish During World War I* (1964); *Analytical Franco Jewish Gazetteer, 1939–1945* (1966); *Jews and the Elihu Root Mission to Russia, 1917* (1969); *Budgeting American Jewish Overseas Relief, 1919–1939* (1969); *Disunity in the Distribution of American Jewish Overseas Relief, 1919–1939* (1969); *Jews in the French Revolution of 1789–1830, and 1848* (1970); *The Attitude of American Jews to Refugees from Germany in the 1930's* (1971); *Jews, Wars and Communism, Vol. I* (1972); *Jews, Wars and Communism, Vol. II* (1974); *East European Jewish Workers in Germany During World War I* (1975); *Jews and the French Foreign Legion* (1975); *Kolchak, Jews and the American Intervention in Russia* (1977); *The Mirage of American Jewish Aid in Soviet Russia, 1917–1939* (1977); *An Illustrated Sourcebook of Russian Antisemitism; An Illustrated Sourcebook on the Holocaust* (1977); honored by the Amer. Academy for Jewish Research.

GLANZ, RUDOLF, author, historian; b. Vienna, Austria, Dec. 21, 1892; d. N.Y.C., July 18, 1978; in U.S. since 1938; mem.: Viennese Bar; Internatl. Mark Twain Soc.; research assoc. YIVO, N.Y.C., since 1938; mem.: advisory research council and bd. dirs., YIVO; Labor Zionist Org. of America; Poalei Zion; Vienna Jewish Community: chmn. Law Com.; mem. exec. com.; mem. bd. dirs.; contributor to English and Yiddish periodicals; editor, *Der Jüdische Arbeiter;* author: *Yiddish Elements in German Thief Jargon* (1928); *Lower Classes of German Jewry in the 18th Century* (1932); *Immigration of German Jews up to 1890* (1947); *Jews in Relation to Cultural Milieu of Germans in America* (1947); *Source Material, History of Jewish Immigration to the U.S.* (1951); *Jews in American Alaska* (1953); *Jews and Chinese in America; The*

Rothschild Legend in America; German Jews in New York City in the 19th Century; The Jews of California (1960); *The Jews in the Old American Folklore* (1961); *German Jewish Names in America* (1961); *Jew and Mormon* (1963); *Jew and Irish* (1966); *Geschichte des Niederen Jüdischen Volkes in Deutschland* (1968); *The German Jew in America; Studies in Judaica Americana* (1970); *Jew and Italian: Historic Group Relations and the New Immigration* (1971); *The Jew in Early American Wit and Graphic Humor* (1971); *The Jewish Woman in America* (1973).

GLENN, MENAHEM G., educator, author, editor; b. Merkine, Lithuania, Dec. 27, 1900; d. Philadelphia, Pa., Feb. 26, 1978; in U.S. since 1914; sr. editor, Morris Jacobs, Inc., 1928–68; taught rabbinics, Bible, Hebrew literature, Gratz Coll., Philadelphia; principal, Hebrew High School, Trenton, N.J.; dir. Hebrew Inst., Waterbury, Conn.; mem.: Topographical Union of Philadelphia; PEN; Higher Inst. of Learning; Amer. Jewish Historical Soc.; Amer. Academy of Jewish Research; Moses Hess Camp, Sons of Zion; Natl. Assn. Hebrew Professors; Histadrut Ivrith; Hebrew Teachers of N.Y. and Vicinity; Temple Israel, Wynnfield, Mass.; columnist, *The Jewish Exponent*, Philadelphia, since 1951; contributor, Hebrew, Yiddish, and Anglo-Jewish press; assoc. editor, *Jewish Book Annual*, since 1952; co-editor, *New Yorker Wochenblat*; author: *Jewish Tales and Legends* (1927); *Tephilath Jeshurun; Al Gedot-ha Neyeman* (1937); *Rashi der Folklerer* (1940); *Ha Milon Ha Ma'asi*, Hebrew-English Dictionary, Vol. 1 (1947), Vol. 2 (1960); *Rabbi Israel Salanter-Religious Ethical Thinker* (1953); recipient, Alumni Award, Dropsie U., 1963.

GOLDFARB, JACOB A., business exec., philanthropist; b. Warsaw, Poland, June 15, 1895; d. N.Y.C., May 28, 1978; founder, pres., chmn. bd. Union Underwear Co., 1926; advisor, mem. bd. dirs. Philadelphia & Reading Corp.; pres. Goldfarb Investing, since 1955; chmn. bd. CFC, since 1958; dir. Sterling Stores, Little Rock; dir. Underwear Inst.; U.S. Army, WWI; mem.: Palm Beach Country Club; Masons; Harmonie Club; Metropolis Country Club; benefactor: Mass. Inst. of Technology; N.Y.U. Medical Center; Sarah Lawrence Coll.; Albert Einstein Coll.; Brandeis U.

(Jacob A. and Bertha Goldfarb Library); Hebrew U.; Technion of Israel; Jewish Guild for the Blind; Boys Town Jerusalem; Counselling Center of N.Y. Fed. of Reform Synagogues; v. pres. N.Y.U. Jewish Culture Found.; treas.: Amer. Jewish Com., Inst. of Human Relations Fund; Brandeis U.; dir. UJA; trustee: Union of Amer. Hebrew Congregations; Fed. of Jewish Philanthropies; mem.: B'nai B'rith; Temple Emanu-El bd. of trustees; hon. alumnus, Hebrew Union Coll.-Jewish Inst. of Religion; hon. DHL, Brandeis U.; hon. v. pres. Amer. Jewish Com.; Jacob A. Goldfarb Medal awarded annually by Brandeis U.; recipient: Herbert H. Lehman Award for exemplary leadership, Amer. Jewish Com.; Haym Salomon Award, ADL.

GOLDSTEIN, SHMUEL (SHMULIK), actor in Yiddish theater; b. Lodz, Poland, (?), 1908; d. N.Y.C., Nov. 23, 1978; in U.S. since 1953; began acting career in Poland with the Aravat group; performed in such plays as *The Inheritors, Yoshe Kolb, It's Hard to Be a Jew, The Big Winner, The Fifth Season, Let's Sing Yiddish, From Israel With Laughter,* and *Hot a Yid a Landele.*

GOLDWASSER, DAVID, business exec., philanthropist; b. Athens, Ga., June 25, 1911; d. Atlanta, Ga., Dec. 29, 1978; pres. Atlantic Envelope Co., 1935–64; v. pres., dir. Natl. Service Industries, Atlanta, 1964–74; v. pres. Amer. Symphony Orchestra League, 1976–79; dir.: Master Packaging; Trimble House; Fisher-Haynes Corp.; pres. Atlanta Symphony Orchestra; v. pres, trustee, Atlanta Arts Alliance; chmn.: Direct Mail Advertising Assn. of America; Atlanta Magazine; dir.: Atlanta Chamber of Commerce; Atlanta Funds Appeal Review Bd.; Envelope Manufacturers Assn.; Planned Parenthood of Atlanta; pres.: Atlanta Advertising Club; Atlanta Freight Bureau; Alpha Epsilon Pi Fraternity; Printing Industry of Atlanta; sec. Emory U. Bd. of Visitors; pres. Natl. Com. for Symphony Orchestra Support; Amer. Jewish Com.: mem. bd. trustees, 1976–79; natl. v. pres.; pres. Atlanta Jewish Fed., 1977–78; v. pres. The Temple, Atlanta; recipient: Human Relations Award, Amer. Jewish Com., 1976; Nehemiah Gillteson Award for Community Service, Alpha Epsilon Pi, 1977; Governor's Award for the Arts, 1978.

GOODBLATT, MORRIS S., rabbi, author; b. Mlawa, Poland, Sept. 18, 1901; d. Philadelphia, Pa., March 21, 1978; chmn. Jewish Law Com., Jewish Law Soc.; pres. Philadelphia branch, Jewish Law Soc.; dir., dean, Academy for Judaism, Rabbinical Assembly of Philadelphia; mem. com. on Law and Standards, Natl. Org. of Conservative Rabbis; mem.: Zionist Org. of America; Jewish Natl. Fund; chmn. com. on Jewish Law and Standards, United Synagogue of America; past pres. Bd. of Rabbis of Greater Philadelphia; rabbi, rabbi emeritus, Congregation Beth Am Israel, Philadelphia, since 1927; author: *Jewish Life in Turkey in the 16th Century* (1952); numerous articles in Jewish magazines; awarded hon. DD, Jewish Theological Seminary, 1963.

GOROG, FREDERIC, attorney, communal leader; b. Budapest, Hungary, March 13, 1890; d. N.Y.C., Dec. 2, 1978; in U.S. since 1948; bank dir; mem. Budapest Bar, 1918–48; attorney with firm of Loeb, Rhoades, Hornblower & Co.; pres. Hungarian Branch, Amer. Jewish Joint Distribution Com., 1945–48; founder, first pres., hon. pres. World Fed. of Jews of Hungarian Descent, 1950 on; dir. Hungarian Jewish Welfare Bd.; author, several articles on law and economics for European periodicals; recipient, Man-of-the-Year Award, UJA.

GOUDSMIT, SAMUEL A., physicist, educator; b. Hague, Netherlands, July 11, 1902; d. Reno, Nev., Dec. 4, 1978; in U.S. since 1927; prof. of physics, U. of Nev.; co-discoverer of electron spin theory, 1925; instructor, assoc. prof., prof. physics, U. of Mich., 1927–46; mem. MIT radiation lab mission to England, WWII, 1943; civilian chmn. mission to Europe, 1944; faculty mem. Northwestern U., 1946–48; Brookhaven Natl. Lab: sr. scientist, 1948–52; chmn. dept. physics, 1952–67; visiting lecturer, Rockefeller Inst., N.Y., 1954–75; Morris Loeb lecturer, Harvard U., 1975; fellow: Amer. Physics Soc.; Netherlands Physics Soc.; Natl. Academy of Science; editor-in-chief, Amer. Physics Soc.; editor, *Physical Review Letters* (1951–74); author: *Alsos* (1947); co-author: *Structure of Line Spectra* (1930); *Atomic Energy States* (1932); *Time* (1966); recipient: Rockefeller fellowship, 1926; Guggenheim fellowship, 1938; Medal of Freedom, 1945; Order of the British Empire, 1949; Research Corp. Science Award, 1954; hon. DSc, Case Inst.

of Technology, 1958; Max Planck Medal, German Physics Soc., 1965; hon. DSc, U. of Chicago, 1972; hon. DSc, Utah State U., 1972; Carl T. Compton Medal, Amer. Inst. of Physics, 1974; hon. DSc, Northwestern U., 1975; Natl. Medal of Science, 1977.

GROSS, REUBEN E., business exec., attorney, communal leader, author; b. N.Y.C., Aug. 6, 1914; d. N.Y.C., July 7, 1978; in Israel since 1968; law practice, since 1938; banking and finance exec., since 1961; U.S. Army, 1944–45; Israel Air Force, 1948–49; a founder, pres. Natl. Jewish Commission on Law and Public Affairs; natl. chmn. Amer. Veterans of Israel; founder, Staten Island branch, Mesivtha Tifereth Jerusalem; natl. sec. Union of Orthodox Jewish Congregations, since 1954; chmn. Union of Orthodox Jewish Congregations Youth Commission, 1974–78; contributor: *Jewish Life; The Jewish Observer.*

HALPRIN, ROSE L., communal leader; b. N.Y.C., Apr. 11, 1896; d. N.Y.C., Jan. 8, 1978; Hadassah: natl. pres. 1932–34, 1947–52; chmn. Natl. Aliyah Com., 1976–78; Jewish Agency: mem. since 1946; chmn. Amer. section, 1955; chmn. 1960–68; mem.: Bd. of Jewish Telegraphic Agencies; Zionist Action Com.; Zionist Gen. Council; World Zionist Org.; United Israel Appeal: life trustee, natl. co-chmn., natl. v. chmn.; World Confederation of United Zionists: co-chmn., hon. life pres.; World Confederation of Gen. Zionists: founder, hon. life pres.; a founder, Hebrew U.-Hadassah Medical School, Jerusalem; lifetime mem. bd. dirs., UJA; mem. bd. dirs. Jewish Natl. Fund; a founder, Amer.-Israel Public Affairs Com.; World Jewish Congress: hon. chmn. Amer. section; mem. bd. govs.; hon. mem. gen. council.

HORWITZ, LOUIS D., social work exec.; b. Cleveland, Ohio, Nov. 29, 1908; d. N.Y.C., Jan. 4, 1978; in Israel since 1974; caseworker, supervisor, N.Y. State, 1931–45; dir. Amer. Jewish Joint Distribution Com.: Italy, 1945–50; Tunisia, 1950–53; emigration dept., 1953–54; Israel, 1957–63; Geneva, 1964–74; gen. dir. since 1967; dir. Europe and N. Africa sections, United HIAS Service, 1954–57; dir. dept. Overseas Studies-Services, Council Jewish Federations and Welfare Funds, 1963–65; consultant on absorption, United Israel Appeal, 1965–67; v. pres. European chapter, Natl. Assn. Voluntary Workers; trustee, Paul Baerwald School of Social

Work, Hebrew U.; chmn. Refugee Commission, Internatl. Council Voluntary Agencies; mem. planning com., Internatl. Conf. Jewish Communal Service; mem.: Natl. Council Jewish Communal Work; Natl. Conf. Social Work; author of papers on: "Jews in Tunisia" (1953); "World Refugee Situation" (1961); "Care of the Aged in Israel" (1964); recipient, Hazuni Award, Israeli Ministry of Welfare.

JACOBS, PAUL, author, social activist; b. N.Y.C., (?), 1919; d. San Francisco, Ca., Jan. 3, 1978; organizer, Internatl. Ladies Garment Workers Union, 1941–43; U.S. Air Force; internatl. rep. Oil Workers Internatl. Union; staff mem., Center for Study of Democratic Institutions, Santa Barbara, Ca., 1956–69; research staff, Center for Study of Law and Soc., U. of California at Berkeley, 1964–72; assoc. fellow, Inst. for Policy Studies, Washington, since 1970; race relations specialist, Amer. Jewish Com.; co-producer, "The Jail," 1972; author: numerous magazine and newspaper articles; *Is Curly Jewish?* (1965); *Prelude to Riot; Between the Rock and the Hard Place* (1970); *The State of the Unions;* co-author: *The New Radicals; To Serve the Devil;* recipient, award from Sigma Delta Chi for public service to journalism.

JACOBSON, IRVING, actor, producer, director; b. Cincinnati, Ohio, (?), 1899; d. N.Y.C., Dec. 17, 1978; owned and operated Natl. Theater and Second Ave. Theater, N.Y.C.; appeared in such productions as *Yiddisha Mama, Abi Gezunt, Man of La Mancha, The Art of Love,* and *So Long 174th Street;* honored as "Man of the Year," East Side Hebrew Inst., 1966.

JACOBSON, MAE SCHOENFELD, actress, producer; b. (?), 1906; d. N.Y.C., March 28, 1978; owned and operated Natl. Theater and Second Ave. Theater, N.Y.C.; appeared in such plays as *The Kosher Widow* and *Enter Laughing.*

KATZ, BENNE, business exec., philanthropist; b. Jaroslaw, Austria, Feb. 9, 1902; d. N.Y.C., June 23, 1978; in U.S. since 1923; founder, pres. Williamsburg Steel Corp., 1926; pres., bd. chmn. Brookdale Hosp. Medical Center; founder, Albert Einstein Coll. of Medicine; benefactor, Kingsbrook Jewish Medical Center; mem.: bd. trustees, Isaac Albert Research Inst.; Greater N.Y. Com. for Israel Bonds; UJA-Fed. of Jewish

Philanthropies; a founder, Boys Town Jerusalem; pres. Manhattan Beach Jewish Center; honored by: Manhattan Beach Jewish Center; UJA of Greater N.Y.; Boys Town Jerusalem; Yeshiva U.; Brookdale Hosp. Medical Center; Fed. of Jewish Philanthropies.

KAUFMAN, ISIDORE, author, editor; b. (?), Austria-Hungary, March 14, 1892; d. N.Y.C., Apr. 30, 1978; in U.S. since 1900; lieutenant, U.S. Army, WWI; reporter, *Brooklyn Eagle,* 1919–22, 1925–55; chmn. Brooklyn Newspaper Guild; editor, N.J. section, *The New York American,* 1922–25; editor, *Frontpage,* N.Y. Newspaper Guild, 1955–73; author, *American Jews in World War II;* awarded Phi Beta Kappa, Princeton U., 1915.

KLEIN, STEPHEN, business exec., philanthropist; b. (?), Austria, (?), 1907; d. N.Y.C., Dec. 17, 1978; in U.S. since 1938; founder, bd. chmn. Barton's Candy Corp.; past dir. Manhattan Day School; active in Vaad Hatzala refugee work, after WWII; mem. Agudath Israel; founding natl. chmn. Torah Schools for Israel; mem. Advisory Council, N.Y. Bd. of Rabbis; bd. mem. Beth Medrash Govoha; mem. bd. govs. Congregation Ohab Zedek, Belle Harbor; trustee, Westside Institutional Synagogue; a founder, v. pres., mem. bd. dirs. Torah Umesorah, Natl. Soc. for Hebrew Day Schools; patron, Yeshiva R'tzahd; founder, Yeshiva U. High School for Girls; a founder, Chinuch Atzmai, Torah Schools for Israel; v. pres. Jewish Ed. Com.; recipient, Heritage Award, Torah Umesorah.

KLEINBARD, MARTIN, attorney, communal leader; b. N.Y.C., Oct. 26, 1919; d. N.Y.C., Dec. 16, 1978; partner, law firm of Paul, Weiss, Rifkind, Wharton & Garrison; mem. bd. trustees, Rye Country Day School, since 1971; U.S. Army; N.Y. Assn. for New Americans, Fed. of Jewish Philanthropies: dir. since 1951; pres. 1965–68; chmn. exec. com. 1968–71; mem. Temple Emanu-El, N.Y.; fellow, Amer. Coll. Trial Lawyers, 1977.

KOLISH, THEODORE J., communal leader; b. (?), 1909; d. N.Y.C., June 27, 1978; Amer. Jewish Congress: mem. since 1945; past pres. Brooklyn Div.; chmn. N.Y. Metropolitan Council; natl. sec. 1958–64; natl. v. pres. 1964; hon. v. pres. 1976.

KOWALSKY, CHAIM NACHMAN, rabbi, communal worker; b. Warsaw, Poland, (?),

1893; d. Baltimore, Md., Jan. 3, 1978; in U.S. since 1927; fund-raiser: Meah Shearim Yeshiva, Jerusalem; Ner Israel Rabbinical Coll., 1938–78.

KRULEWITCH, MELVIN L., attorney, communal leader; b. N.Y.C., Nov. 11, 1895; d. N.Y.C., May 25, 1978; private law practice, 1920–78; U.S. Marine Corps: WWI; WWII; private, 1916; brigadier gen., 1955; maj. gen., 1956; dir. N.Y. Marine Corps Reserve: consultant: Public Service Commission of N.Y.; N.J. Public Utilities Commission; mem.: N.Y. Bar Assn., 1920–78; State Labor Relations Bd.; benefactor, Columbia U.; chmn. N.Y. State Athletic Commission, 1959–67; v. chmn. bd. USO of Metropolitan N.Y.; campaign chmn. USO, 1961; co-chmn. Gen. Douglas MacArthur Memorial Com., 1964; dir. USO, Washington, D.C.; dir. Columbia Law School Alumni Assn.; established Krulewitch Fellowship Program in graduate legal studies, Columbia Law School; mem. Armed Forces and Veteran Services Com.; supporter, Girl Scout Council of Greater N.Y.; mem. Greater N.Y. Com. for Israel Bonds; bd. mem.: UJA; Fed. of Jewish Philanthropies; hon. bd. mem.: Jewish Welfare Bd.; 92nd St. YM-YWHA; Park Ave. Synagogue: past v. chmn. bd.; hon. trustee; author, *Now That You Mention It* (1973); recipient, Hatan Bereshit award, 1953; recipient, 22 medals and commendations.

KUHN, MARSHALL, communal leader; b. San Francisco, Ca., (?), 1916; d. San Francisco, Ca., May 18, 1978; helped organize nature trail, Golden Gate Park; exec. dir. Jewish Community Center; dir. Jewish Welfare Fed. community endowment fund; honored as "Environmentalist of the Year," John Muir Historical Soc.

KUMMEL, FLORENCE M., communal worker; b. Paterson, N.J., May 17, 1895; d. Morristown, N.J., June 21, 1978; pres. Deborah Consumptive Relief League; chmn. No. N.J. chapter, Friends of N.Y. Philharmonic; benefactor, Metropolitan Opera; organizer, Essex County Book Review and Art Study Groups; life mem. Natl. Women's Com., Brandeis U.; founding mem. Assn. Reform Zionists of America; charter life mem. since 1968, Natl. Council of Jewish Women; Hadassah: v. pres. S. Orange chapter; life mem. since 1952; active supporter: UJA; Bonds for Israel; mem. Technion Soc.; recipient, award

for bringing largest number of new members to Friends of N.Y. Philharmonic.

LASDON, MILTON S., business exec., philanthropist; b. Brooklyn, N.Y., Nov. 13, 1906; d. Miami, Fla., June 1, 1978; chmn. Warner Lambert Pharmaceutical Co. for more than 30 years; patron: Metropolitan Opera; N.Y. Philharmonic; established: Lasdon Colonnade, Lincoln Center for the Performing Arts; Lasdon Clinic, N.Y. Hosp.; trustee: Inst. for Advanced Studies in the Humanities; Temple Israel, White Plains; mem. bd. overseers, Jewish Theological Seminary; a founder: The Greater Seminary; Truman Inst., Hebrew U.; recipient, Natl. Community Service Award, Jewish Theological Seminary.

LEFF, PHILLIP, business exec., philanthropist; b. N.Y.C., Oct. 19, 1895; d. N.Y.C., Apr. 13, 1978; pres., bd. chmn. Natl. Spinning Co.; mem.: Palm Beach Country Club; Beach Point Club; Congregation B'nai Jeshurun; America-Israel Cultural Found.; ADL; a founder, bd. mem.: UJA; Albert Einstein Coll. of Medicine; Jewish Theological Seminary; ADL Appeal; Brandeis U.; mem. Amer. Friends Hebrew U.; established Leff Families Chair in Modern European History, Brandeis U.; Jewish Theological Seminary: recipient, Natl. Community Service Award, 80th Anniversary Medal, membership in Soc. of Fellows; elected to Soc. of Fellows, Brandeis U.; hon. life mem. Metropolis Country Club.

LEVIN, GEORGE, real estate exec., philanthropist; b. N.Y.C., Feb. 22, 1903; d. N.Y.C., Apr. 8, 1978; v. pres., treas. Brookdale Garden Apartments; cofounder, pres. Garden Construction Co.; mem.: Mountain Ridge Country Club, N.J.; Temple B'nai Abraham, N.J.; gen. chmn. UJA of Essex County; benefactor, Albert Einstein Coll. of Medicine; trustee, mem. exec. com. Jewish Community Fed. of Metropolitan N.J.; Jewish Community Found. of Essex County: v. pres., gen. co-chmn. Building Fund Campaign; donated Physics Building to Hebrew U., Jerusalem; endowed George and Frances Levin Chair in Psychology, Brandeis U.; fellow, Brandeis U.

LEVIN, HERSCHEL, rabbi, author; b. Baltimore, Md., July 19, 1916; d. Flushing, N.Y., Feb. 6, 1978; rabbi: Temple Emanuel, Lawrence, Mass.; Sinai Temple,

Springfield, Mass.; Temple Beth Sholom, since 1953; treas. N.Y. Bd. of Rabbis; past pres.: North Shore Clergy Assn.; Hebrew Union Coll. Student Body; Bayside Council of Churches and Synagogues; past v. pres., co-chmn. chaplaincy com., N.Y. Bd. of Rabbis; past v. pres. Rabbinical Assembly, Queens; past exec. bd. mem. Central Conf. Amer. Rabbis; mem.: Israel Bond Org.; Queens Rabbinic Cabinet; author, *The American Jew and the State of Israel* (1953); editor, *Directory of New England Liberal Congregations;* recipient, citation as community service leader in Greater Lawrence, Local Council of Churches.

LEWIS, SALIM L., business exec., philanthropist; b. Brookline, Mass., Oct. 5, 1908; d. N.Y.C., Apr. 29, 1978; dir.: Bear, Stearns, & Co.; Deltec Internatl.; Madison Sq. Garden Corp.; Midland Glass Co.; Republic Corp.; Warner Communications; chmn. City of Life Fed. Building Fund; club membership: Century Country; Harmonie; Hollywood Golf; Madison Sq. Garden; N.Y. Stock Exchange Luncheon; Tres Vidas; endowed Hattie and Max Lewis Campgrounds; active in fund drives for: Amer. Red Cross; Beekman Downtown Hosp.; N.Y. Urban Coalition; mem. N.Y.C. Bd. of Ed., 1968; founder, hon. chmn. Appeal for Human Relations, Amer. Jewish Com.; a founder, first pres. Associated YM-YWHA's of Greater New York, 1957–59; Fed. of Jewish Philanthropies: assoc. chmn. bd.; pres., 1954–75; supporter, Fund for Higher Ed. in Israel; benefactor, Mt. Sinai Medical Center; recipient, Herbert H. Lehman award, Amer. Jewish Com.

LIEBERMAN, JUDITH, author, educator; b. Mosheik, Latvia, Aug. 15, 1903; d. N.Y.C., Dec. 21, 1978; in U.S. since 1940; head teacher, principal, Shulamith School for Girls; bd. mem. Mizrachi Women's Org.; hon. pres. Manhattan chapter, Amer. Red Magen David for Israel; author: numerous magazine articles; *Robert Browning and Hebraism* (1934); "Spiritual Autobiography" (1953).

LINDHEIM, IRMA LEVY, communal leader; b. N.Y.C., Dec. 9, 1886; d. Berkeley, Ca., Apr. 10, 1978; first lieutenant, Motor Corps of America, WWI; dir. U.S. Volunteer Land Corps, WWII; pres. 7th District, Zionist Org. in N.Y., 1919; active in Jewish Natl. Fund; v. pres. Zionist Org. of America, 1926–28; pres. Hadassah, 1926–28;

mem. Actions Com., World Zionist Org., 1926–28; mem. Hashomer Hatzair, 1930; helped organize League for Labor Palestine, 1932; mem. Histadrut, since 1933; mem. Kibbutz Mishmar Haemek, Israel, 1933–78; creator, Palestine Fellowships, 1935; author: *Immortal Adventure* (1928); *Parallel Quest: A Search of a Person and a People* (1962).

LINFIELD, HARRY S., rabbi, author; b. (?), Lithuania, (?), 1888; d. Riverdale, N.Y., Nov. 23, 1978; in U.S. since 1905; exec. dir. Jewish Statistical Bureau; mem. N.Y. Bd. of Rabbis; author, several books on Jewish demography.

LUBIN, ISADOR, economic consultant, communal leader; b. Worcester, Mass., June 9, 1896; d. Annapolis, Md., July 6, 1978; statistician, U.S. Food Admn., 1918; consultant, U.S. War Industrial Bd., 1918–19; asst. prof. economics, U. of Michigan, 1920–22; staff, Brookings Inst., 1922–23; teaching staff, Graduate School, 1924–30; advisor, Ed. and Labor Com., U.S. Senate, 1928–29; chmn. labor advisory bd., Public Works Admn., 1933–36; mem. U.S. Central Statistics Bd., 1933–37; U.S. Commissioner of Labor Statistics, 1933–46; statistical asst. to Pres. Roosevelt, 1941–45; U.S. assoc. rep., Allied Commission on Reparations, 1945; mem.: U.S. Economic and Employment Com., 1946–50; U.S. Commission on Reconstruction of Devastated Areas, 1946; UN Economic and Social Council, 1950–53; advisory com. to U.S. Korean Reconstruction Agency, 1951–53; Industrial Commission, N.Y. State Dept. of Labor, 1955–59; Natl. Commission on Money and Credit, 1958–61; prof. public affairs, Rutgers U., 1959–61; dir. Eastern Life Insurance Co., 1959–70; consultant, 20th Century Fund, since 1962; chmn. President's Commission on Railroad Labor Conditions, 1962; consultant, officer, Statistical Standards, U.S. Bureau of Budget, 1963–67; delegate, UN conf., 1963; founder, Internatl. Statistics Inst.; trustee, New School for Social Research; consultant: Jewish Agency for Israel; United Israel Appeal, since 1960; mem.: bd. govs. Amer. Jewish Com.; exec. com., Joint Distribution Com.; dir.: United HIAS Service; Amer. ORT; trustee: Brandeis U.; Weizmann Inst. of Science; author: *Miner's Wages and the Cost of Coal* (1924); *The British Attack on Unemployment* (1934); *Our Stake in World Trade*

(1954); *U.S. State in the U.S.* (1954); co-author: *The British Coal Dilemma* (1917). *Government Control of Prices During the War* (1919).

MARROW, ALFRED J., psychologist, author, business exec.; b. N.Y.C., March 8, 1905; d. N.Y.C., March 3, 1978; lecturer, psychologist, New School for Social Research; chmn. Mayor's Commission on Intergroup Relations; pres., bd. chmn. Harwood Manufacturing Co.; consultant: U.S. State Dept.; City of N.Y.; pres. Natl. Academy Professional Psychologists; mem. bd. of trustees: New School for Social Research; President's Assn. of the Amer. Management Assn.; founder, Amer. Psychology Assn.; mem.: Eastern Psychology Assn.; N.Y. State Psychology Assn.; Amer. Sociology Assn.; N.Y. Academy of Sciences; Amer. Assn. for the Advancement of Science; Internatl. Soc. of Mental Health; Natl. Training Lab in Group Development, Topological Psychologists Soc.; Soc. for Psychological Study of Social Issues; Soc. of Industrial Psychologists; Authors Guild; Palm Beach Country Club; dir.: New School for Social Research; Antioch Coll.; Gonzaga U.; consultant, bd. mem.: Amer. Found. for Management Research; Marshall Fund; chmn. Amer. Council for Behavioral Science in Kibbutz Management; founder, Center for Human Development, Hebrew U., Jerusalem; chmn. natl. exec. com., Amer. Jewish Congress; chmn. Amer. Com. Mental Hygiene for Israel; mem. Temple Emanu-El of Palm Beach; mem. exec. council, Stephen Wise Free Synagogue; benefactor, Rabbi Jacob Joseph School; natl. v. pres., chmn. Commission on Community Interrelations, Amer. Jewish Congress; author: articles for professional publications; *Living Without Hate* (1951); *Making Management Human* (1957); *Management by Participation; Changing Patterns of Prejudice* (1962); *Behind the Executive Mask* (1964); *A Life in Psychology-Biography of Kurt Lewin* (1969); *The Failure of Success* (1972); *Making Waves in Foggy Bottom* (1972); recipient, Kurt Lewin Memorial Award.

MAZER, CEIL, communal worker; b. (?), 1908; d. N.Y.C., March 22, 1978; fundraiser: Hadassah; UJA; mem. Park Ave. Synagogue; a founder, Women's Div., Albert Einstein Coll. of Medicine; mem. Amer. Associates of Ben-Gurion U.; mem.

The Jewish Center; contributor, Beth Israel Medical Center; active in: Amer. Friends of Hebrew U.; Israel Bond Program.

MEYERS, PHILIP M., business exec., philanthropist; b. Cincinnati, Ohio, June 25, 1899; d. N.Y.C., Dec. 27, 1978; founder, chmn. Standard Wine & Liquor Co.; U.S. Army, WWI; pres.: Natl. Assn. Direct Selling Cos., 1939–41; Fashion Frocks, 1942–67; chmn. finance com., trustee, Cincinnati Zoological Soc., since 1946; mem. advisory com., Citizens School Com., since 1948; dir. First Natl. Bank of Cincinnati; dir. Cincinnati School Found., 1950–55; mem. exec. bd. City Charter Com., 1951–61; mem. advisory com., Bureau of Government Research, since 1952; mem. bd. trustees, U. of Cincinnati, since 1954; sec., mem. bd. fellows, Brandeis U., since 1956; bd. chmn. Meyers Development Corp., since 1958; mem.: Losantville Country Club; Bankers Club; Cincinnati Club; founder, Grand Central Athletic Club; mem. Sky Ranch for Boys; pres. Jewish Community Center, 1942–44; co-founder, chmn. Cincinnati chapter, Jewish Welfare Fund, 1944; v. chmn. Union of Amer. Hebrew Congregations, 1944–52; co-chmn. Natl. Council Christians and Jews, 1946–50; charter mem. Cincinnati chapter, Amer. Jewish Com., since 1950; mem.: Central Synagogue; UJA; Fed. of Jewish Philanthropies; natl. chmn. Jewish Defense Appeal, 1953–54; chmn. Jewish Community Relations Com., 1953–54; pres. Jewish Hosp., 1953–67; chmn. Cincinnati Com. for Amer. Jewish Tercentenary, 1955; mem. adv. com. U.S. Technical Assistance Program to Israel, 1956.

MUSTER, MORRIS, business exec., communal leader; b. Sarajevo, Austria-Hungary, Nov. 27, 1900; d. N.Y.C., Apr. 17, 1978; in U.S. since 1909; dir., sec. Home Furniture Assn. of N.Y.; a founder, Furniture Div., Histadrut; founder, furniture div., B'nai B'rith; mem. Home Furnishings Div., Greater N.Y. Com. for Israel Bonds; a founder, Furniture, Bedding and Allied Trades Div., UJA-Fed. of Jewish Philanthropies; mem.: ORT; Amer. Jewish Congress; pres. emeritus, Israel Sachs Lodge of B'nai B'rith; dir. Pine Lake Park Synagogue, for 17 years; recipient: plaque from Israeli government for assistance in the United War Effort, 1943; awards from Histadrut,

UJA, Bonds for Israel, and ADL; honored annually by Pine Lake Park Synagogue; "Furniture Man of the Year," 1974.

PERLMUTTER, MILTON, business exec., communal leader; b. Newark, N.J., 1928; d. Short Hills, N.J., March 15, 1978; pres. Supermarkets Gen. Corp.; bd. mem.: Gen. Mills; Super Valu Stores; INA Investment Securities; Public Service Electric & Gas Co.; Interracial Council for Business Opportunity; natl. sales promotion manager, Colgate-Palmolive Co.; trustee, Rutgers U.; pres. Jewish Community Fed. of Metropolitan N.J.; past gen. chmn., Metropolitan N.J. Div., State of Israel Bonds; past pres. B'nai Jeshurun, Short Hills, N.J.; mem. UJA-Fed. of Jewish Philanthropies; benefactor, Hebrew U.; natl. chmn., commerce and industry, State of Israel Bonds; trustee: Hebrew Youth Academy; Jewish Community Development Corp.; recipient: Israel's Prime Minister's Medal; annual Brotherhood Award, N.J. Region, Natl. Council Christians and Jews, 1977.

PINS, ARNULF M., author, educator; b. (?), Germany, Dec. 14, 1926; d. Jerusalem, Israel, Feb. 8, 1978; in U.S. since 1939; faculty mem. U. of Illinois School of Social Work; consultant; Paul Baerwald School of Social Work; U.S. Dept. of Health, Ed., and Welfare; Natl. Inst. for Mental Health; dir. personnel and training, Natl. Jewish Welfare Bd., 1960–64; exec. dir. Council on Social Work Ed., 1964–71; visiting prof. Hebrew U., 1971–72; dir. Middle East Region, Joint Distribution Com.; exec. dir. Memorial Found. for Jewish Culture; exec. dir. Jewish Material Claims Against Germany; a founder, Joseph J. Schwartz Program, School of Social Work and School of Ed., Hebrew U.; faculty mem. Hebrew Union Coll. School of Ed.; consultant: Israel Ministry of Social Welfare; a founder, past pres. Internatl. Conf. Jewish Communal Service; chmn. Natl. Youth Conf., Jewish Welfare Bd.; active mem. Assn. Jewish Center Workers; program dir. Jewish Community Centers of Chicago; past chmn. Amer. Zionist Youth Found.; chmn. ESHEI, the Assn. for Planning and Development of Services for the Aged in Israel; author of several books and numerous articles for professional journals; honored with establishment of Dr. Arnulf Pins Program for the Training of Professional Supervisors, Hebrew U.

ROSENBERG, IRWIN H., attorney, philanthropist; b. N.Y.C., March 12, 1913; d. N.Y.C., Apr. 25, 1978; partner, Lynton, Klein, Rosenberg, Opton, & Handler; gov. Sunningdale Country Club; founder, pres. Jewish Assn. for Services to the Aged, 1976–78; bd. mem., sec. Associated YM-YWHA's; bd. mem. Fed. of Jewish Philanthropies; author, numerous real estate and tax articles.

ROTHSTEIN, SAMUEL, rabbi, author; b. (?), Poland, (?), 1912; d. Brooklyn, N.Y., Apr. 17, 1978; in U.S. since 1947; editor, *Dos Yiddishe Togblatt;* contributor, *The Jewish Morning Journal;* author of weekly column, *The Daily Forward,* 1970–78; mem. editorial bd., an encyclopedia dealing with the Bible and its commentaries, 1958–78.

RUBIN, GAIL, photographer; b. (?), 1939; d. Maagen Michael, Israel, March 11, 1978; contributed wildlife photos to *Lilith* magazine; exhibitions of her work shown at Images, A Gallery of Contemporary Photographic Art, and Jewish Museum (1977); active in Holy Land Conservation Fund.

RUBIN, SAMUEL, business exec., philanthropist; b. Bialystok, Russia, (?), 1901; d. N.Y.C., Dec. 21, 1978; in U.S. since 1905; founder: Fabergé, Inc., 1937; Samuel Rubin Found.; benefactor, Sydenham Hosp.; a founder, NYU-Bellevue Medical Center; donated six-room house to Community Nursery School of Croton-on-Hudson, 1948; endowed Samuel Rubin Chair in Anthropology, Brandeis U., 1951; founder, bd. chmn., first pres. Amer. Symphony Orchestra, 1963; benefactor, Research Inst. for Study of Man, 1967; established fund to guarantee American participation in Spoleto Festival, 1967; established scholarship fund for needy medical students, NYU-Bellevue Medical Center, 1972; bd. chmn., donated medical library, Fordham Hosp.; donated five-story building for Post-graduate Center for Psychotherapy, NYU; established cultural centers in the Negev and Galilee; established scholarship fund to enable Arabs to study in Israel; past pres. America-Israel Cultural Found.

SALTZMAN, SAMUEL, ophthalmologist, communal worker; b. Keene, N.H., Feb. 19, 1898; d. N.Y.C., Nov. 16, 1978; private practice for more than 50 years; consultant, Albert Einstein Coll. of Medicine; dir. ophthalmology, Seaview Hosp., Staten Island, for 20 years; asst. clinical prof. N.Y.

Medical Coll.; mem.: Amer. Israeli War Veterans; Zionist Org. of America; Assn. Orthodox Jewish Scientists; author: numerous papers on the history of medicine; *History of Eye Glasses* (1979); awarded honorary medal by Israeli government, for work in establishing eye hospitals during War of Independence.

SLUTSKY, YETTA RUBIN, communal leader; b. Vilna, Russia, (?), 1890; d. Ellenville, N.Y., Jan. 4, 1978; in U.S. since 1902; owned and operated Nevele Country Club, Ellenville, N.Y.; built and gave Ellenville residents community center for educational and recreational use; life mem. Hadassah; hon. pres. sisterhood, Congregation Ezrath Israel; awarded "Woman of the Year," UJA and State of Israel Bonds.

STEINBACH, ALEXANDER A., rabbi, author; b. Baltimore, Md., Feb. 2, 1894; d. Hollywood, Fla., Nov. 12, 1978; bd. mem. Asthma Research Center and Hosp. in Denver; mem.: Order of Bookfellows; Amer. Poetry League; rabbi: Congregation Ahavath Sholom, Bluefield, W.V., 1921; Temple Beth El, Norfolk, Va., 1922–34; Temple Ahavath Sholom, Brooklyn, 1934–66; U.S. Army Chaplain, WWII; past pres.: Brooklyn Assn. Reform Rabbis; N.Y. Bd. of Rabbis; Brooklyn Bd. of Rabbis; Jewish Book Council of America; mem.: Central Conf. Amer. Rabbis; Synagogue Council of America; Amer. Jewish Historical Soc.; Ed. and Culture Com., Jewish Agency for Israel; bd. mem.: Internatl. Synagogue, Idlewild; Jewish Ed. Com.; Brooklyn Jewish Community Council; editor, *Jewish Book Annual; In Jewish Bookland;* author: poems for New York *Times* and poetry journals; *When Dreamers Build; Treatise Baba Mezia; Sabbath Queen; What is Judaism?; Musings and Meditations; In Search of the Permanent; Bitter-Sweet; Faith and Love; Through Storms We Grow;* hon. chmn. Natl. Poetry Day; recipient: first prize, Amer. Poetry League Contest, 1949; hon. DD, Hebrew Union Coll., 1956; first prize, Bookfellow Poetry Annual; hon. membership, Mark Twain Soc.; hon. membership, Eugene Field Soc.; "Outstanding Jewish Educator of the Year," Annual Educators' Council, 1963; Frank L. Weil Award "for distinguished contributions to the advancement of Jewish culture in America", Jewish Welfare Bd., 1970; first prize, Seven Lively

Arts Competition for a Shakespearean Sonnet, Hollywood, Fla., 1973, 1974.

STEINBERG, JULIUS, business exec., philanthropist; b. Brooklyn, N.Y., (?), 1915; d. N.Y.C., May 3, 1978; founder, Utility Tire Co., 1947; a founder, Leasco Data Processing Equipment Co., 1961; dir., exec. com. mem. Reliance Group, Inc.; pres. Ideal Rubber Co. of Brooklyn; mem.: Seawayne Club; Congregation Sons of Israel; trustee, Long Island Jewish Hosp.; bd. mem., benefactor, Inst. for Community Health, L.I. Jewish Hillside-Medical Center; recipient, Louis Marshall Award, Jewish Theological Seminary, 1971.

STITSKIN, LEON D., educator, author, rabbi; b. Cracow, Poland, July 2, 1910; d. (?), Nov. 6, 1978; in U.S. since 1919; mem.: Amer. Academy for Jewish Research; N.Y. State Bd. for Equality in Ed.; rabbi: Beth Israel, Warren, Ohio, 1932–42; Beth Joseph, Rochester, N.Y., 1942–50; Community Center, Philadelphia, Pa., 1950–53; dir. community relations and special publications, prof. Jewish philosophy, Yeshiva U., since 1953; Rabbinical Council of America: treas., 1949; sec., 1958; founder, acting dir. W. Coast Inst. of Jewish Studies, Yeshiva U.; 1962; founder, exponent, philosophy of Jewish personalism; mem.: Alumni Assn., Yeshiva U.; Zionist Org. of America; Amer. Jewish Congress; Mizrachi; B'nai B'rith; N.Y. State Bd. of Rabbis; author: *Judaism as a Religion* (1937); *Judaism as a Philosophy* (1960); *Anthology of Studies in Torah Judaism* (1968); *Personalism—A Definition of Jewish Philosophy* (1969); articles for religious journals; editor: *Sermon Manual* (1948, 1956); *Studies in Torah Judaism,* since 1960; *Studies in Judaica;* co-editor, *Tradition,* since 1959; recipient, annual award, Jewish War Veterans.

STORCH, ADOLPH, business exec., philanthropist; b. (?), 1921; d. N.Y.C., March 12, 1978; pres., bd. chmn. Purepac Laboratories Corp.; trustee, Arnold and Marie Schwartz Coll. of Pharmacy, Long Island U.; bd. chmn., hon. dir. Natl. Assn. Pharmaceutical Manufacturers; trustee, Optometric Center of N.Y.; mem. Alpine Country Club; Hebrew U.: mem. bd. dirs.; hon. fellow; established School of Pharmacy; bd. chmn. Drug and Toiletries Div., UJA; mem. exec. bd.: Mizrachi; Jewish Natl. Fund; trustee, Sutton Place Synagogue.

SUDRAN, ABE L., communal worker; b. Hoboken, N.J., May 14, 1909; d. W. Orange, N.J., March 12, 1978; taught course in "Vocational Adjustment Problems," School of Applied Social Science, Western Reserve U., Cleveland; mem. Governor's Commission on Vocational Adjustment, Ohio; v. pres. Occupational Planning Com., Cleveland; bd. mem. Health and Welfare Council, Kansas City, Mo.; mem.: Natl. Assn. Social Workers; Jewish Communal Service Assn.; consultant: Council of Jewish Federations and Welfare Funds; UJA; United Jewish Community of Bergen County; exec. v. pres. Jewish Community Fed. of Metropolitan N.J.; first exec. dir.: Chicago's Bureau on Jewish Employment Problems; Cleveland Jewish Vocational Service; assoc. dir. Jewish Welfare Fed. of Detroit; exec. dir. Jewish Fed. and Council of Greater Kansas City, 1947–63; mem. exec. com. Natl. Conf. Jewish Communal Service; sec. *The Jewish News;* dir. Dept. Campaign Services, CJF; awarded medal for 25 years of service, UJA, 1963.

TUROVER, ISADOR S., business exec., philanthropist; b. Sochachov, Poland, July 8, 1892; d. Washington, D.C., Oct. 16, 1978; in U.S. since 1912; founder, pres. I.S. Turover Lumber Co., 1923; worked with Office of Price Admn. and War Production Bd., WWII; chmn. Community Chest of Montgomery County; v. pres. United Givers Fund of Greater Washington; dir.: U.S. Chess Fed.; Amer. Chess Fed.; helped finance the purchase of the steamer "Exodus" which attempted to carry Jewish refugees to Palestine through the British blockade, 1946; Zionist Org. of America: past. natl. treas.; hon. v. pres.; dir. Louis D. Brandeis Zionist District; dir. Seaboard Zionist Region; pres., campaign manager, UJA of Greater Washington; representative to Jewish Community Council of Washington; delegate, World Jewish Congress; trustee: Hebrew Home for the Aged; Congregation Adas Israel; a founder, natl. v. pres. Amer. Assn. for Jewish Ed.; bd. mem.: Jewish Natl. Fund; Jewish Theological Seminary; v. pres. Jewish Community Center, Washington, D.C.; chmn. of several Zionist national conventions; chess champion of Washington, D.C., 1918–21; honored for leadership in WWII Bond Drives; forest in Israel established in his honor, Jewish Natl. Fund; recipient: Shem Tov Award, Adas Israel Congregation,

1966; Natl. Community Service Award, Jewish Theological Seminary.

UDELL, SOPHIE S., communal worker, philanthropist; b. N.Y.C., June 6, 1900; d. N.Y.C., May 30, 1978; chmn. Foster Home Com.; dir. and chmn. Pleasantville Cottage School Com.; dir. and chmn.: Women's Div., Fed. of Jewish Philanthropies; Women's Div., UJA; N.Y. Assn. for New Americans; CJF; bd. mem., v. pres. Jewish Child Care Assn.; trustee, Jewish Communal Fund; bd. mem. Family Day Care Service of the Eisman Day Nursery and Jewish Child Care Assn.; honored by: Comprehensive High School; Fed. of Jewish Philanthropies; N.Y. Assn. for New Americans; Jewish Child Care Assn.; recipient, Naomi and Howard Lehman Memorial Award for "significant contribution to the welfare of children."

UNTERMEYER, LOUIS M., author, editor; b. N.Y.C., Oct. 1, 1885; d. Newton, Conn., Dec. 29, 1977; v. pres., manager, jewelry business, 1923; poetry editor, *The American Mercury,* 1934–37; poet-in-residence: Knox Coll., 1937; Amherst Coll., 1937; U. of Michigan, 1939–40; U. of Kansas City, 1939; Iowa State Coll., 1940; sr. editor of publications, Office of War Information, 1942; editor: Armed Services Editions, 1943–44; Decca Records, 1944–57; consultant in poetry, Library of Congress, 1961; mem. Natl. Inst. Arts and Letters; author: *Modern British Poetry* (1920, 1962); *Modern American Poetry* (1921, 1962); *This Singing World* (1923); *Moses* (1928); *The Book of Living Verse* (1932); *From Another World* (1939); *A Treasury of the World's Great Poems* (1942); *Doorways to Poetry* (1951); *The Magic Circle* (1953); *Makers of the Modern World* (1954); *Lives of the Poets* (1959); *Britannica Library of Great American Writing,* 2 vols. (1960); *Long Feud: Selected Poems* (1962); *The World's Great Stories* (1964); *Labyrinth of Love* (1965); *Bygones: An Autobiography* (1965); *The Firebringer and Other Great Stories* (1968); contributor of prefaces, translations, critical reviews to: *New Republic; Yale Review; Saturday Review of Literature;* editor, various magazines; recipient: hon. DHL, Union Coll.; hon. D. Litt., New England U.; Gold Medal, Poetry Soc. of America; hon. Phi Beta Kappa: Harvard U.; Tufts U.

WARSHAUER, SAMUEL, business exec., philanthropist; b. West N.Y., N.J., March 18, 1915; d. Tel Aviv, Israel, July 1, 1978; sr. v. pres. Melnor Industries, N.J.; chmn. Hardware Div., UJA of Greater N.Y., 1963, 1967; gen. chmn. Englewood Area Campaign, Israel Bonds, 1970, 1971; pres. Englewood Area Prime Minister's Club, Israel Bonds, 1975, 1976; chmn. bd. govs., trustee, Jewish Community Center of Englewood, N.J.; trustee, UJA of Englewood and Surrounding Communities; v. pres., trustee, Amer. Friends of Hebrew U.; mem. bd. govs. Hebrew U. of Jerusalem; trustee, Temple Emanu-el, Englewood, N.J.; bd. mem. Givat Haviva Ed. Fund; awarded Scroll of Honor, UJA of Greater N.Y., 1965.

WEINBERG, HAROLD M., business exec., physician, philanthropist; b. N.Y.C., Sept. 23, 1889; d. N.Y.C., March 22, 1978; founder, hon. chmn. bd. Amer. Tack & Hardware Co.; U.S. Army surgeon, WWI; v. pres. Hebrew Inst., Boro Park, 1930–37; a founder, mem. bd. dirs., UJA, 1939; pres. Flatbush Jewish Center, 1951–52; v. pres. Hebrew Immigrants Aid Soc., 1965–78; founder, Notions Div., UJA; chmn. Notions Div., Fed. of Jewish Philanthropies; chmn. Fifth Ave. Synagogue; exec. v. pres., hon. pres. Flatbush Jewish Center.

ZUCKER, ISAIAH O., attorney, communal leader; b. (?), 1909; d. N.Y.C., June 19, 1978; pres. West Side Institutional Synagogue; founder, first pres. Williamsburg Jewish Natl. Fund Council; pres. Clymer St. Synagogue, Brooklyn; active in UJA-Fed. of Jewish Philanthropies; benefactor, Rabbi Herzog World Academy; bd. mem. Brooklyn Jewish Community Council.

Calendars

SUMMARY JEWISH CALENDAR, 5740–5744 (Sept. 1979–Sept. 1984)

HOLIDAY	5740 1979	5741 1980	5742 1981	5743 1982	5744 1983
Rosh Ha-shanah, 1st day	Sa Sept. 22	Th Sept. 11	T Sept. 29	Sa Sept. 18	Th Sept. 8
Rosh Ha-shanah, 2nd day	S Sept. 23	F Sept. 12	W Sept. 30	S Sept. 19	F Sept. 9
Fast of Gedaliah	M Sept. 24	S Sept. 14	Th Oct. 1	M Sept. 20	S Sept. 11
Yom Kippur	M Oct. 1	Sa Sept. 20	Th Oct. 8	M Sept. 27	Sa Sept. 17
Sukkot, 1st day	Sa Oct. 6	Th Sept. 25	T Oct. 13	Sa Oct. 2	Th Sept. 22
Sukkot, 2nd day	S Oct. 7	F Sept. 26	W Oct. 14	S Oct. 3	F Sept. 23
Hosha'na Rabbah	F Oct. 12	W Oct. 1	M Oct. 19	F Oct. 8	W Sept. 28
Shemini 'Azeret	Sa Oct. 13	Th Oct. 2	T Oct. 20	Sa Oct. 9	Th Sept. 29
Simhat Torah	S Oct. 14	F Oct. 3	W Oct. 21	S Oct. 10	F Sept. 30
New Moon, Heshwan, 1st day	S Oct. 21	F Oct. 10	W Oct. 28	S Oct. 17	F Oct. 7
New Moon, Heshwan, 2nd day	M Oct. 22	Sa Oct. 11	Th Oct. 29	M Oct. 18	Sa Oct. 8
New Moon, Kislew, 1st day	T Nov. 20	S Nov. 9	F Nov. 27	T Nov. 16	S Nov. 6
New Moon, Kislew, 2nd day	W Nov. 21			W Nov. 17	M Nov. 7
Hanukkah, 1st day	Sa Dec. 15	W Dec. 3	M Dec. 21	Sa Dec. 11	Th Dec. 1
New Moon, Tevet, 1st day	Th Dec. 20	M Dec. 8	Sa Dec. 26	Th Dec. 16	T Dec. 6
New Moon, Tevet, 2nd day	F Dec. 21		S Dec. 27	F Dec. 17	W Dec. 7

	Year 1			Year 2			Year 3			Year 4			Year 5		
	Day	Mo.	Date	Day	Mo.	Date	Day	Mo.	Date	Day	Mo.	Date	Day	Mo.	Date
New Moon, Shevat	Sa	Jan.	19	T	Jan.	6	M	Jan.	25	Sa	Jan.	15	Th	Jan.	5
Hamishshah-'asar bi-Shevat	Sa	Feb.	2	T	Jan.	20	M	Feb.	8	Sa	Jan.	29	Th	Jan.	19
New Moon, Adar I, 1st day				W	Feb.	4							F	Feb.	3
New Moon, Adar I, 2nd day				Th	Feb.	5							Sa	Feb.	4
New Moon, Adar II, 1st day	S	Feb.	17	F	Mar.	6	T	Feb.	23	S	Feb.	13	S	Mar.	4
New Moon, Adar II, 2nd day	M	Feb.	18	Sa	Mar.	7	W	Feb.	24	M	Feb.	14	M	Mar.	5
Fast of Esther	Th	Feb.	28	Th	Mar.	19	M	Mar.	8	Th	Feb.	24	Th	Mar.	15
Purim	S	Mar.	2	F	Mar.	20	T	Mar.	9	S	Feb.	27	S	Mar.	18
Shushan Purim	M	Mar.	3	S	Mar.	21	W	Mar.	10	M	Feb.	28	M	Mar.	19
New Moon, Nisan	T	Mar.	18	S	Apr.	5	Th	Mar.	25	T	Mar.	15	T	Apr.	3
Passover, 1st day		Apr.	1	M	Apr.	19	F	Apr.	8	T	Mar.	29	T	Apr.	17
Passover, 2nd day		Apr.	2		Apr.	20		Apr.	9	W	Mar.	30	W	Apr.	18
Passover, 7th day		Apr.	7		Apr.	25		Apr.	14	M	Apr.	4	M	Apr.	23
Passover, 8th day		Apr.	8		Apr.	26		Apr.	15	T	Apr.	5	T	Apr.	24
Holocaust Memorial Day		Apr.	13		May	1		Apr.	20	S	Apr.	10	S	Apr.	29
New Moon, Iyar, 1st day		Apr.	16		May	4		Apr.	23	W	Apr.	13	W	May	2
New Moon, Iyar, 2nd day		Apr.	17		May	5		Apr.	24	Th	Apr.	14	Th	May	3
Israel Independence Day		Apr.	21					Apr.	28	M	Apr.	18	M	May	7
Lag Ba-'omer		May	4		May	22		May	11	S	May	1	S	May	20
New Moon, Siwan		May	16		June	3		May	23	F	May	13	F	June	1
Shavu'ot, 1st day		May	21		June	8		May	28	W	May	18	W	June	6
Shavu'ot, 2nd day		May	22		June	9		May	29	Th	May	19	Th	June	7
New Moon, Tammuz, 1st day		June	14		July	2		June	21	Sa	June	11	Sa	June	30
New Moon, Tammuz, 2nd day		June	15		July	3		June	22	S	June	12	S	July	1
Fast of the 17th of Tammuz		July	14		July	19		July	8	T	June	28	T	July	17
New Moon, Av		July	22		Aug.	1		July	21	M	July	11	M	July	30
Fast of the 9th of Av		Aug.	12		Aug.	9		July	29	T	July	19	T	Aug.	7
New Moon, Elul, 1st day		Aug.	13		Aug.	30		Aug.	19	T	Aug.	9	T	Aug.	28
New Moon, Elul, 2nd day					Aug.	31		Aug.	20	W	Aug.	10	W	Aug.	29

CONDENSED MONTHLY CALENDAR
(1979–1981)

1978, Dec. 31—Jan. 28, 1979] ṬEVET (29 DAYS)   [5739

Civil Date	Day of the Week	Jewish Date	SABBATHS, FESTIVALS, FASTS	PENTATEUCHAL READING	PROPHETICAL READING
Dec. 31	S	Tevet 1	Ḥanukkah, seventh day; New Moon, second day	Num. 28: 1–15 7: 48–53	
Jan. 1	M	2	Ḥanukkah, eighth day	Num. 7: 54–8: 4	
6	Sa	7	Wa-yiggash	Gen. 44: 18–47: 27	Ezekiel 37: 15–28
9	T	10	Fast of the 10th of Ṭevet	Exod. 32: 11–14; 34: 1–10	Isaiah 55: 6–56: 8 (afternoon only)
13	Sa	14	Wa-yeḥi	Gen. 47: 28–50: 26	I Kings 2: 1–12
20	Sa	21	Shemot	Exod. 1: 1–6: 1	Isaiah 27: 6–28: 13; 29: 22, 23 *Jeremiah 1: 1–2: 3*
27	Sa	28	Wa-era'	Exod. 6: 2–9: 35	Ezekiel 28: 25–29: 21

*Italics are for
Sephardi Minhag.*

1979, Jan. 29–Feb. 27] SHEVAṬ (30 DAYS) [5739

Civil Date	Day of the Week	Jewish Date	SABBATHS, FESTIVALS, FASTS	PENTATEUCHAL READING	PROPHETICAL READING
Jan. 29	M	Shevaṭ 1	New Moon	Num. 28: 1–15	
Feb. 3	Sa	6	Bo'	Exod. 10: 1–13: 16	Jeremiah 46: 13–28
10	Sa	13	Be-shallaḥ (Shirah)	Exod. 13: 17–17: 16	Judges 4: 4–5: 31 *Judges 5: 1–31*
12	M	15	Ḥamishsha-'asar bi-Shevaṭ		
17	Sa	20	Yitro	Exod. 18: 1–20: 23	Isaiah 6: 1–7: 6; 9: 5, 6 *Isaiah 6: 1–13*
24	Sa	27	Mishpaṭim (Sheḳalim)	Exod. 21: 1–24: 18; 30: 11–16	II Kings 12: 1–17 *II Kings 11: 17–12: 17*
27	T	30	New Moon, first day	Num. 28: 1–15	

Italics are for Sephardi Minhag.

1979, Feb. 28–Mar. 28]   ADAR (29 DAYS)   [5739

Civil Date	Day of the Week	Jewish Date	SABBATHS, FESTIVALS, FASTS	PENTATEUCHAL READING	PROPHETICAL READING
Feb. 28	W	Adar 1	New Moon, second day	Num. 28: 1–15	
Mar 3	Sa	4	Terumah	Exod. 25: 1–27: 19	I Kings 5: 26–6: 13
10	Sa	11	Tezawweh (Zakhor)	Exod. 27: 20–30: 10 Deut. 25: 17–19	I Samuel 15: 2–34 *I Samuel 15: 1–34*
12	M	13	Fast of Esther	Exod. 32: 11–14; 34: 1–10	Isaiah 55: 6–56: 8 (afternoon only)
13	T	14	Purim	Exod. 17: 8–16	(Book of Esther is read the night before and in the morning.)
14	W	15	Shushan Purim		
17	Sa	18	Ki tissa' (Parah)	Exod. 30: 11–34: 35 Num. 19: 1–22	Ezekiel 36: 16–38 *Ezekiel 36: 16–36*
24	Sa	25	Wa-yakhel, Pekude; (Ha-hodesh)	Exod. 35: 1–40: 38; 12: 1–20	Ezekiel 45: 16–46: 18 *Ezekiel 36: 18–46: 15*

Italics are for
Sephardi Minhag.

1979, Mar. 29—Apr. 27]   NISAN (30 DAYS)   [5739

Civil Date	Day of the Week	Jewish Date	SABBATHS, FESTIVALS, FASTS	PENTATEUCHAL READING	PROPHETICAL READING
Mar. 29	Th	Nisan 1	New Moon	Num. 28: 1–15	
31	Sa	3	Wa-yikra'	Lev. 1: 1–5: 26	Isaiah 43: 21–44: 23
Apr. 7	Sa	10	Ẕaw (Ha-gadol)	Lev. 6: 1–8: 36	Malachi 3: 4–24
11	W	14	Fast of Firstborn		
12	Th	15	Passover, first day	Exod. 12: 21–51 Num. 28: 16–25	Joshua 5: 2–6: 1, 27
13	F	16	Passover, second day	Lev. 22: 26–23: 44 Num. 28: 16–25	II Kings 23: 1–9; 21–25
14–17	Sa-T	17–20	Ḥol Ha-mo'ed	Sa Exod. 33: 12–34: 26 Num. 28: 19–25 S Exod. 13: 1–16 Num. 28: 19–25 M Exod. 22: 24–23: 19 Num. 28: 19–25 T Num. 9: 1–14 28: 19–25	Ezekiel 37: 1–15
18	W	21	Passover, seventh day	Exod. 13: 17–15: 26 Num. 28: 19–25	II Samuel 22: 1–51
19	Th	22	Passover, eighth day	Deut. 15: 19–16: 17 Num. 28: 19–25	Isaiah 10: 32–12: 6
21	Sa	24	Shemini	Levit. 9: 1–11: 47	II Samuel 6: 1–7: 17
24	T	27	Yom ha-sho'ah weha-gevurah		
27	F	30	New Moon, first day	Num. 28: 1–15	

Civil Date	Day of the Week	Jewish Date	SABBATHS, FESTIVALS, FASTS	PENTATEUCHAL READING	PROPHETICAL READING
Apr. 28	Sa	Iyar 1	Tazria'; Mezora'; New Moon, second day	Levit. 12: 11–15: 33 Num. 28: 9–15	Isaiah 66: 1–23
May 2	W	5	Yom ha-'Azma'ut		
5	Sa	8	Ahare Mot, Kedoshim	Levit. 16: 1–20: 27	Amos 9: 7–15 *Ezekiel 20: 2–20*
12	Sa	15	Emor	Levit. 21: 1–24: 23	Ezekiel 44: 15–31
15	T	18	Lag Ba-'omer		
19	Sa	22	Be-har, Be-hukkotai	Levit. 25: 1–27: 34	Jeremiah 16: 19– 17: 14
26	Sa	29	Be-midmar	Num. 1: 1–4: 20	I Samuel 20: 18–42

Civil Date	Day of the Week	Jewish Date	SABBATHS, FESTIVALS, FASTS	PENTATEUCHAL READING	PROPHETICAL READING
May 27	S	Siwan 1	New Moon	Num. 28: 1–15	
June 1	F	6	Shavu'ot, first day	Exod. 19: 1–20: 23 Num. 28: 26–31	Ezekiel 1: 1–28; 3: 12
2	Sa	7	Shavu'ot, second day	Deut. 15: 19–16: 17 Num. 28: 26–31	Habbakuk 3: 1–19 *Habbakuk 2: 20– 3: 19*
9	Sa	14	Naso'	Num. 4: 21–7: 89	Judges 13: 2–25
16	Sa	21	Be-ha'alotekha	Num. 8: 1–12: 16	Zechariah 2: 14–4: 7
23	Sa	28	Shelah lekha	Num. 13: 1–15: 41	Joshua 2: 1–24
25	M	30	New Moon, first day	Num. 28: 1–15	

Italics are for Sephardi Minhag.

1979, June 26—July 24]   TAMMUZ (29 DAYS)   [5739

Civil Date	Day of the Week	Jewish Date	SABBATHS, FESTIVALS, FASTS	PENTATEUCHAL READING	PROPHETICAL READING
June 26	T	Tammuz 1	New Moon, second day	Num. 28: 1–5	
30	Sa	5	Korah	Num. 16: 1–18: 32	I Samuel 11: 14–12: 22
July 7	Sa	12	Hukkat, Balak	Num. 19: 1–25: 9	Micah 5: 6–6: 8
12	Th	17	Fast of the 17th of Tammuz	Exod. 32: 11–14; 34: 1–10	Isaiah 55: 6–56: 8 (afternoon only)
14	Sa	19	Pinehas	Num. 25: 10–30: 1	Jeremiah 1: 1–2: 3
21	Sa	26	Mattot, Mas'e	Num. 30: 2–36: 13	Jeremiah 2: 4–28; 3: 4 *Jeremiah 2: 4–28; 4: 1, 2*

Italics are for Sephardi Minhag.

1979, July 25—Aug. 23]   AV (30 DAYS)   [5739

Civil Date	Day of the Week	Jewish Date	SABBATHS, FESTIVALS, FASTS	PENTATEUCHAL READING	PROPHETICAL READING
July 25	W	Av 1	New Moon	Num. 28: 1–15	
28	Sa	4	Devarim (Ḥazon)	Deut. 1: 1–3: 22	Isaiah 1: 1–27
Aug. 2	Th	9	Fast of the 9th of Av	Morning: Deut. 4: 25–40 Afternoon: Exod. 32: 11–14; 34: 1–10	(Lamentations is read the night before.) Jeremiah 8: 13–9: 23 Isaiah 55: 6–56: 8
4	Sa	11	Wa-etḥannan (Naḥamu)	Deut. 3: 23–7: 11	Isaiah 40: 1–26
11	Sa	18	ʿEḳev	Deut. 7: 12–11: 25	Isaiah 49: 14–51: 3
18	Sa	25	Re'eh	Deut. 11: 26–16: 17	Isaiah 54: 11–55: 5
23	Th	30	New Moon, first day	Num. 28: 1–15	

1979, Aug. 24–Sept. 21]   ELUL (29 DAYS)   [5739

Civil Date	Day of the Week	Jewish Date	SABBATHS, FESTIVALS, FASTS	PENTATEUCHAL READING	PROPHETICAL READING
Aug. 24	F	Elul 1	New Moon, second day	Num. 28: 1–15	
25	Sa	2	Shofeṭim	Deut. 16: 18–21: 9	Isaiah 51: 12–52: 12
Sept. 1	Sa	9	Ki teze'	Deut. 21: 10–25: 19	Isaiah 54: 1–10
8	Sa	16	Ki tavo'	Deut. 26: 1–29: 8	Isaiah 60: 1–22
15	Sa	23	Niẓẓavim; We-yelekh	Deut. 29: 9–31: 30	Isaiah 61: 10–63: 9

1979, Sept. 22–Oct. 21]   TISHRI (30 DAYS)   [5740

Civil Date	Day of the Week	Jewish Date	SABBATHS, FESTIVALS, FASTS	PENTATEUCHAL READING	PROPHETICAL READING
Sept. 22	Sa	Tishri 1	Rosh Ha-shanah, first day	Gen. 21: 1–34 Num. 29: 1–6	I Samuel 1: 1–2: 10
23	S	2	Rosh Ha-shanah, second day	Gen. 22: 1–24 Num. 29: 1–6	Jeremiah 31: 1–19 (2–20)
24	M	3	Fast of Gedaliah	Exod. 32: 11–14; 34: 1–10	Isaiah 55: 6–56: 8 (afternoon only)
29	Sa	8	Ha'azinu (Shuvah)	Deut. 32: 1–52	Hosea 14: 2–10 Micah 7: 18–20 Joel 2: 15–27 *Hosea 14: 2–10* *Micah 7: 18–20*
Oct. 1	M	10	Yom Kippur	Morning: Levit. 16: 1–34 Num. 29: 1–11 Afternoon: Levit. 18: 1–30	Isaiah 57: 14–58: 14 Jonah 1: 1–4: 11 Micah 7: 18–20
6	Sa	15	Sukkot, first day	Levit. 22: 26–23: 44 Num. 29: 12–16	Zechariah 14: 1–21
7	S	16	Sukkot, second day	Levit. 22: 26–23: 44 Num. 29: 12–16	I Kings 8: 2–21
8–11	M-Th	17–20	Ḥol Ha-mo'ed	M Num. 29: 17–25 T Num. 29: 20–28 W Num. 29: 23–31 Th Num. 29: 26–34	
12	F	21	Hosha'na Rabbah	Num. 29: 26–34	
13	Sa	22	Shemini 'Azeret	Deut. 14: 22–16: 17 Num. 29: 35–30: 1	I Kings 8: 54–66
14	S	23	Simḥat Torah	Deut. 33: 1–34: 12 Gen. 1: 1–2: 3 Num. 29: 35–30: 1	Joshua 1: 1–18 *Joshua 1: 1–19*
20	Sa	29	Be-re'shit	Gen. 1: 1–6: 8	I Samuel 20: 18–42
21	S	30	New Moon, first day	Num. 28: 1–15	

Italics are for
Sephardi Minhag.

1979, Oct. 22–Nov. 20] HESHWAN (29 DAYS) [5740

Civil Date	Day of the Week	Jewish Date	SABBATHS, FESTIVALS, FASTS	PENTATEUCHAL READING	PROPHETICAL READING
Oct. 22	M	Heshwan 1	New Moon, second day	Num. 28: 1–15	
27	Sa	6	Noaḥ	Gen. 6: 19–11: 32	Isaiah 54: 1–55: 5
Nov. 3	Sa	13	Lekh lekha	Gen. 12: 1–17: 27	Isaiah 40: 27–41: 16
10	Sa	20	Wa-yera'	Gen. 18: 1–22: 24	II Kings 4: 1–37 *II Kings 4: 1–23*
17	Sa	27	Ḥayye Sarah	Gen. 23: 1–25: 18	I Kings 1: 1–31
20	T	30	New Moon, first day	Num. 28: 1–15	

1979, Nov. 21–Dec. 20] KISLEW (30 DAYS) [5740

Civil Date	Day of the Week	Jewish Date	SABBATHS, FESTIVALS, FASTS	PENTATEUCHAL READING	PROPHETICAL READING
Nov. 21	W	Kislew 1	New Moon, second day	Num. 28: 1–15	
24	Sa	4	Toledot	Gen. 25: 19–28: 9	Malachi 1: 1–2: 7
Dec. 1	Sa	11	Wa-yeze'	Gen. 28: 10–32: 3	Hosea 12: 13–14: 10 *Hosea 11: 7–12: 12*
8	Sa	18	Wa-yishlaḥ	Gen. 32: 4–36: 43	Hosea 11: 7–12: 12 *Obadiah 1: 1–21*
15	Sa	25	Wa-yeshev; Hanukkah, first day	Gen. 37: 1–40: 23 Num. 7: 1–17	Zechariah 2: 14–4: 7
16–19	S-W	26–29	Ḥanukkah, second to fifth day	S Num. 7: 18–29 M Num. 7: 24–35 T Num. 7: 30–41 W Num. 7: 36–47	
20	Th	30	Hanukkah, sixth day; New Moon, first day	Num. 28: 1–15 7: 42–47	

Italics are for Sephardi Minhag.

1979, Dec. 21–Jan. 18, 1980] TEVET (29 DAYS)   [5740

Civil Date	Day of the Week	Jewish Date	SABBATHS, FESTIVALS, FASTS	PENTATEUCHAL READING	PROPHETICAL READING
Dec. 21	F	Tevet 1	Hanukkah, seventh day; New Moon, second day	Num. 28: 1–15 7: 48–53	
22	Sa	2	Mi-kez; Hanukkah, eighth day	{Gen. 41: 1–44: 17 {Num. 7: 54–8: 4	I Kings 7: 40–50
29	Sa	9	Wa-yiggash	Gen. 44: 18–47: 27	Ezekiel 37: 15–28
30	S	10	Fast of 10th of Tevet	Exod. 32: 11–14; 34: 1–10	Isaiah 55: 6–56: 8 (afternoon only)
1980 Jan. 5	Sa	16	Wa-yehi	Gen. 47: 28–50: 26	I Kings 2: 1–12
12	Sa	23	Shemot	Exod. 1: 1–6: 7	Isaiah 27: 6–28: 13; 29: 22–23 *Jeremiah 1: 1–2: 3*

1980, Jan. 19–Feb. 17]   SHEVAT (30 DAYS)   [5740

Civil Date	Day of the Week	Jewish Date	SABBATHS, FESTIVALS, FASTS	PENTATEUCHAL READING	PROPHETICAL READING
Jan. 19	Sa	Shevat 1	Wa-era' New Moon	Exod. 6: 2–9: 35	Isaiah 66: 1–24
26	Sa	8	Bo'	Exod. 10: 1–13: 16	Jeremiah 46: 13–28
Feb. 2	Sa	15	Be-shallah (Shirah)	Exod. 13: 17–17: 16	Judges 4: 4–5: 31 *Judges 5: 1–31*
9	Sa	22	Hamishsha-'asar bi-Shevat Yitro	Exod. 18: 1–20: 23	Isaiah 6: 1–7: 6 9: 5, 6
16	Sa	29	Mishpatim (Shekalim)	Exod. 21–24: 18 30: 11–16	II Kings 12: 1–17 *II Kings 11: 17–12: 17*
17	S	30	New Moon, first day	Num. 28: 1–15	*I Samuel 20: 18, 42*

Italics are for Sephardi Minhag.

1980, Feb. 18-Mar. 17] ADAR (29 DAYS) [5740

Civil Date	Day of the Week	Jewish Date	SABBATHS, FESTIVALS, FASTS	PENTATEUCHAL READING	PROPHETICAL READING
Feb. 18	M	Adar 1	New Moon, second day	Num. 28: 1–15	
23	Sa	6	Terumah	Exod. 25: 1–27: 19	I Kings 5: 26–6: 13
28	Th	11	Fast of Esther	Exod. 32: 11–14 34: 1–10	Isaiah 55: 6–56: 8 (afternoon only)
Mar. 1	Sa	13	Tezawweh (Zakhor)	Exod. 27: 20–30: 10 Deut. 25: 17–19	I Samuel 15: 2–34 *I Samuel 15: 1–34*
2	S	14	Purim	Exod. 17: 8–16	Book of Esther (night before and in the morning)
3	M	15	Shushan Purim		
8	Sa	20	Ki tissa' (Parah)	Exod. 30: 11–34: 35 Num. 19: 1–22	Ezekiel 36: 16–38 *Ezekiel 36: 16–36*
15	Sa	27	Wa-yakhel, Pekude (Ha-hodesh)	Exod. 35: 1–40: 38 12: 1–20	Ezekiel 45: 16–46: 18 *Ezekiel 45: 18–46: 15*

Italics are for Sephardi Minhag.

1980, Mar. 18-Apr. 16]   NISAN (30 DAYS)   [5740

Civil Date	Day of the Week	Jewish Date	SABBATHS, FESTIVALS, FASTS	PENTATEUCHAL READING	PROPHETICAL READING
Mar. 18	T	Nisan 1	New Moon	Num. 28: 1–15	
22	Sa	5	Wa–yikra'	Levit. 1: 1–5: 26	Isaiah 43: 21–44: 23
29	Sa	12	Zaw (Ha–gadol)	Levit. 6: 1–8: 36	Malachi 3: 4–24
31	M	14	Fast of the Firstborn		
Apr. 1	T	15	Passover, first day	Exod. 12: 21–51 Num. 28: 16–25	Joshua 5: 2–6: 1, 27
2	W	16	Passover, second day	Levit. 22: 26–23: 44 Num. 28: 16–25	II Kings 23: 1–9, 21–25
3	Th	17	Hol Ha-mo'ed	Exod. 13: 1–16 Num. 28: 19–25	
4	F	18	Hol Ha-mo'ed	Exod. 22: 24–23: 19 Num. 28: 19–25	
5	Sa	19	Hol Ha-mo'ed	Exod. 33: 12–34: 26 Num. 28: 19–25	Ezekiel 37: 1–15
6	S	20	Hol Ha-mo'ed	Num. 9: 1–14; 28: 19–25	
7	M	21	Passover, seventh day	Exod. 13: 17–15: 26 Num. 28: 19–25	II Samuel 22: 1–5
8	T	22	Passover, eighth day	Deut. 15: 19–16: 17 Num. 28: 19–25	Isaiah 10: 32–12: 6
12	Sa	26	Shemini	Levit. 9: 1–11: 47	II Samuel 6: 1–7: 17
13	S	27	Holocaust Memorial Day		
16	W	30	New Moon, first day	Num. 28: 1–15	

1980, Apr. 17–May 15]   IYAR (29 DAYS)   [5740

Civil Date	Day of the Week	Jewish Date	SABBATHS, FESTIVALS, FASTS	PENTATEUCHAL READING	PROPHETICAL READING
Apr. 17	Th	Iyar 1	New Moon, second day	Num. 28: 1–15	
19	Sa	3	Tazria', Mezora'	Levit. 12: 1–15: 33 Num. 28: 9–15	II Kings 7: 3–20
26	Sa	10	Ahare Mot, Kedoshim	Levit. 16: 1–20: 27	Amos 9: 7–15 *Ezekiel 20: 2–20*
May 3	Sa	17	Emor	Levit. 21: 1–24: 23	Ezekiel 44: 15–31
4	S	18	Lag Ba-'omer Israel Independence Day		
10	Sa	24	Be-har, Be-hukkotai	Levit. 25: 1–27: 34	Jeremiah 16: 19– 17: 14

1980, May 16-June 14]   SIWAN (30 DAYS)   [5740

Civil Date	Day of the Week	Jewish Date	SABBATHS, FESTIVALS, FASTS	PENTATEUCHAL READING	PROPHETICAL READING
May 16	F	Siwan 1	New Moon	Num. 28: 1–15	
17	Sa	2	Be–midbar	Num. 1: 1–4: 20	Hosea 2: 1–22
21	W	6	Shavu'ot, first day	Exod. 19: 1–20: 23 Num. 28: 26–31	Ezekiel 1: 1–28 3: 12
22	Th	7	Shavu'ot, second day	Deut. 15: 19–16: 17 Num. 28: 26–31	Habbakuk 3: 1–19 *Habbakuk 2: 20– 3:19*
24	Sa	9	Naso'	Num. 4: 21–7: 89	Judges 13: 2–25
31	Sa	16	Be-ha'alotekha	Num. 8: 1–12: 16	Zechariah 2: 14–4: 7
June 7	Sa	23	Shelah Lekha	Num. 13: 1–15: 41	Joshua 2: 1–24
14	Sa	30	Korah New Moon, first day	Num. 16: 1–18: 32 Num. 28: 9–15	Isaiah 66: 1–24 *I Samuel 20: 18, 42*

Italics are for Sephardi Minhag.

1980, June 15-July 13]   TAMMUZ (29 DAYS)   [5740

Civil Date	Day of the Week	Jewish Date	SABBATHS, FESTIVALS, FASTS	PENTATEUCHAL READING	PROPHETICAL READING
June 15	S	Tammuz 1	New Moon, second day	Num. 28: 1–15	
21	Sa	7	Ḥukkat	Num. 19: 1–22: 1	Judges 11: 1–33
28	Sa	14	Balak	Num. 22: 2–25: 9	Micah 5: 6–6: 8
July 1	T	17	Fast of the 17th of Tammuz	Exod. 32: 11–14 34: 1–10	Isaiah 55: 6–56: 8 (afternoon only)
5	Sa	21	Pineḥas	Num. 25: 10–30: 1	Jeremiah 1: 1–2: 3
12	Sa	28	Mattot, Mas'e	Num. 30: 2–36: 13	Jeremiah 2: 4–28, 3: 4 *Jeremiah 2: 4–28, 4: 1, 2*

1980, July 14-Aug. 12]   AV (30 DAYS)   [5740

Civil Date	Day of the Week	Jewish Date	SABBATHS, FESTIVALS, FASTS	PENTATEUCHAL READING	PROPHETICAL READING
July 14	M	Av 1	New Moon	Num. 28: 1–15	
19	Sa	6	Devarim (Ḥazon)	Deut. 1: 1–3: 22	Isaiah 1: 1–27
22	T	9	Fast of the 9th of Av	Morning: Deut. 4: 25–40 Afternoon: Exod. 32: 11–14 34: 1–10	(Lamentations is read the night before.) Jeremiah 8: 13–9: 23 Isaiah 55: 6–56: 8
26	Sa	13	Wa-etḥannan (Naḥamu)	Deut. 3: 23–7: 11	Isaiah 40: 1–26
Aug. 2	Sa	20	'Ekev	Deut. 7: 12–11: 25	Isaiah 49: 14–51: 3
9	Sa	27	Re'eh	Deut. 11: 26–16: 17	Isaiah 54: 11–55: 5
12	T	30	New Moon, first day	Num. 28: 1–15	

Italics are for Sephardi Minhag.

1980, Aug. 13-Sept. 10]   ELUL (29 DAYS)   [5740

Civil Date	Day of the Week	Jewish Date	SABBATHS, FESTIVALS, FASTS	PENTATEUCHAL READING	PROPHETICAL READING
Aug. 13	W	Elul 1	New Moon, second day	Num. 28: 1–15	
16	Sa	4	Shofeṭim	Deut. 16: 18–21: 9	Isaiah 51: 12–52: 12
23	Sa	11	Ki teze'	Deut. 21: 10–25: 19	Isaiah 54: 1–10
30	Sa	18	Ki tavo'	Deut. 26: 1–29: 8	Isaiah 60: 1–22
Sept. 6	Sa	25	Nizzavim, Wa-yelekh	Deut. 29: 9–31: 30	Isaiah 61: 10–63: 9

1980, Sept. 11–Oct. 10] TISHRI (30 DAYS) [5741

Civil Date	Day of the Week	Jewish Date	SABBATHS, FESTIVALS, FASTS	PENTATEUCHAL READING	PROPHETICAL READING
Sept. 11	Th	Tishri 1	Rosh Ha-shanah, first day	Gen. 21: 1–34 Num. 29: 1–6	I Samuel 1: 1–2: 10
12	F	2	Rosh Ha-shanah, second day	Gen. 22: 1–24 Num. 29: 1–6	Jeremiah 31: 2–20
13	Sa	3	Ha'azinu (Shuvah)	Deut. 32: 1–52	Hosea 14: 2–10 Micah 7: 18–20 Joel 2: 15–27 *Hosea 14: 2–10* *Micah 7: 18–20*
14	S	4	Fast of Gedaliah	Exod. 32: 11–14; 34: 1–10	Isaiah 55: 6–56: 8
20	Sa	10	Yom Kippur	Morning: Levit. 16: 1–34 Num. 29: 7–11 Afternoon: Levit. 18: 1–30	Isaiah 57: 14–58: 14 Jonah 1: 1–14: 11 Micah 7: 18–20
25	Th	15	Sukkot, first day	Levit. 22: 26–23: 44 Num. 29: 12–16	Zechariah 14: 1–21
26	F	16	Sukkot, second day	Levit. 22: 26–23: 44 Num. 29: 12–16	I Kings 8: 2–21
27	Sa	17	Ḥol Ha–mo'ed	Exod. 33: 12–34: 26 Num. 29: 17–22	Ezekiel 38: 18–39: 16
28	S	18	Ḥol Ha–mo'ed	Num. 29: 20–28	
29	M	19	Ḥol Ha–mo 'ed	Num. 29: 23–31	
30	T	20	Ḥol Ha–mo'ed	Num. 29: 26–34	
Oct. 1	W	21	Hosha'na Rabbah	Num. 29: 26–34	
2	Th	22	Shemini 'Azeret	Deut. 14: 22–16: 17 Num. 29: 35–30: 1	I.Kings 8: 54–66
3	F	23	Simḥat Torah	Deut. 33: 1–34: 12 Gen. 1: 1–2: 3 Num. 29: 35–30: 1	Joshua 1: 1–18 *Joshua 1: 1–9*
4	Sa	24	Be-re'shit	Gen. 1: 1–6: 8	Isaiah 42: 5–43: 10 *Isaiah 42: 5–21*
10	F	30	New Moon, first day	Num. 28: 1–15	

Italics are for Sephardi Minhag.

1980, Oct. 11–Nov. 8]   ḤESHWAN (29 DAYS)   [5741

Civil Date	Day of the Week	Jewish Date	SABBATHS, FESTIVALS, FASTS	PENTATEUCHAL READING	PROPHETICAL READING
Oct. 11	Sa	Ḥeshwan 1	Noah, New Moon, second day	Gen. 6: 9–11: 32 Num. 28: 9–15	Isaiah 66: 1–24
18	Sa	8	Lekh Lekha	Gen. 12: 1–17: 27	Isaiah 40: 27–41: 16
25	Sa	15	Wa-yera'	Gen. 18: 1–22: 24	II Kings 4: 1–37 *II Kings 4: 1–23*
Nov. 1	Sa	22	Ḥayye Sarah	Gen. 23: 1–25: 18	I Kings 1: 1–31
8	Sa	29	Toledot	Gen. 25: 19–28: 9	I Samuel 20: 18–42

1980, Nov. 9-Dec. 7]   KISLEW (29 DAYS)   [5741

Civil Date	Day of the Week	Jewish Date	SABBATHS, FESTIVALS, FASTS	PENTATEUCHAL READING	PROPHETICAL READING
Nov. 9	S	Kislew 1	New Moon	Num. 28: 1–15	
15	Sa	7	Wa-yeze'	Gen. 28: 10–32: 3	Hosea 12: 13–14: 10 *Hosea 11: 7–12: 12*
22	Sa	14	Wa-yishlaḥ	Gen. 32: 4–36: 43	Hosea 11: 7–12: 12 *Obadiah 1: 1–21*
29	Sa	21	Wa-yeshev	Gen. 37: 1–40: 23	Amos 2: 6–3: 8
Dec. 3	W	25	Hanukkah, first day	Num. 7: 1–17	
4	Th	26	Ḥanukkah, second day	Num. 7: 18–29	
5	F	27	Ḥanukkah, third day	Num. 7: 24–35	
6	Sa	28	Mi-kez Ḥanukkah, fourth day	Gen. 41: 1–44: 17 Num. 7: 30–35	Zechariah 2: 14–4: 7
7	S	29	Ḥanukkah, fifth day	Num. 7: 36–47	

Italics are for
Sephardi Minhag.

1980, Dec. 8-Jan. 5, 1981]   ṬEVET (29 DAYS)   [5741

Civil Date	Day of the Week	Jewish Date	SABBATHS, FESTIVALS, FASTS	PENTATEUCHAL READING	PROPHETICAL READING
Dec. 8	M	Ṭevet 1	Hanukkah, sixth day New Moon	Num. 28: 1–15 7: 42–47	
9	T	2	Hanukkah, seventh day	Num. 7: 48–59	
10	W	3	Hanukkah, eighth day	Num. 7: 54–8: 4	
13	Sa	6	Wa-yiggash	Gen. 44: 18–47: 27	Ezekiel 37: 15–28
17	T	10	Fast of the 10th of Ṭevet	Exod. 32: 11–14 34: 1–10	Isaiah 55: 6–56: 8 (afternoon only)
20	Sa	13	Wa-yeḥi	Gen. 47: 28–50: 26	I Kings 2: 1–12
27	Sa	20	Shemot	Exod. 1: 1–6: 1	Isaiah 27: 6–28: 13 29: 22–23 *Jeremiah 1: 1–2: 3*
Jan. 3	Sa	27	Wa-era'	Exod. 6: 2–9: 35	Ezekiel 28: 25–29: 21

Italics are for
Sephardi Minhag.

1981, Jan. 6–Feb. 4] SHEVAṬ (30 DAYS) [5741

Civil Date	Day of the Week	Jewish Date	SABBATHS, FESTIVALS, FASTS	PENTATEUCHAL READING	PROPHETICAL READING
Jan. 6	T	Shevaṭ 1	New Moon	Num. 28: 1–15	
10	Sa	5	Bo'	Exod. 10: 1–13: 16	Jeremiah 46: 13–28
17	Sa	12	Be-shallaḥ (Shabbat Shirah)	Exod. 13: 17–17: 16	Judges 4: 4–5: 31 *Judges 5: 1–31*
20	T	15	Hamishsha-'asar bi-Shevaṭ		
24	Sa	19	Yitro	Exod. 18: 1–20: 23	Isaiah 6: 1–7: 6; 9: 5, 6 *Isaiah 6: 1–13*
31	Sa	26	Mishpaṭim	Exod. 21: 1–24: 18	Jeremiah 34: 8–22 33: 25, 26
Feb. 4	W	30	New Moon, first day	Num. 28: 1–15	

1981, Feb. 5–Mar. 6] ADAR I (30 DAYS) [5741

Civil Date	Day of the Week	Jewish Date	SABBATHS, FESTIVALS, FASTS	PENTATEUCHAL READING	PROPHETICAL READING
Feb. 5	Th	Adar I 1	New Moon, second day	Num. 28: 1–15	
7	Sa	3	Terumah	Exod. 25: 1–27: 19	I Kings 5: 26–6: 13
14	Sa	10	Teẓawweh	Exod. 27: 20–30: 10	Ezekiel 43: 10–27
21	Sa	17	Ki tissa'	Exod. 30: 11–34: 35	I Kings 18: 1–39 I Kings 18: 20–39
28	Sa	24	Wa-yakhel	Exod. 35: 1–38: 20	I Kings 7: 40–50 *I Kings 7: 13–27*
Mar. 6	F	30	New Moon, first day	Num. 28: 1–15	

Italics are for Sephardi Minhag.

1981, Mar. 7—Apr. 4]   ADAR II (29 DAYS)   [5741

Civil Date	Day of the Week	Jewish Date	SABBATHS, FESTIVALS, FASTS	PENTATEUCHAL READING	PROPHETICAL READING
Mar. 7	Sa	Adar II 1	Pekude, Shekalim, New Moon, second day	⎰Exod. 38:21–40:38 ⎱Num. 28:9–15	II Kings 12:1–17 *II Kings 11:17–12:17* *Isaiah 66:1,24*
14	Sa	8	Wa-yikra, Zakhor	⎰Levit. 1:1–5:26 ⎱Deut. 25:17–19	I Samuel 15:2–34 *I Samuel 15:1–34*
19	Th	13	Fast of Esther	Exod. 32:11–14; 34:1–10	Isaiah 55:6–56:8 (afternoon only)
20	F	14	Purim	Exod. 17:8–16	(Book of Esther is read the night before and in the morning.)
21	Sa	15	Zaw, Shushan Purim	Levit. 6:1–8:36	Jeremiah 7:21–8:3; 9:22,23
28	Sa	22	Shemini, Parah	⎰Levit. 9:1–11:47 ⎱Num. 19:1–22	Ezekiel 36:16–38 *Ezekiel 36:16–36*
Apr. 4	Sa	29	Tazria', Ha-ḥodesh	⎰Levit. 12:1–59 ⎱Exod. 12:1–20	Ezekiel 45:16–46:18 *Ezekiel 45:18–46:15* *I Samuel 20:18,42*

Italics are for Sephardi Minhag.

Civil Date	Day of the Week	Jewish Date	SABBATHS, FESTIVALS, FASTS	PENTATEUCHAL READING	PROPHETICAL READING
Apr. 5	S	Nisan 1	New Moon	Num. 28:1–15	
11	Sa	7	Meẓora	Levit. 14:1–15:33	II Kings 7:3–20
16	Th	12	Fast of Firstborn		
18	Sa	14	Aḥare (Shabbat Hagadol)	Levit. 16:1–18:30	Malachi 3:4–24
19	S	15	Passover, first day	Exod. 12:21–51 Num. 28:16–25	Joshua 5:2–6:1,27
20	M	16	Passover, second day	Levit. 22:26–23:44 Num. 28:16–25	II Kings 23:1–9; 21–25
21	T	17	Ḥol Hamo'ed, first day	Exod. 13:1–16 Num. 28:19–25	
22	W	18	Ḥol Hamo'ed second day	Exod. 22:24–23:19 Num. 28:19–25	
23	Th	19	Ḥol Hamo'ed, third day	Exod. 34:1–26 Num. 28:19–25	
24	F	20	Ḥol Hamo'ed, fourth day	Num. 9:1–14 Num. 28:19–25	
25	Sa	21	Passover, seventh day	Exod. 13:17–15:26 Num. 28:19–25	II Samuel 22:1–51
26	S	22	Passover, eighth day	Deut. 15:19–16:17 Num. 28:19–25	Isaiah 10:32–12:16
May 2	Sa	28	Ḳedoshim	Levit. 19:1–20:27	Amos 9:7–15 *Ezekiel 20:2–20*
4	M	30	New Moon, first day	Num. 28:1–15	

Italics are for Sephardi Minhag.

1981, May 5—June 2]   IYAR (29 DAYS)   [5741

Civil Date	Day of the Week	Jewish Date	SABBATHS, FESTIVALS, FASTS	PENTATEUCHAL READING	PROPHETICAL READING
May 5	T	Iyar 1	New Moon, second day	Num. 28:1–15	
9	Sa	5	Emor	Levit. 21:1–24:23	Ezekiel 44:15–31
16	Sa	12	Be-har	Levit. 25:1–26:2	Jeremiah 32:6–27
22	F	18	Lag Ba-'omer		
23	Sa	19	Be-ḥukkotai	Levit. 26:3–27:34	Jeremiah 16:19–17:14
30	Sa	26	Be-midbar	Num. 1:1–4:20	Hosea 2:1–22

1981, June 3—July 2]   SIWAN (30 DAYS)   [5741

Civil Date	Day of the Week	Jewish Date	SABBATHS, FESTIVALS, FASTS	PENTATEUCHAL READING	PROPHETICAL READING
June 3	W	Siwan 1	New Moon	Num. 28:1–15	
6	Sa	4	Naso'	Num. 4:21–7:89	Judges 13:2–25
8	M	6	Shavu'ot, first day	Exod. 19:1–20:23 Num. 28:26–31	Ezekiel 1:1–28; 3:12
9	T	7	Shavu'ot, second day	Deut. 15:19–16:17 Num. 28:26–31	Habbakuk 3:1–19 *Habbakuk 2:20–3:19*
13	Sa	11	Be-ha 'alotekha	Num. 8:1–12:16	Zechariah 2:14–4:7
20	Sa	18	Shelaḥ lekha	Num. 13:1–15:41	Joshua 2:1–24
27	Sa	25	Koraḥ	Num. 16:1–18:32	I Samuel 11:14–12:22
July 2	Th	30	New Moon, first day	Num. 28:1–15	

*Italics are for
Sephardi Minhag.*

1981, July 3—July 31]   TAMMUZ (29 DAYS)   [5741

Civil Date	Day of the Week	Jewish Date	SABBATHS, FESTIVALS, FASTS	PENTATEUCHAL READING	PROPHETICAL READING
July 3	F	Tammuz 1	New Moon, second day	Num. 28:1–15	
4	Sa	2	Hukkat	Num. 19:1–22:1	Judges 11:1–33
11	Sa	9	Balak	Num. 21:2–25:9	Micah 5:6–6:8
18	Sa	16	Pinehas	Num. 25:10–30:1	I Kings 18:46–19:21
19	S	17	Fast of the 17th of Tammuz	Exod. 32:11–14; 34:1–10	Isaiah 55:6–56:8 (afternoon only)
25	Sa	23	Mattot	Num. 30:2–32:42	Jeremiah 1:1–2:3

1981, Aug. 1—Aug. 30] AV (30 DAYS) [5741

Civil Date	Day of the Week	Jewish Date	SABBATHS, FESTIVALS, FASTS	PENTATEUCHAL READING	PROPHETICAL READING
Aug. 1	Sa	Av 1	Mas'e; New Moon	Num. 33:1–36:13 28:9–15	Jeremiah 2:4–28; 3:4 *Jeremiah 2:4–28; 4:1,2*
8	Sa	8	Devarim (Shabbat Ḥazon)	Deut. 1:1–3:22	Isaiah 1:1–27
9	S	9	Fast of the 9th of Av	Morning: Deut. 4:25–40 Afternoon: Exod. 32:11–14; 34:1–10	(Lamentations is read the night before.) Isaiah 55:6–56:8
15	Sa	15	Wa-ethannan (Shabbat Naḥamu)	Deut. 3:23–7:11	Isaiah 40:1–26
22	Sa	22	'Eḳev	Deut. 7:12–11:25	Isaiah 49:14–51:3
29	Sa	29	Re'eh	Deut. 11:26–16:17	Isaiah 54:11–55:5 *Isaiah 54:11–55:5 I Samuel 20:18,42*
30	S	30	New Moon, first day	Num. 28:1–15	

1981, Aug. 31—Sept. 28] ELUL (29 DAYS) [5741

Civil Date	Day of the Week	Jewish Date	SABBATHS, FESTIVALS, FASTS	PENTATEUCHAL READING	PROPHETICAL READING
Aug. 31	M	Elul 1	New Moon, second day	Num. 28:1–15	
Sept. 5	Sa	6	Shofeṭim	Deut. 16:18–21:9	Isaiah 51:12–52:12
12	Sa	13	Ki eẓe'	Deut. 21:10–25:19	Isaiah 54:1–10
19	Sa	20	Ki avo'	Deut. 26:1–29:8	Isaiah 60:1–22
26	Sa	27	Niẓẓavim	Deut. 29:9–30:20	Isaiah 61:10–63:9

Italics are for Sephardi Minhag.

1981, Sept. 29—Oct. 28]　　　TISHRI (30 DAYS)　　　[5742

Civil Date	Day of the Week	Jewish Date	SABBATHS, FESTIVALS, FASTS	PENTATEUCHAL READING	PROPHETICAL READING
Sept. 29	T	Tishri 1	Rosh Ha-shanah, first day	Gen. 21:1–34 Num. 29:1–6	I Samuel 1:1–2:10
30	W	2	Rosh Ha-shanah, second day	Gen. 22:1–24 Num. 29:1–6	Jeremiah 31:2–20
Oct. 1	Th	3	Fast of Gedaliah	Exod. 32:11–14 34:1–10	Isaiah 55:6–56:8 (afternoon only)
3	Sa	5	Wa-yeleẖ (Shabbat Shuvah)	Deut. 31:1–30	Hosea 14:2–10 Micah 7:18–20 Joel 2:15–27 *Hosea 14:2–10* *Micah 7:18–20*
8	Th	10	Yom Kippur	Morning: 　Levit. 16:1–34 　Num. 29:7–11 Afternoon: 　Levit. 18:1–30	Isaiah 57:14–58:14 Jonah 1:1–4:11 Micah 7:18–20
10	Sa	12	Ha'azinu	Deut. 32:1–52	II Samuel 22:1–51
13	T	15	Sukkot, first day	Levit. 22:26–23:44 Num. 29:12–16	Zechariah 14:1–21
14	W	16	Sukkot, second day	Levit. 22:26–23:44 Num. 29:12–16	I Kings 8:2–21
15–18	Th–S	17–20	Ḥol Ha-mo'ed	Th Num. 29:17–25 F Num. 29:20–28 Sa Exod. 33:12–34:26 　Num. 29:23–28 S Num. 29:26–34	Ezekiel 38:18–39:16
19	M	21	Hosha'na Rabbah	Num. 29:26–34	
20	T	22	Shemini 'Aẓeret	Deut. 14:22–16:17 Num. 29:35–30:1	I Kings 8:54–66
21	W	23	Simḥat Torah	Deut. 33:1–34:12 Gen. 1:1–2:3 Num. 29:35–30:1	Joshua 1:1–18 *Joshua 1:1–9*
24	Sa	26	Be-re'shit	Gen. 1:1–6:8	Isaiah 42:5–43:10 *Isaiah 42:5–21*
28	W	30	New Moon, first day	Num. 28:1–15	

Italics are for
Sephardi Minhag.

1981, Oct. 29—Nov. 26]   HESHWAN (29 DAYS)   [5742

Civil Date	Day of the Week	Jewish Date	SABBATHS, FESTIVALS, FASTS	PENTATEUCHAL READING	PROPHETICAL READING
Oct. 29	Th	Heshwan 1	New Moon, second day	Num. 28:1–15	
31	Sa	3	Noah	Gen. 6:9–11:32	Isaiah 54:1–55:5 *Isaiah 54:1–10*
Nov. 7	Sa	10	Lekh Lekha	Gen. 12:1–17:27	Isaiah 40:27–41:16
14	Sa	17	Wa-yera'	Gen. 18:1–22:24	II Kings 4:1–37 *II Kings 4:1–23*
21	Sa	24	Hayye Sarah	Gen. 23:1–25:18	I Kings 1:1–31

1981, Nov. 27—Dec. 26]   KISLEW (30 DAYS)   [5742

Civil Date	Day of the Week	Jewish Date	SABBATHS, FESTIVALS, FASTS	PENTATEUCHAL READING	PROPHETICAL READING
Nov. 27	F	Kislew 1	New Moon	Num. 28:1–15	
28	Sa	2	Toledot	Gen. 25:19–28:9	Malachi 1:1–2:7
Dec. 5	Sa	9	Wa-yeze'	Gen. 28:10–32:3	Hosea 12:13–14:10 *Hosea 11:7–12:12*
12	Sa	16	Wa-yishlah	Gen. 32:4–36:43	Hosea 11:7–12:12 *Obadiah 1:1–21*
19	Sa	23	Wa-yeshev	Gen. 37:1–40:23	Amos 2:6–3:8
21–25	M–F	25–29	Hanukkah, first to fifth days	M Num. 7:1–17 T Num. 7:18–29 W Num. 7:24–35 Th Num. 7:30–41 F Num. 7:36–47	
26	Sa	30	Mi-Kez; Hanukkah, sixth day; New Moon, first day	Gen. 41:1–44:17 Num. 28:9–15 7:42–47	Zechariah 2:14–4:7 [*Zechariah 2:14–4:7* {*Isaiah 66:1,23* [*I Samuel 20:18, 42*

Italics are for Sephardi Minhag.

1981, Dec. 27—Jan. 24, 1982] ṬEVET (29 DAYS)   [5742

Civil Date	Day of the Week	Jewish Date	SABBATHS, FESTIVALS, FASTS	PENTATEUCHAL READING	PROPHETICAL READING
Dec. 27	S	Tevet 1	New Moon, second day Ḥanukkah, seventh day	Num. 28:1–15 7:48–53	
28	M	2	Ḥanukkah, eighth day	Num. 7:54–8:4	
Jan. 3	Sa	7	Wa-yiggash	Gen. 44:18–47:27	Ezekiel 37:15–28
5	T	10	Fast of the 10th of Ṭevet	Exod. 32:11–14; 34:1–10	Isaiah 55:6–56:8 (afternoon only)
9	Sa	14	Wa-yeḥi	Gen. 47:28–50:26	I Kings 2:1–12
16	Sa	21	Shemot	Exod. 1:1–6:1	Isaiah 27:6–28:13; 29:22,23 *Jeremiah 1:1–2:3*
23	Sa	28	Wa-era'	Exod. 6:2–9:35	Ezekiel 28:25–29:21

Italics are for Sephardi Minhag.

The Jewish Publication Society of America

REPORT OF NINETY-FIRST YEAR

REPORT OF THE 91ST JPS ANNUAL MEETING

The 91st annual meeting of the Society was held on Sunday, June 3, 1979, at the University of Pennsylvania in Philadelphia. Presiding was Edward B. Shils, president of the Society.

Bernard G. Segal, chairman, presented the report of the Nominating Committee. Five new trustees were elected to the JPS Board: James O. Freedman, Philadelphia, dean of the University of Pennsylvania Law School, former associate provost of the University, and author of *Crisis and Legitimacy: The Administrative Process and the American Government;* Rela Geffen Monson, Philadelphia, associate professor of Sociology at Gratz College, field coordinator of the Netsky Institute, and coordinator of Formal Education Programs for the Ramah Camps; Louis Henkin, New York, Harlan Fiske Stone Professor of Constitutional Law at Columbia University, president of the United States Institute of Human Rights, and contributor to JPS' *Essays On Human Rights: Contemporary Issues and Jewish Perspectives*; Richard Maass, White Plains, NY, president of the American Jewish Committee, bibliophile, and past president of the Manuscript Society; and Jerry Wagner, Bloomfield, CT, judge of the Superior Court of Connecticut, director of the World Council of Synagogues, and president of the Hartford Jewish Community Center.

Returning to the Board are the following former trustees: Mitchell E. Panzer, Philadelphia, an attorney, member of the Board of the Federation of Jewish Agencies, and honorary president of Gratz College; and Harry

Starr, New York, president and treasurer of the Lucius N. Littauer Foundation, president of the American Association of Jewish Education, and member of the Board of Overseers Visiting Committees at the Middle East Center, Near Eastern Languages and Literature Department, and Kennedy School of Government, Harvard University.

The following trustees were re-elected for an additional 3-year term: Arlin M. Adams, Philadelphia; Harold Cramer, Philadelphia; Edward E. Elson, Atlanta; J.E. Goldman, Stamford; Irwin T. Holtzman, Detroit; Jack Lapin, Houston; Martin Meyerson, Philadelphia; Robert S. Rifkind, New York; Harry Silver, Baltimore; and Marvin Wachman, Philadelphia.

All JPS officers were reelected.

Following the reports of the treasurer, president, and Nominating Committee chairman, Jerome J. Shestack, honorary president, described an exhibition of JPS books at the Jewish National and University Library, Hebrew University in Jerusalem in May 1979. Maier Deshell, editor, then introduced Professor Yosef Yerushalmi, chairman of the Publication Committee, who read a paper entitled "The Holocaust and the Historians" by Lucy S. Dawidowicz, our scheduled speaker. Mrs. Dawidowicz was unable to attend because of the death of her husband.

From the Annual Report of JPS President Edward B. Shils

On this 91st anniversary of the founding of the Society, I note with pride that since 1888 we have published the finest Jewish books in the English language and distributed some eight million copies of these books all over the world. Our publishing program has steadily accelerated over the years: the records of 1928 show that JPS published six books that year, whereas last year, in 1978, we published 19 books.

The most significant work published in 1978 was the new translation of *The Prophets—Nevi'im,* the second volume of *The Holy Scriptures*. We are grateful that this volume is now available to the Jewish community, and express our thanks to our fine committee of translators—H. L. Ginsburg, Harry Orlinsky, Bernard Bamberger, Harry Freedman, and Solomon Grayzel.

The new JPS translation of the entire Bible will soon be available, as the translation of the third and final volume, *The Writings-Kethubim*, is nearing completion.

I am pleased to report that the Board of Trustees has voted to issue a Hebrew/English edition of the *Torah* and *Haftoroth*, utilizing the new JPS

English translation. Many synagogues have requested the dual-language volume, and work on that edition is currently in progress.

Furthermore, we have commissioned scholars to provide the commentary on the Torah. Nahum Sarna, of Brandeis University, is chairman of the committee and is providing the commentary to Genesis.

JPS is honored that Professor Salo W. Baron has received the Gerrard and Ella Berman National Jewish Book Award for Jewish History for his cumulative contribution to Jewish historic research and thought. Professor Baron has been a member of our Publication Committee since 1941, and we have been privileged to participate in the publication of several of his works, including the monumental 16-volume *A Social and Religious History of the Jews*.

At the Philadelphia Book Show, three JPS titles for 1978 were awarded first prizes for design. *The Prophets, A Book of Hebrew Letters* by Mark Podwal, and *Behold a Great Image: The Contemporary Jewish Experience in Photographs*, edited by Sharon Strassfeld and Arthur Kurzweil, were the winners. Congratulations to JPS editor Maier Deshell and his staff, to designers Ismar David and Adrianne Onderdonk Dudden, and to the JPS Publication Committee, headed by Yosef Yerushalmi. Congratulations also to Professor Yerushalmi on his appointment to the first Jacob E. Saffra Professorship of Jewish History and Sephardic Civilization at Harvard University.

The Society is grateful for a bequest of $377,000 from the estate of Abraham M. Wolfman of Los Angeles. The funds may be used at the discretion of the Society to publish in English, literature concerning the Jews and Judaism, as well as English translations of the Jewish classics. Mr. Wolfman had deep religious beliefs, and a love of books. We are thankful to him for giving us the means to publish books of Judaica that will honor his name.

Last year at the annual meeting, A. Leo Levin announced the establishment of a JPS Community Trust Program to accept gifts large and small, and to distribute books to community organizations that need them but do not have the means for their purchase. During the year, we received requests from Hillel libraries, and I am able to report that books have been sent to a number of these institutions. We hope that we will be able to fill additional needs in the near future.

During the past year, JPS participated in several events involving Israel. We sponsored a ten-day cultural tour of Israel, where our members had the opportunity to tour the country and to meet our prominent Israeli authors and poets. We displayed our books at the Jerusalem Book Fair, where many Israelis, as well as American visitors, became members of JPS.

Finally, in honor of our 90th anniversary, an exhibit of our books is on display at the Jewish National and University Library at the Hebrew University in Jerusalem. This exhibit represents a fine compliment to JPS, as we are the first publisher ever to be given space for an exhibit in that institution.

JPS Treasurer's Report for 1978

It has been said that the past is prologue to the future.

The Jewish Publication Society of America is now in its 91st year. Nearly 8 million volumes, divided among some 800 titles, have been published and distributed around the world, mainly in the U.S., with a growing reader audience in Israel.

Revenue to the Society in 1978 from sales and membership amounted to $889,716, as compared to $986,679 in 1977.

During this period, expenses amounted to $1,237,443, as compared to $1,145,291. Income from donations, welfare funds, and investments was $183,408, compared to $121,500.

Thus, expenses over income amounted to $164,319. However, the increase in expenses includes the costs of the large printing of the new translation of the Prophets which was completed in the latter half of the year, as well as all expenditures incurred in preparation for the 20 new books which are now being readied for printing and will be out in the very near future. Income from the sale of these books will accrue to the Society in the next years.

We are honored to report a generous bequest of $377,317, which was received from the Abraham Wolfman Trust of California. These funds have been placed in our investment account, which is conservatively invested. This money was bequeathed to JPS to help carry out our stated goal of nearly a century—to provide significantly worthwhile and informative books of Jewish content in the English language, so that the Jewish religion, history, literature and culture will be understood and read and known. If it is true, as previously stated, that the past is prologue to the future, then we at JPS—with the help of brilliant leadership, a dedicated board of directors from across the nation, and an interested membership—indeed look forward to a fulfilling and challenging future.

JPS Publications

In 1978 JPS published the following new volumes:

Title and Author	*Printed*
DEFENSES OF THE IMAGINATION: Jewish Writers and Modern Historical Crisis	4,000
by Robert Alter	
WOLFSON OF HARVARD: Portrait of a Scholar	5,000
by Leo W. Schwarz	
THE RISE AND FALL OF THE JUDAEAN STATE, Volume III	5,000
by Solomon Zeitlin	
THE PROPHETS: NEVI'IM, A new translation of the Holy Scriptures according to the traditional Hebrew text	50,000
BEHOLD A GREAT IMAGE: The Contemporary Jewish Experience in Photographs	5,000
Edited by Sharon Strassfeld and Arthur Kurzweil	
STRANGERS WITHIN THE GATE CITY: The Jews of Atlanta 1845–1915	3,000
by Steven Hertzberg	
A BOOK OF HEBREW LETTERS	6,000
by Mark Podwal	
DONA GRACIA OF THE HOUSE OF NASI	2,000
by Cecil Roth (Paperback reprint)	
A HISTORY OF THE JEWS IN CHRISTIAN SPAIN	2,000
by Yitzhak Baer, Volumes I and II (Paperback reprint)	
THE JEWS IN THE RENAISSANCE	2,000
by Cecil Roth (Paperback reprint)	
TREATISE TA'ANIT OF THE BABYLONIAN TALMUD	2,000
Translated and edited by Henry Malter (Paperback reprint)	
SAMUEL USQUE'S CONSOLATION FOR THE TRIBULATIONS OF ISRAEL	2,000
Translated by Martin A. Cohen (Paperback reprint)	
TULLY FILMUS: SELECTED DRAWINGS	2,000
(Paperback reprint)	
CHELMAXIOMS: The Maxims/Axioms/Maxioms of Chelm	1,500
by Allen Mandelbaum (A joint publication with David R. Godine)	
AMERICAN JEWISH YEAR BOOK- Volume 78	3,000
Edited by Morris Fine and Milton Himmelfarb	
Martha Jelenko, Executive Editor	
(Co-published with the American Jewish Committee)	
THE HARVEST	2,000
by Meyer Levin (Co-published with Simon & Schuster)	
LETTERS OF JEWS THROUGH THE AGES	1,500
Edited by Franz Kobler (Co-published with Hebrew Publishing Co.)	
WANDERINGS: CHAIM POTOK'S HISTORY OF THE JEWS	2,000
by Chaim Potok (Co-published with Alfred A. Knopf, Inc.)	
LIVING WITH THE BIBLE	2,500
by Moshe Dayan (Co-published with William Morrow & Co.)	

1978 Reprints

During 1978, JPS reprinted the following books:

THE HOLY SCRIPTURES (29,000); K'TONTON ON AN ISLAND IN THE
SEA by Sadie Rose Weilerstein (2,000); JEWISH WORSHIP edited by Abraham
E. Millgram (2,000); LETTERS TO AN AMERICAN JEWISH FRIEND by
Hillel Halkin (3,000); LEGENDS OF THE JEWS—Volume VII by Louis Ginz-
berg (1,500); THE FIVE MEGILLOTH AND THE BOOK OF JONAH
(3,000); PESIKTA DE-RAB KAHANA translated by William G. Braude and
Israel J. Kapstein (1,000); THE IMAGE OF THE JEW IN AMERICAN LIT-
ERATURE by Louis Harap (2,000); LEGENDS OF THE BIBLE by Louis
Ginzberg (3,000); THE SECOND JEWISH CATALOG compiled and edited by
Sharon and Michael Strassfeld (15,000); THE JEWISH CATALOG compiled
and edited by Richard Siegel, Michael and Sharon Strassfeld (15,000); THE
TORAH (15,000); HEBREW: THE ETERNAL LANGUAGE by William
Chomsky (2,000); JEWISH COOKING AROUND THE WORLD by Hanna
Goodman (2,000).

SPECIAL ARTICLES IN VOLUMES 51–79
OF THE AMERICAN JEWISH YEAR BOOK

413

OBITUARIES

Index

417

American Physicians Fellowship, Inc. for Medicine in Israel, 325
American Red Magen David for Israel, Inc., 326
American Sephardi Federation, 319
American Society for Jewish Music, 297
American Sociological Review, 32n, 33n
American Students in Israel, 60n
American Technion Society, 326
American Veterans of Israel, 319
American Zionist, 355
American Zionist Federation, 326
American Zionist Youth Foundation, Inc., 326
American Zionist Youth Council, 326
Amery, Jean, 234
AMIA (see Asociación Mutual Israelita Argentina)
Amin, Mustafa, 253
Amit, Meir, 266, 267
Among Men and Beasts, 185
Amorai, Adi, 221
Ampal—American Israel Corporation, 326
Amsterdam News, 78, 81
Anatoly Shcharansky Day, 123
Andrews, Donald, 177
Angola, 274
Annette White Lodge (Great Britain), 201
Ansprenger, Franz, 231
Anti-Boycott Coordinating Committee (Gt. Britain), 200
Anti-Defamation League of B'nai B'rith (see B'nai B'rith)
Anti-Nazi League (ANL; Great Britain), 197
Anti-Semitism and Reactionary Utopianism, 231
Antonovsky, A., 53n
Appleyard, R. T., 53, 53n
Arab-Israel conflict, 87–117
Arab League, 88, 190
Arabian American Oil Company (Aramco), 180
Arafat, Yasir, 90, 97, 226, 227
Archbishop of York, 203

Arens, Moshe, 260
Argentina, 188–196, 226, 265
Foreign Ministry, 188
Argentine Council of Jewish Women, 192
Argentine-Jewish Institute of Culture and Information, 195
Argentine League for the Rights of Man, 188
Argentine Zionist Organization (OSA), 190, 191
Argonne National Laboratory, 128
A.R.I.F—Association Pour le Rétablissement des Institutions et Oeuvres Israélites en France, Inc., 301
Aris, Helmut, 235
Arizona Post, 352
Arkes, Hadley, 15n, 17, 17n, 18
Armenia, 241
Arms Export Act, 92
Arnsberg, Paul, 234
Aron, Raymond, 209
Aronowitz, Cecil, 206
Arrow, Kenneth, 104
Arts National Program (Canada), 185
Arvon, Henri, 212
As If We Lived In Peace, 232
Asociación Comunidad Israelita Sefaradí de Buenos Aires (ACIS), 191
Asociación Filantropica Israelita (AFI), 192
Asociación Israelita Sefaradí Argentina (AISA), 191
Asociación Mutual Israelita Argentina (AMIA), 191, 193, 194
Aspen Institute for Humanistic Studies, 121
al-Assad, Hafez, 92, 94, 218, 237
Assalam, 192
Assimilation in American Life, 33n
Associated American Jewish Museums, 297
Associated Hebrew Schools (Canada), 183
Association for Computer Machinery, 128

Levesque, René, 172, 177
Levi, David, 266, 267
Levich, Valentin, 245
Levin, George, 368
Levin, Herschel, 368
Levin, Nora, 205
Levin, Rhonda, 186
Levy, Harold, 281
Levy, Herbert, 186
Lewin, Boleslao, 195
Lewis, Salim L., 369
Lewis, Samuel, 107
Liacouras, Peter, 122
Liberal Party (Canada), 173
Liberal Party (Great Britain), 197
Liberal Party (Israel), 260, 265, 266
Libya, 93, 190, 200, 237
LICA (see International League Against Antisemitism; France)
Lieberman, Judith, 369
Liebeschuetz, Hans, 206
Lieberson, Stanley, 32n
Liebman, Charles, 5n, 29n, 41, 41n
Life for Jerusalem, A, 233
Lifshitz, Mendel, 246
Likud Party (Argentina), 191
Likud Party (Israel), 95, 105, 265–268, 271
Likud-Herut Party (Israel), 267
Likud-La'am Party (Israel), 265, 266, 267
Likud-Liberal Party (Israel), 267, 270
Lilith—The Jewish Feminist Magazine, 357
Linath Hazadak Aid Society (Gt. Britain), 201
Linden, Allan, 185
Lindheim, Irma, 273, 369
Linfield, Harry S., 369
Lipavsky, Sanya, 120
Lipkin, Aileen, 279
Lipman, Vivian David, 205
Lipshitz, Lippy, 279
Lipton, Marcus, 206
Liptzin, Sol, 231
Lipworth, Esther, 281
Lischka, Kurt, 224
Littell, Franklin, 182
Littell, Robert, 205

Litvinoff, Emanuel, 205
Liverpool City Council (Gt. Britain), 202
Living at Gurs, 212
Lobanov, Igor, 178
Loeser, Franz, 237
London Board for Jewish Religious Education, 204
London School of Economics, 206
London Times, 199
Long Island Jewish Press, 357
Long Live the 100-Year Anniversary of the French Communist Party, 208
Long Way Back: Attitudes of Israelis Residing in the U.S. and in France Toward Returning to Israel, 55n
Looking For Mr. Goodbar, 75
Lord's Day Act (Canada), 178
Lord's Prayer, The, 233
Los Angeles Bar Association, 127
Los Angeles Committee of Concerned Lawyers for Soviet Jews, 127
Lookstein, Haskel, 138n
Lourie, Arthur, 273
Lourie, Norman, 281
Louvish, Misha, 107, 273
Lover, The, 212
Lowe, Heinz-Dietrich, 230
Loyalty and Utopia, 212
Lubavitch Movement, 78
Lubetkin-Cukierman, Zivia, 273
Lubin, Isador, 369
Lukas, J. Anthony, 19n, 20n
Lukianenko, Lev, 240
Luna Park (Argentina), 190
Lunenfeld, Joseph, 187
Luria, Aleksandr, 247
Lurie, Harry, 29n
Lurie, Note, 246
Lustgarten, Edgar, 206
Lutheran Church-Missouri Synod, 72
Lutheran Church of East Germany, 235
La Luz (Argentina), 195
Lyons, Lord, 206

Maariv (Israel), 273
Maass, Richard, 125
Macabi (Argentina), 192
Maccabi (South Africa), 281

Missouri Jewish Post and Opinion, 354

Mitterrand, François, 207, 208

Mizrach, Isaac, 196

Mizrachi-Hapoel Hamizrachi Organization of Canada, 335

Mizrachi Party (Argentina), 191

Mizrachi Party (Gt. Britain), 202

Mizrachi Party (Israel), 271

Moczarski, Kazimierz, 232

Moda, Yitzhak, 262

Modai, Yitzhak, 260, 266, 267

Modern Jewish Studies Annual, 355

Mogge, Birgitta, 231

Molodezh Moldavii (Soviet Union), 243

Moment, 6, 29n, 30n, 104

Moncton *Times* (Canada), 177

Mondale, Walter, 93, 103, 105, 107, 127, 257

Montreal Inter-Faith Task Force for Soviet Jewry, 180, 181

Montrose, Lawrence, 8, 24

Moonman, Eric, 199

Morning Freiheit, 357

Morocco, 191, 253, 257

Moroz, Valentin, 240n

Morris, Elaine, 139n

Morris, Horace, 77

Morris, Solly, 280

Morris/Sussex Jewish News, 354

Morrison, Marvin, 9

Moscone, George, 14, 25

Moscow Chamber Choir, 181

Moscow Collegium of Lawyers, 125

Moscow Dramatic Ensemble (Soviet Union), 246

Moscow Watch Committee, 119

Mosre, Roger, 233

Mostert, Anton, 274

Mother Russia, 205

Movement Against Racism and Antisemitism and for Peace (MRAP; France), 209, 210

Movement for a Secure Peace (Israel), 256

Movement for the Defense of Human Rights (Poland), 248

Movimiento Sionista Apartidario (General Zionists; Argentina), 191

Movimiento Sionista Renovador (Shinui; Argentina), 191

Moynihan, Daniel P., 33n, 75, 126

MRAP (see Movement Against Racism and Antisemitism and for Peace; France)

Muffs, Judith H., 25n

Mugavero, Francis, 74

Mulder, Connie, 274

Multicultural History Society of Ontario, 184

Mundo Israelita (Argentina), 195

Munk, Eli, 206

Mussner, Franz, 233

Muster, Morris, 370

My Judaism, 234

My Life, 53n

My Origins, 246

NAACP (see National Association for the Advancement of Colored People)

Nachmann, Werner, 226, 234

Nahir, Moshe, 185

Narodnoe Obrazovanie (Soviet Union), 244

Natal Zionist Council, 281

Nathan, Abie, 256

Nathani, Itzhak, 206

National Academy of Sciences of the U.S., 128, 129, 24

National Association for the Advancement of Colored People (NAACP), 76, 79, 82, 83, 85

Legal Defense and Education Fund, 122

National Association of Jewish Family, Children's and Health Professionals, 323

National Association of Jewish Homes for the Aged, 323

National Association of Jewish Vocational Services, 151, 323

National Broadcasting Corporation (NBC), 25, 26, 85, 86, 178

National Catholic News Service, 82

Raab, Earl, 13, 13n
Rabat summit conference, 109
Rabbi, Z., 54n
Rabbinical Alliance of America (Igud Harabonim), 311
Rabbinical Assembly, 182, 311
Rabbinical College of Telshe, Inc., 311
Rabbinical Council of America, Inc., 311
Rabbinical Council Record, 357
Rabin, Yitzhak, 267
Rabinovitch, N. L., 203
Rabinowitz, Dorothy, 78
Rabinowitz, Louis, 280
Rafi Party (Israel), 265
Rakah (see Communist Party, Israel)
Ramah Hebrew School (Canada), 184
Rand Corporation, 79
Randburg Hebrew Congregation (South Africa), 280
A. Philip Randolph Institute, 122
Rangel, Charles, 77
Ranulf Association (Gt. Britain), 201
Raphael, Marc Lee, 29n
Ras, Shmuel, 227
Rassco Israel Corporation and Rassco Financial Corporation, 329
Rathje, Friedrich, 224
Ratner, Sabina, 184
Ratzinger, Joseph Cardinal, 229
Rayner, John, 205
Rechtman, Shmuel, 270
Reconstructionist, 357
Reconstructionist Rabbinical College, 311
Redcliffe-Maud, John Primatt, 199
Reform Judaism, 357
Reicher, Benno, 227
Reinartz, Wilhelm, 224
Reisman, Simon, 186
Religion and Politics in 20th Century Society, 232
Religion of Reason Out of the Sources of Judaism, 232
Religious Zionists of America, 329
  Bnei Akiva of North America, 329
  Mizrachi-Hapoel Hamizrachi, 329
  Mizrachi Palestine Fund, 330
  National Council for Torah Educa-

tion of Mizrachi-Hapoel Hamizrachi, 330
  Noam-Hamishmeret Hatzeira, 330
Remmers, Werner, 215
Rendtorff, Rolf, 232
Report of Work Conference on Current Concerns in Jewish Education, 136n
Reporter, 355
Representation of the People (Deposit and Nominations) Bill (Gt. Britain), 198
Research Foundation for Jewish Immigration, Inc., 300
Research Institute of Religious Jewry, Inc., 311
Resnizky, Nehemias, 191, 193
Response, 29n, 30n, 357
Revista Culturui Mosaic (Rumania), 251
Revue Française Sociologie, 31n
Rhea Hirsch School of Education (see Hebrew Union College-Jewish Institute of Religion)
Rhetoric of Hate, 231
Rhode Island Jewish Historical Notes, 359
Rhodes, John, 125
Rhoodie, Eschel, 274
Ribicoff, Abraham, 125
Ribner, Sol, 141n
Ricardo Rojas Biennial Literary Competition, 195
Richarz, Monika, 230
Richmond, A. B., 53, 53n
Rifkind, Malcolm, 199
Right To Life Party, 73, 74
Rigner, Gerhard, 251
Rimalt, Eliezer, 265
Riseman, Mervin, 125
Ritterband, Paul, 30n, 205
Rivlin, Joseph, 246
Rizzo, Frank, 80
Roberts, John, 179, 182, 183
Rocard, Michel, 208
Rockwell, George Lincoln, 3
Roeder, Manfred, 214
Roettger, Norman, 86
Rohwer, Uwe, 216